the ***madness*** *of* **money**

To Ravi
Be a long term
investor in a short-
term world!

Love
N C xx

And with thanks and
love from me!
Jan /xoxo

the *madness*
of
money

The misunderstanding & mayhem of modern money markets

Neil F Chapman-Blench & Alistair Crooks

www.theMadnessofMoney.co.uk

author HOUSE®

AuthorHouse™
1663 Liberty Drive
Bloomington, IN 47403
www.authorhouse.com
Phone: 1-800-839-8640

Published by AuthorHouse   12/07/2011

ISBN: 978-1-4678-7957-6 (sc)

INDEX OF CONTENTS

Preface   May 2009—The Credit Crunch—
                A Short History of Tomorrow!.................................. ix

Introduction   October 2009—The Credit Crunch—The Plot; A
                Squid and an Octopus Wrestling In a Barrel of Oil! xix

Chapter 1   April 2007—New Century:
                100 Years of Mortgage Mayhem................................. 1

Chapter 2   May 2007—The Federal Reserve:
                The Bankers' Charity Ball 23

Chapter 3   June 2007—The Alchemy of Aggressive Arithmetic:
                The "Wizards" of Light and Dark............................. 45

Chapter 4   July 2007—The Currency of Illusion:
                The Sovereign Nation of Gold.................................. 67

Chapter 5   August 2007—Wallet or Wheelbarrow: The
                Specter at the Feast—The Glutton in the Famine..... 89

Chapter 6   September 2007—I'm for ever Blowing
                Bubbles! 110

Chapter 7   October 2007—Intellectual, Marxist or Fabien:
                The IMF—Something for Everybody?.................... 133

Chapter 8   November 2007—A Scotsman, a Frenchman and
                an Englishman . . . . went into a Bank! 154

Chapter 9   December 2007—The Emperor's New Clothes 177

Chapter 10   January 2008—A Loan Sweet Home:
                Castle or Prison!.. 199

Chapter 11   February 2008—A Girl's Best Friend—And
                Her Husband, Boyfriend and Lover Too! 218

Chapter 12   March 2008—J. P. Morgan:

              Man to Megabank 1907 to 2007 239

Chapter 13   April 2008—A Bull in a China Shop! 260

Chapter 14   May 2008—Bear Stearns:

              It's All In The Name! 280

Chapter 15   June 2008—Currency Convertor:

              The Warp Drive of Speculation! 302

Chapter 16   July 2008—The Rise of the Conquistadors 320

Chapter 17   August 2008—Cod Moves in Mysterious Ways;

              Island Records! 345

Interlude   The Politics of Illusion,

              the Policies of Delusion! 366

Chapter 18   September 2008—Belgium Bombshell:

              The Bailout without Borders! 389

Chapter 19   October 2008—Rag & Bone Men:

              Junking the Market! 410

Chapter 20   November 2008—Florence to Milan:

              The History of Art-Full Lending 428

Chapter 21   December 2008—Pirates to Ponzis 449

Chapter 22   January 2009—Marchia Orientalis:

              Last Man Standing 470

Chapter 23   February 2009—Sex, Drugs, Rocky Markets

              & Rolling Indexes! 486

Chapter 24   March 2009—Slippery Road:

              Oxford Brogues to Silk Slippers 506

Conclusion   October 2009—A Circle Has No End! 523

Dedication

For My Father

Clive William Chapman

1931-2010

The example I strive for, but will never attain.

Acknowledgements

Jan—My one, only and forever love!

"Love is composed of a single soul inhabiting two bodies."

Aristotle

You truly understand the complexities of my world—and love me anyway!

To My Mother—Audrey Margret Chapman

A mother's heart is a child's fortress.

To My Brother Ian

Your successes as a younger brother are a reflection of my failings as an elder brother!

To My Closest Friends

Adversity thins your friends, but strengthens your bonds!

To All My Other Many Friends—Thank You

"We are each of us angels with only one wing, and we can fly only by embracing each other."

Lucian de Crescenzo

For all my enemies along the way . . . . and there have been a few!

I forgive you all!

In the words of Benjamin Franklin; "Love your enemies, for they tell you your faults."

For Those That I will Always Love—Your Love Is Without Reserve

Mien *"Mr Waggy"*—1996 to 2009   Bellezza—*"Tippy Tip Toes"*

Preface

May 2009—The Credit Crunch—A Short History of Tomorrow!

"A great building must begin with the unmeasurable, must go through measurable means when it is being designed and in the end must be unmeasurable."

Louis Kahn,
American, Architect

December 2008—An investor and trader have dinner or in the words of Winston Churchill; "Always remember that I have taken more out of alcohol than alcohol has taken out of me."

What was the credit crunch? Where did it come from? Who survived?

The Credit Crunch; History is long periods of boredom broken up by *pivot points.* For those not in the financial markets and maybe unfamiliar with the phrase—*pivot points*—the trader's or investor's definition is; *A technical indicator which is used to predict a change in resistance or support levels for a stock, currency, commodity or index.*

In plain English one would say that matters are going along smoothly and, in general, boringly, in one direction and then at a certain point they are interrupted and head dramatically in an alternative direction. Pivot points could simply be explained as *"points of interruption"*. In history, as in investment and trading, the more dramatic the event the more likely we are as humans to recall it; a famous battle, the death of a powerful king or emperor, the invasion of foreign soil. We are less likely to recall the exact timing of the invention of paper or the first coal powered spinning machine as we are to know the dates of the Battles of Waterloo, Thermopylae or Lepanto, the assassinations of J. F. Kennedy and Caesar.

In trading parlance and illustrated on a graph of humanities' activities, the invention of paper and its effects would be a slow upward trend whereas the Battle of Waterloo would be a dramatic, violent and easily seen interruption—a spike—of existing events; indeed popular legend has it that Nathan Rothschild made a fortune in government securities following the immediate and sudden euphoria in financial markets following news of Wellington's victory over Napoleon!

Every generation recalls events in its own unique way. As those events are real and in live time then the perceived impact and actual impact are the same, thus imprinting themselves forever on the memory banks of that generation. The well understood "I lived through it" syndrome.

In the modern era, thanks to the technology of television and the Internet, we have visual imagery to reinforce our memory. My parents' generation will recall the declaration of war with Germany, the bombing of Pearl Harbor and that fatal day in Dallas in November 1963. I, in my time, see vividly in my mind the stock market crash of 1987, the 9/11 abomination and the invasion of Iraq.

The dichotomy I have with "the Credit Crunch" is that it is the most significant economic and financial event of my lifetime and yet it does not have an absolute start date or indeed one of conclusion. In my mind, as an investor and trader, it should have a *pivot point*, yet it does not. I was the Director in charge of a dealing desk for the world's leading fund management company in the 1980's so I can remember instantly Black Monday, October 19, 1987. My mind sees the vivid and terrifying image of screens filled with a sea of red as the index proceeded to fall 26%. At the end of the week I spent time with my father and brother, who were not involved in the financial markets. The strange thing to me, who was exhausted following a harrowing week, to put it mildly, was that they were totally unaffected by the turmoil in the world's stock markets. It was of only mild curiosity to them; a lot of loud young men shouting into house-brick size phones, in unintelligible jargon, wiping millions off the values of companies at random; nothing to do with the real world! Indeed, it took nearly two years for the toxic damage of that particular crash to hit the economy and topple property prices.

It appears that the Credit Crunch, although having no defined start point, affected everybody in short order with devastating consequences. It was similar to one of those disaster movies whereby a man-made bug from a germ warfare base gets into the general populace and multiplies exponentially. By the end of the month the world is displayed in red as the whole of the earth is infected—*except for the two heroes, one of whom is always an attractive female scientist!*

Still I digress.

The Credit Crunch thus is both a *pivot point* and yet it is not! How do we solve this curiosity?

Lightening fast traders, such as my friend and co-author Alistair, seek an unmistakable meeting of defined indicators to deal, either by buying or selling, at clearly defined *pivot points* on a charting system. *How then to make this event more clearly defined?*

The answer lies in extrapolating the graph.

By lengthening the time period of the graph the movement of, or more correctly, *because of*, the Credit Crunch, becomes more abrupt. If we could track humanity's graph back through history then the variation or Credit Crunch adjustment would become sharper and more apparent until it finally emerged as a spike; the metamorphosis from a slowly unwinding event to pivot point finally accomplished.

This throws up a second question; *are we justified in going back thousands of years in order to find a contextual position for our very own "Credit Crunch"?*

As a private individual living in a free society I am of course allowed to think, express and explore whatever I want or, more succinctly, in the words of John Steinbeck: *"This I believe: that the free, exploring mind of the individual human is the most valuable thing in the world. And this I would fight for: the freedom of the mind to take any direction it wishes, undirected. And this I must fight against: any idea, religion, or government which limits or destroys the individual."*

As the author of a book though I feel I must justify my reasoning; an intellectual argument on which to hang my hat. How do we excuse looking at two thousand years of economic and financial history in order to satisfy my selfish trading idiosyncrasies, the urge to place a few squiggly lines on a graph? Well I think I have the link. When researching the credit crunch I sought traces of the oldest evidence of a "Credit Crunch".

The Roman Credit Crunch

Although as humans we like to feel that every sensation and occurrence is unique to ourselves, we are doomed to be disappointed. Father time, the master of all, proves us wrong. Everything major in life has already been experienced by a different generation. If we tumble back through history we pass through many significant years of economic turmoil; 1987, 1929, 1907, 1893, 1873, 1857, 1837, 1819 and 1720, and so on until we arrive back at 1345.

Like Doctor Who, we finally arrive at the time of the Emperors, when Rome ruled the known world. I fully expect that the historians amongst you will be able to cite even older examples but I have used the Roman Empire, as at that time it covered most of the western civilised world so hence it allows an element of "globalisation" into the example. Rome was the leading hegemony both geographically and economically as well as demonstrating longevity, being the dominant power for 800 years.

In year of AD 32, in the reign of Tiberius we find evidence of a financial whirlwind about to raise the togas of the Senate members. In Book VI of *The Annals*, Tacitus, translated from the Latin by Alfred John

Church and William Jackson Brodribb, we find evidence of excessive mortgage lending, government intervention on interest rates to control the economy and borrowing terms and conditions that all resulted in an ancient world's "credit crunch" and an eventual collapse in real estate prices.

All sound so very familiar?

Read on and draw your own conclusions;

"Meanwhile a powerful host of accusers fell with sudden fury on the class which systematically increased its wealth by usury in defiance of a law passed by Caesar the Dictator defining the terms of lending and of holding estates in Italy, a law long obsolete because the public good is sacrificed to private interest. The curse of usury was indeed of old standing in Rome and a most frequent cause of sedition and discord, and it was therefore repressed even in the early days of a less corrupt morality. First, the Twelve tablets prohibited any one from exacting more than 10 per cent, when previously the rate had depended on the caprice of the wealthy. Subsequently, by a bill brought in by tribunes, interest was reduced to half that amount, and finally compound interest was wholly forbidden. A check too was put by several enactments of the people on evasions, which, though continually put down, still, through strange artifices, reappeared. On this occasion, however, Gracchus, the praetor, to whose jurisdiction the enquiry had fallen, felt himself compelled by the number of persons endangered to refer the matter to the Senate. In their dismay the senators, not one of whom was free from similar guilt, threw themselves on the Emperor's indulgence. He yielded, and a year and six months were granted, within which everyone was to settle his private accounts conformably to the requirements of the law.

Hence followed a scarcity of money, a great shock being given to all credit, the current coin too, in consequence of the conviction of so many persons and the sale of their property, being locked up in the imperial treasury or the public exchequer. To meet this, the Senate had directed that every creditor should have two thirds of his capital secured on estates in Italy. Creditors however were suing for payment in full, and it was not respectable for persons when sued to break faith. So at first there were clamorous meetings and importunate entreaties; then noisy applications to the praetor's court. And the very device intended as a remedy, the sale and purchase of estates, proved the contrary, as the usurers had hoarded up all their money for buying land. The facilities for selling were followed by a fall of prices, and the deeper a man was in debt, the more reluctantly did he part with his property, and many were utterly ruined. The destruction of private wealth participated the fall of rank and reputation, till at last that Emperor interposed his aid by distributing throughout the banks a hundred million sesterces, and allowing freedom to borrow without interest for three years, provided the borrower gave security to the state in land double the amount. Credit was thus restored, and gradually private lenders were found. The purchase too of estates was not carried out according to the letter of the Senate's decree, rigor at the outset, as usual with such matters, becoming negligence in the end."

I think it is not only remarkable that we see clear evidence of a financial quagmire so similar to the one we have all so recently experienced, but more remarkably the Emperor and Senate used exactly the same methods as our modern day central bankers and national governments to lift themselves out of the mess; *a massive capital injection into the banking system and reducing interest rates to effectively zero for three years!*

Whilst I was mulling this depressing conundrum over in my mind I stumbled over even earlier data of a *previous* Roman credit crunch! It seems that in 88 BC there was a credit crunch caused by a massive increase in monetary liquidity and an "Asian" economic slump created by ongoing war with Mithradates of Pontus. Cicero, famed orator and first consul of Rome, in 66 BC alluded to the 88 BC crisis in a speech given before the Senate; *"Defend the republic from this danger and believe me when I tell you—what you see for yourselves—that this system of monies, which operates at Rome in the Forum, is bound up in, and is linked with, those Asian monies; the loss of one inevitably undermines the other and causes its collapse."*

Much as when we were at the lowest point of the current credit crunch we looked back to 1929 with the Great Wall Street Crash and the Depression that followed, so must Tiberius have looked back 100 years or so to the previous crisis of Cicero's era; indeed maybe that is how the Senate forced him to take swift and effective measures so promptly.

Despite having found evidence on which I could justify my desire to ink in *pivot points* on my own mental graph I found myself mildly depressed.

Is humanity stuck in a global version of ground hog day? Are we not masters of our own universe but rather a giant galactic joke? Can we ever leave this fiscal and economic trap we ourselves have created?

From being a justification, the thin thread that I could keep the whole unwieldy process together, the evidential investigation of history became the substantial core of the book. The twin pillars upon which I have constructed the book, by looking at economic and financial history, are firstly what the confluence are of circumstances that came together to create the Credit Crunch. Secondly, not could it have been prevented, because that is an academic argument, but rather what do we need to do to prevent any future occurrences? The second is a thorny but stimulating question, as we seem, on the face of it, unable to have prevented comparable financial disasters for the last two thousand years.

The third pillar, the basis of capitalism—or in trader's parlance—"*show me the money*" is to be covered by my co-author Alistair in our follow-up book.

Why write another book on the Credit Crunch?

> *"Only barbarians are not curious about where they come from, how they came to be where they are, where they appear to be going, whether they wish to go there, and if so, why, and if not, why not."*
>
> **Isaiah Berlin**

It began on a wild and windy night . . . . in November 2008.

Alistair and I were staying at the Celtic Manor in Newport. Along with another friend Kurt, we have the privilege of teaching share trading and investment once or twice a month, normally over a three day weekend at a luxury hotel—*life's tough but somebody has to do it!* After a long day and a good meal we were all in relaxed mood and after the obligatory discussion on sport but before we reached the point of "the meaning of life", the conversational lines crossed the subject of the credit crunch. It stayed there for the next four hours and numerous drinks.

It seemed to the three of us that the more we thought we knew the less in fact we actually did. In financial market terms we embraced a broad spectrum of monetary knowledge. Although we were all traders, we came at it from different directions; Alistair was a brilliant trader who had always worked for himself, Kurt had worked for a hedge fund manager and I had spent 17 years in the unit trust and mutual fund arena. That conversation piqued my interest and I spent many subsequent hours researching the *credit crunch* as a result, including the leading question; *if all the nations in the world are in the debt, where did all the money go?*

Kurt, who is an expert on the gold and commodities markets, and I were focused on the reasons for the Credit Crunch and trying from the sidelines to *"football coach"* the most recent global initiatives to correct the sinking ship. Being a true trader, not a diluted hybrid like me, the burning question in Alistair's mind was; *who were the winners? Who made money in the Credit Crunch and by what methodology?*

Thus were the twin seeds of an idea for a book planted and left to germinate. For my part I was drawn to what are the historic reasons that come together on a regular basis to drive humanity to its economic knees and can we possibly break the cycle. Alistair is drawn to the fact that there are always winners and losers in any crisis and how one can end up on the winning side of the coin—or indeed just end up with the coin!

So, this book neatly encapsulates that never ending battle between bulls and bears! Or rather more correctly the twin gods that inhabit those fearsome beasts; Hermes the Greek God of Flight who often takes on the bearish aspect and Dionysus the Greek God of merriness and madness who plays the bull! In modern traders' parlance we more often just say trading and investment is a battle of:

FEAR v GREED

Thus we have chosen to explore three areas of interest during the course of writing this book; the historic mix of economic and human behavioral patterns that bought us to the point of economic turmoil, how the winners and losers were separated, and what we can do to prevent a reoccurrence.

If we can send a man to the moon and to the greatest depths of the sea, if we can split an atom and paint the Mona Lisa surely we can control and harness economic and financial markets for the good of all of humanity? Let's see!

The Madness of Money; A Word of Warning!

Having studied at high school the subjects of economics, economic geography and economic history—*I volunteered, which puts me into that strange territory of guilty of self harm*—I am well acquainted with the anesthetic properties of those triple branches of learning. It goes a long way to explain the fact that I joined all the sports teams at the school in order to escape the class room; including the girls net ball team where unfortunately I was discovered after one match! Based on this formative experience my own personal definition of economic history is; *the supply of numerical data verses the demand of insomniac students!*

Dante Alighieri's Hell has nothing on economics badly or indeed flatly explained. Purgatory, also well covered by Dante, did not mention two hours of economic geography tuition on a cold November's day, covering how many cabbages were produced by the average medieval peasant and how many soups they went into during the following winter! When I next meet Dante, or indeed when I first meet him, hopefully not in one of his delightfully described holiday destinations, I will mention he missed a trick in satisfying the humorous yet sadistic desires of his Florentine audiences by not adding a verse covering my education.

Thus I have attempted to make the book factual yet interesting, serious yet open to humour and, although wide ranging, focused on those points I feel both salient and important to our quest. As a reader you will have to judge whether the correct balance of ying and yang was struck!

Most authors say when writing a book that the conclusions that have been drawn are their own. I would like to enhance that statement by saying that not only is the reasoning my own but the unique direction we may travel on this journey is of my own creation. I am afraid if you like your books to be journey upon well laid railway tracks, moving smoothly from A to B, then you will be disappointed. Think rather of the explorer moving into unknown territory. For ease and safety he may follow the banks of a major river that meanders through the jungle, but at times he will break off his journey to satisfy his curiosity; an interesting tributary, a mountain range, half hidden buildings covered in creepers, all may draw him from his path.

> *"We shall not cease from exploration and the end of all our exploring will be to arrive where we started . . . and know the place for the first time."*
>
> **T. S. Eliot**

So it will be with us. We are on an expedition, a march into the financial jungle.

So let's begin.

Neil Chapman-Blench   **Alistair Crooks**

May 2009

Introduction

October 2009—The Credit Crunch—The Plot; A Squid and an Octopus Wrestling In a Barrel of Oil!

"The charm of history and its enigmatic lesson consist in the fact that, from age to age, nothing changes and yet everything is completely different."

Aldous Huxley

History; *The luxury of interpretive hindsight applied to the actions and suffering of the participants.*

Neil Chapman-Blench

"The lunatics are running the asylum!"
1987 Stock Market Crash Expression

The Credit Crunch—The key question one may ask is what is a credit crunch?

It is an unexpected tightening of the financial liquidity that enables global trade, commerce and nearly all economic activity to take place. In short it is a catastrophe.

It is, though, a catastrophe of mankind's own making.

Evolution has allowed us to replace the burdensome task of barter and swaps with the exchange of a symbol—money. Money in all its glorious forms—coins, notes, credit cards, debit cards, the internet—has facilitated and fueled human development across the eons. Like a loyal dog it has walked side by side with us from our early beginnings in the Indus Valleys to the vast canyons of glass and steel where the once mighty bankers of Wall Street resided. *Just occasionally on that journey it has turned and bitten us on the arse!*

Maybe it wants to remind us, just as dogs are descended from wolves, that it too is dangerous in nature and temperament. What we saw in those first few months of 2007, and onwards for the next two years, was a tightening of lending between financial institutions. The money that was normally available in the money markets to facilitate trade and commerce was gradually withdrawn back to the originating lender. In effect the banks and other lenders looked at each other, decided they did not like what they saw and chose not to lend to each other.

> *"Look in a mirror and one thing's sure; what we see is not who we are."*
>
> **Richard Bach**

What started as a slow process picked up speed as mass hysteria finally took over. Pandemonium reached its peak as former financial greats Bear Stearns and Lehman Brothers went to the block. Like a patient who has suffered a nasty bout of flu and totters on weakened legs, the world's lenders—specifically bankers—still remain, some few years later, slow to lend despite the heavy hints from their respective governments.

> *"Money is the most egalitarian force in society. It confers power on whoever holds it."*
>
> **Roger Starr**

How could humanity get in such a mess? Have we learned nothing over some six thousand years of civilisation?

Surely it was only a few short years ago that we were told that the newest breed of financial alchemist has been able to eliminate risk. The politicians told us that it was an end of the *"boom to bust"* economic cycle. Surely politicians tell the truth. Ah . . . . so early on we have already found the problem!

"90% of the politicians give the other 10% a bad reputation."
Henry Kissinger

Unfortunately politicians are like the seamen on the Titanic, easy to blame but perhaps not the root cause of the disaster. I have read many interesting articles and a few great books on the credit crunch. In particular those that have focused on the struggle for survival of the great financial firms are especially captivating, mixing human emotions with the momentous economic events that took place in a relatively short period of time.

Can the credit crunch be easily explained?

The answer is, **yes it can.**

The caveat is that is can be answered in two forms. The short term explanation would be what I would term the obvious answer. The answer that rests within the framework created by our generation and which probably has a time span of approximately ten years. There are seven specific major causes:-

1. **Direct Home Ownership**

2. **Securitisation of Risk**

3. **Commission Driven Remuneration**

4. **Ratings Agencies**

5. **Government Sponsored Enterprises**

6. **Regulatory Regimes**

7. **Intellectual Ability**

In this opening chapter we are going to look at these seven factors in detail. It should be remembered that these factors are short term and are like the waves lapping on a beach after a violent storm out at sea. The true story of our banking and economic collapse has its origins in the vast, powerful economic and financial "oceanic" currents that actually control our lives.

1. Direct Home Ownership

At the turn of the millennium politicians in many countries became enamoured with the concept of property ownership. There are a number of sound reasons that home ownership is good for the community and, indirectly, the economy. The benefits put forward by advocates of home ownership are simply that:

-   Those that own their own property will care for that possession better than those who rent it. In fairness to tenants across the globe this tends to be true. Well cared for property enhances the community and lowers the crime rate.

-   The financial benefits of owning your home are substantially greater than other alternative investments. Over a 120 year period property has risen on average between 6 to 7% per annum. This is slightly less than the returns from stock markets but home ownership has the added benefit that it does not require great intellectual work and it is possible to obtain leverage which further enhances the return.

The overall political and social atmosphere at the time was that people should take more care of their financial well being and be less reliant on the state. Of course, for politicians this has the added benefit of removing or reducing the burden of social services and medicare that had been put in place by previous generations and on which payment would soon fall due in a big way. For home ownership it would be easy to transpose the word *"pension"!*

As a property and real estate investor myself I believe strongly in ownership and would encourage it within a controlled environment.

There are a number of variables in home ownership which effect the decision to buy or rent including but not restricted to:-

- *Age*

- *Sex*

- *Parents (if they were themselves home owners)*

- *Race*

- *Education*

- *Family income*

- *Number of children.*

In the United States the policy of increasing home ownership was supported by both the Clinton and Bush administrations. Not only did they support it, they enacted policies to push home ownership downwards into socioeconomic groups that had formally been less owner orientated. This lead to initiatives including the American Dream Downpayment Initiative (ADDI), signed into law in December 2003 and making the month of June, National Home Ownership Month in 2002.

These policies were successful. In ten years white ownership of property rose by 8.28% to over 75%. It was in other less traditional groupings that the policy had most impact within the same time period—Asian-American ownership rose by 17.5%, Native-American rose by 12.57%, African-American rose by 13.59% and Hispanic by 20.14%

The bad news is that, as Karl Marx says: *"The road to Hell is paved with good intentions."*

To achieve this admirable goal of making home ownership more accessible to all and to make the American Dream a reality for the next generation, the US Government both pushed and pulled the financial institutions responsible for home loans to a new reality of financial lending. Not that they needed much encouragement. Drunk on the latest alchemic brew of how to turn base metal into gold or, in this case, risk into securitisation, they were as rats to the Pied Piper.

In effect lending criteria was weakened and relaxed to allow more and more groups to qualify for loans. The boring "red tape" and petty regulations that make up the obstacle course of loan applications were swept aside with an imperious Presidential wave of the hand. In a speech on home ownership by George Bush in June 2002 he said: ***"The third problem is the fact that the rules are too complex. People get discouraged by the fine print on the contracts. They take a look and say, well, I'm not so sure I want to sign this. There's too many words. There's too many pitfalls . . . ."***

In a rather surreal way he blamed the small print lurking at the bottom of mortgage contracts—all those seemingly boring warnings about interest-rate risk, late payments, foreclosure orders, repossession, buyer beware and so on—for locking minorities in America out of home ownership.

Well, if the President wants to encourage the spread of weak, uncontrolled lending who are the banks to stand in his way?

The peak of this President led lending ended with the design of the now infamous **"NINJA"** loans.

N - **No**

I - **Income**

N - **No**

J - **Job**

A - **(or) Assets**

"No Income No Job or Assets"—was there anything more stupid? . . . . and yet at the time it was an accepted lending practice to those without anything to support the loan. These loans formed part of the famous subsection of lending called *"subprime"*; a concept we explore in more detail later in this chapter and deeper within the book.

A New Dawn had arrived.

A financial age of no paperwork, or at least contracts with words no longer than two syllables—thus understandable by a President or Prime Minister! It was all so well suited to an era of fast moving financial products but it proved to be a double edged sword for the lenders. During the eight years leading up to the crisis 80% of US mortgages issued to subprime borrowers were adjustable-rate mortgages. This meant that borrowers paid little or no interest at the beginning of the mortgage but at a certain point they went on to a higher interest rate. It is clear from ongoing litigation in the United States that in many cases this was not clearly explained to the borrowers when they took out their loans.

The balloon of home ownership was close to fully inflated so should we be surprised that it eventually burst? Or perhaps the question we may be thinking is:- *should we blame the United States for the global collapse!*

Of course not!

This was not a limited phenomenon. The majority of the world's governments encouraged their populations to take up direct home ownership but it was most heavily pushed in the United States and the United Kingdom. In short this policy triggered three separate dynamics:-

- **Globally house prices rose as an asset group.**

   In the seven years from the start of the millennium countries were reporting amazing gains in residential homes. This was not just confined to the UK and US but included countries as diverse geographically and physically as Norway, Denmark, Iceland, Australia, South Africa, Estonia, Philippines, Malaysia and Thailand. By 2007 it was estimated that 60% of the United Kingdom's entire net wealth was held in property!

- **Banks created more money.**

  It may seem impossible for banks to just "create" more money. For most of us we assume that money is a limited commodity dependent, or rather controlled, by normal rules of the universe. As you read this book the true secret of banking will be revealed to you. At this point you will have to trust me that money can be created by the stroke of a pen or a computer keyboard—*it is of unlimited supply!*

  To meet the unprecedented demand for mortgage funds to acquire residential property the banks, with the tacit approval of central bankers, created more money that was feed enthusiastically into the voracious maw of the global economy.

- **Housing stock and mortgages ended up in weak hands.**

  In 2006/07 the total US housing mortgage market was estimated at US$6.5 trillion, of which US$1.3 trillion was in subprime mortgages. In effect 20% of the total mortgage market was in the hands of those who had no history of home ownership i.e. the weakest financial sector of society. Leaving aside the possibility of fraudulent mortgages, the vast majority of this new mortgage sector had no financial reserves with which to weather any downturn in their own or their community's finances. *This is the financial equivalent of trying to cross the ocean on a lilo.*

Even if you look at it through rose tinted spectacles, the conclusion one would draw is that by 2007 the well intentioned policies of enlightened politicians and planners over ten years or so, depending on which country you view, had created the world's largest asset bubble.

2. Securitisation of Risk

Risk, in finance, is defined as the possibility of loss in an investment or speculation. A banker's task, and I use the word banker to cover lenders of every hue, is to reduce or eliminate the risk in every transaction they undertake to an *acceptable* level.

Why is the word *acceptable* in italics?

By definition all investments carry risk so it is up to the individual or institution to determine the level of risks that they are comfortable with. There are two main criteria for bankers when they evaluate the risk attached to any loan:-

- **The collateral upon which the loan will be secured.**

  Property has been viewed historically as a safe investment. Although there have often been real estate crashes, the long term trend of property prices is upward. Banks, therefore, take the view that if a lender defaults they will be able to seize the physical property and sell it themselves to repay the loan obligation. This has an inherent advantage over other forms of lending, including loans to businesses, in which liquidation is a more difficult and costly operation. The amount lent against any form of property is known as the loan to value or LTV. Most commonly this ranges from 70% to 100% of the current value of the asset or the purchase price, whichever is the lower. A simple rule of thumb is that the more buoyant the overall market, the higher the LTV rate will be i.e. more will be loaned against it.

- **The ability of the borrower to make repayments of the loan principal and to sustain payment of the agreed interest rate over the set time period of the loan.**

  The lender needs to be confident the borrower can sustain any payments, primarily those of interest that will be required during the period of the loan.

As we can see from the above, the banking systems adopted a policy of a more tolerant lending practice during the years from 2000 onwards. This was strongly encouraged by their respective governments. ***Bankers took less account of a lender's ability to repay than the value of the collateral!***

Although this may appear to be risky, bankers were reassured by the growth of securitisation of banking products. The broad theory is that if loans were bunched together the risk was substantially reduced. This was viewed as a form of diversification. It works as follows:-

- A bank would place a number of loans together.

- These loans would be transferred to a special purpose entity (SPE).

- Tranches of these SPEs would be sold to other investors including other banks. These tranches contained various forms of mortgages and had different risk profiles. The investment returns to investors varied according to the type of risk they were willing to purchase.

- These tranches are commonly known as Collateralised Debt Obligations (CDOs).

The first of these CDOs was issued in 1987 but they became more prolific after the invention of risk pricing modules, including the Black Scholes Theory and the Gaussian Copula models. Although these theories are tricky for the lay person to understand, and indeed for most bankers, they give lenders the appearance of ***reassurance*** that they can price risk. Of course history proves that, despite people gaining Nobel prizes for economics for these types of formulas, they are in fact nonsensical. For those who would disagree with me I refer you to the Credit Crunch 2007 to 2009!

So far so good! We have a situation whereby banks lend to the general public, secured on residential property and they are then able to subdivide those loans into thin slices of risk which they can sell to other investors. Sounds great; a sound business with the risk spread over a number of investors.

The first apparent weakness to appear was that a ***moral hazard*** had been created. Before securitisation the banks were in effect lending their own money or reserves but now they were passing the risk onwards, or worse sideways, to other financial institutions. Thus in their own minds they could take larger/higher risks as they were not in the final event going to pick up the tab if everything went wrong. Lending criteria slipped further towards the garbage bin.

The next problem for the banks was if circumstances should dictate a situation when they could not securitise the debt and sell it onwards. It was in effect a giant game of musical chairs with everybody trying to guess when the music would stop.

The next major problem was who was buying these newly created CDOs? The answer of course is mutual funds, pension funds, investment companies and finally ***other banks!***

As if the whole lending structure was not already complex enough, the banks, in particular JP Morgan, invented Credit Default Swaps (CDS) to add to the explosive mix. A CDS is a complex form of insurance that banks and other financial institutions use to "reduce" risk. Unlike traditional insurance this instrument has a number of unique points:

-   They are generally unregulated.

-   The buyers of CDSs generally do not keep "reserves" or indeed are not obligated to keep reserves as one would normally expect in a prudent risk business relationship. They tend to sell on or create further CDSs to alleviate their own risk.

We discuss CDOs and CDSs in detail in the forthcoming chapters but I am sure you can see the apparent difficulty. Everyone was selling to everybody else in the financial arena so in reality the risk was not leaving the system; ***it became the system!***

3. Commission Driven Remuneration

In business the benefits of commission driven remuneration over traditional pay scales are obvious. For a higher output you are rewarded accordingly i.e. you receive more money. It is good for the individual who is earning more as they feel they are getting a direct reward for putting in more effort. For the business it is a win / win situation as well. Whilst they are paying more out in pay the company is getting more from their employees in terms of effort, output, sales, etc.

It is only in the financial arena that this self-evident mutually beneficial set of circumstances manages to take this simple concept, put it through the Alice in Wonderland's Looking Glass and come up with its own distinctive process for remuneration. This is the "Heads I Win, Tails You Lose" system found in the small print of the HR employment manuals of all investment banks.

Let's have a quick glance at some of the highest paid bankers in 2006:-

Lloyd C. Blankflein	Goldman Sachs	US$54.3 million
E. Stanley O'Neill	Merrill Lynch	US$46.4 million
John J. Mack	Morgan Stanley	US$41.4 million
James E. Cayne	Bear Stearns	US$40.0 million
James Dimon	JP Morgan	US$38.3 million
Richard S. Fauld	Lehman Brothers	US$28.2 million
Charles O. Prince	Citigroup	US$24.9 million

There is a moral argument on whether you should reward people with 1,200 times the average annual income in the United States but that is outside the remit of this book. If you take the capitalist view, then these high earnings are surely the reward for the individual's major contribution and heavy responsibility for growing their companies in outstanding fashion over the financial year. Let's see what happened to the share price of those companies in the same period:-

Lloyd C. Blankflein	Goldman Sachs	US$54.3 million	**+91%**
E. Stanley O'Neill	Merrill Lynch	US$46.4 million	**-0.7%**
John J. Mack	Morgan Stanley	US$41.4 million	**+43.5%**
James E. Cayne	Bear Stearns	US$40.0 million	**-0.7%**
James Dimon	JP Morgan	US$38.3 million	**+24.7%**
Richard S. Fauld	Lehman Brothers	US$28.2 million	**-3.0%**
Charles O. Prince	Citigroup	US$24.9 million	**-6.8%**

So, out of seven leading bankers it could be strongly argued that three of them Blankflein, Mack and Dimon earned their just rewards, producing a total increase in stock price of a minimum of 24.7%. Of the others, who took home a total of US$139.5 million between them, they could not even get their stock price to remain at the same level as 12 months earlier.

It should be noted that in the next 12 months Bear Stearns went broke and was sold for US$10 per share to JP Morgan, Lehman filed for the largest bankruptcy in history and E. Stanley O'Neill left Merrill Lynch after it posted a record third quarter loss of US$2.3 billion due to taking a staggering US$8.4 billion write down on subprime mortgages and other toxic debt.

What of Citigroup you may ask?

By November 2008 it was insolvent and had to rely on the government to pump over US$45 billion of direct aid and US$306 billion of disguised aid into its dying corporate body. In the end the US Government became its largest shareholder in order to prevent its total failure.

Think all that is bad, wait till you hear this!

And what of E. Stanley O'Neill, the former CEO of Merrill Lynch—he got a **US$161 million** dollar severance package for his part in his company's overall negative performance. It begs the question—*what would he have got if they had done well under his leadership!*

This may seem pretty weird to the average man in the street—that bad performance is rewarded with riches beyond the dreams of most mortal men but this is how the financial world functions. Unfortunately a system like this is pervasive. It is the insanity of acceptable behavior. It is why no one questions the Emperor's new clothes!

This system of **"Commission Driven Remuneration"** saturates the entire system and although it encourages hard work it makes people do things that they would not normally do. In the investment banks the dealers and their supervisors on trading desks, take bigger risks knowing that those risks are underwritten by the strength of linked balance sheets. Bankers, with PhDs in mathematics, design and create bigger CDOs and CDSs and sell them to unsuspecting fund managers for the pension portfolios they administer. They do this in the full knowledge that those risks are not minimised but rather they will be rewarded by the total amount of debt they can shift from their balance sheet onto somebody else's.

Even right at the bottom of the pyramid we find the same problem. Those that arrange/sell mortgages are paid on commission. Thus we find as more and more mortgage products are forced down the chain, the salesmen at the sharp end are often deceiving the mortgage applicant by failing to point out the full implications of mortgages, such as the often fatal reset mechanism. On the other side they were often seen to be encouraging deception of the mortgage lender by falsifying, or at least turning a blind eye, to misleading data provided by the borrowers.

So we have a system whose work force is motivated by commission driven sales. Not the best suited to ensure rigorous self control.

4. Ratings Agencies

Ratings agencies include famous companies like Moody's, Dun & Bradstreet, Standard & Poor's and Fitch. Their principal role is to attach a risk rating to the products created and financially engineered by banks and financial institutions. They analyse a company or a bond, looking at the creditworthiness of the lender and the relative credit risk that can be ascribed to that individual instrument. In the case of debt offerings they will also look at a particular tranche of debt in relation to its position in the overall debt of a company or institution i.e. is it subordinated?

Using these assessments the Credit Rating Agencies then attach a rating to the debt. These are fairly industry standard ranging from AAA to D. ***Why is this important?***

Institutions, investors, banks, insurance companies and market makers view these ratings as independent and an easy to use guide to the risk attached to any particular instrument or institution. A new bond issue will always have a minimum of one rating and more often as many as three ratings so investors can clearly see what they are getting. It means that bond issues, including CDOs, can be clearly valued, quickly priced and safe for all to use. It makes the capital markets easy to read and understand.

Or does it?

There is, as always in the financial arena, a hidden problem. The half glimpse of the dorsal fin before it sinks beneath the choppy sea some 100 meters away from where you are swimming. In my office I have a picture of a convict and a jailer talking between the bars of a cell:

The convict says: *Do you think I should be buying stocks at these prices?*

The jailer answers: *I have no idea! All I know is never to buy them from a man who sells you the advice!*

Or to put it more succinctly*:*

> **"No one wants advice—only corroboration."**
> **John Steinbeck**

The Credit Rating Agencies suffered from one serious problem; they are in business. Thus, they had to earn monies from the operation of their businesses. In the market place they chose to be paid by the issuer of the debt. A logical choice given that the other side of the equation would be very difficult to enforce i.e. the recipients of the information.

I am sure you can see a classic conflict of interest.

This conflict of interest was further compounded by the fact that the Credit Rating Agencies were in competition with each other for the debt issuers' business. It was in their commercial interests to attach the *highest* rating to a bond issue in order that their client, the debt issuer, was able to sell and issue the largest amount possible of that particular issue.

The best possible interpretation is that in most cases the Rating Agencies will lean towards giving the highest possible ratings to even dodgy debt whilst the more cynical amongst us would say they would give the rating they are paid to give.

A little known fact is that many Credit Rating Agencies run advisory arms. These offer investors services which include advising on the structure of debt issues. It would seem impossible for a Credit Rating Agency to advise a client on a debt issue and then fail to give it the highest possible debt rating!

On the eve of the Credit Crunch a number of reviews and investigations by the SEC in the United States had started to identify these structural weaknesses in the risk assessment system. Changes were made based on those reviews but it was too little too late. Not only had the horse bolted but the stable was on fire!

5. Government Sponsored Enterprises (GSEs)

In this section I am talking primarily about the **Federal National Mortgage Association**, known as *Fannie Mae* and also its brother agency the **Federal Home Loan Mortgage Corporation**, commonly referred to as *Freddie Mac*. We cover both these agencies in detail in Chapter 10 but it is important I touch upon them now. You may wonder, if this is a global experience we all went through, why we are now focusing on two domestic US agencies.

Well the answer to that is:-

-   the US is the largest nation on earth in terms of its economic GDP

-   the US dollar is the world's de facto reserve currency

-   the US has the largest value of residential housing stock in the world.

Like all things in life, the Credit Crunch had to start somewhere and like fire investigators we are trying to trace its original origins.

> *"Your own property is concerned when your neighbour's house is on fire."*
>
> **Horace**

In short, following the Great Crash of 1929 President Roosevelt needed to introduce safety measures to prevent similar exploitation of monetary instruments leading to another fiscal disaster and also stimulation measures to ensure the great American business bandwagon started rolling once more. Leaning towards the side of stimulation, in 1938 Congress passed a charter to allow the formation of the Federal National Mortgage Association which was set up as a stockholder enterprise but with the added status of a government sponsored agency.

This simple and well intentioned charter led to the misleading understanding that the US government was ultimately guaranteeing the whole enterprise. Indeed, ultimately it did have to guarantee the whole shebang but that was not the original intention.

The purpose of this hybrid was to expand the secondary mortgage market by allowing an early form of securitisation to take place with mortgages. The agency was to take over a vast number of mortgage backed securities thus removing them from lenders' balance sheets and allowing the lenders to relend their balance sheets. A sort of wholesaler lender to the banks' retail lending.

Very clever, very smart and generally successful as a stimulation measure after the austerity and reverse gearing effects of the Great Depression!

As you read Chapter 10 you will also see that in 1968 the Government National Mortgage Association known as "Ginnie Mae" was spun out of "Fannie Mae". In 1970 the US government created the Federal Home Loan Mortgage Corporation known as "Freddie Mac" to compete with its original creation just in case it was slacking in the lending market. In the same time span it also chose to make a change to full private share ownership which neatly removed it from the Federal budget. Smart but not smart enough.

God bless Capitalism!

> *"However beautiful the strategy, you should occasionally look at the results."*
>
> **Winston Churchill**

In short the perfect storm was sweeping into the hallowed halls of the GSEs and everybody had left the shutters open! Having been forced into the private sector like a crying child on its first day of school it found that the only thing the private investor is truly interested in is . . . . profit!

> *"As one digs deeper into the national character of the Americans, one sees that they have sought the value of*

everything in this world only in the answer to this single question: how much money will it bring in?"
Alexis de Tocqueville

The agencies had to learn to compete with the market forces and expand their business which they did.

By the middle of 2008 Fannie Mae and Freddie Mac owned or guaranteed about half or 56.8% of the US's $12 trillion mortgage market.

I would like you to pause and read over the above sentence again as it is so mind boggling!

By the middle of 2008 Fannie Mae and Freddie Mac owned or guaranteed about half or 56.8% of the US's $12 trillion mortgage market!

This is unreal.

"One man alone can be pretty dumb sometimes, but for real bona fide stupidity, there ain't nothin' can beat teamwork."
Edward Abbey

In order to compete with the private sector and answer the call of at least two presidents, Clinton and Bush, these agencies had lowered their lending standards and loaded up securitised mortgages, primarily in the subprime sector, like a starving man at a free eat-all-you-can buffet!

Then the tidal wave of foreclosures arrived and the boat was swamped. Given the GSE's amazing hold over the lending market it was inevitable that the US government, through its left and right finance hands—the US Treasury and the Federal Reserve, would have to step in to preserve the agencies. It did this through the twin measures of granting access to Federal Reserve low-interest loans to both agencies—access to the print room in effect—and removing the prohibition on the Treasury Department to purchase GSE stock.

On October 21 2010 Federal Housing Finance Agency estimated the bailout of Freddie Mac and Fannie Mae will likely cost US taxpayers $224-360 billion in total. ***Happy Thanksgiving!***

6. Regulatory Regimes

The Credit Crunch was avoidable.

Logic would dictate that we may expect extreme over exuberance from retail bankers, investment bankers and stockbrokers when in the epicenter of an asset boom. Simple history shows us that markets, in particular stock and bond markets, suffer from extreme booms and slumps. We should expect those that work at the coal face, as a multimillionaire trader of my acquaintance likes to call it, of investment banking to become locked in the excitement of the moment. Indeed their whole basis of remuneration revolves round riding these upward trends for as long and hard as possible. The problem for them is to know when to get off the ride before the animal dies underneath them!

So if we cannot expect the participants of the party to exhibit good and sensible behavior who should we turn to? Who is the designated driver?

The logical answer must be the regulators and those who appoint them; the political body. It would seem that those who are paid to regulate would indeed carry out that function and would have been able to at least pick up warning signals even if they were unable to prevent the eventual avalanche!

Did they do that? Absolutely not!

In the worse case of negligence since the Roman fire brigade went off to listen to Nero play his fiddle whilst the greater part of their metropolis burnt to the ground, the various regulatory bodies did nothing to prevent the crash or indeed highlight the perils appearing. Indeed to stretch the "Rome burning" analogy further they were like firemen who tried to put fires out with kerosene. ***They were as useful as an ashtray on a motorcycle!***

Here are a few classic examples:-

-   In the United States the regulatory bodies were not supported and paid for by central government. They were paid for by those that they supervised. So the more institutions they supervised the stronger and more financially viable the regulatory body would be. In the era of global mega-banks and a plethora of regulatory bodies to choose from, these institutions could literally select which body they would like to be supervised by. Human nature and greed being what it is, they were bound to select the body that had the lightest touch!

    In just such an era we have the vivid picture of James Gilleran, head of the US Office of Thrift Supervision, being pictured in 2003 holding a chainsaw to a pile of paper wrapped in red tape. The visual representation of the removal of regulatory control was a great photo shoot opportunity—my question would be, if you—a generally sane reader of this book—saw a man using a chainsaw as a plaything would you entrust him with the supervision of one of the most vital areas of the economy. I think not!

-   The Federal Reserve is the arch-bastion of conservative banking and the primary supervisor of the banking sector. This institution is the final word in the US financial arena, unlike in the UK where we have a very handy system of pass-the-parcel. It was amusing, in a surreal way, to watch UK television documentaries where the blame for the eventual collapse of the Barclays bid for Lehman Brothers was passed about like a proverbial hot potato! The Treasury, under Alistair Darling, passed the question (and blame) to Mervyn King at the Bank of England. Mervyn King then deftly passed the same question and blame attachment to Hector Sants, Chief Executive of the FSA. Sants, with dexterity worthy of a full time politician as opposed to a public servant, neatly returned it back to Alistair Darling so the whole process could start again. It was a mesmerising performance more worthy of a New Zealander All Black rugby side passing the ball down the line than a serious economic documentary!

The "Fed" is covered and mentioned in detail throughout the book, in particular in Chapter 2, so we will not go into it in a big way now other than to consider the role of Alan Greenspan. His philosophy of regulatory control over the vast financial arena under his watch was to exhibit a "light touch" to the reins of control. Admirable if you mix with bankers and are not paid on results.

- The phenomenal growth of the OTC derivatives markets from 2000 to 2007 alarmed many market participants, the most famous being Warren Buffett who termed such instruments *"financial weapons of mass destruction"*. In a noted speech to the Federal Reserve Bank of Chicago's Forty-First Annual Conference on the 5th May 2005 Alan Greenspan stated he thought that the market would successfully absorb and embrace these new instruments without need of supervision.

Not content with this rather lame response to a financial market that had already grown to $220 trillion in June 2004, Greenspan then actively fought against anyone else who attempted to force any form of regulation on the market participants. The most concerted attempt was by the CBOT, the Chicago Board of Trade, who wanted to assume the role of regulator to this burgeoning financial market. Established in 1848 the CBOT is the largest and oldest futures and options exchange and therefore had direct experience in these more esoteric instruments. Over a three year period they lobbied for tighter control of these instruments and to be the chief regulatory body. They were fought off successfully by a combination of politicians, bankers, the US Treasury and most fervently by the Federal Reserve Bank of New York under Alan Greenspan. It is possible to have some sympathy with those undertaking the job of head of the Federal Reserve. It is a complex job made more difficult by balancing both growth and restraint in the economy through the banking system whilst fending off nearly every politician and interest group in the country. However it is not an obligation to accept the job. Secondly, if somebody comes along who offers to regulate a growing, fast moving and complex financial area it would sensible to embrace them with open arms rather than show them the closed door.

It is said that people get the government they deserve so maybe our own greed and mental outlook during that era led us to elect governments around the world who embraced less legislation and sought to cut regulation rather than increase it. A sweeping generalisation is dangerous!

It seems that in the UK where financial services were the paramount contributor to GDP, banks and financial institutions where able to hold sway or at least resist Government intervention. Yet in nearly every other aspect of our lives regulation and government intervention has grown not diminished. A simple measure is the Tolley's UK Tax Guide which over 10 years of Labour Government grew from one volume to six! The UK can now boast the longest tax code in the world to add to its list of other memorable financial achievements, including selling off its gold reserves at a 20 year low. History will look back and record that a UK government that had time to regulate against a lollipop lady wearing a Christmas hat was unable to regulate the largest financial market that had ever been created in capitalist history.

Shame on you and shame on politicians of every hue, everywhere!

> *"O shame! Where is they blush?"*
>
> **William Shakespeare**

7. Intellectual Ability

People always assume they are cleverer than they actually are. I know this because I am cleverer than other people and so able to judge—*see it can happen to anyone!*

> *"It's only hubris if I fail!"*
>
> **Julius Caesar**

Comparing me to Julius Caesar is of course hubris in itself!

"I have been called many things, but never an intellectual."
Tullulah Bankhead

Joking apart, having worked in the financial arena for many years it is easily possible to adopt an air of arrogance and superiority in relation to the outside world. The environment, and in particular, the high monetary rewards are geared towards producing a feeling of elitism.

Few knew and really understood the new financial world's instruments including CDSs and CDOs to name a few. Yet they were quite willing to actively sell those instruments and, if they were on the opposite side of the fence, stuff their investment funds and pension accounts full of high risk instruments. Their forlorn cry now would be:-

"Everyone else was doing it"!

Or alternatively . . .

"I was made to do it"!

Whichever one of the above the guilty participants adopt then it shows a remarkable simplicity in their intellectual ability. If everyone else was doing it that does not make it right or correct. As mother used to say *"would you jump off a cliff if everybody else was doing so?"* Lemmings need not reply! If you do not question what you are doing then my intellectual ability argument always holds water.

The second argument that *"I was made to do it"* is normally the last bastion of defence in a war crimes trial and we know how they normally end up.

In every facet of the financial arena from mortgage brokers and potential home owners sitting on sofas and going through NINJA loans, to the double-cuffed bankers who bundled them up into securitised loans and sold them to fund managers, who bought them with money released into the system by the regulators sitting in central banks and government departments across the nations, no one stopped to ask what they were doing.

Nobody in that cast of thousands had the intellectual ability to understand what they were dealing with and the risks inherent in the products they handled!

"Since it is seldom clear whether intellectual activity denotes a superior mode of being or a vital deficiency, opinion swings between considering intellect a privilege and seeing it as a handicap"

Jacques Barzun

Conclusion

For many the Credit Crunch of 2007 can be summed up, blamed or at least attributed to the seven deadly sins mentioned above. That is true . . . . but it is not the real story.

Fascinating as the account of the last ten years is, it is like the light of a candle next to a burning building when compared to the story of humanities' epic battle to control the financial beast it has created. As I delved back further in time it seemed that not only had we created this beast but every time we felt we were its master it broke free and wreaked havoc.

The true financial beast is so vast, complex and powerful that we truly have little real control over it—*even those who feel they are in charge are deluding themselves!*

The true story is to understand how this potent beast evolved. How it became the dominant force of our everyday lives and yet remains invisible to the considerable majority of the world's population. How even those who work within it do not truly comprehend its immeasurable power!

We speak of it as a living entity yet it has no body, no head, and no life force as we understand it, yet it is wrapped around our society tighter than ivy on a tree.

That is the true story we hope to uncover within this book—to understand and to comprehend how we have appointed our own master and live by its dictates.

So lets us explore the true Madness of Money.

> *"It is good to have an end to journey towards but it is the journey that matters in the end."*
>
> **Ursula K Leguinn**

Chapter 1

April 2007—New Century: 100 Years of Mortgage Mayhem

"It is the beginning of the end!"

Talleyrand

April 2nd 2007—New Century Financial Corp declares bankruptcy.

The word mortgage was first used in 1390 but was not formally defined until 1590. The word mortgage comes from the mort—which is derived from the Latin word mori—for death and—gage is from the sense of that word meaning a pledge to forfeit something of value if a debt is not repaid. So mortgage is literally a death pledge!

What is a mortgage? Why do we use it? And why does it matter for us if it is toxic?

Mortgage Meltdown, the mayhem begins: On March 5, 2007 an ominous ripple swept through financial markets. New Century Financial, the United States' second largest lender of so-called 'subprime' mortgages, suffered a 69 percent decline in shareholder value, which sparked a virtual run on similar companies that specialised in providing financing to buyers with less than perfect credit. By April 2 of that year, New Century would be forced into bankruptcy, losing over 98 percent of its value after suffering devastating losses from rising loan defaults.

How did the second largest lender in this industry succumb to such a fate? Not only did the mortgage giant collapse, causing the immediate

1

loss of 3,200 jobs and billions of dollars in losses, company executives including CEO Brad Morrice were investigated on criminal charges relating to dealings in company securities and accounting irregularities. How does a once-high flying firm such as New Century go from trading at $64 per share in December 2004 to being de-listed from the New York Stock Exchange and trading for mere pennies only three years later?

In many ways, the rise and fall of New Century Financial would pre-sage the implosion of the housing and credit markets in the years to come. As we shall see in this chapter, the exponential growth and success of the firm and its subsequent collapse directly paralleled the economic conditions not just in the United States but globally as well; the manner in which it rose to such heights and then fell just as quickly serves as a potent lesson for investors and consumers alike, and is telling of the problems that have plagued—and continue to affect—markets across the world.

In this chapter, we will detail New Century's growth and collapse, from its founding in 1995 to its eventual demise in 2007. We will also explore the issue of debt securitisation, which contributed both to the success of firms such as New Century but also of Wall Street and the financial industry more generally. All of this is directly related to the massive growth in the housing market and the insatiable appetite for consumer debt of all types, and was due at least in part to the economic policies of the Bush Administration in the early years of this decade. Lessons to be learned from the implosion of New Century are many, but none perhaps more critical than the interrelated nature of the capital markets of today. Importantly, this is not just an American phenomenon, and investors around the globe need to be aware of these issues so they can protect themselves from future shocks.

New Century Financial—A Giant Emerges

> *"In all realms of life it takes courage to stretch your limits, express your power, and fulfill your potential, it's no different in the financial realm"*
>
> **Suze Orman**

Three former executives of Option One Mortgage founded New Century Financial in 1995. Bob Cole, Brad Morrice and Ed Gotschall were veterans of the mortgage lending industry, and after making their first loan in 1996, took their new company public a year later. Its rapid success led to rapid growth and immense profits, and in 1998 New Century earned the Ernst & Young Entrepreneur of the Year award for financial services in Orange County, California. By 2002, New Century was added to the NASDAQ Financial 100 index, and in 2003 was ranked twelfth on Fortune Magazine's list of the 100 fastest growing companies. Only two years later in 2005, it would rank third on the Wall Street Journal's list of best performing companies, and a year later, it would become the second largest originator of subprime mortgage loans.

New Century was able to expand so rapidly because it concentrated on what was at the time an underserved section of the mortgage market. The term 'subprime' refers to lending that is associated with borrowers with less than perfect credit. In many cases, loans were made to borrowers with little or no credit history, or who may not have qualified for traditional loans based upon their income or ability to afford a down payment. Lenders typically charged higher rates of interest for loans of this type, and over the next decade innovations in finance led to the advent of new products such as interest-only and adjustable-rate mortgages. These provided an avenue of lending for new home purchases and refinancing as a result of the inbuilt flexibility of their payment terms and borrowing rates.

Interest-only mortgages allowed borrowers to defer the repayment of their mortgage principal, usually for a period of up to five years. As the largest component of the monthly mortgage payment, this offered significant flexibility and greatly increased the affordability of home purchases, whether for first-time buyers or those looking to refinance. Adjustable-rate mortgages came in an even wider variety of flavours. Some of these featured balloon payments with higher borrowing costs that would take effect several years after a loan was originated. Others even offered an extremely low 'teaser' interest rate, at or even below prime borrowing rates; in some cases, borrowers could even pay less than what they owed for some initial period, with the difference between what was owed and what was repaid being added onto the principal of the loan each month. Interest-only and adjustable-rate mortgages were often combined as hybrid products, seemingly offering the best of both worlds.

It is easy to see how New Century enjoyed such phenomenal success. In California, where they were headquartered, 60 percent of all new mortgages in 2005 were interest-only or negative-amortisation. These loans were, in essence, gambles that prices would continue to rise. The record high numbers of home sales at record high prices continued unabated. At the same time, and due to various new forms of riskier mortgages, more than 40 percent of first-time buyers—and 25 percent of all buyers—made no down payment on their home purchase, making them especially vulnerable to a downturn in resale prices. New Century went from its fledgling beginnings, originating some $2 billion in mortgages in 1998 to over $60 billion in 2006. Profits soared as the company tapped a seemingly endless stream of fees from new buyers and existing homeowners refinancing their loans.

One can see why these new, more flexible loans were so attractive. In the early 2000's, interest rates were at historical lows. Since the attacks of 9/11 and the bursting of the technology bubble, the US economy was in rough shape. Federal Reserve Chairman Alan Greenspan pushed for very low interest rates and then maintained them for a very long time. Whether we like it or not, our economies depend upon lending for growth, because consumers and businesses alike need access to borrowed funds in order to buy expensive items. For regular consumers, this usually means high-priced goods such as appliances, automobiles and houses. All this added up to a good time for first-time homebuyers to enter the market. It also meant a new wave of refinancing, as current owners sought to capture these new low borrowing rates by refinancing their existing mortgages. The new Bush Administration in the White House needed to stoke the fires of growth to pull the economy out of recession, and they openly encouraged a new boom in housing and finance. It seems even Presidents can suffer from short term memory failure.

> *"Debt is the fatal disease of republics, the first thing and the mightiest to undermine governments and corrupt the people."*
>
> **Wendell Phillips**

By 2005, by all rational measures the housing market had become overheated. The bubble was getting ready to burst. In many areas, local economies were wholly concentrated in housing and urban development. Homeowners repeatedly refinanced their mortgages in order to tap the equity that had been rapidly built up, and this fed into ever more consumer spending. This wasn't a Ponzi trap or pyramid scheme *per se*, but while it wasn't illegal, it certainly wasn't sustainable. Principal payments on mortgages would inevitably have to be made, but by that time, rates would be on the rise, making an untenable situation even more precarious. Homeowners who had already financed too much were invariably saddled with even higher payments, as their interest-only periods expired and higher interest rates quickly kicked in.

As interest rates had been kept artificially low for so long, inflation became a primary risk to the economy. Fed Chairman Ben Bernanke inherited this challenge as Greenspan's successor, and began a steady process of raising rates, in order to stave off further price increases. Commodities were booming as a result, chief among them oil, which put even greater pressure on consumer spending. This made it even harder for the average person to afford their escalating mortgages and other credit obligations.

The credit crisis that began in 2007 was in many respects the perfect storm, but it was reminiscent of the wave of calamities that struck seemingly independent markets in 1998. Housing prices were grossly overvalued; in relation to rents, prices had grown as much as 35% higher than they should have been. The ratio of homeowners to renters had risen as well, but was not supported by an equivalent increase in household incomes, meaning that housing debt-to-income ratios were out of line. Disposable income continued to be drained away by high consumer prices elsewhere in the economy. This is how the economic downturn began.

When the crunch came, it would prove to be more severe and more prolonged than most people had thought it would be. The Economist had predicted in 2005 that even a leveling of house prices would have drastic consequences for the economy. By this time, consumer spending and residential construction accounted for 90% of the total growth in the American GDP from 2001-2005, and more than 40% of all private-sector jobs created since 2001 were in housing-related sectors, including construction and mortgage brokering. As prices leveled, investors began to sell the homes they had speculated upon. Once the extent of over-supply in homes truly became known, it put even more downward pressure on housing prices. Many homeowners had repeatedly refinanced their mortgages and effectively turned their homes into ATM machines to support unsustainable spending. The reality of their precarious position began to set in—they owed more than their homes were worth.

> *"If you think nobody cares if you're alive, try missing a couple of house payments".*
>
> **Anonymous Home Owner**

As the wave of selling continued, it began to reverberate throughout the wider economy. The sharp decrease in consumer spending in every sector of the economy meant a lack of demand for manufactured goods, which put further downward pressure on prices and quickly affected corporate earnings across the globe.

The effects on New Century were catastrophic. New Century's approach to the mortgage business was predicated on the explosion in mortgage financing, and they concentrated on serving those individuals that were not able to obtain financing through traditional means. As we've seen, this most often meant that these were borrowers with imperfect credit histories or income levels. Predictably, as the housing market cooled and began to implode in many areas around the United States, New Century also began to feel the squeeze. As the nation's second largest subprime lender, they were heavily exposed and had little, if any, insulation against the downturn and the subsequent surge in loan defaults by their subprime clientele.

It is no surprise that this flew in the face of the once-infallible credit rating models that sought to explain away the inherent risk of these mortgages. In addition to this, companies such as New Century had made wide use of 'advanced' automated underwriting methods that made fast work of what should have been a complex decision-making process, based upon the creditworthiness of each individual applicant. Looking back, the risks of New Century's business model were monumental, and indeed, they and millions of investors would end up paying the ultimate price for their gamble.

These risks, of course, seemed to be explained away on virtually every level. As it happens in every bubble, investors were certain that the good times would have no end. Homeowners, mortgage companies, and investors who bought the 'end product' of mortgage securities on the secondary market were all making money, and it seemed that the rise in home prices could and would go on forever. There seemed to be an endless ability to refinance, which in large part continued to influence the downplaying of the inherent risk of these new mortgage products. However, as Ben Bernanke's Fed began to raise interest rates in June 2004, the cooling of the housing market soon fed into a rising tide of mortgage defaults. As homebuyers continued to suffer under the weight of higher energy prices and rising rates for all manner of consumer debt, mortgage defaults began to skyrocket. In the fourth quarter of 2006, late payments on subprime mortgages hit a four-year high, according to the US Mortgage Bankers' Association, and it was reported that one in five high-risk mortgages taken out that year would end in repossession, easily eclipsing any previous foreclosure experience in modern financial history.

Despite the apparently obvious change in the weather, New Century continued to originate ever riskier mortgages under what had been previously 'valid' assumptions about their subprime clientele's ability to both take on debt and continue the pace of refinancing. By the end of 2006, their models began to fail under the mounting pressure of mortgage defaults. Investor demand for the high-yielding mortgage securities in turn dried up, and as this process played out, New Century began to face calls from their own creditors. Without the ability to repackage and sell the risky mortgages, New Century became abruptly unable to service its own credit lines. Without financial backing for its operations, New Century announced on March 8, 2007 that it would stop accepting new loan applications. A week earlier, it had also announced that it faced a criminal probe into its accounting practices, and without critical financing from its Wall Street bankers—the "lifeblood" of non-bank mortgage companies like New Century—the doors quickly slammed shut and abruptly ended the party.

By March 12, 2007, New Century's shares had lost 90% of their value and $1.5 billion in market capitalisation was wiped out; trading on the NYSE was halted, and soon thereafter, the company was de-listed altogether. In the words of CEO Brad Morrice, "Given the sudden and significant challenges facing our industry and New Century specifically, bankruptcy is the best means available to allow the company's assets and operations to be sold through an orderly process." New Century filed for bankruptcy on April 2, 2007, and with its assets sold off piecemeal, the saga came to an abrupt end.

What had gone wrong? What had occurred behind the scenes to bring this mortgage giant to its knees in such swift and punishing fashion? Part of the answer lies in how New Century ran its business. As we have seen, it was built upon servicing a particular subset of the borrowing population, which exposed it to extreme amounts of risks that, in the end, could not be explained away by complex credit rating models or automated analytical underwriting techniques. New Century's lending standards were, in retrospect, wholly inadequate. It is said that a rising tide floats all boats, and they were literally only kept afloat by the seemingly endless rise in housing prices and apparently unending supply of mortgage refinances. New Century was also highly leveraged, controlling over $25 billion in assets with little more than $2 billion in equity, which left little margin for error. The combination of rising defaults on their mortgages and the inability to sell its bundled mortgage portfolios to government sponsored enterprises such as Fannie Mae and others would prove toxic for New Century. The rest of the answer can be found in the complex and intricate web of the secondary debt market, to which we now turn.

Securitising the Mortgage Industry

"*Finance is the art of passing currency from hand to hand until it finally disappears.*"
Robert W. Sarnoff

Prior to exploring the issue of securitisation of mortgage debt, let's briefly return to the issue of housing in the greater picture of the overall economy. As we know, what led to the housing boom, just as much as the historically low rates, was the unprecedented access to easy financing for so many borrowers. We all know that Wall Street's appetite for risk is insatiable, and this hunger—measured by the demand for high-yield investments—seemingly had no bounds in the early 2000's. Lending standards of companies such as New Century were relaxed, enticing those with low incomes, poor credit, and often little or no down payments to borrow too much. The new innovations in the mortgages themselves meant that borrowers no longer would be required to pay their interest, at least for some initial period, and in some cases, even the principal could be deferred. The mortgages themselves were then 'bundled' together, packaged up and sold off to institutional investors as complex debt instruments in the bond markets.

This process of securitisation was truly at the heart of the problem, and would later lead to the larger credit crisis that has gripped the global economy since 2007. There are several steps and important players that we need to recognise, in order to fully grasp the extent and depth of this debacle. To begin with, banks and brokers that work with individual clients in order to process their loans, originate mortgages. These loans are typically funded through lines of credit from so-called warehouse lenders, who in turn buy up mortgages and keep them in their 'inventory' until they have enough to package and sell. Mortgage originators profit from the fees they charge individuals in order to process their loans, whether these are new loans or refinancing of an existing mortgage, and they also profit from the difference between what they charge a borrower and what the secondary market will pay for a loan.

Second, these mortgages are then pooled together, or 'aggregated,' from the smaller originators, often by the warehouse lenders who extend initial credit to fund the loans. This is the beginning of the bundling of mortgages that are then sold off to investors at larger institutions, and it may involve the hedging of interest rate risk for protection against rising rates. Hedging against interest rate risk can cause the aggregators to incur losses or reap profits, prior to the eventual sale of these pools of mortgages to the bigger players. It is an enormously complex process, especially in periods of uncertainty or rising rates, but for much of the early years of this decade, the economic policies in the United States seemed to mitigate this risk.

It is at this point that these pools of mortgages become what are known as Mortgage-Backed Securities, or MBS. MBS are bought by brokerage firms and then further dissected and repackaged into several different types of 'end user' investment products. These include Collateralised Mortgage Obligations (CMO), Asset-backed Securities (ABS), and Collateralised Debt Obligations (CDO), each of which have different risk and yield characteristics depending upon their assumed prepayment and interest rate risk profiles. Institutions such as investment banks, insurance companies, pension funds, hedge funds and government agencies all act as 'consumers' of these debt instruments, as they seek yields for their own clients' investments. Depending upon their own investment objectives, these buyers of mortgage securities had the ability to seek out virtually any level of risk, and correspondingly higher yields, in order to satisfy their aims.

As we know, though, buyers of bonds will only hold onto instruments of debt if they continue to receive regular interest payments. Investing in debt securities is all about the purchase of a cash flow or stream of payments. As we've seen, through the use of complex mathematical modeling, the inherent risk of mortgage *prepayment*—and the potential loss of those regular interest payments for bond holders—could not only be factored in, it could seemingly be eliminated. Mortgage bonds were repackaged in ever more complex ways, with correspondingly diverse yields, in order to account for these varying levels of risk.

What this all meant was that the traditional methods for assessing the risk of default, not only on the bonds themselves, but also for the individuals that held the mortgages that backed those bonds, was altered. It was this 'feedback loop' that kept the mortgage mill churning out new and ever more complex products, enticing new borrowers into the market and encouraging existing debtors to further refinance their loans. Financing for new home loans from investment banks and other institutions was continually extended, at the same time as these institutions continued to purchase more and more mortgage securities. It was a seemingly endless cycle.

As the investing world's thirst for higher yields and a deeper supply of them continued to climb, typical methods for assessing credit risk fell by the wayside. As we mentioned above, borrowers were given increasingly greater access to credit that was often well beyond their means (this occurred not just in housing, but in the market for all manner of consumer debt). At the same time, rating agencies such as Moody's and Standard & Poor's began to assign to these mortgage bonds credit ratings that implied a much lower level of risk than was truly there; many of these came to be seen as virtually equivalent to US Treasury bonds, the safest instruments we know.

Isn't it common knowledge, though, that a high credit rating must necessarily correspond to low volatility and high liquidity? Indeed, this has been and always will be the case. How, then, could an inherently risky bond that was backed by an equally risky bet on an unpredictable income stream, be given an AAA rating? The truth is that through the use of complex modeling, the high credit rating was really only *'implied.'*

The credit crunch itself was precipitated by several other notable financial innovations. The first is the process of securitisation as described above. Mortgages were first pooled together in the 1970's; prior to this, mortgages were typically originated by banks and then held until maturity. Loans were funded mostly by deposits, and were the financial obligations of the banks that held them. Thus, it fell to the lenders to assess the creditworthiness of their clients, and it was they who would absorb any losses in the event of defaults, so they were much more careful with their underwriting criteria. However, traditional lenders simply could not keep pace with the rapid demand for housing in the post-World War II era, and government agencies in the US such as the Government National Mortgage Association soon introduced the securitisation process and sold mortgage-backed bonds to investors that facilitated it.

The second innovation was what has become known as the 'shadow banking system.' Financial institutions the world over essentially created offshore funds that raised capital by issuing short-term commercial bonds, and then used the proceeds to buy longer-term bonds. These funds were not shown on the banks' balance sheets, and invested heavily in 'asset-backed securities' that had at their heart the risky mortgages and other credit instruments that Wall Street had sold so feverishly. Investment firms pocketed the difference between what they borrowed on the short-term bonds and what they earned on the longer-term ones; because they were so highly leveraged, they could do this over and over again. In the same fashion, firms such as New Century operated with similarly high leverage, which allowed them to immediately re-sell their mortgage portfolio and continue to originate higher volumes of loans.

While this is a highly simplified explanation of an enormously complex occurrence, what's important to realise is the *extent* to which it happened. Some of the most prolific investment banking institutions would soon fail as well. As the market for mortgage securities dried up, investors began to bail out and cash in. With no accurate method by which to judge their worth, the mortgage securities were no longer accepted as collateral for the loans that these institutions needed to sustain them. As bank after bank strained and began to collapse, they threatened to take the entire global economy with them. What happened within New Century itself was repeated over and over, from the smallest of firms to the largest of institutions.

Closely related to these is the system of accounting that forces firms to provide accurate valuations of the assets that provide their capital bases. This is a thorny issue. So-called 'mark-to-market' or fair value accounting was a practice that actually originated in the derivatives markets, as a result of computerised models that determined pricing, where market prices were perhaps not always readily available. The standards were later adopted more widely. It has been argued that fair value accounting helped precipitate the recent subprime crisis, by forcing firms to provide 'real time' values for the assets they held and for which markets might have been illiquid. It continues to be felt in the ongoing process of asset write-downs, as banks around the world try to account for and absorb their subprime-induced losses.

We've noted previously that New Century itself was investigated for accounting irregularities. In addition to criminal charges in relation to dealings in the company's shares, executives were accused of inaccurately accounting for potential defaults on the loans they had originated. Even though they quickly resold their mortgage portfolios, part of the securitisation process that we've outlined above involves the levy of penalties for early defaults on these loans. For example, if a borrower defaults on their mortgage within the first few months, investors can go back to the lender who originated the loan and force them to buy it back in what's known as a repurchase agreement. The Securities and Exchange Commission initially charged that New Century had not made proper allowances in their corporate accounting for potential repurchase losses, and bankruptcy courts later judged that "significant improper and imprudent practices related to its loan originations, operations, accounting and financial reporting processes," had occurred and even accused auditor KPMG with helping the company conceal the problems during 2005 and 2006.

Returning to the issue of securitisation, it is evident that this innovation was at once both cause and solution to a wide range of problems. As we've mentioned above, without the pooling of mortgages in the 1970's, there simply would not have been any way to supply adequate financing in light of the high demand for housing in the post-World War II period. Securitisation allowed for that demand to be met, and allowed for investors on all sides to profit. Consumers could more easily obtain financing for home purchases, allowing them to invest their savings in a tangible asset that they could then build equity in. It also allowed lenders to somewhat diversify their own risk, and the development of the secondary market provided an even deeper source of funding, as investors of all sizes could buy mortgage bonds, earn the corresponding yields, and facilitate further lending.

The fact that securitisation provided somewhat easier sources of funding for consumer debt, however, was both blessing and curse. As with all things Wall Street, this development was taken beyond any rational expectation and by the late 1990's the rampant pace of securitisation served only to promote reckless lending. The unending quest for yield meant that riskier mortgages such as those we've discussed earlier were developed and offered to consumers that previously would not have qualified, whether this was due to their lack of credit or inability to afford an adequate down payment. The development of no or low documentation loans, for example, where an individual no longer even had to produce traditional financial records to prove their ability to make payments, can be traced to the desire for debt investors to earn equity-like yields from bond-like securities. Mortgage-backed securities of all types emerged as a consequence of this unquenchable thirst for yield on the part of investors in the secondary markets.

As we know, the slicing and dicing of mortgage-backed securities could not go on *ad infinitum*. Eventually the bubble had to burst.

"Finance, like time, devours its own children"
Honore De Balzac

As the credit crisis unfolded, the banking system began to strain as creditors began to default on their mortgages and other credit obligations. What's more, hedge funds and larger institutions had invested heavily in these risky securities, not just offshore in the shadow banking system, but as part of their traditional capital structures. These assets were used as collateral for a wide range of activities, from traditional lending and investment financing to daily operations. As debtors the world over began to default on their loans, credit markets literally froze; fearing that these securities might themselves default on their interest payments, investors quickly sought the safety of US Treasuries, and they did so in record numbers. Regardless of who was holding them or how many they had, investors quickly shied away from using these securities as collateral, *and lending dried up*.

Even now, though, the extent of the damage caused by securitisation as a whole is difficult to estimate. While it originated with the 'simple pooling' of assets in the 1970's, it has been transformed into a vital source of funding across the globe. Some estimates place the overall size of this market at well over $10 trillion, with mortgage-related instruments likely occupying the largest single proportion of that total. As the pace of securitisation increased, so did innovations relating to the issuance of new instruments as means of financing our borrowing activities. Chief among these was the aforementioned 'shadow banking system,' which had at its heart the creation of offshore funds that issued securities in order to finance the purchase of higher-yielding assets. These came to be known as Special Purpose Vehicles, or SPVs. When structured in this way, securitisation allowed for a firm with a lower credit rating but with more creditworthy cash flows to obtain financing at lower costs. It also allowed for the reduction in balance sheet risk, as institutions could 'off-load' these riskier assets from their books but continue to reap the benefits. And at the same time, it allowed for the same institutions to record the earnings and the profits, as if they *were* still on their balance sheets.

However, the extent to which the securitisation process has become wrapped up in our everyday funding activities has been problematic, to say the least. Mortgage-backed securities such as those mentioned earlier were used to finance all manner of financial transactions, and as the loans that comprise them began to default, the cascading effect meant that SPVs were next to fail. This is how the credit freeze began, and as of this writing, it is only now beginning to thaw as a result of significant and perhaps even unsustainable government intervention. Ironically, one proposed solution, in which governments have guaranteed many of these risky assets, involves a process very similar to securitisation itself! For example, as the Federal Reserve has effectively underwritten these assets, it has had to do so by issuing further debt of its own. A prudent observer might see the issuance of more AAA-rated government debt, when only backed by the full faith of the US Government to pay that debt (and when essentially comprised of the much lower-rated securities now in the central banks coffers) as somewhat unsustainable as well! While the very definition of these transactions makes them legal and 'guaranteed,' it would be hard to argue that they don't also resemble a Ponzi scheme of their own.

Risk—A Wolf in Sheep's Clothing?

"Beware geeks bearing gifts!"

Warren Buffett

The saga of New Century exposes us, the investing public, to the issue of risk in its many variations. In its simplest form, risk is the measurement of the potential for loss. As is plainly evident, though, quantifying that measurement can prove almost impossible, for the factors that might come to influence can be nearly limitless. Investors, of course, require higher rates of return as the risk of their capital increases, but as the story of New Century proves, even higher rates of return could not account for all of the risk that investors were eventually exposed to.

At this point, it's worth discussing the different sides of the risk equation, as they relate to New Century. As an individual investor, one must of course take into account the issue of *entity risk*. Simply put, this refers to the risk that a company such as New Century might simply mismanage itself. It obviously did, for it stakes its fortune and that of its shareholders on one single, unsustainable segment of the mortgage industry, the subprime borrower. Beyond this, however, it illustrates the interrelated issues of *liquidity, prepayment and default risk*. New Century built its business on its ability to sell mortgages into the secondary market in rapid fashion, as well as on its ability to operate at high volumes; both of these required it to maintain a significant amount of leverage, but as investors are now painfully aware, the long-term viability of this business model proved untenable as a result. Rising interest rates and energy prices led to a liquidity crisis among the general public, and the subprime borrowers proved to be the first and worst exposed. They in turn 'transferred' these risks to New Century, who was no longer able to pay its own bills and service its own debt.

New Century was, of course, but one of many firms to fail in this fashion. HSBC, the largest subprime lender in the industry, was actually the first to call it quits in 2007; although it left the market for subprime mortgages with its business intact, it suffered nearly $11 billion in losses. Creditors, though, are also beholden to those they lend to. The illiquidity that New Century faced, as it simply ran out of money, meant that the investment banks that had lent it money would also suffer at the hands of their debtor. At one time, New Century had been extended over $17 billion in credit from various Wall Street institutions, but as they quit lending short-term funds, New Century could no longer either service its existing debt or continue its operations to generate new revenues! The effects of this were compounded by the repurchase penalties that New Century was forced to pay, making it even more difficult for it to continue to operate.

These types of risks can be roughly grouped under the rubric of *event risk*. Even though, in retrospect, it might seem obvious that New Century had followed an unsustainable and likely even irresponsible business model, it was still practically impossible to predict when the credit markets might have frozen over. While it is somewhat easier to predict when interest rates would begin to rise, as inflation became a primary concern for the US economy, it is still reflective of the uncertain economic climate which we all inhabited. Interest rate risk is but one type of event risk, and the prudent investor would be wise to factor in other political and economic events as well. Again, these are nearly impossible to predict, and make this type of risk nearly impossible to quantify.

Of final note here is the critical issue of *moral hazard*. Moral hazard is "the prospect that a party insulated from risk may behave differently from the way it would behave if it were fully exposed to the risk." For individuals, this is the risk that they might completely default on their mortgage obligations, and in the case of New Century, this risk was clearly underestimated by the automated underwriting techniques that it made use of. The securitisation process itself underestimated this as well, as the complex mathematical models utilised by institutions and ratings agencies alike sought to explain away the inherent risk in these new mortgage products. New Century operated with impunity for a long time, as evidenced by the improprieties uncovered during the bankruptcy process, apparently judging that it need not lend responsibly or account fully for the risks it faced—the housing market itself had acted for so long as a buffer of the risks faced by the firm.

New Century's eventual collapse into bankruptcy can be viewed in the same way, as it too defaulted on its debts and left its creditors in the lurch. This demonstrates the notion of *counterparty risk*, in which one institution's fate is intertwined with another, and if one should fail then others might go down with it. New Century's failure in many ways sparked the crisis and was but the first of many firms to go under. This eventually forced massive bailout by governments around the world of leading financial institutions and investment banks that threatened to tear down the global financial system as a whole. When counterparty risk such as this becomes *systemic*, it represents risks in its ultimate form.

We can take a view that the officers of New Century believed they were prudent, based on the rational that all other major mortgage lenders operated on similar criteria and economic models.

"In economics, the majority is always wrong"
J. K. Galbraith

Conclusion

As investors, there is virtually no way to eliminate all the risks we might face when we deploy our capital. Even the safe havens of cash or T-bills represent the risk that our investments will underperform in relation to our objectives. After all, at the end of the day, it's all about getting where we want to go. But as Warren Buffett has said, if you aren't prepared to hold a stock for at least ten years, it's not worth spending more than 10 minutes thinking about!

Putting this statement into perspective in the case of New Century is very revealing. As a firm, it rocketed to stardom in very short order. It was a Wall Street favorite, and even by the time that bankruptcy seemed imminent in mid-March 2007, it was still rated favorably by analysts. How was it that the best and brightest of our global financiers did not see the risks and danger inherent in such a flawed business model? New Century did not even last 10 years, the minimum that a successful long-term investor such as Buffett would accept, to say nothing of the total collapse of shareholder value and the bankruptcy that followed!

In retrospect, New Century's failure seemed inevitable. It is a wonder it lasted as long as it did, or was profitable for as long as it was. The profits that they reaped, however, were somewhat of a façade. Just as so many homeowners or real estate speculators made easy money with little or no effort, successes that were short-lived and attributable for the most part to luck rather than investment skill, New Century only profited from the exploitation of market conditions. Those market conditions were beyond their control, of course, but in the end they were beholden to them and suffered devastating and total losses at their hands.

What's more, New Century's profits were not generated because they ran a "good business." In contrast to Warren Buffett for example, who invests heavily in companies that provide goods and services that everyday consumers want and need, New Century concentrated on an industry space that was inherently unsustainable. It would be tough to argue, as the Center for Responsible Lending reported at the time, that this type of lending model was providing any sort of lasting value for consumers. The rampant pace of repossessions and foreclosures that followed the failure of New Century sadly proves this to be true.

So, what can we learn from the story of New Century? When we look at the risks described above and how they played out in this sorry example, we must again remind ourselves that we cannot insulate ourselves entirely from these potential catastrophes. However, careful research might have shown several key things. First, it would have revealed the extent to which New Century was so heavily concentrated in the subprime space; indeed, their SEC filings plainly show that they were almost entirely focused on this segment of the industry. Any firm that is so heavily dependent on one slice of the market is bound to suffer when things go wrong. And it is interesting that even as New Century built its business upon such a rocky foundation, concentrating as it did on extending loans to borrowers with faulty credit, it too should have been rated much higher! Analysts too had the wool pulled over their eyes, apparently fooled by the seemingly endless stream of cash flows from new entrants to the housing market and those that ended up repeatedly refinancing. It seems unbelievable that no one saw that it all had to come to a halt at some time, and as is most often the case, the company's own credit ratings—a key measure of risk for investors—were not downgraded until it was far too late. New Century was yet another example of the failure of industry analysts and credit rating agencies to accurately predict even a modicum of the risk of collapse of a firm such as this.

But, as with all things Wall Street, investors and analysts alike view the good times through rose-tinted lenses. When profits come so easily, no one seems to care about the potential risks; indeed, for many investors the high returns they earned, whether on New Century or the mortgage-backed securities that it helped originate, were too attractive to forego. Perhaps it is easy for us to say that the writing was on the wall. Ratings agencies and stock analysts the world over continued to place their faith in the overheating mortgage market, and the securitisation of mortgage-backed securities extended the damage. What started as a ripple, when defaults began to rise and New Century's loans began to be called back, soon turned into a tidal wave that would topple not just New Century but some of the largest, most prestigious global financial power houses. So while no-one was to blame for the specific bankruptcy of New Century except the firm itself, they certainly were not alone in acting as they did.

When a company such as New Century is revealed to have acted inappropriately with their own capital, deceiving shareholders by misstating their financials, there is little that we as investors can do to prevent this or insulate ourselves from it. However, the high degree of leverage that New Century employed should have signaled at least some caution. This was not an issue as long as they continued to churn out high volumes of loans, and indeed, Wall Street was happy to continually extend to them astronomical lines of credit to foster those high volumes. In turn, Wall Street firms and institutions the world over greedily bought up all the mortgage-backed securities they could for their own portfolios, hungry for high yields that seemed so safe. Trust was placed in mathematical models that equated these inherently risky securities with AAA-rated Treasury bonds, and when the walls fell down, that trust was abrogated. Even as all this was unfolding, never did New Century adjust its practices and tighten its lending standards; even as the subprime market began to collapse, it continued to further loosen its already lax lending standards, making what was a monumental risk and even bigger disaster waiting to happen.

In many ways, New Century was hit by the perfect storm, in much the same way as the broader credit crisis that has gripped the world. As the housing market overheated and the bubble burst, mortgage defaults skyrocketed. New Century was forced to buy back loans at the same time as they had no funds with which to do so—these were soon estimated to have amounted to more than $8 billion! As the firm began to default on its own credit obligations, investor appetite for mortgage-backed securities also began to evaporate, meaning that it could no longer off-load its own deteriorating loan portfolio. Without a way to sell its loans, New Century was no longer able to tap the credit it so needed to operate, and bankruptcy was soon the only option. What started as such stellar, exciting and profitable performance by this new, dazzling upstart quickly collapsed in upon itself, ending in catastrophe and failure. It is unfortunate that it had to happen in this way, but in retrospect, it seemed destined to do so.

Perhaps most unfortunate was the fact that very little adjustment was made by the financial industry as a whole, either by lending companies or by the investment banks and institutions that funded them, until it was far too late. So much of the mortgage meltdown and the collapse of the housing market could have been prevented, had lending standards been maintained at appropriate levels. What's more, if less faith had been placed in the seemingly infallible mathematical models that fed those lending standards, or the complex methods employed to re-engineer the credit ratings of the mortgage-backed securities that resulted from the securitisation of these risky loans, the damage to the greater economy would likely not have been so great. Of course, the securitisation process was not limited to the housing market; all manner of consumer debt, from secured loans for automobiles to unsecured credit card debt, is still pooled, bundled, packaged and sold in place of 'real' assets that can credibly serve as collateral for our funding needs. If nothing else, the story of New Century's collapse teaches us that we have much to learn and a long way to go until our balance sheets are once again rational.

"Credit is a system whereby a person who cannot pay gets another person who cannot pay to guarantee that he can pay".

Charles Dickens

You may be wondering how, in a rational free world with strong central governments and two thousand years of history to learn from, we were unable to have simple rules and controls in place to prevent the spread and adoption of securitisation and toxic debt. Surely this could have been prevented you may ask? In a quick reference to the Praetorian Guard of the late Roman Emperors;

"Quis Custodiet Ipsos Custodes?"

Who are the guards that guard the guardians? In **Chapter 2** we will show that those responsible for the control of our financial destiny have a vested interest in having a weak and overstretched banking system, in the same vein the Praetorian Guard preferred a timid Emperor to a robust one!

Chapter 2

May 2007—The Federal Reserve:
The Bankers' Charity Ball

"The system is private, conducted for the sole purpose of obtaining the greatest possible profits from the use of other people's money."

Charles August Lindbergh

May 17th 2007—Federal Reserve Chairman Ben Bernanke said the growing number of mortgage defaults will not seriously harm the U.S. economy.

What is the Federal Reserve? Who owns it? What is its true function?

Over the course of the credit crunch the Federal Reserve and its Chairman Ben Bernanke moved from a low key, "below the radar" profile to one of the lead actors in the unfolding financial drama. This is a repeat of its role in the many financial crises that have taken place since its formation less than one hundred years ago. When it was formed one of the Fed's publicly stated objectives was to prevent financial instability, yet this institution seems on the surface to always be seeking to treat the symptoms of our financial diseases rather than cure the root cause. *Why is that?*

Let's investigate this mysterious organisation and the dichotomy of its stated objectives with its public and active participation in the world's financial system.

On September 29, 2008 the Dow Jones Industrial Average plunged 777 points, the largest single-day point loss in the history of the index. Although in percentage terms this was not even among the Dow Jones' top-ten largest declines, in the space of a day it erased $1.2 trillion dollars in shareholder value. The drop in the value of the index, which correlates to the market value of the thirty bellwether companies of the American industrial sector, was precipitated by the failure of Congressional legislation aimed at stabilising the US economy. Several days later, when a revised bill was eventually passed, the Dow Jones would drop by an even larger margin, heralding an unprecedented period of stock market volatility.

The damage done to investors was almost incomprehensible in its scope. Ironically, these massive and punishing moves by stock markets around the world were taken in response to the continued efforts of financial regulators to stem the flow of damage from the accelerating credit crisis gripping the global economy. At the helm and steering the course through these rough, uncharted waters was Ben Bernanke, Chairman of the US Federal Reserve. The Fed has countered the credit crisis with actions unprecedented in monetary value in its 95-year history, but it is too soon to tell if they will be enough to pull the US economy, and by default the global economy, out of the deepest contraction in six decades and move it onto a path of growth. For now it seems that global financiers and bankers are in favour of the course he has set, but what about the effects on the Main Street investor.

Very few countries have had such a varied or controversial experience with their central banks as the United States. The Federal Reserve Bank, created in December 1913 by President Woodrow Wilson, is actually the third central bank in US history, but as it stands today it is the sixth monetary regime in the country's two hundred some years of independence. Reflective of the populist sentiments that prevailed when it opened for business—feelings that still resonate far and wide today—the Federal Reserve, or Fed, was set up in order to ensure that the tyranny of government would not adversely affect monetary policy. But would it do so to the benefit of the ordinary consumer?

Acting in the 'Public Interest'?

"Most Americans have no real understanding of the operation of the international money lenders. The accounts of the Federal Reserve System have never been audited. It operates outside the control of Congress and manipulates the credit of the United States."

Sen. Barry Goldwater

The Fed's actions in recent months highlight a number of important roles that it plays in the US banking sector and, more widely, in the US economy. More crucially, however, these actions bring into sharp focus many key questions about the Federal Reserve System itself and whether it is not only adequate but also even appropriate. Popular opinion has it that it was created in order to serve the public interest. However many critics charge that it has done anything but, acting only to protect the narrow interests of the financial and banking elite. This chapter will examine the history of the Federal Reserve since its inception in 1913, and in looking at the varied responses to financial crises since then, hopes to answer some of the growing number of questions and doubts that swirl around it. Chiefly, we'll show how the Fed pursues its own agenda—and that of its member banks scattered around the country—and that in nearly every financial crisis it has failed to act in the 'public interest'—at least how most of us would define this. Even as the Fed has tried to mitigate losses in times of distress, it has failed to do so in the interests of the general populace. Ironically, it too may succumb to this latest crisis; if it were to do so, this time it would be at its own hands.

Six Generations of Central Banking

The first steps towards central banking in the United States came as a response to the American Revolution. Between 1775 and 1791, the Continental Congress printed the nation's first paper money in order to finance war efforts, but it did so in such quantity that it led to rapid inflation. In 1781, the first attempt to set up a national bank, in the mould of the Bank of England, was initiated, but it later failed due to allegations of foreign influence and improper governance. Distrust of the central government was pervasive, and it was felt that smaller

25

state banks, with the power to issue their own notes, were less corrupt. Congress eventually established the First Bank of the United States in 1791. Headquartered in Philadelphia, it was at the time the largest corporation in the country and was dominated by big banking interests, and as such it ran afoul of public sentiment. It failed in 1811, when its twenty-year charter expired and was not renewed by Congress. Surprisingly at the point of its failure important British interests were found to be connected with its control—the exact opposite of why it had been created!

A second attempt at a central bank was undertaken five years later, but it too would fail in short order. The political climate shifted once again in favour of a national bank in 1816, and Congress agreed to charter the Second Bank of the United States. History would repeat itself with this regime, though, as political and financial interests clashed at the highest levels. President Andrew Jackson was an opponent of the central bank, and upon his re-election to the presidency he withdrew not just government support for the bank but its funds as well! The Bank responded to this opposition by contracting the money supply and effectively forcing the US into a recession, but it would ultimately fail, as did its predecessor, when its charter was not renewed in 1836.

> *"The real truth of the matter is, as you and I know, that a financial element in the large centers has owned the government of the US since the days of Andrew Jackson."*
> **Franklin Delano Roosevelt**

At this point, the US entered a period of 'free banking,' which lasted from 1837 to 1862. During this era there was no central bank. State-chartered banks and unchartered 'free banks' issued their own paper notes, redeemable in gold. This period saw a rise in the volume of commerce and banks began to expand their range of services, but it would be fair to say that without a central bank to provide for important centralised functions such as cheque clearing, the 'system' struggled under its own weight. In 1863 a national bank came into existence, with the passage of the National Banking Act. This provided some measure of currency stability, as the new nationally-chartered banks had to back their notes by US government securities, but a series of bank panics gripped the nation from 1873 to 1907 and once again stoked demand for a centrally administered banking system.

Of particular note were the financial panics in both 1893 and 1907. These plunged the US economy into deep recessions, and it was only through the intervention of financier J.P. Morgan that the economy was able to stabilise. In 1907 it was particularly severe, caused by rampant Wall Street speculation that triggered widespread banking panic. Calls for reform divided the American public, with opinions split largely along regional lines; conservative big-money interests in the east clashed with progressives in the west, but all seemed to agree that a single unitary regulatory system was needed in order to control banking across the country.

Once again, though, the powerful banking interests won out. In 1908 Congress passed the Aldrich-Vreeland Act, which provided for emergency responses to financial crises, but more importantly it led to the development of a banker-controlled plan to reform the regulatory framework of the financial sector. By the time Woodrow Wilson was elected in 1912 the stage was already set for a new, decentralised banking regime. In 1913, the Federal Reserve System was born with the passage of the Federal Reserve Act, which created a new system of regional Reserve banks in order to try to balance the competing interests of private banks and populist sentiment.

This was a new and untried system, reflective of not just populist sentiment but of the regional divisions of the American union and the bitter mistrust between the classes. Even as the previous regime had engendered the many banking panics, because of a lack of flexibility for responding to the crises, it still came down to Wall Street to pull the country out of crisis. Progressive interests argued that the Aldrich plan was captive to the interests of the financial elite, such as J.P. Morgan and John D. Rockefeller. The system envisioned at that time was one that was still essentially private and had little government influence. In the end, a compromise was reached with the idea of regional Reserve banks, but perhaps not one that would remove as much control from the powerful money interests as its Democratic proponents would have imagined. The balance of public and private control would not end up as effective as the progressives had intended.

Before we discuss this, let's look at the system itself. Twelve regional Reserve banks and 25 branches make up the Federal Reserve System, under the general oversight of a Board of Governors; these regional banks are the operating arms of the central bank, with each serving a different geographical area of the country. Often called a "banker's bank," the Federal Reserve provides financial services to its member banks, who are shareholders of the Reserve Bank in their district. Each Reserve Bank also has a Board of Directors, intended to represent the diverse interests of each district and to impart private-sector perspectives, expertise and involvement in the affairs of the overall central banking system. While member banks are shareholders in their respective regional Reserve Bank and receive dividends for their 'investments,' they cannot sell or trade their membership interests.

This is perhaps where the interests of the public and the private begin to diverge. Not all banking institutions are required to be members; in fact, less than four in ten of the more than 8,000 commercial banks in the US are. Nationally chartered banks must be members, and state-chartered banks may join if they meet certain requirements. Even though the Fed as a whole provides important payment systems, cheque clearing and currency circulation, and all financial institutions are subject to System regulations such as reserve requirements, non-member banks, savings and loan associations and credit unions represent a large constituency that is not represented in its governance.

The enactment and supervision of financial services is, broadly speaking, one of the four main roles that the Fed is called upon to fulfill. In providing these payment systems, it also supervises and regulates banking institutions to ensure their safety and the soundness of the overall financial system. It also acts as a bank for the federal government, maintaining accounts for the Treasury and redeeming government securities such as Savings Bonds and Treasury bills. And finally, it carries out monetary policy for the federal government, "influencing money and credit conditions to promote the goals of high employment, sustainable growth and stable prices." This is what the

Fed is best known for, and it is in this role—through its control over the supply of money—that it is able to wield such formidable power.

"Give me control of a nation's money and I care not who makes it's laws."

Mayer Amschel Bauer Rothschild

Of course, this was not a development that happened overnight. In order to understand it, one must grasp the complexities of our present global financial system as well. The functioning and the effectiveness of the new Federal Reserve were soon tested by the growth in world trade following the Second World War. Even as politicians and economists argued that the new system would result in greater financial stability, it was just 22 years later that the stock market crash of 1929 again plunged the country into financial chaos. The Great Depression was the worst downturn the country had experienced; not only was the Great Depression painful, and protracted, it was global. As a result of the interdependency of world trade, what could have been a series of local phenomena quickly spread throughout the world's economies. As international trade grew, and gold remained the standard commodity backing the world's currencies, changes to the supply of money were contagious; prices in one country translated into prices in another, and changes in the amount of money circulating around the world—even though they are denominated in different currencies—affected the value of money itself.

World economic powers tried several mechanisms to remedy this situation and insulate themselves from the 'shocks' that periodically bounced around the globe. One method was through exchange rates; currency values were 'pegged' and exchangeable into other local currencies at certain fixed rates. This proved difficult, if not impossible, when each country's currency remained tied to its fixed reserves of physical gold—especially when each country could literally print as much paper money as it liked. In order to maintain exchange rates in relation to the amount of gold they possessed, central banks would be required to buy or sell foreign currencies in order to keep the supply and demand equation intact. The complexities of this mechanism would eventually result in its failure.

To solve the problem, it was seen as necessary to peg one currency, the US dollar, to the value of gold at a fixed rate, and allow other currencies to 'float' in relation to the US dollar alone. From 1944-1968, this worked at least somewhat, but eventually began to unravel as the value of gold in terms of US dollars, and the value of gold on the free market, diverged. By 1971, the decision came to 'delink' the value of the US dollar to gold at a fixed price. As a central bank acts as a 'bank for banks,' it can influence the interest rates that banks charge each other. Additionally, individual banks are required to hold in reserve a certain quantity of government bonds, essentially acting as collateral for lending activities. Central banks sell, or buy, government securities to individual banks, who themselves resell them to their clients or use them as additional reserves to increase lending and liquidity. Central banks can purchase, or sell, their currencies on the open market as well, which will affect the value vis-à-vis the currencies of other nations. Now that the US dollar had become the *world's* reserve currency, the Fed's job had become monumentally more difficult, and elevated the role of the Fed as the arbiter of the money supply to the highest priority.

> ***"1930 will be a splendid employment year."***
> **US Dept. of Labor,**
> **New Year's Forecast, December 1929**

Looking back at the Great Depression shows this to be true. American economists Milton Friedman and Anna Schwartz argued that it was the ***"Fed itself that bore the primary responsibility for turning the crisis of 1929 into a global depression"***, and once again it was as a result of the inadequate response to widespread banking failures. Under the leadership of Benjamin Strong, a "reasonable balance had been struck between the international obligation of the United States to maintain the restored gold standard and its domestic obligation to maintain price stability"; with the death of Strong in 1928, however, the Federal Reserve Board in Washington came to dominate monetary policy and too little was done to ensure the stability of the financial system as a whole. It was the Fed's inability to ensure adequate liquidity and availability of sufficient credit, by buying and selling government securities on the open market, which spurred a near-collapse of the banking sector.

We now know that the effects of the Fed's failures to avert the Great Depression led to an enormous decline in the welfare of the US consumer. Over $15 billion in deposits were lost, even as surviving banks were somehow able to increase their own reserves—the wave of bank failures also resulted in a surge in mergers between banks, as stronger institutions took over weaker ones, but this did not seem to benefit the consumer. Economists, including Friedman, have charged that the Fed inappropriately refused to lend money to small banks during the bank runs of 1929—the very reason for its inception in the first place. It did, however, lead directly to the inception of the Federal Deposit Insurance Corporation, created in 1933 to guarantee bank deposits, even though the Fed itself was already the "lender of last resort" and should have been able to provide this measure of security.

Conflicts of Interest

> *"Whoever undertakes to set himself up as judge in the field of truth and knowledge is shipwrecked by the laughter of the Gods."*
>
> **Albert Einstein**

The above early events since the Fed's inception illustrate the problematic structure of this hybrid system. It takes a little understanding to fully capture its essence, however. Does the Fed act so because it fails to recognise its public utterances or is it successfully answering the commands of its true masters which are different to those of the public who surround it?

The Fed admits that it is an "unusual mixture of public and private elements," aimed simultaneously at providing financial services to its member banks and serving a supervisory and regulatory function. The seven Governors of the Federal Reserve Board are appointed by the President and are confirmed by the Senate; they are tasked with overseeing the operations of the financial system as a whole and make regulatory decisions such as setting reserve requirements. We've seen previously that it is the member banks in each region that contribute capital to their respective Reserve Bank, and they also elect six of the nine directors for each region. These directors then appoint the president of each regional Reserve Bank, who in turn appoints members to the Federal Advisory Council that advises the Board of Governors.

If this seems like circular logic, in many ways it is. How can a bank regulate or supervise itself, particularly when one of the chief concerns of the Fed is the protection of the consumer? As it turns out, this is by no means an easy answer. To begin with, the Fed is an independent federal agency and doesn't receive funding from Congress, even though it is subject to Congressional oversight. In the modern democratic age, control over an agency's budget is one of the primary methods of authority in the public domain. The Fed accepts no true government control.

> *"The few who understand the system, will either be so interested from its profits or so dependent on its favours, that there will be no opposition from that class."*
> **Rothschild Brothers of London, 1863**

The US Senate has long held that the Fed is not transparent enough in the way that it operates, but because it is independent it really doesn't have to answer to Congress in this respect. Critics have argued that increased transparency achieves many aims: it helps clarify policy objectives, improves the workings of financial markets, enhances credibility, reduces the chances of policy manipulation for political purposes, and complements important oversight responsibilities. Many in Congress still believe that the Fed lags behind the progress made in these areas by its counterparts around the world.

Qui bono?

The Fed, of course, counters that its position as a regulator and supervisor means that it better able to make policy decisions.

One might ask: *in whose name are these policy decisions made?*

Looking once again at the structure of the Fed, we've already seen that the private member banks play an important advisory role for the federally appointed Board of Governors. Of course, much of this is related to the important research function that the Fed provides; indeed economic theory dictates that the health of the economy and the effectiveness of monetary policy depend on a sound financial system. Member banks certainly contribute valuable economic data, bringing first-hand information to the policymaking table. The key question, at its most basic level, is whether the Fed should be involved in banking supervision at all?

In effect, the member banks own their own regulator. They are required to own stock in their regional Reserve Bank, and receive a hefty 6% dividend for doing so. Each regional Reserve Bank is independently incorporated, and as we've seen earlier, six of the nine directors on each bank's board are drawn from the member banks themselves, meaning that they are in a position to importantly influence public policy in light of their own narrowly-defined private interests! They also comprise five of the twelve members of the Federal Open Market Committee, which helps set lending rates and overall economic conditions. They are thus in a position, however indirectly, to influence their own profitability! Brian Doherty describes it succinctly:

"One method is 'open market operations,' that is, buying and selling US government securities. Another is regulating the amount of its financial reserves a bank must hold, as opposed to being able to lend out. Yet another is setting the federal funds discount interest rate, also known as the overnight rate—the rate at which Fed branch banks loan money to each other (generally overnight). The federal funds rate affects the amounts of money banks lend to the public, and it influences other interest rates, such as those for mortgages, home equity loans, and consumer credit."

It is easy to see how the member banks are in a position to profit greatly from the policies they themselves have a heavy hand in creating. As part of the Fed's open market operations, the Open Market Committee implements monetary policy by targeting what's known as the federal funds rate; this is the rate that banks charge each other for overnight loans, which are the capital reserves held by banks at the Fed. In addition, the Fed directly sets the 'discount' rate, which is the rate at which banks can borrow directly from the Fed itself. Both of these rates in turn influence the prime rate, which is the basic rate at which it will lend to consumers. Economist Milton Friedman explicitly criticised this shadowy system of targeting interest rates as a means of controlling inflation, since nowhere in the widely accepted money supply equation are interest rates found. The careful observer will notice a multitude of ways that the member banks can influence policy strongly in their own favour.

This problem is compounded when we dig a little deeper into the role of the regional Reserve Banks. While it may have made sense at the time of the Fed's inception in 1913, it is clear that regional disparities are no longer adequately represented: "Missouri has two Fed banks, and a drive from Philadelphia to Boston passes three more, but the entire West Coast reports to the San Francisco Fed . . . The distribution of banking and economic activity, as well as population density, across the country was very different when the Fed was set up than it is now." It is hard to see how the interests of the economic elite, congregated as they are still, are not unequally concentrated as well.

A look at the Reserve Banks' Boards of Directors shows this to be the case. The nine-member board of directors of each district is made up of 3 classes: A, B and C. Member banks choose the A and B class of directors, the former of which is chosen from and representative of the member banks, and the latter of which is chosen to "represent the public with due but not exclusive consideration to the interests of agriculture, commerce, industry, services, labor, and consumers." Importantly, while class B directors are prevented from being an officer, director or employee of any bank, they are most often chosen from the financial elite; as such, it is likely that their definition of the 'public interest' is not on par with that of the average consumer. Douglas Landy, a former lawyer at the New York Fed, says that the real issue is confusion over this very point: ***"Is it a macro public interest like, 'Don't crash the system?'... Is it a public interest like, 'Don't lose taxpayer money?'... More direction on what these people should be doing makes sense."***

The New York Fed in particular shows this to be the case. Long viewed as the Fed's watchdog on Wall Street, as a result of its proximity to this nexus of financial power it acts as the eyes and ears into markets for the bank's governing board. Former New York Fed chairman Stephen Friedman resigned in April 2009 amid questions about conflicts of interests: *"Friedman is a former top executive at Goldman Sachs & Co., which is now regulated by the New York Fed, and remained on the holding company's board of directors. Fed policy bars officers of banks from the type of board seat Friedman held, and the New York Fed sought a waiver for him. While the request was being considered, Friedman bought 37,300 shares of Goldman stock, raising conflict-of-interest questions."* What's more, Friedman was a class C director, which meant that he was prevented from even owning stock in a bank, let alone being a director of one!

This example shows the inherent problem in having a member bank own its regulator. Even as it is a servant to the public as a regulator, it is this "elbow to elbow" position with Wall Street that has lead to numerous calls for its reform. According to Milton Friedman, this should be one of our greatest concerns: ***"One unsolved economic problem of the day is how to get rid of the Federal Reserve. The most unresolved problem of the day is precisely the problem that concerned the founders of this nation: how to limit the scope and power of government. Tyranny, restrictions on human freedom, comes primarily from governmental institutions that we ourselves set up."***

Bubble Machine: The Fed's Responses to Financial Crisis

It is in the run-up and responses to financial crisis that we see the true nature of the Fed's power. Nowhere is this more evident than in its primary role as a fighter of inflation. The postwar period, it should be recalled, was a period of unprecedented growth that lasted for decades. This economic expansion was really only threatened by the twin specters of inflation and unemployment that crept into the system in the 1970's. Even though it is supposed to be independent, the Fed has always remained beholden to political pressure to promote conditions that foster sustainable economic growth.

The 1973 'oil shock' led to perhaps the first economic contraction since the end of the Second World War, as oil exporting countries located primarily in the Middle East quickly ratcheted up the price of oil. Inflation increased rapidly and economies around the world shrank. The economic consequences were far reaching, and the Fed initially tried to counteract these effects by raising borrowing rates. History shows that the Fed didn't act aggressively enough, because high interest rates are bad for business! Since 1980, oil prices increases have been shown not to affect the economy negatively. Evidence now suggests that it was the inappropriate price control strategies of then Fed Chairman Paul Volcker that led to the double-misery of inflation and unemployment that plagued the US economy during his tenure.

> *"The market may be bad, but I slept like a baby last night. I woke up every hour and cried."*
>
> **Unknown Stockbroker,**
> **September 1987**

In 1987, when 'Black Monday' crippled stock markets around the world, the Fed initially responded by easing the supply of money and preventing the type of liquidity crisis that had caused bank runs in the past. In the wake of the crisis, new Fed Chair Alan Greenspan has been criticised for holding interest too low for too long, which has only engendered a series of asset price bubbles. The first was the 'dot-com' bubble, which made profits out of thin air as investors rushed to capitalise on the promise of the internet revolution. The second was of course the housing bubble, whose effects are still being felt. Greenspan coined the term "irrational exuberance" in 1996, in response to the rapidly inflating dot-com bubble, but he failed to raise rates and control the deployment of capital to so many ill-fated firms, which only served to make his Wall Street compatriots wealthy at the expense of the ordinary consumer.

Greenspan, it seems, has always been beholden to the financial elite. In 1984 as a private economist, he argued for deregulation of the Savings and Loan industry, which at the time represented a growing constituent of several regional economies in the US. Greenspan and others felt that if the industry could diversify its mix of business by adding more short-term lending, savings institutions would be cushioned from the potentially disastrous effects of rising interest rates. Even though he acknowledged the inherently risky nature of the direct investments involved in this industry, he advocated for its deregulation. He continued to maintain similar views once he took the helm of the Federal Reserve just three years later.

In the mid-1990's, the United States had begun to recover from a recession, and in order to curb the threat of inflation, interest rates were again raised. The US thus became more attractive to investors relative to the Asian economies, while a host of other factors put downward pressure on these currencies. The result, in short, was a wave of bankruptcies, currency devaluations, and defaults on debt that threatened to engulf not just the East Asian countries but their creditors in the Western world as well. The international community's response was ad hoc and perhaps ill suited to contain the crisis, and the 'Asian flu' quickly spread throughout the globe. Importantly, it threatened to drag down not just the economies where it had been incubated, but the larger financial superpowers—chiefly the US and Japan—that had been the main buyers of the developing world's debt. The turmoil in the East Asian debt markets roiled stock markets worldwide. At the same time, policy changes at the Fed negatively impacted pricing in the commodities markets, which in turn fed back into the ability of many nations whom depended upon these markets for revenues, to service their financing obligations.

Perhaps it is easy to see, especially in retrospect, how intertwined the world economies had become. Private bankers and public monetary authorities alike, though, singularly underestimated the extent of the interconnectedness. The extreme policies of *laissez faire* economics, promulgated by Greenspan, were essentially 'philosophical' in nature and effectively amounted to a willful ignorance to the conditions that nearly caused the collapse of Wall Street in 1998. Where banks are regulated by the Federal Reserve, and most other investments in traditional equity markets are overseen by the Securities Exchange Commission, much of Wall Street remains largely free to trade as they please. Greenspan's reasons for this regulatory freedom are not all that complex: in essence, so long as the numbers of members are significantly limited, and of sufficient wealth to allow them to withstand the inherent risks, then they could do as they pleased. Greenspan, moreover, felt that the regulations already imposed upon lenders, through the facilities of the Federal Reserve and in concert with the United States Treasury, would mean that Wall Street's investors would effectively police themselves. If banks had limits upon whom they could lend to and in what quantities they could do so, then investors in turn would be limited in how much they could borrow.

After the catastrophic events of 9/11 as well as the bursting of the bubble in technology stocks, Fed Chairman Alan Greenspan once again dropped interest rates. These historically low rates persisted for several years, which spurred yet another asset bubble, this time in residential housing. As Nobel laureate Joseph Stiglitz has commented, one bubble was simply replaced by another. Stiglitz has also argued that it was Greenspan's failure to control liquidity, by keeping rates artificially low for too long, as well as his failure as a regulator by not curbing leverage, that in turn led to wider systemic risk. What's ironic in all this is that it was Greenspan that had argued a decade earlier to keep the derivatives market relatively free from regulation.

The credit crisis in 2007-2008 was in many respects the perfect storm. It was reminiscent of the wave of calamities that struck seemingly independent markets in 1998. Like a boxer on the ropes in the last rounds, following the attacks of 9/11 and the bursting of the technology bubble, the US economy was in rough shape. As Chair of the Fed, Alan Greenspan not only pushed for very low interest rates but also kept them there for a very long time. Our economies depend upon lending for growth, because consumers need access to borrowed funds in order to buy expensive items such as appliances, automobiles and houses. The new Bush Administration in the White House needed to stoke the fires of growth to pull the economy out of recession, and it encouraged this new boom in housing and finance. As interest rates had been kept artificially low for so long, inflation became the primary risk to the economy. Fed Chair Ben Bernanke inherited this challenge as Greenspan's successor, and began a steady process of raising rates, in order to stave off further price increases. Commodities were booming as a result, chief among them oil, which put even greater pressure on consumer spending. This made it even harder for the average person to afford their escalating mortgages and other credit obligations.

It's ironic that the demise of financial giant Bear Stearns mirrored the collapse of trading firm Long-Term Capital Management in the wake of the Asian economic crisis just a decade earlier, showing that the Fed had not applied anything it might have learned from that crisis. Bear Stearns was sold off, and its toxic assets guaranteed by the Federal Reserve, because it raised once again the specter of systemic risk. It was too big, and had gone down too fast, for it to be allowed to fail, for its unmanaged collapse would have taken virtually the rest of Wall Street down with it. This most recent crisis continued despite the emergency measures undertaken by the Federal Reserve and its backing of Bear Stearns' sale to JP Morgan Chase.

That backing did not have the results that they intended, which was to restore confidence to the financial system and ensure that liquidity was maintained. Experience in earlier crises had shown that often it was the lack of liquidity and access to credit and lending facilities that allowed those crises to continue unabated. The illiquid nature of the toxic mortgage assets was intractable. Large lenders began to fail, such as Countrywide and IndyMac, two of the largest providers of subprime mortgages. Freddy Mac and Fannie Mae, the quasi-government agencies that owned or guaranteed nearly half of all US mortgages, were taken over by the Federal government, causing a worldwide panic. Last but certainly not least, Merrill Lynch agreed to be taken over by Bank of America, and Lehman Brothers filed for bankruptcy.

Alan Greenspan felt at the time that even though some degree of moral hazard had been created by the orchestrated bailout of Long-Term Capital Management, it paled in comparison to the "serious distortions to market prices had Long-Term been pushed suddenly into bankruptcy." Now, a decade later, they judged that one bailout was enough; Bear Stearns could not be allowed to fail, because of its swift decline and the danger that posed. Lehman Brothers, it was felt, had had ample time to make arrangements, and capital markets were well aware of the risk of its failure. Nevertheless, Lehman's bankruptcy put tremendous downward pressure on stock markets and further accelerated the decline in real estate securities. Creditors around the globe faced massive losses, with little chance of recouping them.

Merrill Lynch's sale to Bank of America, on the same weekend in September 2008 as Lehman Brothers' bankruptcy filing, was judged to be the result of catastrophic losses across many of its business units. These owed in large part to the firm's exposure to mortgage-backed securities, but blame has also been laid upon the system of executive pay in place at the time. CEOs and top-level executives have incentives to take excessive risk because of investors' focus on short-term profits, rather than creating long-term shareholder value. As a result, many argue that CEOs have an inherent conflict of interest as they chase short-term profits in order to generate exorbitant bonuses for themselves: "The incentive is always short-run, because Wall Street enjoys low interest rates. They see it as a positive sign psychologically, and it plays a role in keeping stock prices high. The majority of people still believe this is the road to prosperity, that with lower interest rates businesses do better and banks do better and everyone is going to be happy. What the Fed does is just a form of central economic planning that this country and its business community have come to accept."

The initial response to the 2007-2008 crises may have much wider consequences than we can even realise. The $700 billion bailout orchestrated by the Fed in response to the subprime mortgage crisis was originally intended to remove toxic mortgage assets from bank balance sheets, allowing them to continue critical business and lending activities: "The freezing up of short-term financial markets called for more borrowing. The Fed's response was creative and correct. It recognised that its responsibility as lender of last resort required bold action to maintain the payments system; and it delivered. The rush to bring real short-term interest rates to negative values is an unseemly and dangerous response to pressures from Wall Street, Congress and the administration. *The Federal Reserve became 'independent' in 1913 so that it could resist pressures of that kind.*

In the postwar years, although it often failed to do so, the Fed was expected to safeguard the purchasing power of our money and maintain economic growth.

What's more, when the Fed stepped in to guarantee the sale of Bear Stearns to rival JP Morgan Chase, it did so by buying assets from the collapsing financial giant in order to facilitate the sale. Who did this benefit? Certainly not the everyday consumer or taxpayer, who will foot the bill; but JP Morgan Chase, who saw one of its chief competitors quickly eliminated. This move was part of the strategy promulgated by former Goldman Sachs executive Hank Paulson, as Treasury Secretary, but it was endorsed and backed by Ben Bernanke at the Fed. *It seems that private interest once again trumped public responsibility*. Since the beginning of the crisis, the Fed has spearheaded over **$9 *trillion*** in federal government commitments—lending or spending at least $3 trillion and pledging at least another $6 trillion. Only about $800 billion of that was voted on by lawmakers.

Returning to the issue of transparency that we raised earlier, one can readily see reason for concern: "When Congress approved the TARP on Oct. 3, Fed Chairman Ben S. Bernanke and then Treasury Secretary Henry Paulson acknowledged the need for transparency and oversight. The Federal Reserve so far is refusing to disclose loan recipients or reveal the collateral they are taking in return." Perhaps the largest recipient of government aid has been insurance giant AIG. Heavily involved in the unregulated derivatives market, AIG virtually bankrupted itself and exposed the entire financial system to collapse as a result of overexposure to credit-default swaps; judged too big to fail as well, the Fed bailed out AIG and nationalised the firm. In doing so, over $100 billion was paid out to counterparties around the globe, including Treasury Secretary Paulson's former firm, Goldman Sachs, which received over $10 billion.

Conclusion

It should be evident by now that far from being independent from influence, the Fed has proven itself beholden to political and financial interests that it was created to guard against.

"We have, in this country, one of the most corrupt institutions the world has ever known. I refer to the Federal Reserve Board. This evil institution has impoverished the people of the United States and has practically bankrupted our government.

> *It has done this through the corrupt practices of the moneyed vultures who control it."*
> **Congressman Louis T. McFadden in 1932**

The seeds of its own confliction lie not in the narrow confines of the actions of its public face—its successive Chairmen—although they themselves are compromised by the selection process—but rather in the nature of its birth. At the turn of the 20th century, on the eve of the 1907 Crash, the world's monetary system was in the hands of a few interlocking dynasties and allied groups. In Europe the lead bankers were the Rothschild's, who were aligned with the House of Morgan. In the US the leading rivals to J. P. Morgan's absolute control of the financial system were the Rockefeller and Mellon families. At the Federal Reserve's incorporation the shadowy control of its shares and appointment of its officers rested in the various, but not equal, pockets of these titans of finance. You may think that is nearly one hundred years ago and those men have long since passed to a place where money has no value. *Yes all true, but what of their descendants*?

As you may recall from the above chapter the amount of Federal Reserve stock held by each member is proportional to is size. The Federal Reserve Bank of New York owns the majority, 53%, of the shares in the Federal Reserve System. The largest New York banks control the Federal Reserve Bank of New York. *Would you care to venture who are the largest banks in New York?*

In 1997 the largest three were Chase Manhattan, Citibank and Morgan Guaranty. In 2000 JP Morgan and Chase merged creating the second largest US bank after . . . . Citibank! Citibank, through its various name changes and mergers was originally the foundation of the Rockefeller's financial empire. Thus control of the Federal System rests not in the hands of public shareholders, not even in the hands of the US government but it rests with the heirs of the Robber Barons who originally created it for their own purposes. *The creation, manipulation and control of money lies with those who profit from it most, but the burden, guarantee and cost of that money lies with those who are enslaved by it . . . . the taxpayer!*

In the aftermath of the credit crisis, calls for reform have been many. Some in the new Obama administration have called for a comprehensive review of the Fed's structure, including the dismantling of the Fed's responsibilities as guardian protector of consumer credit, because the Fed has proven either unable or unwilling to do fill this role. Instead of being immune to the prevailing winds of political change or financial lobbying, the Fed has shown itself remarkably captive to the will of its member banks, directors and staff—many of whom have strong ties to Wall Street. As a result of these apparent conflicts of interest, the Fed has proved unable to consistently control inflation; its recent intervention in the bailout of the financial sector, seemingly to the great benefit of a precious few on Wall Street, will likely only further the prospects of long-term economic uncertainty.

Even though people have the illusion of safety now, with the Fed in place as the lender of last resort and the apparent regulator of the financial industry, this may only mean that the mistakes made by government are magnified. Certainly, there is much overlap with other banking regulators, and importantly these are not owned by any such members, that they regulate, as the Fed is. Given its focus on monetary policy, it is highly debatable that the Fed should be involved in supervisory activities at all. This is especially the case when we look once again at the role of the New York Fed, which has long been involved on the ground level and at the center of so many financial rescue efforts. Law makers are once again calling for a re-evaluation of the mechanics of this system and renewed efforts to increase transparency in its operations.

In the coming years, economists, historians and journalists alike will debate the relative merits of the Fed's response to this most recent financial crisis. The financial sector has so far survived, but the shape it will take when all this is over is certainly not known. We are already witnessing a wave of consolidation unseen since the days of the Great Depression, when cascading failures led to the big banks getting bigger and the smaller ones simply disappearing. It is unclear how this will impact us as taxpayers or consumers. What is clear, however, is that the costs will be overwhelming in proportion to any benefit that was gained in the run-up to it. This is likely always the case when bubbles burst. It should also be evident that the Fed is perhaps in the unique position of being able to undertake research that nobody else can. Even as conflicts of interest plague the system and the Fed's influence on public policy has grown exponentially, the benefit of its ability to act quickly in times of crisis so far remain relatively unchallenged. That, though, may change, as the true costs of its programs become known.

Once again, we must ask the question, *qui bono*? The risk faced by taxpayers, at the hands of the Fed, is nothing new. Decades ago, Congressman Wright Patman famously remarked, "You can absolutely veto everything the President does. You have the power to veto what the Congress does, and the fact is that you have done it. You are going too far." Forty-five years later, calls to end its secretive ways and nebulous dealings with Wall Street persist. As they did then, businesses and bankers especially will lobby hard against any further regulation, for it will surely come at their expense. *It should be obvious to us now that the Fed continues to pursue its own agenda, one that is closely aligned with the concentrated, narrowly drawn interests of the financial elite, rather than in the 'public interest' as it should be defined.*

Our story so far has shown how money is created and controlled for purposes other than the general interest of our society. Henry Ford once said *"It is well that the people of the nation do not understand our banking and monetary system, for if they did, I believe there would be a revolution before tomorrow morning."* Well, if only a few people do indeed understand the manipulation of money within that narrow circle, it will be those who excel in its use. In the next chapter we are going to look at the role of these money masters and explore the golden world of the "New Alchemy" of aggressive arithmetic; the wizards of light and dark, or as they are more commonly known . . . . *the Hedge Fund Mangers*!

Chapter 3

June 2007—The Alchemy of Aggressive Arithmetic: The "Wizards" of Light and Dark

"Scholasticism with its subtle argumentation,

Theology with its ambiguous phraseology,

Astrology, so vast and so complex,

are all children's games,

when compared with alchemy."

Albert Poisson

June 7ᵗʰ 2007—Bear Stearns informs investors that two of its hedge funds were heavily involved in subprime mortgages, and halts redemptions.

What are Hedge Funds? Where do they get their money from? What do they do with it?

Risk; It is a word that imparts a sense of danger, to be sure, but in the world of investing it has a counterpart. That counterpart is of course return. One cannot be had without the other; no matter how we try to rearrange the equation, they are inextricably linked. Peter Bernstein details the 'story' of risk in his pivotal book *Against the Gods.* In the book he chronicles our modern-day fascination with the taming of this chaotic element through statistics and probability. However, Bernstein's mathematical muses Bernoulli, de Fermat and Pascal would in all likelihood be rolling in their graves had they been witness to the events of June 2007.

> **"I hear that you dropped some money in Wall Street. Were you a bull or a bear?"**

> **"Neither, just a plain simple ass!"**
>
> **Anonymous**

This month in time heralded, in many respects, the beginning of the credit crunch. On June 7, investment banking giant Bear Stearns informed investors that two of its hedge funds were heavily involved in subprime mortgage bonds. These particular bonds, esoteric instruments called collateralised debt obligations or CDOs, had proven highly profitable until the downturn in the housing market effectively pulled the rug out from underneath them. Within the space of just a few weeks, these once high-flying hedge funds collapsed, and shocked investors around the world watched billions of dollars in value simply evaporate.

Their collapse would eventually lead to the spectacular failure of Bear Stearns, a chapter in itself, which proved unable to calm the 'bank run' panic that came in their wake. While the failure of Bear Stearns is not the issue of this chapter, what is at the heart of this discussion is the far-reaching—and in many respects wholly unpredictable—effects of the hedge fund industry itself. In this chapter, we'll delve into what exactly a hedge fund *is*, and in doing so, we'll expose some of the systemic dangers that they pose for the global economy. Although very much at issue here is the failure of 'risk management,' this takes us far beyond just that critical concern; rather, what is most important is what risk management has *come to mean* for so much of the finance industry.

"It doesn't work to leap a twenty-foot chasm in two ten-foot jumps."

This chapter will shed light on the key role that *quantitative analysis* now plays in so much of modern finance. Forbes describes it as *"a business or financial analysis technique that seeks to understand* behavior by using complex mathematical and statistical modeling, measurement and research . . . [by] assigning a numerical value to variables, quantitative analysts try to replicate reality mathematically." In the world of investing, where so much of it still seems to represent the gamble that Bernstein artfully speaks of, is it really possible to employ complex mathematical models in order to manage risk—or as some seem to believe, eliminate it altogether? As the collapse of Bear Stearns' hedge funds, and later Bear itself, would painfully demonstrate, the answer seems to be a resounding *no.*

To be sure, the failure of hedge funds is neither new nor really all that remarkable—a closer look at the history of this demographic of the finance industry is very revealing in that regard. On average 14% of the hedge fund industry goes belly up in any one year with hardly a ripple on the wider world of finance. This, perhaps, *is* the critical concern; this chapter will peer into the depths of the hedge fund industry, showing exactly what they are and how they came about. Of course, in doing so, we'll uncover what the real problem is, which speaks to what hedge funds are not: **regulated!**

Despite—or perhaps because of—both their lack of regulation and near-unequivocal reliance on complex mathematical models, they have rapidly become a significant risk. Prudent investing and fundamental analysis have roundly been replaced by styles of aggressive arithmetic alchemy. Consequently and when combined with their lack of regulation, they have become not just a risk to themselves or their own investors but also to the wider economy as well.

> *"Arithmetic is one of the oldest branches, perhaps the very oldest branch, of human knowledge; and yet some of its most abtruse secrets lie close to its tritest truths."*
>
> **H. J. S. Smith**

In The Beginning . . .

. . . there was fundamental analysis. This is a method of evaluating a security or investment by attempting to measure its intrinsic value, done by examining a number of related economic financial factors.

47

The end goal is to produce some measure of 'value' that an investor can use to compare the **current** price of a company's stock to some eventual *future* price. Fundamental analysis utilises pieces of real data from company balance sheets including revenues, cash flows and profit margins to forecast stock prices. The belief here is that the present market conditions are reflective more of feelings, emotions and a 'herd mentality' than they are of concrete, tangible 'facts' about a company's performance. Perhaps the most famous and public investor to rely upon this method is **Berkshire Hathaway's Warren Buffett; he has said that if a business does well, the stock eventually follows. As a result, this type of analysis is usually associated with traditional 'buy and hold' strategies.**

Naturally, there is an element of both the **qualitative** and the **quantitative** in this type of analysis. The former has to do with judgments and conclusions drawn from the economic and financial conditions that may affect a stock's future price; the latter, on the other hand, has at its heart the 'pure' rationality that comes with crunching hard data. Fundamental analysis occurs at the intersection of these two techniques. In the real world, neither tells the whole story, and prudent investors carefully weigh each against the other as part of their decision-making process.

Certainly there is value to be extracted from either approach, right? Most of us that reside in the real world would agree. Accordingly, we place our trust in our investment advisors, believing that a thorough accounting of all the relevant factors and considerations will result in the right call when it comes to buying, selling or holding onto a particular security. Up until the mid-1970's this might have been the predominant belief among investors and also their advisors on the opposite side of the table. In the United States the passage of the 1974 Employee Retirement Security Act in America, ERISA, brought about an important paradigm shift in the field of finance. This shift brought about a measure of accountability against which investment choices could be judged, whereas previously there was little to be had for the lackluster returns that often accompanied bad judgment.

This change was very much brought about by innovations in financial accounting that led to the advent of investment benchmarks, primarily through the use of 'indexing.' The Dow Jones Industrial Average (DJIA), the S&P 500, and the MSCI Europe, Asia and Far East (EAFE) are some of the most widely referenced indices, which provide a snapshot of the value of a specific type of asset in relation to some predetermined starting point. By comparing the performance of one's portfolio against the performance of these indices one could, generally speaking, construct a measure of *relative return* by which one could judge the effectiveness of an investment manager. Indices provide a 'passive' measure of asset-class performance, because they are not managed by anybody and are merely representative of a weighted collection of stock values, for example.

> *"Ask a philosopher 'What is philosophy?' or a historian 'What is history?' and they will have no difficulty in giving an answer. Neither of them can pursue his own discipline without knowing what he is searching for. But ask a mathematician 'What is mathematics?' and he may justifiably reply that he does not know the answer but that this does not stop him from doing mathematics."*
>
> **François Lasserre**

A rising tide floats all boats.

The problem, of course, is that it can be difficult to separate man from machine. When the economy is doing well, most companies share in that and profits tend to surge across the board *even in the face of poor management*. We all instinctively know this to be true, but when it comes to investing one's wealth; we all seek something more accurate than a dart, a steady hand, and a multi-colored board on the wall by which to make our choices. We all instinctively *want* to follow the advice and the lead of investors such as Buffett, or at least to be assured that our trusted advisors are utilising a similar approach when acting on our behalf. Through benchmarking, one now had the ability to judge the 'active' component of a manager's input, rather than just looking at the effects of the tide.

At the same time as all of this, the world of investing witnessed an explosion in the growth of the *mutual fund*, a type of investment pool that gave ordinary investors access to the services of professional money managers but on a reduced risk basis. Two developments in America are important for our purposes here: the first was the Investment Company Act of 1940, which defined and regulated this new class of investment fund. Prior to this, there was virtually no limit upon what the managers could or couldn't do with their clients' money. This new act effectively governed the strategies that they could follow and the disclosures that they were obliged to provide to their clients, and to the public as a whole. The second development was the 1975 change in US tax law that allowed individuals to direct their own assets that were earmarked for retirement, whereas previously the nation's savings were concentrated largely in the hands of private pension funds and Social Security.

Standing in stark contrast to the regulatory scheme that governed the mutual fund industry is the ***hedge fund.*** Hedge funds came into existence at roughly the same time, as the investment world was struggling to cope with the aftermath of the 1929 stock market collapse and the devastation caused by the Great Depression. The 1940 Act actually served to augment two previous laws, the Securities Act of 1933 and the Securities Exchange Act of 1934, both of which governed the issuance and trading in many public stocks. They also required that funds register with the new Securities Exchange Commission (SEC) and mandated that they must issue a prospectus that disclosed to investors information about the fund, the securities it would buy, and the manager. Since mutual funds were heavy purchasers of many publicly traded securities, the 1940 Act was seen as a necessary complement to the earlier two, and set forth further guidelines with which all funds must comply.

By almost every measure, hedge funds are the polar opposite of their cousin the mutual fund. Hedge funds are also a form of pooled investment, but in contrast to mutual funds most are not required to register with the SEC. As most of them are not required to register, they are not compelled to disclose information about their strategies, the securities they buy, or even about the managers themselves. They can literally invest in any type of asset they like, such as private companies that don't trade on an exchange, debt, derivatives, commodities and precious metals. They can follow many investment strategies that are judged too risky or complex for average investors to participate in such as short-selling and options. It is from here that they take their name, as some of the strategies employed seek to *hedge* the risk of buying certain securities through the use of complex offsetting tactics. We'll discuss some of these below.

> **"He that diggeth a pit shall fall into it; and who so breaketh an hedge, a serpent shall bite him."**
>
> **The Bible**

There are some limitations to the scope and function of hedge funds. Unlike mutual funds, which continually issue shares to new investors and have no predetermined limit on the number of investors they'll admit or the *type* of investor that is allowed to invest in the fund, hedge funds are somewhat 'required' to take the opposite approach. They are virtually unlimited as too what they can or cannot invest in so federal law provides that hedge funds limit entry to no more than 100 investors. Moreover, that investor participation was limited to those with a net worth of at least $1,000,000 USD or investors who have earned at least $200,000 in each of the last two years. Institutional investors such as banks, pension funds, or other corporate entities must have a net worth of at least $5,000,000 to gain entry to these funds.

For much of their history, hedge funds were only available to a privileged few. By seeking to rely mostly on net worth and income requirements, it was judged that these participants—deemed 'accredited investors'—would by definition be better able to understand the often complex strategies the managers employed, and would subsequently be able to withstand the inherently risky nature of these strategies. These days, however, a million dollars doesn't go as far as it once did, and many more consumers have the financial wherewithal to gain access to these funds.

Dr. Evil: *Let's just do what we always do. Hijack some nuclear weapons and hold the world hostage. Yeah? Good! Gentlemen, it has come to my attention that a breakaway Russian Republic called Kreplachistan will be transferring a nuclear warhead to the United*

Nations in a few days. Here's the plan. We get the warhead and we hold the world to ransom for ...

ONE MILLION DOLLARS!

<u>Number Two</u>: Don't you think we should ask for *more* than a million dollars? A million dollars isn't exactly a lot of money these days. Virtucon alone makes over 9 billion dollars a year!

<u>Dr.Evil</u>: Really? That's a lot of money!

<u>Dr.Evil</u>: Okay then, we hold the world to ransom for ...

<u>Dr. Evil</u>: One ... Hundred ... BILLION DOLLARS!
Austin Powers the Movie

The Best of Both Worlds: It was the widespread application of Harry Markowitz' pioneering academic work, published in 1952 and known since then as Modern Portfolio Theory, that influenced the rise to prominence of the hedge fund and other 'alternative' investments that were previously viewed as inapplicable to mainstream investing. Modern Portfolio Theory showed how the ***diversification*** of a portfolio through careful security selection could result in both an increase in returns *and* a decrease in risk—at the same time! Could you really have your cake and eat it too? According to proponents of this theory and its outgrowths, it seemed that you really could but it is questioned by many leading investors.

"Wide diversification is only required when investors do not understand what they are doing".
Warren Buffett

The Quants Take Over

Let's return for a moment to the post-1974 period, and the paradigm shift that swept the investing world with the widespread acceptance of benchmarking as the predominant means by which to judge a manager's performance. Through Modern Portfolio Theory, numerical values could be ascribed to the extent to which a company's stock, for example, performed in relation to an appropriate index; Microsoft's stock value could be compared to the Dow, such that a historical accounting of the company's stock price in relation to that index could be created. Statistical analysis of the standard deviation of historical returns and the volatility of those returns resulted in a measure of the stock's *correlation* to the index, which came to be known as *beta*. Greater or lesser values were then observed, with a one-to-one relation of movement in one vs. the other ascribed a value of 1.0.

It's fair to say that if you could collect enough good companies that tended to consistently outperform their competitors, and pool these together in the same portfolio, you'd probably be a pretty good manager! *Alpha* was the term used to convey this 'active' component of a manager's input, rather than simply relying upon the rising tide of a good economy, for example. When all of these complexities are factored together, Modern Portfolio Theory gave investors a precise accounting of how the managers they hired were performing *relative* to not only their peers but also in relation to the market as a whole.

Confusing? We'd say so!

These terms—standard deviation, volatility, *alpha*, *beta*, and many more—became commonplace in financial parlance. Relative return was all that really mattered, and the question for most investors quickly became not just "how am I doing?" but "how am I doing against everybody else?" Not just in the US but also globally, personal finance expanded in endless waves of growth, innovation and access. Complex investing became commonplace and part of the fabric of our everyday lives; how your portfolio performed was something everyone talked about at cocktail parties and neighborhood barbeques. Institutional investors that had the skill and resources to apply the academic models and deploy their own capital in new and profitable ways, moreover, quickly embraced hedge fund investing. Wall Street investment banks, large pension funds, university endowments, and other large investors brought this once obscure and little-known animal into plain view. Human evolution being what it is, what once was the purview of the privileged soon became accessible to the masses through investment advisors the world over—*and not just at exclusive brokerages.*

How does this relate to the issue of quantitative analysis and risk management? As more and more investors piled into mutual funds and entered the investment market *en masse*, the ability of a given manager to outperform their respective benchmarks soon began to decline. By the late 1990's, seeking relative return had become a zero-sum game; it soon became evident that most managers were simply unable to outperform the benchmark indices, especially when you factored in fund expenses. The fees they charged soon ate up any *alpha* they were able to produce. Informational advantages were also increasingly more difficult to come by, and a fund manager's ability to exploit qualitative factors was slowly but surely overcome by the ability to perform more complex quantitative analysis, which itself seemed to overrule the art and intuition that previously characterised the role of the manager.

Benchmarking also spawned the invention of the 'index fund,' a particular type of fund that chose *not* to actively seek additional returns, or *alpha*, above and beyond a given index's performance. Index mutual funds became a popular feature in employee pension plans and self-directed investment accounts, because of their low cost and easy accessibility. Beating the market almost seemed to be a thing of the past; if it was not, it was again something that was attainable only by the giants of Wall Street, who had made use of complex mathematical 'black box' strategies; a leading part of the trading they undertook for their own accounts.

Several factors dispelled the 'myth' of relative returns and poked holes in the curtain of relative performance that managers could hide behind when charging fees. The first, of course, was the widespread use of benchmarking and the advent of the low-cost index fund, as described above. The second was a series of catastrophic events, beginning with 1987's Black Monday when stock markets around the world crashed. Much of the blame for this event has been placed on 'program trading' that had become commonplace at brokerages on Wall Street and elsewhere; the articulation of the Black-Scholes stock option pricing model had, for instance, led to the widespread belief that portfolios could be "insured" through the use of complex hedging strategies.

Other models simply dictated the buying and selling practices based upon external factors, such as predetermined market levels.

The second event was the bursting of the dot-com bubble, which lasted from 1998-2001 and peaked in March 2000. Speculative buying of unproven internet-based companies led many, among them the much-lauded Federal Reserve Chairman Alan Greenspan, to proclaim that a new era in stock valuation had begun. Much of this, of course, was also directly related to the rapidly advancing ability of analysts to crunch numbers in new and profitable ways that seemed to explain away traditional conceptions of risk. The third event was the 2003 mutual fund scandal, in which some of the largest mutual fund companies were involved in illegal after-hours trading of mutual fund shares. Due to the regulations covering mutual fund pricing, it was possible to exploit certain aspects of the rules governing those trades. Traders could place trades 'late,' essentially right at or even just after the close of the exchange upon which those shares traded; hedge fund Canary Capital and brokers at Bank of America were charged with collusion in this respect. Others were implicated in 'market timing' strategies that sought to illegally profit from buying and selling of the same shares across different time zones, trades that were often in contravention of the fund's own prospectus to say nothing of issues of exchange rules or tax law.

The confluence of these factors brought the deficiencies of the relative return paradigm into sharp focus. Painful economic declines occurred as a result of these events and billions of dollars of shareholder value were erased almost overnight. Investors, regardless of how big or small, took no comfort in the fact that everyone else was suffering too; *performance relative to the rest of the market no longer carried the same significance, especially when investors factored in the escalating expenses they had paid in order to be subjected to these losses of wealth*. The direct outgrowth of these factors was the advent of a new paradigm: almost instantly, *absolute* returns became the new game in town.

The Best of Both Worlds, Redux

While certainly not the only type of investment to employ these complex tactics and strategies, hedge funds are perhaps the best known, although possibly the least understood as well. Recalling the tenets of Modern Portfolio Theory, it was believed—and still is today—that proper analysis could result in both the reduction of risk and a simultaneous enhancement of returns. Markowitz' study was one of the first to systematically adapt mathematics to finance, and it pioneered new statistically-driven methods of security selection; it's important to realise as well that this is by no means confined to equity assets. Indeed, all manner and classes of investments could be analysed for potential inclusion in investment portfolios in light of their diversification benefits. While it might seem contrary to common sense, even historically more-risky assets such as commodities and real estate could be combined with 'traditional' equities and bonds in order to 'optimise' a portfolio. *The inherent trade-off between risk and return could thus be tilted solidly in the latter's favour through the precise combination of asset weightings within a given portfolio.*

The absolute return paradigm grew from this, because it allowed such precision in the analysis of investments. The overriding concern for funds that employed this strategy, then, was to generate positive returns—or at least, lose significantly less—regardless of which way the market was trending. If the market was going up, a manager either generated *alpha* or in the least, participated in the *beta* that everyone else saw too. *Beta* is not synonymous with returns, at least not in the sense of percentages, but over time it earned the same connotation because it effectively determined performance relative to a given benchmark.

When fund managers of all stripes get paid in percentage terms on the basis of their fund assets, rather than just according to profitability, the incentive exists to take undue risk with clients' funds. That risk, moreover, was not confined solely to the realm of security selection; as the market timing scandals demonstrated, it took on a deeper, legal meaning as well, as some fund managers were tempted to act fraudulently, or at least unethically, in order to generate a bigger paycheck for themselves. *In a zero-sum game, one man's gain is another's loss; investors suffered at the expense of managers, who got paid regardless of whether they won or lost.*

In one sense, this is actually one way that hedge funds trump mutual funds, because most hedge fund managers *don't* get paid just on the basis of their fund's assets. Investors and managers both share in profits, and often the managers are subject to predetermined hurdles, or 'high-water marks,' that they must eclipse in order to keep getting paid. The incentive exists for them to keep working hard in order to generate returns, which is what their clients are paying them exorbitant fees to do! Many hedge funds managers earn 2% of a fund's asset values, much like mutual funds do, but they also earn as much as 20% or more of any positive returns. Particular hedge funds also specify how much return they will generate over and above a selected benchmark yield, prior to allowing managers to be paid. These fee structures and constraints are intended to align the interests of investors and managers more closely than a flat percentage fee alone might do.

The real question, then, becomes *how* the fund manager seeks to generate those returns. As with fundamental analysis, which has at its core the consideration of qualitative factors as well as quantitative concerns, there is an important judgment component that managers try to exploit in order to gain their edge. Research, access to information, and proprietary modeling of the ways in which different securities interact in varying economic conditions are the primary determinants of returns here, and they help to characterise hedge funds into six main types or strategies. The first is by style, which can be further broken down into sub-types such as global macro, event-driven, arbitrage and futures trading. Here, managers seek to exploit global financial market conditions including changes in interest rates or currency values, or event-specific consequences such as unexpected bankruptcies or political decisions. These can have dramatic consequences and can generate substantial and spectacular profits or losses.

Managers can exploit these developments in a variety of ways. One way they do this is through market selection, which is the second type of fund. Managers specialise in equities, bonds, commodities, currencies, derivatives, real estate or virtually any other type of asset that can be bought or sold. An alternative way that managers seek to generate profits or avoid losses is through the instruments or specific investment techniques that they employ; they might buy and hold, they might sell short, or they might utilise a variety of financial derivatives in order to hedge risk and/or enhance returns. A fourth and related way, is the concept of exposure. While some managers seek that elusive *alpha* by following the market up, trying to beat the market by picking more wisely than their peers, others want to force it down and profit from its decline. Short-selling is not the only way that they profit from the directionality of the markets; another method is called the 'market neutral' strategy, and involves the careful pairing of securities that are often in the same industry or likely to be influenced by the same market conditions. Managers hope that one will go up and the other will go down, and when combined with other tactics described above, the can profit from the difference.

The term market-neutral points to the fifth strategy, which is related to the type of exposure that managers subject their portfolios to. ***Just as important as what, when, and how a fund is invested are the issues of where and why***. The particular geographic region or industry sector that they focus on, while very much related to and by no means divorced from the other strategies they employ, are themselves indicative of a different type of fund category. Finally, and following this line of thought, it is possible for funds to diversify and be invested in multiple strategies, in multiple markets, and even for them to invest with other managers in a fund-of-funds, multi-manager structure.

It should be readily apparent that the scope and function of even your average 'run of the mill' hedge fund could reach far beyond the comprehension of even the most gifted investment advisor, analyst or academic. Quantitative analysis of the multitude of complex, interrelated factors that could form the basis of an investment decision is therefore at the heart of the operation of these funds. Robust mathematical models often, although not always, replaced any qualitative input from the manager—the art and intuition of investing that in many respects formed the myth of the successful investor subsequently went out the window. Advisors that relied on traditional methods, as Buffett has and still does, were marginalised by the financial industry and relegated to a secondary role as analysts only.

The impact on global finance came to be monumental in its breadth and depth. While estimates vary on size and number, most peg the size of the hedge fund industry as eclipsing $2.5 trillion USD at its peak in mid-2008, with the potential number of funds usually approximated at well over 7,500. By contrast, the mutual fund industry in the US reached perhaps $12 trillion, with about 8,000 funds. The lack of hedge fund regulation makes it difficult to fully grasp their enormous reach and potential impact on the market. Many of them exist in secrecy, closed to all but a few investors; they argue that this is precisely how they maintain their competitive edge and have been so profitable, because they are not required to disclose their trading strategies in the same way that mutual funds do.

This also reveals an important factor in their rise to prominence: the profit incentive. In the early 1970's Wall Street began to attract a new breed of financier, the academic. Mathematicians were the hot commodities, because of the high demand for the proprietary models they could create and employ, primarily through the use of arbitrage strategies. These exploited minute differences in the price of stocks or bonds, for example, and often carried out these trades by buying and selling the securities on different exchanges. Complex equations could crunch the necessary numbers with increasing efficiency and effectiveness, even given the ever-present advances in market liquidity. The best and brightest of academia, such as award-winning mathematician James Simons, left their university careers behind in search of massive profits—Simons earned an astonishing $2.5 billion in 2008 after his flagship Medallion fund recorded 80% returns, and that's *net* of his 5% management fee and 44% performance fee!

Simons' Renaissance Technologies is indicative of the extent of this mathematical infiltration into the world of finance: "Simons won't discuss his strategy except to say that it is based on rapid-fire trading across almost every possible market and that it relies on computer-driven programs designed by an army of more than 100 Ph.D.s. Publicly disclosed information is limited largely to quarterly reports of equity holdings, which amounted to $27.6 billion at year-end 2008, down from $57.4 billion 12 months earlier." It is a far cry from the single-page sketches employed by Warren Buffett in making his investment decisions! It is also no wonder that the lure of such wealth has proved so irresistible to so many managers; Simons' is by no means alone, as 2008 saw the top four managers in the hedge fund universe each earn over $1 billion, and the top 25 taken together raked in nearly $12 billion. Following the bursting of the dot-come bubble and the 2003 mutual fund scandal, the ranks of these managers swelled considerably and a virtual exodus took shape as many sought to escape the tightly regulated, highly scrutinised world of mutual fund investing.

But is it better investing?

Certainly the experiences of the most famous and profitable hedge fund managers would suggest that the 'Quants' held an important edge. As competition in the mutual fund industry and rapid changes in market liquidity as a result of technological innovation decreased profit margins for everyone, the rise of quantitative analysis as the premier investment methodology heralded another change in the minds of the investment world: quantitative analysis drastically altered our conceptions of what constituted adequate returns. Even more important, it distorted our perceptions of what constituted appropriate risk.

One of the best examples of hedge fund investing, and possibly the most famous hedge fund manager, is George Soros. Soros earned $1.1 billion in 2008 for his management services, placing him in the fourth spot that year, but perhaps more compelling is his record of success. In 2008, Soros also ranked 97th on the Forbes' annual list of the world's most wealthy individuals, and has decades of experience with generating almost unheard-of returns through his well-timed investments. One of his most famous was when he 'broke' the pound sterling in 1992 by betting $10 billion that the rising costs of German reunification following the fall of the Berlin Wall would force the Bank of England to devalue the British currency. Soros was right, and the swift decline of the pound sterling resulted in Soros' Quantum Fund earning more than $1 billion on that one trade alone! From the Fund's inception in 1969 until Soros effectively exited the 'risk business' in 2000, it had returned in excess of 30% year upon year, more than three times the annual returns of the S&P 500.

Soros, while perhaps less of a 'Quant' than many of his peers, is nevertheless a follower of highly unorthodox, hugely complex trading strategies. Soros relied upon 'informational advantage' and is famous for his disbelief in the 'efficient market hypothesis,' choosing rather to base his strategies upon contrarian positions that seek to factor in the bias, ignorance and irrationality of the millions of other investors. For these and other key hedge fund strategies to succeed, however, they depend upon two critical factors: the lack of transparency that is facilitated by regulatory laxity, and massive amounts of leverage. Looking first at transparency, the regulatory framework that has prevailed up to this point has allowed hedge funds to operate with seeming impunity. They can effectively do whatever they want, whenever they want, and however they want, because this is exactly what they are paid to do. Clients turn over their capital to these managers precisely because they are hopefully able to generate returns in unconventional ways, and to do so regardless of the present market conditions that might otherwise hobble their trades or produce lackluster returns. Hedge fund managers argue that they could not do what they do if they were required to disclose their strategies in the same way as mutual funds do.

Second, many of these trades involve massive amounts of leverage, which is also facilitated by this regulatory opacity. Especially when it comes to tactics such as short-selling and derivative-based trading strategies in the commodities or futures markets, leverage is an integral part of the investment process. Former Fed Chair Alan Greenspan is infamous for his position that adequate regulation already imposed upon the hedge funds' lenders, through the facilities of the Federal Reserve and in concert with the United States Treasury, would mean that Wall Street's newest breed would effectively police itself. If banks had limits upon whom they could lend to and in what quantities they could do so, then hedge funds in turn would be limited in how much they could borrow. The collapse of Long-Term Capital Management in 1998 showed the world the colossal error of this line of thinking, but little has since been done to correct it—leverage, while enhancing investment opportunities and the potential for greater returns, also exponentially compounds risk and loss. Without access to the balance sheets of hedge funds, which typically control double-digit multiples of the actual assets on their books, their ability to quickly and massively move the markets is unparalleled.

> *"Often the difference between a successful man and a failure*
> *is not one's better abilities or ideas, but the courage that one*
> *has to bet on his ideas, to take a calculated risk, and to act."*
> **Maxwell Maltz**

Quantitative analysis thus represents somewhat of a double-edged sword. The idea that you could pursue absolute returns is not new; in fact it is much older than the idea of benchmarking. Quantitative analysis, simply put, made it easier to be done by more people. It elevated the game of active management to the utmost level, and ushered in a new paradigm that has influenced the investment strategies of all investors, regardless of how big or small. However, the flip side is that the concomitant effect was a distortion in perceptions of risk, both for the individual investor and for the financial system as a whole.

When transparency is reduced to the point where any disclosures that do occur are meaningless, such as their quarterly or yearly equity holdings reports, our ability to understand the amount of risk being taken is critically handicapped. Volatility, one of the key considerations when trying to gauge investment risk, is very likely to be critically understated, *despite* and perhaps *because of* the predictable manner in which these funds are supposed to behave—roughly half of the main strategies detailed earlier are argued to display extremely low volatility, low correlation to the market, and to reduce portfolio risk. At the same time, a large proportion of these still predict better than average returns and diversification benefits.

It is easy to see why institutional investors including pensions and endowments eagerly sought out these investments and have deployed billions of dollars to participate in these strategies; many of the larger players in this space now devote large percentage allocations of their overall investments to absolute return strategies. One measure of the performance of diversified hedge funds has shown that from 1990-2008, hedge funds returned double-digit performance gains in 10 out of 19 years, with only three out of the remaining years experiencing declines;

most tellingly, those declines were but a fraction of the losses incurred by traditional equities, and never entered double-digit territory. ***This shows how these funds have played an important part in protecting capital for investors with a long enough timeline to withstand their risk, and good investors know that insulation from loss is just as important as participating in returns.***

In the wake of the credit crisis, hedge funds proved just as unable to adequately explain away or manage risk as traditional investments. In 2008 hedge funds lost as much as 18% and losses were recorded at two out of three funds. When investors try to pull their funds out, it can often upset the delicate balance built into the complex models that underpin them, and most funds impose tight restrictions on how and when investors can withdraw their capital. Of course, losses are simply not supposed to happen, so when declines such as these occurred, the wave of redemptions forced many funds to close up shop. By the end of 2008 at least 15% of all funds had been forced to close.

Of course, if we could hedge away all risk, this would be reflected in diminished returns. Certainly these strategies have a place for those that can bear them out over the long term, but what is less clear is how far their impact does in fact reach. The story of Long-Term Capital Management in 1998 and the collapse of Bear Stearns' two mortgage funds in 2007 showed that when left unchecked, the size and scope of hedge funds in general threaten the entire system as a whole. It is fair to say that these latest failures led directly to the collapse of Bear Stearns itself, and heavily influenced the sale of Merrill Lynch, one of Bear's main creditors. It is this snowball effect that illustrates the dangers of leverage and the risks of a weak regulatory framework; and just like in 1998, nothing has yet been changed to compensate for the risks we are all painfully aware still exist.

Conclusion

"In the business world, the rearview mirror is always clearer than the windshield."

Warren Buffett

What does all this mean for investors, whether on Wall Street or Main Street?

In an age when hedge funds alone account for one-third of all bond trading, it's not a consideration that should be taken lightly. Problems certainly exist with respect to the regulatory framework that hedge funds are still subject to; the US Treasury Secretary has stated his intention to bring hedge funds and other investors that are similarly less regulated under the umbrella of federal supervision. Federal Reserve Chair Ben Bernanke has called for a systemic-risk regulator in order to monitor and hopefully counter any potential future crises like the one we are in now, a new 'resolution authority' with the power to seize and wind-down non-bank institutions that could threaten the entire system.

The Obama administration has also made clear that hedge funds should in future be subject to registration with the SEC, much as the mutual fund industry has been since the Great Depression. This would likely result in increased levels of transparency and making them subject to inspections by agency staff. They have also advocated for a new centralised clearinghouse for unregulated derivative contracts and stricter limits on the size and number of positions that traders can hold.

Seemingly absent, however, has been the issue of leverage. Long placed at the center of this issue, the debate over reform is less about the type of risk than the magnification of it. Indeed, Modern Portfolio Theory has at its heart the assumption that investors are risk averse: given a choice between assets that offer the same expected return, they will inevitably choose the one that is less risky. The problem, though, is that this assumption also implies that only expected return and volatility matter. Most investors likely find little solace in the fact their funds, while losing 18% or more in 2008, still outperformed the S&P 500, which lost nearly 40% of its value. If most investors could really see what went on 'behind the hedge,' it's fair to say that many would be running for the door even faster than before.

Recalling the position of Greenspan, and his belief that adequate regulation already imposed upon the hedge funds' lenders would result in the 'self-regulation' of the industry itself, it is now painfully evident that this approach has not worked. More to the point, what if the lenders themselves don't behave? Perhaps most troubling is not the hedge fund industry, which is for the most part, only exposing to 'undue' risk those investors that are *willfully* participating in it; if these investors are judged to be able to withstand the ride, and have the capital to commit to this adventure, then by all means they should be able to get on the rollercoaster! The real issue, though, is the investment banks and big institutions such as AIG, which were hedge funds in disguise.

Goldman Sachs, for example, effectively used the non-recourse bailout loans from the TARP program in order to continue operating just as a hedge fund would. Generating stronger-than-expected profits in the first quarter of 2009, the company bounced back after their worst quarter as a public company. According to the firm, their exceptional results were driven by big profits in its fixed income business, where revenue surged to $6.56 billion, which was 34% above the previous record. ***Sound familiar?*** It should, for it is reflective of their continued reliance on risky trading for their own accounts, but this time they did it with funds borrowed from the taxpayer rather than just their own clients. Rather than scale back the risk they were taking, especially given their own acknowledgement of the difficult economic environment, when revenues in their primary lines of business declined by as much as 30%, they took on *more* risk.

How can they not have learned? How can they continue to justify behaving in such a way, especially given the intense scrutiny that they receive as a public company? The answer to these questions may never be fully known. What we do know, however, is that managers—unlike investors—always seem to choose the more risky course, rather than the less risky one. The profit incentive, it seems, is simply too great or at least too poorly aligned with the interests of their clients. Even though quantitative analysis should make the investment decisions easier, it has in many respects only served to engender systemic risk that threatens us all. In the case of Goldman Sachs, they've done so with taxpayer-funded bailout money. They've continued to take enormous risks, not just on behalf of their own clients but also by leveraging their entire balance sheet in order to do so.

Hedge funds are inherently risky, and they have always been so. As their standard disclosures maintain, they are suitable only for those investors in a position to bear their limited liquidity and complex strategies. As a result, they were always only intended for those with long-term investment horizons and capital enough to suffer heavy loss. Curiously, however, as quantitative analysis supplanted qualitative considerations, timelines for investment tactics—if not their strategies—have become increasingly shorter. As it has proceeded to do so, traditional conceptions of risk have been significantly distorted. Perhaps the models are still not complex enough; alternatively, perhaps we should be paying even more attention to the ignorance and bias that Soros believes still plague the markets. If we did this, perhaps investing would once again be more reflective of game theory, rather than gambling—because sooner or later, **everyone's luck runs out**!

Hedge funds lie on the knife edge of capitalism, at the point where maximum risk meets highest returns, in the void of regulatory control. In 2007 when hedge fund manager John Paulson earned US$3.7 billion, 14% of his industry's fellow funds closed down. The question for hedge fund investors perhaps lies in quantifying the track record of the selected manager and predicting his future returns. Rather than regulate the industry, an easier control mechanism would be for regulators to limit the proportion of net wealth a single individual investor may place in these vehicles.

In the next chapter we move from hedge funds, the newest and rawest form of capitalism back to where it all began; *the glamour and glitter of gold!*

Chapter 4

July 2007—The Currency of Illusion: The Sovereign Nation of Gold

"Curst greed of gold, what crimes thy tyrant power has caused."

Vergil

May 2007—Gold Price resumes an upwards only price trajectory.

What is the allure of Gold? That hypnotic spell of all that glitters, yet does it draw us ever closer to disaster!

Gold. The very mention sparks visions of wealth and grandeur. Has anything else ever captured the imagination and the resources of so many in its pursuit? Empires have been created purely in order to source it, and wars have been fought over it. Even today, gold prices continue to be among the most widely reported of all financial assets in the financial press, and many investors continue to seek out gold as a store of their wealth. In today's tough economic times, one doesn't have to look far to see that gold still captures our attention; global demand for this precious metal has surged and prices have seemingly climbed into the stratosphere. ***Contemporary economists and policymakers are even advocating a return to the gold standard***.

The history of gold as an economic item stretches back over seven millennia. It was first adopted by ancient civilisations in the Middle East and Northern Africa as sacred and ornamental, but did not gain use as a monetary instrument for several thousand years. Even then, gold did not become the standard currency for several thousand more. Today, and despite many popular myths to the contrary, it plays virtually no part in our modern economic system. Yet, gold continues to hold our focus. It is not simply a commodity like any other, with its value determined *solely* by supply and demand.

> *"The desire for gold is the most universal and deeply rooted commercial instinct of the human race."*
>
> **Gerald M. Loeb**

Since the earliest discovery of gold refining, this precious metal has done more than stand in the place of other items of value. Gold has also played an important role as a social item, which in many respects goes beyond relative measures of its scarcity. Indeed, because of its central place throughout much of modern economic history, gold has been a transmitter of societal values. It has played a key role in the socioeconomic development of many nations, and continues to do so even today.

In this chapter, we'll delve into these issues and explore the essential question: *why gold?*

Of course, in doing so, we'll also reveal the flipside to that question! We'll begin by discussing the rise of the 'gold economy,' why it came to play the role that it did as a representation of the wealth of nations, and why it soon lost favour. Even though it is no longer the backer of the world's currencies, gold still exerts influence over monetary policies and investment behaviour. We'll also examine some of the critical *human* impacts that gold has had on nations around the world, which helps to show how the 'value' of gold—and why we need to understand it—goes beyond its monetary uses. In today's tough economy, gold is still as precious as ever, and it is our hope that by the end of these pages we'll understand why this continues to be so.

The Rise and Fall of the Gold Economy

> *"Those entrapped by the herd instinct are drowned in the deluges of history. But there are always the few who observe,*

reason, and take precautions, and thus escape the flood. For these few gold has been the asset of last resort."
Antony C. Sutton

Going back thousands of years, we know from the first human settlements and cities that people have used anything that was scarce in nature as a means of simplifying their purchases of goods and services. If it was scarce, it had value, a simple concept that all of us learn as children. Many physical items have been used in this way, including shells, agricultural produce, and precious metals.

However, the use of these commodities as a form of what we now call money did not emerge until civilisations had begun to coalesce as distinct from simple tribes or hereditary groups. Previous to this, physical commodities such as wheat or barley were used primarily in exchange for other vital goods, a system known as barter. Simply put, something that one person had, was traded for something that she or he wanted that someone else possessed. In its simplest form, this was an adequate arrangement, with people trading what they had for what they wanted or needed, and vice versa.

As human societies progressed and grew, it became much more difficult to arrange. Transactions in their purest form of exchange are difficult, because in order to trade their goods, they need to be in the same place, at the same time. Buyers need sellers; a person looking to exchange their grain for something else, for example fruit or livestock had to find someone else that wanted to buy it and *that valued it to the same degree as they did*. Economists call this a 'coincidence of wants,' and it shows the inherent difficulties and inefficiencies of the barter system. If one person had grain and another had fruit, they both needed to be harvested at the same time for an exchange to take place, to say nothing of establishing some measure of equivalency between these two goods!

It is easy to see why people chose to use basic commodities as a substitute for other goods. Taking the example of precious metals, for example, it was easier for a wider range of people to agree on them as an item of value, one that could be used on its own to build tools or weapons as well as something that could be easily exchanged for other things, such as food. If everyone could agree on a given commodity as something of value, then it could be measured and standardised, and thereby treated as an intermediary between buyers and sellers. As well, commodities were often easier to transport, and helped solve some of the problems posed by time and place.

The use of basic commodities, whether precious metals, agricultural produce, livestock or anything else with inherent value, still did not completely solve these key issues. As societies grew and developed, most often under some form of aristocratic rule, new principles of organisation aided in the creation of 'representative' money. With the advent of various forms of writing, for example in ancient Mesopotamia, receipts for deposits of grain at royal warehouses came to be seen as a form of money. From this point forward, money was seen not as a substitute for a particular thing with inherent value, *but as a symbol of trust*. So long as one's receipts were backed by a physical deposit of your valued commodities, one could even transfer that promise to another person, in exchange for something else of value.

Representative money did many things. It solved the problem of transportation, of time and of place. In this way, and most importantly, it allowed the idea of borrowing and lending to be formalised. This enterprise quickly expanded and while most often it still needed the seal of approval of the ruling elite, a new class of citizens undertook the new 'business of money'. They in turn created their wealth through the settlement of accounts. However, it must be remembered that 'new money' still had to be created—by growing it, farming it, producing it, or digging it up from the ground. Trust in the value of money was still tied to the promise of its backing by physical goods on deposit, which in turn held their own *intrinsic* value.

As trade grew and expanded beyond just the immediate locales of cities and states, the issue of time became central to the issue of money. The enterprise of banking grew out of the need to solve this issue of time, with families such as the Medici in Italy acting as brokers for transactions between merchants. Bills of exchange were another form of representative money that could be used as a means of payment upon the conclusion of a transaction at some time in the future; these bills could also be exchanged for cash in advance, albeit at some discount. Despite the religious prohibition against charging interest, brokering the deal and absorbing that discount could still make profits.

It is easy to see how money came to be created, rather than simply farmed, produced or mined. As banks became more involved in issues of trade, they developed the business of deposit taking and currency exchange. With the introduction of fractional mathematics to the European continent in the Middle Ages, bankers quickly learned the lesson of money creation: not all deposits were likely to be called for at the same time, and as a result, they could write more receipts than were actually backed by physical deposits. It was usually only during times of crisis that banks would fail, when depositors demanded their assets and forced a liquidation, or if one large creditor demanded payment for a debt.

This example shows the power of money, or more importantly, the power that comes with the ability to control money. Since the advent of representative money, governments have sought to monopolise its issue and circulation. Empires were formed purely for the ability to capture the natural resources that were converted into paper bills, such as silver and gold, and it was not until the 1970's that money itself was 'de-linked' from precious metal. Hundreds of years previously before this time, the world's powers learned a most important lesson; *that money could embody its own power too!*

Throughout most of the latter half of the millennium, and up until the middle of the 20th Century, money, in the form of currencies, was still backed by precious metals in particular, but not exclusively gold, on deposit and owned by sovereign states. For much of that time, the aspirations of empires were driven not just by the need to support their growing populations and to find new sources of cheap, raw materials, but by the need to find new sources to back their currencies. Territorial expansion, like every other trade that held the promise of a future transaction, allowed countries to print money, because sooner or later the goods to back it would enter the markets. Unfortunately, the world also found that when they did so, supply and demand took over, and prices adjusted accordingly. While it may seem elementary to us, the concept and process of inflation was a tough one for many to grasp.

What we see here is the delicate balance between supply and demand, and how it relates to the issue of money. Money could literally be 'created' out of thin air, but there was a limit to this excess, and its circulation as well as its issue had to be controlled. The monopoly to do this usually—although not always, as was the case in the United States for much of its history—rested with the central government. As international trade grew, and gold remained the standard commodity backing the world's currencies, history also shows us that like the flu, changes to the supply of money can be contagious. Prices in one country translate into prices in another, and changes in the amount of money circulating around the world—even though they are denominated in different currencies—will affect the value of money itself.

> *"For more than two thousand years gold's natural qualities made it man's universal medium of exchange. In contrast to political money, gold is honest money that survived the ages and will live on long after the political fiats of today have gone the way of all paper."*
>
> **Hans F. Sennholz**

World economic powers tried various methods to remedy this situation and insulate themselves from 'shocks' such as the Great Depression that periodically transmitted throughout the global financial system. One method was through exchange rates: currency values were 'pegged' and exchangeable into other local currencies at certain fixed rates. This proved difficult, if not impossible, when each country's currency remained tied to its fixed reserves of physical gold. This is especially the case when each currency could literally print as much paper money as it liked! In order to maintain the exchange rates in relation to the amount of gold they possessed, central banks would be required to buy or sell foreign currencies in order to keep the supply and demand equation intact. The complexities of these mechanisms in turn contributed to its failure.

Another method was to peg one currency, the US dollar, to the value of gold at a fixed rate, and allow other currencies to 'float' in relation to the US dollar alone. From 1944-1968, this worked at least somewhat, but eventually began to unravel as the value of gold in terms of US dollars, and the value of gold on the free market, diverged. By 1971, as we have mentioned before, the decision came to de-link the value of the US dollar to gold at a fixed price. Once this decision was made, the value of a country's currency would no longer represent the quantity of gold that it possessed, and could not be converted into gold at fixed prices. No longer was money the symbol of a valued commodity, but now, it was a commodity itself. Trading in this commodity continued because money became a symbol of trust, in that governments and their central banks promised to honour it as a means of payment and exchange for all payments and debts, not just deposits.

At long last, we can see how money has come full circle. It began as a substitute for a basic commodity, something of value that could be exchanged for something else, in order to solve the problems that existed between buyers and sellers. Transportation, time and place were all problems that could be solved with relative ease, when something other than the goods and services that were desired was used in its stead. Money as a separate commodity did not exist when societies operated under the barter system, but quickly grew into one of the utmost importance when human progress and economic development grew and went global. Many things have stood for money, the most important of which was one of our most precious metals, gold.

A little under forty years ago the limits of physical convertibility were reached under the strain of international trade and the foreign exchange of so many currencies. Money, as a symbol of the trust we place in our governments and banks to maintain its value, has now literally become a commodity itself.

Why (or, Why Not) Gold?

> *"Gold would have value if for no other reason; than that it enables a citizen to fashion his financial escape from the state."*
> **William F. Rickenbacker**

Once a physical commodity no longer supports a currency, that money is no longer **representative**; it becomes what's known as *fiat* money. Once this break is made, money is itself a commodity, just like any other. So, if money is—like gold—now 'just' a commodity, does that mean that it's as good as gold? **Paper currencies are backed by the 'full faith and credit' of their sovereign governments, so why does gold persistently hold our collective attention?**

In order to address this question, we must step back in time once more, and explore the gold standard itself.

Why gold? To begin with, it is exceedingly rare. Its scarcity, of course, increases its demand, and according to the laws of economics we know that when the supply of such a thing is severely limited, its price will inevitably reflect that. It has been estimated that the total amount of all the gold *ever* mined is only about 150,000 tonnes—and over 60% of that has been produced since 1950. Gold was adopted as the backer of currencies for precisely this reason, **because it is so much scarcer than other metals.** Yet a further plus is that gold has its own intrinsic value because it can be used for other purposes, such as jewellery and various industrial applications.

The use of paper money backed by gold was originally introduced by China. It was not adopted in this manner in Europe until the early 1700's, and even then, it was only used alongside other forms of coin currency, namely silver. Silver was used as currency because of its relative abundance, but nations such as Spain that pursued its acquisition quickly discovered the phenomenon of inflation: as more silver was mined, minted and introduced into the 'money supply,' the relative worth of it as a currency soon declined.

Arguably the first nation to adopt a true gold standard was the United Kingdom. In 1717, the UK fixed the value of gold to the shilling, but this only served to overvalue gold relative to silver when compared to valuations in other countries. Over time the result was outflows of silver from the UK. Silver was sent abroad and gold flowed in, which created a *de facto* gold standard. The gold standard did not become law in the UK until 1844, when the Bank Charter Act established that Bank of England notes—fully backed by gold—were the legal standard. Other countries in Europe slowly followed suit throughout the 1800's; the United States was one of the last nations to adopt a *de jure* gold standard, in 1900.

In the absence of a co-ordinated international financial system, however, countries were free to fix the value of their currency to gold however they saw fit. This led to an informal system of fixed exchange rates. The outgrowth of this, however, was that the money supply in each country was thus indirectly determined by the balance of their imports and exports, vis-à-vis other nations. Even though for a time this could mean some measure of price stability for trading purposes as well as a long-term 'anchor' for price (or inflation) expectations, it also meant that countries gave up their ability to control their own money supply; in effect, it meant a choice between free trade and an independent national monetary policy.

> *"With the exception only of the period of the gold standard, practically all governments of history have used their exclusive power to issue money to defraud and plunder the people."*
> **F.A. von Hayak**

Trying to maintain the system of fixed exchange rates that was necessitated by 'pegging' many currencies to a single commodity eventually eroded the system. The First and Second World Wars caused sharp fluctuations in the effective exchange rates between the major economic powers, which in turn caused most countries to devalue their currencies versus the US dollar. This gave the US a strong competitive advantage, especially following the devastation of the Second World War. In the immediate post-war period, it was recognised that free trade—which was necessary to rebuild the world's shattered economies—required freely convertible currencies. The compromise was reached with the Bretton Woods system.

The architects of Bretton Woods realised that gold production itself was not sufficient to meet the demands of growing international trade. In order to remedy the problems posed for exchange rates that were fixed to predetermined gold reserves they choose to use the US dollar as the reserve currency. Countries would instead peg their currencies to the US dollar, which was in turn backed by and convertible into gold at a predetermined price of $35 per ounce; in order to maintain exchange rate stability, countries would buy and sell US dollars and thereby remedy any trade imbalances. The US dollar thus became the 'world's currency,' and the International Monetary Fund became the *de facto* mechanism for managing the new liberal economic order.

As the world swung into recovery following the Second World War, the United States was able to run massive trade surpluses; they exported much more than they imported. Dollars were flowing into the US, but in order to maintain the proper functioning of the new economic system, the country had to ensure that there was enough liquidity, paper dollars, for use around the world. In order to remedy this potentially destabilising dynamic, the US promoted competitive industry in Europe and Japan, and provided financial aid to the lesser-developed areas of Europe, Asia and the 'Third World.' Three reasons were expounded for this:

"Bretton Woods, then, created a system of triangular trade: the United States would use the convertible financial system to trade at a tremendous profit with developing nations, expanding industry and acquiring raw materials. It would use this surplus to send dollars to Europe, which would then be used to rebuild their economies, and make the United States the market for their products. This would allow the other industrialised nations to purchase products from the Third World, which reinforced the American role as the guarantor of stability. When this triangle became destabilised, Bretton Woods entered a period of crisis that ultimately led to its collapse."

This also highlights another often overlooked justification for supplying US dollars as the world's currency: the need to counteract the rising might of the Soviet Union. The Soviet Union, it must be noted, had significant gold resources of its own, and without the constraints imposed by the Bretton Woods system, the Soviet Union would be better able to finance its expansion. In addition, if the US were able to take a leadership role as the guarantor of stability throughout the world, it would be in a better position to pursue its own foreign policy agenda.

Bretton Woods thus provided an indirect means of economically isolating the Soviet Union.

However, from 1958-68, the United States' efforts became self-defeating, and the country soon began to run trade deficits. What's more, in order to maintain the smooth functioning of this economic order, it *had* to do so. Only the dollar was convertible into gold, so it soon became more worthwhile to hold dollars; by 1960, the price of gold on the open market began to diverge from the fixed Bretton Woods price. There was thus a temptation to buy gold at the Bretton Woods price and sell it on the open market in order to deal with internal monetary policies, and this threatened to erode confidence in the US dollar.

It soon became impossible to enforce the system of pegged exchange rates, and when coupled with increased speculation in currency markets by investors, the system became untenable. In 1971, the ten countries with the largest economies agreed to devalue the US dollar to $35 per ounce and allowed the currencies to float more freely. The collective inability of the US government, Treasury and Federal Reserve System to stem the outflow of dollars from the US continued to put downward pressure on the dollar, resulting in increasingly higher prices of gold; by 1973, the decision was made to completely de-link the dollar from gold, and the world economic order entered a new regime of freely floating currencies. When this decision was made, the gold standard finally came to an end.

From this reading of history, one can readily see that the very finite supply of gold in the world could not keep up with the almost limitless demand for dollars, as a result of the growth in global trade.

When the Bretton Woods system ended, currencies and gold floated freely; exchange rates were determined by the forces of supply and demand, based upon the need to finance imports and exports, and there would now be only one price—the open market price—for gold. Gold prices began a seemingly inexorable march upward, jumping immediately from $44 to $70 overnight. A year later, it had nearly doubled to $126, and ten years later it was nearly *ten times* greater, at $647; adjusting for inflation, gold hit an all-time high of $850 in

January 1980—a price it has yet to eclipse, at least in nominal terms if not in monetary inflationary terms.

The 'Gold Economy' Today

We've seen thus far how gold rose and fell as the backer of the world's currencies, most notably the US dollar. During the time of the gold standard, the public could not hold gold or engage in gold transactions, as these were reserved for central banks. Today, no country bans private ownership of gold. Investors and speculators are free to buy, sell and trade gold, just as any other physical commodity.

Even though it no longer backs any of the world's currencies, gold has retained its primacy as one of the most important assets. Certainly, gold is still widely used for industry, medicine, computers, electronics and jewellery. Gold's properties make it valuable because it can be refined in many ways. Beyond this inherent worth, gold is still regarded as a *store of value*, and consequently its attractiveness has only grown for investors. Emerging countries have once again turned to holding gold as a part of their foreign currency reserves, as a means of diversifying against the dollar. China, for example, has increased its gold reserves by more than 75% since 2003, during which time the price of gold has tripled. As a result, even though developed countries are continually offloading their own supplies of gold, it is unlikely that the prices will fall.

Gold has traditionally been viewed as a hedge against political and economic instability, and this phenomenon has continued—or even accelerated—in the present economic downturn. It has been able to keep up this somewhat paradoxical position in the global economy because of its scarcity, of course, but also because it is a 'hard' asset. Like real estate, commodities or other precious metals, investors and speculators buy, sell and trade gold because it seems to embolden us with a sense of physical security. Not only is its price level indicative of this, but we also see this in the recent development of gold recycling. Gold demand has skyrocketed recently, up nearly 40% in the first quarter of 2009, and this has almost entirely been attributable to investment demand among non-Western buyers.

These activities are demonstrative of a ***flight to quality***, above and beyond the usual moves from riskier assets such as stocks and bonds to US Treasury securities. One of the reasons why the Bretton Woods system collapsed was because it encouraged a crisis of confidence for the US dollar, which came under threat in a time of economic uncertainty. Now, the same dynamic is playing itself again; as the massive stimulus plan and monetary interventions by the US policy have drastically increased the supply of dollars in circulation around the world, many countries such as China—which remains the largest buyer of US dollar-denominated securities—are beginning to lose confidence in the 'full faith and credit' of the almighty dollar! Even the European Central Bank has begun to curtail its planned sales of gold, choosing instead to hold onto its reserves as a means of hedging against the uncertainties to come.

> *"If ever there was an area in which to do the exact opposite of that which government and the media urge you to do, that area is the purchasing of gold."*
>
> **Robert Ringer**

The careful observer, however, might continue to wonder why this investment behaviour persists? If gold is 'just another commodity,' and notwithstanding its relative scarcity, why has demand for gold continued to increase? The answer is not a simple one. Warren Buffett famously stated: ***"[Gold] gets dug out of the ground in Africa, or someplace. Then we melt it down, dig another hole, bury it again and pay people to stand around guarding it. It has no utility. Anyone watching from Mars would be scratching their head."*** To Buffett, perhaps the world's most famous investor, the ***absence of utility*** limits its value.

Moreover, it is arguable that gold really represents the store of value that most people think it does; in January 2008, gold broke the $1000 price barrier and briefly reached $1032 per ounce, one must recall that this was only a *nominal* price—when adjusted for inflation, gold would have to reach $2,200 to reach a new record in 'real' terms. Anyone who invested in gold in 1980 would have had to wait 28 years in order to break even, and with gold trading near $950, would now still be only slightly ahead! In fact, the esteemed professor of business Roy Jastram, who studied the behaviour of gold prices since 1560, deemed that gold moves independently of other commodities which in turn dictates the level of inflation—like every other asset, it goes through periods of both appreciation and depreciation that are much less correlated to inflation as popular belief suggests. While it may exhibit a high level of price stability, it is arguable that it protects against inflation in the true sense of the word.

The Social Value of Gold

These arguments, however, have diminished neither the relevance of gold today nor its demand. Some economists and policymakers even advocate for a return to the gold standard. Former Fed Chair Alan Greenspan, testifying before Congress in 1999, stated, *"Gold still represents the ultimate form of payment in the world. It's interesting that Germany could buy materials during the war only with gold. In extremis fiat money is accepted by nobody and gold is always accepted and is the ultimate means of payment."* Again, we see in this argument the fact that gold is a real asset, whereas fiat currency is not; in the absence of trust in its backer, fiat money is worth less than the paper it is printed upon.

> *"If you don't trust gold, do you trust the logic of taking a beautiful pine tree, worth about $4,000-$5,000, cutting it up, turning it into pulp and then paper, putting some ink on it and then calling it one billion dollars?"*
> **Kenneth J. Gerbino**

Much of the criticism of the 'fiat money economy' emanates from this very stance, and has at its core the belief that private life should remain free of government influence. Objectivists such as Greenspan, libertarians such as Ron Paul in the US, and economists from the so-called Austrian School of thought all have at one time advocated for a return to the gold standard. In fact, the Austrian School argues that governments actually pursue inflationary monetary policies as a means of funding their activities; recalling that the gold standard effectively made independent monetary policy impossible, one can see why they would continue to believe in the relative safety of gold.

Gold, it is argued, should act as a constraint on the potentially abusive encroachment of government into our private lives and consequently, it protects our economic freedom.

We see evidence of this in historical accounts of the 'gold rush.' Perhaps the first of these began in 1848 in California, when gold was discovered on the shores of the American River. These spurred the largest mass migration in US history, with nearly half a million people travelling to the territory from across the US and abroad. Not yet a state, the gold rush led directly to a massive economic and social boom. The territory was made a state in 1850 as a result, the economy and government were transformed, and California was propelled to the financial forefront of the United States and in many respects, the world.

The Californian gold rush, it could be said, came to embody the American dream itself. The notion of the American entrepreneurial pioneer, staking his claim and creating instant wealth, became a part of the nation's mythos. The US became known as a land of opportunity around the world, and far from only involving the many immigrants that travelled to the new state, the resulting boom heavily influenced patterns of trade throughout North and South America. The flip side of this, though, was that the gold rush resulted in significant social and racial stratification. Over time, it also substantially altered labour relations, as the mining and finance industries developed and innovated in order to absorb the influx of wealth. It is impossible to divorce the system of banking that developed in the US from the economic and social developments that preceded it and spurred its own growth.

The Australian gold rush of 1851 had similar effects on that country, and the development of the nation as a whole cannot be separated from it. Australia was also a colonial possession at the time so the gold rush had a substantial impact on the national psyche and the development of Australian culture. Part of the identity of the nation is tied to the 'digger' mentality and the often-open disdain of authority and the English 'superiors.' As gold discoveries swept from territory to territory, over 300,000 immigrants arrived in Australia, and markedly transformed the continent from an island of convicts and their descendants to a nation of explorers. Multiculturalism, reflective of the massive population inflows from well beyond the boundaries of the Commonwealth, took root and in turn influenced the national identity. In short order, the gold rush itself laid waste to the prison system that had founded the island.

The gold rush in the southern African territories presented an equally powerful force for socioeconomic development, and more importantly, the potential for political freedom for the Boer settlers. The potential 'loss' of colonial trade routes around the Cape and recently discovered mineral deposits was a major source of British aggressiveness, and prompted the annexations that led to the Boer Wars. In 1877, Britain annexed the Transvaal territory but the Boers revolted and formally declared independence in December 1880. The Republic government under Kruger had also realised the economic impact of the territory, which could catapult them to a position of economic and political leadership—and independence—in southern Africa. The resulting brushfire war was fought mainly in order to maintain British superiority in the region, a truce was reached in 1881 and self-government—but not independence—was granted to the territory.

In 1886, massive gold deposits were discovered in the Transvaal region, which could have made it the richest and most powerful nation in southern Africa. Huge inflows of immigrants threatened the balance of power between the old Boer order and the new, foreign *uitlanders*. Cecil Rhodes, founder of mining giant DeBeers and an ardent believer in colonialism had used his influence to lobby the British government to come to the aid of the uitlanders and to again secure annexation of the Transvaal. Human rights became the pretext for the British-backed incursion, which resulted in a siege of the region and a guerrilla war that ended in defeat for the Boers in 1902.

Rhodes had been hugely successful in obtaining mining concessions from tribal leaders throughout southern Africa. He used the economic leverage of his virtual monopoly in the region to significantly expand British colonial possessions. Rhodes was able to unite the English-speaking mining firms into a cartel that was a powerful political force in London and was viewed as an enemy within the Boer-controlled territory. It was the growth of the gold mining industry that justified the British invasions, but these huge profits were in turn reliant on the employment of a large proportion of native African workers, which comprised up to 90% of the mining industry's workforce. Rhodes, it must be noted, used his economic and political influence to forcibly expand his version of an English-speaking empire, and this served as the basis for the long-standing racial divides that prevailed in southern Africa until the final years of the 20th century.

What the gold rush developments tell us, more than anything else, is that gold *is* different from other commodities. Gold is produced *not* primarily for ***consumption*** but for ***accumulation***. It is this dynamic that influences the demand for gold, and endows gold with its key trait as a store of value. The scarcity of gold, of course, influences its price, but unlike oil and other commodities, we do not really exhaust our supplies of gold because it is not consumed. Thus, gold is mainly produced when there is a need to accumulate it—and when there is a growing need to do so.

> *"Better an ounce of happiness than a pound of gold."*
> **Yiddish Proverb**

Conclusion

In this chapter, we have discussed the rise and fall of the gold economy—and its seeming rise once again. The introduction of gold as an economic good came after the discovery of methods to refine it, which allowed the minting of coins and the birth of commodity money. As societies grew and developed and economic transactions became more complex, the advent of representative money solved some of the problems of transportation, time and space that commodity money could not. As trade and finance continued to multiply at exponential rates, representative money itself came under siege. Gold, the ultimate backer of the world's currencies until just a little less than forty years ago, ceased to keep up with the demands placed upon it. Fiat money was thus created, and money itself became a commodity.

What we have seen in this discussion, however, is that gold is not 'just another commodity.' Its relative scarcity does more than drive up prices because it is in short supply. Gold is, in many respects, the *ultimate* commodity: in contrast to other hard assets, we don't really consume gold, and produce it only to accumulate it because it is regarded as the ultimate form of stored value. Gold has retained its relative importance in the world economy and is still one of the most sought after commodities, even though it is common knowledge that it no longer plays a central role in monetary policy.

With the fall of the Bretton Woods system and the move to a floating exchange rate regime, the world's economic powers finally embraced the idea that free trade and independent monetary policy management were more important than holding gold. The US dollar became the *de facto* reserve currency of the world under the global gold standard, and it has effectively retained this position today. Two thirds of the world's foreign exchange reserves—the funds that countries use in order to repay foreign debt and for currency defense—are held in US dollars. For much of the 20th century and up to the present day, the US dollar has mostly been regarded 'as good as gold,' because it is backed by the full faith and credit of the US government, still the most powerful economic player in the world.

However, it is possible that we are beginning to see a shift in this dynamic. The ability of the US to sustain trade deficits and outflows of dollars, it seems, has begun to wane. The rise of China and the ascendancy of the European Union have also 'threatened' the primacy of the US, which in recent years has seen its competitiveness slip and its ability to assert both dominant foreign and economic policies around the world come under fire. Of late, many emerging economies have begun to diversify away from holding the US dollar in their foreign exchange reserves, opting to hold Euros instead; some have even begun to redeploy their capital into the commodities markets and are once again buying gold.

>   *"When we have gold we are in fear, when we have none we are in danger."*
>
>   **English Proverb**

These tectonic shifts are, to be sure, only nascent developments. They are important to recognise nonetheless, as many observers have noted the inevitable decline of the US as the guarantor of economic stability throughout the world. Were this to be true, we would argue that we are now seeing signs that the pace of that decline is accelerating. The massive fiscal stimulus and monetary policy actions undertaken over the past two years by the US government, in order to maintain liquidity in the financial system, unfreeze the credit markets, and jumpstart economic growth, are beginning to take their toll. Many holders of US dollars are now beginning to lose confidence in it, and its 'good as gold' status is now somewhat less certain.

As we have seen earlier, one of the reasons why the Bretton Woods system failed was that the gold standard imposed an unwanted monetary discipline upon governments, in that they had to choose between pursuing free trade and maintaining an independent monetary policy in a regime of fixed exchange rates. Monetary policy is a means by which countries can adjust their money supply, in order to control inflation; when a currency is tied to gold, the only way to adjust the supply of money is to alter the 'value' of the currency. This can have undesirable consequences for trade, as changes to the value of the currency—relative to those of other currencies—can impact the balance of imports and exports. In the post-war era, the supply of gold simply could not keep up with the demand for dollars, and currencies had to float relative to each other rather than being fixed, however indirectly through the US dollar, to a finite quantity of gold.

It is this very dynamic that some critics argue is desirable: many now advocate for a return to the gold standard precisely *because* it imposes discipline upon national governments and removes their control over the money supply. Inflation is by all accounts the most insidious destroyer of wealth and value; when governments no longer have the ability to create money in order to fund their own financial objectives, they cannot destroy wealth. Gold, as the ultimate commodity, is thus the guarantor of economic security because without it, money is not even worth the paper it is printed upon.

> *"I see a great future for gold and silver coins as the currency people may increasingly turn to when paper currencies begin to disintegrate."*
>
> **Murray M. Rothbard**

What these critics fail to realise, however, is the absolute size of the fiat money supply currently in existence. Even at present market prices, all the gold ever mined would be dwarfed in value by the amount of money in circulation just within the US! The extreme scarcity of gold would mean that its value would inevitably skyrocket. While this is not altogether disadvantageous, for it is simply a reflection of the forces of supply and demand, it is not enough; returning to the gold standard would also imply an end to fractional reserve banking and would remove many of the macroeconomic tools that policymakers rely upon to manage our financial system. Many economists argue, for example, that it is the ability to inject liquidity into the financial system that provides the stability we need to fight economic downturns. With the gold standard, we would not have this option.

What this means then, is that monetary policy would be determined by the rate of gold production. We have seen that this was indeed the case in the gold rush eras across three continents, in that the accumulation of gold was the primary driver of economic and political expansion. *Would we once again return to an age of empires, where nations seek wealth and the ability to grow and develop purely through territorial aggrandizement?*

It is not altogether clear but it certainly would be ill advised to once more inadvertently link gold to military might. What this might hold in store for the system of international relations that we live in today is similarly unclear.

However, what we do know is that gold is still one of the most highly sought after commodities, despite what Warren Buffett suggests is its lack of 'utility.' Still, and as a result of its scarcity, trading in gold is highly speculative. Gold is still regarded as an important component of global monetary reserves, and even though many countries in the developed world are now seeking to offload their stores, many emerging economies are looking to increase their own supplies. This is a reflection of the declining confidence in the US dollar, to be sure, but perhaps there are other dynamics at play: sovereign wealth funds, state-owned investment companies formed to invest excess currency reserves, are now seeking to deploy capital in many financial markets.

The ascendancy of these funds is deserving of exploration because their sheer size and ability to impact markets across the globe is nearly unrivalled.

Gold, despite its limitations and partly because of them, still plays an important part in the monetary policies of the world's economies. Most of the world's gold is owned and controlled by the major economic powers. *No longer at the head of this list, the US is likely to see its ability to enforce its own policies upon the world decline in the coming years, and perhaps this is a reflection of its waning ability to manage one of the most precious resources that we know.*

What is interesting to note here is the rising influence of the investor as a player in the global financial system: the seventh largest holder of gold is the Gold Trust, an exchange-traded fund that owns physical gold and that allows individual investors to own fractional shares of its holdings. Whether this means that individual investors or groups of investors will one day be able to control world events because of their ability to assert control over the supply of gold, is anyone's guess; it does, however, call to mind the gold rush cartels that were formed over a century ago and that were able to highly influence the political and economic balance of power.

So is gold 'just' another commodity?

No. In many respects it is not just another commodity, it is the ultimate commodity.

Looking back upon history, we see that gold has not fulfilled the promise that many investors see in it, that it is the ultimate store of value; but this, perhaps, is what keeps the illusion of gold alive. Indeed, the truth is that the price of other commodities actually follows gold, such that movements in the open market for gold will influence the markets for other goods! This paradox persists despite arguments to the contrary, and despite the fact that gold is really only produced so that we can accumulate it. Some would suggest that in absence of a 'real' demand for it, we shouldn't seek to hold it, but this is precisely what endows gold with the illusion of utility! So long as the major players on the world economic stage continue to foster these beliefs, the illusion of gold as the ultimate store of value will remain alive and well.

> *"There are about three hundred economists in the world who are against gold, and they think that gold is a barbarous relic—and they might be right. Unfortunately, there are three billion inhabitants of the world who believe in gold."*
>
> **Janos Fekete**

In the next chapter we will look and explore the effects on a nation's currency and wealth when rampant inflation is allowed and indeed encouraged in an economy; one that had depleted its gold reserves to close to zero. For those of us who now feel depressed we do not own a gold mine I will console you with the words of Napoleon Hill: *"More gold has been mined from the thoughts of men than has been taken from the earth."*

Chapter 5

August 2007—Wallet or Wheelbarrow: The Specter at the Feast—The Glutton in the Famine

""Lenin is said to have declared that the best way to destroy the Capitalist System was to debauch the currency. By a continuing process of inflation, Governments can confiscate, secretly and unobserved, an important part of the wealth of their citizens."

John Maynard Keynes

6th August 2007—The German bank IKB has been the recipient of an $11 billion bailout.

Why do Governments always focus on inflation even during periods of massive financial upheaval? Why is inflation always at the forefront of monetary policy? Is inflation truly the evil it is portrayed to be or is its reputation undeserved?

Inflation; When is a dollar not a dollar? Whether they know it or not, this seemingly simply question has confounded consumers, economists and politicians for hundreds of years, perhaps since the birth of money itself. The "true" answer to it, however, is not so simple: *anytime!*

Except for right this moment, the "value" of a dollar, or euro, or pound sterling, is not as constant as we might think.

Due to the ever-present specter of inflation, the price of the goods and services that we rely on daily are prone to change. While we all "know" this to be true, very few of us realise that it is not just a matter of changes in price, simply because the cost of raw materials has risen. To be sure, the supply and demand of commodities will play a leading role in the rise or fall of prices, but what is often unknown is the fact that it is the **supply or demand of money** itself that can influence the number on the sticker!

This is a "fact" that most of us probably take for granted, but it is one that has only recently begun to be understood in the field of economics. It is usually only during times of crisis that we pay much attention to it, although it is of central concern to policymakers because of its long term effects on economic growth and stability. While some level of "uptick" in prices is not necessarily a negative thing, assuming it happens concurrently with or as a result of an increase in our standard of living, the "unseen" consequence of unchecked inflation is that it can very quickly erode our savings. Indeed, inflation is actually one of the most insidious destroyers of wealth.

>*"The nation is prosperous on the whole, but how much prosperity is there in a hole?*
>
>**Will Rogers**

One of the most infamous examples of inflation in the annals of history occurred in Germany following its defeat in World War I. The "hyperinflation" of the Weimar Republic was set in motion in the years following the Treaty of Versailles, as a result of the burden of war reparations. The economic consequences of these enormous debt payments are well known, but what are not as well understood are the political consequences. Many have attributed the rise of Hitler and the onslaught of World War II to the burden of reparations, but the economic conditions that saw the Nazi regime come to power were not the singular cause.

A less contentious result of Germany's interwar history is of course that its experiences in this period strongly influenced the character of its financial institutions once peace was restored in the postwar years.

Certainly, the devastating impact of reparations on the one hand and World War II on the other engendered within the German nation a sense of *"fiscal conservatism"* and reserve. Thus, Germany serves as a fitting backdrop for the discussion of global inflation. In this chapter, we will explore the reasons for and outgrowths of the hyperinflation that occurred in the interwar period. As well, we'll delve into the impact that this has had on Germany's banking system. Just as important, though, we'll show what the current economic crisis and the responses by the German government mean for that country's financial health going forward, for it seems that inflation may once again be on the rise.

Inflationary Pressures

> *"Inflation is as violent as a mugger, as frightening as an armed robber and as deadly as a hit man".*
>
> **Ronald Reagan**

Economics, simply put, is about the production and distribution of goods and services. As Lionel Robbins described it, it is *"the science which studies human behaviour as a relationship between ends and scarce means which have alternative uses."* When most of us think about economics, we think about supply and demand, but as the eminent British economist points out, there is much more to the equation. Indeed, it would behoove us to recall Robbins' definition, for we will return to its precepts in short order.

The "ends and scarce means" to which Robbins refers, of course, are what determine the supply and demand for goods and services. Mainstream economics teaches that we must consider both inputs and outputs to these market equations, however, and one of the most critical inputs is price. As the study of economics gradually developed beyond the narrow confines of the classical economics of Smith and Ricardo, the science began to incorporate the notion that *"value"* was a perceived notion and not altogether determined by rational calculations.

The normative bias in mainstream, or neoclassical, economics leaves much to be desired. Even though it does not fit well into many—or even most—economic models, human behaviour is one of the most important contributors to the functioning of the markets. As we are all too aware, human behaviour is not always rational, but this constraint makes the predictive value of many economic models less meaningful.

One of the more influential offshoots of neoclassical economic theory is widely known as the "Chicago School." Collectively, this refers to a body of work and method of analysis developed and popularised by the faculty of the University of Chicago. While still adhering to the tenets of neoclassical theory, this approach favours the free market as the lynchpin of economic analysis but in doing so, it seeks to do so through the relative absence of mathematical models.

Perhaps the most important contribution of the Chicago School has been the development of the "monetarist" approach. Monetarism is concerned with the impact that variations in the supply of money has on the economic output of a country in the short term and on price levels in the long term. Milton Friedman, one of the most influential economists of the 20th century and a proponent of the monetarist approach, famously argued that when the money supply expanded, people would not simply wish to hold the excess but would choose to spend it. The opposite was also true, and as a consequence, Friedman concluded that the *economic demand was influenced by the supply of money*.

Any discussion of inflation must therefore include the work of Friedman. In his 1971 work, ***Monetary History of the United States 1867-1960***, Friedman famously argued that:

"Inflation is always and everywhere a monetary phenomenon."

Inflation can be defined as a rise in the general level of prices of goods and services over time. When prices rise, each dollar, euro or pound sterling buys fewer of these, so inflation is thereby construed as an erosion of purchasing power. Usually, inflation is measured through a "basket" of consumer items, usually weighted to reflect their relative importance and the number of those items one would typically purchase. From these prices, an index value for a given year is constructed, which is then compared to a benchmark year in order to establish the rate of inflation:

$$\left(\frac{211.080 - 202.416}{202.416}\right) = 4.28\%$$

In the United States, the most commonly referenced measure of inflation is the Consumer Price Index, or CPI. In the European Union, however, a different measure is used, called the Harmonised Index of Consumer Prices; a similar measure has recently been adopted in the UK in order to make coordination of monetary policies easier.

When Friedman wrote his **Monetary History**, he, and co-author Anna Schwartz, greatly influenced public policy around the world. Inflation, they argued, was created by excessive increases in the money supply by central banks; the reverse was also true, in that deflation resulted when policymakers failed to support the supply of money during a liquidity crunch, such as occurred in the Great Depression or most recently in the 2007/09 Credit Crunch. This differs from the work of Keynes, for example, who had argued that the Great Depression was the result of a lack of investment.

In many respects the monetarist approach was a response to the failure of Keynesian macroeconomic policies that seemed unable to solve the dual problems of unemployment and inflation that plagued global finance during the Bretton Woods era. Following World War II, many central banks had adopted a strong bias towards fiscal policies, or demand management. It is not a usual occurrence that high unemployment and high inflation will coexist, but in the early 1970s they did; in the United States, price stability became the primary concern of central bank policy at the Federal Reserve from this point forward, and this inflation-targeting orientation has come to dominate policy at the European Central Bank as well.

Arguably the most striking difference between the Keynesian and monetarist models has to do with government intervention in the economy. Keynes advocated a stronger role for government, and called for increased spending in times of unemployment in order to stimulate economic growth. From this, the concept of the "social safety net" was born. Moreover, the Keynes' ***General Theory of Employment, Interest and Money*** did not consider inflation over the long term, and focused primarily on prices that were stable in the short run. Monetarists sought the opposite, choosing instead to focus on growth in the money supply as the key determinant of fiscal stimulus by the government. Increased spending by central governments was seen as both unnecessary and harmful, because it raised long-term interest rates and "crowded out" private sector investment.

A third argument can be found in opposition of both Keynesian economics and monetarist policy, with the so-called "Austrian School." Practitioners of this school of thought hold that due to human behaviour, mathematical modeling is inherently flawed, and advocate a strict *laissez faire* approach to economic policy. The Austrian School would agree with the monetarist approach that inflation is "always and everywhere" related to the money supply, leading to increases in nominal interest rates and the eroding purchasing power of a nation's currency. The key difference between the Austrian and Chicago schools, though, concerns the role of the central bank: ***they postulate that it is the ineffectual central bank policies that engender volatile swings in the economy, or business cycles, with inflation as the by-product***:

"Those who pretend to fight inflation are in fact only fighting what is the inevitable consequence of inflation, rising prices. Their ventures are doomed to failure because they do not attack the root of the evil. They try to keep prices low while firmly committed to a policy of increasing the quantity of money that must necessarily make them soar. As long as this terminological confusion is not entirely wiped out, there cannot be any question of stopping inflation."

Thus it is the central bankers, as extensions of the central governments, which are the real culprits. Austrian School economists argue that inflation is a distinct action taken by the government, and is one of three main tools that governments use to finance its activities—taxation and borrowing being the others. Many proponents have advocated for an end to the fractional-reserve system of banking and a return to the gold standard as necessary outgrowths of curtailing this purported intervention by the central government into our private lives.

"Inflation is the senility of democracies."
Sylvia Townsend Warner

Of course, as we all know from history and personal experience, times of economic distress call for government action. The fact that we "know" this today is an outgrowth of these relatively recent "discoveries" in the world of economics, especially as they relate to the issue of inflation! Friedman, Keynes, and others have greatly impacted our understanding of this phenomenon and how it relates to economic activity more generally, and it is not well known that these conclusions have mostly been drawn within *the past seventy years*.

All is not what it seems, however, and there is still much to be learned about the relationships between inflation, investment and unemployment, for example. In 1960, economists Paul Samuelson and Robert Solow expanded upon the idea originally developed by William Phillips, which described the inverse relationship between inflation and unemployment. Friedman later showed that the tough period of the 1970's, when economies around the world experienced "stagflation"—the coexistence of high inflation, high unemployment, and stagnant economic growth—disproved Phillips' theories. Much like Keynes' General Theory, Phillips' model did not adequately account for differences between short-term and long-term rates of inflation. More recently, Robert Gordon has theorised that a "triangular" relationship between short-term inflation, long-term or built-in inflation, and increases in the cost of goods themselves determine the "actual" rate of inflation and thus, the "natural" rate of unemployment.

"Only one person in a million understands the inflation question, and we meet him every day."
Anonymous

Clearly, there is no single "right" answer when it comes to fiscal or monetary policy. Nobel Prize winning economist Joseph Stiglitz has recently argued that the inflation-targeting policies of central banks are permanently flawed. He believes that we must not target price levels *in isolation from their source*, considering that many countries effectively "import" their inflation as a result of rising commodity prices:

"Inflation in [developing] countries is, for the most part, imported. Raising interest rates won't have much impact on the international price of grains or fuel. Indeed, given the size of the US economy, a slowdown there might conceivably have a far bigger effect on global prices than a slowdown in any developing country, which suggests that, from a global perspective, US interest rates, not those in developing countries, should be raised. So long as developing countries remain integrated into the global economy—and do not take measures to restrain the impact of international prices on domestic prices—domestic prices of rice and other grains are bound to rise markedly when international prices do."

In the absence of a co-ordinated global financial regime, in which inflation targets and expectations are agreed upon and equal, Stiglitz maintains that these monetary policies will only engender weak economies and lead to higher unemployment, especially in the developing world. This is compounded by the fact that International Monetary Fund and World Bank policies are very much predicated on economic performance, including inflation targeting. He has also argued that the relationship between inflation and money supply growth—the mainstay of the monetarist approach—is equivocal for ordinary inflation, as opposed to rapid inflation, meaning perhaps more than 10% year-over-year—which is almost universally regarded as an effect of government spending at a time when output growth cannot absorb it.

Now that we have a primer on the subject of inflation and monetary policy, we can begin to understand the evidence in the real world. This last point is a fitting one, given that our backdrop for the discussion of global inflation is the historical experience of Germany! It is to this that we shall now turn.

Germany's Hyperinflationary Past

"The first panacea for a mismanaged nation is inflation of the currency. The second is war. Both bring a temporary prosperity. Both bring a permanent ruin!"
Ernest Hemingway

Germany's history in the interwar period is one of the most well known stories about inflation and its devastating effects. It begins with the Treaty of Versailles in 1919, which was the culmination of six months of deliberations at the Paris Conference following the victory by the Allied Powers at the conclusion of World War 1. In the Treaty, sole blame was laid upon Germany for the war, and as a result, the Allied Powers, to varying degrees, demanded reparations to pay for the economic damage thus inflicted.

Between 1919 and 1921, the "war bill" presented by the victors, actually remained unspecified. When combined with insufficient taxation and excessive spending this created enormous deficits for Germany. When the Reparations Commission finally presented the liability to the Weimar Republic, it amounted to 269 billion gold marks, which is an astronomical sum even by today's standards—it would amount to nearly $400 billion! The enormous scale of the reparations burden prompted economist John Maynard Keynes to resign prior to this, out of protest for the exorbitant amount that the Reparations Committee was trying to extract from the German republic. Indeed, and despite the heavy costs and millions of lives lost, this was seen by many as too high a cost to impose.

Keynes resigned from the Reparations Commission as Britain's representative. In protest at what he saw as an injustice he wrote ***The Economic Consequences of the Peace***. In this bestselling book, he criticised the notion of reparations, which many thought treated Germany unfairly, especially considering that extreme damage was inflicted on and by both sides. The book would go on to heavily influence the Bretton Woods system that was established in 1944 *as well as underpinning the Marshall Plan that was created in order to help rebuild war-torn Europe following World War II.*

Later in 1921, the reparations were reduced to 132 billion gold marks. This amount, too, did not hold. When Germany first defaulted on its war debt in 1923, this prompted France and Belgium to occupy the Ruhr Valley across the German border, the center of the country's coal and steel industry.

Perhaps as importantly, but less visual, was that 1923 saw the beginning of Germany's hyperinflation. More than one third of all government expenditures between 1921 and 1922 were earmarked for reparations, which discouraged any foreign investment except for highly speculative purposes. The German government saw no alternative but to print excessive amounts of money in order to finance the deficits they were forced to run, and this immediately caused a rapid depreciation in the value of the mark. The roots of this, however, are not solely *economic* in nature:

"Inflation is a monetary phenomenon, as Friedman said. But hyperinflation is always and everywhere a political phenomenon, in the sense that it cannot occur without a fundamental malfunction of a country's political economy."

It was a political decision to print money to finance the repayment of the war debt, one that was rooted in the belief that *"runaway currency depreciation would force the Allied powers into revising the reparations settlement, since the effect would be to cheapen German exports relative to American, British and French manufactures."* This conclusion was borne out at first, and inflation had indirectly fueled the initial recovery by German industry, but over the next few years government spending was inappropriately used to support public sector wages, and when combined with the aforementioned weak tax regime, German deficits again soared.

When Germany defaulted on its debt in 1923 and Allied forces occupied the industrial heartland, it further interrupted economic activity and only exacerbated the problem of inflation as the government again financed their resistance efforts by printing money. By the end of the year, the mark collapsed after reaching a peak inflation rate of more than 180 billion percent! Yes that figure again .... *180 billion percent!*

"If inflation continues, the two-car garage will be replaced by the two-family garage."

Anonymous

This resulted in the virtual collapse of the economy, as production dropped and unemployment soared. Money was rendered worthless and the hyperinflation eroded all manner of wealth.

The preliminary solution was found with the introduction of a new currency, called the Rentenmark. The Dawes Plan of 1924 instituted a new repayment plan, a new tax regime, and called for the withdrawal of occupying troops. While it reorganised the German central bank to accommodate the repayments, it is also worth noting that it established the fact that Germany could not succeed without loans from the US. *This was to be the beginning of American leadership in the global economy.*

Under the Dawes Plan, the German currency finally gained stability, and as a result the nation could once again attract foreign investment. It was immediately apparent that even this plan could not last; the Young Plan of 1929 further scaled back the debt to 112 billion gold marks to be repaid over a period of 59 years.

Keynes, it should be noted, foresaw much of this economic catastrophe in *The Economic Consequences of the Peace*. Germany's hyperinflation and subsequent currency collapse did not wipe out the *external* debt imposed by reparations, because this was fixed in pre-war terms, but it did have the effect of destroying the *internal* debt of the country, including government and other bonds. Keynes had written of this very dynamic:

"By a continuing process of inflation, governments can confiscate, secretly and unobserved, an important part of the wealth of their citizens. By this method they not only confiscate, but they confiscate arbitrarily; and, while the process impoverishes many, it actually enriches some . . . Lenin was certainly right. There is no subtler, no surer means of overturning the existing basis of society than to debauch the currency."

Keynes also described the inherently destabilising dynamic between Germany's budget deficits and rising inflation, observing that even without the burden of the war debt; it was not likely to be able to sustain its spending habits. The economic legacy was to be one of weakened banks and chronically high interest rates, due to the inbuilt "inflation risk premium."

Germany's experience with hyperinflation was not the first, nor would it be the last or worst, that the world would witness. What this particular series of events demonstrated, however, was the fact that Germany chose to go down the path of *"least resistance,"* in the sense that fiscal restraint could have prevented much of the damage. Inflation in this period had the effect of discouraging savings, for the value of one's stores of money was inevitably and almost immediately eroded. It is plainly evident, though, that when savings decrease, consumption increases, and while this dynamic might last for a time, it is certainly not sustainable. In Germany's case, it provoked the collapse of not just the currency but the economy as a whole.

Discussions of the political consequences of Germany's hyperinflation are often limited to the rise of Hitler, as a result of popular dissent against their war debt bondage. This, however, is too simplistic a conclusion. It should be recalled that the Great Depression made the Young Plan of 1929 unworkable, because the US was no longer either willing or able to extend credit to Germany. As well, we must remember that reparations payments effectively mandated a balance of payments surplus, whereby Germany exported more than it imported. The only way that reparations could be collected was by appropriating foreign currency or gold, which necessitated a trade surplus on the part of Germany; the hoped-for social consequences of reconstruction, then, fundamentally clashed with the desire for repayments on the part of the Allied powers.

The Great Depression itself was the result of a classic stock market bubble; this bubble may have actually been worse, had the Federal Reserve Bank in New York not acted prudently and adhered to strict monetary policy while maintaining its obligation to the renewed gold standard. It is debatable as to whether the Federal Reserve Board in

Washington did not do enough to ensure **the stability of the financial system as a whole**; it was the Fed's inability to ensure adequate liquidity and availability of sufficient credit, by buying and selling government securities on the open market, which spurred a near-collapse of the banking sector.

> *"We have two chickens in every pot, two cars in every garage, and now we have two headaches for every aspirin".*
> **Fiorello H. La Guardia**

The economic decline in the 'epicentre' that was the US quickly spread to other countries, many of which were also similarly impoverished. Protectionist trade policies restricted free trade, chiefly through the Smoot-Hawley Tariff Act, and it is this factor that many observers point to that made the Great Depression a global one. The worldwide gold standard also exacerbated the spread of the economic crisis; as international trade grew, and gold remained the standard commodity backing the world's currencies, changes to the supply of money were contagious. In Germany, unemployment rose to 40% by 1932. Through the Young Plan, the reparations bill was yet again modified, but the moratorium on payments contained therein eventually led to a second default; **the Nazi party seized upon the enormous popular discontent with reparations and swept to power soon thereafter.**

The economic and social consequences of World War II are well known. It should be recalled, however, that the interwar period strongly influenced the character of the German banking system after 1945. In the wake of the devastation of the war, a new currency, the Deutschemark, was introduced. A new banking system was created as well, based in large part on the US Federal Reserve system. **What is most notable about this system was the "political independence" granted to the new central bank, which was a direct outgrowth of the negative experiences of the previous decades.**

In 1957, the Bundesbank formally came into existence, and became the country's central bank. It would perform banking functions for its regional *Lander* banks, which carry out business independently but do not issue notes or currency on their own. This task fell only to the

Bundesbank, which would also provide monetary policy. It proved remarkably successful in maintaining price stability throughout the remainder of the 20th century, making the Deutschemarks one of the most solid world currencies. The Bundesbank became the model for the European Central Bank that was created with the Treaty of Maastricht, as part of the European Union.

German Banking Today

"Law of inflation: whatever goes up will go up some more."
Anonymous

Despite the independence of the central bank, though, the German state has remained heavily involved in the banking system. The German banking sector is often described as a "three pillar" system: public sector banks, which are split between state-owned *Landesbanken*, local government-owned *Sparkassen*, or savings banks, and development banks; cooperatives, which are owned by their depositors; and commercial banks, which are publicly listed.

This system served Germany well through much of the postwar period, especially during the 1960's and 1970's that was a period of prolonged growth and industrial expansion. Recently, however, the complex system of state and mutual ownership stakes has resulted in high costs, inefficiencies, and low profits. As a result, banks in Germany have not kept up with the pace of modernisation prevalent throughout much of Europe, because banking has historically been viewed in the same vein as a utility that involves state ownership.

It is this tangled web of ownership that harks back to Germany's disastrous interwar experience. While on the one hand, political independence was a necessity at the federal level in order to prevent heavy-handed government influence on monetary policy, the three-pillar structure is nevertheless clearly reflective of the need to maintain control and to influence economic policy by German politicians. The *Landesbanken* and *Sparkassen* are some of the largest employers regionally, so they have historically been an important source of political influence.

The *Landesbanken* sometimes referred to as universal banks for their role in wholesale banking and broad-based financial services are often said to have been instrumental in the country's industrial development. These banks have historically had close ties to large industrial players in their regions, and have held large ownership stakes in them. Up until very recently, German firms have traditionally not tapped international capital markets, depending rather on their banks as the main funding source. Not surprisingly, these ties have made it difficult for reform measures to go through, because of the financial influence that this nexus has historically been able to wield.

Crisis and Reform

> *"Inflation is bringing us true democracy. For the first time in history, luxuries and necessities are selling at the same price."*
>
> **Robert Orben**

As a result of the credit crisis, the German banking system has now been forced to reform itself. Trouble in the banking sector began, as it has done elsewhere, with the near-collapse of a single entity, commercial lender IKB. IKB had invested heavily in US subprime mortgage securities. It bore the full brunt of the subprime crunch as a result of a credit line tied directly to securities that it held in a conduit vehicle called Rhineland Funding.

As a result of Germany's history of economic devastation, the banking system has evolved to incorporate a "guarantee" system that effectively socialises potential losses. In order to mitigate systemic risk, bank losses are essentially pooled and funded by the *Landesbanken,* spreading the burden across the banking sector. Thus, the bailout of IKB quickly ballooned from its original price tag, and is likely to continue to plague the system far after the peak of the credit storm.

If ever there was a case to let a bank fail, it seems on the surface that it would be IKB. Relatively small in stature, the bank exposed itself to risky assets and to some, should be allowed, even required, to pay the price: economist William Buiter argued, *"I can think of no better way of encouraging more appropriate future behaviour towards risk by German banks than letting IKB go into insolvency now. The institution gambled recklessly and irresponsibly. It lost. Liquidation and sale of its assets would be the market-conform reward for its failures."*

The initial bailout began with a €3.5 billion capital infusion, two-thirds of which came from government-owned development bank KfW on August 1, 2007. Four months later, new risks at IKB forced KfW to contribute an additional €2.3 billion; two days later, this amount was increased by an additional €350 million. By February 2008, a third round was undertaken, this time necessitating a capital infusion of €1 billion by the federal government, with other private banks making up the balance of an additional €500 million. The total cost, when all was said and done, was a bailout package of nearly €8 billion.

This bailout could potentially become even greater, based upon the aforementioned guarantee mechanism, *"a trigger of which would cost German banks €24bn", according to Peer Steinbrück. "Consider also that IKB has loans to more than 1 in 10 German companies, and maybe a case for systemic risk."* All of a sudden, the seemingly insignificant IKB has been catapulted to the front of the line! In retrospect, allowing the firm to fail, as US regulators did with Lehman Brothers, would likely have caused further damage—especially in light of its loan exposure throughout the German economy; *it seems that systemic risk knows no bounds!*

The IKB story is also highly illustrative of the interconnectedness of the German political and financial elite. Many have criticised the bailout for being politically driven. KfW's CEO Ingrid Matthaus-Maier, who orchestrated the bailout of IKB, is well connected:

"A lawyer by profession who was a financial expert for the SPD for many years, she would not have been able to get on the board of a private bank in 1999, the year she joined the board of KfW—she lacked the banking experience required by law. But KfW is not subject to the same regulations as other banks, which explains why Matthäus-Maier doesn't owe government auditors an explanation—not even now,

in the wake of recent public accusations that she botched the IKB crisis."

IKB is not alone, of course. The state of North Rhein-Westphalia was prompted to bail out WestLB to the tune of €1 billion, and in Saxony the state was forced to issue guarantees of €2.3 billion; other state-owned banks have provided another €14 billion in guarantees. Critics have declared that these losses are *"perfect examples of the fatal mix of amateurism, greed and political protection that is symptomatic for many of Germany's state-owned, partially state-owned and public sector banks. It is an environment that can only thrive in the shadow of the state—and that has drained more than €20 billion from the public treasury within the last decade."*

The state banks are supposed to bail each other out when necessary, but in a climate where their health is threatened, the system itself has been called into question. When the *Sparkassen* savings banks are factored in, the problem multiplies due to the fact that they too are closely interlinked. This situation is made all the more precarious by the pressures of financial integration within the European Union, which required that the German federal government withdraw its bank guarantees in 2005; this has had the effect of raising borrowing costs and decreasing their competitive advantage in lending at lower rates. More poignantly, it gave the banks an incentive to take on excessive risk:

"Hard up for funds, many of the public-sector banks began speculating with high-risk securities. According to a former bank executive, many 'literally stocked up on these investments' shortly before the cut-off date. Others even continued to do so after the cut-off date. Lacking a functioning business model, they turned to what was essentially gambling—and lost."

Bailouts of this magnitude are never popular, or politically expedient, because inevitably it is the taxpayer that will bear the burden. The tangled web of the German banking sector demonstrates yet again that if one firm fails, others will be damaged in its wake. It seems that this is particularly the case here, given the extent and degree of interconnection between the three pillars of the German system:

"If that happened, the corporate customers of the affected banks could end up without access to their money for weeks, possibly even months. Despite the fact that the customers' deposits are in fact guaranteed, any bank insolvency is preceded by a moratorium on all bank transactions. This, Weber argued, would only lead to further bankruptcies, especially since the remaining savings banks in North Rhine-Westphalia, as their association presidents conceded, would have trouble satisfying the regional economy's liquidity requirements, because they already have a total of €43 billion in WestLB loans on their books. Furthermore, many of these banks also invested in American subprime mortgage securities, which they too would have to write off."

It is questionable that this could lead to a collapse of the entire economy, but some have argued that the risk is not worth the cost of the bailout. As a result of this heavy exposure, the federal government had to take extraordinary—and almost unprecedented—measures to ensure this did not occur.

In reality, this process was set in motion in 2005 when the government removed the safety net, but clearly, it did not adequately account for the risks involved in this withdrawal of the guarantee mechanism. Now that the federal government had to come to the rescue of IKB, and others as a consequence, it proposed to create a "bad bank" fund in order to remove toxic assets from bank balance sheets in return for government bonds with a known value and guaranteed return. The aim was to ensure the confidence of the banking system as a whole, an approach that bears some similarity to that taken in Sweden in the 1990s.

These extraordinary measures are likely to have an extraordinary cost: a recent government report estimated that in addition to €850 billion in toxic assets, the weakened banks are exposed to more than €800 billion in corporate loans—these are likely to put additional downward pressure on the banks' balance sheets as the economy continues to tread through the downturn. Thus far, it has guaranteed perhaps half of these troubled loans, and has taken a 90% stake in real estate lender Hypo. It is unknown how long it might take to absorb these assets and make the banks profitable, or what the eventual cost may be to do so.

Conclusion

"How is the human race going to survive now that the cost of living has gone up two dollars a quart?"
W. C. Fields

What is clear, however, is that there is much work to do. This scheme has recently garnered EU approval, but concerns about the banks still persist. Neelie Kroes, EU Competition Commissioner, has continued to express concern about the ways in which these firms are structured, arguing that taxpayers should not be content with the status quo. She has called on the banks to change their business models, perhaps reorienting towards the retail sector; this is an approach that has paid significant dividends in France, one of the few countries that has come through the credit crisis relatively unscathed. Italy has itself undergone similar changes within the past twenty years: *"'In 1990, 70 percent of the Italian bank sector was publicly owned and now it's 7 percent,' said a London-based analyst. 'They have done it and massively improved the performance of their business.'"*

In a related vein, the **Landesbanken** have been called upon to consolidate, perhaps even further than they have already been forced to do. Their number has already fallen from thirteen to six in a wave of mergers, but further consolidation in this area has been demanded by the Savings banks. As they are not beholden to the capital markets in the same manner as listed commercial banks are, so they have been able to resist further calls for reform. This presents somewhat of a conundrum, given the dynamic that exists across the Atlantic and elsewhere; *banks' predilection for excessive risk has been attributed to shareholder pressure to continually create higher profits. Clearly, the German experience with state control has shown that the reverse is true as well.*

This illustrates one of the more salient points, and it is a judgment that is not particular to the German case: ***nothing yet exists that prevents banks from undertaking this type of speculation, essentially gambling with taxpayers' funds***.

Germany's banking system sets a tough standard for reform, because of the unique nature and dominance by the state. The elimination of bank guarantees in 2005 only exacerbated the crisis when it hit, although this could not have been foreseen and was nevertheless mandated by the financial integration of the European Union; costs were raised, and in a climate of declining profitability, the outlook for the banks was perhaps already a grim one.

As was the case elsewhere in the world, the wave of bailouts that started with IKB was undertaken in order to ease fears and in an attempt to buoy confidence in the banking sector as a whole. However, given the pressure from the European Union, this may yet amount to an illegal use of state aid. As the German saga plainly illustrates, it is a sad fact that true reform can only come when the economy emerges from the credit crisis. This too will only truly happen when the full costs of the crisis have become known; some have said the eventual price tag could reach 1 trillion euros.

At the end of the day, the German variant of the credit crisis harks back to the hyperinflation of the 1920's: above all else, both the problems and the solutions have been and will remain political in nature. Vested interests throughout the federation will want to maintain the status quo, whether for political expediency or some other narrowly construed economic gain. The burden for doing so, however, will inevitably be shouldered by the taxpayer. Given the astronomical costs involved in what might have been a confined bailout of a small firm, the German taxpayer is likely to shoulder that burden for years to come.

Adding to the conundrum is the direct outgrowth of those experiences some eighty-five years earlier: the hyperinflation of the 1920's *did* engender the federal government with a deep sense of financial restraint. Even in the midst of this crisis, it has remained wary of stimulus spending, preferring to adhere to its fiscal conservatism. It is in precisely this type of climate that Keynes had argued for demand-driven public policy in order to foster growth and recovery, yet the federal government has been reluctant to embrace it, at least to the same extent as the US and other nations have.

However, they may yet prove to be correct: it is possible that we are already seeing yet another bubble on its way to bursting. The credit crisis has uncovered a shaky foundation of corporate indebtedness, with heavy domestic exposure on the part of the already weakened banking sector. *Will the contagion spread beyond Germany's borders, as the US subprime crisis has?*

We have already seen on so many occasions that where one fails, others—if not all—seem destined to follow. Only time will tell if this will be the case, but perhaps the German fiscal prudence that is lamented today will prove to be a boon for the future, when yet another crisis hits.

> *"It does not at all encompass the role that Germany plays and should play. Europe urgently needs a Germany that is in good form again."*
>
> **Neelie Kroes,**
> **EU Competition Commissioner**

As we have seen inflation is a necessary, though insidious, result of economic activity but also is linked closely to demand for *money* as a commodity in its own right. In Chapter 6 we are going to reverse engineer by having a look at commodity prices directly and the effects of trying to manipulate those market forces—*so let's try and corner the market!*

Chapter 6

September 2007—I'm for ever Blowing Bubbles!

"When you ascend the hill of prosperity, may you not meet a friend!"

Mark Twain

"We are persistent in the face of boom and bust."

Bill Beck

Date—September 2007—Fed Symposium blames the artificially low interest rate policies of Alan Greenspan for the housing boom and bust; economist Robert Shiller warns of looming price drop of 50%!

Boom and bust—when the price of a particular commodity rises, a severe downturn inevitably follows. This is known as a 'boom and bust'.

Bubbles; During a classic 'boom' scenario consumers pay more and more money to buy a particular commodity. The price goes up and up, even beyond what the item is reasonably worth, but people keep paying—right up until the bottom suddenly drops from the market and the price, as well as the value, of the commodity crashes.

If you hunt around online or at your local library, you will find mention of some classic cases of boom and bust going into effect around the world. One example—perhaps the most striking—has been documented quite extensively. *The Tulip* by A. Pavord (1999), *Tulipomania: The Story of the World's Most Coveted Flower and the Extraordinary Passions it Aroused*, by M. Dash (1999), and *Tulipmania* by A. Goldgar (2007) all describe and analyse the circumstances that lead to the incredible peak in the price of tulip bulbs in 17th century Holland.

Although each of these three accounts documents their share of quirky stories, emphasising the feverish speculation of February 1637, it is perhaps most interesting to consider that the degree of irrational behaviour was so extreme and some investors were so overcome, that many people were forced into bankruptcy as a result of the serious and widespread consequences of the craze and its subsequent crash. Often mentioned is the fate of the artist Jan van Goyenm who died in poverty as a result of his losses and despite his talent.

Of course, we might look back on this event and call the particular crisis a needless tragedy. However the tulip crisis was hailed as one of the most significant events in Dutch history in the 17th century and it remains one of the primary examples of boom and bust—the causes, the elements, and the far-reaching effects.

> *"All nations with a capitalist mode of production are seized periodically by a feverish attempt to make money without the mediation of the process of production."*
>
> **Karl Marx**

Perhaps modern society could never sanction or conceive of this mass hysteria and irrationality. We might dismiss the tulip craze as something that modern society could neither facilitate nor tolerate. There are other more recent cases of the 'boom and bust' cycle in the market place, all of which have causes and effects decidedly similar to the madness caused by the tulip frenzy. Like it or not, investors almost always chase the value of commodities, whether it is as a result of mass hysteria or as a result of an actual, devastating event that spurns a real sense of crisis. People can also manipulate the market to manufacture 'boom and bust' cycles if they think it is to their advantage.

On Black Friday, September 24, 1869, for example, two speculators, James Fisk and Jay Gould, cornered the gold market on the New York

Gold Exchange. Fisk and Gould manufactured financial panic in the United States by taking this action, and the two men took advantage of the fact that the government had issued a large amount of money during the Civil War period to try and make a substantial profit.

After all, the money issued by the government was backed by nothing but credit and this worried people; a concept we explore in other chapters. People commonly believed that the US Government would buy back the paper money once the war was over. Everyone believed, moreover, that they would buy it back with gold.

Gould and Fisk began their efforts to control the market by reaching out to those they believed would have influence over the government's actions. They recruited President Grant's brother-in-law, a financier named Abel Corbin, and used him to get close to the President in social situations. Taking advantage of the relationship, they argued against government sale of gold and persuaded Corbin to support their arguments. Ultimately, Corbin convinced President Grant to appoint an associate of Gould and Fisk, General Daniel Butterfield, as assistant Treasurer of the United States. Butterfield agreed to tip the men off when the government intended to sell gold.

Late in the summer of 1869, Gould began to buy large amounts of gold. This action caused the prices to rise. The stock market also began to plummet. Quick to appreciate what was going on President Grant responded to the situation. The federal government sold $4 million in gold and on September 20, 1869, Gould and Fisk started hoarding gold, driving the price higher.

By September 24, four days later, the premium of a gold Double Eagle, which represented 0.9675 troy ounce of gold bullion at $20, was 30 percent higher than when Grant took office. Government gold hit the market shortly after, however, and the premium plummeted within minutes.

As the value of gold dropped, investors raced to sell their holdings. Most of them, including Abel Corbin, Grant's brother-in-law, were financially ruined. Notably, Fisk and Gould escaped significant financial harm but they were certainly implicated in the subsequent Congressional investigation into the fraud.

> *"Entrepreneur: A high rolling taker who would rather be a spectacular failure than a dismal success."*
> **Jim Fisk**

In the 1970's, a similar scandal was orchestrated by two brothers who belonged to one of the richest families in the United States. In 1973, the Hunt family bought precious metals as a hedge against inflation. They couldn't buy gold because, at the time, it wasn't possible for private citizens to own gold. Instead, the Hunts bought silver in enormous quantity. By 1979, Nelson Bunker and William Herbert, the sons of patriarch H.L. Hunt, were conspiring with some wealthy Arabs to form a silver pool. Relatively quickly, they amassed more than 200 million ounces of silver, which was the equivalent to half the world's *deliverable* supply.

> *"To be successful, you must decide exactly what you want to accomplish, then resolve to pay the price to get it".*
> **Bunker Hunt**

The Hunts began accumulating silver in 1973. At that time, the price of silver was around $1.95 per ounce. By early 1979, the price had risen to about $5. By late 1979, heading into early 1980, the price had risen to over $50 per ounce. It eventually peaked at $54 per ounce.

With the silver market effectively cornered, outsiders began to join the chase but a combination of changed trading rules on the New York Metals Market (COMEX) and the intervention of the Federal Reserve undercut the chase. The price of sliver began to slide. On March 27, 1980, the value dropped 50% in one day; the price plummeted from $21.62 to $10.80.

As with the collapse of the gold market with Fisk and Gould, the collapse of the silver market resulted in catastrophic losses for speculators. In fact, the Hunt brothers declared bankruptcy, and by 1987, their liabilities had grown to nearly $2.5 billion against assets of $1.5 billion.

In August 1988, the Hunts were convicted of conspiring to manipulate the market.

There were many other knock on effects of the silver crash. For many traders the collapse in silver was the final straw for a stock market already under siege from worries as diverse as the Iranian hostage crisis, the Russian invasion of Afghanistan, and soaring interest rates. The consumer price index climbed at a rate of 13% for 1979 and the prime lending rate hit 22% in early 1980. By the year's end, however, the whole decline was almost forgotten. The Dow ended the year at 963.99, thanks in large part to the euphoria over the election of Ronald Reagan.

What triggers such absurd behaviour in otherwise sane investors and businessmen?

Ultimately, the boom and bust cycle is often triggered by uncertainty and fear. The World Trade Center attacks on September 11, 2001, for instance, created much uncertainty and made two points immediately clear. First, the human toll was tremendous, and second, there was a potential for serious economic instability. The human toll was something everyone began to appreciate as the numbers of victims and casualties were reported. The economic destabilisation was something that, psychologically, most of us picked up on watching television footage on the day.

The destruction of the twin towers was symbolic to everyone around the world. The towers had been an iconic symbol of American capitalism since their construction. Their destruction cast a dark shadow over the United States and over the global market because their strength and prowess were so literally destroyed. The terror attacks and the subsequent wars in Afghanistan and Iraq also drove investors to do what they have done so many times before—clamor after certain commodities. As everyone's mind ran to the prospect of a lengthy and bloody war in the Middle East, oil was one of the first things investors were thinking of; the United State's reliance on the Middle East for this commodity presented a tenuous reality.

Then there was the real estate market!

The subsequent 'boom and bust' of subprime mortgages has been hailed as the latest example of this particular economic cycle in motion. In his 2007 economic study of the crisis, Gramlich outlined how the subprime mortgage market initially had positive effects, increasing homeownership from 64% to 69%, benefiting minorities and those on low incomes, and simplifying the loan application process. On the downside, however, Gramlich also discussed how the widespread abuse of the largely unregulated mortgage sources and the dramatic rise in default rates created such enormous losses in financial markets around the world. As a result of the crisis, about 45% of low-income home owners and 57% of renters are now spending over half their disposable income on housing.

This instance offers a perfect example of our generation's 'boom'. In periods of uncertainty, commodity prices rise and investors grab at tangible, hard assets to create a kind of security blanket. As far as the value goes, it's like a child with an old and familiar toy. The toy may actually be totally worn out, but it's not going anywhere until there is some psychological breakthrough for the child; until they don't feel that they need the security blanket and comfort the toy provides.

Another way to look at it is to consider the concerns of investors after 9/11. Leading up to the close of the year, the political climate in the United States and around the world was certainly tense. The Bush Administration was poised for war in the Middle East and, as we've mentioned, that got many people thinking about the types of commodities that would be in particular demand. Oil and other raw materials were definitely on that list.

Since late 2001, however, a global recovery appeared to be under way. After an initial downturn immediately following the attacks, trade and industrial production picked up around the world. However, concerns about the pace and sustainability of the recovery soon came into play.

Financial markets had weakened by early 2002 and equity markets had fallen sharply by the second quarter. This fall in equity was also accompanied by a depreciation of the US dollar and weak financing conditions in emerging markets, particularly in South America and Turkey.

A global recovery was still apparently under way, led by the United States and underpinned by a pickup in global industrial production and trade. The global slowdown in 2000 and 2001 had also proven to be more moderate than most previous downturns; even allowing for the substantial downward revision to GDP growth in 2001 in the United States. This owed much to an aggressive policy response, particularly following the events of September 11, which in turn was made possible by the improvement in economic fundamentals during the 1990's. Other contributing factors included the decline in oil prices in 2001; the resilience of the global financial infrastructure to a variety of substantial shocks; and a degree of good luck, in that the impact of the terrorist attacks on confidence proved surprisingly short lived.

So how do these boom and bust crises affect the economy? What effects do these crises—real, imagined, or orchestrated—have on the economy?

When the stock market crashes, for the most part, it is as a result of sudden and dramatic revisions in expectations about future economics and financial variables. The classic example of our time we have already mentioned: the September 11 attacks. Another good example, although perhaps less widely known, is the Russian default.

The events that trigger the revised expectations often vary. They have unique causes and features. One thing most have in common, however, is that they are followed by some degree of liquidity crisis in financial markets. Real or perceived, there is always some likelihood that these events will disrupt economic activity; that they threaten the stability of prices. Most busts are caused by some combination of physical disruption to the financial system and sudden uncertainty about what economic conditions are really at play. Both of these conditions tend to lower asset prices and create balance sheet problems for financial institutions—namely banks, hedge funds, and the like.

Since most financial institutions survive on a day to day basis, thanks to a complex systems of payments, they are, for the most part, vulnerable to the failure of larger banks or hedge funds. Most Wall Street firms and hedge funds are highly leveraged as well. Most of their assets are purchased with borrowed money, so their financial stability is actually very precarious.

If, or rather when, asset prices drop dramatically, the value of your average Wall Street financial firm drops. The value of their liabilities, including their loans, perhaps most obviously, increases exponentially. Liabilities can exceed the value of assets in heavily leveraged firms, causing the value of the firm to drop to a negative and putting the firm on the point of bankruptcy if additional capital is not available. When a hedge fund goes bankrupt, moreover, it has something of a ripple effect in the financial markets at large. The bankruptcy of your average hedge fund firm means that banks will not receive payment on money they have lent. If the borrowed money was a sufficiently large amount, the lending bank might face insolvency as well.

An alternative scenario, when the value of certain assets drops dramatically and leaves financial institutions relatively cash-poor, is for these businesses to ration their scarce liquidity. In other words, the firms, out of necessity, determine only to make the most important payments while they remain insolvent. Some debts, ultimately, are not settled on time.

Looking at the financial institutions that keep the markets afloat, the fear of counterparty risk is almost as severe as fear of bankruptcy. When a counterparty might not be able to settle a transaction, it is common for fear of this counterparty risk to create a kind of financial gridlock; other firms and individuals are less likely to enter into financial transactions. A classic example is the bankruptcy unwinding of thousands of individual trades that took place between Lehman and its competitors.

Failure of counterparties to make payments can create *systemic risk*. When there is a systemic risk, there is a chance that the health of the entire financial system is in danger. More particularly, there is also a perceived risk that there will be a kind of domino-style string of bankruptcies running throughout the system. The biggest problem, of course, has to do with the interconnectivity of the financial institutions and the economy at large. If the financial system—the banks, investment firms, hedge funds—breaks down, the whole economy is immediately affected because economic activity depends on the efficient functioning of the payments system. *If people suddenly think that they will not be paid, then there is little incentive to work or to sell!*

Financial breakdowns, including those that are the result of a bust, tend to cripple the economy because the financial system typically matches people looking to save money with firms who want to invest that money in productive activities. When the financial system stops functioning, the people who were looking to save can no longer be matched with investors. As people lose faith in the concept of investing—entrusting their money to the professional investors—investment falls in every sector and people revert to putting their money under their pillows at night.

Back to the boom and bust cycles, it is important to understand that a fall in stock prices or in the price of a particular commodity, will also affect the real economy. When the price of a stock or a commodity falls, it has an influence on the credit-worthiness of the owners of those items. When a stock price falls, most often, it influences the credit-worthiness of financial firms, but a drop in the value of real estate, for example, will mean that ordinary, everyday people also find their credit-worthiness is undermined.

A disparity exists, however, in the riskiness of the decision-making once creditworthiness is lost. When the stock price of a firm drops, the value of the firm also declines. The owners of the firm typically have a limited financial liability, however. This means that they retain any gains without experiencing particularly drastic losses. This creates a kind of security net, if you will; it means that the owners of firms have an interest and an active incentive to borrow money and make risky decisions with that money in the hope of achieving sizeable profit.

Of course, the risk of firms taking extreme risks to try and recover profits is only applicable if they can actually borrow the money to take those risks. Few businesses and even fewer individuals want to lend money to firms with low equity. Often, they choose not to lend money to these firms because they know the borrowed money is likely to be used to take risky gambles. Drops in equity also undermine economic activity by affecting what is known as trade credit. Trade credit involves buyers taking delivery of goods and paying for them later. As you might expect, however, most firms with low equity will not receive trade credit. Unfortunately, without it, continuing to operate becomes particularly difficult during a financial crisis.

All of these issues come into effect during a boom and bust cycle because the credibility of affected businesses is always decidedly undermined, along with their actual perceived creditworthiness.

The next question to ask, now that we have a clear impression of the factors that affect investors and the stability of the market in the boom and bust cycle, concerns the role of the Federal Reserve.

Does the Fed facilitate or work to control the boom and bust cycle? What role, if any, does the Reserve play in facilitating or controlling a boom and bust cycle and the subsequent crisis?

We have explored the Federal Reserve Bank in Chapter 2 but let's have a look at its role relative to the boom bust cycle.

After 9/11, the boom and bust of commodity prices was directly related to the actions of the Federal Reserve. In fact, if we go back a bit further, we can acknowledge that, in 1914, the Federal Reserve was formed as a response to the financial crises of the United States that exacerbated recessions in the 19th century.

Before the Federal Reserve System, the US economy was beset by occasional banking panics. One of the most notable of these was the crisis of 1907, which directly motivated the creation of the Federal Reserve System in 1914. Although the Fed has many responsibilities, one of the most important was initially to provide an elastic supply of currency to banks. It was believed that this backup money supply would help to meet temporary increases in currency demand, such as those that occurred during banking panics. A primary goal of the Federal Reserve System was, in fact, to prevent or at least minimise, banking panics.

To a large extent, the Federal Reserve has actually lived up to its primary purpose. It has made banking panics almost unheard of and nonexistent since the Great Depression, thanks to deposit insurance, prudent regulation, and the Fed's own preparedness to lend money as a last resort.

The Fed is no miracle worker, though. Extreme conditions, such as the terrorist attacks of September 11, 2001, still have the potential and the power to destabilise the system. These kinds of crises can still threaten the health of the economy due to the effects they have upon the financial markets.

A valid question, then, pertains to the role of the Federal Reserve in minimising the severity of these crises when they occur. Do the Fed's actions actually help to minimise the instability or, as some have suggested recently, have the Fed's actions, after events such as 9/11, actually undermined the financial well being of the country and create a sense of crisis?

If we consider some of the conditions we discussed earlier in this chapter—the type of psychological shifts that occur for investors and for lenders when there is even a hint of financial crisis—we can perhaps begin to question the behaviour of the Fed as a last resort lender to the financial system, intent on maintaining a stable environment for businesses.

Perhaps one of the most interesting things about how the Federal Reserve reacts to crises is how it *should* react. Most people assume the Federal Reserve should try to prevent drastic changes in asset prices when there's a strong likelihood that those changes are going to harm the economy. *In fact, the Fed shouldn't try to prevent possible problems in this way!*

There is a need to distinguish between preventing problems all together and preventing problems in the financial markets from affecting other aspects of the economy. It is rarely a good idea for the Fed to try and directly control asset prices, and most policymakers hold to this.

When it comes to the level of prices in asset markets, it is very easy to be wrong about what level is actually the appropriate level. As William Poole, President of the Federal Reserve Bank of St Louis said in 2001, *"this judgment ought to be left to the market"*.

The Federal Reserve has two methods for influencing stock prices. Either it can apply open market operations to influence prices by affecting interest rates, or it could exert its authority to adjust margin requirements for the markets. There are a number of problems with both of these methods. First, it would be very hard to control the effect of changes applied to interest rates because large changes might be needed to change equity prices enough to create the required impact. Second, when it comes to margin requirements, the Fed would be dealing with requirements that have rarely been changed and it would also be dealing with a fairy unpredictable tool. It would be very difficult to accurately predict the impact of changes to these requirements.

Ultimately, it is far easier for the Fed to work to control the disruptive effects that stock market prices can have on the real economy when they rise and fall dramatically, as is the case with boom and bust cycles. *But what exactly can it do?*

The Fed can and does take action to curb the effects of dramatic changes in the value of stock market prices. The policy reactions also have varying effects—some are short-term while others are considerably longer-term. Others fall somewhere in between.

The uncertainty most crises produce—taking 9/11 as an example—often necessitates immediate provision of additional liquidity to the financial system. In the medium term, the Fed can maintain lower interest rates than they otherwise would, to safeguard business conditions and keep banks and other financial institutions on solid ground.

Most of the crises that spurn economic instability have long-term effects on the economy. After 9/11, for example, people looked for increased defense and security. Instead of prioritising for funds to be directed to health care, durable goods, and investments, resources were directed towards preventing further attacks.

Financial crises also tend to be synonymous with a lack of liquidity. Individuals and businesses both tend to have assets—and they don't necessarily lose those assets in a crisis—but it is rare that those assets can be quickly converted to cash to facilitate a payment of debts when there is an instability in the market, real or imagined. Traditionally, central banks like the Federal Reserve, step up to provide extra liquidity in times of crisis, getting around this problem. The Federal Reserve can buy assets, usually Treasury securities, to give banks greater reserves and lower the federal funds rate. It can also lend directly to banks through the Federal discount window and encourage banks to loan money more freely with regulatory forbearance.

Following the stock market crash of October 19, 1987, the actions of the Federal Reserve received particularly close scrutiny. There has also been considerable debate and discussion as to the causes of the crash and how the central banks might have prevented it.

In particular, the Brady Commission considered portfolio insurance and program trading the central catalysts of the 1987 crash—the primary elements that created the problem.

The Commission also found that specialists were partly to blame for selling into the crash instead of buying. Santoni (1988) suggested that the crash was a rational reaction to fundamental news about stocks, though no specific inference was made as to what the news might have been. Other analysts blamed monetary policy, although there was little agreement on the particulars. Either tight monetary policy caused the crash (Roberts, 1987) or the monetary policy was too loose (Canto and Laffer, 1987).

Short-term interest rates were certainly rising before the crash of 1987. Moreover, the stock markets do tend to fair poorly when interest rates rise (Jensen, Mercer, and Johnson, 1996; and Thorbecke, 1997). This concept supports Roberts's (1987) viewpoint that rising interest rates alone do not cause stock prices to crash. They are, however, just one factor in the bust.

Two months prior to the crash, stock markets experienced significant losses. Between August 25 and October 16, 1987, the S&P 500 lost about 16% of its value. The S&P 500 plunged by 20% and the Dow Jones Industrial Average sank more than 500 points on October 19, 1987. *This was the largest one-day decline in stock market history.*

Immediately after the crash, however, Alan Greenspan, Chairman of the Reserve, announced that the Reserve System was ready to serve as a source of liquidity to support the economic and financial system. The Fed then began pouring liquidity into markets by lending directly through the discount window, purchasing Treasury securities, and persuading banks to lend to Wall Street.

There was also considerable flexibility facilitated by the policy of the reserve. Several times, the Open Market Desk entered the market early to provide reserves. As a measure of the degree of liquidity in the period, we can look to the excess reserves, which rose to the unusually high level of almost $1.6 billion in the reserve period ending November 4, 1987.

The Federal Reserve also continued to lower interest rates as a means of easing pressure in the money markets. The Fed lowered the federal fund's target to influence all short-term interest rates, several times in the four months following the crash. The total reduction of that period was about 80 basis points.

The stock market crash of 1987 reduced the wealth of shareholders in the medium term. Reducing their consumption, the reduction in wealth also reduced the extent of business investment and employment. It was also noted that the general uncertainty about future economic activity reduced output in general because non-investors were still concerned about their financial standing, particularly their future employment.

Despite the perceptions and opinions held at the time, however, the crash of 1987 had relatively little impact on consumption directly. Recovery was quick; stock prices were back to pre-crash levels within two years. The limited reduced consumption is actually better explained by the fact that the rapid recovery happened early in the year; not realising the reality of their financial situation, that they were, for the most part, financially sound, people had not bothered to adjust their consumption.

Now we are going to develop a second point of comparison for our focus, which is the Federal Reserve's actions after the 9/11 attacks and the part these actions may have played in creating the subsequent boom and bust of the housing market. Our second point of comparison is the Russian Default, which with the October 1987 crash, gives us two points of reference for how the Federal Reserve acts in the wake of possible economic crisis and instability.

The term, Russian Default, however, refers to the fact that Russia experienced major economic struggles during the mid-1990's. The Russian economy was hampered by negative economic growth, massive debt inherited from the Soviet era, and an inefficient tax system. At the same time, the Russian government was also trying to maintain a target zone exchange rate against the US dollar.

The generally unfavourable conditions, combined with the July Asian crisis in 1997 meant that international investors were extremely cautious about investing in Russia and other developing economies. Russia's fiscal situation then worsened in 1998 when the oil prices fell and the Russian government failed to pass appropriate tax reform legislation that might have alleviated the problems of the inefficient tax system.

Overall, the fiscal concerns with respect to Russia created a serious international problem. At the very least, the concerns posed a real problem for the maintenance of the exchange rate because of the need for the fiscal deficits to be financed by some combination of borrowing and monetisation. The money supply had to be expanded somehow or other and there was certainly a limit to the appetite of foreign investors for this type of activity.

Basically, investors were not too keen to continue to manage the Russian debt, given the general conditions of the economy there. The deficit, moreover, began to create an expanded money supply and caused the Russian price level to rise. Russian goods became more expensive on world markets. The subsequent fall in demand for Russian goods, which were deemed overpriced, increased pressure for a devaluation of the ruble. In turn this was risking the capital of the foreign investors who had already invested in Russian assets.

Many investors began to wonder whether the Russian government would be able to honor its debts. Given that most considered it unlikely, many investors began withdrawing their capital from the country's economy as well. Finally, there was a vicious and negative progression in play: demand for Russian assets fell, Russian interest rates rose, and stock prices fell.

By August 11, 1998, the Russian government had decided to stop trying to fix the value of the ruble. The government also decided to default on domestic debt and halt payments on its foreign debt. International investors shied away from Russia after the Asian crisis and the Russian Default. These two events also implied a greater risk in emerging market debt and lead any investor to look for safer ways to invest their money. Many investors completely revised their assessment of the danger of investing in developing countries, and this increased the spreads between yields on more-safe and less-safe assets around the globe.

Still, the severity of the changes and loss of confidence linked to the Russian default alone were not entirely organic. An important factor in altering the perceptions of risk was the refusal by the International Monetary Fund (IMF), to provide bailout to Russia. This decision must be set in context, however, as the IMF had chosen to provide bailout to Bulgaria, Thailand, and Mexico when those countries had been at similar points of economic distress.

In fact, the IMF had considered Russia too important to ignore right up until August of 1998. The IMF had even been reluctant to forego assisting the country in a payments crisis because of Russia's importance to the global economy. In August, 1998, however, many of the emerging market funds sold some of their positions in profitable countries to meet margin calls on their Russian positions, further increasing the disparity between securities in emerging and developed countries.

The Russian default had particular implications for US economic policy, as well. After the default became apparent, many investors rushed to find safer assets, causing a fall in the yields on 10-year US bonds for the period. Equity prices also declined in the US as implied volatilities rose, and the foreign exchange value of the dollar rose briefly after the default, only to decrease again, and quite considerably, as uncertainty in US equity markets increased.

What is most interesting, however, is the action of the Federal Reserve, and the Fed certainly took action, shifting policy decisions, in the wake of the default. Most notably, the Fed lowered short-term US interest rates to try and minimise the consequences of the international financial conditions for the US economy. This policy decision was also intended to try and ameliorate conditions abroad.

Lowering short-term interest rates on loans from central banks was designed to facilitate the creation of a greater demand for imported goods and to lower international borrowing costs. The Fed also hoped that lower interest rates for emerging economies would raise US exports and the earnings of US firms in the long-run. Two rate-hikes later, however, in November of 1998, people were beginning to worry that unrealistically high US equity market valuations might be encouraged by the Fed's manipulation of the interest rates. The equity market had had several years of very strong performance and there was some overvalue by traditional measures such as price-earnings ratios.

Reductions of the FOMC by 75 basis points over the four months following the Russian default were persistent in the wake of the 1998 Russian default and helped to insulate the US economy from the asset market turbulence of the default. The fund's target remained consistent, moreover, with a very low US inflation target and the financial markets remained volatile throughout 1998 until interest rate reductions by the central banks of several developed countries took effect.

The Long-Term Capital Management (LTCM) was one of the most notable casualties of the Russian default. This was a highly leveraged hedge fund whose strategy was to make money from extremely small disparities in prices. As it was so highly leveraged, however, the LTCM was vulnerable to small losses. The strategy was very profitable for several years and led to the narrowing of these disparities in prices, but the risk assumed by the strategy proved to be a two-way risk.

The price difference for similar assets resulted from differences in liquidity. The differences would only increase in times of stress, such as when there was a default, and indeed, the Russian default caused very large, protracted differentials in the prices of the assets for LTCM. Of course, the failure of a single financial firm and the bankruptcy of its owners is rarely a matter that concerns a central bank or, indeed, any other organisation with a similar capacity and responsibility within the broader market place. LTCM, however, was so large and deeply leveraged that its downfall risked the failures of its many creditors as well.

The Federal Reserve Bank of New York, in an effort to keep the market stable, facilitated a meeting of LTCM creditors on September 23, 1998, and encouraged an agreement to facilitate a controlled end to the company. The creditors present agreed to provide additional capital in exchange for 90 percent of the firm's stock. No public money was used or put at risk in the transaction but the purchase did achieve its objective, allowing an orderly dissolution of LTCM's assets. The new investors also supplied the original owners with a 10 percent stake in the firm to induce them to assist in the liquidation of LTCM's assets.

Now we have two points of comparison, we can begin to take a closer look at the effects of 9/11 and the possibility that the actions taken by the Federal Reserve were directly or indirectly responsible for the subsequent booms and busts of the housing market.

The immediate effects of the attacks on 9/11, beyond the human cost and the physical destruction to downtown New York and the Pentagon, included the disruption of the payments system, a temporary closure of the NYSE, and a grounding of commercial air flights in the United

States. Following the attacks, there were also a number of specific economic changes. First, US stock prices fell. Second, the implied volatility of equities rose and remained high for several months.

Both direct physical disruption of the financial system and the liquidity problems hit after 9/11. As is often the case, the falling asset prices and heightened uncertainty lead the banks and other intermediaries to reduce lending in the wake of the crisis.

The response of the Federal Reserve was something of a knee-jerk, however. Initially, the Federal Reserve sought to restore confidence and avoid significant disruption to the payments and financial system. It took steps, therefore, to support liquidity. It made repurchase agreements by the New York desk, facilitated direct lending through the discount window, allowed for foreign central banks to meet liquidity needs in US dollars, and repeated reductions in the federal funds rate for several weeks after the attacks. Ten-year bond yields fell and the foreign exchange value of the dollar also fell and then rose strongly for several months.

Perhaps most notably, the Fed took steps to float money so that when a bank presented a cheque to the Fed for clearing, the presenting bank was often credited with the amount before the paying bank was debited. This floating step was taken because the 9/11 attacks had, among other things, caused a suspension of air transport, which significantly slowed the process for cheque-clearing.

On September 12, the level of deposits at Federal Reserve Banks was $102 billion. This was more than five times the average of the previous ten Wednesdays. Within three weeks, however, the available liquidity figures were back to pre-attack levels.

At the time it was difficult to make an accurate assessment of the exact effects of the 9/11 attacks on the US and world economies. It was also difficult, then, to gauge the appropriate response; assuming the Fed was going to take active steps, it was near impossible, in the short to medium term, to figure out exactly what measures would help to facilitate stability and what steps might, given the history of events in the wake of the 1987 crash and the Russian default of the 1990's, make the economy less stable.

With the benefit of hindsight, analysts have identified three factors that bolstered the value of the dollar in the period immediately after the attacks. These factors were (1) better-than-expected US economic performance, (2) short-term interest rate cuts by the world's major central banks, and (3) apparently successful military operations in Afghanistan.

The attacks caused tremendous uncertainty about a whole range of outcomes. There was great concern about further attacks in the short to medium term and doubts about the measures that might be necessary to prevent further attacks. Most of these concerns and fears manifested themselves quickly. They were instrumental in the creation of a sharply higher implied volatility for stocks and depressed consumer confidence represented by a significant reduction in consumption and investment that exacerbated the general economic slowdown.

The immediate effects of the attacks, however, were almost unanimously predicted by forecasters. Most agreed that the attacks would exacerbate the developing slowdown by sending consumer confidence and asset prices into a tailspin. Macroeconomic Advisers was one prominent group to revise their pre-attack forecast for 2001 growth, reducing their expectations from 0.9 percent to -0.6 percent in the wake of the attacks.

What complicated the Fed's policy decision problem, however, was the unusual nature of the disruption to the payments systems, air transport, and other sectors. The September and October economic statistics ultimately provided less information than usual regarding longer-run trends.

In the first three months after the attacks, the FOMC lowered the federal fund's rate target by 175 basis points. These reductions served primarily to maintain the accommodative stance of the general monetary policy, however. The Taylor rule, a guiding principle for these policy decisions, did call for lower rates, but the actual rate reductions only kept pace with what the rule actually prescribed. It did not go beyond.

The long-term effects of the attacks had much to do with these and other related policy decisions undertaken in the immediate aftermath. The long-term effects, in general, can be classified into wealth effects and taste technology shocks.

First, with regard to wealth and economic factors, it is notable that investments needed to rise, and consumption likewise needed to fall somewhat. This would help to replace much of the destroyed physical and human capital.

Writing approximately a year after the attacks, Bram, Orr, and Rapaport (2002) estimated that the property damage, cleanup, and earnings losses of the destruction of the World Trade Center ranged from about $33 to $36 billion through to June 2002. Obviously, since that time, the spending on law enforcement and defense activities has risen considerably and much of the United States, with the subsequent market crash of 2008 and the ensuing general financial crises, has found itself struggling.

In addition to these direct losses, the attacks imposed more subtle costs on the economy. By raising the costs associated with travel, security, and insurance, the attacks have shifted resources among industries. To an extent, they are a negative productivity shock, as more resources were required to produce the same product, at least in the immediate aftermath and short to medium term. Travelers require more security to fly about the country and companies like IBM pay a higher cost for a given level of property insurance for a downtown office building.

What of the boom and bust phenomenon discussed at the beginning of the chapter?

Certainly, the stock market crash of 1987 and the 9/11 attacks posed substantial potential dangers to the economy through disruption of the payments system and financial markets. Consumers were sent into tailspin psychologically, their confidence in the market severely undermined. The stock market crash of 2008 has also caused the markets to destabilise somewhat and in a similar way. This most recent crash can also be traced, in part, to the sudden fall out of the rise in the cost of housing across the US, indirectly linked to 9/11 and its aftermath.

After the stock market crash of 1987 and, indeed, after the 9/11 attacks, liquidity problems were created by the dramatically lower stock prices and increased uncertainty about the future, both political and economic. While the implications of the 9/11 attacks became clear, investors and consumers grasped at commodities that provided the proverbial security blanket of hard assets. The housing market was undoubtedly part of this. After all, what is more securing than a home?

Banks and other financial institutions sought to feed the ballooning bubble by offering unusually competitive loan agreements and financing options, particularly for low-income buyers who were also grasping at housing as a viable security in the uncertain times. By 2008, however, seven years after 9/11, the bubble was ready to pop—and it did.

Stock market crashes and other similar disasters on the economic front, tend to generate liquidity problems, as we have suggested. When the price of stocks is dramatically lowered and uncertainty greatly increased, it becomes difficult for even large organisations to maintain liquidity of cash flow. The attacks of 9/11 had a similar effect to past stock market crashes, resulting in lower asset prices and much higher uncertainty, as well as physically disrupted payments and financial systems.

After 9/11, as it has done in many similar circumstances, the Federal Reserve provided immediate liquidity to ensure that the payments system continued to function and eased short-term interest rates to reduce the pressure on the financial system. Their actions were intent on protecting real economic activity and limiting the extent of the residual damage to the global financial markets.

On the downside, though, the monetary policy response offered by the Fed after 9/11, and in the other two instances discussed, was similar to the response to bank panics that the Federal Reserve System was created to handle.

Faced with falling asset prices and considerable uncertainty, banks often decide to cut back on or stop customary lending to financial markets. Despite the need for capital, which is at its most pronounced during such times, the banks often assist in creating the liquidity problem. The stock market crash of 1987, the Russian Default of 1998, and the attacks of 9/11 all impacted and undermined the stability of the US economy because of how they impacted the financial system. In response to these recent financial crises, the Fed has functioned as a lender of last resort. However, its role in manipulating interest rates and other financial factors in an effort to mitigate liquidity problems has often served only to send mixed messages to consumers at large. Those mixed messages, moreover, feed into the bubble pattern discussed at the beginning of the chapter, sometimes, if not often, creating the impression that there is a greater impending crisis. Consumers typically then run to hard assets, causing the prices to rise in response to demand; the rise becomes artificial; **as the crisis mentality is validated**.

We're forever blowing bubbles in the midst of moderately difficult economic situations, at least in part, because the Fed supports the crisis mentality of financial situations and consumers.

In this Chapter we looked at the role of the world's shadow bank in the creation of booms and busts. In Chapter 7 we will look at the creation of the official World Bank and the IMF. *Do they do what they claim to do or do they really carry out the murky and hidden instructions of their creators?*

Chapter 7

October 2007—Intellectual, Marxist or Fabien: The IMF—Something for Everybody?

"It is the growing custom to narrow control, concentrate power, disregard and disfranchise the public; and assuming that certain powers, by divine right of money-raising or by sheer assumption, have the power to do as they think best without consulting the wisdom of mankind."

W. E. Du Bois

October 2007—"The credit squeeze will force governments worldwide to make substantial changes to their budget plans," warns Rodrigo Rato, outgoing Managing Director of the International Monetary Fund.

What is the International Monetary Fund? Where does its money come from? Where does its money go?

Financial Crisis; Once upon a time, it was believed that major financial crises occurred only a few times a century: big ones, like the Great Depression, seemed to happen once every 100 years, and "little" ones, like the 1987 Black Monday stock market crash, about every fifty. Now like everything in the modern world they are speeding up, gaining momentum and generally arriving quicker than ever before; *it seems that they plague us more than once a decade; the present credit crisis was preceded by the bursting of the dot-com bubble only*

six years prior, which itself followed closely on the heels of the Asian financial crisis of 1998.

It would seem from this cursory look at relatively major financial upheavals that the international economic regime has not been able to keep up with the pace of world events. Perhaps this is due to the myriad advancements in technology and financial innovations that have transformed the speed at which economic shocks are transmitted throughout the system. At the same time, it is possible that the depth and breadth of economic integration makes it virtually impossible to predict and pre-empt these occurrences. It is likely that there is more than just some truth in each of these views.

An alternative reading of our recent economic history, however, might suggest a more radical conclusion: ***that we have become increasingly adept at mismanaging the international economic order, rather than the opposite!***

Instead of growing more capable of handling these crises and moving towards a regime that is not only responsive to these shocks but that also actively manages them prior to their outbreak, thereby discouraging the formation of bubbles and blowups, growth spikes and recessions, we are travelling in the opposite direction. The invention of Collateralised Debt Obligations (CDOs) and Credit Default Swaps (CDSs) are discussed in detail elsewhere in this book but they were introduced to ***lessen*** risk on the balance sheet of banks and financial institutions. In truth they ended up being used to circumnavigate the 1988 Basel Accord (Basel 1), a form of limitation of lending based on capital reserves; a rough guideline is for every US$100 lent banks must have reserves of US$8, a 12.5 debt to equity ratio on non sovereign debt. Thus our once prudent bankers were able to load up on unregulated high risk debt like a starving man at an eat all you want buffet! They could claim to all and sundry that their balance sheets were both within regulatory requirements and "insured" against risk but in the deepest depths of their souls they must surely have known they stood on the edge of a precipice.

Like all disasters everybody denies responsibility and more often places blame elsewhere so we need to ask ourselves a key question;

Who truly controls the international banking system?

At the heart of the present global monetary order is the International Monetary Fund. It was instituted in response to the effects of World War II, as well as the need to both manage international monetary transactions and promote economic growth and recovery as a result of the war. The IMF was given the heady tasks of first; assisting in the reconstruction of the world's international payment system and second, managing foreign currency flows between nations in order to prevent further crises as a result of trading imbalances. However, and despite the fact that it has grown to encompass nearly every country on the planet, it has remained controversial with respect to these objectives, ever since its creation in 1944.

This chapter seeks to explore the formation and evolution of the IMF in order to assess not just its history but also its future, as it relates to the present economic crisis now in play. In particular, we will look at the reasons for its design as well as some of the criticisms of that structure and its programs; we will also examine the IMF's 'sister' organisation, the World Bank. In many respects, these groups have grown in ways that were not foreseen, which in turn has had, by some accounts, unanticipated substantial impacts on the economic development of many nations. As such, and putting them into the present context, many questions arise about what the next crisis might bring. And to many, the answers leave much to be desired.

Out With the Old?

> *"If only God would give me some clear sign! Like making a large deposit in my name at a Swiss Bank!"*
> **Woody Allen**

The IMF was formed in 1944 with the goal of stabilising exchange rates and assisting in the reconstructing of the world's international payment system; it describes itself as ***"an organisation of 186 countries,*** *working to foster global monetary cooperation, secure financial stability, facilitate international trade, promote high employment and sustainable economic growth, and reduce poverty around the world."* As part of the new liberal economic order created under the Bretton Woods system, the IMF's overriding purpose was to promote methods by which countries could maintain exchange rate stability, thereby fostering free trade, economic growth, and development.

Much of the blame for the Great Depression, and indeed the two World Wars, has been blamed on problems of trade and economic relations between the world powers. While nationalistic aggression and a tangled web of alliances certainly contributed to the outbreak of World War I, much of the blame for the war has also been put upon the imperialist ambitions of the major powers. As natural resources were being depleted on the European continent, overseas colonies were viewed as both necessary and an expedient means of aggrandising national wealth. This upset the balance of trade and created tensions between the major powers in Europe, which in turn fanned the flames of aggression and eventually sparked the conflict itself. Economic and military rivalries were correlated and interdependent, and because of their effects on industry and trade, must be considered as key factors in the outbreak of war in 1914.

In the interwar period, the Treaty of Versailles attempted to place the financial burden of the war on Germany. While it is often noted that the Treaty stipulations forced the German state into an untenable economic situation, and thereby further destabilised the already weak country, some scholars have recently argued that the material burdens imposed by reparations were less onerous than originally believed. Rather, it was other drastic economic consequences that were less apparent that would end up dispelling the peace. *What was not envisaged was the extent to which the collection of reparations would lead to a balance of payments crisis, the depreciation of Germany's currency, and rapid inflation; moreover, the financial chaos caused by the uncertain repayment terms would inevitably spread throughout global foreign exchange markets, and would affect other countries as well.*

As well, the only way that reparations could be collected was by appropriating foreign currency or gold which necessitated a trade surplus on the part of Germany; the hoped-for social consequences of reconstruction, then, fundamentally clashed with the desire for repayments on the part of the Allied powers. The destabilising effect of these huge trade imbalances, when combined with the ineffective monetary and social policies of the German government, resulted in the well-known hyperinflation of the German mark and the eventual collapse of the currency, as documented in Chapter 5.

It can be argued that the Great Depression had its roots in the global "economic dislocations" that had arisen since 1914. Shifts in industry and production away from Europe led to a "chronic over-capacity" that, when coupled with the massive war debts and rising labour demands, made it extremely difficult for the more developed countries of the world to generate foreign currency to pay for imports.

> *"Nothing did more to spur the boom in stocks than the decision made by the New York Federal Reserve Bank, in the spring of 1927, to cut the rediscount rate. Benjamin Strong, Governor of the bank, was chief advocate of this unwise measure, which was taken largely at the behest of Montagu Norman of the Bank of England . . . . At the time of the Bank's action I warned of its consequences . . . . I felt that sooner or later the market had to break!"*
>
> **Bernard Baruch,**
> **re the 1929 Stock Market Crash**

What's more, technological and financial innovation created a classic stock market bubble; this bubble may have actually been worse, had the Federal Reserve Bank in New York not acted prudently and adhered to strict monetary policy while maintaining its obligation to the renewed gold standard. *The Federal Reserve Board in Washington did not do enough to ensure the stability of the financial system as a whole!*

It was the Fed's inability to ensure adequate liquidity and availability of sufficient credit, by buying and selling government securities on the open market, which spurred a near-collapse of the banking sector. The

sharp fluctuations in the effective exchange rates between the major economic powers, which in turn caused most countries to devalue their currencies versus the US dollar. This gave the US a strong competitive advantage, especially following the devastation of the Second World War. *In the immediate post-war period, it was recognised that free trade—which was necessary to rebuild the world's shattered economies—required freely convertible currencies. That compromise was reached with the Bretton Woods system.*

The architects of Bretton Woods also realised that gold production itself was not sufficient to meet the demands of growing international trade. In order to remedy the problems posed by exchange rates that were fixed to predetermined gold reserves they choose to use the US dollar as the reserve currency. Countries would instead peg their currencies to the US dollar, which was in turn backed by and convertible into gold at a predetermined price of $35 per ounce; in order to maintain exchange rate stability, countries would buy and sell US dollars and thereby remedy any trade imbalances. The US dollar thus became the '*world's currency*', and the International Monetary Fund became the *de facto* mechanism for managing the new liberal economic order.

Following the Second World War, the United States was able to run massive trade surpluses as the world's economies began to recover; they exported much more than was imported and used the convertible financial system to trade at a tremendous profit with developing nations, expanding industry and acquiring raw materials. Dollars were flowing into the US, but in order to maintain the proper functioning of the new economic system, the country had to ensure that there was enough liquidity—dollars—for use around the world. Under the Marshall Plan, the US would use this surplus to send dollars to Europe, which would then be used to rebuild their economies, and make the United States the market for their products. So that this dynamic did not become destabilising, the US promoted competitive industry in Europe and Japan, and provided financial aid to the lesser-developed areas of Europe, Asia and the 'Third World.' This in turn reinforced the American role as the guarantor of stability.

"Open the books . . . and you will be staggered to see how much American money has been taken from the United States Treasury for the benefit of Russia. Find out what business has been transacted for the State Bank of Soviet Russia, by its correspondent, the Chase Bank of New York."

Louis McFadden

This also highlights another often-overlooked justification for supplying US dollars as the world's currency: the need to counteract the rising might of the Soviet Union. The Soviet Union, it must be recalled, had significant gold resources of its own, and without the constraints imposed by the Bretton Woods system, the Soviet Union would be better able to finance its expansion. In addition, if the US were able to take a leadership role as the guarantor of stability throughout the world, it would be in a better position to pursue its own foreign policy agenda. Bretton Woods thus provided an indirect means of economically isolating the Soviet Union or so it was assumed.

The Liberal Agenda

The IMF began life with 45 member countries, but rapidly expanded its membership throughout the 1950's and into the 1960's, as African and Asian countries gained independence. When the Bretton Woods Agreement later collapsed in 1971, under the weight of accelerating trade deficits in the US, the influence of the IMF grew as it became more relevant in managing the international economic order. In an area of freely floating exchange rates, or where countries attempted to peg their currencies to a basket of foreign currencies, the IMF became instrumental in assisting with a policy of independence for its member nations.

Of course, the Bretton Woods system and its institutions, the IMF and the World Bank, were created to reflect the dominant foreign policy agenda in the Western world. At the helm was the new economic superpower, the US. It would not, however, be fair to characterise the IMF and the World Bank as simple extensions of US politics by other means. A growing body of evidence has linked economic growth to the institution of democracy as part of the development agenda. However, that development assistance was not without strings. IMF members were routinely required to take on loans in order to facilitate the policy moves required for them to participate in free trade, but these loans were not given freely. In line with the IMF's overarching, liberal *raison d'être*, these loans were 'conditional' on member nations adopting specific free-market economic policies. These 'structural adjustment programs' had many components; *that countries substantially liberalise their economies, denationalise their industries, and pursue 'monetarist' economic policies such as those favoured in the US and much of the Western world*.

As a result of these and other controversial policies, such as raising taxes and interest rates in order to manage inflation, it is often argued that the IMF and World Bank have helped to make inherently weaker economies even weaker—even though they existed in order to help these countries develop and pay back their debts. IMF policies have been blamed for economic crises that were invariably worsened by governments' inability to sustain critical sectors such as health care, education and security. At the same time, valuable national resources and industry were sold off to powerful corporate interests in more developed nations. IMF policies are thus criticised for leading to the simultaneous impoverishment of its debtor nations and their inability to escape the vicious monetary policy circles that keep them weak.

Of course, these policies were invariably tied to the prevailing beliefs that economic development in emerging nations had to occur along the same lines as it had in the industrialised world, although this theory has been the subject of much debate. Doing so would serve to solidify the basis for globalised free trade on the one hand and, as mentioned earlier, to prevent more countries from falling onto the socialist path and thereby isolate the Soviet Union on the other. With the IMF and the World Bank, economic development and the provision of foreign aid became inextricably linked to *democratic development*.

> *"Capitalism is based on self-interest and self-esteem; it holds integrity and trustworthiness as cardinal virtues and makes them pay off in the marketplace, thus demanding that men survive by means of virtue, not vices."*

Alan Greenspan

These debates are not new; indeed, they go back to the time of Adam Smith, if not further. The authoritarian model has been drawn upon frequently, especially in light of the success of the "Four Dragons" of East Asia—Hong Kong, Singapore, South Korea and Taiwan. No longer confined to the developing world, these newly industrialised economies have succeeded in bridging the gap to the developed world, with standards of living that in many ways rival "older" economies. These four states have in common the fact that they all, in varying degrees, have relied upon authoritarian political systems. This attribute is hailed as *the* characteristic that has enabled them to outpace most every country in the world in terms of economic growth rates, surpassing even the advanced economies of Japan and the US.

These states have industrialised and raised their standards of living to nearly the same degree as the advanced economies of the West faster than any other set of countries before them. However, one crucial difference along this path is that these achievements were done in non-democratic systems. It is this distinction that has made the difference, allowing them to develop at such a rapid pace and achieve such high levels of economic growth. *Why should authoritarianism lead to higher levels of growth and better economic performance?*

Singapore's first prime minister stated *"what a country needs to develop is discipline more than democracy, the exuberance of democracy leads to indiscipline and disorderly conduct which are inimical to development."* Similar arguments come from other Asian countries. Until recently Indian politicians had viewed their country's slow growth as the price of democracy, in that *"having to justify policies to an electorate . . . made it harder to get things done."* Taiwan's government, it is argued, was *"able to intervene intelligently in economic management partly because it was spared popular pressure to intervene unintelligently."*

Central to the authoritarian thesis is the claim that stability, above all else, is required for development, which can only be supplied by a strong central government. This is precisely because of the aforementioned pressures: ***"The result is that national energy is often spent on dividing the pie rather than on increasing its size. Governments that do not rely on votes, by contrast, are better placed to make the difficult choices."*** Furthermore, it is argued that political instability reduces the supply of both capital and labour, by discouraging investment and causing "brain drain" and capital flight. It has been found that political instability in Africa severely hampered economic growth, which is consistent with these claims. Moreover, it does not appear that extensive civil and political liberties, characteristic of democracy rather than authoritarianism, are strongly associated with higher rates of growth with respect to gross domestic product. Rather, it seems that, at least in the case of Asia, political repression is positively associated with economic growth.

Contrary to the aforementioned claims, there are several arguments that can be made for democracy. First, it is argued that ***"democratic political structures foster private investment by bolstering belief in the political system's durability."*** While authoritarian regimes may provide certain freedoms, such as property rights, they cannot be guaranteed. They can be suspended at any time, which decreases the credibility of the promises; moreover, it is "plausible to believe that, over time, democracy entrenches economic freedoms, making them more stable and credible . . . in this way, political freedom makes a contribution in its own right to economic growth." Furthermore, democracy permits a more efficient allocation of resources in the economy, because a climate of open debate is allowed. This is quite the opposite of the earlier arguments. Perhaps most importantly, democratic systems foster freedom of choice and ***"tend to unleash people's creative energy."*** These become particularly important when economies enter the later stages of development, which require extensive innovation to continue along the growth path.

However, it is also important to consider empirical evidence, rather than just rhetorical claims, as convincing as they may be for either side in this debate. To that end, it is instructive to consider several studies that have analysed the relationship between economic growth and democracy. In the first, the impact of political and property rights on economic growth was examined in 59 less developed and transitional countries. It concluded that *"higher levels of democracy . . . are associated with faster growth"*—the implication is that political freedom contributes to rising economic output. It was also observed that countries with uncertain property rights tended to grow less; the view that democratic institutions, and thus secure property rights, promote economic growth is supported by the analysis. In the second study, the relationship between economic growth and democracy was investigated through an examination of 90 countries over 17 years. One of the most important findings was that both civil and political freedoms promote economic growth. This is due to the fact that in democratic political systems, people can be assured, to a greater extent than in authoritarian regimes that important freedoms such as property rights and contract enforcement, will not soon disappear.

A third study investigated several questions with respect to development and democracy. It was observed that in the last thirty years, the developing world has become significantly more democratised. It found that *"democratic regimes grew more rapidly and redressed their external imbalances more effectively than did their authoritarian counterparts,"* and it was suggested that democracies were better able to adapt their economic strategies than was believed. Interestingly, "older" more established democracies outperformed both "newer" democracies as well as non-democratic regimes. ***The catching up for lost time theory!***

Most important for our purposes, it has been shown that democratic countries that undertook the structural adjustment programs of the IMF and the World Bank were able to improve their GDP, export growth, and external balance more than their non-democratic counterparts. In fact, the non-democratic countries that did not undertake structural adjustment programs performed the worst of those under study, while democratic governments performed the best of all groups. The conclusion was that while democracies ***"must contend with greater political vulnerability than more authoritarian forms of government, they are also bolstered by a greater resilience, superior flexibility, and a broader political base, which allow them to institute changes more readily."***

It is possible that more rapid economic growth produces democratic institutions. Some have observed that economic factors, both international and domestic, "appear decisive in shaping a nation's democratic future." It is very interesting to note that it seems most likely that democracy does not cause economic development, and that the "causal arrow most probably runs from economic development to democracy", but not the other way.

World of Debt

> *"No pecuniary consideration is more urgent, than the regular redemption and discharge of the public debt: on none can delay be more injurious, or an economy of time more valuable."*
>
> **George Washington**

More problematic for the current debate, however, is the long-term uncertainty of the economic recovery achieved by countries that did undertake these structural adjustment programs. While these countries did return to a path of growth, it is not clear that this growth will be sustainable in the long run: *"They appeared to generate their growth by substituting external resources for domestic ones and in doing so substantially increased their debt burden."*

At this point, we must draw a distinction between the different types of financial aid that are available to countries in crisis. First, the IMF's structural adjustment programs are intended to address the economic problems that countries face, taken as a whole. Most often these are concerned with issues stemming from trade imbalances. Loans are intended to be temporary in order to establish sufficient currency reserves so that countries can begin to address the problems plaguing their economies.

When countries become members of the IMF, they pay a subscription in order to do so, based upon their relative contribution to the overall world economy. They can pay up to one quarter of their subscription, or quota, in one of the major currencies such as the US dollar, the yen, the euro, or the pound sterling; alternatively, they can pay this quota with Special Drawing Rights, which is neither a reserve currency nor a claim on the IMF, but a "potential claim on the freely usable currencies of IMF members." The value of an SDR is determined daily through a weighting of the four major currencies listed above. SDRs were originally created in order to replace gold and silver in international transactions, and are sometimes referred to as "paper gold." Through the allocation of SDRs, the IMF determines interest rates for loans based on a weighted average of representative interest rates on short-term debt in the money markets of the SDR currencies basket.

For the World Bank, however, financial aid is provided through a more complex network of institutions; chief among these are the International Bank for Reconstruction and Development (IBRD) and the International Development Association (IDA).

The IBRD's original purpose was to finance the reconstruction of war-torn Europe and Japan following World War II, but it has since expanded its mission to fight poverty on a global scale. Once the European and Japanese economies had sufficiently recovered, the IBRD's mandate was expanded to include Asia, Africa, and Latin America. Loans are funded through the issuance of bonds on the traditional capital markets, backed by the creditworthiness of the largest donor nations. The IDA was instituted in order to serve the poorest nations and facilitate long-term, interest-free lending to address basic development needs such as primary education, basic health services, environmental safeguards, infrastructure and institutional reforms.

Arguably the largest criticism of the IMF and the World Bank organisations has to do with the debt burdens that they have incurred. In the immediate decades following World War II and the wave of decolonisation that followed, the policies favoured by the IMF and the World Bank centered upon the development of massive infrastructure projects as well as import-substituting industrialisation. As such, the lending policies represented somewhat of a convergence of ideologies promulgated by capitalists, communists and nationalists alike. However, in most of these countries the domestic markets were too small and lacked the requisite natural resources or raw materials to follow the same path towards industrialisation the more developed nations had.

Import-substituting industrialisation essentially promotes the targeting of specific sectors of the economy in an attempt to increase domestic production and thus cut imports, and for most nations this was not a viable option. It was soon realised that these strategies were unable to attract significant capital and generate significant savings, both of which were necessary ingredients for economic development.

The structural adjustment programs discussed earlier were a response to the threat of default from the developing world, as a consequence of the inefficiencies of the import-based models. In the 1960's, there was a fundamental reorientation towards export-oriented industrialisation: the provision of infrastructure so as to provide the necessary inputs for manufacturing operations; few restrictions on foreign ownership, entry and exit, or repatriation of profits; and finally, diversification of trade in order to reduce competition and increase profit motives. However, many of these policies—aimed at making the investment climate more attractive to foreign capital—had the result of increasing capital outflows. Investments in the public sector, moreover, were discouraged as a consequence, which often made it difficult for countries to provide the necessary savings to get out of debt. These economic adjustments were made the precondition for IMF and World Bank loans, and saddled much of the developing world with massive debts that they had no hope of repaying.

Much of the focus of IMF and World Bank loan programs is aimed at reducing barriers to trade and investment. According to neoliberal theory, protectionist policies were argued to have made a heavy contribution to the economic crises and military conflicts of the first half of the 20th century. Indeed, both the IMF and the World Bank exist to perform surveillance and a research function, with the goal of not just providing technical expertise for developing countries but also with the objective of pre-empting crises before they strike. *Has this new institutional framework actually succeeded in preventing further crisis?*

Part of the institutional framework that was envisaged at Bretton Woods was the World Trade Organisation, which began life in 1948 as the General Agreement on Tariffs and Trade (GATT). Originally intended to be a part of the United Nations, the GATT grew out of the failure of the International Trade Organisation. Since then, it has had an equally contentious history. In the absence of an international organisation governing trade, the GATT became the de facto institutional mechanism aimed at removing tariffs and other economic factors indirectly related to trade, such as government policies on business, finance, investing and employment.

When the WTO was officially instituted in 1995, it formalised many of the treaty provisions that had been only provisional up to that point. The GATT, moreover, had no real enforcement protocol, so the WTO expanded its mandate to include a dispute settlement mechanism. The WTO also put in place new agreements governing intellectual property, service industries, investments, and government trade policies. Critics charge, though, that the WTO merely institutionalises the asymmetrical power relationships that already existed between industrialised nations and developing economies; even though it has a democratic mandate, decisions about trade policies are generally taken by consensus, as the outgrowth of *back-room negotiations* between aligned blocks of nations. As a result, what we have witnessed with the WTO is less the promotion of free trade and economic liberalisation but a systemic bias away from the developing world and in favour of the industrialised nations. The WTO is one of the most inclusive global organisations but it is criticised for being unrepresentative and undemocratic, serving only to further impoverish the developing world that needs it most.

It seems apparent, though, that changes may be on the horizon. In May 1995 negotiations among the world's wealthiest nations were begun with the aim of further liberalising global rules on investment. While not secret, there was little public awareness of what these talks entailed or what the consequences of their institution might mean for the developing world. When they became public, they were roundly criticised: *"they appeared to establish a new body of universal investment laws to guarantee corporations excessive powers to buy, sell and undertake financial operations all over the world, severely diluting national laws, e.g., on environmental protection, regulation of labour standards and human rights established in developed countries."*

This prompted a massive worldwide campaign against the proposed agreement, and public protests were eventually successful in killing the entire proposal, despite the attempt to incorporate it into the broader WTO framework.

This speaks to one of the primary problems with the WTO system: *"The opening of national financial systems has created a globalised financial market, but we have not developed the market infrastructure at the international level to make it work. This is fundamentally what has generated the new crises. We have created a world in which devastating financial crises in developing countries have become endemic. The trouble is that the international community is seeking to push the world economy still further in this direction."*

The Asian financial crisis of 1997 was particularly damaging for the IMF, which was accused of worsening the crisis through the implementation of economic reforms that engendered further political instability in these already damaged countries. Currency devaluations caused their dollar-denominated debts to skyrocket.

The conclusion that follows is perhaps even more damaging: with each new crisis, and even in the face of different causal factors, the international system's response has been just the same as in the 1980's and 1990's, based on loans to the government concerned from international agencies and developed countries, subject to conditions on economic policies. The policies themselves have barely changed. In the case of the Asian crisis, the preconditions serve only to further undermine the internal stability of the countries in question.

To prevent currency values collapsing, these countries' governments raised domestic interest rates to exceedingly high levels primarily to help diminish flight of capital by making lending more attractive to investors. They also intervened in the exchange market, buying up any excess domestic currency at the fixed exchange rates with foreign reserves. Neither of these policy responses could be sustained for long. Very high interest rates, which can be extremely damaging to an economy that is healthy, wreaked further havoc on economies in an already fragile state, while the central banks were hemorrhaging foreign reserves, of which they had finite amounts. When it became clear that the tide of capital fleeing these countries was not to be stopped, the authorities ceased defending their fixed exchange rates and allowed their currencies to float. As a result the value of those currencies depreciated which meant that foreign currency-denominated liabilities grew substantially in domestic currency terms, causing more bankruptcies and further deepening the crisis.

Similar crises, like the situation now underway in Iceland following the collapse of the banking sector, only confirm this judgment against the IMF. Not only have they not adjusted their policies but, worse, they have staunchly adhered to them in the face of so much evidence to the contrary.

Conclusion

What to do in the face of crisis? If our international institutions have failed us, what choices do we have in order to help manage the economic order?

We have seen in this chapter how the Bretton Woods system came about in response to a wave of earlier massive economic shocks, and the perceived need to lessen their impact. Prior to this, the world's economies adhered to a stricter version of the gold standard, but as a result of this, they were forced to choose between independent monetary policy and free trade; under the gold standard, they could not have both. Fixed exchange rates were not the answer as they tended to translate economic shocks through the international system to an even greater extent.

The compromise solution at Bretton Woods involved the creation of the IMF and the World Bank group on the one hand, and the designation of the US dollar as the world's reserve currency on the other. Interestingly, economist John Maynard Keynes had advocated for the creation of a new international reserve currency to be called the *bancor*, which could have achieved several substantial 'gains' for the global economy. Chief among these would have been the removal of the tension that perpetually faces the US dollar, in that it has been used as an instrument of both national *and* global monetary policy; in order for it to be effectively used for the latter, it must flow out of the former, thereby placing the US in a perpetual balance of payments problem; a problem that has grown ever more visual in every decade since the agreement was signed. Within the confines of the Bretton Woods system, the economic consequences of this fundamental dilemma were simply untenable, and the system fell apart.

In the absence of the gold standard, the IMF and World Bank seemed to have 'lost' the battle for a new reserve currency for the world economy. This is most likely due to the overwhelming economic and thus political influence of the US at the birth of these organisations. The US dollar was effectively designated the world's reserve currency because this placed the US in the position as the guarantor of global security. Of course, it has paid the price for this in times of recession and by facing similar constraints on its monetary policy. ***Even though the gold standard was abolished formally in 1971, the US has remained the de facto reserve currency since that time.***

Recently, there have been calls for important reforms to these institutions, the IMF, World Bank and WTO and their economic underpinnings. We have seen how the liberal economic policies have in many respects failed the nations of the world during times of crises, serving only to force national governments into unsustainable debt burdens and economic policies that only make the situation worse. In response, many countries have begun to accumulate their own foreign currency reserves in so-called Sovereign Wealth Funds, and have now begun to deploy this capital throughout the global economy. Rather than 'investing' these reserves with the IMF and increasing their quotas, for example, countries such as Dubai, Singapore and China have chosen to invest these funds for further profit. They are now estimated to be over $3 trillion, which ranks them close to or perhaps even above the size of total hedge fund assets, and have become an important source of diversification and stability for these countries.

There have also been numerous proposals for a re-evaluation of the *bancor* concept, most notably emanating from the new economic superpower, China. Recently, China has agitated for a move away from the US dollar as the world's reserve currency, perhaps through an expansion of the IMF's Special Drawing Rights. As we've seen earlier, SDRs are a unit of accounting similar to the ideas behind the *bancor*, but as presently constructed they are only reflective of four currencies. It is argued that SDRs could be exchanged for foreign reserves in order to provide a measure of currency stability in the face of economic crisis. If the basket composition of the SDRs were more reflective of the broader global economy, and updated regularly to better represent each country's relative contribution to the global economy, they could prove more viable as a reserve currency.

The IMF recently approved a special allocation of $250 billion in SDRs, in order to pre-empt further concerns over a shortage of global liquidity. This will have the effect of increasing foreign currency reserves and may provide an important buffer for further economic dislocations. Unfortunately, it comes just a year too late to save the economy of Iceland, which will continue to contend with the extraordinary burdens of IMF loans that are conditional on sweeping reform of the island nation's monetary policies. Whether these policies will have the effect of prolonging the country's currency crisis remains to be seen. However, this would still not remove the ever-present specter of inflation, because this would still be indirectly influenced by the monetary policies of its member nations. Therefore, an inflation-indexed currency unit is still regarded as beneficial by some of the world's leading economists.

Yet another method for addressing the volatile currency markets has been proposed by economist James Tobin, and essentially imposes a minute tax on currency trades in order to discourage short-term currency speculation. While some argue that currency speculators serve a critical purpose and actually inject liquidity into a system that might otherwise dry up or become even more volatile, proponents of the 'Tobin tax' argue that it will create a cushion for exchange rate fluctuations, preventing the need to raise interest rates and providing "a measure of opposition to the dictate of the financial markets."

What is clear from this discussion is that the present system is still on a collision course with economic crises. When all is said and done, it seems that the IMF and World Bank, as presently construed, have not served their original intent. In all likelihood, they have made them worse, and many of these crises have not been solved until countries took their fates into their own hands in order to fundamentally reorient their economies and return themselves to a path of stability. That is not to say that they have not achieved great good; the abolition of poverty and promotion of economic growth and development are indeed of pivotal importance, so they should not be written off altogether.

However, as the influence of the US begins to wane towards the end of the first decade of 21st century, it is clear that alternate solutions must come to the fore. Looking at the policy responses to the credit crisis in the US, for example, we are forced into sober considerations about the future of the almighty dollar, and whether its present position as the world's reserve currency is even sustainable—**to say nothing of whether it is advisable!**

In many respects, the US is acting as the ultimate emerging market economy, trying to borrow its way out of crisis when reckless borrowing was what got it into the present predicament in the first place. For a variety of interrelated reasons, the dollar has not slid far in the face of rampant monetary expansion, but only time will tell if the massive fiscal stimulus from the US Treasury and the exponential balance sheet expansion for the US Federal Reserve will result in any significant devaluation. *If the dollar were to collapse, this would truly test the mettle of the IMF, for who else would—or could—come to the rescue!*

On that sobering thought in Chapter 8 we will look at one national government that appears to have balanced well the twin demands of private profit and public service with its banking system and so been less buffeted by the financial hurricane that has enveloped the world. *Is this possibly a blue print for a new and stronger global banking system?*

Let's see!

Chapter 8

November 2007—A Scotsman, a Frenchman and an Englishman . . . . went into a Bank!

"When a government is dependent upon bankers for money, they and not the leaders of the government control the situation, since the hand that gives is above the hand that takes. Money has no motherland; financiers are without patriotism and without decency; their sole object is gain."

Napoleon Bonaparte

November 2007—the French Banking Crisis comes to a head. The French banking sector rallied after the government agreed a deal to inject around 10.5 billion Euros ($14 billion) into the country's top six firms in the form of loans.

"French Banking"—That very phrase summons images of well padded, elegantly dressed Parisian bankers drawing up and arranging beautifully constructed loans with clients over leisurely eight course lunches. What though is the reality?

Vive La Banque Universelle; with the world in financial turmoil, no country has been immune from the crisis. That is not to say, however, that all parties have fared equally! In many respects France has remained above the fray. Looking to the future, it would seem a safer bet than most countries. For the most part, the French banking sector has remained strong, and many are now looking to France as the potential 'successor' model for successful and resilient banking. This is in so many ways a direct mirror of the position the French central bank was able to achieve under its then Chairman Emile Moreau following the 1929 crash.

While other governments around the globe run to the aid of national banks in trouble, there is an air of cautious optimism in France that their national banks will weather the storm better than most. What's more, they may well emerge from the credit crisis in a stronger position, and will be able not just to maintain their standing in the international marketplace but to bolster it. Others, of course, will not be so fortunate.

"Never ascribe to malice, that which can be explained by incompetence!"

Napoleon

To date, the only significant intervention by the French national government has come with its participation in the bailout of Dexia, a Belgian bank specialising in public finance; a situation covered in a later chapter. Of course, one must consider that Dexia's lending activities supported approximately half of the local governments in France, but significantly it did not have any retail operations there. French Finance Minister Christine Lagarde said the capital infusion was essential *"to guarantee the stability of the financial system,"* and as a result Dexia is likely to emerge as one of the better-capitalised banks in Europe. Considering that the French government secured nearly a one-third equity stake in the Belgian firm, this intervention may prove to be even more valuable financially than the less-tangible political dividends might initially suggest.

What distinguishes the French banking system from its counterparts, both in Europe and globally?

There are several factors that seem to engender stability in French banks. Taken together, these should reassure French savers—and taxpayers—that their banks are made from tougher stuff than those elsewhere. While France is not yet out of the woods, and like much of the global financial system is still facing a severe economic downturn, there are several reasons to believe that the French banking system will prove more resilient than those in many other parts of the world.

This chapter will discuss these factors, and in doing so we hope to illustrate some of the dangers inherent in today's debt-based economies. What's more, we will look at some of the particular *cultural* factors that reinforce the health of the French financial system. This should not imply, however, that everything has come up roses in France, or that the continuing credit crisis does not pose significant risks to the *future* health of the French financial system; here, we'll detail some of the damage done to the French banking system, and what this bodes for the future. However, if they are able to maintain their solid footing, we may all just have a more robust model upon which to build.

France's Economic Climate—the Formative Years

For us to understand the French financial system, it's necessary to first put it into the broader socioeconomic and political context that has prevailed in the country. France is often used as a strong example of the *dirigiste* economic model, in which the central government exerts relatively greater influence than in other, more liberal systems. In France, it would be apt to characterise the economy as one that is essentially capitalist in nature, but with strong economic participation by the central government. Of course, most modern economies display similar characteristics, although many commentators tend to downplay these. For example, in the United States there is a relatively high degree of government intervention in the economy shielded by a perceived "spin" of laissez faire capitalism.

> *"Endless money forms the sinews of war."*
>
> **Cicero**

The foundations for the banking system in France today came into being in 1716, when the ***Banque Generale Privee*** was set up by John Law. Law was a Scottish economist who had gained prominence on the continent through currency and securities speculation in Amsterdam, Genoa, Venice and London. Observing the frenzied activity of the traders in these exchanges on the one hand, and the limited involvement and conservatism of the banking systems on the other, Law saw the promise of a new system altogether: ***"The idea was already taking shape in Law's mind of a breathtaking modification of these institutions, which would combine the properties of a monopoly trading company with a public bank that issued notes in the manner of the Bank of England."***

In 1705 Law proposed the creation of such an institution in his native Scotland; this new bank would issue interest-bearing notes rather than minting coins. Notably, and well ahead of his time in this regard, Law observed that **confidence alone** was the basis for public credit; with confidence in the issuer, bank notes would serve equally as well as coins.

> *"Thus, our national circulating medium is now at the mercy of loan transactions of banks, which lend, not money, but promises to supply money they do not possess."*
> **Irving Fisher**

Law's proposal was turned down by the Scottish Parliament; likely due in part to the pending union with England, but the dire economic circumstances in France following the War of Spanish Succession gave the financier the opportunity he needed to try out his new system. Law convinced the French crown to institute his new **Banque Generale**, which was given license to issue notes backed by gold or silver for a fixed twenty-year period.

Law's Banque Generale was further built upon the consolidation of the French royal debt, which by this time had nearly pushed the treasury into default. He viewed the absolutist monarchical French state as a means by which to both extend credit further and to do so at lower interest rates, precisely because of its monopoly control over the financial system. Moreover, when that bank issuing **monopoly** was combined with a **monopoly** trading company, the entire financial system would be centralised for the benefit of the royal coffers; to that end, from 1718-19 Law convinced the French rulers to grant his new 'Company of the West' a monopoly over commerce in the new French territory of Louisiana, a land mass Law believed contained untold riches.

Law believed that his new 'System' had created a coherent, self-reinforcing financial model that incorporated the previously disjointed efforts of the royal mint, taxation, trading and currency. For a time, this worked as a means of injecting much-needed liquidity into the devastated French economy. In addition, the *Banque Generale's* notes were guaranteed by the King, which effectively made it the first French central bank. The problem came with the fact that Law had obtained a majority of the government debt, and since his System heavily encouraged trading in his Company shares, it encouraged an asset bubble that had no real basis in reality. Expansion was funded not by profits but by issuing new shares, but Law offered new shares at increasingly higher prices because of the promise of future profits from the territories in the Americas.

Speculation in the dividend-paying Company shares led to inflation and a decline in the all-important confidence in the paper currency. As Law had pumped so much liquidity into the money supply, effectively doubling the amount of currency in circulation, as a result of the continued issuance of shares to fund the Company's not-so-profitable trading activities in Louisiana, people began to revert to payment in gold or silver rather than royal banknotes. Government led efforts to curtail the public supply of gold and silver on the one hand, and to unilaterally devalue the banknotes on the other, were unsuccessful and in short order the trading and banking arms of the Company collapsed. The effects on the French financial system were catastrophic:

"Law's bubble and bust fatally set back France's financial development, putting Frenchmen off paper money and stock markets for generations. The French monarchy's fiscal crisis went unresolved and for the remainder of the reigns of Louis XV and his successor Louis XVI the crown essentially lived from hand to mouth, lurching from one abortive regime to another until royal bankruptcy finally precipitated revolution!"

It was Law's monopolistic control over both stock and credit markets, and the Ponzi-like nature of the bubble that he engendered from the false promise of the Louisiana territory, that proved his undoing and caused such financial devastation.

Sound familiar?

It should, as it calls to mind the present economic crisis and the unsupported housing bubble that was brought upon us as a consequence of the extreme overlapping of capital markets today! Uncontrolled lending led to a collapse in confidence upon which Law's entire System was based, and even though he was perhaps hundreds of years ahead of his time as an innovator in paper money, without the proper backing it would prove worthless. It is astonishing that one man could have gained so much control through the promulgation of his ideas as he did, given that there was really no basis for the demand that he created virtually out of thin air. Of course, within a period of four years, the bubble burst and it all went up like so much Louisiana tobacco smoke!

> *"When speculation has done its worst, two and two still make four".*
> **Samuel Johnson**

It must be recalled that the innovations that Law offered to the economically crippled and vulnerable French monarchy were not entirely unreasonable. He succeeded in re-inflating the French currency and spurring growth in trade and finance by injecting liquidity into the financial system.

Sound familiar once more?

At its root, it is no different from the actions many governments are taking today in response to the present economic crisis gripping the world. Law was correct in observing that confidence was at the heart of the financial system. Law was also incorrect; he proved his own undoing by creating an asset bubble that had no backing. When the public grasped the fact that Law's System could not support itself, that confidence was shattered and the bubble quickly burst.

The collapse of Law's System engendered in the French populace the wider distrust and reticence for capital markets that exists today. We can see the vestiges of this eroded confidence in the public bank that Law created, and perhaps this is why French citizens are much more accepting of the interventionist actions of French governments. Devolving economic power to the private financier as completely as they did resulted in a devastating impact upon the French economy; *it is likely that this distrust discourages the use of capital markets for fundraising activities by banks, which is what we see in the United States and the UK but is relatively absent from the present French system.*

What is clear is that France learned a hard lesson from the entrepreneurial activities of Law; that one man cannot control so much and a system of banking must be built upon a solid foundation that has at its heart a strong consumer base. Law was ahead of his time, and contributed several important innovations to the system of paper money which would eventually take hold throughout the world, but based as it was upon so many false promises, it was bound to collapse. *The extent to which it damaged the French financial system and influenced economic behaviour in the nation is still prevalent today.*

Jumping forward several generations, we note that there has been somewhat of a 'convergence' of political influence within the broader economic system since the Second World War. Prior to this, it would be fair to characterise France's economy as much more traditionally 'laissez faire' in its capitalist tendencies; in the postwar period France generally sought to enforce the economic direction of the country through what has been called 'indicative central planning'. This should not be confused with the type of central planning undertaken by socialist or authoritarian states, such as in the Eastern bloc or the Soviet Union; rather, the French state simply favoured maintaining minority stakes in a range of key industries and economic entities.

Most of us are familiar with the leading role that French governments have played in infrastructure, transportation and telecommunications. Much of the modernisation of the French economic system can be said to have coincided with a particular concentration of political and financial elites, as a result of the heavy influence of educational institutions such as l'Ecole Polytechnique and l'Ecole Nationale d'Administration. During the three decades from 1945-75, France experienced high levels of economic growth and a demographic boom, and much of this was attributed to this 'middle path' approach to economic planning and resource allocation.

Since the 1980's, a large proportion of the French economy has denationalised, but it still possesses a strong measure of *rigueur* in terms of economic and consumer centralisation. While much of French political and economic life has since evolved away from the ***dirigiste*** model, especially after the Mitterrand era, many of its traits remain and are distinctive aspects of French culture. These are particularly evident in the banking sector, and have a number of salient qualities that serve to distinguish this industry from its peers abroad.

Of course, much of this was undertaken by French financial and political authorities in order to specifically address the fragmented nature of French industry, and in order to counteract the growing ascendancy of the United States. In order to do so, they generally sought "rational, efficient economic development, with the long-term goal of matching the highly-developed and technologically-advanced economy of the United States." In turn, broader efforts aimed at European integration had the same end goal, which began with economic co-ordination with the European Steel and Coal Community and have thus far culminated in economic policy convergence through the European Central Bank.

Cultural considerations have played a significant role in the development of the modern financial sector in France. As a result, we'd argue that France in general, and the French banking industry in particular, is better positioned to weather the credit crisis. Several key characteristics of French banking, which can only be said to be part and parcel of the broader socioeconomic context within which they operate, distinguish it. The following section will discuss these in greater detail.

Banking in France Today

In the wake of the current credit crisis, economists, politicians and taxpayers alike are looking for answers; *what went wrong in the global financial system that allowed such widespread devastation and loss?*

Part of the answer, of course, lies with the subprime credit crisis itself, the dynamics of which are largely understood and well-documented elsewhere. *What appear to have been less well discussed are the reasons that some firms, countries, and regions have fared better than others!*

France, in particular, has weathered the crisis particularly well. Many attribute this to the specific nature of the French banking system and the many cultural factors that reinforce its resilient character. The traditional model of the French bank is often referred to as *la Banque Universelle*, or universal banking model, which differs substantially from those abroad. To begin with, French banks in general are much more broadly based, pursuing a much more diversified range of activities than their peers in other countries. By contrast, institutions in the US and the UK tend to be more focused and specialised in a particular product or service area, such as investment banking or home loans—*these are noteworthy, of course, because it was the interrelation of these activities that has caused the present difficulties!*

In France banks are less reliant on investment banking, with retail banking accounting for around two-thirds of their business activities. BNP Paribas, one of the strongest performers during the credit crisis, attributes its strength to its retail focus and critical attention to detail at the consumer level. BNP is one of the ten largest banks in the world, and engages in a range of activities that include everything from retail banking to commercial and investment banking. Roughly half of the activities are concentrated at the retail level—only about a third of the bank's operations emanate from the commercial end of the spectrum. What this has meant for the bank is a remarkable level of consistency, regardless of market conditions. Other banks display similar attributes, and this has made France one of the most mature and consolidated banking markets in Europe, with one of the highest ratios of products per client in the region.

This approach has clearly paid dividends for BNP, and has elevated it to a position where it can continue to capitalise on past successes. Its huge deposit base, for example, has allowed it to continue to operate safely in difficult market conditions and to remain profitable at the same time. This is in marked contrast to the experience of US investment banks Goldman Sachs and Morgan Stanley, both of which were forced to convert into bank holding companies in order to fortify their weakened positions and buttress their deposit-taking abilities. Had they not done so, it is doubtful that they would have survived the credit crisis as well as they have.

Numerous acquisitions within the French banking industry in the 1990's and early 2000's have served to strengthen their consumer bases and, at the same time, made them more competitive on a global scale. BNP Paribas was created from the merger of three smaller firms in 2000, making it the largest bank in France and one of the largest in the Eurozone, always close on the heels of Swiss rival UBS. Societe Generale similarly acquired a smaller retail-banking rival in 1999, which catapulted it into the second place position in the country, prior to the merger of Caisse d'Epargne and Banque Populaire. These two banks began merger talks in February 2009 that have only recently been finalised; it is interesting to note that French financial authorities played a large role in encouraging this merger as a means of dealing with the spreading crisis.

These and other larger financial institutions are constituted in broadly similar ways to their US bank holding company counterparts. What separates them, however, is that each has developed a particular specialisation and expertise in their investment banking operations. As a result, they tend to focus more in particular areas than institutions in the US and UK might. For example, Societe Generale has developed expertise in asset management and private banking; BNP has concentrated more on commercial and investment banking, as somewhat of an extension of their retail banking dominance.

This distinctive expertise in specialist areas relies on a thorough mastery of each discipline, as is apparent from the performances and ratings achieved in international classifications by the specialist companies concerned. This expertise is reinforced by the marketing undertaken by retail banking networks, which frequently underpins such companies and has led to a transformation of the model; this innovative, well-defined, long-term relationship between producer and distributors is indeed the envy of its American rivals, where the ratio of products and revenues per client has traditionally been lower.

What this means for the universal bank is a different conception of risk management. In relying on a larger mix of businesses, they have remained diversified and less subject to market downturns. Societe Generale's Charles Pierron describes it this way: *"The key also for me is to have not only a universal banking model but a focused business approach. It differentiates us from other competitors who spread themselves too thin without the critical mass thus taking unnecessary risk."* Thus, it is the combination of a strong domestic market, coupled with conservative and selective risk management that has kept them strong when others have suffered.

This type of risk management extends into key areas of the retail-banking sphere, especially in lending. Ideas about consumer credit differ significantly from other countries. As one French banker put it, *"It's true that you can note a big difference in consuming behaviours between the French and the English . . . People here don't believe you can just put your debts together and get them refinanced. But in London, it was as if wealth was something you could get from a bank; it's a sort of miracle people seem to believe in England. It seems to me people there are very keen to use up all the money they have, and that's a worry when you wonder how people are going to have money for retirement for instance."*

In France, credit is simply not extended in the same ways or to the same degree as it is elsewhere, such as in the United States or the UK. Household debt, for example, was 47% of Gross Domestic Product in 2008, whereas in the UK it was over twice that. Banks are extremely careful about whom they lend to. French banks enforce strict standards in their lending practices, and consumers must face a tough test of their ability to repay before loans are entered into. French banks have generally been far more wary about lending to homebuyers. In 2007 French mortgage debt represented only 35% of GDP, according to the European Mortgage Federation, less than in Germany (48%) and way off that in the housing-bubble economies of Britain (86%), Ireland (75%) and Spain (62%). French banking regulators, moreover, prevent banks from making loans in which interest payments represent more than *one third of a borrower's income*, and banks are under a legal obligation not to push borrowers into more debt than they can manage.

Retail credit in France is similarly curtailed, but this seems to be as much of a cultural artifact as a business model. Some have pointed to an innate 'prudence' among consumers: *"But it is very difficult to spend money you do not have in France. French credit cards are little more than debit cards, so there is no question of simply sticking a couple of flat screen TVs on your credit card and hoping to pay for them later—if there are insufficient funds in your account, your bank will immediately block the transaction."* The country as a whole simply seems to take fewer risks, and a culture of living within one's means keeps runaway spending in check. This of course, is in direct contrast with the recent American and English experience:

"Local homeowners pumped more and more capital out of their houses as well, taking out home-equity loans and injecting money into the local economy in the form of home improvements and demand for retail goods and low-level services. Cities grew, tax coffers filled, spending continued, more people arrived. Yet the boom itself neither followed nor resulted in the development of sustainable, scalable, highly productive industries or services. It was fueled and funded by housing, and housing was its primary product. Whole cities and metro regions became giant Ponzi schemes."

While this example is an extreme one, it is illustrative of the harder, economic data that now points to an alarmingly low household savings rate in the US, which is now near zero. In addition, the reluctance to tie the French economy into the housing market, in direct contrast to the US, has also meant that when the American subprime market collapsed, it did not drag the French market with it. French Finance Minister Christine Lagarde, commenting on the banking crisis, recently outlined the lending regulations that have helped minimise the crunch: *"Expect two conditions—a down payment of 20% of the value of the house plus mortgage repayments which will not exceed 30% of income. You already have a pretty good safety net there and clearly no real estate financing similar to the sub-prime market that has existed in the US and which has hurt the financial system so much."*

Clearly there are cultural factors at work, and the extensive social safety net in France likely serves as a large source of economic cushioning. To begin with, France's public spending accounted for 52% of GDP in 2007, next to 45% in Britain and 37% in America. Over 20% of France's workers are employed in the public sector, and nearly 50% of the entire workforce is only moderately vulnerable to the recession. Other aspects of the social safety system, such as extensive unemployment and health care benefits, act as "automatic stabilisers" and help to support consumer demand.

Economist Alexander Law puts it this way: *"In the US and the UK, the economy has been driven by household spending, consumption has been driven by credit, and a lot less in France, so that's why when there were periods of expansion France grew a lot more slowly than the UK and the US but conversely when it's slowing down, it will slow down in a more moderate fashion than the UK or the US."* France's economy has been less hard hit than many during this crisis: GDP is expected to shrink by 3% this year, according to the IMF, against 4.1% in Britain, 4.4% in Italy and 5.6% in Germany. However, this model has not been without its detractors—including President Sarkozy—or its downsides; these are generally regarded as *"disappointing macroeconomic performance, with low growth and high unemployment."*

Performing Under Duress: How the French Banking Industry Has Held Up

Clearly, no country or geographic region can remain wholly untouched by the current crisis but it seems as though the French banking system is positioned ideally to weather the credit storm. Part of this relative immunity stems from the dynamic just described above: even though France tends to grow less quickly than many of its peers in Europe and abroad, it also tends to experience a more moderate decline in tough times. If we were to graph this dynamic, we'd see the peaks and valleys of France's growth rates demonstrate less volatile swings. This has very likely contributed to the resilience of France's banking sector as well. The IMF recently noted that in addition to France's generous social safety net, the country's limited reliance on exports has shielded it from the worst effects of the global recession.

However, the ongoing nature of the crisis means that today's stability may be replaced by tomorrow's upheaval. The Bank of France Governor Christian Noyer noted in mid 2008, ***"In today's globalised financial world, there are many channels through with financial turbulence can spread. We therefore need to remain very vigilant."*** In July 2009, IMF officials also warned that even as France's banks have performed better than their overseas rivals, French authorities still need to remain at the ready to inject capital into the banking sector. The continuing nature of the economic crisis means that the pace of loan defaults, for example, may still accelerate; the third quarter of 2008 saw a sharp rise in loan defaults, which were up 75% from a year earlier. As transportation, construction and property sectors continue to be affected; banking sector performance may still decline before the economy improves.

These observations recall President Sarkozy's statements in October 2008 following the bailout of Belgium's Dexia Bank, in which he declared "***no French depositor would lose a euro in savings,***" signaling his intention to follow through on state-funded rescue efforts if need be. Even though it was not strictly necessary, the government chose to act preemptively by injecting €10.5 billion into the banking system in December 2008, in order to ensure the adequate supply of credit and prevent unwanted tightening. What's more, the French government has proactively addressed public outrage at executive bonuses at failing banks; March 2009 saw over three million workers on the streets to protest against the government's policies towards unemployment, living standards, and their general handling of the steep recession.

How has the industry performed?

According to George Pauget, Chairman of the French Banking Federation, the results and reasons are unequivocal:

"The leading French banks occupy top 10 positions in several international classifications and, although the level of losses on certain activities may have been substantial, the financial crisis has impacted upon them less severely than other players. The resistance of this model stems from two factors: a high level of diversification; and targeted expertise in certain areas of derivatives and structured finance. In-depth knowledge of a particular area does not provide complete protection from the consequences of a, generally regarded, unprecedented crisis. However, the effects are less severe and owning such in-depth knowledge allows the consequences to be absorbed and the necessary changes to be implemented more rapidly."

These statements echo the observations of Alexander Law and others. Going beyond these general observations, however, we see from the economic data that as a result of the universal model, French banks have maintained more robust performance and continuity in their banking practices. Tough conditions in the credit markets have only marginally impacted lending in France, which is in direct contrast to the experience in the US and other areas of Europe. As French banks tap the capital markets less than their overseas competitors, the strength of their capital bases has tended to offset any loan refinancing difficulties; any slowdown in mortgage lending has been offset by the strength in both household liquid investments and corporate lending. This effect is as much a "self-regulatory" mechanism of already tough lending standards in France, as opposed to a "correction" in runaway growth as it is in the United States or the UK.

"The human species, according to the best theory I can form of it, is composed of two distinct races: the men who borrow, and the men who lend."

Charles Lamb

Looking at banking sector performance more specifically, we see a range of results. In this section, we will highlight some of the ways in which France's six largest financial institutions have been affected by the credit crisis, and how they have in turn dealt with the challenges. Overall, this 'report card' on France's largest banks yields mixed results, but is revealing because of their varied experiences. France has certainly not been immune from the global downturn, but in contrast to the results in the US and the UK, for example, we find markedly different results.

Credit Agricole is France's largest retail bank and was hard hit by the credit crisis. By the third quarter 2008, it had reported losses of approximately €6.5 billion. These losses were attributed to its trading activities as well as the depreciation of assets in its investment banking division, Calyon. Calyon itself reported subprime mortgage-related losses in excess of €1 billion, and Credit Agricole moved swiftly to restructure the firm and refocus its business along more traditional—and less risky—lines. The bank was then forced to raise nearly €6 billion from shareholders in order to shore up its capital base, making it the largest capital call to date for a French bank.

Societe Generale, France's second biggest listed bank, announced write-downs of more than €2 billion related to the global credit crunch in January 2008. Bad luck following bad luck meant that unfortunately only days later the bank announced a further loss of €4.9 billion. This was as a result of fraud caused by a single trader. Already reeling from the credit crisis, the fraud would only make it more difficult for the bank to recover; it was then forced to raise €5.5 billion through a capital increase to shore up its balance sheet. By the end of third quarter 2008, Societe Generale reported that its net profit was still down 63% from a year earlier.

The bank, due to exposure to its deteriorating loan portfolio in Eastern Europe as well as continued heavy losses in its commercial and investment banking division, recently revealed further losses. The fraudulent trading in 2008, moreover, prompted credit rating agencies to scrutinise the firm more highly, and has put more pressure on it to raise capital. This is in contrast to its more retail-minded domestic competitors, who have been able to avoid similar difficulties, and underscores the political as well as financial costs of engaging in risky trading operations.

However, where Societe Generale may yet benefit from the global downturn is in relation to its highly developed and specialised knowledge of key areas, in particular emerging markets. Where its global competitors such as Merrill Lynch and Lehman Brothers were forced early on to retrench their efforts within their domestic markets, Societe Generale is now able to fill the void they have left in key areas such as South Korea. The fact that it has been a leader in the innovation of the universal model, moreover, and the critical input of a diversified business mix, means that it is able to weather the credit storm where its global competitors have failed.

Clearly the hardest hit has been investment bank Natixis. Formed in December 2006 and jointly owned by Banque Populaire and Caisse d'Epargne, Natixis was forced to seek a bailout from its parent companies of over 1 billion euro as a result of losses at its bond insurance unit CIFG. While it initially remained profitable in 2007 as a result of asset sales and limited write-downs, the firm swung to heavy losses only a year later, reporting a net loss in the fourth quarter 2008 of €1.6 billion. Continuing losses in the first quarter of 2009 of €1.85 billion forced Natixis to seek further capital from its parent companies of €3.5 billion.

In addition to losses from its bond insurance unit, Natixis suffered heavy losses as a result of the collapse of Lehman Brothers in the US as well as its exposure to Icelandic banks, which have been among the hardest hit globally. Natixis was forced to restructure and undertake extreme cost cutting measures, and the outlook for its recovery continues to be difficult; Natixis still has investment banking assets that are expected to further drag down its performance, with further write-downs expected.

Natixis' parent companies Banque Populaire and Caisse d'Epargne were forced to merge as a result of their exposure to their troubled subsidiary. This was seen as a marriage of necessity and, reflective of the strong interventionist policies of the French government, was highly managed by French banking regulators. This merger will make the new BPCE group the second largest banking group in France. Criticism has been aimed at President Sarkozy for his role in the merger because of the appointment of his former financial aide to head to the new company.

One of the best performers throughout the crisis has been BNP Paribas. It is the only French bank that has significant investment banking activities and has remained profitable. In fact, it has even attracted customers and has increased its assets, while its domestic rivals have struggled with losses. Much of its continued ability to perform has been as a result of the strength of its capital base, which has not only been maintained but also fortified; this has allowed it to maintain its credit rating, which has in turn fortified its credit-related businesses, such as derivatives.

BNP believes that it can export its successful business model to other areas. The bank owns BancWest in the US, which has been a consistent performer throughout the credit crisis. Its subsidiaries have reported strong revenue and deposit growth, in line with the successes of their parent company. BNP acquired Italy's Banco Nazionale del Lavoro and has been able to 'export' its success: *"That means maintaining the conservative approach to lending and balance sheet management that have steered them through the recent crisis, kept their CDS spreads stable and their bondholders happy. It also means keeping an eye open for the growth opportunities and potential delivery of enhanced shareholder value from the continued turmoil in the financial services sector, which is leaving many competitors vulnerable."*

However, BNP's recent acquisition of Belgium's Fortis has not been without issue. Shareholders blocked the deal twice and sued to secure their rights to vote on the sale, and the court case even brought down the Belgian government as a result of conflict of interest claims. BNP would also gain Fortis' insurance businesses and secured a €1.5 billion guarantee from the Belgian government to cover losses for up to 3 years. BNP's success in negotiating the deal thus helped protect not only its own shareholders but those of Fortis as well.

Recent financial results seem to bear out that BNP has the right model and a successful corporate culture that engenders further success. Its acquisition of Fortis contributed strongly to its own profits, which were up over 6% since a year ago. As a result, it has continued to look for strategic partners abroad and to expand its market share in countries such as Italy, where it already owns BNL. BNP now has presence in 35 emerging markets and 85 countries world-wide.

Conclusion

"I have made all the calculations; fate will do the rest"
Napoleon

In Europe more generally, it is possible that the worst of the credit crisis is over, as nearly 80% of banks are no longer tightening credit. Some analysts warn that the present model, as much as it has provided a solid measure of stability for the banks' domestic operations, is not the only solution. While having a dependable and extensive retail base is important for addressing liquidity concerns, and trading scandals such as those at Societe Generale call into question the risky trading businesses that banks still undertake, quality is just as important as quantity. Banks still need to expand their products and services and increase their market penetration, not just their market share. As the experience of BNP Paribas suggests, it is as much about striking the right balance between risk management, balance sheet stability, and growth into new areas.

Congressional enquiry question: "Is not commercial credit based primarily upon money or property?"

"No sir," replied J. P. Morgan. "The first thing is character."

It is impossible to divorce the cultural aspects of French life from the system of banking. The ingrained sense of prudence that seems to prevail not only meshes well with the more restrictive lending practices, but they tend to reinforce each other. In the United States and the UK credit is freely available, and financial institutions have certainly played a large part in the persistent belief that debt is a part of life. Living beyond our means, as measured by household debt as a percentage of GDP, for example, is ample evidence that this myth is alive and well. The fact that France was able to avoid a housing bubble was likely due to tough loan standards, and this clearly played a part in decreasing the demand for real assets in the first place.

Does it have to be this way?

Lending standards in the United States and the UK have tightened considerably in recent years, and we are only beginning to see signs that the supply of credit is starting to ease. It appears that the underlying conditions are likely to persist for much longer, and that much of the world will lag France's banks in getting back on the road to recovery. The costs of that recovery, as witnessed by the massive government interventions into the financial system and the numerous bailouts of so many financial institutions in particular, are almost impossible to comprehend.

Much of this, as well, has to do with the differences in the overall socioeconomic and political climate in France, in contrast to other countries and regions of the world. French citizens are much more accepting of government intervention, and expect it as part of daily life. The prevalence of so many 'automatic stabilisers', as part of a broad social safety net, has helped to buoy consumer demand and remove at least some of the downward pressure that otherwise would have been placed on the banks and their balance sheets. In the United States, by contrast, public debate over the radical overhaul of the health care system has come under extreme criticism because of its enormous costs; implementing such a system is likely to be extremely difficult in the coming months and years, especially in light of the already-astronomical cost of the financial bailout. In this sense, even though France's health care system—a mix of public and private provision—is similar to what has been recently proposed in the US, it is likely that its long-standing entrenchment sets it too far ahead to serve as an applicable model.

The public, it seems, is thus much more willing to endure government intervention when it is deemed to be in the public good. France's financial services regulators extended their ban on the short-selling of financial securities, in order to quell public fears and provide some measure of market stability during the crisis. The US and the UK removed similar bans much earlier, which reflects the differing conceptions of economic freedom that prevail in these very different countries—even though the days of extreme volatility in capital markets seem to be behind us now, it seems that France is still taking no chances.

The government has moved for strict supervision of executive pay at the banks, even though those in the US dwarf the scale of bonus payments in France for example. Finance Minister Christine Lagarde said on Europe 1 radio that international rules are needed to ensure bonuses don't encourage excessive risk-taking. Perhaps the rest of the world is catching up to the French model; notably, the G-20 agreed on April 2 2009 on *"principles for sound compensation practices to avoid 'perverse incentives' that contributed to the financial crisis."* France's overall political climate seems to make this type of intervention and discourse much more readily 'saleable' than in other regions and only time will tell whether similar reforms are indeed adopted.

The performance of France's largest banks is also very revealing, especially when compared against each other domestically. It is no surprise that it was those that pursued riskier practices, such as Credit Agricole, Societe Generale, and Natixis that elicited poorer results, in contrast to BNP Paribas and the newly formed BPCE group. Each of the banks profiled here share similar attributes, and diversified their businesses and investments to an extent that is much less common in other areas of the world. *However, what is evident is that the banks that emphasised commercial and investment banking to a greater degree than their competitors were indeed the ones that have suffered the most; it is no secret that this is precisely the same pattern that has occurred in the US and the UK.*

The reluctance of others, however, to be overly tempted by quick profits is very revealing. What's more, those that have *maintained* their conservatism have been rewarded for it; BNP Paribas is now regarded as one of the best banks in Europe and has secured for itself a position as one of the leading banking franchises in the world. Now greater attention is being paid to the French banking system as a model that can be more widely exported and translated to other regions of the world.

Analysts caution, however, that an overemphasis on the retail-only model can also backfire: ***"Gathering retail deposits in bulk will be of limited value if it fails to generate much in the way of ancillary business . . . The other snag is that in a highly competitive market there is a limit to the volume of secure and potentially profitable deposits swirling around the market."*** The experience of Northern Rock in the UK, for example, which fell as a result of a rapid bank-run panic that saw £1 billion in customer deposits withdrawn in a single day, should be ample evidence that this is not enough either.

In hindsight, it seems obvious that prudence and risk management are what we've always expected from our banks, and it is almost incomprehensible that such a model is not more commonplace. It is as well almost unbelievable that in most regions of the world, there is a strong disequilibrium between risk management/balance sheet stability and shareholder value. We all intuitively know that this cannot be the case, for you cannot truly have one without the other! In today's rapid-paced, globalised financial world, in many respects quantity *does* trump quality, at least in the short term; shareholders are all too willing to demand quick profits, which often come at the expense of long term value.

What does the future hold? If the success of BNP Paribas and other similar institutions is any evidence, banks will need to re-engineer not just their balance sheets and corporate structures but the corporate *culture* as well. Even though it seems like commonsense, the scope and scale of these changes will require significant financial innovation if they are to be successful. More to the point, these changes will have no chance of taking hold if shareholders don't recognise that short-term profits cannot forever trump long-term value. In this sense, just as is the case in France, wider changes to the broader culture of public and private life need to take hold as well.

While one cannot expect the wholesale exportation of every aspect of the French socioeconomic sphere to other countries and regions, it is clear from this exposé that significant change in *some* of these areas will go a long way. Of course, France is not yet out of the woods either; it still faces a difficult road to recovery, and, as we've seen, the very 'automatic stabilisers' that have played such a key role in the resilience of the French banking system, may yet prove to be a detriment to the economy as a whole. As Keynes said; ***"If, however, a government refrains from regulations and allows matters to take their course, essential commodities soon attain a level of price out of the reach of all but the rich, the worthlessness of the money becomes apparent, and the fraud upon the public can be concealed no longer."***

Striking the appropriate balance is the key, and it seems that no country has yet to find the exact right answer. Time and history will tell whether France has got it *more right* than others.

From the relative safe harbour and calm waters of French banking we now move in **Chapter 9** to the turbulent high seas of the global insurance market. Already reeling under the combined assault of a wave of natural and manmade disasters would it finally sink beneath the tidal wave of financial instability about to be unleashed in the credit crunch?

Chapter 9

December 2007—The Emperor's New Clothes

"Dine on little, and sup on less."

Miguel de Cervantes

December 2007—At December 31, 2007, AIG's consolidated assets were $1.061 trillion and shareholders' equity was $95.80 billion. December 2008—US Government revises original loan package to AIG, increasing the original $85 billion to over $150 billion, in exchange for the issuance of a stock warrant to the Federal Reserve Bank for 79.9% of the equity of AIG.

Insurance: An arrangement by which a company gives customers financial protection against loss or harm in return for payment premium.

How are insurance companies and banks connected? What is a shadow bank? What is risk and who can measure it correctly?

Insurance, good news for once: on August 20, 2009 shares of American International Group (AIG) jumped more than 20% as markets reacted favorably to the appointment of Robert Benmosche as CEO. Benmosche, a veteran of the insurance industry, promised a "radical" change in the corporate culture of the battered insurance giant, which had struggled since it was nationalised in late 2008. The new CEO will have to succeed where his most recent predecessors have foundered; *to reverse the decline of the virtually bankrupt insurer, return it to*

profitability, and instill it with the discipline it needs for long-term viability.

The story of AIG is one of stunning decline. Once one of the largest corporations in the world, in 2006 it was eighteenth on balance sheet strength and the 90-year old firm witnessed its market value plummet by 95% by the time of the federal bailout in autumn 2008. It lost its vaunted AAA credit rating and was de-listed from the Dow Jones Industrial Average; ever the bellwether of the US economy, this member of the Dow indeed showed the world the extent of the damage sweeping the nation and the globe. *AIG would go on to receive the largest taxpayer-funded bailout in history, receiving loan after loan from the federal government once they had judged the firm was "too big to fail." That cost now stands at over $180 billion!*

The "facts" about AIG's bailout have been well documented. Federal Reserve Chairman Ben Bernanke stated in congressional testimony that the company had exploited huge gaps in the regulatory system, made "irresponsible bets" and had suffered monumental losses as a result. Due to its extreme size and the degree to which it was integrated into the global economy, as a result of a complex web of financial derivative contracts, federal officials had "no choice" but to nationalise it. The results: three rounds of capital infusions that have ballooned the Federal Reserve's balance sheet and made the government an 80% shareholder in the debilitated firm.

It is not the size of the bailout or its extent, however, which is most revealing. While certainly remarkable in absolute terms, the financial commitment to AIG by the government has exposed just how little we knew, and indeed the regulators knew, about the operations of this hugely important company. As the layers were peeled back to reveal just how deep the trouble ran, it became increasingly hard to fathom just how the firm got to this point. What's more, the saga has drawn into sharp focus some of the most contentious issues surrounding Wall Street regulation, executive pay, and the risks we collectively face as a result of the interplay between these seemingly unrelated factors.

In this chapter, we will explore the evolution of the business of insurance, and in particular, how a firm such as AIG could become so interrelated with other firms that it posed a threat to the entire financial system. We will then discuss the extent of the bailout by the US government, and some of the more divisive issues that have been raised as a result. These include the lack of regulation on key financial derivative instruments as well as the public outcry against the excesses of executive compensation at firms similar to AIG.

As one can imagine, AIG is not the only company that faces harsh criticism. However, as the largest single recipient to date of federal aid, it certainly remains at the forefront of our attention. In the months and years to come such attention is not likely to diminish, unless and until the company can return itself to a sustainable path. During such time, it is likely that even more questions will be raised about the insurance giant, in particular, and the insurance industry more generally. How these concerns play out in the public domain will be of great consequence.

Institutionalising Risk

> *"We risk all in being too greedy!"*
>
> **Jean de la Fontaine**

Prior to delving into the history and recent exploits of AIG, this section will briefly look at the broader universe of the business of insurance. Insurance began to emerge as a part of commercial enterprise generally with the extension of "forgivable" loans to merchants in the fourteenth century. As most trade was carried out by sea routes this activity centered on merchant shipping. The first true insurance contracts appeared around the middle of the fourteenth century, and were gradually standardised and incorporated into mercantile law.

Insurance as we know it today, as the "assumption of risk" due to "whatever loss, peril, misfortune, impediment or sinister event that might occur". It emerged out of the informal exchange of information at Edward Lloyd's coffee house in London between the 1730's and 1760's; it is here that the first true "market" for insurance was formed, as those exchanges became more frequent and routine. In 1774, the Society of Lloyd's was formed at the Royal Exchange as an unincorporated association of market participants who bore ***unlimited liability*** for the contracts that they underwrote.

It was the application of probability and statistical analysis to this practice, rather than generally observed averages, that catapulted the business of insurance into its modern age. Aside from the insurance of shipping vessels, other types of specialty insurance such as fire, health and life insurance had been offered since as early as 1666, but the first true insurance fund was created by Robert Wallace and Alexander Webster in 1744. Using actuarial tables constructed by Edmund Halley, Wallace and Webster sought to create a fund that would provide pension benefits for the widows of Scottish ministers, based upon predictions of the life expectancies of the ministers and their spouses. Premiums were collected from all and invested profitably in order to cover "death" benefits and administration costs for the fund. Within twenty years, the Scottish Ministers' Widows' Fund had become the benchmark fund for life insurance, and became the model upon which many others were founded.

Insurance, then, is all about the assumption of risk by underwriters and the distribution of that risk to the insured via the payment of premiums. Even though we can't know when a catastrophic event or loss might occur, the probability of its occurrence may be estimated with relative certainty. The law of large numbers makes this estimation somewhat easier and more predictable, for as the size of a group increases, the probability that certain events will occur at regular intervals tends to increase. ***In the language of statistics, as the sample size gets larger, things tend to "revert to the mean."***

Insofar as insurance is concerned, the collection of small premiums from insured parties serves to "spread" the risk of paying for a large loss among many individuals or entities. The Scottish Ministers' Widows' Fund showed how these principles could be utilised for the provision of life insurance benefits, paid upon the death of an insured minister to his spouse and that they could be applied to virtually all types of specialty insurance.

Over time, as the number of insured parties grew, insurance funds and the companies that ran them turned to the capital markets in order to profitably invest the premiums. Innovation turned the business of insurance into an important avenue for savings and investment. The reverse is also true, the growing size and number of investment companies needing to invest their funds quickly made them one of the largest and most influential actors in financial markets around the world. Growth in the number of insured parties as well as in the size and complexity of insurance policies meant that underwriters soon had to seek out new avenues of capitalisation.

This is the uniqueness of the original Lloyd's exchange, formed as it was as a meeting place where financial backers could come together to pool resources and spread risk. Lloyd's, it should be recalled, is not itself an insurance company, but exists as a "society" of members that form together in syndicates to contribute the necessary capital to fund insurance operations. Parliament passed the First Lloyd's Act in 1871, which legally established the Society and set out its objectives. Syndicates were formed for a period of one year, although it was not uncommon for membership to be carried over from one year to the next. While members themselves act as underwriters for insurance policies, it is also the case that the syndicates will further 'underwrite' members' business, which is referred to as *reinsurance*. This helps to further spread risk amongst Society members.

Importantly, though, it serves to allow members to assume greater risk than they otherwise would. The financial health of the reinsurer is critical as well. In this sense, insurers are essentially trading insurance risk for credit risk, although it is common practice for reinsurance to be purchased from multiple parties in order to share that risk. Lloyd's is now one of the largest markets for reinsurance, but in the late 1980's it was on the verge of collapse because of its failure to adequately manage its reinsurance risk. As mentioned above, Lloyd's syndicates band together on a yearly—if often recurring—basis. As claims can often take some time to be reported and paid out, financial results were most often declared after three years; syndicates would purchase reinsurance in order to pay any future claims. Thus the syndicates could transfer liability to pay future claims to a reinsurer, the syndicate could be closed, and a profit or loss declared.

Unfortunately, the eventual result of this transfer of risk was the creation of a "spiral": because the reinsurer was always another syndicate, the transfer could not be passed off indefinitely, and eventually a member would become liable for losses incurred years earlier. *Sooner or later, we all know that you have to pay the piper!*

Due to the long term liability that Lloyd's had assumed in connection to asbestos, pollution and health hazard policies, the Society suffered several waves of massive financial losses as old liabilities came due: *"Lloyd's had suffered multiple blows, the hardest of which was its huge exposure to US asbestos and other pollution and health related claims. The volume of these long-tailed liabilities—so called because of the time they take to emerge and be settled—was increased by big US court judgments. In five disastrous years of account, from 1988 to 1992, the cumulative losses at Lloyd's climbed to almost £8bn. Each Lloyd's "name"—individual underwriter—lost an average £287,000 but because losses were spread unevenly, some lost far more."*

Lloyd's was forced to restructure. In 1996 it established a separate reinsurance vehicle called Equitas that would be liable for all business written prior to 1993. To a certain extent, this allowed members to start underwriting with a clean slate, but Equitas was able to aggressively negotiate settlements related to the pollution-related claims with some of the world's largest corporations. Critics charge that this has only transferred the risk back to the very companies that were insured by Lloyd's in the first place. As part of its long-standing tradition of "reinsurance-to-close" as described above, Lloyd's was successful in moving the Equitas vehicle off its own books and shirking its claims-paying responsibilities, despite the fact that the law had no provision for such actions; regulators in the UK and the United States stood idly by as these dynamics played out, to the likely detriment of claimants and corporations that should have been more fully covered by Lloyd's.

Lloyd's, of course, successfully argued that these actions were necessary for its long-term survival. Without a new reinsurance vehicle such as Equitas, and without starting with a clean slate, as it was able to do, Lloyd's would have been unable to attract new capital and would likely have collapsed under the weight of the "long-tailed" liabilities. What is evident, however, is that the Lloyd's market carried *itself* to the point of collapse because it operated in an opaque accounting environment, where members' liabilities were unclear or unknown, and in a loosely regulated framework that did not police such over-extension of risk. While the particular dynamics are different, as we shall see shortly, the same problems were to repeat themselves in 2008 with AIG's collapse.

An American International Giant

"Want is a growing GIANT whom the coat of Have was never large enough to cover!"
Ralph Waldo Emerson

AIG began life in 1919 as American Asiatic Underwriters in Shanghai, China as a "sub-agent" for other American insurers. The company was started by Cornelius Vander Starr, and was moved to its current headquarters in New York City when the Chinese People's Liberation Army took over the country in 1949. The company expanded rapidly, mainly through acquisitions, but also by going where new opportunities presented themselves; by the end of the 1950's, the company had grown to include subsidiaries in 75 countries.

AIG truly became a "success story" under the leadership of Maurice "Hank" Greenberg, who took the helm from Starr in 1968. Starr had named Greenberg to head the North American operations of AIG in 1962, and Greenberg became his eventual successor. It was Greenberg that transformed the company from an "insurance backwater" into the financial giant that we know today. Under Greenberg, the company went public in 1969 with a market capitalisation of just over $900 million, and steadily grew in size and stature over the next four decades as its focus shifted from personal insurance to more lucrative corporate finance.

In large part, the story of AIG is also a story of political influence and elite association. This began under Starr but was perfected under Greenberg: *"A glance at AIG's board of directors during Greenberg's AIG days illustrates the company's ties to the political realm. Board members included U.N. Ambassador Richard C. Holbrooke and former U.S. Defense Secretary William S. Cohen. "'They gave the company prestige, opened doors, and helped solve problems and never questioned Greenberg's authoritarian rule.'"* Greenberg himself was a Director of the New York branch of the Federal Reserve from 1988 to 1995, and had held numerous high-level advisory positions for the United States government.

Presently, AIG operates in four core areas: general insurance, life insurance and retirement services, financial services, and asset management. While a cursory glance of the company's holdings shows that they are—at least in number—primarily insurance-related, there are a number of very large, high-profile holdings that are of particular interest for our purposes. Expanding as it did beyond the core business of insurance underwriting, AIG secured its footing in global real estate markets, port operations, aircraft leasing, mortgage financing, and corporate debt underwriting. *It was the creation in 1987 of the little known AIG's Financial Products unit that proved to be the undoing of the firm.*

Known as AIGFP, the unit got its start when three former traders from investment bank Drexel Burnham Lambert convinced Greenberg to create a division that would focus on complex derivatives trading. AIGFP was able to "piggyback" its operations on its parent company's AAA credit rating, and negotiated to receive the profits from its trades upfront, even though they could take years to play out in the markets. Under CEO Tom Savage, a mathematician who had pioneered the use of computer models for collateralised debt obligations which, as discussed throughout this book, played a heavy hand in causing the present credit crisis, AIGFP created the first credit default swap in 1998:

"That year, JP Morgan approached AIG, proposing that, for a fee, AIG insure JP Morgan's complex corporate debt, in case of default. According to computer models devised by Gary Gorton,

a Yale Business Professor and consultant to the unit, there was a 99.85 percent chance that AIGFP would never have to pay out on these deals. Essentially, this would happen only if the economy went into a full-blown depression, in which case, the AIGers believed, the counter-parties would be wiped out, and therefore would hardly be in a position to demand payment anyway. With the backing of Cassano, then the CEO, Savage green lighted the deals. Credit default swaps were born."

As this shows, credit default swaps, or CDSs, are complex derivative instruments that essentially insure a particular debt. They are written against the risk of default: like life insurance. A buyer of a CDS contract pays a premium to the seller, who agrees to provide a payoff to the buyer in the event that a bond issuer, for example, defaults on its obligations to repay its principal. In their infancy, these instruments were used in order to hedge against default risk, but predictably, and because of the extraordinarily weak regulation of the derivatives market, their use quickly became overwhelmingly speculative in nature—*under the Commodity Futures Modernisation Act of 2000, CDS contracts became largely exempt from regulation in the US!*

Far from being confined to the market for just *corporate debt*, the CDS market rapidly expanded to include all manner of debt, including the now infamous and mushrooming subprime mortgage debt. As there exists no central clearinghouse for CDS contracts, all trades are done *"over the counter,"* which has made the overall size and scope of the market difficult to estimate. By the end of 2008, it was widely reported that the entire CDS market equaled upwards of *$30 trillion*! It is hard to even imagine how far their impact extends.

Their impact on AIG, however, began to be felt in 2005 when Hank Greenberg was ousted as CEO of the company. Due to allegations of conflicts of interest, illegal payoffs to other insurance firms and bid rigging for insurance contracts, and under pressure from New York Attorney General Eliot Spitzer, Greenberg was forced to resign from AIG. These potentially fraudulent business practices and irregularities resulted in AIG's credit rating being downgraded, which in turn triggered provisions in some of AIGFP's swap contracts, and required the parent company to post over $1 billion in collateral. That same year, AIGFP determined that its potential exposure to subprime losses could result in further losses, and they stopped writing CDS contracts; this, however, did not undo the contracts they had already written, which by that time were estimated at up to *$80 billion!*

CDS contracts on subprime-related securities, however, amounted to only a small proportion of the total size of the firm's exposure to the derivatives market as a whole. It has been reported that by September 2008, when AIG was on the brink of collapse, AIGFP had written contracts *totaling over $400 billion*—this number itself is perplexing for the very fact that much of the CDS market can be said to vastly eclipse the total debt that these contracts are said to insure! While some contracts stipulate the physical delivery of the underlying security, much as stock options do, others provide for cash settlement.

As the credit crisis accelerated in the late months of 2007, AIG began to hemorrhage. When the housing market collapsed, AIG was required to post additional collateral to cover its exposure to subprime mortgage losses. Under Joseph Cassano, it was found that AIGFP had not accounted properly for the value of its CDS portfolio and that CDS transactions had not been properly audited; Cassano maintained that its exposure to the US residential housing market had been accurately identified. However, AIG continued to suffer huge losses, and by September 2008, had its credit rating cut again. When this happened, it triggered a liquidity crisis for the firm.

That liquidity crisis exposed just how interconnected AIG had become with the rest of Wall Street and with investment banks and financial institutions the world over. Once the potential cost of AIG's fall was realised, and fearing that AIG posed a threat to the entire financial system, the Federal Reserve orchestrated a massive bailout package. In exchange for an 80% ownership stake, on September 16 2008 the Fed provided an $85 billion loan to AIG in order to prevent its collapse, effectively nationalising the company and putting US taxpayers on the hook for the cost. *It is notable that Lehman Brothers filed for Chapter 11 bankruptcy protection on September 15, 2008, the previous day, despite being the fourth largest bank in the US, and was unable to elicit support from the Federal Reserve despite having been brought to its knees by a similar but not identical tangled web of subprime mortgage instruments!*

> *"Play not with paradoxes. That caustic which you handle in order to scorch others may happen to sear your own fingers and make them dead to the quality of things."*
>
> **George Eliot**

In the wake of its collapse, we have learned much about the extent to which AIG had been mismanaged. Only days prior to its takeover, AIG had sought a $40 billion bridge loan from the Fed in order to cover its capital commitments and to prevent its stock from sliding further. As it would turn out, the company had vastly underestimated its own exposure to the CDS market, causing it to lose over $13 billion in the first half of 2008. By the first quarter of 2009, AIG posted a $61.7 billion loss, the largest in history. *What's more, commitments by the Fed to the firm in order to keep it afloat have now ballooned to $182 billion!*

How did one firm wreak such devastation?

Greenberg, for one, swears off on the entire CDS debacle. Since his ousting in 2005, Greenberg has claimed that he was unaware of the extent of involvement by AIGFP in the derivatives markets, and has sued his former firm for tying him to those losses. Joseph Cassano, who had been CEO of AIGFP, and Martin Sullivan, CEO of AIG, had both painted a rosy picture and downplayed the losses as not just minimal but almost non-existent. It was later discovered in October 2008 that AIGFP had $2.7 trillion worth of swap contracts and positions, and 50,000 outstanding trades with 2,000 different firms around the world. Even though he had left in 2005 it is hard to imagine that Greenberg had not been aware of the direction and focus of AIGFP's dealings during his period of office, especially considering that he was the sole creator of the unit: *"AIG FP from the way it operated to its compensation were all set up under Greenberg, and AIG was well into it by the time he left,"* said Nicholas Ashooh, a spokesman for AIG, "Greenberg's diversification plan paid off handsomely at first.

AIG Financial Products contributed $5 billion to the insurer's profits from the time it was formed in 1987 through 2004, Greenberg's last full year as CEO."

"You Break It, You Buy It!"

Toys R US

Moral Hazard: *is the prospect that a party insulated from risk may behave differently from the way it would behave if it were fully exposed to the risk.*

The Fed's bailout of AIG has of course raised significant concerns, not the least of which is the extraordinary and unprecedented size of the capital commitment itself. When the Fed first stepped in to extend the lifeline to AIG, it was accomplished through an $85 billion credit line that was granted in exchange for an 80% ownership stake in the failing firm. Judged as being too extensively intertwined with the global financial system for it to fail, AIG was first bailed out in relation to toxic mortgage-related assets and capital calls to other institutions. While the Fed, under Chairman Ben Bernanke, was the primary actor in the bailout, Congress did approve it as part of the overall bailout of the nation's banking system in the Emergency Economic Stabilisation Act of 2008.

Not even one month after receiving this first $85 billion infusion, AIG was forced to borrow an additional $37.8 billion, as most of the original capital had been used to settle transactions with counterparties. By March 2009, the original terms had been altered for a third time; the US has now committed $182.5 billion to rescue the insurer, including an investment of as much as $70 billion, a $60 billion credit line and $52.5 billion to buy mortgage-linked assets owned or backed by AIG.

While it was expected that much of the original $85 billion credit line would be used to cover capital calls to counterparties, this has nonetheless drawn intense criticism from the public and lawmakers. After initially refusing to disclose the recipients of these payments for fear of further spreading AIG's "infection," the company and the Fed finally did so. Among the largest recipients were nearly a dozen US financial institutions that had also received federal assistance through the Troubled Asset Relief Program (TARP). Many have criticised Goldman Sachs, for example, for having taken taxpayer's money in order to continue funding their own trading activities, acting as hedge funds in disguise and without regard to the risks they are taking with public funds.

Just as important, though, it illustrates how the decision to save AIG was reflective of the *perception of systemic risk*. Had AIG's counterparties not been paid, it could have precipitated the fall of the European banking system as well, in light of the fact that some of Europe's largest banks—Deutsche Bank in Germany, Societe Generale and BNP Paribas in France, HSBC, RBS and Barclays in the UK, Rabobank in the Netherlands, and many more—had received billions in the deal. Perhaps they were correct in their assertions about AIG's importance—especially considering that the financial authorities including the US Treasury and the FED had let Lehman fail and have since been proven wrong or at least un-defendable.

One of the most contentious issues relating to the AIG bailout has been the subject of executive compensation. The week following the initial extension of credit to the firm, AIG sponsored a retreat as a reward for top-earning employees and distributors of its life insurance products; while they maintained that the trip was planned well before the bailout, it didn't stop them from further spending on a lavish hunting trip in the English countryside. Just prior to the third wave of federal assistance, the company was reported as having spent nearly $350,000 on another luxury retreat in Arizona. While these may seem exorbitant, especially given the dire circumstances facing the company and the fact that it had recently taken such massive taxpayer-funded handouts, those accustomed to Wall Street dealings know that these are not out of the ordinary.

"I get so tired listening to one million dollars here, one million dollars there, it's so petty!"

Imelda Marcos

Indeed, we would learn soon enough that AIG had made such practices routine. In March 2009, it disclosed that executive compensation for the entire firm could amount to $1.2 billion, with perhaps $450 million going directly to the very professionals at AIGFP that had brought the company to its knees. The public and Congress were, not surprisingly, shocked and outraged upon learning of this, considering the scale of federal aid already committed to the embattled firm. What's more, Senate Banking Committee Chairman Christopher Dodd admitted to weakening language that dealt with executive bonuses for firms receiving bailout funds. The Washington Times later reported that Dodd had sought political contributions from AIG, and that these bonuses were expressly encouraged by none other than Joseph Cassano, when he was CEO of AIGFP: *"The message in the Nov. 17, 2006, e-mail from Joseph Cassano, AIG Financial Products chief executive, was unmistakable: Mr. Dodd was "next in line" to be chairman of the Senate Banking, Housing and Urban Affairs Committee, which oversees the insurance industry, and he would 'have the opportunity to set the committee's agenda on issues critical to the financial services industry.'"*

While this type of fundraising in the workplace is legal in the US, these incidents clearly bear witness to the heavy influence that AIG wielded in political circles. One must ask whether Greenberg's association with other financial and political heavyweights made a difference to AIG's receipt of the bailout itself, given that he was himself a former director of the New York Fed—the branch of the Federal Reserve that played the most active part in facilitating the extension of credit. In part due to the fallout from the so-called "Dodd amendment," the Obama Administration named Kenneth Feinberg as Special Master for Compensation in June 2009 and quickly moved to develop new guidelines for executive compensation in companies receiving federal bailout funds.

The government now finds itself in new territory. Although similar efforts had begun to be developed under the outgoing Bush Administration, the law is unclear on the matter and companies have yet to receive full explanations or direction. Feinberg oversaw payouts to victims of the September 9/11 attacks, which totaled over $7 billion, and reportedly reviewed every single claim that was to be paid from Treasury funds. Of course, companies have cried foul, arguing that "retention bonuses" are standard practice in the industry and are necessary in order to attract and keep key talent. In the case of AIGFP, critics argue that it is hard to fathom how these individuals should receive any bonus, given the devastation that their recklessness has caused.

AIG, or so it would seem, is a classic example of what has been called *"lemon socialism."* This points to a breakdown in the free-market capitalist system, which would normally allow defective companies to fail, but because they are seen to threaten overall economic stability they receive government support. Often referred to as socialism for the rich and capitalism for the poor, in the case of AIG we can see how the notion of privatising profits and socialising losses, has been carried out through the continuation of executive bonuses on the one hand, and the massive taxpayer-funded bailout on the other.

Of course, lucrative executive compensation was nothing new to AIG or particular to its AIGFP unit. Greenberg has sued his former firm for misrepresenting him, but he is now also defending himself against potential improper arrangements said to have been put in place to induce executives to join the firm. Greenberg now runs C.V. Starr & Company, and from this position he also controls a second firm, Starr International. Both of these firms are reported to control $4.3 billion in AIG stock which had been intended to fund a retirement trust for AIG executives; Greenberg is charged with improperly removing these shares, despite a long-standing arrangement in which they were held in trust for key employees: *"But while its structure and legal status have been shrouded in mystery, A.I.G.'s executive retirement plan was well known in the insurance industry. It was seen as a potent recruiting tool, allowing A.I.G. to poach top talent away from go-go Wall Street firms, something normally beyond the reach of a staid insurance company. The plan is thought to have been an important factor in A.I.G.'s becoming the world's largest insurance conglomerate."*

While it seems that AIG has recently returned itself to profitability, it is too soon to tell whether this trend will take hold. It would appear that the market has stabilised somewhat for AIG, which recently reported its first quarterly profit since 2007. However, it will likely face continued scrutiny as a result of its commitment to controversial executive compensation plans, having recently said that it would spend another $1.1 billion in bonuses to retain key staff members while the company unwinds its financial positions and sells off businesses. Some believe that the bonuses are justified, as the company must retain high-performing employees to oversee the successful winding down of AIG's assets.

Indeed, the selection of Benmosche as the firm's new CEO, highlights the issue: *"The selection sets up a test for how the Obama administration will determine the proper level and structure of CEO pay at a company essentially controlled by the government but that needs to pay enough to attract someone talented to run, and fix, the firm. AIG's board approved a pay package worth between $7 million and $10 million for Mr. Benmosche, people familiar with the matter said. The package is heavily tilted toward equity grants and contains relatively little cash."*

Pay for Play?

Of course, the problem with this type of equity grant as part of an executive compensation package is that it can encourage individuals to take undue risk in order to inflate their own pay or bonus. Certainly, when we look back at the history of AIGFP, we see that its founders were able to convince Greenberg to pay them up front for deals that would not even play out for years to come. One cannot but think that the recklessness with which AIGFP wrote such massive amounts of CDS contracts had much to do with this, a direct correlation between pay and market share instead of pay and profitability. Individuals had further incentive to take on excessive risk given the elite nature of Greenberg's off-balance sheet employee stock plan. One must ask why AIG would have subscribed to such an unusual arrangement, but Greenberg was notorious for his heavy-handed rule during his 38-year tenure, and when the going is good, those receiving bonuses of this magnitude had little to complain about.

When we look back at the history of Lloyd's, we see a similar situation. Even though the circumstances were markedly different, the practice of *"reinsurance-to-close"* encouraged members to write more business than they had reserves to cover. By passing the buck from syndicate to syndicate they were transferring the reinsurance risk from year to year, but as we've seen, this spiral soon caught them up and proved their undoing.

Are other insurance businesses any different?

It seems they may be. In 2006, Berkshire Hathaway's National Indemnity unit secured a deal to reinsure the assets, liabilities and operations of Lloyd's Equitas reinsurance vehicle. Once again, it seems that Warren Buffett has ridden to the rescue and stepped in where others—such as AIG—could not. Some have argued that this is precisely because Buffett focused almost exclusively on the long-term, and has chosen managers for his subsidiaries that have shown they can do the same; what's more, shareholders in Berkshire Hathaway have shown they are willing to wait, and have long proven reluctant to pressure the firm's management into short-term profit chasing.

Unless and until Wall Street executives are similarly "encouraged" by their shareholders, *they will continue to chase short-term profitability at the expense of long-term viability*.

Despite the fact that Greenberg, for example, is still the largest single owner of AIG shares, it seems apparent that profit chasing has always been a part of the business. AIG is certainly not alone in enticing executives with massive pay packages as a reward for short-term performance, but the arrangements now under public scrutiny seem to bear out the judgment that it did things differently than other insurers.

Conclusion

On the day of the AIG bailout, economist Joseph Stiglitz proclaimed:

"America's financial system failed in its two crucial responsibilities: managing risk and allocating capital. The industry as a whole has not been doing what it should be doing—for instance creating products that help Americans manage critical risks, such as staying

in their homes when interest rates rise or house prices fall—and it must now face change in its regulatory structures. Regrettably, many of the worst elements of the US financial system—toxic mortgages and the practices that led to them—were exported to the rest of the world. It was all done in the name of innovation, and any regulatory initiative was fought away with claims that it would suppress that innovation. They were innovating, all right, but not in ways that made the economy stronger."

Even though this was not strictly related to the saga about to play out with AIG, it is telling and applicable nonetheless. Stiglitz highlights the most salient issues that AIG's collapse helped bring into the public eye. While none of these issues are new, it also shows that the public perhaps shares some blame as well; when the going is good, and everyone is fixated on the trappings and illusions of wealth, no one wants to blow the whistle and cry foul.

Insurance was created in order to help manage the risks that are inevitable in life. The application of complex mathematics to the practice transformed it from what was effectively a gamble on the unknown and into a thriving, exponentially growing and immensely profitable business. Reinsurance, moreover, helped further that business and transferred those risks from one entity to another, but it neither eliminated the risks faced by individuals or insurers nor did it make it easier to manage. In the case of Lloyd's, it did free up capital that should have been held in reserve for future claims, but this only encouraged further reckless behaviour that eventually brought the firm to the point of collapse.

> *"My special pleasure in mathematics rested particularly on its purely speculative part!"*
> **Bernhard Bolzano (1781-1848)**

AIG's Financial Products unit behaved similarly. Chasing short-term profits led these professionals to throw caution to the wind, and encouraged them to write almost incomprehensible numbers of credit default swap contracts. The particulars of their compensation packages overtly promoted recklessness, and as we are so painfully aware, nearly tore the global financial system asunder. Had federal officials not intervened and understood the threat that the firm's unmanaged collapse would pose to the entire world financial system; complete economic ruin would certainly have followed.

The case of AIG brings these seemingly unrelated factors into sharp focus. Truly, it is at their intersection that crises occur. Hank Greenberg built AIG into a massive and diverse empire, but his inability to foster the same type of long-term focus as Warren Buffett has done at Berkshire Hathaway certainly led AIG down a road that eventually brought it to its knees. AIGFP exploited massive regulatory loopholes and operated with impunity, either unaware or with complete disregard for the risks they had exposed not just their own unit to but to the parent firm as well. Because these risks were inadequately capitalised and managed, and in light of the virtually non-existent regulatory framework that has persisted in the commodities market, AIG's recklessness nearly brought down the entire global financial system.

Now, federal officials are faced with the task of returning the US economy to stable footing. Part of that task now entails the payback of $182 billion in federal funds from the struggling insurer. AIG's new CEO is credited with turning around another industry giant, MetLife, and is widely regarded as having successfully changed the corporate culture at that firm: ***"Mr. Benmosche is credited with changing the culture of MetLife, turning what was seen as a bureaucratic, mutually owned company into a more competitive and profit-focused publicly traded company."*** He is well renowned for his deal-making prowess as well, having taken MetLife public in 2000 and presiding over several acquisitions that made that firm the largest life insurance company in the country.

This very dynamic, however, points once again to what has been one of the key issues in the present economic downturn: the interplay between short-term profits and long-term viability. It is more than interesting that Benmosche transformed MetLife from a "mutual" insurance company into a publicly-traded stock insurance company. In contrast to stock insurance companies, which are owned by investors, mutual insurance companies are actually owned by their policyholders. While consumers that do business with mutual insurance firms have similar interests in making sure that they remain healthy and that their claims-paying ability remains on solid footing, stock insurance companies will always face pressure from shareholders to produce profits—importantly, though, those shareholders need not even be customers!

It is at this point that the interests of policyholders and shareholders diverge. Stock insurance companies may be enticed to take on excessive risk in order to return profits to their shareholders, but this very behaviour can—and has—put their claims-paying ability at risk. The Hartford, for example, has been punished by capital markets because of massive losses in their variable life insurance unit; these losses threatened the overall financial health of the firm as a whole. The damage to its capital reserves could very likely have meant that it would not have survived, had it not received TARP funds in June 2009; the company had to buy a bank, however, in order to qualify.

Mutual insurance companies, however, may prove to be more responsive to the needs of policyholders and the liability they have for paying claims, and this may entice them to maintain better capital standards and take less risk than their stock insurance counterparts:

"While stock-owned insurance companies showed higher growth rates and better earnings than Mutuals at the turn of the decade, according to an August report by Moody's Investors Services. However, mutual insurance companies experienced less severe credit downgrades than stock-owned companies during the latest recession. Mutuals, the report says, are better capitalised, have a less risky business focus and are not as subject to the investor panics created by newspaper headlines. 'Mutual insurers are typically more focused on life insurance and other protection products, which tend to stay in force for long periods and have a very stable earnings profile with a low degree of risk,' the report says."

Mutual insurance companies also pay dividends to their policyholders, which represents the return of profits in much the same way as traditional shareholders would receive them. Mutual insurance companies represent a different approach to the business of insurance, and as such it is not necessarily the case that one is "better" than the other. However, it is telling that many of these firms have not only remained somewhat insulated from the effects of the credit crisis but have actually seen their profitability increase.

AIG's new CEO is confident that he will not just return the firm to profitability but also pay back the bailout funds. Flatly stating, *"I don't liquidate things, I build them,"* Benmosche seems poised to take a vastly different approach than his predecessor Edward Liddy had, and seems willing to wait for favourable economic conditions to return rather than divesting assets at fire-sale prices. Whether his stock-focused compensation package puts him at odds with the long-term interests of the taxpayer—his firm's new owners—remains to be seen; one must hope that his track record, like that of Buffett's, speaks to his abilities to successfully navigate these treacherous waters. This was once a mighty company that served the aims of both its stockholders and policyholders equally efficiently so who is too blame for its public collapse:

> *"The way to stop financial "joy-riding" is to arrest the chauffeur, not the automobile."*
>
> **Woodrow Wilson**

Beyond this, of course, the saga of AIG's collapse highlights the task still left to the Federal Reserve: returning the country to profitability. The assets and liabilities of AIG are now on its balance sheet, currently held in purpose-built vehicles named Maiden Lane II and III; these call to mind the "run-off" reinsurance entity Equitas that Lloyd's established in order to ring-fence the massive liabilities the company was sure to face as a result of its excessive risk-taking and ineffective risk management. As we are all too aware, though, Warren Buffett cannot rescue everyone. Profits at AIG were indeed privatised and the losses were effectively socialised when the Fed bailed out the failing company, so it is the taxpayer that ultimately bears the burden of the risks undertaken by AIG. It is not yet clear how the Fed's exit strategy will play out, but if one thing is certain, it will only be to the detriment of the US consumer.

This mighty giant fell to earth because of its exposure to CDSs, and to a lesser extent CDOs, primarily covering asset based securities in the sub-prime mortgage market. In Chapter 10 we look at the two largest players in the mortgage market and see if they are just . . . . ***too big to fail!***

Chapter 10

January 2008—A Loan Sweet Home: Castle or Prison!

"As Safe as Houses!"

Anonymous

January 2008—on the 24ᵗʰ January 2008 the National Association of Realtors announced that 2007 had the largest drop in housing sales in 25 years, and perhaps the first decline in prices since the Depression

Is housing the bedrock of wealth? When is a risk worth taking?

The American Dream: For many people, a home of their own is a central tenet of the American Dream, but the costs of homes in the Western World, not just America, has vastly outstripped the ability of the average wage earner to save up and buy a place of their own.

"He who overlooks a healthy spot for the site of his house is mad and ought to be handed over to the care of his relations and friends."

Varro

Between 1996 and 2006, the cost of the average American home doubled. Over the same time span, house prices in Ireland quadrupled; in the UK, they more than tripled and Spain saw house price growth of 2.8 times. According to the American Census Bureau, over this period the poorest 20% of American households saw their income rise by just

6% whereas the richest 5% of households saw incomes rise by 14%. In other words, even the richest segment of the American community has not found their income keeping up with property inflation; by a very wide margin.

There are only a limited number of solutions to the problem of the affordability of homes:

i) reduce the price of a new home such that the average worker can realistically afford to save up and buy one;

ii) increase average wages such that home ownership becomes affordable;

iii) provide loans so that an average worker can take possession of a new home and pay for it over many years.

Of these options, the third offers a lucrative solution to the financial sector, realtors and the construction industry alike and provides the illusion that everybody, almost irrespective of their financial means, can aspire to become a home owner. This belief was ultimately responsible for the provision of sub-prime loans which was the trigger point of the global financial crisis of 2007. In this chapter, we will look at the history of the Savings and Loan industry in the USA and the reasons for its spectacular collapse twenty years ago which are echoed in the 2007 crash.

Savings and Loan: The Philadelphia Story

"Home is the place where, when you have to go there, they have to take you in!"

Robert Frost

The Savings and Loan movement in the USA can be traced back to Philadelphia in 1816 when the Philadelphia Savings Fund Society opened its doors for business. The Society was the first savings bank, a mutual, to be established in America and was founded by Condy Rauget, a merchant, diplomat and a strong advocate of free trade; it is likely that Rauget found his inspiration for the venture from literature on English savings banks. Within 15 years, such institutions had become widespread in the USA.

The utility of savings in the 19th century, from a national perspective, was that it was the basis of "capital formation" from which economic growth could spring. It must be recalled that this was an age when the gold standard was at its zenith, meaning that growth from international trade was based on the money in circulation. On a personal basis, it meant that individuals started to put aside money for making major purchases, such as buying a home, to tide them over rough patches when work was scarce, perhaps, or to make provision for their old age. By the year 1850, savers at the Philadelphia Savings Fund Society were typically saving between 10 and 15% of their annual income with the Society.

The intention of the Philadelphia Savings Fund Society was to encourage thrift amongst the poor—this is why modern savings and loan institutions are sometimes referred to as "thrifts". When the Society was created, the working man had very few opportunities to accumulate wealth. Cash could be kept under the mattress or in the "cookie jar"; invested in jewellery, furniture and other largely illiquid property that could be re-converted into cash by selling it or taking it to the pawnshop, but there were no alternatives that would provide a return on investment. Although there was no injunction barring the working man from owning land or property, such acquisitions required relatively large sums of cash which were not readily available to him. Commercial banks and the stock market were available to wealthier people as channels for investment, of course.

The Society allowed ordinary people to save part of their income against a rainy day. When the Society, and the organisations that followed it, came into existence, social security, Medicare, unemployment insurance and pension provision were unheard of and these needs had to be met from savings and family sources. In addition to being able to save for major purchases, the savings and loan institutions permitted "life-cycle" saving (saving for old age); precautionary saving (savings to cover unforeseen circumstances such as unemployment, sickness or death of the bread winner) and target savings (saving to buy a major item, such as a home). The savings and loan banks initially saw themselves as charitable, benevolent institutes; indeed, in its first public statement, the Philadelphia Saving Fund Society stated that its aim was *"to promote economy and the practice of saving amongst the poor and labouring classes of the community".*

By 1850, the Philadelphia Saving Fund Society held $1,700,000 on deposit and had 10,299 active accounts. On average, an account held $172 which represented approximately 75% of the average annual wage of a labourer. The funds on deposit at the Society were substantially more than those held by a typical US savings bank, being around $400,000. The Philadelphia Saving Fund Society adopted prudent, conservative investment practices for at least the first hundred years of its existence. It maintained a substantial proportion of its deposits in liquidity to protect investors at the bank from any eventuality. The size of the contingency fund was larger than that of other similar banks and this meant that the Society offered less competitive rates, but the policy brought the Society through some turbulent times that saw a number of their competitors go to the wall. Typically, the Society paid its depositors between 4% to 5% interest per annum. The majority of the bank's investment portfolio was in mortgages.

> *"Chance fights ever on the side of the prudent"*
>
> **Euripides**

In its heyday in 1917, the Philadelphia Saving Fund Society was the largest savings fund in the USA in terms of the accounts held and was the second largest bank in terms of deposits. Amidst the carnage of the Great Depression, the Society was reckoned to be the 34th largest savings bank in the world. Towards the end of the century, the world of personal finance had changed irrevocably. The fund was obliged to merge with the troubled Western Saving Fund Society under a Federal government plan to strengthen troubled banks by merging them with strong institutions. The plan also allowed for an expansion of the Society's activities. This resulted in the conversion of the Society from a mutual to a corporate entity in 1983. In 1985, the Philadelphia Saving Fund Society changed its name to reflect the more diversified nature of its business, becoming Meritor Financial Group. By the 1990's the group was in trouble. Within two years, the group was in receivership, under the control of FDIC which eventually sold the 27 surviving branches to Mellon Bank for $181 million.

The Federal Role: Savings and Loans during The Great Depression

> *"No Congress of the United States ever assembled, on surveying the state of the Union, has met with a more pleasing prospect than that which appears at the present time. In the domestic field there is tranquility and contentment . . . and the highest record of years of prosperity. In the foreign field there is peace, the goodwill which comes from mutual understanding."*

> **Calvin Coolidge**
> **December 4, 1928**

By 1911, the Savings and Loan industry counted some 6,000 institutions with a combined membership of 2 million members and total assets under management of $925 million. The interest paid on these accounts was typically as much as 5% whereas the interest demanded on a loan was just 6%—nobody with good security in America needed to pay more to secure a mortgage. Federal law dictated what securities the Savings and Loan institutes were permitted to invest in and required them to have a liquid reserve fund that held not less than 5% of their assets. The accounts of members were exempt from taxation and the members could not be held liable for the debts of the institute were it to fail.

At the height of the Great Depression, the Federal Home Loan Act was voted into being. The act was sponsored by President Herbert Hoover with the intention of reducing foreclosures on home loans; stimulating the US housing construction industry; and to support the concept of widespread home ownership in America. Some action was imperative: the Great Depression had seen a 40% default rate in America's home mortgages; at that time, the home mortgage value of the USA was believed to be $20 billion. Some 1,700 of the nation's 12,000 savings institutions had failed.

Before President Hoover's initiative, financing for home purchases in America tended to be handled through insurance firms. The terms of these loans were often as short as five years, attracted variable interest rates and typically incorporated a final "balloon" payment that often triggered a refinancing or even foreclosure when the home owner had to meet the payment. The Great Depression saw real estate values fall dramatically and there were very limited means for owners to refinance their loans. This contributed to the very high number of defaults seen at this time. The Federal Home Loans Bank (FHLB) was established under the Federal Home Loans Act; it was an association of 12 co-operatively owned wholesale banks and their principal function, at the time and for the next fifty years, was to be a reliable provider of long-term funding to the "thrifts" and some insurance companies. The aim was to promote the use of long-term fully amortizing residential mortgages which were to be offered at fixed rates.

The 1930's also saw the creation of the Federal Housing Authority, under the National Housing Act, 1934, which was to run a mortgage insurance programme. The act was instrumental in restoring confidence within the banking industry, leading to the resumption of lending. The 1934 Act also lead to the creation of the Federal Savings and Loan Insurance Corporation (FSLIC) which ensured the protection of deposits held at Savings and Loan institutions. Only one organisation, the National Mortgage Association of Washington, took advantage of a provision in the Federal Housing Act to become a chartered national mortgage entity within the Federal government. The National Mortgage Association of Washington eventually became the Federal National Mortgage Association and is better known as Fannie Mae.

The Saving and Loan Scandal

"The largest and costliest venture in public misfeasance, malfeasance and larceny of all time."
John Kenneth Galbraith

The reason that many Savings and Loan institutes found themselves in financial difficulties in the 1980's was due to the fact that they were required to offer cheap mortgages and had to attract investors by paying competitive interest rates. Furthermore, as we have seen, the operational scope of the Savings and Loan institutes was strictly limited, in line with their original purpose of being mutual community societies designed to sponsor thrift and increase public ownership of real estate. However, these facts alone hardly explain why the savings and loan scandal of the 1980's became one of the world's most expensive financial disasters of all time.

When the legislation that covered the Savings and Loan industry was drafted in the 1930's, there had been a general backdrop of stable interest rates. As we have seen, thrifts typically offered fixed mortgages at 6% for the lifetime of the loan. Originally, the loan period was five years, but it was extended to 15 and then 25 years, locking the thrifts into long-term arrangements. The deposit accounts that savers held with the thrifts typically attracted 4% interest rates. However, the financial environment altered out of all recognition from its traditional state in the twenty years between the 1960's and the '80's.

The Road To Hell

A proverb that could have been designed explicitly to refer to the savings and loan scandal is *"the road to hell is paved with good intentions"*. The good intention behind the savings and loan movement was, of course, to open up the possibility of becoming a home owner to many poorer and working class families. However, the machinations behind how this principle was supported against a sea of changes and the creation of a climate where some unscrupulous individuals plundered the system for their own gain, led the USA into a veritable financial hell that cost tax payers *in excess of $150 billion dollars!*

A key factor in the savings and loan scandal was the good intent which lay behind the FSLIC promise to underwrite funds on deposit with the thrifts. The concept, against the backdrop of the Great Depression, was simple enough; the savings and loan institutes needed to be able to attract deposits. In part this was achieved by the Federal government providing a guarantee, through FSLIC, that funds deposited with the thrifts were backed by a national insurance plan that would safeguard depositor's money should the thrift get into financial difficulties. Deposits were guaranteed up to a ceiling of $40,000 on an individual account. At the time, the guarantee was essential to calm a very nervous financial sector. The promise remained in force throughout the 1980's savings and loan debacle. However, the FSLIC concept was flawed from the very start since all thrifts were charged the same premium irrespective of the risk associated with a given institute getting into difficulties. It is standard practice in insurance that the premium charged for a policy is directly proportional to the perceived risk in the venture being insured. Under FSLIC, unsound financial structures at some thrift's were tolerated for decades.

Another measure that was designed to help the savings and loan industry was the introduction in 1966 of a cap on the amount of interest that any thrift could pay for funds on deposit. The measure, known as regulation Q, also prevented banks from paying interest on any "demand deposit". A demand deposit is the term used to describe an account where the funds on deposit are immediately available for withdrawal, such as a checking account. As a consequence of the legislation, having savings in any thrift should have become more attractive since they were a demand deposit facility that could command an interest payment. The move had become necessary since, by the early 1960's, it had become evident that the savings and loan institutes were not competing successfully with the commercial banks or the securities market for funds. This meant that the amount of money available for mortgages was likely to be inadequate to meet demand. However, the relief that the measure brought only provided a temporary solution and was eventually to prove a hindrance.

In the 1970's, players within the money markets began to compete strongly to attract investors and offered interest rates that were set by the markets. The thrifts could not compete—particularly as their maximum interest rates were now capped. A problem that faced the savings and loan industry was that their business activities were usually local to the area where a given thrift had been established and was almost exclusively geared to residential finance activities, in line with their original business purpose. The thrifts faced a fundamental problem because of the very nature of their business model. After the re-invention of the thrifts during the Great Depression, their mortgage lending took on a much longer-term nature with repayments scheduled over twenty or more years. The interest rates that the thrifts could charge on these debts were fixed and relatively low. Savers were able to get substantially better returns in the financial markets which led to a hemorrhaging away of savings and loan deposits. Ultimately, the thrifts had to pay more interest to attract funding than they were able to charge for their lending. Clearly, this was an untenable situation. A bad problem intensified as first, market interest rates rose and then inflationary pressure took its toll.

With higher market interest rates, the economic value of the existing savings and loan portfolios fell sharply, threatening many of the thrifts with insolvency. By the end of the decade, the world had experienced another oil price shock which pushed inflation into double digits. As a reaction to curb inflationary pressures within the market, central banks around the world pushed up the cost of borrowing. In 1980, the interest rate on US Treasury bonds hit 16% which was fabulous news for savers, but a disaster for the savings and loan sector.

In a bid to allow the Savings and Loan industry to be able to attract more investment, the regulation Q requirements were relaxed, and subsequently removed, between 1980 and 1982. However, the move backfired. The thrifts started to offer commercial and / or higher interest rates to attract savers, but since the return from their income stream, residential mortgages, was still fixed, all it did was to drive them further into the red. By any normal accountancy measures, many of the thrifts were insolvent by this stage and should have been forced to cease trading at the start of the decade. However, this didn't happen; largely because of the special nature of the thrift industry and its potential social costs, but also because the regulators lacked the political, financial or human resources to tackle the problem at that stage. A policy of rigorous enforcement would have bankrupted the FSLIC fund; literally hundreds of thrifts should have gone under in the early '80s. Naturally, there were also many political obstacles at state and federal levels that would have had to be overcome, if fiscal rectitude was to rule the day. It didn't. The pain was put off for almost another decade and the magnitude of the scandal when it finally emerged was that much greater.

Rearranging the Deck Chairs

"Professionals built the Titanic, amateurs the Ark!"
Frank Pepper

Rather than address the heart of the problem, the government sought ways of postponing the day of reckoning in the hope that it might never arrive. If interest rates fell back to more modest levels, they reasoned, the thrifts could get themselves out of the mess. A condition known as "regulatory forbearance" was allowed to prevail. Regulations were altered to permit the thrifts a wider scope of business opportunities which were both more lucrative than traditional residential mortgages, but also considerably riskier. At the same time, the requirements for holding capital, the thrift's liquidity, were also relaxed. Significantly, the FSLIC guarantee was more than doubled to $100,000. This new level of insurance meant that even insolvent Savings and Loan institutes could attract depositors by offering rates marginally higher than the market rate because savers knew that their deposits were guaranteed by the government in the unfortunate event that the institute did go under.

A number of measures were brought in or altered during the early eighties when the plight of the Savings and Loan industry was too obvious to ignore. One practice that did come to an end in the early 1980's was the non-enforcement of due-on-sale clauses in residential mortgages. Prior to the change, some householders were allowed to transfer their low interest rate mortgage to the purchasers of their home; locking the thrifts into lower than market rates for more years. Many states had usury laws, designed to prevent unscrupulous lenders from charging extortionate rates of interest on the loans that they offered. These laws were also applied to the thrifts, preventing them from increasing rates when market forces elsewhere pushed commercial rates higher. The US Congress outlawed this practice in 1980, providing some relief to the sector. The federal ban on the thrifts preventing them from applying variable interest rates was finally lifted in 1981.

In order to address the problems of certain thrifts being exposed to the consequences of regional economic downturns, that reduced the value of their real estate collateral, Savings and Loan institutes were allowed to trade across state lines from the early 1980s—a privilege denied to banks until 1994.

A highly questionable accounting practice that was adopted in the 1980's, with the likely intent of portraying the state of the Savings and Loan industry in a better light, was "supervisory goodwill". Under this system, a firm that took over a troubled and / or insolvent Savings and Loan institute could use the difference between the values of its assets and the value of its obligations as "goodwill" which was subsequently treated as capital. For example, if the assets of a subsumed thrift were $500 million and its obligations were $1 billion, the acquiring firm could count $500 million as new capital. The tactic was also referred to as "push-down" accounting since losses were pushed down the balance sheet into the goodwill category. The acquiring firm was allowed to post apparently stronger accounting and capital figures for up to 10 years following the merger. At the same time, the capital standards required for any thrift to operate were also debased, meaning that the liquidity requirements were softened.

The FHLB also relaxed its requirement in 1983 that the maximum loan to value ratio should not exceed 75% of the market value of the property, thereby permitting 100% mortgages. They also allowed excessive lending to individual borrowers without the former scrutiny that had been given to their ability to maintain repayments; but of course, home owners that failed to meet their repayments were still subject to foreclosure.

These moves were about as effective a rescue measure as rearranging the deck chairs on *The Titanic* after it hit the iceberg, *as they did nothing to address the fundamental problems of the industry!*

Other changes made by FHLB ultimately worsened the crisis. It became easier for small groups of investors or individuals to gain control of any thrift under new FHLB regulations in the early 1980's. By leveraging the risk and potential return from an initial investment, a modest capital base could be used to expand a savings and loan institution rapidly. This modality attracted the wrong type of management and owners into the industry. Despite the desperately weak fundamentals, the relaxed rules brought new thrifts into the market place between 1982 and 1985, and the asset base grew by 56%. In 1984 alone, 133 new thrifts were created.

The mid-1980's saw a property boom in the USA in which house prices rose by approximately 20%. This is significant but pales in comparison with the boom between 1997 and the start of the 2007 global financial crisis, where the house prices almost doubled. Under the relaxed regulations, the thrifts were able to cash-in on the boom and to fuel it by the provision of lending. Changes in the rules which governed the Savings and Loans industry now allowed riskier and higher return investments; this included lending to, and investing in, real estate development, construction and service companies. 40 Texas Savings and Loan institutes tripled in size between 1982 and 1987, a pattern repeated elsewhere in the country, most notably in California.

The riskier lending practices of certain thrifts were exposed in the second half of the 1980's when a series of regional crises hit the industry. The regional problems were triggered by collapses in the property, farming and oil sectors. Notably, the construction boom in Texas had been funded on the back of the oil boom, when this came to a grinding halt and the bubble burst, thrifts were left hugely overexposed since they had financed and invested in the construction boom; when the value of real estate fell, their assets plummeted in value. The problem was exacerbated by a reversal of the federal tax policy in 1986 which had stimulated construction in the early eighties. By the end of the decade, the housing bubble had burst and real estate prices were falling, shedding approximately 12%.

Biting The Bullet

"I had learnt early in my career that when someone says "don't worry", it's time to worry."

Max Markson

By the end of the eighties, the Savings and Loan situation could not be ignored any longer, although it did not feature in the election campaign of George Bush senior in 1988.

In January 1987, the General Accounting Office (GAO) had declared that FSLIC was insolvent by at least $3.8 billion. The following month, FHLB insisted that direct investment by Savings and Loans that exceeded 2.5 times their tangible capital needed prior approval; the technical term for this should have been *"closing the stable door after the horse had bolted"*. By August 1987, a $10.8 billion recapitalisation plan was put in place for FSLIC by the federal government.

In February 1988, a plan was put together under the auspices of FHLB to resolve insolvencies amongst the Southwest Savings and Loan institutes. 205 thrifts were disposed of, with assets totaling $101 billion, by means of consolidation and selling them off to the highest bidder. The shortfall between assets and liabilities of the failed thrifts was paid for through FSLIC notes; tax incentives; income; capital value and yield guarantees, measures designed to conserve FSLIC's scarce cash reserves.

In August 1989, the Financial Resources Reform and Recovery Act (FIRREA), which had been unveiled by President Bush in February, came into force. Under FIRREA, the FHLB and FSLIC were abolished, with deposit insurance responsibility passing to Federal Deposit Insurance Corporation which is responsible for insuring all banks and saving association deposits. The Resolution Trust Corporation (RTC) was created to deal with insolvent thrifts and went on to liquidate hundreds of Savings and Loans. RTC dealt with 318 thrifts in 1989 with assets of $135 billion; 213 in 1990, with assets worth $130 billion; between 1990 and 1992 it wound up a further 59 with assets worth $44 billion and a further 13 between 1993 and 1995 which was acknowledged as the year the scandal ended.

The cost of the Savings and Loan debacle was in excess of $150 billion, excluding on-going legal actions. Of this sum, the brunt, $124 billion, was met by the US tax payer with the industry itself contributing $29 billion. Approximately 1,000 thrifts were closed between 1986 and 1995, the greatest number of institution failures since the Great Depression.

The Keating Five

> *"There is no greater fraud than a promise not kept."*
> **Gaelic Proverb**

One of the more infamous chapters of the Savings and Loan scandal involved criminality and what, in the UK, is called sleaze. This is the failure of the Lincoln Savings and Loan. For many, it typifies what was wrong with the thrifts in the 1980's.

Charles Keating was a banker and the head of American Continental Corporation, a real estate construction company based in Phoenix, Arizona. In 1984, it bought Californian based Lincoln Savings for $51 million; on paper Lincoln had assets of $1.1 billion and was one of the State's biggest thrifts. Within four years of the take-over, Lincoln's paper worth had climbed to $5.5 billion. The regulation of Savings and Loans under Californian State law was regarded as lax, a point that may have strengthened Keating's interest in Lincoln.

Keating brought in his own management team to run the thrift and set about what was later described as a "systematic pillaging" of Lincoln's assets through the use of accounting gimmicks. Money was channeled into the parent company's coffers to cover losses on real estate deals. The thrift was also used as a conduit to sell hundreds of millions of dollars worth of American Continental Corporation Stock to depositors at Lincoln. This was not covered by any Federal guarantee, of course; indeed these were high yield "junk" bonds.

Keating used political contacts and other means to lobby against a cap that the FHLB board introduced restricting direct investments to 10% of an institute's assets. In the end, it is clear that he simply ignored the cap once it was imposed. Keating's activities had attracted the scrutiny of Savings and Loan regulators, but he had support from a group of five US Senators that he had given political contributions to over the years, totaling almost $1.4 million. The most famous of the five were John McCain (who ran for the Presidency in 2008) and former astronaut, John Glen. The others were Alan Cranston, Donald Riegle and Dennis DeConcini. The Keating Five, as they became known, lobbied the board of the FHLB on behalf of Lincoln in two meetings in 1987. It was suggested that, at the time, Lincoln was the target for a criminal investigation. The meetings delayed action by the board for a further two years, buying Keating valuable time.

Eventually, the FHLB board used its authority and appointed a conservator to take over Lincoln, thus depriving American Continental Corporation of further access to Lincoln's funds. American Continental Corporation was declared bankrupt in 1989 with debts of $285 million, costing 21,000 investors their life savings, many of whom were elderly.

The FHLB board appointed conservator eventually established that Lincoln was insolvent by in excess of $600 million. The cost to the tax payer of the Lincoln Savings and Loan debacle was the greatest single failure of any thrift; costing $3.4 billion on its own.

Charles Keating was charged with 18 counts of securities fraud linked to the sale of American Continental Corporation junk bonds and misrepresenting them as being protected under federal insurance by the State of California. He was convicted on 17 counts. In a second trial, he was convicted on 73 counts of fraud, racketeering and conspiracy. In total, he was sentenced to fifteen years in jail, but the convictions were overturned on technical grounds. In a plea bargain, he pled guilty to fraud charges and was sentenced to time already served being 4 years 2 months. He was also the subject of many civil suits resulting in fines totaling several hundred thousand dollars.

The Keating five were eventually reprimanded by the Senate Ethics Committee in 1991 for their actions.

Fannie Mae and Freddie Mac

"If people are worried about the size of their trailers, I kind of say their priorities are off!"

Taylor Hackford

Fannie Mae and Freddie Mac are the two largest mortgage companies in the USA today; between them, the two companies guarantee or hold a staggering $5.5 trillion of mortgage debt; about 50% of the USA mortgage market. To give it a sense of scale this is the equivalent, roughly, of the combined gross domestic product of France and the UK.

As we have seen, Fannie Mae has been in existence since 1938 and is a Government Sponsored Enterprise (GSE). A GSE is protected by financial support from the federal government, should this be necessary. A GSE enjoys freedom from state and national taxation; they are exempt from SEC oversight and have a line of credit through the US Treasury. Fannie Mae's role, in the aftermath of the Great Depression was to provide liquidity to the banking and Savings and Loan industry by buying up mortgages from primary lenders and so injecting further liquidity into the system. It is engaged in providing funds for single family homes; community developments and capital markets. Fannie Mae does not deal directly with the general public, but rather it works in the secondary mortgage market.

Its start-up capital was $1 billion, but the corporation is credited with helping to create a new generation of home ownership in America. Its actions helped to extend loans to low-and middle-income buyers who would otherwise have had difficulties in obtaining credit. It became a private, share-holder owned company in 1968. The privatisation occurred against the backdrop of the economic pressures of the Vietnam War and removed Fannie Mae's debt portfolio off the government balance sheet.

Freddie Mac or, as it is more formally known, the Federal Home Mortgage Corporation is also a GSE and was created in 1970 in order to avoid giving the newly privatised Fannie Mae a monopoly in the secondary mortgage business. It was privatised in 1989 in its turn and, obviously, has a similar mission to its rival; the provision of *stability, affordability and liquidity* within the mortgage industry.

Fannie and Freddie can and did raise cheap funding on the international money markets because of their privileged positions with the US government and their GSE status; in essence, foreign investors treat them in a similar way to US government bonds: a low risk investment with a guaranteed yield. This means that they can facilitate the provision of low interest mortgages, requiring low initial down payments, to home buyers, very much as the original Savings and Loans did.

One mechanism that both Fannie and Freddie exploited to generate profits for their shareholders was the "securitisation" of the mortgages they held. This involved pooling a large number of mortgages into a financial instrument that investors can purchase parts of. This evened out the risk implicit in a single mortgage. It was appealing to investors since mortgages are usually a safe field to invest in as during normal circumstances most home buyers do not default. Fannie and Freddie also had the backing of the US government behind them, after all.

As touched upon in the introduction the housing boom started in 1997 and ended ten years later. Wall Street, and other financial centers around the world, started to offer a wide range of mortgage products tied to short term—one year—interest rates. The adjustable-rate products were often designed so that the borrower could re-finance before the rates increased or higher payments fell due. Products included "interest only" loans; "negative amortisation" and often had lax underwriting requirements meaning that a stated income or stated assets were not always insisted upon.

It was a logical extension to also tap into the ready market of people aspiring to buy their own home who would not traditionally qualify for a loan because they had few assets, low income or a chequered credit history. This area of financing became known as the sub-prime mortgage market. Equally, credit was extended to people with good credit histories but little documentation of income or assets. These sub-prime mortgages were referred to as "Alt-A" loans. As the risk associated with these loans was higher, borrowers were required to pay higher interest rates than their "prime" counterparts. In contrast to the traditional US mortgage model, sub-prime mortgages had variable interest rates. Since 1986, US taxation had been changed to remove interest deduction from commercial loans, but it remained in place for mortgage borrowing. According to the Federal Reserve board, sub-prime lending saw an average 25% annual increase between 1994 and 2003. It is estimated that sub-prime loans brought more than 9 million families into home ownership. The volume of Alt-A loans peaked in 2006 when they accounted for 48% of new residential mortgages worth $1.4 trillion. It should be noted that not all of this lending was to "bad risk" borrowers, rather it reflects loans which incorporated an Alt-A component such as a 100% loan i.e. no down-payment; variable interest rate; low starting rate, etc.

Low interest rates helped to fuel the inevitable sub-prime crisis. In 2003, the US Federal Reserve rate had drifted down to just 1%—borrowing had never been so cheap! Wall Street had adopted the "securitisation" model used by the two GSEs. The mortgages, asset backed securities, that they marketed contained a mixture of high quality prime and very dubious quality sub-prime loans within the bundle. These securities were granted A+ (or better) standard by the ratings agencies which meant that they were regarded as high quality investments with a very low probability of default. Pension and hedge funds, foreign governments and insurance companies were attracted to the new range of financial products on offer, including the bundled sub-prime loans.

Freddie and Fannie were faced with a loss of market share and started to take on more and more loans and securities of low credit quality themselves. Due to their size, such loans were quickly a significant part of their portfolios. Their share in this market from overseas investment grew from about $107 billion in 1994 to approximately $1.3 trillion in 2008.

The trigger for the sub-prime crisis was the bursting of the US housing bubble in 2006 and higher interest rates. By the end of 2006 the number of home owners being forced into foreclosure was becoming very significant. As a result of falling house prices, some borrowers were faced with "negative equity" meaning that the debt on the home was greater than its market value. These borrowers could simply relinquish their homes and debt burden, and move into rented accommodation rather than struggle to make payments, leaving them with more disposable cash. Such a move exerted further downwards pressure on house prices because of a glut of properties on the market. The year-on-year decline in house prices to January 2008 was 10%.

Freddie and Fannie are the only two members of the Fortune 500 that are not required, due to their GSE privileges, to declare any financial difficulties they are experiencing. This meant that they were able to hide losses due to defaults on sub-prime loans. As the storm clouds of the global financial crisis gathered it became impossible to disguise the fact that the two corporations were heavily over-exposed to sub-prime mortgages; both within the securitised instruments and because they guaranteed the original mortgage that was the subject of the default.

Whilst, for instance, Fannie Mae's Alt-A loans represented just 9% of its loan guarantee business, they were responsible for 40% of the company's losses in Q4 2009. More than a fifth of the Alt-A loans, taken out in 2007, were 90 or more days in arrears by the end of last 2009. The situation at Freddie Mac was comparable.

Ultimately, the US government had to step in and take over both businesses in the autumn of 2008 to avoid a meltdown of the financial system—the two companies were too big to be allowed to fail. As Hank Paulson, then US Treasury Secretary put it *"Fannie Mae and Freddie Mac are so large and so interwoven in our financial system that a failure of either of them would cause great turmoil in our financial markets here at home and around the globe."*

In Chapter 11 we will look at alternatives to housing. *As money floods out of a falling asset class like housing where does it go? Are there any really safe "stores of wealth"?*

We look at the surprising world of alternate investments and the links between them.

Chapter 11

February 2008—A Girl's Best Friend—And Her Husband, Boyfriend and Lover Too!

"Diamonds Are Forever" . . . *forever* . . . *forever* . . . *forever!"*

Shirley Bassey

February 2008—The carat price of diamonds goes up 27% between February 2008 and August 2008. The price subsequently loses the same percentage between September 2008 and February 2009.

Why are diamonds valued as a store of wealth? Are they truly a hedge against financial meltdown? Are we so blinded by their brilliance we cannot see their true value clearly?

Diamonds; There is an invisible link between diamonds and blood. Diamonds are lusted after the world over; an ego salving outward reflection of riches and prosperity. Seen as a safe haven in times of war and peril, being small and lighter than gold coins, they are easily transportable upon one's person. Beneath the glamour, fashion and wealth of these brilliant stones is a history of greed, death, bloodshed and wars to topple kings and shake empires. The carat price of diamonds is quoted daily in pounds and dollars for international buyers, but its true weight lies unmeasured on the scales of human suffering.

In January 2002, Sierra Leone emerged hesitantly from over a decade of civil war. Tens of thousands died and millions more became refugees, forced to flee into neighboring Guinea and Liberia; the burden of hosting these refugees in turn threatened the stability of these fragile states. The "structural elements" that allow for renewed conflict still remain intact; the link between small arms proliferation and clear access to diamonds.

> *"With future mineral concessions in question, the very survival of the state and its citizens was at the mercy of questionable corporate players interested in the protection of commercial interests."*
>
> **Dena Montague,**
> **Arms Trade Research Center,**
> **World Policy Institute**

At the same time Sierra Leone was tentatively reaching for peace and stability, a conflict that has become known as the "PlayStation War" has been smoldering half way across the continent, in the Congo region. When the war started, it was believed that Rwanda had invaded the Democratic Republic of the Congo, their neighbour to the west, in search of retribution and justice for the Rwandan genocide of 1994. In 2001, a UN investigation revealed that rebels were actively engaged in a war for natural resources, namely an obscure mineral called *coltan* that was a valuable input to electronics manufacturing; the UN alleged that the war was directly and indirectly fueled by multinational mining companies in order to *"keep the coltan flowing freely out of the Congo"*.

To a large extent, Western nations have turned a blind eye to these conflicts and the costs, both human and economic. The simple, difficult-to-deny, yet unpalatable fact of the violence that has devastated the African continent since it emerged from colonial rule following World War II; *is that it is good for business*.

Due to the high demand for consumer items like diamond rings and electronics, trading in the raw materials that support their manufacture is booming. Like oil, consumer demand puts tremendous pressure on the supply of these natural resources, driving prices sharply higher. Even if the demand for these were to fall, and prices along with them, it is likely that some other resource will only take their place as the "hot commodity," with the emergence of another African resource war not far behind.

> *"I never hated a man enough to give him his diamonds back."*
> **Zsa Zsa Gabor**

The dynamics behind these conflicts are nothing new. Since the discovery of Africa's natural resource wealth centuries ago, the continent has been a target for aggrandizement and exploitation at the hands of colonial powers and corporations. The history of conquest, settlement, development and independence in Africa parallels the discovery and exploitation of these commodities; *one of the most important examples of this has been the diamond.*

In this chapter, we will explore the discovery of diamonds in South Africa. In particular, we will delve into the consolidation of the mining industry and the influence of Cecil Rhodes in the late years of the 19th century, and the monopoly over the diamond industry that has persisted since then, at least until recently. The many wars of conquest and territorial conflict that have raged since then cannot be divorced from these historical developments. We will discuss the more recent outgrowths of the political and economic stability across the continent and the problems that these pose for international order. For, as we shall see, these problems and their root causes are relevant far beyond the borders of Africa.

There Be Gold (and Diamonds) In Them There Hills

> *"The real fact is that I could no longer stand their eternal cold mutton."*
> **Cecil Rhodes**

The first colonial settlements in southern Africa were established by the Netherlands. The Dutch East India Company founded Cape Town as a trading post and naval station in 1652. It was a critical waypoint for trade routes around the Cape of Good Hope. Due to its strategic importance, it gradually developed into a community of settlers, as farming was established in order to supply Dutch shipping. Local populations had no political or economic organisation, and as such the Dutch farmers were able to rapidly expand inland; often, this was accomplished through military means.

When France invaded the Netherlands in 1795, Britain occupied the Cape Colony in order to prevent Napoleon from gaining access to these important trade routes. By this time, nearly 150 years of settlement had made the ethnically Dutch "Afrikaner" into a strong and distinct community. After control of the colony was briefly relinquished to the Dutch state, which was by then under the influence of Napoleon's France, Britain once again occupied the Cape in 1806. British settlement and expansion inland and eastward thus began.

The "diamond rush" in southern Africa, as it came to be known, can be said to have provided much of the impetus for the political and economic development of the colonies in the region. Indeed, because of the discovery of gold in what is now present day South Africa, in such close proximity to the diamond fields, it is virtually impossible to divorce the growth of the colonies from the diamond trade itself. It is not known when trading in these minerals began, but they have been revered for thousands of years because of their extreme rarity. Some ancient records seem to indicate that diamonds were traded between China, India and the Mediterranean; with the advent of polishing and finishing techniques the diamond has maintained its premier status among gemstones.

In South Africa, the first diamond was discovered on the banks of the Orange River in 1866. This region, as well as sites on the Vaal River, became the center point of one of the two major diamond rushes in the region; the second occurred near a site that would become famous as Kimberley. Kimberley is situated well inland, in what was then a contested area on the joint borders of the South African Republic, the Orange Free State, and the Cape Colony. Mineral wealth in the area presented a powerful force for socioeconomic development, and more importantly, the potential for political freedom for the Boer settlers.

It should be noted that the South African Republic and the Orange Free State had gained their independence between 1852 and 1854, but the diamond rush in the area caught the attention of the British and reignited the imperialist drive.

The potential 'loss' of colonial trade routes around the Cape and the recently discovered mineral deposits was a major source of British aggressiveness, and prompted the annexations that led to the Boer Wars. In 1877, Britain annexed the Transvaal territory but the Boers revolted and formally declared independence in December 1880. The Republic government under Paul Kruger had realised the economic impact of the territory, which could catapult them to a position of economic and political leadership—and independence—in southern Africa. The resulting brushfire war was fought mainly in order to maintain British superiority in the region, a truce was reached in 1881 and self-government—but not independence—was granted to the territory.

In 1886, massive gold deposits were discovered in the Transvaal region, which could have made it the richest and most powerful nation in southern Africa. Huge inflows of immigrants threatened the balance of power between the old Boer order and the new, foreign *uitlanders*. Cecil Rhodes, founder of mining giant De Beers and an ardent believer in colonialism, had used his influence to lobby the British government to come to the aid of the uitlanders and to again secure annexation of the Transvaal. Human rights became the pretext for the British-backed incursion, which resulted in a siege of the region and a guerrilla war that ended in defeat for the Boers in 1902.

Rhodes had been hugely successful in obtaining mining concessions from tribal leaders throughout southern Africa. He used the economic leverage of his virtual monopoly in the region to significantly expand British colonial possessions.

> *"I have found out one thing and that is, if you have an idea, and it is a good idea, if you only stick to it you will come out all right."*
>
> **Cecil Rhodes**

Rhodes was able to unite the English-speaking mining firms into a cartel that was a powerful political force in London and was viewed as an enemy within the Boer-controlled territory. It was, though. the growth of the gold mining industry that finally justified the British invasions, but these huge profits were in turn predicated on the employment of a large proportion of native African workers, which comprised up to 90% of the mining industry's workforce. Rhodes, it must be noted, used his economic and political influence to forcibly expand his version of an English-speaking empire, and this served as the basis for the long-standing racial divides that prevailed in southern Africa until the final years of the 20th century.

The story of modern day South Africa really begins with Rhodes and his influence on the diamond trade. Born in 1853 near Hertfordshire, England, he attended Oxford and developed an intense admiration for the imperial system. After an initial failure in cotton farming, Rhodes went to Kimberley in 1871 and began to buy up small diamond mining operations. He was aided in these efforts by a somewhat "natural development" within the mining industry: in the initial gold rush, numerous miners were able to work small individual claims, but as the digging got deeper it became more difficult and miners began to combine into small cooperatives or were bought outright by other companies. By the late 1870's this shift away from the small-scale claimholder and towards larger-scale amalgamation of mining interests was heavily influenced by European capital. The Rothschild family partially financed Rhodes and by 1888 he had succeeded in buying up most of the mining operations in the Kimberley area. This created a virtual monopoly that extended to control of the supply chain both downwards to employment of labour at fixed rate wages and upwards to the eventual retail price of diamonds.

> *"If it were necessary to give the briefest possible definition of imperialism, we should have to say that imperialism is the monopoly stage of capitalism."*
>
> **Vladimir Lenin**

That year, he set up De Beers Consolidated Mines by merging his Kimberley operations with the Barnato Diamond Mining Company. Some have argued that De Beers was founded in order to fund the extension of British imperialism, and it is apparent that the consolidation within the industry was backed by the state, with Rhodes as both Member of Parliament from 1880-90, and Prime Minister from 1890-95. Nevertheless the relationship certainly benefited both sides. De Beers controlled most of the diamond mining in the region until a new site was discovered near modern-day Pretoria in 1902; this "Premier Mine" was very high yielding and by 1907 had equaled the combined output of all the Kimberley mines.

It was not until after World War I that the Premier Mine came under the control of De Beers. 1902, the year the Premier Mine was discovered, was also the year of Rhodes' death. Before De Beers Consolidated Mines was set up, though, Rhodes successfully manipulated the fears of European merchants that South African diamonds would flood the world supply and drive down prices; these merchants actually helped fund the De Beers consolidation efforts, in return for a guarantee that their syndicate would have exclusive rights to the new company's entire diamond output. By this time, the "London Syndicate" was under the control of the Oppenheimer brothers, Bernard, Ernest and Louis.

When the Premier Mine was discovered, De Beers had claimed it a fraud, and this gave the Oppenheimers the opportunity to challenge the virtual monopoly that De Beers had by then developed, by setting up a rival marketing operation in the US. Competition in the marketplace with the Premier diamonds prompted De Beers to attempt to collude with Premier, but these efforts were rebuffed; De Beers was forced to cut production in order to buoy prices, and saw its cartel nearly collapse.

Diamonds were discovered in German-controlled South West Africa in 1908, which further cut into the share of the world diamond trade. Ernest Oppenheimer had realised the key to the diamond trade in 1910, declaring, ***"Common sense tells us that the only way to increase the value of diamonds is to make them scarce, that is to reduce the production."*** A rival syndicate was set up in Antwerp, and despite an apparent agreement between the London Syndicate and the Germans, the latter continued to expand production until the outbreak of war in 1914 prompted them to divide world diamond production between them.

This "peace" was threatened by the outbreak of war, and because the Oppenheimers were of German descent and represented German investors, they found it necessary to court American financial interests in order to dilute their own interests; Ernest set up the new Anglo American Company as a South African entity, with backing from J.P. Morgan among others. When the Treaty of Versailles was signed in 1919, the German diamond trade was ceded to Anglo American in order to protect German financial interests from confiscation by the British. Oppenheimer was able to co-opt the largest shareholders in De Beers by offering them a share of profits from Angolan and Congolese mines, the marketing for which Oppenheimer had gained control of with his threat of a new syndicate that would compete against De Beers' London Syndicate.

In the end, the Oppenheimer Syndicate won over; as a result of the South African government's new Diamond Control Act, which restricted the export of finished gemstones, and the concession of the Barnato Mining Company as De Beers's largest shareholders, Oppenheimer solidified his control over the diamond industry in the country in 1925. De Beers also signed on with the new syndicate, and Ernest Oppenheimer gained a seat on its board. Over the next few years, Oppenheimer bought up large tracts of land and negotiated enough agreements to secure his bid for chairmanship of De Beers as well as control of the London Syndicate, thus unifying their mining and marketing efforts in October 1929. The Oppenheimer family was now firmly in control of virtually the entire diamond trade, which was henceforth carried out under the De Beers name.

Over the next seventy years, De Beers worked assiduously to limit the supply of diamonds on world markets and also to curtail the trade of inferior diamonds, in order to make sure prices remained high; at times, production was halted altogether. Bribery and corruption were alleged in efforts to curb mining in the US prior to World War II, and a Justice Department investigation concluded that a "brick wall" had been erected by *"an alliance of Washington bureaucrats, British diplomats, the Diamond Syndicate and the US War Production Board staffed by men connected to the Diamond Syndicate,"* despite the pressing need for industrial grade stones to support the war effort.

The Diamond "Market"

"Diamonds are nothing more than chunks of coal that stuck to their job"

Malcolm Stevenson Forbes

As it turns out, diamonds are really not all that rare. De Beers has been the most successful commercial cartel in history not only because it controlled the supply of diamonds, but also because it has also succeeded in controlling the *demand* for them.

Following the Great Depression, prices had collapsed in Europe, but in the United States this had not occurred; in fact, by 1938, three quarters of De Beers's diamonds were sold in the US, albeit at lower quality and price. An ingenious and exclusive marketing campaign led by the advertising agency N.W. Ayer—the firm responsible for such slogans as '*When it rains it pours,*' and '*Be all you can be*'—spawned the phrase '*a diamond is forever.*' The links between diamonds, romance, celebrity and fashion were irrevocably drawn and have endured for over seventy years. The marketing campaign was so successful that it eventually swept across the globe, and it is has been credited with reviving an industry that should have been in decline.

South Africa's share of world diamond production, moreover, had seen a steady, albeit uneven, rate of decline, from 98% in 1911 to only 10% in 1936. The Ayer campaign capitalised on the importance of the diamond trade for Great Britain, as London was the virtual center of the diamond trade, and mobilized public opinion around the value of diamonds to the Royal Family. Over the next ten years, Ayer and De Beers mounted a massive effort to influence one of the broadest segments of the public that one could have imagined: "*it defined as its target some 70 million over 15 years and over whose opinion we hope to influence*" and spent millions to secure the image of the diamond as something inextricably linked with visions of love and commitment.

They succeeded, and in the process literally transformed the American psyche. When the campaign was extended internationally, it had similar results. In Japan, for example, De Beers created an entirely new industry in a country that had not even permitted the importation of diamonds until 1959; by the 1980's more than 60% of brides wore diamonds, a radical rewriting of 1,500 years of Japanese marital traditions. With the discovery of huge mineral deposits in the Soviet Union in the 1950's, De Beers realised that its hold on the supply of diamond production was effectively lost, but they nonetheless developed and implemented a successful strategy to sell these new, smaller gems that were about to flood the market:

"De Beers devised the 'eternity ring,' made up of as many as twenty-five tiny Soviet diamonds, which could be sold to an entirely new market of older married women. The advertising campaign was based on the theme of recaptured love. Again, sentiments were born out of necessity: older American women received a ring of miniature diamonds because of the needs of a South African corporation to accommodate the Soviet Union. The new campaign met with considerable success. The average size of diamonds sold fell from one carat in 1939 to .28 of a carat in 1976, which coincided almost exactly with the average size of the Siberian diamonds De Beers was distributing."

The effect on De Beers' sales as a result of these marketing campaigns was monumental: sales increased from approximately $23 million in 1939 to over $2 billion by 1980. Supply of diamonds has never been a problem, but De Beers has made sure of this as well, by restricting both the initial supply of diamonds to the market to its select group of merchants, as well as the "re-entry" to the market of second-hand diamonds. It thus preserves the "illusion of price stability" by cutting back distribution, by buying back diamonds at the wholesale level, and by discouraging their sale at the retail level by the public.

Until recently, De Beers was successful in monopolising the diamond industry, from start to finish. Throughout most of its history, it has done this by controlling the supply of diamonds that go to market; in times when demand has not kept pace, it has held back the supply in order to try to maintain price levels. It was a business model that created the *"perception of scarcity."*

In the late 1990's, De Beers' own supply threatened the viability of its business model, and new diamond deposits have continually been found that have upset the delicate balance they have sought to maintain. When the company was young, it was able to use its political influence as a formidable weapon in the fight for industry dominance. It was also able to wield financial resources that were virtually unmatched, in order to buy up smaller rivals and expand into new areas. Nevertheless, the company saw its overall share of the world diamond trade shrink over time. Two major factors have influenced this decline. The first is the competition that De Beers has faced from new sources and new suppliers; the second relates to disturbing developments in the arena of state security.

> *"A merchant who approaches business with the idea of serving the public well has nothing to fear from the competition."*
> **James Cash Penney**

We've previously mentioned how the flood of new stones onto the world market from the Soviet Union impacted De Beers' highly successful marketing campaign; when the Mir mine was discovered in 1955, it drastically changed the geopolitics of the diamond industry. Although many of these diamonds were small, a relatively high proportion of them were gemstone quality. De Beers was originally the main buyer for the Soviet Union's diamonds. When the Soviet Union collapsed, mining operations were privatised and the *Almazy Rossii-Sakha* Joint Stock Company, or Alrosa, was created as the "capitalist" successor to the previously government owned entities in 1992. Presently, Alrosa controls about one quarter of the world's rough diamonds. The company estimates that it will be able to sustain its mining operations for nearly 20 years.

Perhaps the most significant diamond find of the past 50 years occurred in Western Australia with the discovery of the Argyle mine. Although mineral deposits were well known in the country since the discovery of gold in the late 19th century, diamonds were not found until 1979 after ten years of exploration. This mine, owned by the Rio Tinto Group, is now the largest single producer of rough diamonds by volume, although most are these are not of gem quality. It is also the world leader in the coloured diamonds, such as pink and red, which are especially rare relative to other tones.

"Gems being precious cannot be owned by all and sundry."
Sam Veda

Of particular interest here is the fact that Rio Tinto is not part of the De Beers Empire, and does not sell through their Diamond Trading Company. When the company discovered high-quality diamonds in Canada, it refused to be a part of the De Beers cartel. This decision has its roots in the apartheid era, when De Beers tried to buy its way into the Australian mining firm as a small shareholder—as it had always done. It then tried to corner the marketing rights for the total output of Australian production, but when another minority partner learned that De Beers was attempting to undercut the Australians by offering them 80% less than the current market price, it ignited a firestorm of public and political protest:

"The opposition Labour Party charged not only that De Beers was seeking to cheat Australians out of the true value of the diamonds but that the deal with De Beers would support the policy of apartheid in South Africa. It demanded that the government impose export controls on the diamonds rather than allow them to be controlled by a South African corporation. Prime Minister Malcolm Fraser, faced with a storm of public protest, said that he saw no advantage in 'arrangements in which Australian diamond discoveries only serve to strengthen a South African monopoly.'"

In Canada, Rio Tinto's Diavik Mine is a joint venture with Harry Winston Diamond Corporation, which is a competitor of De Beers on the retail side of the industry. This mine has one of the highest concentrations of diamonds and these are of a very high grade. They are marketed primarily through Rio Tinto's Antwerp-based subsidiary, but Harry Winston also accounts for about 25% of the diamonds sold through Tiffany's retail stores.

In addition to their quality and abundance, one of the most valued characteristics of Canadian diamonds is the fact that they are "issue free." South Africa, of course, is not the only country with diamond reserves. As the African continent decolonised following World War II, De Beers saw its monopoly control begin to slip away. In 1981, Zaire (now the Democratic Republic of Congo) ended its exclusive selling arrangement with the company and became one of the largest sources of so-called *"conflict diamonds."* These diamonds are smuggled out of the war-torn country and sold on the black market, with proceeds used to buy weapons and to fund their struggles. The Congo is not the only party involved in this trade; Sierra Leone and Angola are the other primary sources of this trafficking, with distribution occurring through a number of neighbouring states.

What's more, this illicit trade in diamonds has occurred on both sides of the law, having been pursued by both governments and rebel groups alike. Estimates from outside the diamond industry have put the amount of conflict diamonds at up to 15% of global trade; De Beers had long sworn off its involvement in this illegal trafficking, but has nonetheless profited immensely from its ability to continue to control the supply. De Beers has admitted to buying these diamonds in order to keep them from flooding the market; in 1999, its profits soared by more than 80%.

> *"Profits are like breathing. You have to have them. But who would stay alive just to breathe?"*
>
> **Maurice Mascaranhas**

One of the most concerning elements in this dynamic occurred in Sierra Leone. In 1991, the rebel Revolutionary United Front, or RUF, began a protracted civil war against the government. The movement claimed that the government had sold out to foreigners and demanded the return of diamond revenues to the people of Sierra Leone, whom they claimed to represent. The RUF began a forced labour campaign and by 1992 had occupied the focal point of the country's diamond mining industry, thereby disrupting the state's access to diamond revenues. The RUF then turned the conflict into a guerilla war, and set up a complex network of arms smugglers and diamond buyers: *"Sierra Leonean diamonds labeled as Guinean, Gambian, or Liberian were exported to Europe to finance weapons shipments . . . The exchange of illicit weapons and diamonds was conducted with apparent ease.*"

This had all been accomplished with "apparent ease" because the international community ignored it until 1995, when the RUF had appropriated enough of the country's diamond industry to impede the state's ability to repay loans to the International Monetary Fund. Unable to oust the rebel faction on its own, the government was pressured into finding an alternate solution to the conflict: they contracted what was perhaps the world's most sophisticated private army, South Africa's **Executive Outcomes.**

Formed in 1989 after the dissolution of South Africa's apartheid regime and the dismantling of much of its special operations forces, Executive Outcomes was highly trained and heavily armed. Many of its troops had seen combat in Angola and Namibia, and others had been part of the South African apartheid regime's counterinsurgency as well as the South West African Police Forces, which were disbanded when Namibia gained independence. Some of Executive Outcome's members have been linked to covert operations, including assassinations of political opponents on behalf of the South African Defense Force.

Executive Outcomes' initial foray into the diamond business began with a contract to train security personnel for Debswana, the mining joint venture between De Beers and the government of Botswana. In 1992, Executive Outcomes was contracted by Angola to fight the rebel UNITA forces, and has been credited with securing conditions that lead to a peace settlement. The company was brought to Sierra Leone in 1995, because it was a vastly superior option to the poorly trained and underequipped government troops. It used its preponderance of force to quickly repel the RUF and secure the diamond mines.

Executive Outcomes left after two years when it appeared that the financially ruined Sierra Leonean government proved unable to pay for their services. Part of their contract involved not just the provision of security services and the "liberation" of the crucial diamond-mining region, but also the implementation of a new mining contract for their partner, Branch Energy:

"The problem is not the individual episodes, but the bigger picture which they help form—of a world in which beleaguered and legitimate governments find little formal international protection against internal predators and are forced into Faustian bargains in order to survive . . . Closely connected to mining interests, the phenomenon [of Executive Outcomes] however, is more than just a convenient way to let the international community off the hook. It begins to look like a protection racket, with the payment for assistance made in future mineral concessions—concessions for protection."

It has become cliché to note the resemblance of the Executive Outcomes story to that portrayed in Hollywood, in the film **Blood Diamond**. Yet, as far as the liberation of the diamond fields in Kono, that was exactly the way history played out. Executive Outcomes' contribution to the *"peace and stability"* of Sierra Leone was hailed as a success, and it left the country at a time of relative peace.

However, such dramatisation really only reveals the tip of the iceberg. Executive Outcomes' success virtually created a new industry. Despite a questionable legal framework for their operation, private military companies have become a distinct characteristic of the African landscape; *what's more, the IMF and World Banks have encouraged this development as part of their reform programs, which have advocated for the "disengagement" of the state and widespread deregulation.*

This dynamic is exacerbated by the weak authority of many states on the continent that, like Sierra Leone, have proven either unable or unwilling to provide internal security. It is further troubling that the privatisation of security has now become a "widespread general feature" of the mineral extraction industry in Africa. Where De Beers had previously monopolised the entire trade, it has been supplanted in many areas by smaller firms that have partnered with both local governments and private military companies. While not precisely a new or unique feature of the *"new world order"*—under Rhodes, De Beers controlled security through the British South Africa Company's own police force—it has now spread across the continent and has further contributed to the phenomenon of "enclave development." This involves the separation of mining or other similar projects, such as oil drilling, from the local population, with much of the work going to foreign skilled workers.

These developments have been encouraged by the IMF and World Bank on the grounds of their efficiency and profitability in an economic environment of extreme deregulation. Of course, as these enclaves have come to resemble "*off shore*" extraction projects, so has the extraction of wealth from these vulnerable states, which in the end see little economic benefit from these projects. This dynamic is compounded by the exchange of lucrative mining concessions in exchange for the provision of security, as we saw in Sierra Leone. It has engendered the rise of the **nongovernmental state**, in which security is not a question of national sovereignty but akin to the provision of any other utility.

De Beers, of course, has not been absent from this transformation of the industry. Predictably, in many respects it has led the way. Outside of South Africa, De Beers carries out major operations in Botswana and Namibia. Both of these nations share the same colonial roots as South Africa. As the De Beers Empire began to falter, it was forced to enter into new arrangements with its host governments in order to protect its monopoly control. In Botswana, De Beers formed a joint venture with the government in 1969, after diamonds were discovered in the early 1960's. In order to maintain full control over the diamond industry, De Beers gradually gave increasing ownership to Botswana, beginning at 15% and now standing at 50% each. A similar ownership structure is in place in Namibia.

While Botswana as a whole has been heralded as an economic development success story, with some agencies declaring it the safest credit risk in Africa; the diamond industry has underpinned the country's growth. It has not benefited everyone, though, and the country remains sharply divided between rich and poor. Much of this development has also been at the expense of indigenous people, they have either been displaced or excluded as part of the aforementioned trend toward "enclave" development; it was recently revealed that the Kalahari Bushmen were "*evicted*" to make way for new mining operations. An offshoot of the World Bank allegedly funded prospecting efforts in this region.

Reviving the Diamond Trade: Just a Quick Polish?

"Treason is like diamonds; there is nothing to be made by the small trader!"

Douglas William Jerrold

In the late 1990's, the diamond industry faced a tough onslaught of negative press that threatened to derail its long history of profitability, as a result of the revelations of the trade in conflict diamonds. The international community first imposed sanctions in 1998 on Angola as a result of their involvement in the diamonds-for-arms trade. In 2000, several southern African states met in Kimberley, South Africa, to deliberate on a new scheme to control this trade, which became known as the Kimberley Process.

In December 2000, the United Nations adopted a resolution that supported the creation of an international certification process that would prove the origin of rough diamonds. Essentially, this process restricted shipments of rough diamonds between participating countries; these shipments were to be accompanied by government-validated certificates. According to the Kimberley Process, it imposes *"extensive requirements on its members to enable them to certify shipments of rough diamonds as 'conflict-free.'"*

Despite the apparent widespread support for these measures, with 49 members representing 75 countries, it is not yet clear what the impact will be on the diamond trade. The Kimberley Process was formally endorsed in 2002, but it remains a voluntary program. Member countries are supposed to pass domestic legislation to enforce the accord, but many key governments have been unwilling to take "strong and much needed actions" to strengthen the process and ensure that loopholes are closed and weaknesses are shored up:

"A United Nations Group of Experts on Cote d'Ivoire has recently found that poor controls are allowing significant volumes of blood

diamonds to enter the legitimate trade through Ghana, where they are being certified as conflict free, and through Mali. As well as pointing to the need for stronger diamond controls in the region, the Group of Experts recommends that international trading centre's introduce better systems for identifying suspicious shipments of rough diamonds. Many other diamond-producing countries have weak government diamond controls that cannot guarantee the diamonds they export are conflict-free."

In the US, for example, Congress enacted the Clean Diamond Trade Act, but significant problems exist with it. Through intense lobbying efforts, a tougher version of the bill was dropped in favour of one that was effectively written by the World Diamond Council, a group representing members of the diamond industry. The ensuing legislation was replete with loopholes and exemptions, making enforcement virtually impossible and circumvention almost certain. The World Diamond Council, on the other hand, counters that they wanted to make the law as efficient and practical as possible, and by inserting exemptions on jewelers that handle conflict diamonds, for example, they argue that they are only trying to keep focus on the main problem—the source of conflict diamonds, and not the end product.

The Kimberley Process claims to have significantly reduced the flow of conflict diamonds. The true impact is extraordinarily difficult to assess. As diamonds are easy to smuggle, once illicit stones enter the legitimate supply of diamonds, they are virtually impossible to trace. It is estimated that conflict diamonds still account for between 15-20% of the diamond trade from Sierra Leone. Proponents argue that the "compulsory" nature of the Kimberley Process makes it very costly for countries to violate its terms, for if one is expelled from the group they cannot trade with other members. This has not stopped Zimbabwe's army from operating forced labour mines. National officials argue that the army's involvement in the diamond trade was only undertaken in order to remove illegal miners from the fields, but human rights groups claim that this was in reality a *"systemic attempt to enable key army units, whose support President Mugabe needed following June's elections, to have access to riches."* Some claim that the costs—or illegal profits—from the illegal mining amount to as much as $200 million per month, and largely as a result of the situation in Zimbabwe, the Kimberley Process is on the verge of failing.

Conclusion

> *"Difficulties are meant to rouse, not discourage. The human spirit is to grow strong by conflict."*
>
> **William Ellery Channing**

Like drugs, it is evident that curbing the supply simply will not work. The real issue is with demand. De Beers and others, of course, realised this and have sought once again to transform their business models. Throughout much of the history of the diamond trade, De Beers as the market leader sought to control supply; but by the late 1990's this model was no longer effective. De Beers saw its monopoly slip, but it still maintains a 40% hold on the market through its central selling organisation.

The issue of conflict diamonds put significant pressure on the demand of diamonds. Realising the impact on the industry of conflict diamonds, De Beers was at the forefront of the Kimberley Process, and has tried to serve as a role model for others in the industry. It has recently relocated its diamond-sorting facilities from London to Botswana, which the firm claims *"places us in a position where we are aligned with the needs of the country and where we're the partner of choice for the government. We think that it adds to our competitive advantage."*

As De Beers became increasingly unable to manage the supply side of the trade, it realised that it must transform the way it did business: *"De Beers shifted its strategy from managing supply to driving demand. Under its 'Supplier of Choice' program, De Beers had the goals of stimulating diamond demand by 5% per year; improving the efficiency and margins of all De Beers operations, from mining to sales; and leveraging the De Beers brand by offering De Beers-branded jewelry directly to consumers."*

It has nonetheless remained committed to supply-side management, curtailing supply and curbing production at its mines in order to lift prices. Most other diamond producers, such as Rio Tinto and Alrosa, have similarly cut production or even stopped it altogether as a consequence of the global recession. From December 2007 to October 2008, prices climbed on average 20% across the broad spectrum of weights; interestingly, however, the vast majority of stones are relatively small, and saw virtually no change in price during this period—almost all the price increases occurred for large stones of size greater than 3 carats, with stones greater than 4 carats even appreciating by 40%. *In 2009, prices fell by an average of nearly 6%.*

One can conclude, then, that the diamond industry is subject to the effects of economic cycles, but because of the peculiarities of supply and demand, producers are still much more able—and willing—to fix prices. Whether this dynamic will remain in place in the future is unclear. It is possible that emerging markets such as China and India will cause demand to once again eclipse supply, and it must also be considered that no new or significant diamond reserves have been discovered in more than a decade. It may be that the "natural" forces of supply and demand will come to the fore in the future.

Even so, it is possible that we may yet see resurgence in the monopolistic practices of the major producers. Faced with uncertain economic prospects, we may see De Beers and Alrosa join forces to further control the market, and in light of their combined 70% market share, they would be in a position to significantly influence prices from the supply side: *"Any solutions based on the "stand alone" strategy will inevitably bring the diamond-mining companies to competition which will drive rough prices down and provoke such "surprises" as one-time dumping of huge stocks accumulated by either of them to the market. That would be good if it was grain, but who needs price unpredictability in the luxury symbol?"*

The social inputs to the diamond equation, it should be noted, are still of considerable concern. Where companies like Executive Outcomes have been involved, they have done so to the detriment of the wider citizenry in these countries. The fragile conditions in these countries make the threat of renewed hostilities an ever-present one: *"Mining companies and international institutions that encourage investment in the diamond sector must recognise their role in profiting from a weak state that is unable to enforce legitimacy in diamond mining.*" Even if demand for diamonds were to drop, it is likely that something else—like coltan or oil—will simply replace it. Unless and until the critical inputs of democracy and development have solved these economic and social issues, we are unlikely to see the outcome changing.

When first researching this chapter I was seeking a correlation between economic collapse and the price movement of diamonds. That correlation appears weak in the modern era. More unsettling was that the more I uncovered about these luxury goods the more disturbing the events that swirled about them. Over 100 years ago Cecil Rhodes proposed the following; *"We must find new lands from which we can easily obtain raw materials and at the same time exploit the cheap slave labour that is available from the natives of the colonies. The colonies would also provide a dumping ground for the surplus goods produced in our factories."*

It appears little has changed; blood and diamonds are irretrievably linked.

In **Chapter 12** we turn from monopolies in diamonds to the man who tried to create a monopoly in American banking and finance in the beginning of the 20th Century; **J.P. Morgan.**

Chapter 12

March 2008—J. P. Morgan:
Man to Megabank 1907 to 2007

"A man always has two reasons for doing anything. A good reason and the real reason!"

J P Morgan

14th March 2008—Bear Stearns accesses emergency loan backed by Fed, sold to JP Morgan Chase for $2 per share, avoiding bankruptcy.

Why do some succeed and others fail? Why do some firms have longevity whilst others stumble and fall?

J. P. Morgan; Exactly 100 years before the advent of the 2007 Credit Crunch the world was poised on the edge of a similar financial abyss. The year was 1907 and all hope and expectation of salvation was centered on one man; ***John Piermont Morgan.***

In 2007 the Federal Reserve turned once more to the Bank that bore his illustrious name to stem the financial tidal wave that was threatening to overwhelm Wall Street and the World's financial markets. It's current CEO and Chairman James L. "Jamie" Dimon proved he was up to the job; the mighty mantle he had inherited rested lightly upon his shoulders. JP Morgan Chase the bank was to emerge from the crisis bigger, financially stronger and, perhaps more importantly, with its reputation enhanced whilst all about others had been stripped bare.

Who was this titan of the money markets?

J.P. Morgan, the man: an American investment banker, art collector and philanthropist, considered by many to be the greatest financier in the history of the United States. He dominated corporate finance and industrial consolidation during his time. As a private banker, J.P. Morgan raised millions of dollars in foreign investment to build railroads in the United States and to help pay off the country's enormous debt following the Civil War. He was responsible for the merger of Edison General Electric and Thomson-Houston Electric Company to form General Electric in 1892. However, his greatest accomplishment came in 1907. J.P. Morgan brought bankers together to halt the financial panic that threatened the United States' banking system. Interestingly enough, there was growing concern over J.P. Morgan's control of investment banking, which led the US Government to appoint a commission that recommended the creation of a central bank. ***That central bank is now known as the Federal Reserve.***

John Piermont Morgan was born into a well-to-do family in Hartford, Connecticut on April 17, 1837. His father, financier Junius Spencer, was a partner in Peabody, Morgan and Co., a company initially founded to meet the increasing demand for securities issued by the American railroads. When George Peabody, the founder of the company retired, the company became J.S. Morgan & Co. Junius Morgan achieved great success and raised his son to follow in his footsteps. Junius sent Piermont to private schools in the United States, Switzerland and Germany where, in addition to business, Piermont studied German and art history.

J.P. Morgan to J.P. Morgan & Company

At the age of 20, Piermont went to work for the brokerage house of Duncan, Sherman & Company in New York City. As an accountant, *"Pierpont worked without pay, learning investment banking from the ground up."* Piermont went on to become the American agent and attorney for the London firm of George Peabody & Company in 1860. This was the company his father was a partner of—it later became Peabody, Morgan and Co., and then J.S. Morgan & Co.

By 1864, Piermont was an increasingly influential partner in Dabney, Morgan and Company. In 1871, Piermont partnered with the Drexels of Philadelphia to create Drexel, Morgan and Company. Upon the death of his father in 1890, Piermont inherited J.S. Morgan & Co., which gave him important European connections and enabled him to run a large foreign reserve business. The death of Anthony Drexel in 1893 enabled Piermont to reorganise Drexel, Morgan & Co., to become J.P. Morgan & Company, with branches in London and Paris. Piermont retained close ties with Drexel & Company in Philadelphia. Over the years, Morgan had many partners, but he always remained firmly in charge. The firm J.P. Morgan & Company became recognised in the United States *"and abroad as one of the most powerful financial institutions in the world."*

"Morganisation"

After the American Civil War (1861-1865), J.P. Morgan specialised in marketing American securities to Europe. The war had been tremendously expensive and the US Government sought to refinance its debt at the lowest possible interest rates. From 1873 to 1879, Morgan was a major player in refinancing the post war debt. One specific example of the company helping the government with their finances occurred in 1877. Together with August Belmont and the Rothschilds, they floated $260 million in US Government bonds.

During the 1870's and 1880's, Morgan funded Thomas Edison and laid the financial foundation for the Edison Electrical Company. During this time, with his fortune growing, Morgan also continued making investments and acquisitions. Many small companies and railroads ran into tough times after the war and Morgan saw opportunities and amassed companies with potential. He did this with such intent that *"his process of buying and consolidation of railroads came to be known as Morganisation."* By the mid 1880's, Morgan had significant railroad holdings and by 1900 owned 5,000 miles of rail line. He then consolidated and restructured many of his railroad companies. For the most part the government had failed to regulate the industry, which gave Morgan the opportunity to set the regulations and standards. Through his railroad empire, Morgan saw another opportunity: rails and trains required huge quantities of steel. Therefore, Morgan founded and acquired massive steel-making operations to supply his rail companies. Morganisation continued and by 1901 Morgan established the industry-dominant U.S. Steel Company by merging Carnegie Steel Works with several smaller steel companies.

There is, however, another way of looking at these developments. These historical accounts paint a picture of J.P. Morgan simply acquiring and merging companies. The other side shows a more holistic improvement of businesses; J.P. Morgan had a vision for greater efficiencies. As mentioned above, Morgan raised large sums of money in Europe following the Civil War. He also acquired railroad companies that were in trouble. These funds from Europe were used to help reorganise and achieve greater efficiencies for the railroads. He had a vision of an integrated transportation system. Morgan fought against those interested in purely speculative profits.

> *"Of all forms of tyranny the least attractive and the most vulgar*
> *is the tyranny of mere wealth, the tyranny of plutocracy."*
> **J. P. Morgan**

In order to efficiently regulate the railroad industry, Morgan set up conferences in 1889 and 1890. The conferences brought together railroad presidents to help the industry follow new laws and write agreements for the maintenance of public, reasonable, uniform and stable rates. These conferences were the first of their kind and created a community of interest among competing lines thus paving the way for the great consolidations in the early 1900's.

Morgan's reputation as a banker and financier brought interest to the companies that he took over making the transactions successful. The process of Morganisation was known to return troubled companies to profitability. J.P. Morgan's ascent to power was, as to be expected, not void of interesting accounts. One of those concerned the re-machining of guns for the US Government. Well-established by the time of the Civil War, J.P. Morgan was approached to finance the purchase of antiquated rifles being sold by the army for $3.50 each. The rifles were re-machined by Morgan's partner and sold back to the government for

$22 each. The guns were defective and known to blow off the thumbs of those who used them. Obviously, a scandal ensued as the government refused to pay for defective weapons at an exorbitant markup. Morgan then sued the government twice to collect on his contract. Like other wealthy individuals, Morgan avoided military service by paying $300.

Panic of 1893

Even before the better-known Panic of 1907, there was the Panic of 1893—a national economic crisis in the United States. On occasion, it has been considered part of the Long Depression that began then. The Panic of 1893 was set off by the collapse of two of the country's largest employers, the Philadelphia and Reading Railroad as well as the National Cordage Company. Their collapse resulted in panic erupting on the stock market. Previously, hundreds of companies had financially overextended themselves by borrowing to expand their operations. When the crisis hit, banks and investment firms began calling in their loans, which caused hundreds of bankruptcies throughout the United States. Especially hard hit were banks, railroads and steel mills.

Over fifteen thousand businesses failed during the Panic of 1893 and unemployment rates soared to twenty-five percent during the worst of it. Homelessness skyrocketed as workers lost their jobs and could no longer pay their rent or mortgages. Like other economic or financial crises, the Panic of 1893 followed a period of remarkable economic expansion. However, prior to housing bubbles bursting and dot-coms imploding, excessive growth in previous centuries came in other forms. Like the expansion our modern generation knows, the expansion in the 1880's became *driven by speculation*. In the 1880's, the industry for speculation was railroads. They were vastly over-built, fortunes were made and companies tried to take over others regardless of seriously this would endanger their own stability.

If you were in any of the areas hard hit by the housing bubble of late, you will likely remember an infestation of real estate agents. It seemed as though people could pick up a real estate license with their $4 latte as they hit the drive through in their Hummers. Along with the speculation of housing values rising and investors flooding the market, came the opportunities for everyman to make a commission on a sale—certain things go hand in hand. Like the housing bubble, the railroad bubble affected other industries and in the 1880's it was mines. Many mines were opened and their products, especially silver, flooded the market.

As a result of the railroad companies collapsing, the stock market crashing and unemployment escalating, there was obviously concern about the state of the economy. As the state of the economy continued to worsen, people rushed to withdraw their money resulting in bank runs. Not unlike the recent events in the 21st century, the financial panic rippled through to the United Kingdom and Europe. This caused foreign investors to sell American stocks and obtain American funds backed by gold.

> *"When the house is on fire good girls have to get out as well as the bad ones."*
>
> **J. P. Morgan**

During the depths of the Panic of 1893, the Federal Treasury was nearly out of gold. The nation's gold reserves had already dipped below $100 million in 1892. President Grover Cleveland had already authorised four new government bonds to raise gold between 1894 and 1896. With the threat of defaulting on its international obligations looming, a desperate Cleveland, turned to J.P. Morgan to float the bonds. Essentially, Cleveland arranged for Morgan to create a private syndicate on Wall Street to supply the US Treasury with $65 million in gold and to float the bonds restoring the treasury to a surplus of $100 million. In seeking help from Morgan, *"Cleveland was derided for allying with powerful Wall Street interests instead of helping the average American."* The President, however, felt that he had no choice but to replenish the country's gold reserves and J.P. Morgan came to the rescue. Other historians simply state that J.P. Morgan bought $200 million worth of government bonds with gold that preserved the credit of the United States. Morgan however, was heavily criticised for the harsh terms on the loan.

The Turn of the Century

"Go as far as you can see; when you get there, you'll be able to see farther."

J. P. Morgan

J.P. Morgan's biggest deal was the forming of the US Steel Corporation in 1901. It was the first billion-dollar corporation. In addition to existing assets, Morgan purchased mills from Andrew Carnegie and formed US Steel with an approximate value of $1.2 billion. Morgan's goal for US Steel was to "achieve greater economies of scale, reduce transportation and resource costs, expand product lines, and improve distribution". He also planned for the corporation to allow the United States to compete with Britain and Germany. Once again, critics chimed in claiming that US Steel was a monopoly. The company, in addition to dominating the steel industry, had also been working towards dominating the construction of bridges, ships, railroad cars and associated railroad products along with a host of other products.

Speculation in the early 1900's was rampant. At the time, there was no central bank. This was worrisome because *"the banks were intimately involved in the market, either as underwriters or investors."* In addition to banks, organisations called trust banks were also intimately involved in the market. Trust banks were separate from commercial and investment banks. They administered trust funds, money invested on behalf of estates, wills, etc. Many of the trust banks, in the 1900's made loans to market speculators and took securities as collateral. Therefore, if the value of stocks fell, everyone was hit—investors, commercial and investment banks, and trust banks. Without a central bank in place, *"no one would loan them money if a depositor's run developed or they needed cash to prop up their positions under duress."*

Not surprisingly, the US economy was about to come across a downturn in 1906. At the time, the business community was pressuring President Teddy Roosevelt to ease up on regulatory measures and antitrust prosecutions. Seeing storm clouds on the horizon, Roosevelt threatened to subject all large trusts to federal control. He said that Americans were enjoying unprecedented prosperity with complete disregard to the possible hard times ahead.

The Panic of 1907

"I made a fortune getting out too soon."

J. P. Morgan

The downturn that President Teddy Roosevelt anticipated hit in the spring of 1907. J.P. Morgan had planned to leave for Europe mid-March 2007 but ended up in Washington instead. There were rumours that Roosevelt was going to make a dramatic move against the railroads—this called Morgan to Washington. On March 12, Morgan met with Roosevelt and spent two hours discussing the present business situation. When he left the White House, Morgan informed the press that Roosevelt would meet with the heads of the leading railroads to find solutions to allay public anxiety. As a side note, the then President of Princeton University, Woodrow Wilson, had recently publicly attributed the country's economic troubles to the government's aggressive attitude toward the railroads.

The New York stock market plunged on March 13th, yet Morgan sailed off to Europe. The following day, the market crashed and lost 8.3% of its value. In describing the trading floor at the New York Stock Exchange, *The Brooklyn Daily Eagle* reported, **"Brokers rushed here and there in an effort to unload, and thousands of shares were dumped on the market in less time than the telling of it takes."** This description of the trading floor is not remarkable—it would fit any financial panic that the United States has experienced. Although similar, with symptoms of money supply constriction, each financial crisis is *"part of the fabric of their unique eras."* The Panic of 1907 was a result of a boom in industry and investment in the United States with credit flowing to the point of leaving lenders vulnerable.

The day after the initial crash, the *Brooklyn Daily Eagle* reported that the White House and the Treasury Department had been bombarded by frantic telegraphs, telegrams and mail for the last 24 hours with people begging the government to do something about the tumbling stock values on Wall Street. People knew that there was a great threat of full-blown panic on the horizon. However, there was as yet no Federal Reserve Board to keep excess in check or to direct the economy.

The drain on the money supply was a result of the capital needed to fund the Russo-Japanese War of 1905, the rebuilding of San Francisco following the devastating earthquake and fires in 1906 and several railroad expansions. The banking system had thus over-extended itself. Additionally, speculation had caused *"the stock market to soar to new heights, credit was severely strained and some banks and trust companies had failed. When long-term bonds could not be sold, the constricting money supply plunged New York Stock Exchange prices into a sudden collapse on March 13th."* Regardless of some recovery in April, wild fluctuations continued throughout the rest of 1907 as world markets fell and banks failed. The Bank of England sent specie—coin based bullion—across the ocean to relieve the financial crisis in the United States but it was not enough.

October 1907

Although it was March 13th 2007 that marked the beginning of a four-year recession attributed to the most recent circumstances—easy credit, wild financial speculation and constriction of the money supply—it wasn't until October when things became dire. The tipping point that led to a run on the banks was a failed attempt to corner the market on the stock of a copper company. That copper company was F. Augustus Heinze's United Copper Company and the eventual run on the banks started at the Mercantile National Bank in New York City. Augustus had made a fortune as a copper magnate in Butte, Montana before moving to New York City in 1906.

Cornering the market is a scheme to manipulate the price of a stock. More specifically, if a company has cornered the market, it means they hold a very high market share of a particular stock, commodity or other asset. The basic idea is that by holding enough of the asset, the person initiating the corner has the ability to control the supply of the asset thus being able to manipulate its price. Another financial concept to understand before we continue is that of short selling. If an investor believes that the price of a stock, or any other asset, is likely to drop, they will borrow shares from a third party with the intention of buying those identical shares in the future from someone else to return the initial shares borrowed. For example, investor Ian believes that shares in Acme will drop in the future. Ian goes to Lou who lends him 5 shares of Acme. Ian then sells the shares for $5 each and has $25. A month later, Acme is only worth $4 per share so Ian buys 5 shares for a total of $20 and gives the shares back to Lou. The profit for Ian is the difference between what he sold the borrowed shares for ($25) and what he paid to purchases them ($20) to return them to Lou. Ian has a $5 profit.

Now we move back to 1907. It was Augustus's brother Otto that devised the scheme to corner United Copper. Otto believed that the Heinze family already controlled a majority of the company; however, investors had **borrowed** a significant number of those shares. Otto believed that those investors were gambling that the price of United Copper shares was going to drop, also known as shorting the stock. Otto proposed a short squeeze where the Heinzes would aggressively purchase as many remaining shares as possible. Not only would this make it difficult for the short sellers to find enough stock to repay their loans, it would drive up the price of the shares. When it came time to repay the loans / return the borrowed shares, the short sellers would have to turn to the Heinzes to buy shares because they wouldn't be able to buy them elsewhere. This would enable the Heinzes to charge the short sellers in excess of true market price, thus turning a healthy profit.

In order to finance this scheme, Otto and Augustus met with notorious Wall Street bankers Charles Morse and Charles T. Barney. Augustus had recently formed a close relationship with Morse and Barney, the president of Knickerbocker Trust Company, the city's third largest trust, had provided funding for Morse's previous schemes. Morse cautioned Otto that he needed much more money than he had to attempt the squeeze and Barney declined on funding the venture. Otto however, paid no heed to the warning and attempted the risky squeeze.

On Monday, October 14, 1907, Otto Heinze began to aggressively purchase shares of United Copper. In one day the shares rose from $39 to $52 per share. On Tuesday, Otto issued the call for short sellers to return the borrowed stock. The price of the shares rose to nearly $60 each. Much to Otto's dismay, he had misread the market and short sellers were able to find ample shares from other sources. ***The share price of United Copper began to collapse!***

The sights "on the curb", outside the hall of the New York Stock Exchange where United Copper was traded, had apparently never been so wild. Shares closed at $30 on Tuesday and fell further to close at $10 on Wednesday. Then things proceeded to get even worse. Otto Heinze was essentially ruined. The failed stock manipulation left him unable to meet his obligations and sent his brokerage house, Gross & Kleeberg into bankruptcy. On October 17, the New York Stock Exchange suspended Otto's trading privileges.

As is so often the case with financial disasters, the results of Otto's failed attempt then rippled outwards. The State Savings Bank of Butte Montana owned by Augustus Heinze, held United Copper stock as collateral against some of its lending. The Montana bank was also a correspondent bank for the Mercantile National Bank in New York City where Augustus then resided as president. The collapse of United Copper required the State Savings Bank of Butte Montana to announce its insolvency.

The board of the Mercantile National Bank found Augustus' association with the corner and the insolvency of the State Savings Bank of Butte Montana to be too much. Before lunch, the board immediately forced Augustus to resign as president; however it was already too late. With the news of the collapse spreading, depositors rushed en masse to withdraw their savings from the Mercantile National Bank. The Mercantile bank was able to sustain a few days of rampant withdraws but things worsened when depositors began to pull funds from the National Bank of North America and the New Amsterdam National, both banks of Charles W. Morse. You may recall the Augustus and Morse were close associates.

With severely tainted reputations, both Augustus Heinze and Charles Morse were forced to resign from all banking interests. It was the New York Clearing House that forced the men to step down based on the potential impact their association could have on the banking industry. By the weekend a full-blown panic had yet to set in. Monies withdrawn from Heinze and Morse associated banks were deposited in other banks.

More exuberant boom contributing to bust then came from the Trust sector. In the decade prior to 1907, trust companies boomed with assets growing 244%. The leaders of the trusts were prominent members of New York's financial and social circles. One of the most respected financiers was Charles T. Barney, who, as mentioned above, was an associate of both Charles Morse and Augustus Heinze and whose trust, Knickerbocker Trust Company, was the third largest in New York. On October 18, depositors began to pull deposits. Due to his association with Augustus and Morse, Knickerbocker's board asked Barney to resign on October 21, 1907.

That same day, the National Bank of Commerce announced that it would no longer act as a clearinghouse for Knickerbocker. The news had spread and on October 22, the Knickerbocker faced a classic bank run. From before the doors opened that morning, the crowd grew. The *New York Times* reported, *"as fast as a depositor went out of the place ten people and more came asking for their money [and the police] were asked to send some men to keep order"*. The mayhem resulted in $8 million being withdrawn in less than three hours and shortly after noon, the Knickerbocker was forced to suspend operations—its funds were depleted beyond hope. The bank's president, Charles Barney, shot himself several weeks later, prompting some of the bank's outstanding depositors to commit suicide as well.

Things continued in a downward spiral as the grim news spread. Other banks and trust companies, fearful, were reluctant to lend which sent interest rates for brokers through the roof. With brokers not being able to borrow, stock prices crashed. The panic then hit both the Trust Company of America and Lincoln Trust Company and continued. By the 24th, a smattering of financial institutions had failed including, the Twelfth Ward Bank, Empire City Savings Bank, Hamilton Bank of New York, First National Bank of Brooklyn, International Trust Company of New York, Williamsburg Trust Company of Brooklyn, Borough Bank of Brooklyn, Jenkins Trust Company of Brooklyn and the Union Trust Company of Providence.

J.P. Morgan to the Rescue

"No problem can be solved until it is reduced to some simple form. The changing of a vague difficulty into a specific, concrete form is a very essential element in thinking."

J P Morgan

The United States Treasury had injected millions of dollars into the system, and while this capital helped, it was J.P. Morgan who really came to the rescue. New York City's most famous banker, J.P. Morgan, happened to be attending a church convention in Richmond, Virginia when the chaos really hit Wall Street. On the evening of October 19 following the conference, Morgan took an evening train back to New York City. Not only was J.P. Morgan the city's wealthiest and most-connected banker, he had previous experience rescuing the Treasury back in 1893.

J.P. Morgan was the greatest banker of his era and perhaps of all time. At 70 years old and the height of his power, J.P. Morgan stepped up and did what needed to be done to prevent further crisis. Almost immediately upon his arrival in New York City, Morgan assembled a group in the red room of his famous library on Madison Avenue. His brownstone was like a revolving door of New York City bank and trust company presidents who had arrived to share and seek information in surviving the crisis. Morgan, "was suffering from a bad cold, but got through the following days and nights on heavy doses of Havana cigars".

Another source describes the scene as Morgan *"locking the nation's top bankers into the ornate library at his home for late-night confession sessions. He asked them to lay bare their balance sheets, keeping himself alert with endless Havana cigars"*. This gave J.P. Morgan and his men direct access to the books of the troubled institutions and thus gave them the ability to fairly appraise their value.

Morgan was then able to determine which financial institutions were to die and which ones would live. Morgan rallied Wall Street cronies, the great men of banking to organise a pool of money to save institutions and restore faith in the system. J.P. Morgan's determination was unfaltering—he banged his fist on the table and even locked the door not allowing bankers to leave without getting what he wanted. He was so determined that during one of the meetings he locked up a group of uncooperative New York trust company presidents overnight until they conceded. To get their cooperation, Morgan presented them with a document that spelled out what they were going to contribute to restore confidence. Encountering Morgan's eyes was described as, *"confronting the headlights of an express train bearing down on you."*

On occasion, excited and desperate men burst into Morgan's library reporting leaking assets that needed more and more money to save them from sinking. Assets and liabilities were examined as all the markets were crumbling, respected companies were going into receivership and banks were on the brink of failure as crowds of people lined up to withdraw funds. During one of the initial meetings, with Morgan leading, the group determined that the Knickerbocker was insolvent and did not intervene. In many respects this was similar to the decision of the Federal Reserve not to save Lehman in 2008. The Fed decreed Lehman's had no remaining assets upon which an advance could be made, similar to the position of Morgan and his view of the Knickerbocker Trust and yet the implication of letting it fail were perhaps not thought through well enough!

The failure of the Knickerbocker triggered runs on other more healthy trusts, which prompted Morgan to take charge of the rescue operation. The president of the Trust Company of America approached Morgan for assistance on October 22, 1907. Morgan conferred with two bankers as well as the United States Secretary of the Treasury, George B. Cortelyou. The two bankers were George F. Baker, president of First National Bank, and James Stillman of the National City Bank of New York (the ancestor of Citibank).

President Teddy Roosevelt had tremendous faith in Morgan, and Cortelyou relayed that the government was ready to deposit money into banks to help shore up their deposits. It was extraordinary that, *"the Treasury of the largest emerging economy in the world had to transfer funds to private bankers in order to prevent a financial collapse"*. In order to save the Trust Company of America, the group had pooled $3 million. The bailout was initially effective and restored a measure of confidence but it wasn't yet enough. A run on the Trust Company of America hit, Morgan worked with Stillman and Baker to liquidate the trust's assets to allow them to pay depositors. The trust made it to the close of business that day but Morgan knew it needed more funding to remain solvent the following day.

Morgan had declared this to be the place to stop the trouble; to draw the line in the financial sand. Determined to save the Trust Company of America, that evening Morgan gathered presidents of the other trust companies. They were held in a meeting until they agreed to provide loans of $8.5 million to allow the Trust Company of America to open the following day. Cortelyou deposited $25 million to be parceled out as needed to various New York Banks. John D. Rockefeller, the wealthiest man in America, deposited $10 million into Stillman's National City bank, which gave the bank the deepest reserves in the city. To further instill public confidence, Rockefeller called Melville Stone, manager of the Associated Press and told him that he would pledge half of his wealth to maintain America's credit.

The Stock Market

Although the infusion of cash helped restore calm among the public, it wasn't enough for the markets. Despite ample funds, the banks of New York were reluctant to make the short-term loans necessary to facilitate daily stock trades. The lack of funding on the market caused prices on the exchange to begin to crash. On Thursday, October 24, Ransom Thomas, president of the New York Stock Exchange, exploded into Morgan's office and told him that he would have to close the exchange early. Thomas pleaded for help. Morgan knew that an early close of the exchange would be catastrophic especially given the anxiety in the city.

Morgan summoned the presidents of New York's banks. He was ready to play hardball again. The bankers started to arrive at 2 p.m. and were informed that, *"as many as 50 stock exchange houses would fail unless $25 million was raised in 10 minutes"*. By 2:16 p.m.. $23.6 million was pledged and by 2:30 p.m. the money reached the exchange in time to finish the day's trading. Pandemonium broke out on the exchange. Morgan heard a thunderous noise from his office across the street—it was the members of the NYSE giving him a standing ovation. By market close, $19 million had been loaned out. Yet another disaster was averted. That night when Morgan, who usually eschewed the press, left his offices, he stated to the press, *"If people will keep their money in the banks, everything will be all right."*

The following day, on Friday, panic on the exchange returned. This time Morgan was only able to get $9.7 million out of the bank presidents. Things were getting dire and Morgan decided that the $9.7 million to keep the market afloat could not be used for margin sales. The markets narrowly made it to the closing bell with a great big sigh of relief. The weekend, however, didn't begin for many of the financial district's participants.

Morgan had obviously done some serious tapping of resources. The city's financial leaders would not be able to pool money indefinitely. The US Treasury was even low on funds. Meetings resumed Friday evening after the market's narrow escape. Everyone knew that confidence needed to be restored. The bankers formed two committees for mass communication. One committee was to communicate with the press, and the other to convince the clergy to calm their congregations on Sunday. The press committee was to explain the various aspects of the upcoming financial rescue package. Treasury Secretary Cortelyou returned to Washington to spread the word that the worst on Wall Street had already passed.

Once again, Morgan's leadership achieved some stability. The New York Clearing House issued $100 million in loan certificates to be traded between banks to settle balances. This allowed the banks to retain cash reserves for depositors. The reassurance through the clergy and the newspapers was successful. The combination of bank balance sheets flushed with cash and trusted words was enough to return a sense of order in New York on Monday.

Morgan Hailed as Saviour

Granted, not everyone hailed Morgan as a Saviour, but the overwhelming majority was on his side. Populist politicians claimed that Morgan had done all this only for personal gain. However, even President Teddy Roosevelt, who previously considered Morgan and his ilk malefactors of great wealth, was in awe of what Morgan had accomplished.

The critics were few and far between especially when compared to the mass support Morgan held. Morgan was, *"hailed as the saviour of the banking system, the stock exchange, and even New York City"*. Morgan was such an icon that when he, "rode down to Wall Street in his Brougham," according to one biographer, people shouted: "There goes the Old Man. There goes the Big Chief." He accomplished the unthinkable. J.P. Morgan is credited with single-handedly staving off *"a potential run on U.S. banks—by forcing rivals to come together to save their own."*

When J.P. Morgan died on March 31, 1913 his estate was worth $80 million. In today's terms, that would equate to about $1.2 billion. Compared to his peers, especially Rockefeller, Morgan's estate was not large. Rockefeller even commented, *"And to think he wasn't even a rich man."* J.P. Morgan's power did not lie in the millions he had, it lay in the billions he controlled.

Comparing 1907 and Today

There are striking similarities between the Panic of 1907 and the recent credit crisis. The period before the 1907 panic saw remarkable growth and speculation just as the period before the recent credit crisis in the United States did. It was John Piermont Morgan, the man, who was credited with saving the economy in 1907. Interestingly enough his name has also been recently linked to the bailout of a teetering financial institution. In March of 2008, J.P. Morgan, now J.P. Morgan

Chase & Co. bailed out the near-collapsing Bear Stearns and then later swallowed whole the troubled Washington Mutual Bank.

The scope of J.P. Morgan's individual contribution to the economic crises in 1907 has yet to be matched. He has been credited with, *"single-handedly staving off a potential run on U.S. Banks"* and being *"more effective in his day than the combination of Treasury Secretary Henry Paulson and Federal Reserve Chairman Ben Bernanke have been in ours."* However, perhaps times were different then.

Just like the desperate late night meetings in J.P. Morgan's library, the recent crisis produced dead-tired appearances of the important men of money. This time around it was Treasury Secretary Henry Paulson and Ben Bernanke of the Federal Reserve. There were also dramatic scenes in New York boardrooms and the draining of assets on Wall Street. However, as much as that echoed 1907, there are significant differences as well.

One key difference was that when the presidents of banks and trusts entered J.P. Morgan's library and laid their balance sheets on the table, it was clear. Everyone knew the details of each respective bank. Morgan was able to fairly appraise the value of the troubled financial institutions. Things have changed since then. Today's financial instruments are, ***"so complex that banks are still trying to unravel the different pieces of mortgage-related securities"*** and ***"despite mandated regulatory reporting, it is difficult, if not impossible, for financial decision-makers to know with clarity what is going on.".***

With all of our sophistication, we have managed to make things nearly too difficult to decipher. Now, there are literally hundreds of categories of debt available on a single trading screen. Back then, traders' technology consisted of a pencil and scrap paper. The entire system was fairly simple compared with the masses of derivatives and packaged mortgage equities available today. History tends to repeat itself. The Panic of 1907 was triggered by the unwillingness of some New York banks to make loans. That unwillingness spread across the country. Stock investors were anxious over declining markets. Bank to bank lending ceased. The economy was in a recession. All of that was in reference to 1907, but surely, it sounds alarmingly familiar?

According to the Wall Street Journal, it seems as though we have also forgotten a basic financial concept well known to J.P. Morgan. Morgan, *"who would have recalled the panics of 1837, 1873 and 1897"* knew that *"until prices are established, credit panics will not end and financial firms will remain frozen."* We seemed to have missed the lesson from these previous crises that, *"the sooner new valuations are set for bank assets and liabilities, the sooner recovery begins."*

One of the key holdups in getting past the recent credit crises is the continual unknown value on the remaining mortgage-backed securities. Things were much simpler back in 1907. Morgan was able to determine accurate values by going around the room and evaluating balance sheets. Price discovery nowadays is much more involved. Specifically with the bad debt, auctions need to be held to allow the market to find a new norm. According to the *Wall Street Journal*, *"Getting our arms around the scope of the bad debt would define the capital needs for banks, and there would be prices set that potential private-sector buyers of the debt could consider."*

From the time of cigar smoke in J.P. Morgan's library to today's complex financial derivatives, things have become much more complex. The difficulty in determining the value of assets suggests the need for increased disclosure. This transparency is the goal of regulators. The idea is that with disclosure we have more efficient markets and fewer surprises. What we have seen recently are incorrectly priced financial instruments with no disclosure requirements. In addition to complexity and disclosure, there is also the difference of quantity. The amounts back then were small in comparison to those being bandied about these days: *"Back then, perhaps for the last time, Wall Street could take care of its own panics. Today, only governments have the resources, and it is not even certain that Bernanke and Paulson can pull it off."*

Conclusion

The Panic of 1907 led to important reforms including the formation of the Federal Reserve. Only time will tell what new reforms will come about from the recent financial crises in the United States and how we will get out of this mess. Perhaps one day, we will learn from history and avoid these painful, gut-wrenching crises. It seems, though, that we have yet to fully do so.

Certainly, the general conditions in each of these periods shared striking similarities. Both were preceded by periods of extraordinary economic expansion, and much of this was fed not by growth with a solid foundation but by speculative fervor. That growth, as it inevitably does, became a bubble that was bound to burst; when it did so, panic ensued, markets crashed, and economic regression was the result. In both cases, the resulting market conditions caused credit to tighten significantly. In the earlier case, however, there was no Federal Reserve to step in as the lender of last resort, as there is today.

Of course, the Federal Reserve has since had a long history of joining hands with Wall Street in order to orchestrate such periodic bailouts. Today, this is as often as not seen as capitalism for the rich but socialism for the poor, as the taxpayers end up shouldering the burden, financing the rescue through increased debt and taxes, while the wealthy elite keep the profits from speculation and excess. It is likely that there is some truth to this observation, and elitism certainly characterises much of this.

However, at the same time as one lays such blame, we must consider the repercussions of taking no action in such crises. Capitalism and the workings of the free market, if left to their own devices, might punish that excess even more severely. The threats to the larger economy have, historically, been seen to be worth even the stiff penalties that we are now paying, and will surely be paying well into the future. It seems, then, that there is no right answer and we must continue to learn from our mistakes before we find it.

Despite the close similarities, it must be noted that sharp differences also exist as well. The sheer scope and scale of today's economic activity and the vast number of new, innovative financial products makes it difficult to compare with even a decade ago, let alone a 100 years. Of course, as mentioned above, there was no Federal Reserve to step in, marshal the economic forces at play, and guarantee the recovery process.

What is clear, however, and perhaps most extraordinary, is the simple fact that J.P. Morgan was able to do so much on his own. Whether through reputation or financial power, he was single-handedly able to bring together all the disparate actors on the economic stage and coordinate an effective response. He also had the knowledge and foresight to act when it was necessary, where others, even at the national level, did not. It is remarkable that one man could have been so influential.

Perhaps there is no one factor that distinguishes Morgan from others, either in his time or since, but it is certainly the case that the combination of all his personal characteristics enabled him to achieve not just success in his own businesses but also to have so much influence beyond them. We would do well to learn from his many examples, and perhaps sooner rather than later we will realise the answers to the questions raised in this chapter that still plague us to this day. To those who feel the United States will never recover its position after the Credit Crunch 2008 it is worth recalling another of J P Morgan's famous sayings:—*"Remember, my son, that any man who is a bear on the future of this country will go broke."*

From looking at an ancient banking power that has survived the last one hundred years we look to an ancient superpower that has risen, then fallen and now risen once more to take its place upon the world stage. We look at the power and wealth of China.

Chapter 13

April 2008—A Bull in a China Shop!

"Rise and fall of a nation rests with every one of its citizens."

Old Chinese Saying

Date—April 17, 2008—Xinhua News Agency—Exhibiting at China's largest trade fair may not be a painkiller for tens of thousands of Chinese exporters who have felt a pinch under the spell of the US credit crisis.

"Impatience never commanded success."

Edwin H. Chapin

If the whole world is in debt where has all the money gone?

China; In his seminal book, ***The End of History and The Last Man***, Francis Fukuyama argued that the collapse of communism and the dissolution of the Soviet bloc on the one hand, and the demise of the Apartheid system in South Africa on the other, signaled the triumph of the liberal-democratic mode of governance.

A corollary victory was also won for the capitalist economic system; liberal democracy and capitalism, Fukuyama argued, were interrelated and self-reinforcing. Globalisation and the progressive march of science and technology, furthermore, were seen in a positive light precisely because of their demonstrated effects on bringing about the "utopia" that was within reach for the world—that is, the global entrenchment of the capitalist-backed, liberal-democratic state.

However, China presents a conundrum for this sweeping conclusion. China has continued to "buck the odds" when it comes to the liberalisation that generally accompanies industrialisation and modernisation. What's more, that liberalisation has historically been considered necessary for the type of economic growth and modernisation that China has undergone, especially in the past decade. China is one of the five remaining "official" communist regimes in today's world—three more have communist parties in power but allow multiple parties—but it has clearly navigated its own course in order to maintain this political alignment.

Despite the breakup of the Soviet Union, the dissolution of the Warsaw Pact, and the end of the Cold War, China continued along its communist path. In part due to these events, the early 1990's saw a significant amount of attention paid to "Third World" or Less Developed Countries (LDCs) and their path to economic development. As such, it was argued that this type of model was more useful in describing and understanding economics in China than the "communist party-state" model. An examination of the two models and their applicability to the Chinese experience aids in the resolution of this dilemma.

In this chapter, we will explore how China has developed since World War II. In particular, we will delve into the unique ways that the Chinese Communist Party steered a "middle course" between economic modernisation and political liberalism. As we shall see, these are mutually reinforcing and thus cannot be divorced from each other when understanding how China has reached its present place in the global financial order; *as creditor to the world*.

Just as important, though, we will discuss what China's economic development really *means*: more than just an economic powerhouse, China has vaulted to a priority spot in today's world. In many respects—economic, financial and military—it has reached the critical mass needed to call it a *superpower*, and now plays a key role as informal *"banker"* for much of the rest of the world. How China emerges from the credit crisis will be extraordinarily important going forward, so we shall explore what China's present position means for the future and how it is likely to impact the global financial order in years to come.

From Grassroots to Financial Giant

"Politics is war without bloodshed while war is politics with bloodshed".

Mao Tse-Tung

In 1949, the People's Republic of China was created. This came with the seizure of power by the Chinese Communist Party (CCP) after the defeat of the nationalist Kuomintang. With this came the creation of a new Chinese state, initially modeled along what is known as the communist party-state. The chief characteristic of this model is the constitutionally provided "leading role in government and society" for the Communist Party. China's population of 1.3 billion makes it the largest country in the world. In 1998, it had a GDP estimated at $964 billion, but with growth rates topping 8 percent since then, it has grown nearly five-fold since that time. **It now stands at approximately $4.4 trillion!**

Since 1979, China has been engaged in a continuous effort to reform its economy, by adopting a pragmatic perspective on many political and socioeconomic problems, and reducing the role of ideology in economic policy. This theme has been enforced by the broad political and economic policies promulgated by the Chinese political elite. Much of this is in contrast to the Maoist policies followed until his death in 1976, which provided *"an opportunity for a change in both leadership and the economic development strategy."*

Deng Xiaoping, as supreme leader in China, focused on agricultural reform, opened the Chinese economy to foreign trade and investment and instituted market policies in the urban-industrial sector. Deng's policies have been described as the process of building a *"socialist economy with Chinese characteristics"* and while they were far from complete at the time of his death in 1997, they were able to produce average annual growth rates of 9.8%. In fact, 2008 was the slowest growth that the country has seen in nearly a decade; at 9%, it seems that the credit crisis has only slightly dampened China's output.

Deng Xiaoping called on localities *"to take risks to speed economic development"*, which had the effect of spurring economic growth in the Chinese countryside through the creation of numerous "town and village enterprises," or TVEs. Indeed, rapid economic growth in the Deng era was largely spearheaded by their creation. These rural industries accounted for 45% of China's industrial output by 1995, and in line with the main platform of the Jiang Zemin-Zhu Rongji administration—rapid economic growth—they were encouraged until approximately 2003, when the process of privatisation began. While this gradual process is still underway, it appears that it has resulted in even greater productivity.

The state supported the goal of rapid industrialisation primarily through institutional arrangements, such as the decentralisation of the political economy, to stir up local initiatives and through the creation of growth-oriented and consumerist social norms. Moreover, contribution to rapid economic growth is the lens through which the state defined authority relations: greater authority was vested in those organisations that supported this primary goal. However, it is important to note that this has not always represented a policy of sustainable development. At least until 1992, China continued to regard itself as a developing nation and thus gave explicit priority to economic development; this characterisation meant that other factors such as environmental protection were viewed as economic rather than social issues, and as such would come at the expense of developmental needs.

> *"Dream in a pragmatic way"*
>
> **Aldous Huxley**

The Party initially asserted its control over the economy and industry through the use of *nomenclature* lists of important positions and people qualified to fill them. This reflects the principle of *"democratic centralism,"* and facilitated the Party's continued control over all aspects of the modernisation process. The command economy that is characteristic of the communist party-state initially extended into all aspects of economic life, from central planning of industry and production to control over wages, prices, the press and even leisure activities.

Discrepancies between the contemporary Chinese state and the traditional communist party-state became evident when the CCP let slip its formal monopoly on power. In 1982, Article 2 of the Constitution, which provided this monopoly, was removed. It thus became increasingly difficult to characterise the Chinese economy as simply a command structure. Following the death of Mao Zedong, the Chinese leadership under Deng Xiaoping introduced several reforms into the economy. These were guided by three very non-Marxist principles:

- *private property can play a useful role in a socialist economy*

- *market forces should be used to allocate goods and services and determine prices*

- *material incentives (the possibility of higher wages, personal profit, and the accumulation of wealth) would be the main way to increase productivity and efficiency*

The implications of these reforms were far-reaching, agriculture was essentially privatised which resulted in marked productivity increases, state enterprises became more market-driven and profit-oriented, and the private sector grew tremendously. The most noticeable break from the command economy of the communist party-state model is the establishment of Special Economic Zones, or SEZs. These represented a break from the self-sufficient, closed economies—somewhat the mainstay among textbook communist party-states—and were a clear move towards modernisation and the attraction of foreign trade and investment. Currently, as many as one fifth of China's immense population reside within these SEZs and this number is likely to increase.

Economics: Politics by Other Means?

"Take the ideas of the masses (scattered and unsystematic ideas) and concentrate them (through study turn them into concentrated and systematic ideas), then go to the masses and propagate and explain these ideas until the masses embrace them as their own".

Mao Tse-Tung

How, then, does China fit into the typology of the communist party-state? Politically, the CCP does not enjoy a formal, legal monopoly over the exercise of power. And economically, it does not readily parallel any other communist state or the "typical" centrally planned economy. From these one can conclude that the communist party-state is no longer an accurate description of contemporary China.

Analyses of the Chinese state thus turned to the "Third World" model of development. The first characteristic of this model is the weakness of the state. Many see that the inability of the LDCs to determine their own economic destinies has increased. This is manifested most prominently in the extent and severity of poverty within these countries, as well as their increasing vulnerability to global economic forces. The second characteristic is the "strong symbolic component" to politics within Third World states, in which these countries find it ever harder to close the economic gap between themselves and the advanced industrialised nations.

The third characteristic is that political life is severely restricted. There may be single party or military dominance, and there is little or no freedom to criticise the government or organise opposition to it. Finally, the Third World is characterised by its colonial history. European or North American nations controlled by use of imperial military force most nations in Asia, Africa and Latin America, and those countries current politics and institutions are often reflective of this influence.

The Chinese economy can, at the outset, be explained and understood from this Third World context. The Chinese state has exhibited considerable weakness. This is evidenced by the size and strength of the democracy movement in the late 1970's and 1980's, as well as the state's inability to successfully implement its socialist economic policies. Very much related to this have been the state of China's economic development and the extent of its poverty throughout much of its history. China has a relatively high population growth rate; a staggeringly large population; low GNP per capita of just over $3100; a high proportion of illiterate people, relative to the other industrialised nations; and a relatively low percentage of its geography in the urban sector.

This list is by no means exhaustive, but is indicative of China's historical economic position as an LDC. This is also indicative of the symbolic content of Chinese politics. Chinese political leaders were essentially forced to enact the aforementioned reforms, in order to close this economic gap. Furthermore, the CCP, while not maintaining a formal monopoly on power, does have an informal one. Chinese leaders based this on the continued endorsements of the cardinal principles that called for continued party dominance.

> *"Every good communist should know that political power grows out of the barrel of a gun."*
>
> **Mao Tse-Tung**

Finally, China has been influenced quite strongly by colonial powers, most notably with its defeat by Britain in the Opium War, the subsequent opening of China to missionaries and merchants, and the principle of extra-territoriality. This influence has remained evident in Chinese foreign policy, although it somewhat decreased with the creation of the SEZs in recent decades.

Despite the apparent match between the Chinese state today and the Third World model, two key problems still face examination. The first of these is the prevalence of factors common to both the communist party-state model and the Third World model. The second concerns factors in the Chinese experience that do not fit *either* model, but are nonetheless important. Both share a strong symbolic component to politics; whether communist or LDC, these regimes are forced to operate within a global capitalist system, which constrains and limits their scope of available actions. The communist states, with their internal socialist economies, are still forced to operate externally within a global capitalist economy. LDCs, with their resources often concentrated on primary commodities or natural resources, remain dependent upon the industrialised nations for both exports and imports.

Thus, both models find it increasingly difficult to bridge the gap that separates them from the industrialised world. Furthermore, a severely restricted political life and the personalisation of politics around a single leader are common to both models. These factors, as evidenced earlier, combine to form a weak state regardless of which model one chooses. Finally, both communist party-states and LDCs have continually resorted to repression as a means of maintaining law, order, and the status quo.

The second key problem concerns factors in the Chinese experience that fit *neither* model. The first of these is the existence of patron-client relationships. These continue to survive in the LDCs and are also a key ingredient in the traditional model of the communist party-state, taking the "founding state" of Russia as an example. However, these do not exist to the same extent in the Chinese culture. Moreover, there is continued acceptance, based on Confucian principles, of one's place in the social hierarchy. Also, there seems to be no major ethnic or religious fragmentation in China, which has figured in the political struggles in the former Soviet Union as well as in many LDCs today. The Chinese population is relatively homogeneous with more than ninety percent being ethnically Chinese. The remainder has tended not to be politically significant. Finally, along similar lines, is the strong sense of national identity. There is strong agreement that *"a China"* should exist as well as the existence of some sense of national superiority. The latter may be a common factor among many nations around the world, but there is often strong disagreement about the former.

In these respects China has been somewhat of an enigma. It may be argued that the communist party-state is useful in explaining politics in China, but only to a limited degree. The CCP maintains the traditional party structure, and the Chinese state maintains its autonomy in economic policy. In most respects, China can be described as a communist party-state, except with respect to the Special Economic Zones and the privatisation that is increasingly prevalent. But China also fits the pattern established by the Third World model. It has been historically poor, its state is weak and losing *"social"* legitimacy and its politics are fluid to the same extent found within many LDCs.

So, then, how can this seemingly "rogue" nation be categorised? The fact remains that, despite the many similarities among political attributes in these two models, China *is* a communist state; it has maintained its traditional party structure, including its bureaucracy full of hard-liners.

The Chinese leadership, despite its fluidity and personalised politics, remains willing to use repression to maintain its authoritarian control. There is also no way of telling, based on the Soviet experience at least, when such a regime will unravel, or when the potential crises within it can no longer be repressed.

Why did modest attempts to decentralise the centrally administered Soviet system lead to its collapse, while in China more far-reaching decentralisation left central political and economic hierarchies relatively intact?

On the one hand, organisational reforms in the Soviet Union radically weakened authority links within Soviet hierarchies and accelerated the process of disintegration. Superficially similar reforms in China left fundamental authority linkages intact. It is important to note that bureaucracies in command economies generally faced soft budget constraints: the state covered their operating losses. In practice, this meant that principals were neither profit maximising nor budget balancing. The consequence of this abrogation of managerial discipline is the nullification of almost all downside risk for principals. To put it differently, managers had little incentive to make sure targets were met or to uncover cheating when they weren't.

What occurred in the Soviet Union when reforms were introduced can be likened to events surrounding a bank run. The critical element here is the ***perception*** that the principal can no longer control his resources. This perception could result from several developments, but for the most part, we consider situations in which agents begin to exercise greater autonomy from principals. This can result from less rigorous monitoring, or more flexible performance targets. In both the Soviet Union and China, fiscal reforms that granted local officials limited discretionary control over their budgets had this initial goal. In other words, the motivation for reform is the presumption that the plan has been too restrictive. The earlier problem of hidden information had never been adequately resolved so additional resources were diverted from the plan and an accumulated "safety margin" could give agents the capacity to resist further exercise of authority from the center. Once all parties recognise this, a process of disintegration is unleashed.

In the postwar Soviet case the rare challenges to the authority of the leadership were met quickly with a coercive reply. In the post-Stalin era, however, such shows of force were seen as inappropriate. Corruption by officials was rampant under Brezhnev, and the anticorruption drives of Andropov and Gorbachev were limited in scope. Thus, when local officials began blatantly appropriating the assets of state organisations, few alternatives other than dismissal were available. Even dismissal became an empty threat when the assets removed from these organisations were sufficient to underwrite more lucrative future employment.

China, on the other hand, represents a case of organisational survival in the midst of reforms, rather than disintegration. Beginning in 1979, reforms devolved property rights over many industrial assets and regional fiscal resources from central leaders to lower-level officials. As in the Soviet Union, these reforms opened the door at lower levels of the political and economic hierarchies to defy authority and break hierarchical controls. These controls may have strained, but in contrast to the Soviet Union, in China they have not snapped.

In the early 1980's economic reforms in China transferred significant autonomy to local and regional governments in two ways. First, in a process like spontaneous privatisation, local authorities were granted extensive property rights over economic enterprises under their jurisdiction, triggering an explosion of so-called town and village enterprises. Second, in a shift much like the Soviet fiscal decentralisation, local regions were entitled to keep a significant share of the taxes on regionally "owned" enterprises, passing only a negotiated percentage on to the central government. In many regions local officials were rapidly transformed into rich industrialists, who operated with great independence from those above them in the hierarchy.

By the late 1980's, though, the economy in several regions was in danger of severely overheating. Officials at the center attempted to slow economic growth in precisely those regions whose economic success had made them most independent from Beijing. However, control over regional officials was not administered perfectly and remained incomplete. Certain regions successfully resisted the imposition of a unified tax code and evaded attempts to limit investment levels in overheated regions.

The striking question is, of course, how officials in Beijing managed to maintain any measure of control over thriving local economies when reforms gave local officials access to resources not directly administered by the center. In Russia, external resource flows acquired by those in economic, state and political hierarchies made it possible for them to defy hierarchical authority—a situation that triggered structural disintegration. *In China, although local officials had some success in resisting the intervention of the center, their resistance never triggered the sort of bank run that would render impossible any assertion of authority by leaders in Beijing.*

Chinese reforms *clarified* rather than obscured property rights, and created incentives that addressed rather than exacerbated problems of hidden action and information. The result of economic reforms, which depended critically on empowering regional rural officials as engines of economic growth, was a virtual partnership between enterprise management and local government. This had been described as "local state corporatism," in that it represented a merger of state and economy in which fiscal reform assigned local government property rights over increased income. Moreover, this did not lead to disintegration because local officials profited from reform by collecting higher levels of taxes and by direct profit sharing in quasi-public rural enterprises. Local officials were thus not driven to move assets out of the state sector as they did in the Soviet Union, but faced powerful incentives to keep their privileged position and accept whatever discipline was necessary to retain it.

As a consequence of its economic reforms, China became increasingly open to influence from the private sector. Standardisation, for example, is encouraged to protect people's health and safety, the rights of consumers and the environment, and to promote economic and technological cooperation with foreign entities and foreign trade. What makes China different, however, is that it has almost invariably insisted that foreign investment be done directly, by building factories in SEZs, for example.

At the same time, China has ensured that its economy is geared largely towards exports. The world's largest retailer, Wal-Mart Stores of Arkansas, sources 70% of its products from China, which accounts for $18 billion in sales per year. In fact, the SEZs were specifically designed to encourage China's export orientation. From 1987 on, the number of ports conducting foreign trade was dramatically increased, and tax exemptions were instituted for manufacturers engaging in foreign trade. By 1993, responsibility for foreign trade was devolved to the local governments within the SEZs, giving them freedom to act according to the market, rather than in accordance with the centrally planned economy. Competition and free trade were also allowed, and subsidies were reduced or removed in order to enforce *"market"* discipline.

1994 marked a turning point for China, as it prepared to enter the World Trade Organisation. Liberalisation and the reform of export industries was accelerated. China's free market orientation was solidified and in 2001 the country joined the WTO. Foreign trade had to be consistent with international norms, which meant that trade and competition could potential weaken or bankrupt domestic industries. However, the opposite has proven to be the case, as China has been able to marshal its comparative advantage in traditional labour-intensive production and low-to-middle technology, mechanical and electrical manufacturing. Its ability to provide low cost goods to international markets has in turn driven its imports of high technology and capital-intensive manufacturing, and has continued to feed back upon itself in a self-reinforcing cycle.

Growing Pains

> *"Be resolute, fear no sacrifice, and surmount every difficulty to win victory."*
>
> **Mao Tse-Tung**

China's industrialisation has not been without issue, of course. Crucial to this discussion is the underlying trend in energy consumption. China's rapid economic growth will cause energy consumption to increase exponentially, due to the rapid pace of industrialisation on the one hand and increases in living standards on the other. Even though China's energy consumption per capita is still by all accounts less than one-fifth that of OECD countries, its population growth and overall demography will ensure sustained pressure on energy demand going forward.

It is expected that fossil fuel production will underpin this demand, in large part due to the relatively undeveloped nature of other energy sources. Natural gas production, for example, was supplanted by petroleum production, despite its relative abundance. Despite China's tremendous resources in terms of hydroelectric power, its capacity has remained relatively undeveloped as well, due to high construction costs and its uneven distribution across the country. Overall, these and other energy sources, including nuclear power and biomass energy, represented less than 10 percent of the total energy consumption in 1995.

Since 1993, China has been a net importer of oil; China's energy planners have recognised that China cannot remain isolated from the global oil markets, and oil security is now among their top concerns. Many analysts, moreover, see improved economic efficiency as the key to improving China's economy. In line with this, Beijing has targeted improvements in efficiency and competitiveness of state companies, and has moved to partially privatise them by offering shares to public and private investors, both domestic and international.

Sustainability in terms of economic development represents a clear challenge for China, in many respects. Clean coal techniques are seen as the best ways of reconciling China's high reliance on coal with the need for environmental protection, but the short-term prospects of this are limited. Given the country's huge hydropower potential, China has embarked upon massive construction programs, such as the flagship Three Gorges Dam across the Yangtze, but doubts surround its long-term economic and environmental viability.

In the US, the view has long been held that China has manipulated its currency in order to keep the price of its exports artificially low. China has maintained a trade surplus with the US since the mid

1980's, exporting more than it imports, and the imbalance has grown exponentially in recent years. It has ballooned to record proportions, and in the midst of the credit crisis in 2008 it reached $268 billion. Critics and policymakers in the US charge that China has manipulated the Yuan on the open market:

"Today, the People's Bank of China (PBOC) devalues its currency by purchasing U.S. Treasury securities. In doing so, it must first convert yuan to dollars, thereby releasing more Chinese currency into circulation, devaluing it and increasing inflation in the process. The PBOC "sterilises" the purchase by simultaneously selling yuan-denominated PBOC bonds, which remove yuan from circulation, negating the inflationary effect of the intervention."

While this has increasingly strained relations between the two countries as it has grown, it is not without costs to China. It has not been fully effective, and in part due to the country's rapid economic growth, inflation has remained high at over 8% in 2008, easily surpassing the government's target rate of just under 5%:

"Due to the immense scope of China's past intervention, the amount of PBOC bonds outstanding is now equal to more than half of the total amount of yuan in circulation. Demand for PBOC bonds is low, which means interest rates are rising and relatively high, about 5.31 percent currently, compared with US short-term interest rates near 0 percent. The cost to the PBOC of receiving little or no interest on the US bonds it owns and paying 5 percent interest on its own bonds is more than $4 billion a month, according to estimates by Goldman Sachs. China's foreign currency holdings, which total more than $2 trillion, are growing faster than the Chinese economy. In coming years, these realities will make intervention and sterilisation untenable."

Of course, we know from previous discussions that when a nation pegs its currency to that of another or to an underlying commodity such as gold, it effectively binds its hands in terms of its ability to use monetary policy to manage the economy. China has been able to finance this internally, but it is not clear how long it will be able to continue to do so. Inflation, the pervasive destroyer of wealth, will eventually take its toll, and China will be forced to revalue its currency accordingly.

Industrialisation and an export-oriented economy are not, however, necessarily evident of a "spillover" to the larger economy. Chinese capital markets are still nascent and relatively undeveloped. As a result, they do not display the depth of investment that other industrialised nations do; retail investors dominate domestic trading, with institutional players being relatively absent. Stock markets such as the Shanghai exchange are thus not necessarily reflective of the "smart money" at play in the overall economy. Stock prices have climbed astronomically in the past three years, in part due to easy credit, lending by state-owned banks, foreign investor interest; however, because of the drought in exports as a result of the credit crisis, many firms have taken to investing these low-cost loans in the stock market.

Growth-oriented economic policies such as these, in the absence of stricter securities regulation, may be creating a national asset bubble. State-owned banks have lowered lending rates in order to encourage corporate growth, *but in many cases these loans have been diverted to the purchase of stocks and real estate.* A dangerous state of affairs that the western world now knows so well!

It seems to be the case that China's continued domestic growth in the face of the wider global credit crisis has been mostly attributable to the easy lending policies, rather than concrete asset growth. At present, it seems that the Chinese authorities are torn between stoking growth in the face of worldwide recession and a limited capacity to alter the course of the economy, as a result of their limited monetary policy tools.

There is evidence that these policies may result in the same type of lending bubble as we have seen in other countries, particularly the US. Although the root causes are different, the fact remains that, were a serious shock to disrupt further economic growth, banks could have significant difficulty calling in loans that have been pledged to securities that have substantially fallen in value. Due to the weak regulatory framework that now exists for domestic banking and securities, China may experience drastically negative consequences for its capital markets in the months and years to come:

"The recent sell-off in the Chinese stock market—down 25 percent in the past four months—could also hobble banks because a big chunk of their business comes from equity-related products. A fair amount of corporate lending found its way into the stock markets, and that money might have evaporated already. Chinese banks have, though, raised billions of dollars from capital markets, and this would help them absorb any credit losses. But the question remains: What level of asset quality shock could Chinese banks absorb? 'Chinese banks are largely untested,' said Alex Boggis, director at Aberdeen International Fund Managers. 'They do not have much experience handling the stress and strains associated with open markets. That is why we do not like to own them.'"

Even though Chinese banks have largely avoided any subprime related losses, it appears that the Chinese economy itself is still at risk for principally the same reasons. This dynamic could be compounded by a prolonged downturn, or a delayed recovery, in China's crucial export markets. Economist Nouriel Roubini has observed that there is an increasing probability of such an occurrence:

'If U.S. consumers consume less, then for the global economy to grow at its potential rate, other countries that are saving too much will have to save less and consume more,' he said. 'My concern is that for a number of reasons . . . (it is unlikely that) countries like China, other emerging markets in Asia, Japan, Germany in Europe, will have a significant increase in the consumption rate and a reduction in the savings rate.'"

To this point, one of the key strengths for China as a whole has been its propensity to save. This may now prove to be a weakness for the Chinese economy. Without strong foreign demand for Chinese manufactures, it is unlikely that domestic consumption can rein in the slack. Chinese consumers do not share the same propensity to spend as their Western counterparts, particularly in the US. As a result, the economy is likely to suffer indirectly from the global credit crisis, because it will be unable to reduce inventories and continue to perform at the same pace as it has until now.

From this perspective, some of the statistics about China's growth must be taken with a grain of salt. By the end of 2008, real growth in the economy had probably dropped to near zero, despite official estimates that pegged the economy's performance at 9% for the year. When the effects of monetary easing are factored in, it is likely that the economy had leveled off and it is possible that it even marginally contracted. Official predictions are that China will be the first country to emerge from the crisis, and they may yet be proven correct; at the same time, the present downturn has laid bare some of the problems that are likely to plague the economy going forward—that is, if the government does not get its reforms just right.

Conclusion

Assessing the real, long-term implications of China's economic development to date are inherently problematic. Much of the aforementioned analysis hinges upon statistics that are questionable and often incomplete. In its *China 2020* report the World Bank remained optimistic that China can meet the challenges of continued transformation and sustained rapid growth. Economic development in China, as it is elsewhere, is necessarily path-dependent: *economic growth will be highly dependent on how the political process is played out in the coming years.*

It would be fair to say that China's leadership has exhibited a virtual obsession with growth and industrialisation. While it is gradually shifting towards new means, the high material intensity of production methods, often promoted at the expense of natural resources, will certainly have future costs; they have been able to exert continued high level control over the economic development process, but this has often been to the detriment of public safety, and certainly has occurred in the absence of any measure of *"democratic"* consensus on the process.

As living standards rise and the Chinese economy becomes more highly developed, the question the Chinese will demand of their leaders will likely be *"what have you done for us lately?"* As development and consumption patterns come to resemble those exhibited elsewhere in the world, public demands may prove to be significant challenges for the political leadership; environmental disasters, for example, will only exacerbate the problem. Finally, it is important to recognise and address the security dimensions of energy and the environment, and their potential for both domestic and international conflict.

Of course, the introduction of as-yet-unexploited energies and the development of new technologies may change things altogether. Wind, geothermal and solar energy all exhibit potential for exploitation by the Chinese energy sector, but their future contributions to economic development are uncertain. China has only recently taken up the challenge of new technologies such as the hydrogen fuel cell, continuing to "simply replicate the fossil fuel energy transport pattern found in Europe, North America and North-east Asia." However, if companies such as BYD can attract Warren Buffett to become one of the largest shareholders of this rapidly expanding and innovative automotive and electronics firm, then perhaps the sky is the limit for the overall economy as well.

It is known from the Soviet experience with economic policy that institutions thought to be guiding a reform can be profoundly weakened by the very reforms they unleash. This may, in the long term, prove to be true for China as well. However, the ramifications of the various dimensions presented here are more far-reaching; indeed, they are indicative of the broader political situation in which China now finds itself. It is now facing, or soon will face, distinct challenges to its broader development policies that result from its fixation on "short term" results over long-term sustainability—in terms of economic growth, and also political power itself.

This, then, is the real question: what does China's continued growth *really mean* for the future? China has succeeded in modernising its economy and lifting itself from the realm of the developing world, although it still has some way to go until it fully joins the ranks of the industrialised nations. It has done so by realising exactly what the rest of the world was looking for: cheap goods for export, in exchange for imports of raw materials. This, of course, has proven to be a double-edge sword. Despite the apparently symbiotic relationship between China's imports and its exports to the rest of the world, the end result has been somewhat of a balance of power shift from the center to the periphery.

The result of its successful export-oriented industrialisation over the past several decades is that China now commands what is unequivocally the largest pool of investment funds the world has ever known, through the China Investment Corporation. This is a sovereign wealth fund that holds $2 trillion in foreign exchange reserves; at present, the fund holds mostly US treasury securities, some US$800 billion at last count, preferring to play the role of banker to the US. Many believe, however, that in the coming years it will seek to exert higher levels of influence through the purchase of direct investment stakes in companies, that themselves have the ability to exert political pressure on their host governments. As the largest buyer of US treasuries, the company has levered its way into the position of being able to exert great influence upon the economic policies of the US itself.

> *"A man in debt is so far a slave!"*
> **Ralph Waldo Emerson**

While nothing has yet come of this potential influence, it seems only a matter of time before the implied pressure manifests itself. The US has voiced its criticism of China's currency manipulation, but at the same time, it has not altered its policies in order to remedy this. US competitiveness is really the issue here, not China's low cost of goods or labour. As time passes, and China's influence grows ever greater, there will be little that the US—or other nations—will be able to do, beyond the realms of diplomacy at least. China's size and influence are bound to grow and calls for currency reform, for example, will likely fall on deaf ears.

One way that China may seek to exert its influence is by choosing simply not to hold US dollar-denominated securities. Rather, were it to flood the market with treasuries, it would monumentally impact the US economy and indeed, that of the rest of the world as well. Some have predicted that China may look to diversify into euro-denominated bonds in future years, as it has recently done by buying up gold reserves from the industrialised nations, *or it may continue to agitate for a new global reserve currency*.

Others counter that such a move would only hurt China's fortunes; such actions would only serve to devalue its own sovereign wealth fund's holdings. The corollary effect would be to force the price of the US dollar down, and this would put considerable upward pressure upon the Chinese Yuan as a result.

The important point to consider here, as we've noted earlier, is that sometimes economics *is politics by other means*. China has shown the world that it can succeed on its own terms, and it has charted its own path largely as a result of its policies via its latent socioeconomic potential. It has developed rapidly and now stands as the third largest economy in the world, and that gap to the top is closing fast. It seems unlikely that this trend will change in the coming years, and as it continues along this path, its relevance in the global financial order is only set to increase.

China has in fifty years moved from peripheral player in the global financial arena to one now standing on the verge of greatness. It rivals both the US and Europe in terms of financial firepower and can act quicker and more decisively than both these other monetary blocks. In the final conclusions of the book we will turn to the question of whether that rivalry can be turned into a mutually beneficial and holistic approach to the future of the world's economy and financial markets.

From the bullish rise of a global super power we return in Chapter 14 to the collapse of a bank whose very name reflected the markets forces that destroyed it . . . . *Bear Stearns!*

Chapter 14

May 2008—Bear Stearns:
It's All In The Name!

"The average man doesn't wish to be told that it is a bull or a bear market. What he desires is to be told specifically which particular stock to buy or sell. He wants to get something for nothing. He does not wish to work. He doesn't even wish to have to think."

Jesse Livermore

30th May 2008—JPMorgan Chase completes its acquisition of Bear Stearns at the renegotiated price of $10 per share.

Bear Market;—*The term Bear Market refers to a declining or poor state of the market or trading group, usually a stock market, in which consumer confidence and financial expectations are on a decline and the market continues to lose value, usually at an average loss of 15% to 20% in one or more index over a 12 month period.*

Why listen to experts when experts cannot save themselves?

There is an old saying in the stock market—you're only as good as your last deal! Like athletes who play on beyond their best so great traders and indeed great trading firms go soft and eventually collapse. Bear Stearns; A sad story of decline.

How is it possible that JP Morgan Chase could acquire its rival Bear Stearns at $10 per share? How is it possible that JP Morgan bought Bear, with 14,000 employees, for a third of the price that a much smaller Bear went public for in 1985? How is it possible that just one year prior to the sale, stock in Bear Stearns was trading at $170 per share? Even more remarkable, how is it possible that the initial price for that same deal was *five times lower*, at $2 per share?

The answers to these and other questions can be found in the complex world of mortgages, hidden within the bubble and burst of the US housing market. As previously explored, high default rates on subprime and adjustable rate mortgages led to a rapid decline in the market for these securities. Bear Stearns was perhaps the most prolific casualty of the seizure within this market, but the mortgage crisis was not the only reason that this mighty giant was brought to its knees in such a swift and punishing fashion.

The collapse of Bear Stearns on March 3, 2008 and its subsequent takeover in May of that year by JP Morgan Chase was certainly one of the most prominent examples of the mortgage debacle. Bear Stearns, known to be ahead of the trends, had an astonishing run on Wall Street, surviving the Great Depression and many subsequent stock market collapses. When a bank this big and storied crashes, we must question how deep the financial industry's woes go, and we wonder what other banks might be at risk.

Bear Stearns certainly had an impressive run and outlasted many of its competitors through the worst economic crises, including the 1929 and the 1987 stock market crashes. For the most part, the company was continually growing and acquiring. However, it was not all simple and straightforward, and no single factor accounts for it all. As we shall see, some of the firm's practices—even while innovative—were risky and routinely questioned by regulators and oversight agencies. In the end, it was questionable behaviour such as this that brought about the fall.

In this chapter, we will take a historical look at the rise and fall of Bear Stearns since its inception to May 30, 2008 when JP Morgan Chase completed its acquisition. We will also consider other banks over the same time frame which may help us better understand the scope of the current financial downfall. We will also examine the crucial role played by the United States Federal Reserve in the acquisition. In doing so, we'll shed important light on the practices of Wall Street in general, because many of these same factors remain present to this day, despite the calamitous fallout from Bear Stearns' collapse and the questionable legal framework in which they exist.

History

Bear Stearns was founded during the 'Roaring Twenties' in May 1923 by Joseph Bear, Robert Stearns and Harold Mayer. It started as an equity trading house with $500,000 in capital. Heavy demand for capital during World War I encouraged the public to enter the securities markets en masse, investing heavily in stocks. Then came the speculative boom, and people were even borrowing money to invest in stocks. The young Bear Stearns *"prospered in the frenzied optimism of those markets."* As soon as the company began trading in government securities, it soon became a leader.

> *"A phrase began to beat in my ears with a sort of heady excitement: 'There are only the pursued, the pursuing, the busy, and the tired.'"*
>
> **F. Scott Fitzgerald**

Another company that also benefited from the flooding of government securities as a result of the Liberty Loan Act of 1917 was Solomon Brothers. Also a relatively new company, Solomon profited from the lucrative government bond market but entered the equities market tentatively during the booming 1920's. While Solomon Brothers benefited less from the bull markets in stocks, it also managed to escape serious damage in the 1929 crash.

By August 1929, brokers were routinely lending more than two-thirds of the face value of the stocks they were buying to enable their investors to buy on margin. There was more than $8.5 billion out on loan, which was more than the entire amount of currency circulating in the United

States. There was such frenzy that people were even mortgaging their homes to invest more. Thousands of fraudulent companies were formed to take money from naive investors.

The prices of the stocks in the late 1920's, not unlike housing prices prior to the recent mortgage crisis, were rapidly increasing which encouraged more people to invest. Speculation fueled further increases, and again, not unlike the housing markets of late, created an economic bubble. When the bubble burst and trading fell sharply with the 1929 crash, Bear Stearns suffered setbacks but had previously accumulated sufficient capital to survive quite well. Not only did the company survive, they managed to avoid layoffs and even continued to pay bonuses. Although we are not going to discuss the Great Depression in detail, the fact that Bear Stearns survived as the market continued to tank through 1932 when stocks had lost nearly 90% of their value, is truly extraordinary.

The Great Depression followed the 1929 crash and as the country struggled to resurface, Bear Stearns entered the bond market to promote President Franklin Roosevelt's call for renewed development of the national infrastructure. Roosevelt's reform measures resulted in the country's banking system accumulating a large amount of cash because the demand for loans was very low. At the time, bonds were cheap and Bear Stearns made its first substantial profits by selling large volumes of inexpensive bonds to the cash-rich banks around the country.

Lehman Brothers also survived the crash and did so by shifting focus to venture capital with private equity capital coming from institutional investors or high net worth individuals. The focus here was—and still is—on companies in their early stages of development with great potential for growth. In the 1930's, Lehman underwrote the initial public offering for the first television manufacturer DuMont and helped fund the Radio Corporation of America—both lucrative moves that kept the company in business while the equity markets recovered.

A further company that survived the crash was Goldman Sachs. However, it felt more pain than Bear Stearns and Lehman Brothers. Goldman had been known to heavily recruit from those with MBA degrees from leading business schools—a practice still in place today. In the early 1900's Goldman Sachs was a major player in establishing the initial public offering (IPO) market. In 1906 they managed one of the largest IPOs to date, that of Sears, Roebuck and Company. They then launched Goldman Sachs Trading in 1928, which was a closed-end fund with similar characteristics to that of a Ponzi scheme. The fund failed miserably with the crash of 1929 hurting the firm's reputation for years to come. In order to weather the failed equities markets, the company shifted their focus away from trading and toward investment banking. Goldman Sachs's tarnished reputation was repaired over time.

Charles Merrill and Edmund Lynch, who had formed Merrill, Lynch & Company in 1915, initially became well known in financial circles for financing the newly emerging chain store industry. Merrill was the founder of Safeway Stores and his company underwrote the IPO. Throughout the 1920's, Merrill Lynch reaped the benefits of the prolonged economic boom. However, Merrill became uneasy about the frantic pace of investment and in anticipation of the crash, streamlined the company's operations and adopted a low-risk investment approach. Despite Merrill's foresight, the company decided to sell the firm's retail business and like the other survivors, shifted focus to investment banking.

Building up

> *"You get recessions, you have stock market declines. If you don't understand that's going to happen, then you're not ready, you won't do well in the markets."*
>
> **Peter Lynch**

By 1933, Bear Stearns had grown from its original seven employees to 75 and after buying out the Chicago based firm Stein, Brennan, opened its first regional office in Chicago. By now, the firm had accumulated a capital base of $800,000. In 1933, Bear Stearns hired Salim L. "Cy" Lewis, a former runner for Salomon Brothers to direct a new institutional bond-trading department. Lewis went from partner in 1938, to managing partner in the 1950's, then became Chairman and built Bear Stearns into a large influential firm. With legendary character, outspokenness and drive, Lewis gave Bear Stearns the swagger and style that made it stand out on Wall Street for decades to come.

Bear Stearns continued to grow, opening an international department in 1948 and its first international office in Amsterdam in 1955. From there, and with their international business prospering, the firm opened offices in Geneva, Paris, London, Hong Kong and Tokyo. They also expanded their retail business operations in the 1960's, once again ahead of the trend. Bear Stearns opened an office in San Francisco in 1965 and offices in Los Angeles, Dallas, Atlanta and Boston between 1969 and 1973. This retail business was very successful at attracting and managing accounts for wealthy clients thus laying the foundation for successful margin operations in the future.

In 1975 Bear Stearns took a great risk by investing $10 million in New York City securities. At the time, the city was nearly bankrupt. The firm came close to losing millions of dollars but eventually profited greatly. Following the death of Cy Lewis in 1978, Alan "Ace" Greenberg became Chairman of Bear Stearns. Greenberg joined Bear Stearns in 1949 and moved rapidly up through the company from a clerk to running a risk arbitrage desk and by 1957 trading for the firm. By 1978, Greenberg had earned the reputation of being one of the most aggressive traders on Wall Street. Greenberg was just as successful, perhaps more so than his predecessor. When Greenberg became Chairman in 1978 the firm's total capital was $46 million. By the time the firm went public in 1985, its total capital was $517 million and by 1989 it was $1.4 billion.

> *"Dancing on the edge is the only place to be."*
> **Trisha Brown**

It was Bear Stearns's willingness to take risk that allowed it to venture into corporate takeovers to the extent of being described as a breeding ground for corporate takeover attempts. In 1986 Bear Stearns had a creative and innovative option agreement essentially allowing clients to buy stock under the Bear Stearns name, which facilitated corporate takeovers. The Justice Department and the SEC put an end to this by filing lawsuits against Bear Stearns' clients.

In 1985, Greenberg and Bear Stearns' executive committee wanted to increase the company's ability to raise capital to finance larger trades. They achieved this by making a public stock offering in October of that same year. Bear Stearns also formed a holding company to facilitate the raising of capital, and through this holding company Bear Stearns Securities Corp, they later offered global clearing services to broker dealers, prime broker clients and other professional traders including securities lending. Following the public offering, Bear Stearns reorganised from a brokerage house to a full-service firm serving corporations, institutions, governments and individuals. Bear Stearns's businesses had developed to included corporate finance, mergers and acquisitions, institutional equities, fixed income sales & risk management, trading and research, private client services, derivatives, foreign exchange and futures sales and trading, asset management and custody services.

The Crash of 1987

The 1987 crash hit Bear Stearns hard and numerous positions at the company were eliminated. However, this streamlining actually helped the company when the economy picked up again. The general attitude of the company following the crash is evidenced in a statement made by Alan Greenberg, CEO of Bear Stearns on October 22, 1987. In response to questions about the crash, Greenberg said, *"Stocks fluctuate, next question."*

Similar to Bear Stearns, Merrill Lynch also grew but hit more than a few bumps in the 1980's. For example, scandal broke out in 1986 when one of their brokers was arrested by the FBI for mail fraud. This case "typified for many the money fever of pre-crash Wall Street." Then, in April of 1987 Merrill Lynch was caught speculating on mortgage-backed securities and lost more than any other company in one day in the history of Wall Street. This speculation lost them $377 million. Following the crash later that year, Merrill Lynch was forced to freeze salaries, cut bonuses, dismiss employees and slash commission payouts. However, Merrill Lynch rebounded quickly with profits reaching a record high of $463 million and the retail giant continued to grow throughout the rest of the decade.

During the 1980's Goldman Sachs diversified its business by absorbing the commodities-trading firm, J. Aron & Company, which dealt mainly in precious metals, coffee and foreign exchange. This gave them a strong footing in South American markets, and this proved to be an area of strong growth later on. Goldman also took over the London-based merchant bank First Dallas, Ltd. in 1982. The beginning of 1984 marked yet another craze on Wall Street. Investment companies began engineering leveraged buyouts (LBOs) of entire firms. The practice could be very lucrative but at the same time extraordinarily risky. Goldman Sachs chose to focus on transaction work rather than partaking in the higher-risk LBOs. The 1987 crash proved to be a harsh lesson for Goldman, as transaction profitability took a dive. Many clients left the company in favour of other, more aggressive investment firms. Goldman Sachs was forced to downsize and reduce overheads by eliminating hundreds of positions by the end of the decade.

In the 1980's, Solomon participated heavily in the LBO boom. They were involved in significant transactions including Xerox's acquisition of Crum & Foster, Texaco's controversial acquisition of Getty Oil and the mergers between Santa Fe Industries and Southern Pacific as well as Gulf Oil and Standard Oil of California. Solomon was also retained as an advisor for AT&T as they went through the largest corporate breakup in United States' history. However, Solomon still focused on their core business of underwriting and bond trading with a high-volume, low-margin approach. Prior to the 1987 crash, Solomon announced retrenchment plans because changes in tax laws and interest rates earlier in the decade caused a slump in the bond market, their main business, as well as new competition from Japanese firms that was cutting into profits. Solomon was forced to drastically downsize, but luckily, it wasn't hit as hard as other retail-orientated firms during the October crash.

Recovery in the 1990's

Once the economy had fired its engines again, the revenues from investment banking as well as brokerage activities increased substantially for Bear. By 1991, it became the top equity underwriter in Latin America. In 1992, Bears Stearns' earnings doubled to over $295 million and during that same year, the company managed more than $13 billion in initial public offerings (IPOs) for various US and foreign companies. Bear Stearns also had success in clearing trades for other brokers and brokerages, boasting to brokers that its ratios were among the best in the industry.

In 1993, James E. Cayne succeeded Alan Greenberg as CEO of Bear Stearns. Cayne guided the company towards new profitable opportunities in investment banking and foreign markets. Cayne's executive style and approach, in contrast to that of Greenberg's impulsiveness, was more cautious. He was known to avoid big risks and called upon consultants when making important decisions. Greenberg and Cayne were considered to be a powerful and well-balanced team. Even though Cayne became CEO, Greenberg retained the title of chairman as well as the final word at the company.

Bear Stearns continued to establish itself in the emerging markets of Asia and Latin America in the mid-1990's. In 1994, the company opened a representative office in Beijing in addition to its Hong Kong office. This move was not only pragmatic but diplomatic as it demonstrated respect for, and commitment to China as a world financial power. This move paid off for Bear Stearns Asia Ltd. in 1995 with the significant reward of being chosen by Guangzhou Railway Corporation to be the sole underwriter for its public offering. Bear Stearns' competitors in Hong Kong surely took notice.

Once again, Bear Stearns came under scrutiny but this time by the SEC, and this time it was more serious. In 1997, the SEC investigated Bear Stearns for its role as a clearing broker for a smaller brokerage named A.R. Baron that had defrauded its customers of $75 million and ended up bankrupt in 1996. Bear Sterns was accused of, "overstepping its bounds as a clearinghouse by continuing to process trades, loan money, and extend credit to Baron in the face of mounting evidence that the firm, then in serious financial jeopardy, was manipulating stock prices and conducting unauthorised trading while raiding the accounts of its customers."

After a two-year probe, Bear Stearns settled civil and criminal charges with the SEC and the Manhattan District Attorney in the summer of 1999. The company agreed to pay $42 million in fines and restitution, yet refused to accept or deny guilt. Meanwhile, Bear Stearns assured the public that the settlement was immaterial to the business and well being of the company. It was quite a scandal that not only tainted the records of both Greenberg and Cayne and adversely affected the image of the company, but also negatively impacted share prices, which traded at discounted prices for the next two years.

Other Firms in the 1990's—Different Focus, Different Strategy

Another firm recovering nicely in the 1990's was Goldman Sachs. With new Co-Senior Partnership, the company promised to focus on globalisation and strengthening the Merger & Acquisition and Trading business lines. This focus proved successful and in 1991 Goldman Sachs reported a record high pre-tax profit of $1.1 billion. You were in good hands if you were with the company in 1992, when year-end bonuses were 25 percent of annual salaries. By 1993, Goldman Sachs was one of the most profitable firms in the world, with pre-tax earnings of $2.7 billion. The firm attributed this profitability to offering Japanese securities to US investors and by expanding their markets overseas.

Goldman Sachs' momentum slowed briefly in 1993 when a federal appeals court ruled that an investment-banking firm could no longer advise a company with whom it had a business relationship in bankruptcy proceedings. What this meant is that investment-banking firms could no longer advise corporate clients in bankruptcy reorganisation. This ruling was significant because it signaled the end of a lucrative era for large investment banks. This area alone netted Goldman and similar firms over $100 million a year.

Further setbacks arose with the crash in the market price of Treasury and other bonds in 1994 as well as the drop in the US dollar in foreign markets. Goldman ended up shedding many employees by mid-decade. Even more serious for Goldman Sachs was the mass "retirement" of nearly fifty of the firm's veteran partners. During the rapid expansion in the early 1990's, partner relationships became strained. As discontented partners left the firm, they took equity in the amount of $250 million with them and the firm was forced to raise significant replacement capital.

However, by 1996 Goldman was back on track. Among acquisitions and other notable advancements, Goldman Sachs introduced paperless trading to the New York Stock Exchange, lead-managed the first ever global debt offering by a US Corporation, entered a 50-50 joint ownership of the Rockefeller Center and in 1996 was the lead underwriter in the IPO for internet company Yahoo! *Furthermore, the company went public in May of 1999, which raised $3.6 billion.*

In the same arena another competitor, Morgan Stanley, acquired Van Kampen American Capital in 1996. Then in 1997 it merged with Dean Witter Reynolds and Discover & Co., the spin-off financial services business of Sears Roebuck. This merger created the largest asset management company and the largest securities firm, in terms of equity capital, in the United States. The deal was worth $10.22 billion and the company eventually became known as Morgan Stanley Dean Witter & Co. (MSDW) in 1998.

Part of the significance of this mutually beneficial merger was that it provided Dean Witter access to international markets and considerably expanded their offerings and investment choices through Morgan Stanley. For Morgan Stanley, it was beneficial because it gave them access to Dean Witter's extensive US network of sales offices. Critics spoke addressing the culture of the two companies as not being an ideal fit—the aristocratic culture of Morgan Stanley with the meat and potatoes environment at Dean Witter. For the first time, it was as if Sears and Saks Fifth Avenue shared a storefront! The 1990's were generally volatile across global financial markets but Morgan Stanley performed well with profits in 1998 up 27% from 1997 reaching a record of $3.3 billion. Regardless of the continued weak economic conditions in Europe and Asia, the firm worked to strengthen overseas operations. Their goal was to be a stable force in a turbulent world.

Into the New Century

Indeed, the new century would prove to be perhaps *the* most turbulent era thus far in the world of finance. Come the turn of the century, Bear Stearns got back up on its feet and in early 2000, expanded its London office by 100 employees in a move to grow its European presence. Ironically, some of those jobs were cut after the quickly approaching economic downturn. By mid-2000, Bear Stearns found itself in a precarious situation. Amid the climate of rampant mergers and acquisitions in the securities industry, the company found itself to be one of the last independent financial services firms on Wall Street. Bear Stearns' competitors were merging into global powerhouses and the former maverick's reputation began to dwindle.

In the past, Bear Stearns had weathered various economic downturns with little signs of pain. However, the terrorist attacks on September 11, 2001 proved to be more challenging. Following the terrorist attacks, securities markets had problems due to the burst dotcom bubble and the subsequent recession. Typically, Bear Stearns was the last in the securities industry to cut jobs. However they eventually succumbed to the need to reduce expenses and cut 800 bankers, which amounted to nearly 10% of its work force.

Bear Sterns continued to operate on a different model than the rest of Wall Street, which proved to be advantageous in the early 2000's. As mentioned above, the company wasn't considered competitive in the mergers and acquisitions business in the late 1990's and as a result, was one of the few firms that avoided significant losses from the industry-wide downturn in this arena. The company continued to succeed by *"maintaining its emphasis on clearing operations, honing in on the housing boom by increasing its focus on packaging and selling mortgages, and selling bonds to investors too skittish to buy stocks, Bear Stearns was the only securities firm to report a first-quarter profit increase in 2002, demonstrating its resilience and its competitive edge once again."*

Over the last 85 years or so, which were mostly good times for Bear Stearns, they earned a stellar reputation on the Street. Fortune recognised the firm as the "Most Admired" securities firm from 2005 to 2007. This prestigious list is compiled from an annual survey ranking employee talent, quality of risk management and business innovation. However, as it would happen following such longstanding success, a drastic change was indeed on the horizon.

The Lead Up to Implosion: Mortgages, Credit, the Housing Bubble and the Risk of Financial Innovation

"The four most dangerous words in investing are "This time it's different"".

Sir John Templeton

If you were in any of the US markets where the housing bubble inflated, notably California, Florida, Nevada, Arizona, Oregon, Colorado, Michigan, the Northeast Corridor and the Southwest markets, you saw it firsthand. Underlying causes of housing bubbles are complex, but historically they involve low interest rates, lax lending standards and a speculative fever. Housing and other bubbles are easy to identify in hindsight, and one might recall an increase in loan incentives such as easy initial terms in addition to long-term substantial increases in housing prices. These factors encouraged buyers to assume mortgages that, in the long run, would be difficult to sustain. As interest rates began to rise, homeowners were unable to refinance for more favorable terms. Housing prices started to drop moderately making it more difficult to refinance. Default and foreclosures increased as the initial easy terms of the loans wore off and the adjustable rate mortgages switched to higher rates.

Leading up to the financial crisis was a financial boom. Significant amounts of foreign money flowed into the United States making it easier for the Federal Reserve to keep interest rates artificially low. According to the Taylor rule, a monetary policy rule that stipulates what interest rates "should" be, interest rates in the United States from 2002-2006 were *"too low,"* making it too easy to obtain the unprecedented amounts of debt. These easy credit conditions lead to the United States housing bubble. As a result of the increasing debt, the amount of financial agreements called mortgage-backed securities

(MBS) greatly increased. Mortgage-backed securities are, of course, backed by the underlying asset of the property they've funded. An alternative way of looking at it is to consider the MBS to be a debt obligation that represents a claim on the cash flows from mortgage loans.

In mass quantities, individual mortgages are initially purchased from banks, mortgage companies and other loan originators. Government agencies, government sponsored enterprises and private entities then assemble the mortgages into pools. By "aggregating" the mortgages, it is assumed that the risk is distributed. Through a process known as securitisation, new securities backed by the pool of mortgages are issued. If these securities are structured properly and perform as expected, the credit risk of the structured debt can be said to improve. If they're not structured properly, there will be dramatic credit deterioration and potential for loss. In theory, all assets can be securitised as long as they are associated with cash flow. The financial innovation of these mortgage-backed securities enabled investors from around the world to invest in the United States housing market, and they did so at an unprecedented rate.

The process that followed is now well known. The economy began to overheat from such a prolonged period of low rates and easy credit; inflation began to pose a serious threat, and along with it, commodities' prices dramatically increased. The conglomeration of these factors meant that homeowners now faced new and drastically higher payments for their risky mortgages. The pace of default ramped up, and consequently, the MBS cash flow machine literally ground to a halt. Investors quickly fled from these securities, causing their prices to drop just as fast, but because they had been used so extensively as collateral throughout the financial system, the cascading effect of the housing market's implosion spread much wider than most everyone had anticipated. ***For Bear Stearns, the damage would prove to be fatal.***

Bear Stearns and the Blowup / Implosion

Now, let's take a look specifically how Bear Stearns was involved in all of this. As mentioned above, these mortgage-backed securities are a financial innovation. Bear Stearns pioneered the securitisation and asset-backed securities markets. As the investor losses began to mount in 2006 and 2007, Bear Stearns actually increased their exposure, especially in the mortgage-backed assets that were central to the subprime mortgage crisis.

Rewind back to a time, in very recent history, when Bear Stearns operated as a *"cigar-chomping, suspender wearing culture where taking risks was rewarded."* Taking risks is part of the business especially for Bear Stearns who was never truly considered one of the white-shoe investment banks. In many respects, the firm was an outsider that defied its mainstream rivals. Bear Stearns was a proud, solid and in many eyes a maverick company. In 1998 when the Federal Reserve helped plan a bailout of Long Term Capital Management, Bear Stearns refused to join the effort.

In 2007, those risky moves and innovations started to rear their ugly heads. On June 22, 2007, Bear Stearns pledged a collateralised loan of up to $3.2 billion to *"bail out"* one of its funds, the Bear Stearns High-Grade Structured Credit Fund, while negotiating to loan money against collateral to another fund, the Bear Stearns High-grade Structured Enhanced Leveraged Fund. During the week of July 16, 2007 Bear Stearns disclosed that its two subprime hedge funds had lost nearly all their value amid the rapid decline in the market for subprime mortgages.

On August 1, 2007 investors in these two funds filed arbitration claims with the National Association of Securities Dealers alleging that Bear Stearns misled investors about its exposure to the funds. Several other legal actions were also filed against Bear Stearns in regards to these funds. Co-President Warren Spector, who managed the two subprime mortgage funds that collapsed, was asked to resign on August 5, 2007. There were also civil suits filed by investors including Barclays Bank PLC, who claimed Bear Stearns knew certain assets were worth much less than their professed values. The law suit claimed that Bear Stearns devised *"a plan to make more money for themselves and further use the Enhanced Fund as a repository for risky, poor-quality investments"* and that Bear Stearns told Barclays that the fund was up almost 6 percent when *"in reality, the portfolio's asset values were plummeting."* Matthew Tannin and Ralph R. Cioffi, both managers of the funds, were later arrested on June 19, 2008 in regards to this suit.

On September 21, 2007 the New York Times reported that Bear Stearns posted a 61% drop in net profits due to their hedge fund loses. That November, Bear Stearns was writing down a further $1.2 billion in mortgage related securities and would face its first loss in 83 years. Consequently, Standard and Poor's downgraded the company's credit rating from AA to A. The company's books were not looking good as of November 30, 2007 with notional contract amounts of approximately *$13.40 trillion in derivative financial instruments,* of which $1.85 trillion were listed as futures and options contracts. At year end, Bear Stearns leverage ratio was 35.5 to 1 meaning that the company was highly leveraged with many illiquid potentially worthless assets. This led to rapid diminution of investor and lender confidence. Bear Stearns was forced to call the New York Federal Reserve to stave off the looming cascade of counterparty risk that would ensue from forced liquidation.

The End Draws Near

In March of 2008, the results of the risks Bear Stearns had taken were proving to be drastic. On March 6, 2008 rumours swirled that the *"investment bank's shares had dropped nearly 20% in the previous ten days, and there were murmurs that short-sellers were circling."* It seemed to have blind-sided some executives who were claiming, *"Our counterparties are getting paid, trades are clearing, and business is picking up. It doesn't seem to be the likely scenario for an investment bank's collapse."*

If there's one thing companies hate to do, it's commenting on rumours. The theory behind it is that it confers legitimacy on unfounded gossip. But Bear Stearns had no choice. In a press release on March 10, 2008 they stated, *"There is absolutely no truth to the rumours of liquidity problems that circulated today in the market."* At the time, it seemed to be true: Bear Stearns had some $17 billion in cash. As mentioned above, Bear Stearns was heavily leveraged with $11.1 billion in tangible equity supporting $395 billion in assets that resulted in the leverage ratio of more that thirty-five to one. Furthermore, that $11.1 billion in assets was much less liquid than the assets of the company's competitors.

In reality, the problem had metastasized into something considerably more dangerous than just a rumour. The factual side was that on the preceding Friday, March 7, a major bank had rejected Bear Stearns' request for a short-term, $2 billion loan. This type of loan, a securities-backed repurchase or "repo," is essential for investment banks as they borrow and lend billions to fund their daily business. The denial for the loan sent Bear Stearns executives scrambling trying to find money elsewhere. **The signal was clear; credit was drying up!**

Concerns continued to grow, confidence continued to ebb and Bear Stearns, like a magician whose trick is exposed, again tried to reassure its investors. On CNBC, CFO Samuel Molinaro claimed that if he knew why it was happening, he would do something to address it. He maintained the company's position that the rumours were false and that there was no liquidity crisis or margin call. Regardless of Molinaro's reassurance, though, momentum was turning against Bear Stearns and the body blows kept coming. In previous weeks, Goldman Sachs, and other investment banks, had been agreeing to stand in for institutions that were nervous that companies such as Bear Stearns wouldn't be able to fulfill their obligation on interest rate swaps. Of course, to take on this risk, firms like Goldman Sachs were charging a handsome fee. However, on the morning of March 11, Goldman Sachs told their clients via email that they would no longer step in for them on Bear Stearns' derivatives deals.

This move by Goldman Sachs communicated to the investing world that the risk associated with Bear Stearns was too much. The end was coming, but they weren't there yet. Bear Stearns had to endure more painful blows before all was said and done. The cost for Bear Stearns to insure $10 million in debt via credit default swaps, which was around $350,000 in February, had shot past $1 million. By the end of that horrific day, the rate was irrelevant. The banks refused to issue further credit protection on Bear Stearns' debt.

As the week continued, so did the disaster. When the news of the Goldman Sachs' email leaked, the floodgates opened. Hedge funds and other clients began withdrawing funds at alarming rates. Bear Stearns continued to maintain publicly that everything was fine. CEO Alan Schwartz, who hadn't seen the need to return to headquarters, conducted an ill advised CNBC interview from Palm Beach stating, ***"We're not being made aware of anybody who is not taking our credit as a counterparty . . . We don't see any pressure on our liquidity, let alone a liquidity crisis."***

By Thursday, the weight of the situation finally registered at Bear Stearns. Liquidity had plummeted. CEO Schwartz returned to New York and in desperation, contacted J.P. Morgan CEO Jamie Dimon that evening. As the firm was frantically negotiating a rescue package, Bear Stearns executives continued to try to convince the world that everything was under control. Schwartz went so far as to contact a well-known New York hedge fund manager, and long time Bear Stearns client, begging the manager to appear on CNBC the next morning and express his confidence in Bear Stearns. The fund manager, curious as to why Bear Stearns needed a client to vouch for them, politely declined.

That morning, Bear Stearns announced $30 billion in funding provided by J.P. Morgan and backstopped by the government. CEO Schwartz seemed to be in a state of denial, claiming that Bear Stearns had been subject to a significant amount of rumour and that the new loan facility would restore calm. There was nothing restorative or calm when the company's stock dropped nearly 40% in the first half-hour of trading.

Within a day, the 85 year-old investment banking legend, Bear Stearns, had come to an end. By March 16, 2008, J.P. Morgan Chase had swallowed up Bear Stearns. In the shocking deal, J.P. Morgan Chase agreed to pay a mere $2 per share to buy all of Bear Stearns—less than one-tenth of what the firm's market price was the preceding Friday. The $270 million price tag on Bear Stearns is a third of the price that a much smaller Bear went public for in 1985. Less than a year prior to the deal, shares in Bear Stearns had been trading at $170.

Almost immediately, a class action lawsuit was filed in retaliation to the deal, challenging the fire-sale price that had been hastily arranged by the Fed Chair Ben Bernanke, Treasury Secretary Hank Paulson, and Bear Stearns. Just as quickly, a new agreement was reached that gave investors $10 per share, rather than the original $2 they would have received just a week earlier. This new revised deal was aimed to appease investors, but the real question too many was the seemingly arbitrary process for valuing the once high-flying company. Critics charged that it was not the investing public that was being newly compensated, but the executives at Bear Stearns whose pay packages consisted largely of near-worthless stock.

Many felt that Bear was being punished by competitors such as Goldman, vis-à-vis their alumni in high office such as Hank Paulson. Whether there is truth to these critiques remains to be seen. What is clear, however, is the extent to which the public has taken over the burden of executive excess. When the Fed stepped in to guarantee the acquisition by JP Morgan, it did so by establishing a new LLC to facilitate the unwinding of securities that were judged too risky for the new owner to take on. Justified by the need to prevent wider damage to the economy, were Bear Stearns to fail in an uncontrolled way, the burden for the firm's collapse was thus shifted to the taxpayer, causing a "book loss" of up to $2 billion. In doing so, the defensive argument is it can be said that further damage to Bear Stearns' competitors was averted and markets stabilised.

Conclusion

"Confidence . . . thrives on honesty, on honor, on the sacredness of obligations, on faithful protection and on unselfish performance. Without them it cannot live."
Theodore Roosevelt

In the summer of 2007, Bear Stearns survived one liquidity crisis when two of its hedge funds cratered after the subprime mortgage collapse. The firm managed to somewhat repair its balance sheet, improve its financing and assure its investors that all was well. 2008 was a different story. A look at that week in March 2008 before Bear

Stearns agreed to be acquired reveals the speed at which things tumbled. Bear Stearns' long time customers and counterparties lost their faith in the investment bank that undermined its ability to continue. All of this is a reminder that the business is based on confidence.

When that confidence evaporates, so does the business. Bear Stearns proved unable to survive the second liquidity crisis, and as it succumbed, it became the most prominent example—at that point—of the credit crisis that would soon grip the global economy. Certainly, the collapse of the housing market dealt a fatal blow to Bear Stearns, but in the aftermath of the firm's demise, we have learned that it was not an inevitable ending for this storied establishment.

The collapse of Bear Stearns gave the investment world a rare and unique glimpse into the internal workings of one of the world's oldest and most powerful financial institutions. Sadly, all was not well beneath the surface, perhaps in spite of the bravado of its executives. Indeed, we have seen that throughout its history the firm took exorbitant risks, and while most of the time it, and its investors were handsomely rewarded for it, on more than one occasion they were severely punished as well.

After the collapse of Bear Stearns, it *"seemed almost achingly quaint to recall those warm and hazy days when 'banker' was a synonym for sobriety and propriety—a time when those who worked in finance, as well as those who reported on it, believed that a pinstriped suit connoted one thing and a chalk stripe something else entirely."* The collapse of Bear Stearns signaled the beginning of the worst global financial crisis since the Great Depression.

In the final analysis, the fall of Bear Stearns raises significant questions for the management and regulation of the financial institutions that we depend upon. Recalling the often-caustic and dismissive attitude of its executives, we must ask ourselves to what extent they were aware of the risky behaviour being undertaken on their watch. *Whether they were aware or not, one must consider if even they fully comprehended the enormous risks being shouldered by their traders!*

What is clear, however, is that it is the wider public, not just Bear Stearns' clients, counterparties and investors, that will pick up the tab after all is said and done. Even today, that price tag has yet to be determined. When the Federal Reserve stepped in to backstop JP Morgan's purchase, it did so using the full faith and credit of the United States government. While this may have had the arguably necessary effect of reassuring investors in the soundness of the financial system, at the same time it may have had detrimental consequences for its long-term health.

Bear Stearns was, in that instance, judged to be too big to fail. However, we would see only a short time later that Lehman Brothers, an equally important link in the global financial system, did not receive the same consideration. As we shall see in later pages, this decision was in many respects the *"beginning of the end,"* and marked the onset of the current global financial crisis. One after another, following the sale of Bear Stearns, the giants of the financial sector would fall prey to their own excess: Lehman Brothers would soon be bankrupt, Merrill Lynch was forced to merge with Bank of America, and AIG was nationalised. Moreover, the fall of Lehman marked the true shift into full-blown crisis, for the effects of its failure would ripple not just through the US but to the farthest reaches of the global economy as well.

It is perhaps too easy to look back upon the ways in which these events unfolded and cast blame or attribute cause. However, several conclusions are nonetheless evident. Following the 1929 crash, those companies that resisted the temptation to concentrate their focus on volatile equity markets were those that survived. The parallel today can be seen in those banks that did not stray so heavily into the dangerous arena of mortgage-backed securities; banks such as Wells Fargo have fared much better because they maintained their focus on a healthy and responsible balance sheet. While Bear Stearns was heralded throughout its history as one of the longest-running and most successful financial institutions, it is plainly evident that "success" is relative; *when defined simply as the pursuit of profits, then clearly that success had its price, and in the end the firm succumbed to its own triumphs.*

Finance is all about innovation. Bear Stearns was at the forefront of many of these waves throughout much its life. It was able to continually innovate and indeed re-create itself over the years. In looking deeper at this history, we see now the true character of the risky behaviour that the company undertook at nearly every step of the way. What's more, the imprudence of its executives, while certainly a driving factor in much of its heretofore-successful operations, ended up sounding the death knell for the firm. It made a practice of going against the grain, which would end up bringing about its downfall; in retrospect, we simply cannot overlook the hubris of the CEOs. Clearly, there is no return without risk, but one must believe now that there is a better way to be found. Too many other firms have followed in the same steps as Bear Stearns, but one must hope that as we emerge from the present crisis, that we have finally learned the lessons of history, at least in this respect.

In Chapter 15 we turn from the micro effects of the credit crunch on a single firm to the largest arena of speculation in the globe; *the currency markets!*

Chapter 15

June 2008—Currency Convertor:
The Warp Drive of Speculation!

"There are two times in a man's life when he should not speculate: when he can't afford it, and when he can!"

Mark Twain

June 2008—The UK Pound has embarked on its longest slide in 37 years against the US Dollar.

What is a currency? Why do we use it? And why does it matter for us if it is volatile?

A stable currency is the foundation both of capitalism and of freedom. As Lenin said, the best way to destroy the Capitalist System was to debauch the currency. *But what is currency and how exactly does it work? What is the value of money and how do we assess it?*

In June, 2008, the UK pound sterling embarked on one of its longest slides in thirty-seven years against the US dollar. In other words, the value of the pound, compared to the dollar, decreased dramatically. *So why is this important?*

This chapter will explore the history and evolution of the world's currencies and in particular the last 50 years in respect of Keynesian economics. We will also look at the fact that in the last ten years 95% of currency trading was speculation and only 5% devoted to international trade.

Currency can refer to one of two things, technically speaking. It can, for instance, refer to a particular currency; the US dollar, for example. Currency can also refer to legal tender, such as coins and bank notes that people use on an everyday basis to trade and manage their money supply. One of the most interesting things about currency, however, is the way it is rated or compared. Different nations have different forms of currency, and the wealth or economic standing of each nation is determined by the value of their national currency against or compared to currencies of other nations.

To understand this and other characteristic behaviours of currency, we need to explore its history, and, in particular, its origins. Money, historically, is the most popular form of currency. Gold or silver coins, which have some intrinsic value, are common forms of commodity money. A modern form of currency is fiat money, which is intrinsically worthless.

The origins of currency dates back some 15,000 years to the earliest days of civilization and to about the same time that people began to trade goods. The process of trading initially emerged as the exchange of one valued item for another, a process also known as bartering. As you might expect, trading and bartering emerged at roughly the same time or just shortly after formal communication was developed. In other words, prehistoric people did not purchase goods using money but instead, bartered; they determined the comparative value of two or more items.

Between about 9,000 and 6,000 B.C., for instance, livestock was often used as a unit of exchange. As forms of agriculture began to develop, people also used crops for barter. During the Stone Age, flint was also traded for a material known as obsidian, a volcanic rock. The exchange of these two materials, trading obsidian for flint, was tempered by the respective uses of the materials and the degree of their availability for each party involved.

If an abundance of obsidian was owned by one group and that group had found a use for it, for example as a good building material, then they might decide to control the source of the obsidian. Similarly, group

B might control a source of flint because they have an abundance of it and plenty of uses for it. They can also secure a controlling interest over the source of the material.

Communication between communities led to the discovery of items of different value; products, primarily, and their uses. The group of people that discovered and found a use for flint and were able to stock-pile flint will have become aware of the second group using obsidian. Meeting and exchanging information about the two commodities, the groups decide to make a trade and, at some point, make a determination whether obsidian and flint are worth equal amounts. They determine whether one unit of obsidian is worth one unit of flint. Factors impacting the value of the units include availability of the product, the effort required to extract the product, and the amount of the product required for a standard project.

Of course, bartering and the broader concept of trading were extremely popular since their earliest days. Early on, a number of important trade routes developed linking together different nations of people. The Egyptians, for example, began trading jewellery around 3000BC and a series of long-range trade routes emerged in the third millennium BC. These routes have been used by the major civilizations throughout history, including the Sumerians who traded between Mesopotamia and the Indus Valley, and the Phoenicians who, as far north as Britain, used the sea at ports along the Mediterranean Sea.

Major civilizations emerged around the world in Byzantium, Greece, Italy, and Egypt, and each of them developed an elaborate trading system. Trading not only became more frequent but the volume and number of goods traded increased. Eventually trading became an established practice in most parts of the world. Certain products such as spices and manufactured materials were assigned higher values. Others that were more common were traded at a lower value rate.

Prominent trade routes were also established because of the popularity of certain products. The European spice trade, for instance, established routes between Europe and the East. The trade of spices throughout Europe was also crucial to the emergence of the Age of Exploration, which in turn allowed many individuals, such as Vasco da Gama, to travel to remote areas of the world.

By the sixteenth century, free trade was an emerging principle in Europe, with Holland becoming the center for encouraging the trading of goods without subject to exchange controls on their movement.

More than two centuries later, in 1776, the renowned economist, Adam Smith published a paper exploring the nature and causes of wealth. *An Inquiry into the Nature and Causes of the Wealth of Nations* put forward a lot of information about the benefits of economic specialisation. He argued as well that the principles of mercantilism, the global volume of trade, were unchangeable.

Currency serves as a means of facilitating trade in a manner more sophisticated than the simple trade of goods. As the Master of Ceremonies sings in the musical Cabaret, *"Money makes the world go round"*, and by providing a system for the exchange of goods, this is precisely what money, and currency, as a form of money, allows.

It is a neutral claim, however, although there are a range of negative and positive claims made about money as well. The Bible warns, for instance, that "the love of money is the root of all evil" while George Bernard Shaw argued that it is rather the lack of money which is the root of all evil and what people should fear.

> **"Speculation is only a word covering the making of money out of the manipulation of prices, instead of supplying goods and services."**
>
> **Henry Ford**

Money—a form of currency—maintains an enormous personal and moral significance to society, *despite whether we choose to consider it a negative or a positive influence*. Its importance to the functioning of modern society, moreover, is broader and deeper than can be stressed with an understanding of its basic economic aspects.

Whether we are speaking of money in simple or primitive communities or in much more advanced, complex and sophisticated societies, it is not enough simply to examine the narrow economic aspects of money. Money has traditionally been associated with various degrees of closeness with religion, the psychology of habits, and various attitudes, hopes, fears and expectations.

The taboos that affect spending in primitive societies are similar to the stock market bears that evaluate expenditures by changing subjective assessments of values and incomes; the truth about what money means to people requires the sympathetic understanding of the less obvious motivations as much as, if not more than, the narrow abstract calculations of the computer.

Money is described as the main method by which the *logic of limited resource usage*, money is put to work.

Economics focuses upon how to make the most of one's money, since the allocation of resources and changes in the valuation of assets necessarily involve accountancy and payment systems based on money.

The demands made upon the efficiency of the monetary system vary from place to place and age to age. The close relationship between the development of money and its efficient use in the allocation of resources is both complex and convoluted. One would expect all pre-metallic moneys to be associated exclusively with primitive communities. Similarly, all metallic money should be associated exclusively with more advanced societies.

This is far from being the case, however, and the logical order differs significantly from the chronological. The development of banking in Britain, for example, followed a thousand years behind the introduction and widespread use of coinage. Banking in Babylon, on the other hand, preceded the 'invention' of coinage by a similarly long period.

Some businesses in Birmingham, for instance, were still manufacturing metallic bracelets in the first decades of the twentieth century to use as primitive forms of money among certain Nigerian tribes, in preference to the coinage systems which were readily available for their use and which the state authorities had been trying to enforce with little success for many years.

The best way to begin to understand the role of currency, however, is to look at its development throughout history. There were many early forms of currency deserving of consideration. Many of the earliest types of coins were produced as direct imitations of those primitive types of currency with which the communities concerned had long been familiar.

According to Toynbee's *Study of History*, social anthropologists have categorised over 650 separate primitive societies. Most of them were still in existence in the twentieth century and have used one or more forms of primitive money.

Many hundreds of objects have been used as primitive monies including the cowrie. The cowrie is the ovoid shell of a mollusc widely spread over the shallower regions of the Indian and Pacific Oceans. It comes in various types, colors, and sizes. It can be the size of the end joint of the little finger up to about the size of a fist. The most prolific single source was the Maldives Islands, where, for hundreds of years, whole shiploads were distributed around the shores of Oceania, Africa, the Middle, and Far East.

The value of the cowrie rose as the cowrie became scarcer and people had to move farther from their point of origin. In addition to having religious and ornamental qualities, cowries were popular forms of currency because they were durable, easily cleaned and counted, and impossible to imitate or counterfeit. For modern monies, the cowrie proved to be a formidable rival, particularly for items that were deemed to be of small value. In Central Africa, when cowries were first introduced into Uganda towards the end of the eighteenth century, two cowries in the most remote regions was known to have been sufficient to purchase a woman; by 1860 it required one thousand cowries for such a purchase.

Trade grew and cowries became more plentiful, however, so they naturally depreciated further. They were still officially accepted for payment of taxes until the beginning of the twentieth century. Only when the Uganda Railway began to penetrate the country did coins gradually take over from cowries, and only then for medium and large-sized transactions. By the 1920's several thousand tons of cowries had been brought into Africa, not only from the Maldives but also from other areas. They became progressively more devalued elsewhere which also caused them to depreciate in the internal regions of Africa as well.

In East and West Africa, especially in the remotest districts, it was not until the middle of the twentieth century that cowries virtually disappeared from circulation for the smallest purchases. Their immense circulation and prolonged popularity had seen them not only coexist with modern types of monies, but also, from time to time, push debased coinage from official acceptance in a strange reversal of Gresham's Law.

Many examples of monetary unit representation have been recorded in the long history of Chinese currency. In this, as in many other aspects of civilization, the Chinese offer the longest sequence of authentically recorded development. In contrast to the vast range of the cowrie, two other forms of currency were much more geographically limited: the sperm whale's tooth, also known as the 'tambua' of the Fijian group of islands, and the stone currency of the island of Yap.

For the first of these, the sperm whale's tooth, a particularly high value was assigned. In particular, the teeth were deemed to have ceremonial origins in Fiji, as demonstrated by its continued use as part of the ritual of welcome to visiting royalty, such as on the occasion of the visit of Queen Elizabeth and the Duke of Edinburgh in 1982. The official reception of royalty was deemed unthinkable without the formal presentation of a whale's tooth. Quite simply, it represents the deep-rooted Fijian cultural traditions. In addition to the use in official ceremonies, however, whales' teeth also serve as bride-money and hold a symbolic meaning similar to that of an engagement ring within the Fijian culture. Since so much prestige was derived from the ownership of whales' teeth, which were constantly oiled and polished, as currency they maintained a high value; higher, often, than gold.

The peculiar stone currency of Yap, a cluster of ten small islands in the Caroline group of the central Pacific, was used until the mid-1960's in some areas. Stones known as 'fei' were quarried from Palau, some 260 miles away, or from Guam, even further away. The stone currency increased its value over time. Similar to the whale's teeth, the stones not only served as a form of currency, they also served as badges of rank and prestige, and maintained religious and ceremonial significance within the island communities who used them. Though their use as currency was limited they were nevertheless by far the most acceptable form of money to the Yap islanders.

What can be learned from these, and other examples of primitive currencies which have been used in various parts of the world, is that value is assigned, first and foremost, on how various materials have been utilised.

Metals were eagerly accepted by late Stone-Age men and became increasingly indispensable once man had become accustomed to using them. This indispensability explains their ready transformation into forms of currency. Interestingly, the word for 'silver' and 'money' has remained the same from prehistoric to modern times in a number of languages, including French ('argent') and Welsh ('arian'). Metals used as currency have formed a strong and wide bridge from primitive to modern or coined money. They were, however, often used symbolically in imitation of, and as a more valuable extension of, the age-old primitive monies. The Chinese were insisting on the manufacture of both copper and bronze cowries and imitations of these coins were considered by some numismatists to be among the earliest examples of quasi-coinage.

A shift in usage from the specific as tools to symbolic and more general applications as media of exchange and units of account were observed for a number of metallic objects made of copper, bronze and iron, including things such as axes, spears, knives, swords, hoes and spades. Swords and spears were considered to be of particular value, and were often treasured possessions. Replicas could conveniently be reduced in size as they lost their purpose and became used as money.

Several writers commented on Julius Caesar's castigation of the ancient Britons for still using crudely made iron sword-blades as currency when more civilized Europeans had long used coin.

From Lydia and Ionia, spreading east to the Persian Empire and west through the rest of the Ionian and Aegean islands to mainland Greece, and then to its western colonies, including Sicily, the use of currency in the ancient world also spread northward to Macedonia, Thrace and the Black Sea. Apart from mainland Italy and Lower Egypt, the use of coinage spread rapidly around the countries bordering the central and eastern Mediterranean and over the widespread and growing Persian Empire through Mesopotamia into India.

There is a basic distinction to be drawn, however, between the development of coinage to the east and west of Ionia. The Greeks minted coins almost exclusively in silver, with other metals, including gold, largely overlooked. The Persians and others to the east of Ionia tended to have a different preference. The Lydians, for example, preferred gold and used silver as a subsidiary.

In the Persian Empire, the bimetallic influence of Croesus, King of the Lydians, established a tradition of mixing gold with other metals to establish a form of currency. An interesting administrative division gradually developed, however; the minting of gold coins was the sole right of the Persian emperor.

Between the middle of the sixth century BC to the death of Alexander in 323 BC, the world's first great intermixing of eastern and western cultures began. From the time that money was first used for a variety of purposes up to around the second half of the seventeenth century, some form of physical commodity represented either the only or the main form of money and therefore established the basis for currency. Generally speaking, this meant that during this early period, the limits within which money could become relatively scarce or plentiful were closer than have subsequently been the case. Periodically, the relative quantities and velocities of circulation of money did fluctuate considerably, despite communities being reliant solely or mainly on commodity moneys. Modern fluctuations in the value of money are similar to those that occurred in earlier periods.

The commercial revolution, which occurred between 1160 and 1330, was stimulated by increased supplies of both silver and gold, enabling the creation of multi-denominational currencies, comprising gold coins for very large payments with silver and copper. These currencies were used for the medium and small transactions which made up the vast majority of payments.

The plentiful supplies of money during this period, however, gave way to recurring bullion famines in the later Middle Ages and increasingly frequent shortages of currency in general. During the first decade of the fifteenth century, for instance, there was a notable shortage that drove many monarchs to debase their national coinage. This was especially common practice on the Continent; the Tudor monarchs in England were able to minimise their own need to debase coinage by using other devices such as the dissolution of the monasteries, with the Church's silver plate adding to the proceeds of the sale of monastic lands. Debasement was, however, rendered less necessary after the influx of precious metals into Europe from the Americas, coinciding with the simultaneous rise in the acceptance and circulation of banknotes.

Printed money supplemented and often replaced minted money when the principle and practice of 'convertibility' was adopted. It was used more frequently when governments found it expedient to abandon convertibility despite the inflation risk which was then cured only by re-linking paper money to gold or silver or a combination of the two.

In the history of currency, it is interesting that there have been long periods of reasonably stable prices in times of peace; wars have always caused a rise in prices, for two main reasons. First of all, the government expenditure grows during wars. At the same time, productive factors are diverted into non-productive channels. Second, the normal powers of governments to borrow and to create money are generally stimulated by the state of war. War causes an inflation of money supplies and, even during the post-war periods, these inflated money supplies typically remain in existence to form a new, higher base for the economy to operate. Military ratchet has been the most important single influence in the rise of prices and the reduction of the value of money in the past 1,000 years. Debasement was the most common way of strengthening the 'sinews of war' during this time, if not the only means. To supplement the periodic bouts of official debasement there were the more continuous practices of counterfeiting, clipping, and forgery intended to supplement official money supplies.

Despite the harshest punishments involved throughout history, which included the death penalty, counterfeiting was a widespread practice and points to the reality that the demand for money exceeds the supply. This lead to attempts by the more entrepreneurial elements to try and overcome the constraints of the money supply—wherever the incentives were sufficiently profitable!

As Glyn Davies said, however, ***"Bad money did not always drive all good money out of use but usually supplemented rather than supplanted good money, the latter being kept selectively for high-priority purposes, e.g. for export or for the payment of taxes"***.

Gresham's Law—from Sir Thomas Gresham 1519-1579 the English financier—first worked to increase the quantity and velocity of the circulation of money. Carried to extremes, it also went into reverse: coins became of such poor quality that they were no longer readily accepted. Holders of good coin would no longer part with them. In the further expansion of currency, however, technical improvements to modes of exchange, which have changed dramatically in more than a millennium, have done a lot to promote its development.

For the most part, the changes were small in scale, incremental, too. There were, however, two major changes. The first took place at the end of the Middle Ages when the printing of paper money began to supplement the minting of coins. The second major change has occurred in our time, since electronic money transfer was invented.

The notion of electronic funds transfer is, in fact, only one of a number of major improvements in communications. Other examples include the development of lasers and the use of satellites. Major economies in the midst of the monetary media evolution tend to suffer quite considerable macroeconomic effects. They can, first of all, stimulate growth in the rise of banking. Secondly, they can also be opening the way towards universal and instantaneous money transfer in the modern global village.

"If the world were good for nothing else, it is a fine subject for speculation"
William Hazlitt

Adam Smith, (1776, Book II, 257), described the revolution caused by the introduction of paper money: *'The substitution of paper in the room of gold and silver money replaces a very expensive instrument of commerce with one much less costly, and sometimes equally convenient. Circulation comes to be carried on by a new wheel, which it costs less both to erect and to maintain than the old one.'*

The most important of the two major forms of invention is the reduction of the governmental monopoly over money. When coins were the principle form of money, monarchs were extremely concerned with guarding their sovereign power over their royal mints.

Paper money, on the other hand, has facilitated banks to become increasingly competitive sources of money. This particular development caused not only significant macro-economic changes; it also facilitated contemporary revolutionary constitutional changes.

In England, it was no coincidence that the Whig party, which supported the limited constitutional monarchy under the monarchs, William and Mary, was a key promoter of the Bank of England. It is also worth noting that in an age of electronic banking that 'national' money has become increasingly anachronistic. Millions have eagerly accepted a variety of demand and savings accounts offered by competing financial institutions in competing currencies. It is a buyer's market, so to speak, and national money monopolies are spoiled for choice, despite being in the reality, reduced in effectiveness.

Monetary authorities have consistently tried to reassert their monopolistic power as opposed to the natural creation of money supplies produced elsewhere by working of market forces. The effective working of the international gold standard at the beginning of the twentieth century was most notably dependent on the activities of the Bank of England. Similarly, the evolution of the European Monetary System in the last decade of this century has also been dependent on the discipline imposed by the German Bundesbank.

Traditional boundaries between currencies, banks and other financial institutions continue to dissolve. Real choice in currency is an option only in affluent societies despite the existence of the buyer's market in general. Adolf Hitler was actually somewhat premature in suggesting that there were no longer any islands because it is only since the development of the smart card and the satellite that geographical boundaries have become obsolete as far as the movement of money is concerned.

Nevertheless, the reference to Hitler, when considering currency, is doubly relevant. It was his terrible legacy of war and inflation that caused not only the Schuman Coal and Steel Community to form, which made future European wars much less likely. It also contributed to the historic decision to grant the German central bank an unusually high degree of independence. The Schuman Plan prompted the development of the Common Market, and from early 1993 to the Single Market. These developments also lead to the concept of a Single Currency. The draft treaty on European Union was signed by EC heads of state in February 1992. This treaty included proposals for Economic and Monetary Union (EMU), which were deemed of special significance. It also outlined in detail the path towards a system of independent multi-state central banking for controlling monetary policy throughout the EC.

Towards the end of 1993, the treaty had, for the most part, been accepted by the member states. There were, however, opt-outs for Britain and

Denmark, and exceptions made for coins. The treaty would remain of considerable importance for the greater part of the world's population.

Despite some opposition on the basis that the development of real choice in currency is a surrender of national sovereignty to unelected bureaucrats, there was enough momentum to carry at least twelve member countries towards the 'convergence' and the final stage for the establishment of a single currency.

According to a European Commission report entitled One Market, One Money, the single currency is intended to remove transaction and exchange costs worth up to 1 per cent of GDP annually for the smaller states and around 0.5 per cent for the larger states. The single currency would also save around Ecu 160 billion in the EC's foreign currency reserves, allowing a higher sustainable rate of growth to be achieved (European Commission, Luxemburg, October 1990). Worldwide, opinion has shifted in favour of, and policy has followed, targeted in ending inflation at almost any cost, which is an interesting diversion. In February 1991, for instance, the Bank of Canada and the Government together announced targets for reducing inflation.

Specific targets were designed to reduce the year-over-year rate of increase in the consumer price index to 3% by the end of 1992, 2½% by the middle of 1994, and 2% by the end of 1995. The long-term objective was further reductions until the achievement of price stability. By October 1992 the UK had adopted a similar approach to meeting inflation targets, of 1% to 4%. The Bank of England published its own independent assessment of progress each quarter, amended to 2 ½% in 1997.

The principle recognised by these policies, however, was that worldwide, though at great cost, it is countries with low inflation that have achieved high growth and low unemployment. Even in the leading industrial countries, inflation has looked unstoppable; most particularly, during the sixty-year period immediately following 1933, during which the cumulative effect on the level of retail prices has been enormous, equivalent to 4,000% in the UK and 950% in the United States.

For the UK, however, the two main tenets of the Keynesian economics for the thirty years after the war, the macroeconomic policies affecting taxes, public spending, interest rates, and the like, should be used to keep up the level of demand in the economy and control the level of unemployment. Microeconomic policies, including price controls and incomes policies, should be used to control inflation.

The right-wing Tory party deliberately undertook to reverse these ideas and policy focuses. The macroeconomic policy after 1979 was intended to control inflation, while the microeconomic policy, or supply-side policies, were generally focused on reducing unemployment. The record of this shifted strategy, however, is "patchy" at best. Millions of people lost their jobs in two of the worst recessions in postwar Europe. These recessions undermined the central arguments advanced by the monetarists. The arguments implied that anti-inflationary macroeconomic strategy should produce only a short-lived rise in unemployment. However, in reality, unemployment climbed for seven years. It peaked at more than three million in 1986.

Britain's overall growth record since 1979 has been worse than that of other countries, and worse than the two decades immediately after World War II. Current recovery is very different from that during the eighties, when unemployment did not start falling until the fourth year of recovery. Inflation followed shortly after that. The recovery after 1992 was different, however, and unemployment fell by more than one million, while inflation stayed low. Possibly the underlying rate of productivity also started to increase as these other factors came into play. The combined effect of these two changes determined that Britain's economy might be able to grow at 3 to 4% a year for the next three or four years without taking huge risks with inflation. Realistically it will be at 2.5 to 3% a year compared with an underlying 2 to 2.5% for most of the postwar era.

When the Labour government came to power in the UK in 1997, it was widely held that the financial markets would probably not facilitate a boost in demand spurned by an incoming government, particularly not when the policy would concentrate on increasing borrowing. This feature of Keynesian economics established a case for reducing interest rates. One challenge affecting the Labour Party as it came to power was the test that Britain could grow faster if the tools of demand-management were put to use. The second challenge relates to the same supply-side policies that improved Britain's growth prospects and established weaker trade unions and greater inequality.

Evidence consistently supports the idea that monetary policies, whether expansive or restrictive, can work well only for a limited short—to-medium-term period, without having to be radically readjusted. Whichever single policy is prolonged or applied too broadly, the end result is that the policy tends to suffer from a pernicious form of macro-economic diminishing returns.

The periods of shifting inflation rates have demonstrated that the apparent short-term benefits of inflation are outweighed by long-term costs. The key to a successful economy is control of the money supply in all its changing forms. At the same time, it is important to note that inflation can only be achieved when the sovereignty of national government is limited using independent central banking systems.

Inflation is inextricably linked with the value of currency. With the increased competition among currencies, there has been a change to the ability and the incentives of governments and central banks to pursue high-inflation policies. Such changes have facilitated improvements in central bank independence, governance, and credibility, leading to better inflation outcomes.

Greater central bank credibility has facilitated the development of long-term bond markets in many countries. These markets did not exist before and flattened yield curves around the globe. The ways in which factors such as globalisation, deregulation, and financial innovation affect competition among currencies are numerous. First, there is the issue of the increased circulation of banknotes in dollars or other hard currencies that enable citizens to conduct transactions and store liquid wealth without holding inflationary currency.

The portion of US currency believed to be held in foreign countries rose dramatically from less than 20% in 1980 to almost 50% in the late

1990's. It remained near this high level as inflation rates came down. About $350 billion of US currency was held abroad in around 2007. This constituted an interest-free loan from the rest of the world to the United States.

Various advances in electronic payments and trading systems, both in the retail and wholesale sectors, have allowed consumers, investors, and banks to begin shifting wealth very cheaply and quickly, away from currencies and assets subject to inflation and related risks. Many emerging-market economies are also adopting these technologies, which are already in use in advanced economies.

While financial innovations such as credit card networks and money market mutual funds continue to become more widespread, especially in the various economies that have experienced high inflation, firms have also successfully reduced their holdings of cash and central bank reserves, shrinking the "base" for the inflation tax.

Developments facilitating competition among currencies may combine with a government that pressures a central bank to pursue an inflationary policy and secure much less benefit from increased inflation. Given the nature of currency, people can more rapidly and conveniently switch out of the local currency. The website of the central bank of Brazil, for example, explicitly acknowledges the role of inflation in driving financial innovations. It enabled firms and households to economise on cash balances.

As well as facilitating financial innovation, the rather negative experience of high inflation helped the public to become educated about the costs of inflation. Economists and central bankers have also devoted great attention to understanding the causes and consequences of inflation. They have provided the intellectual underpinning to policies oriented toward price stability.

The development of long-term local-currency bond markets also seems to have enabled governments and firms to establish long-term infrastructure and investment projects designed to promote economic development. Debt markets are only one of many factors which have helped cut the costs associated with long-term planning and enhance companies' abilities to undertake long-term investments. With the establishment of a stable currency, higher and more stable growth can be achieved and combined with an improved ability to undertake long-term plans. It can also help to improve the fiscal outlook for a country.

A strong, positive fiscal outlook can be achieved by increasing confidence and financial market development. A strong currency further boosts growth and, in a cyclical process, reinforces prospects for continued price stability. Prudent fiscal policies, which include programs designed to lower deficits, facilitate longer debt maturities, and reduce foreign-currency debt, can, in turn, reduce the likelihood and potential severity of a financial crisis. Strong currencies, promoted by strong financial policies, also help to make the financial positions of emerging-market governments less vulnerable to movements in interest rates and exchange rates. Reducing the perceived risk of a government defaulting also makes changes in investor sentiment and financial contagion less likely, thereby reducing financial market volatility.

Strong currencies are, in short, the foundation of the global community and, as another famous Russian, Dostoyevsky, said, currency, money, is *'coined liberty'*, providing a universally recognisable form of value and facilitating positive interaction between nations.

> **"When speculation has done its worst, two and two still make four."**
>
> **Samuel Johnson**

Chapter 16

July 2008—The Rise of the Conquistadors

"He who surpasses or subdues mankind must look down on the hate of those below."

Lord Byron

14th July 2008—Banco Santander announces that it intends to take over the UK bank Alliance & Leicester with £24bn in deposits and 254 branches

Conquistador; *A conqueror, especially one of the 16th-century Spanish soldiers who defeated the Indian civilisations of Mexico, Central America, or Peru.*

Why do some thrive and others wilt in times of crisis? What is the difference?

The Spanish Empire, the New World Order; During the course of the credit crisis the banks of Spain, most especially Banco Santander, sailed majestically on, like heavily armed galleons able to fend off the timid attacks of both a cooling national property market and a global liquidity problem. *How was this possible? Did they know something the world did not?*

To uncover the routes of this seemingly impregnable financial position it is necessary to look back at the history of that majestic country. During the 16th and early 17th century, the Spanish Empire quickly became one of the largest empires in world history. This growth occurred at an alarming rate without incorporating various aspects of the Spanish economy. Unfortunately, the implications of that rapid growth were not considered at the time. The excessive amassing of wealth was eventually detrimental for Spain, with Spain becoming a second rate power and has yet again to play a major role in European politics.

Since the fall of Rome, there had been no empire based in Europe extending outside that continent. This situation changed abruptly when Spain and Portugal became the pioneers in a new era of colonisation. Historically, this era was known as the Age of Discovery, or alternately, as the Age of Exploration. During this time, European nations began exploring the world by ocean, searching for trading partners and valuable trade goods.

In this era of discovery and exploration, Spain amassed tremendous wealth and a vast colonial empire led by the Conquistadors, or Conquerors. The rise of the Spanish Empire began just prior to 1500 and was emboldened with strategic, intelligent tactics; alliances were forged throughout Europe and rapid territorial expansion took place. Most often, this was accompanied by brutal destruction of foreign lands and violent colonisation of their native peoples.

Spain's global and imperial expansion was essentially motivated by four factors: to spread its religion; to reinforce national unity and identity by keeping alive a sense of national mission; to compete with Portugal for trade, territory, and glory; and to enhance Spain's international power. Although spreading the Catholic religion was seen throughout Spanish history as a driving force, it is not the main focus for our purposes. The other three motives are pertinent, however, and will be discussed in the following sections, for they form the development of the Spanish banks that exist today.

Laying the Foundation; The Union of Castile and Aragon

> *"Kings fight for empires, madmen for applause!"*
> **John Dryden**

In 1469, the profoundly significant marriage of Isabella I of Castile, at 18 years of age, and Ferdinand II of Aragon, at 17 years of age, united the two kingdoms of Castile and Aragon, and laid the foundation for a period of great success for Spain. This union ended Spain's internal, centuries-long conflicts. In 1474 Isabella I inherited the throne of Castile and in 1479 Ferdinand II inherited the throne of Aragon. The two jointly ruled and became known as ***Los Reyes Católicos***, the Catholic Monarchs.

During the reign of Isabella I and Ferdinand II, there was a perceived threat to the church from Jews masquerading as Christians. Because of this apparent threat, Pope Sixtus IV allowed the Catholic Monarchs to establish a special branch of the Inquisition of Spain. The First Grand Inquisitor, Tomas do Torquemada was appointed in 1480. Torquemada, coming from a family of converted Jews, became legendary and highly respected by the Spanish people. He was the most notorious of the Grand Inquisitors, and epitomised the harshness and cruelty of the Inquisition.

In 1492, the last Muslim stronghold, Granada, was captured and Roman Catholicism was established as the official state religion. The fall of Granada rendered the "re-conquest" of Spain complete. Torquemada convinced Isabella I and Ferdinand II to expel around 160,000 Jews who were unwilling to convert to Christianity. Violating the treaty with the former King of Granada, which guaranteed religious freedom for Muslims, Ferdinand II forced the Muslims to convert to Christianity. Those that did not convert were subsequently expelled in 1502; ***Spain went from being one of the most tolerant countries to one of the least***.

Following the siege of Granada, Isabella I and Ferdinand II debated whether to accept a proposal from the visionary explorer Christopher Columbus. Columbus had been pestering European courts, specifically in Portugal and Spain, to sponsor his expedition for the last eight years. Columbus believed that he had found mathematical proof that it would be easier to reach India by sailing west from the Canary Islands than it would be to travel east via land—in reality, Columbus severely underestimated the circumference of the earth!

Even though Portuguese explorers had notable success at sea, the king of Portugal rejected Columbus' argument. Columbus then presented his theory to the Spanish monarchs who delayed for a few years while a commission investigated his claim. Amid the development of economic competition between nations seeking wealth from the establishment of trade routes and colonies, the Spanish monarchs accepted Columbus' somewhat exorbitant terms and the explorer prepared vessels for the great adventure.

Spain and Portugal

> *"It is the privilege of posterity to set matters right between those antagonists who, by their rivalry for greatness, divided a whole age."*
>
> **Joseph Addison**

Spanish expansion overseas began for a number of reasons. One reason was that the Catholic Monarchs, Isabella I and Ferdinand II, wanted to secure the areas around Spain to defend against Muslim raids originating in North Africa. They also wanted to protect Castile's trade and shipping activities in the Mediterranean Sea and the Atlantic Ocean. Castile's positioning on the Iberian Peninsula was ideal for all travel and trade involving the New World into Europe, thus helping to spread Spanish culture and language. The monarchs also wanted to expand into neighbouring areas for gold and to enslave Africans. Spain wanted to increase its potential trade with the Far East, thereby gaining wealth and international prestige. The underlying motivation, of spreading Christianity, *was the primary reason why exploration of distant areas was politically supported*.

The Portuguese Empire was the first global empire with territory in South America, Africa, India and Southeast Asia. The desire to increase Spanish trade centered on the need to overcome the advantage Portuguese explorers and traders had gained by establishing these overseas bases. Some of the Portuguese bases on the African continent and islands off of its coast had the same advantages to those of the Spaniards. Furthermore, the Portuguese claimed Madeira and the Azores in 1419 and settled them in 1425. Portugal also occupied the Cape Verde Islands, established trading ports in the Gulf of Guinea and sailed around the Cape of Good Hope at the southern tip of Africa, thereby opening a sea route to the Far East. Spain was extremely motivated to match its neighbour's growing international influence.

When Christopher Columbus returned to Spain in 1493 after his first voyage to the Americas, Queen Isabella I and King Ferdinand II were determined to ensure that the valuable discoveries belonged to them rather than Portugal. They had hoped that Columbus' voyage would bring Spain international prestige and fabled riches. Isabella I and Ferdinand II secured from Pope Alexander VI the promise that all lands west of a certain line would belong exclusively to Spain, and all those east of the line to Portugal. In return for this, Isabella I and Ferdinand II claimed they would convert the heathen natives—those not belonging to the widely held religion. The line determined by the Pope extended through the Atlantic 100 leagues, 300 miles, west of the Cape Verde Islands, which were Portugal's most westerly possession.

King John II of Portugal protested that this line trimmed him too tight. Therefore, in 1494 ambassadors from Spain and Portugal met at Tordesillas in northwest Spain to resolve the dispute. The principle of the line had already been accepted, but both sides agreed to move it to a point 370 leagues west of the Cape Verde Islands. This line of declamation was known as the Tordesillas Line. This agreement had a profound significance which no one yet appreciated: this line sliced through the entire eastern part of South America from the mouth of the Amazon to São Paulo.

Both Spanish and Portuguese navigators discovered the east coast of South America in the same year, 1500. The Line of Tordesillas determined that this territory belonged to Portugal. Thus the vast area that is now known as Brazil, the largest territory in South America, is the exception to Spanish domination in the new world. Brazil is the only modern country in Latin America with Portuguese, rather than Spanish as its national language.

> *"Tangled in that ancient endless chain*
>
> *Of profit, power, gain, of grab the land!*

Of grab the gold! Of grab the ways of satisfying need!

Of work the men! Of take the pay!

Of owning everything for one's own greed!"

Langston Hughes

Before examining the increasingly exciting advancements abroad, there were some other noteworthy events occurring in and around Spain that also contributed to the expansion of the Spanish Empire. Specifically, the Canary Islands became part of Spanish Territory in 1495 and to the detriment of France, Spain's military dominance continued in the Mediterranean with the conquest of the Kingdom of Naples at the southern tip of the Italian peninsula. The southern part of the Kingdom of Navarre—a small piece of land along the Atlantic Ocean on either side of the Pyrenees mountain range, thereby forming a massive divide between France and Spain—was absorbed by the Crown of Castile in 1513 and thus became part of the unified Kingdom of Spain.

The Spanish Monarchy

"I shall be an autocrat: that's my trade. And the good Lord will forgive me: that's his."
Empress Catherine the Great 1729-1796

Another strategic move on Queen Isabella's part to ensure long-term political stability in Spain was the arrangement of prudent marriages for each of her five children. Queen Isabella's first daughter, Isabella II, was married to Alfonso of Portugal. This forged an important tie between Spain and Portugal, which was hoped, would release tensions and ensure future alliances. Unfortunately, Isabella II died shortly after the marriage and before giving birth to an heir.

Queen Isabella's second daughter, Juana, married Prince Philip of the Kingdom of Bohemia; Philip was heir to the crown of the Holy Roman Empire. This ensured Spain's alliance with the Holy Roman Empire, which was a far-reaching union of territories in Central Europe, and assured Spain's future political security. Juan, Queen Isabella's only son, married Margaret of Austria, thereby maintaining the ties with the Habsburg dynasty, a relationship Spain relied upon heavily. Queen Isabella's fourth child, Maria, married Manuel I of Portugal, a move that strengthened Spain's link with Portugal. Finally, Catherine, Queen Isabella's youngest child, married Henry VIII, King of England and was the mother to Queen Mary I.

Upon the death of King Ferdinand II, the Spanish crown went to his grandson Charles, son of Juana and her husband Philip. Charles was Charles I of Spain but also, as a direct descendant of the Habsburgs of Austria, went on to become Emperor Charles V of Germany. In 1519, he secured the title of Holy Roman Emperor for the Austrian dynasty. This was the peak of glory for Spain, but was followed by a period of endless wars that drained the country of its wealth and consumed increasing sums of gold and silver from the new world. Additional European wars were waged under Philip II, including the war between Spain and England where the Great Armada—the unsuccessful invasion by Spain of England—resulted in the destruction of Spain's "invincible" fleet in 1588. From here, Spain's political decline became notorious with a series of clumsy politicians and heirs.

The Voyages of Columbus

"Following the light of the sun, we left the Old World."
Christopher Columbus

Columbus and the Pinzón brothers, a family of wealthy fleet owners, set sail from Spain to the Canaries on August 2, 1492. On September 6 the ships set sail westward into "the unknown" and reached the shore of an island in the Bahamas on October 12. They were not the first Europeans to reach the American continent; they were preceded by the Norse, led by Leif Ericson, who established a temporary settlement some 500 years earlier. However, it seems that Columbus and his crew were the first to record their achievement. Columbus planted the royal banner of Spain and claimed the land for Isabella I and Ferdinand II.

The island was named San Salvador, for Jesus the Savior, and although it is not known which island they landed on, one of the Bahaman Islands still bears the name San Salvador. A few days later the explorers sailed past numerous islands giving them each a Spanish name until they reached the most important landfall of the expedition. This was the large island of Cuba—Columbus had convinced himself that it was Cipango, the poetic name for what is now assumed to be Japan, and a place of renowned marvel as described by Marco Polo.

The next significant landfall was the large island Columbus named after Spain—Española, or Hispaniola. On the shores of Hispanolia, Columbus' ship, the *Santa Maria* ran aground and was wrecked. Columbus left a small colony of 40 men with food and ammunition for a year and went back to Spain with a party of kidnapped natives, of which only a handful survived. Columbus was well received at the court of Isabella I and Ferdinand II as he presented the monarchs with a few captured natives ***and some gold!*** This was to be the height of Christopher Columbus' career.

His following three voyages to the Americas were fraught with misfortune, although there were certain exceptions. Columbus' second expedition was on a much larger scale, with the main intent of establishing colonies. The first landfalls proved to be the new discoveries of Guadalupe and Puerto Rico. Unfortunately, the natives massacred the garrison Columbus had left on Hispaniola. When this news reached Spain, doubts began to arise regarding Columbus' judgment.

During this voyage, Columbus and his men implemented a policy that has been referred to by historians as genocide. The native people on the island of Hispaniola, the Tiano, were mostly and systematically enslaved and murdered, while others were rounded up by the hundreds and shipped to Europe to be sold. The remaining population was forced by Columbus to search for gold. The Tiano tried to resist, but with superior weaponry and European diseases ravaging their population, the Tiano fighters were no match for the Castilians. They were hunted down and killed.

In despair, the Tiano engaged in mass suicide, even killing their own children to save them from the Castilians. In two and a half years, the Tiano population plummeted by approximately 250,000; those remaining were taken as slaves to work on plantations but the mortality rate was high. By 1550, less than 60 years after Columbus landed, the native population on the island was down to only a few hundred and another hundred years later, perhaps only a handful remained.

Despite the doubts about his managerial skill, Columbus managed to successfully confront his critics in court and set sail again in 1498. By the time he returned to Hispaniola in 1498, he encountered many of the Castilian settlers, who were discontented for having been misled about the supposedly bountiful riches of the new world. Columbus also refused to baptise the native people of Hispaniola because, as a fierce supporter of slavery, he would not be able to enslave them under Catholic law. Columbus repeatedly dealt with rebellious settlers and natives going so far as to hang his own crew for disobeying him.

Some of the returning settlers and sailors lobbied against Columbus at the Castilian court, accusing him of gross mismanagement and governing tyrannically. This prompted Isabella I and Ferdinand II to appoint Francisco de Bobadilla, a member of the Order of Calatrava, as a governor to supervise Columbus. Bobadilla arrived in Santo Domingo while Columbus was away, and immediately bombarded Columbus and his two brothers with accusations. A Spanish historian even stated that those who loved Columbus had to admit the atrocities that had taken place. As a result of the complaints, Columbus was returned to Spain in chains without being allowed a word in his own defense. He was cast into prison, unable to return to Castile until he was 53 years of age.

King Ferdinand II and Queen Isabella I were sympathetic to his plight, and Columbus set sail on his final voyage in May of 1502. This was an almost unmitigated disaster. At one point, Columbus realised there was a hurricane brewing and attempted to find shelter on Hispaniola at Santo Domingo. Columbus was denied port and the new governor refused to listen to Columbus' prediction of a storm. Columbus' ships found shelter at the mouth of the Rio Jaina and survived the storm with only minor damage. However, the Spanish treasure fleet sailed into the hurricane and did not fare as well. Twenty-nine of the thirty ships were lost in addition to 500 lives and an immense cargo of gold. After numerous other unfortunate events, which included storms, ships damaged by pestilence and stranded at sea, Columbus eventually returned to Spain in November of 1504.

Exploration, Conquest and Colonisation

"How grand is victory, but how dear!"

Anonymous

What resulted next were a series of events that are perhaps unparalleled in history. The half-century that followed Columbus' voyages consisted of a frenzy of activity in the new world, at once part exploration, and part conquest and part colonisation. The Spanish scrambled and struggled to make the most of their unexpected new opportunities. They were successful, and the 16th and 17th centuries witnessed *the birth of a new world power.*

The Spanish Empire became the world's foremost power and European politics were hinged upon their dominance. The Iberian Peninsula was poised for a leap into the unknown both abroad and at home.

By 1506 the entire continental shore of the Caribbean Sea had been explored from Honduras to the mouth of the Orinoco. During the first decade of the 16th century, the only secure Spanish settlement in the new world was in Santo Domingo on the island of Hispaniola. Another equally stable settlement was not achieved in continental America until 1510, when Vasco Núñez de Balboa, Spanish explorer, governor and conquistador, founded Santa María la Antigua del Darién.

Founding Santa María was not as simple as declaring it so. Balboa encountered the native chieftain Cémaco with 500 warriors waiting to battle. It was a difficult battle for both sides, but with a stroke of luck the Spanish came out on top and the natives abandoned the town and headed for the jungles. The Spanish plundered the houses and gathered a treasure trove of gold ornaments. In 1513, Balboa crossed the Isthmus of Panama to the Pacific Ocean and became the first European to see or reach the Pacific from the new world. After discovering the Pacific, Balboa was given the responsibility for "Spain's new ocean."

This enraged Pedrarias Dávila, also known as Pedro Arias de Ávila, and fueled their bitter rivalry. Pedrarias, who married a close friend of Queen Isabella I, was at the time the governor of a neighbouring crown colony and was already furious at being upstaged by his much younger counterpart. Pedrarias had Balboa judicially beheaded on charges of treason. In 1519, within a month of his rival's murder, Pedrarias established a new Spanish municipality and bishopric on the south coast of the isthmus at Panama.

Panama immediately became the place of focal importance for the developing Spanish Empire. Many expeditions to colonise the Pacific set out from Panama and the produce of the Pacific colonies was brought there before journeying back to Spain. The goods came across the isthmus to Portobelo. It became a great scene of trade every year up to 1748. Every year a fleet of Spanish galleons arrived, delivering European goods to the colonies and returning the wealth of Latin America to the colonial center. From this moment forward, the speed of Spanish expansion and consolidation over a vast region was astonishing. As a result of conquering Cuba and founding Havana, by 1515 all of the islands in the Caribbean were under Spanish control and became a launch pad for further expansion.

Rise of the Conquistadors

In this new era of exploration, discovery and colonisation, Spain amassed tremendous wealth and a vast colonial empire through the conquest of the Americas. Many of the new possessions were gained by the work of adventurers and explorers who became known as *Los Conquistadores*—the ruthlessly brilliant Conquistadors. Following Christopher Columbus' discovery of the new world in 1492, the Conquistadors brought much of the Americas under Spanish control in the 16th and 17th centuries. During the half-century following Columbus' voyages, the activity by a single nation, Spain, on the other side of a vast ocean in an age of relatively primitive sailing vessels is perhaps unparalleled in history. There were numerous demonstrations of courage, greed, cruelty and wanton destructiveness by the Spanish Conquistadors.

As mentioned earlier, Spaniards had used the major Caribbean Islands as a base for their expeditions since the early 1500's. It was the Conquistadors who recruited, equipped and led these expeditions, often with the financial backing of merchants in Spain. They were in search of great riches or legendary places such as the Seven Cities of Cíbola where the streets and houses were supposed to be adorned with gold and jewels, and a spring whose waters were said to have the power to restore youth.

The Conquistadors came from an area in Spain where fighting was a way of life and were usually mature men who fought earlier battles with the Muslims in the south of Spain. The wars against the Muslims in Spain had gone on for centuries, and these men were accustomed to achieving their goals of fame and fortune through military endeavour. By taking treasure, territory, and subjects for their country, they won recognition from the king. Many explorers also felt it was their moral responsibility to convert people to Christianity.

> *"It is only mercenaries who expect to be paid by the day."*
> **Teresa of Avila**

The Conquistadors were more mercenaries than actual soldiers. They would have been motivated to take part in hostilities by the desire for private gain that would have been promised, by or on behalf of a party to the conflict. The material compensation would have likely been substantially in excess of that promised or paid to combatants of similar ranks and functions in the armed forces of that party. The authority of the captain was assured by being granted a royal commission, due to his experience and by the fact that he controlled the spoils. The captains would often resort to extreme measures to maintain their authority, thus making them heroes and legendary figures as seen by their soldiers.

Another trait of the Conquistadors was that in comparison to other contemporary military ventures, a very low percentage of them came from nobility. Commoners made up the bulk of the Spanish forces, and joining a Conquistador company was an attractive method of social advancement. With the blessing—but not the financial support—of the Spanish government, these Conquistadors made their way through Central and South America claiming territory for Spain. The Conquistadors' expeditions radically increased Spain's territory, wealth, and power.

The Spanish conquest of the Americas, moreover, has been chronicled as an impressive feat that occurred at an unprecedented pace. The purpose of these conquests was equally to spread the "Word of God" and to bring civilisation to the most obscure parts of the world. This was accomplished with astounding ability, quickly expanding its borders far into other territories. However, the testimony of some indigenous peoples, as well as some contemporary Spanish humanists, has presented the Spanish Conquest of the Americas as a series of unfortunate and morally questionable acts, driven by greed for gold, that resulted in the destruction of several native civilisations.

Specifically, the group of Conquistadors that first voyaged with Cortés went for the sole reason to find gold in the New World. Historians have studied the short time required for the Spanish conquest of vast populations in the Americas. The native populations were conquered with intentional force by the Spaniards, combined with somewhat unintentional fortune for the Spanish. While technological and cultural factors played an important role in the victories and defeats of the Conquistadors, one fatal factor was the disease brought from Europe, especially smallpox, which in several cases destroyed entire nations before the arrival of the Spaniards.

Another key factor in the Spanish conquest of the Americas, was the ability of the Conquistadors to manipulate the political situation between indigenous peoples, either by allying with natives who had been subjugated by more powerful neighbouring tribes and kingdoms, as in the case of the Aztec empire, or by supporting one side of a civil war, as in the case of the Inca Empire. Regardless of the indigenous peoples' established settlements, determination to remain independent and their large numerical superiority—the Spanish population never exceeded 5% of the native population—the Conquistadors ultimately overcame native populations. The advantages of advanced military technology, divide-and-conquer tactics and strategy, and European diseases were unmatched by the natives.

As mentioned above, Vasco Núñez de Balboa was one of the early Conquistadors voyaging west from Spain, however two adventurers in particular caught the imagination of their own time and indeed, of every age since. These two men are credited for the victories won against the greatest odds for the greatest gains. Both Hernán Cortés de Monroy y Pizarro and Francisco Pizarro González each with a handful of Spaniards toppled the great empires of the Aztecs in Mexico and the Incas in Peru. These two conquests were especially significant in Spanish history because of the great wealth found in both Mexico and Peru.

Cortes

> *"Among these temples there is one which far surpasses all the rest, whose grandeur of architectural details no human tongue is able to describe; for within its precincts, surrounded by a lofty wall, there is room enough for a town of five hundred families."*
>
> **Hernán Cortés**

Hernán Cortés de Monroy y Pizarro, known simply as Cortés was a Castilian Conquistador that brought about the fall of the Aztec Empire. He also brought large portions of mainland Mexico under Spanish rule in the early 16th century. Like most of the Conquistadors, Cortés came from a family of lesser nobility. He was a farmer and lawyer who had been in the new world since 1504 and established himself in Hispanolia and Cuba.

In the summer of 1518, a party of Spanish explorers met with the retinue of a local chieftain on the Caribbean coast of Mexico. The two sides were only able to communicate in signs but the mood was amicable and gifts were exchanged. The Spaniards presented glass beads, iron pins and scissors. In return, the indigenous people presented, much to the astonishment of the Spaniards, superbly worked golden ornaments and vessels. The Indian chieftain sent the news of these pale-skinned, bearded strangers to his lord, the Aztec emperor. The arrival of the Spaniards suggested to the Aztecs that the exiled Quetzalcoatl might be about to return. Appropriate measures were taken and this "god-king" was welcomed.

The golden objects were dutifully sent back to the Spanish superiors in Cuba and the King of Spain's share of the treasure was dispatched to Spain. The effect of this gold is catalytic—an expedition is immediately prepared to invade the wealthy kingdom now known as Mexico. The choice of leader fell on Cortés, who set sail in 1519 and rebelled against the recall of his expedition by the governor of Cuba, Diego Velázquez de Cuéllar.

In March 1519, the Spaniards led by Cortés arrived in Mexico with greed in their eyes. The Spanish party arrived with eleven ships carrying 600 men, 16 horses and about 20 guns and was confronted by a large number of Indians ready for battle. The horses and guns, both new to the Indians, proved overwhelming and the battle was rapidly decided. Peace was made and presents exchanged—including 20 Indian women for the Spaniards. One of these women became known to the Spaniards as Doña Marina. Doña Marina became Cortés' interpreter and mistress, and later bore Cortés a son.

Through a strategic alliance of warring indigenous peoples, as well as against the governor of Cuba, Diego Velázquez de Cuéllar, Cortés was successful in conquering Mexico. Furthermore, the fortunate event of the Aztec emperor, Montezuma II—believing Cortés to be Quetzalcoatl—also aided Cortés' success. Recognising the potential danger ahead, Cortés devised a plan to remove the emperor from his palace. The plan was brilliantly controlled with persuasion and threats of violence, while Montezuma II appeared to be in control and protected by the Spanish. A few hundred Spaniards effectively took control of the mighty Aztec Empire.

Pizarro

> *"Many [Indians] came to gape at the strange men, now so famous, and at their attire, arms and horses, and they said, 'These men are gods!"*
>
> **Francisco López de Gómara**

Francisco Pizarro González was a Conquistador of the Crown of Castile and was made famous for conquering the Incan Empire and founding Lima, the modern day capital of Peru. In February 1502 he sailed to the new world with the Governor of Hispaniola and then in 1513 accompanied Balboa in crossing the Isthmus of Panama. Siding with Pedrarias when Balboa was murdered, Pizarro was bestowed the important political office of mayor and magistrate of Panama City.

In August of 1526, Pizarro led the second of three expeditions to Peru from Panama with the intent of extracting wealth. The first expedition was unsuccessful, succumbing to such hardships as bad weather, lack of food, and skirmishes with hostile natives. Upon arrival in Colombia, the party separated and Pizarro stayed to explore the new and often-perilous territory of the swampy Colombian coasts while the other group headed back to Panama for reinforcements and Pizarro's main pilot Bartolomé Ruiz sailed further south.

Bartolomé Ruiz sailed over the equator, found and captured a raft of natives. Much to everyone's surprise, the raft carried a load of textiles, ceramic objects, and some much-desired pieces of gold, silver, and emeralds. Ruiz took some of the natives to serve as interpreters. This chance encounter was the first contact between Europeans and the fabulously wealthy empire of the Incas. Ruiz's findings became the central focus of this second expedition, which only served to pique the Conquistador's interests for more gold and land.

In the spring of 1527, after weathering appalling conditions on a swampy uninhabited island, Pizarro sailed southwards. They arrived at Tumbles, their first Inca city. After a brief expedition, Pizarro's men confirmed that they had arrived at a rich and civilised society. It was not until January 1530 that Pizarro was able to drum up enough support from the Spanish government and sail again from Panama. Unlike Cortés' speedy advancement in Mexico, Pizarro's progress was slow. Finally in September of 1532 Pizarro marched out and attacked the vast empire of the Incas.

Once again, the Spanish had luck on their side. When they marched into the Inca Empire, they found it in a state of turmoil caused by a civil war. Therefore, the small band of strangers was dealt with less forcefully than they would have been. In another stroke of luck, the Spaniard's starting point gave them easy access to Atahualpa's army. The Spanish rode in on their horses to find Atahualpa and the natives relaxing with their women after winning the civil war. Tensions were light until Atahualpa declined Friar Vincent Valverd's proposal that he submit to the Christian rule and contemptuously threw his Bible to the ground.

The Spaniards, relying mainly on the terror inspired by their horses, animals unknown to the Incas, annihilated Atahualpa's army. Atahualpa quickly understood what Pizarro was after. In exchange for their freedom, the Incas offered Pizarro something even Cortés had never dreamed of: Atahualpa offered to fill a room that measured 22 feet by 18 feet and 15 feet tall, once with gold and twice with silver within two months; these riches became one of the enduring images of the Spanish conquest. In the months that followed, the Incas collected 13,420 pounds of 22 carat gold and 26,000 pounds of pure silver. Regardless of their agreement, Pizarro had Atahualpa publicly garroted in August of 1533. The Inca Empire continued to be torn apart with an orgy of Spanish plundering and formally dissolved in 1572.

> *"It is not the want, but rather abundance that creates avarice."*
>
> **Michel Eyquem De Montaigne**

Pizarro's life ended as violently as he lived. He was stabbed to death in Lima in 1541 following a quarrel with a fellow Conquistador. Pizarro's legacy to the Spanish crown however, exceeded even his own dreams. *In 1545, in what Pizarro's men called Upper Peru, an Indian named Diego Gualpa discovered something that changed the economic history of the world.*

With a peak towering 15,827 feet above sea level, the uncannily symmetrical Cerro Rico was the supreme embodiment of the most potent of all ideas about money: a mountain of solid silver ore. Cerro Rico literally translates to "rich hill" and is actually located in Potosí, in modern Bolivia.

"It was not by gold or by silver, but by labour, that all wealth of the world was originally purchased."

Adam Smith

Initially, the Spaniards paid the inhabitants to work the mines, but the conditions were so harsh that by the late 1500's a system of forced labour was introduced. Men from across the provinces were conscripted to work in the mines. The mortality rates were extremely high due to constant exposure to mercury fumes generated by the "patio process" of refinement. Furthermore, the miners had to descend seven hundred feet through the most primitive mine shafts through air that was, and still is, noxious. The silver rush city of Potosí became known as a "mouth of hell," where great masses of people entered every year and were sacrificed for the greed of the Spaniards. When the indigenous workforce was depleted, the Spaniards imported thousands of African slaves to act as human mules.

Interestingly enough, the Inca were, 500 years ago, the most sophisticated society in South America. *The Inca Empire was moneyless!*

The Incas appreciated the aesthetic qualities of rare metals. Gold was considered the sweat of the sun, and silver was considered as the tears of the moon. It was labour that was the unit of value in the Inca Empire. In fact, the Inca could not understand the insatiable lust for gold and silver that gripped the Europeans. For the Inca, it was incomprehensible that Pizarro and his men considered silver to be more than a shiny piece of decorative metal. The Inca didn't see what the Spaniards saw in the silver; *something that could be made into money, a unit of account, a store of value, and portable power.*

Potosí was where Spain struck its riches. Between 1556 and 1783 Cerro Rico yielded 45,000 tons of pure silver that were transformed into bars and coins and shipped to Seville. Despite the horrendous conditions in Potosí, the city rapidly became one of the principal cities in the Spanish Empire; in modern day Spanish, the expression, *valer un potosí,* "to be worth a potosí" refers to Potosí and means to be worth a fortune.

It is argued that money is a medium of exchange with the advantage of eliminating inefficiencies of barter. Money is considered to be a unit of account, facilitating valuation and calculation. It stores value, enabling economic transactions to occur over time and geographical distances. In order for money to function optimally in the way it is designed, it must be readily available, affordable, durable, fungible, portable and reliable. For millennia, gold, silver and bronze were regarded as the ideal monetary raw material.

There were various problems with early monetary systems in Europe one of them being what medieval and early modern governments called the problem of small change. The difficulty of establishing stable relationships between coins made of different types of metal meant that smaller denomination coins were subject to recurrent shortages, yet also to depreciations and debasements. When the Spanish Conquistadors found plentiful silver in Potosí and other places in the new world, notably in Zacatecas Mexico, it appeared they solved this century's old problem.

The Castilian monarchy was of course the first beneficiary because they had sponsored the conquests. The convoys of ships transporting 170 tons of silver a year docked at Seville. One-fifth of all of this went directly to the crown. Spain's newfound wealth was spent in a way that provided the entire continent with monetary stimulus. The Spanish *"piece of eight"* became the world's first truly global currency and financed the protracted wars Spain was fighting in Europe as well as the rapidly expanding European-Asia trade.

Even with immense wealth from the new world, Spain could not get the rebellious Dutch to heel nor could they secure England under the Spanish crown, and most importantly, all of that silver could not save Spain from an inexorable economic and imperial decline. Similar to King Midas, the Spanish monarchs Charles V and Philip II found that such abundance of precious metal could be a curse as much as a blessing.

The Spanish had so much silver dug up so quickly to pay for their conquests that silver declined in value. This was based on its purchasing power with respect to other goods. What resulted from the influx of silver was a price revolution that affected all of Europe from the 1540's to the 1640's. The cost of food, that had shown no sustained upward trend for over 300 years, rose markedly. Within Spain, there was also a resource curse or "paradox of plenty," where the abundance of silver stunted economic growth in other areas. The incentive for more productive economic activity declined. The Spanish failed to understand that the value of precious metal is not absolute. Money is only worth what someone else is willing to give you for it. All other things equal, an increase in the money supply will only make prices higher. *It will not make a society richer; it will just lead to inflation!*

The Conquistadors of Today

One of the historical outgrowths of Spain's exploration, conquest and collapse in this era was that it prevented the country from developing a sophisticated banking system. As we well know, money is really about *credit*. That credit is in itself a form of belief in the ability of the institution—in their case, the monarchy—to pay. Between 1557 and 1696, the monarchy defaulted on its debt not just once, but fourteen times! All the silver from the new world could not ensure that Spain would make good on its debts, and prevented the nation from developing along the same lines as much of Europe had.

Fast forward to the present; it seems that like the explorers of old, Spanish citizens have sought to expand their territory without heeding the potential consequences of over-extension. Spain has seen an almost unprecedented growth in the housing market, which one analyst described as *"the United States on speed!"* Housing prices tripled in the last decade in the credit-fueled expansion, and as in other countries, the market quickly overheated as a result of reckless lending. Consumption was almost entirely credit-driven, as homeowner's extracted home equity at record pace in order to finance a rapidly-expanding standard of living.

As the Spanish property bubble came on the heels of the US experience, warning signs were perhaps more evident. International banks scrambled early to sell off mortgage-related securities, in a pre-emptive move that forced prices down abruptly. Suffering its own property-induced downturn, Dubai's sovereign wealth fund pulled support for Inmobiliaria Colonial, the country's largest lender. Fearing a painful economic downturn, the Spanish government quickly moved to cushion the downfall by injecting 20 billion euro into stimulating spending. Luckily, Spain had saved for rainy day, unlike some of its European neighbours, so it was able to call upon its budget surplus in order to aid the fiscal stimulus.

What is interesting, especially in the context of Spain's historical ambitions, is that the impetus for much of this internal expansion came from outside its territory. In the modern era, it was the need for Spain's acquiescence to the European Union that has, in effect, financed this boom—*and set the stages for its subsequent bust*. When Spain joined the European monetary regime, it lost the independence to chart its own course in terms of monetary policy; this had the effect of halving its interest rate virtually overnight. This had the knock on effect of dropping interest rates below the prevailing rate of inflation, which fuelled an explosive credit boom; now the situation is playing itself in reverse, as the markets have reacted to the collapse in mortgages by ratcheting rates by nearly a factor of two since 2005.

Despite the fiscal stimulus, many believe that Spain's renewed decline is just the tip of the iceberg. Unemployment has risen drastically and banks' capital has seized in recent months, as a result of their inability to absorb the sharp rise in non-performing loans. Much like the "perfect storm" that bankrupted the early Spanish monarchies, Spain faces a convergence of unprecedented economic factors that are forcing its decline: dramatically increased energy prices, rising interest rates, and the country's "home grown" housing collapse. Reflecting Spain's competition with Portugal some 500 years earlier, many have linked this particular circumstance to the "importation" of competitive factors from the European Union. Like before, Spain had little choice but to rapidly expand its economic policies, in the process, unintentionally spurring unsustainable growth.

The *"importation"* of the credit crisis is certainly not the only factor to be considered in the Spanish case. It is widely believed that reckless lending and lax standards led to the housing bubble as much as any other factor; indeed, while Spain has dodged the "subprime bullet," it seems that housing valuations upon which loans were originated were routinely inflated. The "great unknown," then, is how widespread this practice was, and to what extent banks around the world will be exposed to these highly-inflated mortgage values.

Even amid the chaos of rampant decline, the new Conquistadors are on the rise. Two of Spain's largest banks are poised to expand where others have failed:

"In late July, Spain's two biggest banking groups produced results that must have had victims of the global credit crunch weeping. First, BBVA announced a rise in operating profit of 12% to €5.5 billion for the first half of 2008; its return on equity is one of Europe's highest, at 25%, and its return on assets a more than healthy 1.25%. The next day, its main rival Santander produced equally impressive numbers. Its profit rose 22% in 2008, to €4.73 billion. Revenues grew 16% over the period, whereas costs grew by just 5%, enabling operating income to grow 26%."

Like their predecessors centuries earlier, the success of these Spanish banking giants has come not from their internal conquests but from overseas expansion. This has meant that they have avoided much of the dynamic that has brought about the impending collapse of Spain's domestic banks: *"Much of the growth of the banking industry in Spain in the past 20 years has been linked to the construction industry; banks lent to property developers to build homes, and then lent money to homeowners so that they could purchase them, with a period of negative real interest rates this decade adding fuel to the fire."* BBVA and Santander are now poised to assert their dominance once more, even as their domestic counterparts suffer at the hands of their own expansion.

What's more, Banco Santander has emerged as one of Europe's strongest banks. Now the largest bank by market value in the Euro zone, it has earned that success by wholly avoiding exposure to toxic mortgage securities and pursuing a diversified business across Europe and the Americas. Like its successful counterparts in France, Santander turned its focus away from lucrative short-term investment banking activities and instead concentrated on its retail operations; at the same time, it diversified away from its domestic bias, building a strong business in the rapidly expanding banking sector in Latin America and buying distressed real estate assets in the UK. In doing so, it has complemented its own existing strengths and has not overexposed the bank to unforeseen future losses.

However, even though it has accomplished this expansion in a diversified and responsible way, it has nonetheless done so in a concentrated fashion within both Spain and Britain, its two main regional markets. These markets account for three-quarters of its loan assets, meaning that further pain in these areas could result in losses that have not yet been accounted for. The ramifications of further losses, perhaps due to a so-called "W-shaped" recession—one in which the global economy initially recovers from recession but slips again before finally emerging from the crisis—could mean that future losses in Spain will infect the wider Euro zone:

"We've already commented that Spain's banks are fast becoming the country's biggest landlords and estate agents because of the amount of unsold property and the number of property developers and constructors who have gone to the wall—leaving behind unfinished properties and outstanding debts. Rather than take these bad debts 'on the chin', Spanish banks are using every trick in their accounting book to revalue these 'assets', doing anything they can not to declare a debt as "bad." In a desperate attempt to keep their day-to-day balance sheets looking healthy, they have created a fictitious asset base of dubious value. While there is undoubtedly a storm brewing here in Spain, think how France and Germany (and the other stronger nations) are feeling about this particular economic millstone they'll soon be lumbered with. Spain no longer stands or falls alone, and these banking practices are enough to cause severe problems throughout Europe."

This illustrates the as-yet unknown territory that even Spain's most successful banks have entered into. BBVA and Santander have, like the Conquistadors of old, earned success where those before them have failed, but they may yet suffer at the hands of their own expansion. This saga calls to mind the mountain of silver at Potosi, which seemed to be the answer to everything, creating money from nothing. Then before very long the very source of the prosperity eventually led to the downfall and collapse; overvalued real estate assets now held on the books of even the strongest banks may yet unravel in the same manner as the silver market's collapse 500 hundred years earlier.

Conclusion

> *"But in truth, should I meet with gold or spices in great quantity, I shall remain till I collect as much as possible, and for this purpose I am proceeding solely in quest of them."*
> **Christopher Columbus**

In the Age of Discovery, Spain built an empire that was nearly unrivalled in its scope and breadth. It reaped an unprecedented amount of natural resource wealth from the new world, enriching itself and vaulting itself to a privileged and powerful position on the European continent and beyond. As we have explained, this overexpansion and unchecked growth actually prove to be its undoing; without a solid foundation upon which to build, the Spanish monarchy eventually overextended itself; *having built its empire upon the uncertain promise of future riches.*

Where one explorer failed, others succeeded. The Conquistadors took up the exploration and conquest of the new world where Columbus and his followers left off, and indeed, continued the expansion of the Spanish empire. As they were privately funded and richly rewarded with the spoils of their wars of conquest, they were able to succeed where Columbus and others had not, precisely because of their varied experience and methods. Eventually, they too would succumb to the same fate, as unfettered growth soon led to collapse.

In much the same way, albeit five centuries later, Spain's domestic banking industry has engendered its own collapse through overexpansion within its own territory. Reckless lending and lax standards, coupled with monetary policy that was forcibly "imported" from the wider European Union, created a housing bubble rivaling even that of the subprime crisis in the US. Even though some banks have stood strong, too many have come crashing down, as uncertain real estate valuations make the once-strong balance sheets of these new Conquistadors evaporate—*like the silver wealth of the Spanish monarchies!*

It is too soon to tell what many happen in the wake of this renewed crisis in Spain. What makes the scenario even more dangerous than any before it is the inescapable pressure of the European Union; where previously, banks might expand and collapse under their own power and be responsible only to themselves, the new generation presents an as-yet untested dynamic for the wider Euro zone. If these large, diversified banks were to collapse amid these *"fictitious valuations"* and require a rescue, Spain alone will not be able to undertake these measures on their own, and the crisis will inevitably spread across the continent.

Readjustment of the economy to such a shock will be immensely damaging and far more catastrophic than anything before it. However, the Spaniards have had luck on their side before. If they are able to heed the warning signs where their predecessors and counterparts did not, perhaps their aggressive strategy will yet pay off. It may be that luck will triumph over logic or in the words of Christopher Columbus, the man who inadvertently launched the first Spanish Empire: *"For the execution of the voyage to the Indies, I did not make use of intelligence, mathematics or maps."*

From the man who is credited with discovering America we move in Chapter 17 to another seafaring race, the Icelanders who cheerfully, and maybe recklessly, traded their fishing nets for the lure of internet banking!

Chapter 17

August 2008—Cod Moves in Mysterious Ways; Island Records!

"Greed is a fat demon with a small mouth and whatever you feed it is never enough."

Jan Anwillem Van De Wetering

August 2008—The Moment the Icelandic Banking System Collapsed.

Landnámabók; *Iceland was discovered by Naddoddr, one of the first settlers on the Faroe Islands, who was sailing from Norway to the Faroe Islands, but got lost and drifted to the east coast of Iceland. Naddoddr named the country Snæland (Snowland).*

What is it about the allure of money that can drive an entire nation to the brink of fiscal madness? What is the difference between symptoms and the disease?

Alone in a Sea of Debt—An Island Crisis; On November 20, 2008, the deputy managing director of the International Monetary Fund, John Lipsky, stated that Iceland was *"in the midst of a banking crisis of extraordinary proportions."* Faced with astronomical levels of debt, a severe recession, a shattered banking sector, and a collapsing currency, Iceland was forced to secure a $4.6 billion bailout from the IMF and its Nordic neighbours and sought over $5 billion more from Russia that has yet to fully materialise.

Commentators worldwide regarded the virtual collapse of not only the tiny nation's financial sector but also its entire economic base as the first *sovereign* casualty of the credit crisis. A country of some 300,000 people had somehow racked up an impressive debt of up to $70 billion by some accounts, and an economy that shrunk by 10% in 2009. Unemployment hit a 40-year high and substantial financial pain is surely to remain a permanent fixture in Icelandic life for years to come. Politically, the administration of Prime Minister Geir Haarde came under direct fire, and after several failed attempts to form a coalition government, fell under the weight of the economic collapse.

How does a tiny nation historically renowned for cod fishing and geysers go from being one of the richest countries in the world, with one of the highest standards of living according to the United Nations, to national bankruptcy?

Far from being an exaggeration, the central bank is technically insolvent, and the country's financial future is heavily mortgaged. Several factors contributed to Iceland's demise. This chapter will explore these in turn, beginning with the collapse of the banking sector and the dynamics that contributed to its implosion.

Of course, such a discussion would be meaningless without briefly exploring the social and economic context of Icelandic life. The damage will inevitably spread far beyond the island nation's shores for, even as its citizens try desperately to cope with their drastically diminished circumstances, the intricate financial relationships that spawned the economy's collapse will drag down others with it. The costs and consequences, both economic and political, are likely to be far reaching for years to come.

Iceland: The Rising Star of International Finance

"The Candle That Burns Twice As Bright Burns Half As Long!"

Iceland presents a strange conundrum to the world. Its relative size belies the impact that it has had, and the prominent place that it held for many investors around the world. Iceland has one of the longest traditions of democratic rule, which is often strongly tied to a liberal economic order. Despite its thousand-year parliamentary history, the type of liberalisation that one might expect to accompany this political experience only came about within the last twenty years. Yet regardless of its close ties with and proximity to Europe, in many ways Iceland is more comparable to the 'Four Tigers' of Southeast Asia in terms of its economic development.

At least until recently, most economic activity was dominated by fishing and fish production. Although only about 10% of the workforce was actually mobilised in these areas, nearly three quarters of merchandise exports and approximately half of all foreign exchange earnings were derived from them. The economy itself is highly service-oriented, with two thirds of the workforce employed across the public and private service sectors. Travel, tourism, and to a much lesser extent mining and forestry make up the balance of the economy.

The 1990's saw a heavy push by the Icelandic government to liberalise the economic system. In 1994, Iceland joined the free-trade zone of the European Economic Area. Subsequently the government deregulated the state-owned banking sector, allowed the krona to float freely rather than fixing it to a basket of foreign currencies. It simultaneously embarked on a process of large-scale privatisation. As a result of these moves, Iceland's growth rates outpaced its European trading partners and by 2005 it was the fifth richest country in the world. It catapulted the country's financial sector to the forefront of the nation's service-based economy.

As part of the liberalisation and deregulation of the financial system, lending rules were severely relaxed. This further fueled the pace of economic growth and expansion, and household debt levels skyrocketed to at least 220% of GDP. Much as was the case in the US, for example, consumer debt was one of the primary drivers of the economic boom. The consequences, of course, were not altogether predictable: *"A series of interest rate hikes by the central bank, aimed at taming inflation, unwittingly sent the free-floating krona soaring on international markets. That made imports cheaper for Icelanders, further fueling the consumption boom."*

347

Inflation has played a key role in the Icelandic crisis. As a result of the high levels of inflation that were the reflection of this ten-year economic boom, Iceland had high interest rates relative to many European and Asian countries. As a consequence, Iceland became a central fixture in what has become known as the 'yen carry trade.' As Japan had been in a near-permanent recession since the early 1990's, it had maintained borrowing rates close to zero percent; this allowed investors to borrow yen at almost no cost and to invest in foreign currencies and foreign-denominated financial assets, profiting from the difference. The Icelandic economy presented an ideal target for just such a trade, because of its double-digit interest rates. It is because of this dynamic that Iceland came to be regarded as a giant hedge fund:

"Iceland had relatively high interest rates, so investors borrowed heavily in Japanese yen and bought Icelandic bonds. Money flooded into Iceland and its big banks borrowed $120bn (£85bn) on the international markets—six times the size of the country's GDP. This is the sort of leverage normally associated with hedge funds, which borrow money for their speculative plays. The money was recycled into other European economies, including Britain where Icelandic investors bought up large parts of the high street, and all was well while the bubble continued to inflate."

Leverage can thus be regarded as the other primary driver of Iceland's economic boom in the years immediately preceding its collapse. Much as it played out in the US in the run-up to the subprime mortgage crisis, the nation effectively went on a debt-and-leverage-fueled shopping spree:

"Cheap money abroad helped do the rest, as did top-notch credit ratings, hedge funds' appetite for Iceland's high-yielding krona currency, an ever-rising stock market and flamboyant entrepreneurs like Jon Asgeir Johannesson, who installed a 10-foot Viking statue with a sword and electric guitar at his London office. Banks and entrepreneurs went on shopping sprees and created an ever-wider net of companies that bought stakes in each other at ever-higher prices. In the end, the nation itself had become a highly leveraged fund that borrowed foreign money to buy stuff at inflated prices."

What's more, it seems that Iceland's central bank actually encouraged the appetite for risk. Reserve requirements were significantly relaxed, which freed up the banks' capital and allowed them to substantially expand their investment and lending activities both at home and abroad. Iceland's stock prices grew nearly tenfold from 2003 to 2007, and the government began to issue krona-denominated 'glacier bonds' in order to profit from the high demand.

In mid-2006, the yen carry trade began to unravel after the credit rating agency Fitch downgraded their outlook for Iceland; the currency plunged 25% within days. The central bank and the three major Icelandic commercial banks launched a concerted effort to support the value of the currency, and this tactic worked for a time. Former Prime Minister and then head of the central bank, David Oddsson, blamed the temporary crisis on speculators trying to *"bring a healthy economy to its knees."* Investors continued to hold the krona and Icelanders continued to bask in the illusion of wealth that was created as a result.

> *"Though life is made up of mere bubbles, 'Tis better than many aver, For while we've a whole lot of troubles, The most of them never occur."*
>
> **Nixon Waterman**

However, it is in the nature of a bubble for it to burst, and burst it did. Iceland's three main banks—Glitnir, Landsbanki and Kaupthing—pushed the carry trade to its furthest reaches, ballooning their combined balance sheets to as much as *ten times the country's GDP!*

For comparative purposes, the total short-term debt of the banking sector in the US equals only 15% of the GDP. Although this is not a 'fair' comparison, given the absolute differences in size between the two countries, and given the fact that Iceland's banks had grown to international stature—just as they had in many other small European nations. It does though speak volumes about the extreme liberalisation and deregulation that had been undertaken in Iceland. Moreover, it is telling that the government as well as the central bank seemed to have actively encouraged this rapid, unchecked expansion by their three main banks.

> *"Certain signs precede certain events."*
>
> **Cicero**

Warning signs did exist, however. First, early in 2008 Iceland's Landsbanki had commissioned a study on the soundness of the banking sector in general and the policy options that the country might have in the face of a banking crisis. The study found that if Iceland were to maintain its own monetary policy and currency independence, it could not sustain the pace of its foreign currency activities. The three banks had initially each grown as sector-specific entities, but as the economy grew, they had mostly converged and simultaneously expanded internationally. One of the major functions that they carried out was role of 'broker' for these currency transactions, especially after the 'attacks' in 2006.

The second and related warning sign was the huge amount of short-term debt the banks held as a result of their heavy involvement in the carry trade as well as large speculative lending activities. While it is not yet known if, or to what extent, the banks held risky mortgage-related securities on their balance sheets, by some accounts their exposure to these so-called toxic assets was non-existent. What is clear, however, is that the banks had made massive loans to investment funds, 60% of which were abroad, making the banks especially vulnerable to events that would play out beyond Iceland's borders. What's more, these loans were highly leveraged and denominated in foreign currencies.

Even if the banks had relatively healthy capital ratios, the absolute size of their balance sheets dwarfed the central bank itself. When the krona again came under fire for being overvalued, the banks struggled once more to clear the trades. The decision in the United States to let Lehman Brothers collapse had drastic consequences, because almost overnight the Icelandic banks became unable to refinance their heavy short-term debt burdens. Without the credit lines they needed to survive, they tried to get funding from the central bank but were refused, and the government opted instead to nationalise Glitnir on September 29 and Landsbanki on October 7.

The Kaupthing bank initially looked like it might survive the crisis. However, when Landsbanki collapsed, its offshore subsidiary Icesave became insolvent. Icesave had operated as an extension of Landsbanki, rather than as an independent banking entity under the single-market rules of the European Economic Area. This had the effect of creating competing legal jurisdictions for the bank, which had attracted a large number of customers in the UK and the Netherlands with its high-interest, internet-only deposit system. Customers assumed they would be covered by Iceland's deposit insurance, in which all deposits were fully guaranteed by the Icelandic government.

When Iceland's government implied that it would not guarantee the deposits of Icesave to the same extent as its domestic banks, political uproar in the UK prompted Gordon Brown's government to freeze the assets of not just Icesave but also a subsidiary of Kaupthing, the internet-based Edge savings bank. They accomplished this through an arcane application of the UK's antiterrorism laws. This move was politically expedient in the UK, but devastating to the viability of Kaupthing in Iceland; as we shall see in later pages, it would have other, unintended consequences as well, that placed Iceland's future in doubt. As Kaupthing's other overseas subsidiaries were frozen or taken over by their home governments, Kaupthing itself collapsed and became the final bank in Iceland to be nationalised.

As the banks collapsed, Iceland's stock market cratered. The exchange was relatively nascent; having only begun trading in equities in 1990, and in line with the size of the country's economy, it was quite small and illiquid. The OMX Iceland 15 index, a basket of the 15 largest companies in the country, was closed for the better part of the first two weeks in October 2008, due to the highly volatile conditions persisting as a result of the failure of the banking sector. Trading in banking stocks was suspended, and when the exchange reopened on October 14, it had fallen by more than 75%. Glitnir, Landsbanki and Kaupthing made up nearly three quarters of the value of the index.

"Good bankers, like good tea, can only be appreciated when they are in hot water."

Jaffar Hussein

The factors that led to the collapse of Glitnir and Landsbanki are many, and certainly have to do with the extremely lax controls placed upon them, but much blame has been placed on Oddsson, the head of the central bank. Whether or not it was even capable of guaranteeing the two banks, when the central bank refused to step in, it effectively forced the government to nationalise them. In the wake of Lehman's collapse and without credit facilities to fund their overleveraged activities, Iceland faced a downgrade of its sovereign debt. Predictably, this panic swept through the international system, and the value of the krona plummeted; monetary policy, it should be recalled, had kept interest rates extraordinarily high, but the fall of the krona placed the entire regime in jeopardy and caused a now-familiar bank run panic on the banks' offshore subsidiaries. It was this dynamic that caused the collapse of Icesave and others, and which in turn destroyed Kaupthing as collateral damage.

The central bank attempted to mitigate the currency crisis, but mistakenly tried to peg the value of the krona far higher than markets would bear. Without the three banks to clear the trades, the central bank was forced to abandon the currency peg only two days later, on October 8. The currency collapsed, and lost more than two thirds of its value since the start of the year. International trading in the krona virtually ceased, and the government resorted to daily currency auctions in order to try to restore stability to the market.

In order to do so, Iceland had to turn to the international community, and quickly sought loans of over $4 billion from the IMF and four Nordic nations. Political tensions between Iceland and the UK and Dutch governments, though, stalled the provision of these loans; the latter were still outraged that their citizens were not to be insured as Icesave and others went under—Iceland later negotiated a separate $5.5 billion loan from these two governments in order to pay the tab for Icesave. In the meantime, though, Iceland turned its focus east and sought an additional $5.5 billion in emergency funding from Russia.

Although very little of this has yet to materialise, it is nevertheless very instructive of the changes now under way in the realm of international finance; only ten years earlier, Russia had itself been swept up by financial crisis, in which it defaulted on its debt and faced a collapsing currency. Now, flush with its own tremendous foreign currency reserves, Russia's entry to the financial aid game was strongly reflective of its growing economic clout.

As the Icelandic government struggled to keep pace with the crisis and negotiate a solution, social unrest began to climb as jobs were lost and the economy entered a steep recession. Iceland had very low levels of foreign currency reserves to begin with, but these were depleted almost instantly as they attempted to peg the currency and restore stability. Imports of goods became difficult, as firms would not accept the krona and foreign currencies were rationed. Iceland desperately needed external aid in order to rebuild its foreign currency reserves and restore credibility in the economy, especially given its heavy dependence on imported goods.

Bailing Out or Buying In?

Arguably one of the key outgrowths of the banking crisis and collapse in Iceland was the *'re-entry'* of the International Monetary Fund as a force in world finance. The IMF had initially been critical of the monetary policies pursued by Iceland, as they had failed to substantially counter inflation and had resulted in high levels of debt for the government. However, significant debate exists around the role of the IMF and its relative contribution to solving the crisis.

A brief history lesson reveals much about the role that the IMF may play and its potential impact on Iceland's future. The IMF was formed in 1944 with the goal of stabilising exchange rates and assisting in the reconstructing of the world's international payment system; it describes itself as *"an organisation of 186 countries, working to foster global monetary cooperation, secure financial stability, facilitate international trade, promote high employment and sustainable economic growth, and reduce poverty around the world."* As part of the new liberal economic order created under the Bretton Woods system, the IMF's overriding purpose was to promote methods by which countries could maintain exchange rate stability, thereby fostering free trade, economic growth, and development.

As touched upon in other sections of this book much of the blame for the Great Depression, and indeed the two World Wars, has been blamed on problems of trade and economic relations between the world powers. The IMF was created as part of an orchestrated approach to remedying this dynamic. Rather than relying upon a strict interpretation of the gold standard, in which a country's currency value was directly tied to its physical reserves of gold, the Bretton Woods system effectively made the US dollar the world's *'reserve currency,'* which would be the only country whose currency value was pegged to a fixed price of gold. Individual currencies were then priced in relation to the US dollar, based upon their initial input into the system; fixed exchange rates were targeted and countries would buy and sell US dollars in order to remedy trade imbalances. The IMF was the *de facto* mechanism through which the new liberal economic order would be managed.

An often-overlooked justification for supplying US dollars as the world's currency was the need to counteract the rising might of the Soviet Union. The Soviet Union, it must be recalled, had significant gold resources of its own, and without the constraints imposed by the Bretton Woods system, the Soviet Union would be better able to finance its expansion. In addition, if the US were able to take a leadership role as the guarantor of stability throughout the world, it would be in a better position to pursue its own foreign policy agenda. Bretton Woods thus provided an indirect means of economically isolating the Soviet Union, by promoting liberal, *laissez-faire* economics in the rest of the developing world.

The IMF began life with approximately 44 member countries, but rapidly expanded its membership throughout the 1950's and into the 1960's, as African and Asian countries gained independence. When the Bretton Woods collapsed in 1971, under the weight of accelerating trade deficits in the US, the influence of the IMF grew as it became more relevant in managing the international economic order. In an area of freely floating exchange rates or where countries attempted to peg their currencies to a basket of foreign currencies, the IMF became instrumental in assisting with this policy independence for its member nations.

However, that assistance was not without strings. IMF members were routinely required to take on loans in order to facilitate the policy moves required for them to participate in free trade, but these loans were not given freely. In line with the IMF's overarching, liberal *raison d'être*, these loans were 'conditional' on member nations adopting specific free-market economic policies. These 'structural adjustment programs' had many components, but the most important of them required that countries substantially liberalise their economies, denationalise their industries, and pursue 'monetarist' economic policies being those favoured in the US and much of the Western world.

As a result of these and other controversial policies, such as raising taxes and interest rates in order to manage inflation, it is often argued that the IMF has helped to make inherently weaker economies even weaker—and in doing so, it has only strengthened the hand of the already-strong Western economic powers. In countries such as Argentina, IMF policies have been blamed for economic crises that were invariably worsened by the government's inability to sustain critical sectors such as health care, education and security. At the same time, valuable national resources and industry were sold off to powerful corporate interests in more developed nations. IMF policies are thus criticised as leading to the simultaneous impoverishment of its debtor nations and their inability to escape the vicious monetary policy circles that keep them weak.

In the wake of criticism of policy advice and the failures they engendered in the 1990's, the IMF has in recent years played a limited role for several reasons. First, it faced significant competition as a provider of 'economic supervision' by a number of other organisations, such as the OECD and the World Bank. Many countries that had suffered drastic economic consequences as a result of IMF policies in the late 1980's and 1990's were determined never to utilise the IMF's stabilisation mechanisms. These served as an example for others for how *not* to survive an economic crisis, and it called into question the IMF's relevance as a *'lender of last resort'* for countries in serious financial trouble.

The Icelandic banking crisis, though, seems right out of the traditional IMF 'playbook.' Due to the size of the banking sector in relation to the central bank, there was no way that the central bank could step in to guarantee the deposits:

"In normal economic circumstances this is not a cause for worry, so long as the banks are prudently run. Indeed, the Icelandic banks were better capitalised and with a lower exposure to high risk assets than many of their European counterparts. In this crisis, the strength of a bank's balance sheet is of little consequence. What matters is the explicit or implicit guarantee provided by the state to the banks to back up their assets and provide liquidity. Therefore, the size of the state relative to the size of the banks becomes the crucial factor. The relative size of the Icelandic banking system means that the government was in no position to guarantee the banks, unlike in other European countries."

This is precisely what has played out in Iceland's situation. The central bank was caught in the position of being too small to adequately guarantee domestic savings, let alone the additional burden of deposits amassed by the banks' overseas subsidiaries. When the government stepped in to nationalise the banks in exchange for equity stakes, it too suffered a crisis of confidence, as there was virtually no way that it could provide the necessary financial ammunition for the firefight to come. When the country's debt was downgraded by Moody's and other ratings agencies, the downward pressure sparked a run on the currency, which had two consequences: it not only made the banking crisis itself worse, it threatened the stability of the central bank, which had itself amassed very little in the way of foreign currency reserves that would be necessary to run the import-dependent economy.

The IMF was able to step in, and Iceland became the first industrialised country in thirty years to request assistance. With the help of the IMF, Iceland was able to negotiate extensions of credit from several countries. However, as we have seen earlier these loans were stalled—in part because of political tensions between Iceland on the one hand, and the UK and Dutch authorities on the other, in regards to deposit guarantees for their citizens. What's more, the role of the IMF in Iceland's rescue is likely to be controversial because of the "*conditionality*" that tends to accompany the extension of aid.

It is somewhat paradoxical that the IMF initially criticised the Icelandic government's monetary policies. Iceland continued to pursue extremely liberal monetary policies, which led to very high levels of inflation, and at the same time, it kept interest rates extraordinarily high. This was done not only to counter inflationary pressures, but also to attract foreign investors, which only served to further increase demand in the economy and for the krona. Both of these, in turn, led to ever-higher price pressure. Iceland was caught in somewhat of a monetary 'catch 22' in which it likely had limited policy options, but in retrospect it is clear that the government and central bank did little to discourage the activities of the banking sector or the speculation in currency markets.

Following the collapse of the banking sector, the IMF is likely to implement high interest rates once again as part of their lending program. It will be difficult for the krona to float freely, a consequence that will be made even more difficult as a result of the structural adjustments that the IMF loans will entail. Without significant financial aid, it will be difficult for the krona to reach a point of stability and to allow the economy itself to stabilise, because of the simple fact that the capital is not in place to support any type of viable currency peg.

Another policy option did reveal itself prior to the banking crisis, but it has yet to be fully committed to and carries with it a variety of high-level economic and political consequences. In the study commissioned by Landsbanki in early 2008, the authors argued that Iceland had several competing policy choices: it could either maintain its monetary policy and currency independence, or it could relocate its foreign currency lending to the Eurozone. Icelanders have long resisted integration into the European Union.

The fall of the Haarde administration, a direct casualty of the banking crisis, brought this long-standing and contentious issue to the forefront once again. Iceland had previously been a member of the European Free Trade Area and was already a member of the European Economic Area, which created a single market for capital and labour in the European region. Iceland has acceded to other agreements that form the backbone of the European Union, but since 1995 further integration had been opposed by two of the three main political parties. The former Prime Minister Geir Haarde had formally opposed membership in the EU, stating that there were no special interests that demanded it and maintaining that adopting the euro currency would be detrimental. ***How wrong he has been!***

In 2007, a commission was created to monitor and explore the impacts that EU developments might have on Iceland, although it maintained at the time that it was not created in order to explore membership. Although Iceland has never held a referendum on the subject, opinion polls in recent years have shown significant divisions among the public on joining or even starting negotiations. One of the major factors influencing public opinion has been the perception that EU membership will negatively impact the country's fishing industry, which has historically dominated the economy. Even in light of the economic disaster that Iceland is now trying to emerge from, public opinion remains sharply divided, albeit with only a narrow majority remaining opposed to joining the EU.

Iceland's political stance in the first days of the crisis, in which it publicly declared that it would not give UK and Dutch depositors the same protection afforded to its domestic constituents, has continued to cause considerable friction. Iceland only agreed in June 2009 to take on $5.5 billion in loans from the UK and the Netherlands in order to cover the repayment of these deposits, and this heavy burden has fostered further resentment and skepticism over joining the EU; membership has in fact been made conditional on the Icelandic parliament's agreement to the repayment scheme.

The country's new Prime Minister, Johanna Sigurdardottir, has made joining the EU a priority. In late July 2009, the Icelandic parliament narrowly agreed to pursue membership, apparently acquiescing to the fact that the particular circumstances of Iceland's economy can no longer be sustained through the independence of its monetary and currency policies. Since the size of the banking sector outweighed the scope and reach of the central bank, Iceland was effectively left without a lender of last resort—joining the European System of Central Banks, or simply the Eurosystem, would endow it with this much needed backstop. While certainly limiting some of Iceland's economic freedom, the euro will provide it with a measure of stability that it would find exceedingly elusive to obtain otherwise.

After joining, Iceland would still need to meet stringent economic and currency stability demands that the Eurosystem places upon its member nations before it can adopt the euro. Even with help from the IMF, it is far from reaching these performance-based demands, particularly price stability. The EU itself has said that Iceland's accession will be not be problematic, given that it is one of the oldest democracies in the world and because it was one of the founding members of NATO. It was initially the position that it will not be given special treatment, but under the current presidency of the EU, which is held by Sweden, it was announced that Icelandic membership would be given priority. Germany and France, though, have stated that until the Lisbon Treaty is ratified—which formalises key parts of the EU such as the European Central Bank—they do not want new members admitted.

Underneath the Ice

> *"Fishing is much more than fish. It is the great occasion when we may return to the fine simplicity of our forefathers."*
> **Herbert Hoover**

Looking at the crisis with the benefit of hindsight, and even though Iceland has yet to effectively begin the process of economic recovery, many factors have become evident. Although it was not made public at the time, the stated reason being that it might undermine confidence in the banking sector, the Landsbanki study revealed that the Icelandic system was not viable:

"The fundamental reason was that Iceland was the most extreme example in the world of a very small country, with its own currency, and with an internationally active and internationally exposed

financial sector that is very large relative to its GDP and relative to its fiscal capacity. Even if the banks are fundamentally solvent . . . such a small country—small currency configuration makes it highly unlikely that the central bank can act as an effective foreign currency lender of last resort/market maker of last resort."

This assessment was right on the money. In the absence of a central bank that could function as the lender of last resort, and because the central bank depended on the banks to clear currency trades, the banking sector fell prey to both a liquidity crisis and a run on the currency. It really didn't matter if the banks were solvent, and by most accounts they were better capitalised and had lower exposure to risk than many of their European counterparts. Due to its small size relative to the banks, there was virtually no way that the Icelandic government could realistically underwrite the recapitalisation of the banks without threatening its own credibility.

What has come to light, though, are some of the more damaging allegations that may have contributed to the banks' collapse. The Icelandic government has now opened a special investigation into several highly unusual and potentially criminal relationships between the banks, their majority shareholders and certain investment funds. The Gudmundsson brothers, who had built an empire through their food manufacturing empire, controlled Kaupthing and it is apparent that Kaupthing had made questionable loans:

"Kaupthing's loan book, which was leaked on to the internet last week, shows that around one third, or €6bn (£5.1bn), of its €16bn corporate loan book was going to a small elite of men connected to the bank's owners and management. Several investigations into Kaupthing centre on share ramping, where the bank would allegedly give loans with no interest or security in order to buy shares in that same bank—boosting the share price."

It is also alleged that through some "particularly murky" transactions, Kaupthing was effectively buying its own shares surreptitiously, and that loans made to key employees were written off just days before the collapse. Further potentially criminal activity, centering upon inappropriate business loans among connected financial entities and *"related parties"* stretching from Iceland to the UK, are being investigated at Glitnir and Landsbanki as well.

Many have questioned why financial regulators remained unaware of these activities. The answers are not encouraging: *"One headache that may have caused the regulators to back away was the banks' complex ownership structures involving a constantly shifting mess of investment vehicles and holding companies. All the banks appear to have sold and re-sold stakes, shifted around top management staff and lent each other's owners large amounts."* While it was not known at the time, it also seems that the UK government's decision to apply anti-terrorism statutes in order to seize Icesave and Kaupthing Edge's assets may be proven correct:

"It looked like the Icelandic banks were finding it even more difficult than most to raise money on the international markets, turning instead to more European depositors to fund their loan operations. This gave birth to Landsbanki's Icesave and Kaupthing Edge. Per Lofgrem, an analyst for Morgan Stanley wrote at the time: "New funding has not come from traditional sources. The acquisitions of Derbyshire Building Society and Robeco [a Dutch bank] were made in order to get hold of their deposit bases. We also believe that the bank would have used better-known markets than Mexico to issue debt if more conventional markets were open."

If these assessments prove to be correct, Icesave and Kaupthing Edge were almost the equivalent of Ponzi schemes, purchased and operated only to attract deposits that were then overleveraged to fund the potentially improper investment activities of their majority shareholders. What's more, the government has so far been unable to completely eradicate conflicts of interest among former employees; *even as it ordered them to be released from duty, they've only been immediately rehired as consultants by the banks!*

Conclusion

"If the chief party, whether it be the people, or the army, or the nobility, which you think most useful and of most consequence to you for the conservation of your dignity, be corrupt, you must follow their humour and indulge them, and in that case honesty and virtue are pernicious."

Machiavelli

Iceland would not be the first country to experience widespread corruption that led to economic disaster, and it certainly will not be the last. The collapse of the banking sector reveals much about the liberal economic order and the problems that we still face. Certainly, the Iceland saga has played out in a particular fashion that is reflective of the uniqueness of the island nation itself. There is much to be learned from the specific dynamics that Iceland succumbed to.

Beginning with the banks themselves, we have seen how the collapse of the entire sector was brought about. Blind adherence to extreme laissez-faire economic policies encouraged over leverage and created an asset bubble; both a liquidity crisis and a run on the currency consumed the banks, once the central bank proved unable to fulfill its role as the lender of last resort. Political expediency on the part of Icelandic officials as well as the UK and Dutch governments hastened the crisis, and the friction that has resulted has yet to be fully resolved. This may yet prove to weigh heavily on the prospects for the country's recovery.

In retrospect, many observers have noted that the decision by US Treasury Secretary Hank Paulson and others to let Lehman Brothers collapse—where they had come to the rescue of Bear Stearns months earlier—was a mistake. The same can be said for the decision by the UK, for example, to enforce anti-terrorism statutes in order to justify the seizure of the Icelandic banks' assets. The resulting political tensions are likely to make the critical process of Iceland joining the EU more difficult. Many now see this as a logical and necessary next step in Iceland's 're-entry' into the international financial order: without a central bank that can act as a lender of last resort for its banks and a market maker of last resort for its currency, Iceland needs to adopt the euro in order to survive.

Iceland is now caught in what could play out as several vicious and interrelated cycles. If it chooses to forego its debt to its foreign creditors, its accession to the EU is likely to be blocked; if it repays all its creditors in full, it is not likely that it will be able to rebuild its economy for decades. At the same time, Iceland is dependent upon financial aid from the IMF, which may also be blocked if Iceland does not fully back the repayment scheme; without this financial aid, there is little chance that Iceland will be able to stabilise its currency and restore confidence in its economic viability. This is especially important for a tiny nation such as Iceland, which is so dependent on imports.

While some have said that the involvement of the IMF has signaled its renewed relevance in international finance, it is too soon to tell whether the IMF has truly been reinvigorated. It is paradoxical that the IMF had been critical of the high interest rate policies pursued by the Icelandic government in trying to tame inflation, when it is most often the case that its structural adjustment programs call for the very same prescription. Raising taxes when the economy is so severely debilitated is also likely to prove harmful.

The Iceland saga shows the fallacy of blindly adhering to *laissez-faire* economics, or rather, the application of them in extremis: ***"Iceland got its regulations from the EU, which was basically sound . . . But the government had no understanding of the dangers of banks or how to supervise them. They got into the hands of people who took risks to the highest possible degree."*** Divergent opinions on the extent to which that recovery is underway are already appearing:

Olafur Isleifsson, a professor of business at the University of Reykjavik and former advisor to the IMF, believes the banks are already in recovery mode. *"Some of the information that has already been revealed is quite shocking,"* he says. *"But an important step consists of recent decisions that place the new banks on a secure financial footing."* Dr. Danielsson disagrees, arguing that the financial system is still crippled by bad banks and a lack of trust in the authorities. *"Things have not been able to progress and are getting worse,"* he says. *"The government needs to act to try to find anyone who is guilty and punish those people. That is important for the country to heal."*

Prevailing economic theories hold that free markets are self-regulating, but the Iceland saga shows that there are limits to their application. The events that played out demonstrate the disastrous consequences that inexperienced policymakers can have on the economic wellbeing of a nation. It is for these reasons that many economists argue for the independence of central banks. Oddsson himself was a former politician, and it seems that the central bank was beholden to the government, and perhaps pursued a more liberal set of policies than it otherwise might have. Nonetheless, the political actions by Oddsson made the crisis worse at every point.

Above all else, though, the Icelandic banking collapse illustrates two things: first, it shows the severity of the dangers that still may lie hidden in the emerging markets of the world. If commentators such as David Smick are proven correct in this assumption, which he presciently argued only months before this crisis, the economic impact may be even more devastating than we've previously believed.

Second, when the sum of the parts are added together in the Iceland equation, we see that even though the worst seems to be over for the credit crisis, there is still a significant danger of even large countries succumbing to the same dynamics that felled Iceland. In the financial bastions of the UK and Switzerland, for example, bank debt exceed GDP just as it did in Iceland; excessive leverage in Germany could mean that even a small percentage drop in the value of all bank assets would wipe out the net worth of the entire banking system. There is still the danger of a rapid decline in the value of the US dollar, in light of the massive bailout in 2008 and the fiscal stimulus that followed shortly thereafter. If the dollar were to fall precipitously, the IMF may be the only savior.

When all is said and done, the prospects for Iceland do seem to be relatively good. The long-run potential for the economy's recovery is strong: it is resource rich, has the potential to diversify, and has a well-educated workforce; even though savings have been negatively impacted, the country is likely to weather the crisis well as a result of its already high standard of living. Clearly, though, the tiny island has a significant amount of work to do and is in for a long haul if it is to rebuild its shattered system and indeed, its confidence.

In Chapter 18 we move to mainland Europe when the fall of a major bank leads to the first of many international financial rescue missions—*we look at the Belgium bombshell!*

Interlude—The Politics of Illusion, the Policies of Delusion!

"It is natural for man to indulge in the illusions of hope. We are apt to shut our eyes against a painful truth, and listen to the song of that siren till she transforms us into beasts. For my part whatever anguish of spirit it may cost, I am willing to know the whole truth, to know the worst, and to provide for it."

Patrick Henry

Delusion*; An idiosyncratic belief or impression maintained despite being contradicted by reality or rational argument, typically as a symptom of mental disorder.*

Oxford Press

"Politics is the art of looking for trouble, finding it whether it exists or not, diagnosing it incorrectly, and applying the wrong remedy!"

Ernest Benn

September 15th 2008 Lehman Brothers files for the largest bankruptcy in US business history.

Lehman Brothers; On September 15, 2008, over $600 billion in value vanished, virtually in an instant, when a famed Wall Street institution collapsed. That institution was Lehman Brothers, then the 4th largest investment bank in the United States. Preceding the eventual demise of the firm, it's own stock value had plummeted over 90%, but the ripple effects would extend much further; on that fateful day, the Dow Jones closed down over 500 points, which at the time represented

366

the largest single-day drop since the terrorist attacks on September 11, 2001.

For Lehman Brothers, there was no remedy, recourse or rescue. No bailout was forthcoming. Six months to the day earlier, however, rival Bear Stearns *had* been saved when another competing firm, J.P. Morgan, extended it a $30 billion loan—and, critically, the US Government backstopped this lending facility, providing not just the liquidity that was needed to keep Bear Stearns running but also ensuring that the entire financial system did not grind to a halt overnight. Judged "too big to fail" in light of the risks posed to so many other institutions were it to default on its obligations, Bear was sold at the fire-sale price of $10 per share to J.P. Morgan in a deal that was orchestrated by the US Treasury and again guaranteed by the Federal Reserve. For a longer review check out Chapter 14!

Lehman Brothers would not be so lucky. When the Fed stepped in to guarantee the acquisition of Bear Stearns by J.P. Morgan, it did so by establishing a new LLC to facilitate the unwinding of securities that were judged too risky for the new owner to take on. Justified by the need to prevent wider damage to the economy were Bear Stearns to fail in an uncontrolled way, the burden for the firm's collapse was thus shifted to the taxpayer. In doing so, it can be said that further damage to Bear Stearns' competitors was averted, although it meant that the public has taken over the burden of executive excess. When Lehman Brothers found itself on the brink of bankruptcy, however, once its collateral had evaporated and its losses had escalated to the point of no return, it had no choice but to look for outside suitors to inject capital into it. When none could be found, even under the supervision of the New York Fed, rescue efforts collapsed.

Simply put, Lehman was *allowed* to collapse where Bear Stearns was not. This illustrates the issue of ***moral hazard***, a fuzzy term used to convey that if one firm is rescued, rather than being allowed to fail, it will encourage other firms to take undue risks because they too will expect to be rescued. It was judged that one bailout was enough; Bear Stearns could not be allowed to fail, because of its swift decline and the danger that posed. Lehman, it was felt, had had ample time to make alternative arrangements, and capital markets were well aware of the risk of its failure.

Nevertheless, Lehman's bankruptcy put tremendous downward pressure on stock markets and further accelerated the decline in real estate securities. For the first time, a money market fund was forced to "break the buck," with assets falling below $1 per share. The Lehman brokerage operations, which were very critical for many investors worldwide, were frozen. Creditors around the globe faced massive losses, with little chance of recouping them. The ripple effects would indeed spread far and wide, and continue to be felt several years later.

In this chapter, we will explore the issues surrounding the Lehman Brothers' collapse. We shall start with a closer look at the history of this legendary, if not venerable, institution from its humble beginnings in the mid-nineteenth century up to and including its eventual demise in late 2008. As one can imagine, much criticism has been levied for the decision to allow Lehman to fail; the economic distress that followed in its wake forced the adoption of over $700 billion in bailouts that spread across the entire financial system. Controversy still surrounds the firm, even despite the fact that its liquidation has been well underway for nearly 4 years. On a final note, we'll examine the wider ramifications of the Lehman bankruptcy and what it means for the economy more generally. In many respects, it remains to be seen whether the inherent flaws that this collapse exposed have been remedied, and what still needs to be done to shore up those faults.

Humble Beginnings, Humbling End

"Arrogance diminishes wisdom!"
Old Arabian Proverb

Undoubtedly, the story behind the rise of this giant of Wall Street is less well known than is the story of its demise. Existing variously as a storefront family-run shop, a commodities trading firm, an investment partnership, and a publicly traded brokerage house, Lehman Brothers represents in many respects the culmination of the American Dream.

Indeed, its story is one of remarkable transformation, from its humble beginnings to its equally humbling end.

1844 was the year in which Henry Lehman came to America, the son of a Bavarian cattle merchant, and opened his dry-goods store in Alabama. With the arrival of his brother Emanuel three years later, the firm became H. Lehman and Bro, and when they were joined by a third brother in 1850, the company finally became what we know it as today: Lehman Brothers. At the time, it was the high and rising cost of cotton that prompted the brothers to accept this important commodity as payment for other goods, and they soon began a side business trading cotton. These secondary operations quickly took on primary importance, and it was in this manner that the firm established its commodities trading and brokerage roots.

At the same time, the US economy witnessed the rise in stature of New York City, which soon became the financial hub of the country. Lehman Brothers opened their first branch office in New York, but the Civil War caused them difficulty, forcing them to merge their operations with cotton trader John Durr. Following the war, the company's headquarters were moved from Alabama to New York, where they helped to establish the New York Cotton Exchange in 1870. Railroad financing and other advisory services propelled the firm into prominence in the late nineteenth century. It would not take on the role of investment banker, transitioning away from its commodities-trading and brokerage operations, until 1906.

The next two decades would see Lehman Brothers became one of the largest providers of stock offerings. Lehman Brothers survived the stock market crash of the Great Depression by shifting focus to venture capital with financing coming from institutional investors or high net worth individuals. The focus here was on companies in their early stages of development with great potential for growth. In the 1930's, Lehman underwrote the initial public offering for the first television manufacturer DuMont and helped fund the Radio Corporation of America—both lucrative moves that kept the company in business while the equity markets recovered.

Up until this time, the firm had been run largely as a family business. The first non-family member joined the firm in 1924 but it was not until the death of Robert Lehman in 1969 that this traditional partnership structure would change. With no clear successor in place and facing financial difficulties in the tough times of the early 1970's, Pete Peterson was brought in to save the firm in 1973. A series of mergers and acquisitions soon transformed the company into the fourth largest investment bank in the United States, and under Peterson's leadership the next five years saw record profits. The resurrection seemed well in hand.

It is here, however, that the seeds of destruction were sown. A divide had opened up between the bankers and the traders, the latter of whom had been driving the firm's recent string of successes. Peterson chose to promote a former trader, Lewis Glucksman, to the position of co-CEO, but his management style served to increase tensions and eventually resulted in the ousting of Peterson himself. Bankers left the firm in droves, the company suffered, and Glucksman was forced to sell the firm in 1984.

> *"Acquisition means life to miserable mortals!"*
>
> **Hesiod**

This rift between the bankers and the traders widened when Shearson/ American Express acquired Lehman Brothers. Shearson/American Express was a securities firm oriented primarily towards brokerage rather than investment banking. Ten years later, American Express began to divest itself of these subsidiary operations, selling its retail operations and spinning off its institutional securities business as well, which eventually became an independent publicly owned company: Lehman Brothers Holdings. The brokerage business was thereafter the primary focus of new CEO, Richard Fuld. Under Fuld, Lehman Brothers again expanded its operational base; it acquired a private-client services branch, it deepened its securities underwriting business, and grew its institutional asset management and private equity divisions. However, it seems evident that trading operations still dominated. Not only were they highly lucrative, they were a part of the culture where excessive risk-taking prevailed.

Hazardous Materials: Handle with Care

So that we can fully understand the collapse of Lehman Brothers itself, we need to take a step back in time and re-examine the run-up to the financial crisis of 2007-2008 more generally. It should be recalled that after the terrorist attacks of September 11, 2001, as well as the bursting of the bubble in technology stocks, Fed Chairman Alan Greenspan dropped interest rates and kept them at historically low levels for several years. This spurred yet another asset bubble; this time in residential housing; as Nobel Laureate Joseph Stiglitz commented later, one bubble was simply replaced by another.

Stiglitz asserted that it was Greenspan's failure to control liquidity, by keeping rates artificially low for too long, combined with his failure as a regulator, by not curbing leverage, amongst others, which in turn led to wider systemic risk. What's ironic in all this is that it was Greenspan who had argued a decade earlier to keep the derivatives market relatively free from regulation. Recall that innovations in finance had led to the advent of "subprime" and interest-only mortgages, which were then "securitised," repackaged and sold off to institutional investors as complex debt instruments in the bond markets. The underlying asset of the property, often through many permutations, was mortgage-backed securities. Another way of looking at it is to consider these securities to be a debt obligation that represents a claim on the cash flows from mortgage loans.

All of this prompted record numbers of first-time homebuyers to enter the market. It generated a new wave of refinancing, as current owners sought to capture these new low borrowing rates by refinancing their existing mortgages. What led to the housing boom, even more than the historically low rates, was the unprecedented access to easy financing for so many borrowers. Lending standards were relaxed, enticing those with low incomes, poor credit, and often little or no down payments to borrow too much. New innovations in the mortgages themselves meant that borrowers would no longer be required to pay their principal, at least for some initial period, and in some cases, even interest could be deferred. The use of complex mathematical models implied that the inherent risk of mortgage prepayment—and the resulting end to those regular interest payments for bond holders—could not only be factored in, it could seemingly be eliminated. Thus, mortgage bonds were repackaged in ever more complex ways, many with correspondingly higher yields, in order to account for this 'reduction' in risk.

Mathematical models altered the traditional methods for assessing the risk of default, not only on the bonds themselves, but also for the individuals that held the mortgages that backed those bonds. As the investing world's thirst for higher yields and a deeper supply of them continued to climb, typical methods for assessing credit risk fell by the wayside. As we mentioned above, borrowers were given increasingly greater access to credit that was often well beyond their means. This occurred not just in housing, but in the market for all manner of consumer debt. At the same time, rating agencies such as Moody's and Standard & Poor's began to assign credit ratings that implied a much lower level of risk than was truly there; many of these came to be seen as virtually equivalent to US Treasury bonds, typically regarded as the safest instruments in the world! A high credit rating must necessarily correspond to low volatility and high liquidity.

Wall Street's appetite for risk was insatiable, and this thirst—measured by the demand for high-yield investments—seemingly had no bounds. This engendered an endless, downward spiral in which the demand for credit from homeowners was given a seemingly endless supply of financing. This, in turn, fanned the flames of demand, and prompted those that were extending that credit to relax their standards even further, making the growing problem even worse. At the same time, however, investors in mortgage bonds demanded even more of them, which continued to drive the extension of loose credit and the securitisation of even lower quality mortgages and mortgage bonds. Demand fed upon demand, and supply was endlessly offered up to meet that demand.

By 2005, by all rational measures, the housing market had become overheated. A bubble of unseen proportions was getting ready to burst. In many areas, local economies were wholly concentrated in housing and urban development. Homeowners repeatedly refinanced their mortgages in order to tap the equity that had been rapidly built up, and this fed into ever more consumer spending. Although it wasn't illegal, it certainly wasn't sustainable. Principal payments would inevitably have to be made, but by that time, rates were on the rise, making an untenable situation even more precarious. Homeowners who had already financed too much were invariably saddled with even higher payments, as their interest-only periods expired, higher interest rates quickly kicked in, and balloon payments came due.

As interest rates had been kept artificially low for so long, inflation became the primary risk to the economy. Fed Chair Ben Bernanke inherited this challenge as Greenspan's successor, and began a steady process of raising rates, in order to stave off further price increases. Commodities were booming as a result, chief among them oil, which put even greater pressure on consumer spending. This made it even harder for the average person to afford their escalating mortgages and other credit obligations.

The credit crisis in 2007-2008 was in many respects the perfect storm. It was reminiscent of the wave of calamities that struck seemingly independent markets in 1998. Housing prices were grossly overvalued; in relation to rents, prices had grown as much as 35% higher than they should have been. The ratio of homeowners to renters had risen as well, but was not supported by an equivalent increase in household incomes, meaning that housing debt-to-income ratios were out of line. Disposable income continued to be drained away by high consumer prices elsewhere in the economy. This is how the economic downturn began and warning signs were everywhere.

When the crunch came, it was more severe and more prolonged than most people had thought it could ever be. The Economist had predicted in 2005 that even a leveling of home prices would have drastic consequences for the economy, and as they did so, investors began to sell the homes they had speculated upon. Once the extent of over-supply in homes truly became known, it put even more downward pressure on housing prices. Homeowners, many of whom had repeatedly refinanced their mortgages and effectively turned their homes into ATM machines to support their spending, began to realise that they owed more than their homes were worth. The wave of selling continued, and began to reverberate throughout the wider economy. The sharp decrease in consumer spending in every sector of the economy meant a lack of demand for manufactured goods, which put further downward pressure on prices and quickly affected corporate earnings across the globe.

> *"Content makes poor men rich: discontent makes rich men poor."*
>
> **Benjamin Franklin**

The credit crunch itself was precipitated by two other notable financial innovations. The first is what has become known as the "shadow banking system." Financial institutions the world over essentially created offshore funds that raised capital by issuing short-term commercial bonds, and then used the proceeds to buy longer-term bonds. These funds were not shown on the banks' balance sheets, and invested heavily in 'asset-backed securities' that had at their heart the risky mortgages and other credit instruments that Wall Street had sold so feverishly. Investment firms pocketed the difference between what they borrowed on the short-term bonds and what they earned on the longer-term ones; because they were highly leveraged they could do this over and over again.

The second innovation was a relatively new and very esoteric derivative called a credit default swap, or CDS. These contracts were created to insure against the default on debt, but because the markets for them are largely unregulated they quickly came to be used for more speculative purposes than was the original intent. In fact, there was really *no* regulator for them at all; Greenspan, for example, had felt that they could police themselves. In contrast to stock options, where the options clearing houses ensure an orderly marketplace and enforce limits on the number of contracts that investors can hold, CDS contracts had no such limits. In contrast to the commodities markets, regulated by the Commodities Futures Trading Commission, investors in CDS contracts were not required to meet any net worth or reserve requirements. As a result, speculation had become rampant, ballooning the size of this market to as high as *$30 trillion*. In actuality, no one really knew the size of this market.

As the credit crisis unfolded, the banking system began to strain as creditors started to default on their mortgages and other credit obligations. What's more, hedge funds and larger institutions had invested heavily in risky asset-backed securities, not just offshore in the shadow banking system but as part of their formal capital structures. These assets were used as collateral for a wide range of activities, from traditional lending and investment financing to daily operations. As debtors the world over began to default on their loans, credit markets literally froze; fearing that asset backed securities might themselves default on their interest payments, investors quickly sought the safety of US Treasuries, and they did so in record numbers. Regardless of who was holding asset backed securities or how many they had, investors quickly shied away from using these securities as collateral, and lending dried up.

While this is a highly simplified explanation of an enormously complex occurrence, what it is important to realise is the *extent* to which it happened. Some of the most prolific investment banking institutions ended up failing as a result. The first among them was Bear Stearns, but it proved to be only the first of many casualties. As the market for asset-backed securities dried up, Bear Stearns was forced to try to bail out two of its own hedge funds that had invested heavily in them. With no accurate method by which to judge their worth, the asset-backed securities were no longer accepted as collateral for the loans that Bear needed for its rescue. The hedge funds collapsed, and threatened to take the entire investment bank with them.

It was the classic scenario of a run on a bank. James Cayne, the CEO of Bear Stearns, viewed the collapse of his firm as a virtual conspiracy. It was as if his competitors, sensing the imminent collapse, had circled for the kill and forced its downfall. Bear Stearns had shocked that tight knit Wall Street world with the extent of its concentration in and exposure to the very same "toxic" asset-backed securities that it had helped create, manufacture, and sell. It was the bank's own strategies that served up its downfall; Bear was also leveraged, to the tune of more than 30 to 1, but unlike regular banks that were required to hold certain levels of capital in reserve, the investment bank had financed its operations with the now-illiquid mortgage-backed bonds. They did this almost purely through the lending facilities in the so-called overnight markets which we cover in detail later.

Once it became known that they could not post the much-need collateral, their financing evaporated, literally overnight. On March 14, 2008, the Federal Reserve orchestrated a 28-day emergency loan from JP Morgan Chase, and on March 17, Bear Stearns was sold at the fire-sale prices. Bear Stearns was sold off, and its toxic assets guaranteed by the Federal Reserve, because it raised the spectre of systemic risk. It was too big, and had gone down too fast, for it to be allowed to fail. Its unmanaged collapse would have taken virtually the rest of Wall Street down with it.

The crisis in the credit markets continued, however, despite the emergency measures undertaken by the Federal Reserve and its backing of Bear Stearns' sale to JP Morgan Chase. That backing did not have the consequences that they intended, which was to restore confidence in the financial system and ensure that liquidity was maintained. Experience in earlier crises had shown that often it was the lack of liquidity and access to credit and lending facilities that allowed those crises to continue unabated.

The illiquid nature of the toxic mortgage assets was intractable. Large lenders and providers of subprime mortgages began to fail; Freddy Mac and Fannie Mae, the quasi-government agencies that owned or guaranteed nearly half of all US mortgages, were taken over by the Federal government, causing a worldwide panic. Last but certainly not least, Merrill Lynch agreed to be taken over by Bank of America, and Lehman Brothers was forced to file for bankruptcy.

Lehman's Demise

"The truest characters of ignorance are vanity, and pride and arrogance."

Samuel Butler

As the investor losses began to mount in 2006 and 2007, Bear Stearns actually increased their exposure, especially with the mortgage-backed assets that were central to the subprime mortgage crisis. Bear Stearns failed in its bid to rescue its hedge funds as a result of its creditors' rejection of its request for a certain type of short-term loan, a securities-backed repurchase agreement or "repo." Such financing is essential for investment banks as they borrow and lend billions to fund their daily business. The denial for this loan sent Bear Stearns' executives scrambling elsewhere to find the money, but they failed to secure what they needed.

The fall of Bear Stearns raises significant questions for the management and regulation of the financial institutions that we depend upon. Recalling the often-caustic and dismissive attitude of its executives, we must ask ourselves to what extent they were aware of the risky behaviour being undertaken on their watch. Whether they were aware or not, one must consider if they fully comprehended the enormous risks being shouldered by their traders. Perhaps even more important, we must ask why others did not learn from their mistakes and indeed, from their epic failures.

We know now that Lehman Brothers also held onto large numbers of these securities, but the reasons why it did so are less clear. *Long after virtually every market had turned against them they continued to pursue the same aggressive strategies that had brought about the collapse of Bear Stearns.*

The company was forced to take heavy losses in the first half of 2008, and its stock value plummeted by nearly 75%. It was forced to undertake massive cost-cutting measures, but over the third quarter of 2008 it seemed that nothing could stop the financial haemorrhaging. Rumours abounded that Lehman was being put up for sale.

When news reports dispelled those rumours in the first weeks of September, it seemed clear that the end was near for Lehman Brothers. Bear Stearns was, six months earlier, judged to be too big to fail. However, we would see only a short time later that Lehman Brothers, an equally important link in the global financial system, did not receive the same consideration. This decision was in many respects the beginning of the end. The fall of Lehman marked the true shift into full-blown crisis, for the effects of its failure would ripple not just through the US but to the farthest reaches of the global economy.

Internally, Lehman Brothers was rife with tension, and seemed like a disaster waiting to happen. Just prior to its collapse, it was suggested by some executives at Neuberger Berman, one of Lehman's investment management businesses, that top executives at their parent company should forego their large multi-million dollar bonuses in order to stave off the impending failure. This assertion that they were shirking their responsibility as managers was met with scorn by those at Lehman Brothers itself, dismissed as an absurd notion without any merit; it saw its stock price slid even further as a result, and found itself once again looking for a buyer. Later, during the bankruptcy proceedings, members of the US Congress would hear testimony that pointed to a crisis of confidence within the firm, and that portrayed a company in which there was no accountability for failure.

When the time came for Lehman to reach out to the Federal government for help, no rescue was forthcoming. On September 13, 2008 New York Fed President Timothy Geithner met with potential private-sector suitors, but none could be found. The next day, special derivatives trading took place so that investors could offset various positions in light of the impending bankruptcy. On September 15, it finally happened: Lehman filed for Chapter 11 bankruptcy protection, and the liquidation got into full swing. What's interesting here is that Fed *did* choose to step in, but only to facilitate the sale: *"A group of Wall Street firms agreed to provide capital and financial assistance for the bank's orderly liquidation and the Federal Reserve, in turn, agreed to a swap of lower-quality assets in exchange for loans and other assistance from the government."*

Was the Fed playing favourites? It backstopped the loans provided to J.P. Morgan when it acquired Bear Stearns six months earlier, and provided similar assistance in order to facilitate the dismembering of Lehman. It seems as though a political killing was taking place. One month after the bankruptcy filing, Fed Chairman Ben Bernanke commented that the US Treasury did not have sufficient authority to bail out the firm and absorb potentially billions of dollars of losses. And yet, *only one day later,* the Fed provided an $85 billion credit line to insurance giant AIG! **How could there be such a difference?**

Despite Lehman's key role as a leading broker on Wall Street and more globally, the Fed argued that all they could do was provide support for the orderly dissolution of the firm. With AIG, the story was different: *"the Federal Reserve and the Treasury judged that a disorderly failure would have severely threatened global financial stability and the performance of the U.S. economy. We also judged that emergency Federal Reserve credit to AIG would be adequately secured by AIG's assets. To protect U.S. taxpayers and to mitigate the possibility that lending to AIG would encourage inappropriate risk-taking by financial firms in the future, the Federal Reserve ensured that the terms of the credit extended to AIG imposed significant costs and constraints on the firm's owners, managers, and creditors."* For the regulators, it is evident that the key difference was to be found on each firm's balance sheet: AIG was judged to have more collateral with which to provide *"reasonable assurance"* that a loan would be repaid, whereas Lehman, it seems, did not.

Of course, this was not to be the end of the story. Not even one month after receiving this first $85 billion infusion, AIG was forced to borrow an additional $37.8 billion, as most of the original capital had been used to settle transactions with counterparties. By March 2009, the original terms had been altered for a third time; the US had now committed $182.5 billion to rescue the insurer, including an investment of as much as $70 billion, a $60 billion credit line and $52.5 billion to buy mortgage-linked assets owned or backed by AIG. The US government effectively nationalised the insurer, and continues to hold its majority stake.

While it was expected that much of the original $85 billion credit line would be used to cover capital calls to counterparties, this has nonetheless drawn intense criticism from the public and lawmakers. After initially refusing to do so for fear of further spreading AIG's *"infection,"* the recipients of these payments were finally disclosed by the company and the Fed. Among the largest recipients were nearly a dozen US financial institutions that had also received federal assistance through the Troubled Asset Relief Program (TARP). Many have criticised Goldman Sachs, for example, for having taken taxpayer money—to the tune of $13 billion—in order to continue funding their own trading activities, acting like a hedge fund in disguise and without regard to the risks it was taking with public funds.

Returning to Lehman's bankruptcy, we saw that indeed the sharks were circling prior to its collapse and in the days that followed, they moved in for the kill. Barclays Bank had been a party to the emergency discussions held by Tim Geithner over that fateful weekend, but declined, along with Bank of America, to buy the entire company. Barclays would go on to purchase the majority of Lehman's North American operations for about $1.3 billion—in the bankruptcy proceedings it was argued that it was the only available option, and so it was approved just 5 days later. Nomura Holdings of Japan agreed to buy Lehman's Asia operations and parts of its European division for about $225 million, despite the fact that these divisions contributed to nearly 50% of Lehman's global revenue. Neuberger Berman was effectively privatised, purchased by that firm's management, prevailing over a competing bid by a pair of private equity firms.

Without a doubt, Lehman's collapse pushed the global economy over the brink. Only days later, the US Treasury approved the still-contentious $700 billion TARP bailout plan, and was later forced to inject $250 billion in capital into the banking system in order to shore up its foundations, giving it equity stakes in nine leading banks. In the week prior to Lehman's bankruptcy filing, the federal government had also taken over the quasi-independent agencies Fannie Mae and Freddy Mac; it would later pledge $800 billion to buy mortgage bonds issued by these agencies. Trillions have since been injected into the financial system to ensure liquidity and to promote economic growth. *We must now ask, would things have been different had they given Lehman Brothers the same consideration?*

The Road to Recovery

While it may be easy to judge in hindsight, it is evident that Lehman's plunge into insolvency and the Fed's decision to let it fail threw the global financial system into a panic. Governments on both sides of the Atlantic were forced to undertake costly efforts to recapitalise their most important financial institutions to prevent further failures. It was the largest bankruptcy in the world, by some accounts ten times the size of the Enron case, and cost upwards of 5 million lost jobs when all the counts were tallied. But what has happened in the aftermath of Lehman's bankruptcy filing? The answers to this question are surprising.

First, let's revisit the issue of Lehman's failure. We've already seen how Ben Bernanke had initially insisted that providing a bailout to Lehman Brothers would have been unlawful. Former CEO Richard Fuld has testified that it only needed short-term financing so that it could unwind its toxic positions and survive this liquidity crisis. It seems that Bernanke's position was that the panic gripping the financial system in light of Lehman's potential failure meant that a bailout was a moot point, and that no amount of lending would have prevented the bank run that ensued. The result would have been the same, Lehman's failure was all but certain, and it would have left the Fed holding billions of illiquid, toxic assets.

This then points to the issue of viable alternatives. The US bankruptcy judge presiding over the case argued that the eventual purchase by Barclays of Lehman's core North American business was the only transaction available. We must now ask whether the Fed could have sent a different signal to the financial markets:

What if the Fed and the Treasury had made a public announcement that they had approved a takeover by Barclays and were willing to provide Lehman with bridging finance until the deal could be completed? Wouldn't that have been enough to reassure the firm's creditors and counterparties?

It isn't immediately obvious that the answer is no.

Perhaps this was part of Barclays' strategy, and it seems in retrospect that Barclays made out quite well by not agreeing to a takeover and instead, waiting for the Lehman to go under on its own. And who could blame them?

Was there another message, however? Another former Lehman executive has argued that it was indeed a political killing. Others, such as Richard Fuld, have contended that Lehman Brothers was not given the same consideration as others, such as Bear Stearns and AIG, and the result is that more politically connected firms such as Goldman Sachs have banked the windfall. Bernanke pointed to problems within the firm for justification for letting it fail:

"It was a combination of general fear, certainly, but also some legitimate concerns about both the asset position of the company, its balance sheet, but also some concerns about the longer term viability of the firm, its business model," said Bernanke, who expressed hope that future failures could be contained through new laws requiring big institutions to have "living wills" outlining steps for an orderly wind-down. In a thinly veiled attack on Wall Street bosses such as Fuld, who enjoyed pay of more than $310m over seven years, Bernanke told the commission: *"It seems like a lot of people who drove their companies into the ditch walked away with a lot of money and that's not good capitalism—it's not a good ethical outcome, either."*

Moreover, employees were highly rewarded for entering into transactions that booked short-term profits but put the firm at long-term risk. It is possible that charges will still be brought in conjunction with the failure. This, then, points to some of the problems that plagued Lehman Brothers and brought about its collapse, to which we will now turn. Many have argued that, indeed, it was financial mismanagement the led to the failure. At firms such as J.P. Morgan and Goldman Sachs, there was a direct line of communication between the CEO and CFO; at Lehman, there were at least four layers between them, which contributed to its dysfunction. Senior executives were excessively self-confident in their understanding of financial markets, and chose to exceed reasonable limits on leverage, diversification and concentration:

"Although Lehman conducted stress tests on a monthly basis and reported the results of these stress tests periodically to regulators and to its Board of Directors, the stress tests excluded Lehman's commercial real estate investments, its private equity investments, and, for a time, its leveraged loan commitments. Thus, Lehman's management did

not have a regular and systematic means of analysing the amount of catastrophic loss that the firm could suffer from these increasingly large and illiquid investments . . . Lehman's management decided to exceed risk limits with respect to Lehman's principal investments, namely, the "concentration limits" on Lehman's leveraged loan and commercial real estate businesses, including the "single transaction limits" on the leveraged loans. These limits were designed to ensure that Lehman's investments were properly limited and diversified by business line and by counterparty. Lehman took highly concentrated risks in these two business lines, and, partly as a result of market conditions, ultimately exceeded its risk limits by margins of 70% as to commercial real estate and by 100% as to leveraged loans."

It was the pervasive use of "accounting gimmicks" that proved Lehman's undoing. Chief among these was the use of so-called repurchase agreements. A repurchase agreement is a type of ultra short-term loan used heavily by large financial institutions. Known as a repo, the loan works like this: *"A bank borrows money from an investor. The bank backs that loan by lending the investor assets and promising to repurchase them at a set time at a slightly higher price (hence "repo"). The bank doesn't really sell these assets; it just posts them as temporary collateral, so for reporting purposes they're still part of its balance sheet."* This however, is not the whole story for many investment banks, especially Lehman Brothers, who utilised this technique even more aggressively than others.

Lehman made extensive use of what is known as Repo 105, which differs from other types of repurchase agreements. With Repo 105, if Lehman over collateralised these short-term loans they could classify them as sold and thereby remove them from their balance sheet, despite the fact that they were still obligated to repurchase them in the future. Thus, Lehman's management could claim a clean balance sheet and report reduced leverage. By doing this, they could shift up to $50 billion in assets off their books, although the legal justification has come under fire. What's more, when they coordinated these strategic "sales" with the release of quarterly reporting, it even allowed them to *increase* their leverage in the meantime.

One should rightly ask, how did Lehman, and other financial firms, get away with this? In the case of Lehman, they relied upon an obscure legal ruling obtained from an offshore law firm. In essence, Lehman Brothers needed a legal opinion that would classify their use of Repo 105 as asset sales, which they obtained from the UK firm Linklaters LLP. All the while, and since 2001, Lehman's domestic auditors Ernst & Young were aware of what was going on and, according to New York Attorney General Andrew Cuomo, understood that these techniques were designed to manipulate the firm's balance sheet. With the help of their external auditors, Lehman hid these transactions from the public by aggregating them with groups of other derivates and burying them in the footnotes. Ernst & Young reaped at least $150 million in accounting fees in the years preceding the bankruptcy for its role in hiding the facts from the investing public, and faces several lawsuits for its role in this potential accounting fraud.

Even more troubling, though, was the apparent complicity of the New York Fed, and at its helm, Tim Geithner. The New York Fed is tasked with ensuring the safety and soundness of the banking system and by extension should have known what was going on behind the scenes at Lehman. It has since emerged that when the New York Fed reviewed Lehman Brothers, it should have seen the impending insolvency and insisted upon winding it down as a "bad bank." Anton Valukas, the bank examiner appointed to investigate Lehman's failure, notes: *"the Examiner questioned Lehman executives and other witnesses about Lehman's financial health and reporting, a recurrent theme in their responses was that Lehman gave full and complete financial information to Government agencies, and that the Government never raised significant objections or directed that Lehman take any corrective action."* The New York Fed carried out stress tests to determine the bank's health—it failed, but no action was taken because Lehman conducted its own stress tests with its own standards, and passed.

One must then ask to what degree should Tim Geithner be held accountable for this regulatory failure?

Prior to the collapse of the firm, CEO Richard Fuld had raised the possibility of converting the company to a bank holding company rather than an investment bank. This option was dismissed as "gimmicky" by Tim Geithner, who stated *"You can't solve a liquidity/capital problem by becoming a bank holding company."* However what is particularly telling in the aftermath is that other institutions including Goldman Sachs and Morgan Stanley did just that, once the financial crisis was full-blown. Yet again, the public was told one thing, and another happened; and yet again, Lehman Brothers' competitors received preferential treatment at the hands of the regulators, implying once more that indeed, Lehman was simply ***allowed*** to fail.

Conclusion

The Lehman Brothers case file is still far from closed. The price tag for the bankruptcy has already climbed past $1 billion, and the lawsuits are far from settled. As Lehman Brothers is unwound and its assets sold off, it continues to face a number of legal challenges. Hedge fund manager Paulson & Co. has filed a competing reorganisation plan, citing preferential treatment of Lehman's banking creditors over those of at least ten hedge fund creditors. California's Public Employees' Retirement System, CALPERS, has accused Lehman Brothers and former top executives of fraud related to the false reporting of mortgage-related losses.

The "new" Lehman Brothers Holdings however, doesn't behave much like a bankrupted firm. To be sure, as the largest bankruptcy in history, it can't very easily be judged against any other—nor should serve as a precedent for future insolvencies. Bryan Marsal, a restructuring expert acting as Lehman's CEO, has delayed certain asset sales in anticipation of more favourable pricing; Lehman won approval to manage sales of illiquid real estate assets for as long as five years. Some of the firm's creditors want to recover their assets sooner, but in delaying those divestitures, Marsal plans to raise nearly $58 billion as property values recover. The implication, however, is that *"the liquidating estate is acting like an ongoing investment concern,"* holding nearly $20 billion in cash and even injecting further capital into some of its distressed properties.

If we are to learn from the past, it seems evident that the financial system still faces a regulatory void that needs to be filled. Lehman Brothers failed the Fed's stress tests, but nothing was done. If the Fed also knew about the improper accounting practices that masked the excessive risk being taken by Lehman, they took no action. In the meantime, it remains to be seen whether the financial system is any less fragile than it was before. It is possible that the US government might even *make* money after the bailout has settled when all is said and done. However, the prolonged economic and societal costs are far less certain.

What has changed since the collapse of Lehman? One such possible preventative measure has been the passage in July 2010 of the so-called Dodd-Frank Act in the US. This legislation aims to restructure the regulatory regime that governs the financial system, chiefly by creating a new consumer protection agency, a council to monitor systemic risk, new regulations to govern derivatives, and restrictions on executive compensation. Financial institutions are said to face new standards for increased capital requirements, leverage limits, liquidity requirements, concentration limits and credit exposure. Importantly, it also aims to make the government more accountable for its emergency lending practices.

Critics of these measures, though, are not so convinced of their likely impact. Federal Reserve Bank of Kansas President Thomas Hoenig has argued that even though firms that engender systemic risk are supposed to be identified and wound down by the new legislation, it would be impossible to do so because of the tangled web of interconnection between them. He cites the extreme concentration of derivatives still held by Wall Street firms, with the top 5 investment banks still accounting for more than 95% of the derivatives held by all the companies of the S&P 500. Knowing that there's always someone else on the other side of these trades, Hoenig feels that we may even be *worse off* now than before the crisis occurred.

On a positive note, the Dodd-Frank Act has already resulted in a significant increase in so-called "whistleblower" tips to financial regulators: "the number of 'high-value' tips on fraud and other violations of securities law numbered about two dozen a year before the law. Since July, the agency has sometimes been receiving one or two a day, Thomas Sporkin, chief of the SEC's Office of Market Intelligence, told the SEC Speaks event sponsored by the Practicing Law Institute. Whistleblowers who provide 'original information' about large frauds could net as much as 30 percent of the penalties and recovered funds collected by the SEC under the Dodd-Frank act."

The Federal Deposit Insurance Corporation, FDIC, has also been given a new mandate under the act, and has recently proposed strict curbs on executive compensation in order to discourage excessive risk-taking. Some firms have already implemented similar reforms, and now aim to delay bankers' bonus payments over a period of at least three years and to tie compensation to future—rather than just present—performance. With a focus on the long-term, it is argued that speculation will be less rampant and should help contribute to the prevention of future crises.

Will it all work? What was clear, in the aftermath of the Lehman Brothers collapse, was that many more options than were previously disclosed were in fact available to executives and regulators and could have prevented—or at least lessened—the financial crisis. Lehman was not the only investment bank to utilise the Repo 105 technique; it has been alleged that Bank of America has similarly manipulated its balance sheet. It is clear, then, that accounting rules still need to change. Regulators should now move to a system in which firms are judged by the substance of what they are trying to do, rather than simply whether they followed the letter of the law. It was not just Lehman Brothers that encouraged excessive risk-taking among its bankers, traders and executives. We have yet to see significant change here, and banks are still able to compensate their top employees in nearly any way they please—despite having taken billions in taxpayer funded bailouts.

In the final analysis, it is not just the institutions that must change but also the system itself, something we look at in the final chapter. If the New York Fed had been more proactive, it might not be culpable for the financial crisis—the jury is still out on the extent of the Fed's involvement, or to what extent it should be held accountable for the failure of Lehman, in particular, or the financial crisis more generally. Certainly, history will be the judge, but that will no doubt be little consolation for those that lost their jobs, or saw their personal investments vanish overnight, or face further economic and societal challenges that continue to crop up in the wake of this latest financial crisis.

In every crisis there is a defining moment that stands out clearly as a visual record of the overall event. The collapse and bankruptcy of Lehman Brothers was that moment. Its impact was devastating and we can debate forever as to whether it was preventable but the key is—*have we learnt from our mistake!*

Chapter 18

September 2008—Belgium Bombshell: The Bailout without Borders!

"The truth is I've never fooled anyone. I've let people fool themselves. They didn't bother to find out who and what I was. Instead they would invent a character for me. I wouldn't argue with them. They were obviously loving somebody I wasn't. When they found this out, they would blame me for disillusioning them—and fooling them."

Marilyn Monroe,
the Original Bombshell

Sept 2008—Belgium bank Dexia collapses.

"The years of slavery are past, The Belgian rejoices once more; Courage restores to him at last The rights he held of yore. Strong and firm his grasp will be—Keeping the ancient flag unfurled To fling its message on the watchful world: For king, for right, for liberty."

Louis A. Dechez
La Brabanconne, Belgian National Anthem
written during the revolution of 1830

A Market Analyst; "A market analyst is an expert who will know tomorrow why the things he predicted yesterday didn't happen today!"

Who are these mysterious market analysts who hide in ivory towers? What strange and exotic power do they wield over the international money markets?

One of the largest concerns of the credit crisis came in the wake of accelerating failures in the United States, as the 'Bear Flu' quickly spread and infected its counterparties in the investment banking system specifically, but throughout the financial system more generally. It is this issue of systemic risk that has proven so difficult to protect against. As the case of Dexia Bank shows, while systemic risk might be easy to define, limiting its scope and insuring the system against failure are remarkably difficult and costly tasks for policymakers.

The case of Dexia Bank is also very illuminating in several other key ways, because it is perhaps the first and best example of spillover of systemic risk beyond the wider investment banking system in the US. Even though Dexia was not the first European bank to encounter difficulty, and the scope of its bailout package was not as extensive as its rival Fortis received, it is perhaps more important precisely *because* it is the second bank in this important region to require intervention. Dexia is also markedly different than Fortis in that its 'infection' meant that the contagion was not being contained, and it threatened to spill over into other areas of the financial system as well. The effects of this spillover are still very uncertain, but will affect not only shareholders but many other citizens around the world as well; this, however, is not as a result of the intervention, as many might predict, but because of the impact on Dexia's businesses themselves, as we shall shortly detail.

In this chapter, we'll investigate the main reasons why Dexia Bank required financial intervention in late September 2008. More important than just this, however, it is what that intervention means, on several different but interrelated levels. Dexia's rescue was the first large-scale intervention to cross international borders, and thus is demonstrative of the contagious nature of systemic risk. Moreover, it sheds light on some of the problems that now plague us as a result of the interconnected nature of the global financial system; at issue here is the role of the European Central Bank, which heretofore had confined its role to fighting inflation. With the bailout of Dexia, the ECB was called on to play a role that *did not previously exist*!

We will discuss these ramifications and what they mean, for the trickle-down effect of this intervention will invariably affect everyone, but for reasons that most observers will not realise. For the first time, the spillover effects of a bank bailout would reach beyond the federal level, where the effects are somewhat diffuse. Certainly, this is not to diminish the burden on present and future generations of the enormous costs of the US federal bailout, or of other nationally funded interventions. The impact of the credit crisis on Dexia's businesses will mean a declining ability for its subsidiaries to carry out the critical role of providing lending to local governments around the world, especially in France, as well as its key role as a bond insurer. For all these reasons, it's important for us to understand the case of Dexia, and what it may mean for our *everyday quality of life* in the future.

The Collapse of Dexia

Dexia was not the first Belgian bank to need a bailout. It was not even the biggest bailout. *So what is interesting about this bailout amidst so many others?*

What is interesting about the case of Dexia is the speed with which it followed the bailout of rival bank Fortis. On September 28, 2008, Fortis received 11.2 billion euro from the three Benelux nations; Belgium, the Netherlands and Luxembourg. Very much a part of the fabric of Belgian life, Fortis is one of the largest non-state employers and traces its roots back almost 300 years. Fortis faced collapse after it depleted its capital base by being part of a consortium that acquired ABN AMRO earlier in the year. As a result of this and the worsening economic conditions around the world, Fortis was judged by the Belgian and Dutch financial authorities to be too big to fail.

Like Fortis, Dexia was an integral part of the financial life of this region. Dexia is also markedly different from Fortis, for in addition to its retail operations it is also one of the largest lenders to local governments. As well, a significant portion of its revenue at that time came from its bond insurance business in the US. As such, analysing the bailout and its consequences must take into account this multinational, multi-line business.

> **"He that will not sail till all dangers are over must never put to sea"**
>
> **Thomas Fuller**

Dexia was created in 1996 out of the merger of Credit Communal de Belgique and Credit Local de France. This was a significant achievement, considering the pace of European integration at the time; monetary union was still nascent, with the process having only formally begun six years before this merger. It is demonstrative of the economic convergence that was well under way. Dexia was initially founded as a dual-listed corporate entity, but in 1999 the Belgian side effectively acquired the French side to form one single company, to be headquartered in Brussels.

Through a series of key acquisitions, Dexia grew rapidly through the late 1990's and early 2000's, and by the time of the bailout was the largest provider of financial services to local governments, and the fourth largest bank in Belgium overall. One of these key acquisitions was the purchase of Financial Security Assurance, or FSA, in 2000. FSA provides default insurance on municipal government bonds. This is not to be confused with bond underwriting, however, but is nevertheless an integral part of the funding process for many local governments in the United States.

Similar to Fortis, Dexia's potential collapse would have been economically devastating for Belgium. Only two days after Fortis nearly failed, the panic that nearly toppled that bank threatened to take down Dexia as well. Then-CEO Axel Miller stated that the bank was the victim of "*very nervous markets*," which prompted clients to hastily withdraw savings from Fortis, and the threat that this would carry over to Dexia led the bank to ask for state intervention. Dexia's shares traded down some 30% on Monday, prior to being suspended on Tuesday when the bailout was announced. Fortunately, the ever-present specter of political failure that seems to plague Belgium, as it continues to be gripped by regional and cultural struggles that routinely threaten the survival of governments, was vanquished only days earlier. The Belgian coalition government itself nearly collapsed the previous weekend, as it struggled under the weight of declining economic conditions and fallout from the deepening credit crisis.

> *"Half a truth is better than no politics!"*
> **Gilbert K. Chesterton**

The bailout itself was noteworthy not simply because of its price tag, but because it involved so much political coordination, both within Belgium and across its borders. In contrast to Fortis, which had also received a capital infusion from three nations, the Dexia package necessitated the involvement of France. This, in and of itself, is compelling as evidence of the breadth and depth of the widening credit crisis. Dexia consequently received the 6.4 billion euro bailout, which involved the coordination of Belgium's federal and regional governments, France and the largest shareholders of the multinational company. Belgian Prime Minister Yves Leterme said: *"Given the crisis situation around the Dexia group we took concrete and correct decisions to reinforce Dexia's health so that the group can face the events playing out in financial markets."* French Finance Minister Christine Lagarde said the capital infusion was essential *"to guarantee the stability of the financial system,"* and points to the central role that Dexia played in the area of public finance more generally.

The bailout itself stemmed from the firm's declining financial health, as a result of its businesses that were almost entirely concentrated outside Belgium. Dexia had made a multi-billion loan to German bank Depfa, a unit of one of Germany's largest lenders, Hypo Real Estate. Hypo had been hit particularly hard by the credit crisis, having earlier taken on substantial debt and as a result was itself seized by German authorities. Dexia was also significantly damaged by the collapse of Lehman Brothers in the United States; at the time, they expected to incur losses of 350 million euro in the wake of its failure. This made it more difficult for Dexia to access the funds that it needed for daily operations.

Dexia's FSA unit, moreover, was also hit hard by the subprime mortgage crisis. As bonds backed by risky mortgages suffered heavy losses, FSA suffered over $300 million in initial losses by June 2008. Dexia was forced to set aside an additional $500 million to cover potential additional losses, and extended to FSA an unsecured credit line of $5 billion to cover further write-offs. Losses due to the Lehman collapse would later double, and an additional 500 million euro in losses was booked due to trading losses as well as from the collapse of the Icelandic banking system.

> *"Show me a good loser and I will show you a loser"*
> **Paul Newman**

As a result, Dexia was forced to sell FSA to rival Assured Guaranty, owned by New York financier Wilbur Ross. Markets initially smiled on this news, but later turned sour as the company continued to face "headwinds" from restructuring, higher financing costs, and exposure to the risky asset-management business and investment portfolio that was not part of the deal with Assured Guaranty. In addition, half of the capital that Dexia received in the FSA sale was in stock of Assured Guaranty, meaning that it remained exposed to the troubled bond-insurance business.

While the subsequent streamlining in its operations and renewed focus on its core business of public finance was heralded, it is anything but certain how the effects of Dexia's near collapse will play out. Dexia's bailout shows how the systemic risk imposed by the tangled web of financial markets and institutions was all too real, and reveals some of the problems that we will face in the wake of the credit crisis. We will explore each of these in turn below.

Financial Integration in Europe

> *"Unity, not uniformity, must be our aim. We attain unity only through variety. Differences must be integrated, not annihilated, not absorbed".*
> **Mary Parker Follett**

Dexia's formation in 1996 was heralded as one of great significance. Due to the central role that its two predecessors played in the public finance system in France as well as in the Benelux region, this merger was important because it spoke to the deepening financial and political integration on the continent. It should be recalled that European integration more generally was pursued as a consequence of the rising power of the United States following the Second World War. In order to remain competitive and to counter the rise of the US, European elites began the gradual process of economic and political integration.

Integration began in more functional areas of economic coordination. The development of a common market accomplished the free movement of goods, services, people and capital within and among member states; most important for our purposes, the free movement of capital was intended to remove restrictions on the flow of investments across borders. Customs union and common economic policies followed, and as early as 1969 the development of a single European currency became one of the highest priorities. The Maastricht Treaty in 1993 legally bound the member states to start the monetary union by January 1, 1999, and the euro currency was born on this date. It remained an *"accounting currency"* until January 1, 2002, when national currencies among twelve member states at the time were phased out. The currency zone has since grown to sixteen countries.

The adoption of the euro meant that monetary policies among member states had to be synchronised. This was achieved in three stages, beginning with the complete freedom of capital transactions and increased cooperation between central banks in order to foster economic convergence. The second stage involved the establishment of the European Monetary Institute, the predecessor to the European Central Bank, or ECB, and required a move toward independence of national central banks in order to increase the coordination of monetary policies. In the third stage, exchange rates were fixed with the introduction of the euro, and a single monetary policy was adopted under the auspices of the European System of Central Banks, which together with the ECB are now known as the Eurosystem. The Eurosystem is the singular monetary authority in the Eurozone, and has as its primary function; *the maintenance of price stability in the area.*

Headquartered in Frankfurt, Germany, the continent's largest financial center, the ECB traces its heritage to the German Bundesbank. Although its primary function is to control inflation in the region, the ECB is politically independent from its sixteen member states. This, of course, has been a source of continued tension. Member states do appoint the six members of the Executive Board to the ECB's Governing Council, but they serve non-renewable eight-year terms; national central bank governors also sit on the Council but are required to serve at least five years in their home states. Of late, the ECB's independence has come under fire from French President Nicolas Sarkozy, who has argued that the ECB should expand its influence in several critical areas.

This points to one of the key constraints within the European Union as it relates to monetary policy. *The ECB is notable not simply because it is the singular authority for maintaining price stability, but because this is in fact its only statutory function.*

Sarkozy has argued that the ECB should play a larger role in economic growth and job creation, and has criticised the ECB's stance on interest rates. The 2007 Treaty of Lisbon would make the ECB a formal institution of the EU and would formally ensure its independence, but all European Union members have not yet ratified it.

Moreover, this reveals a major difference between the US Federal Reserve system and the ECB, in that the ECB *does not function as a lender of last resort*. This task still devolves to the national central banks, which should prove adequate when a private bank has a clear 'nationality.' As the Dexia bailout displays, however, there was no role for the ECB. It fell to the national fiscal authorities in each member country to coordinate their policies, which could reasonably have led to its failure. At present, the ECB lacks a clear mandate to deal with troubled institutions, and in its absence national governments have had to step in.

Part of the blame for the panic that threatened to topple Dexia lay with the rejection by the US Congress of the Bush Administration's $700 billion bailout plan. This sent the Dow Jones spinning into one of its largest trading losses ever, and quickly spread to markets around the globe. Nothing is more evident of systemic risk than this! In Europe, even as Dexia marked the fifth nationalisation within the Eurozone and the UK, it was felt that not enough was being done to stop the bleeding. These events underline the urgency of cross-border cooperation and coordination, and critics point to the ECB's missing mandate as a critical means of fixing this problem in the future.

This also highlights the 'missing link' of financial regulation, both within the EU and globally. National central banks in the Eurozone still suffer this critical disconnection and must separately coordinate actions such as the Dexia bailout, although in this case they were able to do so quickly and effectively despite the tripartite nature of the plan. The swift worldwide stock market declines that followed the initial failure in the US to adopt a comprehensive bailout are further evidence of this; market reactions show the necessity of an urgent response on how to remove bad debt from bank balance sheets and thaw the frozen credit markets. These losses showed the *real* risk of a system-wide crash, as trillions in value were wiped out in the space of a few days.

> *"Government is not the solution to our problem, government is the problem."*
>
> **Ronald Reagan**

Dexia's former CEO Axel Miller goes one step further: *"The management of the crisis has at times been a little chaotic and the markets just don't accept that . . . It's time for regulators globally to get together to find some kind of global solutions to a situation where banks essentially are not lending to each other anymore."* Indeed, there has been much discord between the Fed and the ECB, in terms of their preferred responses to the crisis. In recent months, ECB president Jean-Claude Trichet stated that more spending was not the answer, throwing the bank's weight behind Europe's governments in their battle with the US over how to overcome the worst recession in a generation: *"Nothing will really work until the financial sector is back on track and ready to lend on a sustainable basis. I would say exactly the same with the budget. Decisions have been taken; they are very important. Let's do it! Quick implementation, quick disbursement is what is needed."*

Even as many private-sector economists have criticised the lack of fiscal stimulus emanating from the ECB and its delayed response in dropping key lending rates to restart growth, Trichet's arguments stand in contrast to the US stimulus package, which has in many respects proceeded in "fits and starts." This also illustrates some of the key differences that make cross-border coordination virtually impossible. Key measures of the economy are judged differently on each side of the Atlantic; inflation for example, is targeted in different ways, and results in large diversions in base lending rates at the Fed and the ECB.

In addition, Trichet argues that spending responses must be divergent, because of the different nature of bank funding in Europe: *"Mr. Trichet said most euro-zone private-sector funding comes from banks—not from securities markets as in the U.S.—and hinted that the ECB is preparing new programs to help banks further. But he suggested purchasing government assets wouldn't fit the euro-zone financial system."* This, he says, would result in a "blending of responsibilities" between the central ECB and the Eurozone's sixteen national central banks and a blurring of the ECB's mandate.

In the United States, one of the driving factors behind the federal bailout package was the need to cleanse bank balance sheets of toxic assets that were preventing them from weathering this storm. Even though this process has been applied at best unevenly in the US, the Fed has pressured the ECB to accept "junk mortgage paper" as collateral in its lending operations. The ECB, however, was more reluctant because of its lack of mandate in this area; moreover, at present this would involve agreement among each separate national government.

These divergent views have hampered a coordinated effort to solve the widening crisis. In fact, policies pursued by the Bank of England and the Fed, for example, may have had the unintended consequences *of deepening the credit crisis or creating one of the elements of a future one!* In seeking to remove these toxic assets from bank balance sheets, they have effectively set a "floor" for mortgage-backed securities, and according to some commentators, these prices are too low and imply unrealistic levels of mortgage defaults. It is argued that new accounting rules have actually exacerbated the credit crisis, by requiring 'mark to market' pricing in real time.

This is a thorny issue. So-called 'mark-to-market' or fair value accounting was a practice that actually originated in the derivatives market, as a result of computerised models that determined pricing, where market prices were perhaps not readily available. The standards were later adopted more widely. It has been argued that fair value accounting helped precipitate the recent subprime crisis, by forcing firms to provide 'real time' values for the assets they held and for which markets might have been illiquid. Erratic market behaviour caused pricing calculations to break down; human behaviour and judgment filled in the gaps and prices jumped accordingly. This continues to be felt in the ongoing process of asset write-downs, as banks around the world try to account for and absorb their subprime-induced losses.

This also points once again to the problem of systemic risk: what does it mean for a bank to be too big to fail?

Most often, when we conceptualise this issue, we have in our minds an entity such as Bear Stearns or Lehman Brothers. In the case of the former, Bear was judged too big to fail, and a fire sale of its assets was hastily arranged; the US Fed brokered the deal and guaranteed the assets that JPMorgan assumed when it agreed to buy Bear. In the case of Lehman, however, it was judged that Lehman was allowed to collapse where Bear Stearns was not. Policymakers felt that one bailout was enough; Bear Stearns could not be allowed to fail, because of its swift decline and the danger that its unmanaged collapse posed. Lehman, though, had had ample time to make arrangements, and capital markets were well aware of the risk of its failure.

Nevertheless, Lehman's bankruptcy put tremendous downward pressure on stock markets and further accelerated the decline in real estate securities. Lehman's brokerage operations were frozen. These were critical for many clients worldwide and creditors around the globe faced massive losses, with little chance of recouping their losses. Dexia was one such firm that suffered in the aftermath of the Lehman bankruptcy. Indeed, as we've seen earlier, the costs to Dexia were in fact significantly higher in the end than were previously envisioned at the time. The argument that capital markets could 'price' the effects, virtually overnight, seems to be without merit.

Was Dexia too big to fail?

As the fourth largest bank in Belgium, the impact of putting 35,000 out of work, at home and abroad, would clearly have had drastic, negative consequences. The same arguments have been offered for US carmakers, which is why they have received such significant intervention and assistance in recent months. Some economists argue that the very term is too difficult to quantify, and isn't really about size—even small, "seemingly innocuous" firms can pose substantial threats to the financial system. Recent efforts in the US to 'predetermine' which banks *are* too big to fail, may even engender more risk—creating such a list could encourage the very type of risky behaviour that regulators are trying to eliminate.

The ECB's approach, though, has not yet worked either. In July 2009, the ECB injected half a trillion Euros into cash markets in efforts to ensure that liquidity concerns have been met, but this has been seen as only a short-term solution. The problem, however, goes beyond liquidity and recent ECB efforts have yet to address the issue of capital: without cleansing their balance sheets, banks have simply been unable to lend out the funds the ECB has provided to them. As a result, credit markets have remained tight and banks have as yet been unable to 'spend' these funds in ways that will help them over the long-term—they are thus caught in a vicious cycle.

Not only are regulators caught in the dilemma that public money provided to banks has not in turn been lent out quick enough, they are faced with the vicious circle of "too big". If they break up the financial institutions into smaller units then those self same units have less protection against further, inevitable and future financial hurricanes. If they merge them into mega-banks then they are faced with public outcry and moral outrage when, as always happens, one becomes "too big" to fail.

"If I see you have a staff, I will give it to you. If I see you have no staff, I will take it away from you."

Zen Riddle

The Business of Bonds

One of the most compelling issues in the wake of Dexia's near collapse and bailout concerns the restructuring that was required in the aftermath. As a result of the massive losses that Dexia suffered, it was forced to sell its US bond insurance business, FSA. We've previously discussed the costs associated with the sale, but what is also at issue is the bond insurance industry as a whole; FSA's purchase by Assured Guaranty may in fact have a negative impact on both bond issuers and consumers as a whole.

First, let's take a closer look at the world of bonds, and specifically as it relates to Dexia, the world of municipal bonds. Cities, local governments, or their agencies, issue these bonds in order to finance public works projects. Funds raised from the issuance of these bonds are used for a variety of purposes, from infrastructure improvements to financing student loans. Interest and principal payments are usually funded through general tax revenues, although they may also have a more specific revenue source such as from a particular venue or infrastructure project.

As with any bond, the issuer is assigned a credit rating by a variety of different credit rating agencies, such as Moody's, Fitch and Standard & Poor's. These agencies assess the creditworthiness—the ability to repay—of the issuing body, and take into account whether the bonds are a general obligation or whether they are to be backed by revenues from specific sources. Rating agencies can be hired by the issuer in order to issue a 'bond rating,' which is most useful to investors buying the bonds directly from the issuers rather than on the secondary market.

Information about a specific issue of bonds is contained in an official statement that details the terms of interest and principal payments, any security pledged as collateral for repayment, and material financial information about the issuer. In the US, the Municipal Securities

Rulemaking Board governs rules concerning the required disclosures; in recent years, there has been a trend towards requiring further annual disclosures as well, such as notices of events that could affect the creditworthiness of the issuer.

In addition to their own inherent creditworthiness, many localities will try to enhance the attractiveness of their bond offerings through the purchase of bond insurance. In 1971 Ambac Financial created the 'monoline' insurance industry, so named because they provide insurance to only one type of industry. Their goal was to help bond issuers get better access to cheaper funding, through the purchase of additional 'insurance' against default. These insurers must themselves be of high credit quality in order to provide this back-up guarantee, often to lower-rated borrowers.

While not automatically or always the case, the end result of this dynamic was that issuers could effectively *purchase* a higher-credit rating in exchange for insurance premiums, and the bonds themselves would then effectively *assume* the credit rating of the bond insurer. Higher credit ratings are for obvious reasons more attractive to investors, who want to lessen their exposure to default and continue to enjoy timely payments of interest and principal. The nature of these insurance policies also means that if the bond insurer itself suffers a credit downgrade, this effect will filter through to the underlying bonds.

Unfortunately, the small capital base that most of these insurers operated with meant that when the subprime crisis hit, the effects were devastating. Many insurers were heavily exposed to mortgage-backed securities, including collateralised debt obligations or CDOs, which were among the riskiest of these types of bonds; default rates on these bonds soared, and the insurers began to suffer heavy losses as they now had to pay policy benefits far in excess of what their capital bases could support. When Fitch reduced Ambac's credit rating in January 2008, it triggered the simultaneous downgrade of over 100,000 bond issues, totaling more than $500 billion. Much like a bank run, this brought other insurers under review as well, and the municipal bond market declined substantially, to the point where many insured bonds were trading as if they had no official rating.

Prior to the credit crisis, bond insurers had an important part to play in the $3 trillion municipal bond market. Since the crisis hit, their role has subsequently declined, and their economic value to the issuers has been drastically affected. Bond insurance is perhaps of lesser value to larger localities, but it plays a key role in obtaining access to capital markets for smaller issuers. Prior to 2007, more than half of all public issuers in the municipal bond market carried insurance, but in recent months, this has declined to just 10%; the crisis, moreover, has prompted an industry consolidation, the effects of which are as yet unclear. Consolidation is, as we all know, a two headed monster.

> *"The ultimate plan, which proved too visionary, was to consolidate under one control a vast network of (railway) lines extending all over the continent."*
>
> **John Moody**

The sale of FSA by Dexia to rival Assured Guaranty was one such merger. As with every insurance company, premiums are invested and managed in order to perpetuate their ability to pay policy claims. Of course, much of their portfolio would have been invested in government and agency securities which themselves likely suffered heavy losses as a result of the credit crisis. Dexia and its government backers will still be responsible for significant potential losses in this respect. Having exited the asset-backed securities business in the third quarter of 2008, the company expects to be able to weather the storm while still earning premiums on their existing portfolio and adding to their capital base.

How will this all affect consumers, as the end users of municipal bond fundraising?

It is perhaps too early to tell. At present, the effect on bond insurers of absorbing these losses has meant that pricing has been elevated. This means that bond issuers will have to pay more in order to access higher credit ratings, and this limits the ability of smaller municipalities and those with lesser credit ratings of their own to find adequate sources of capital. If local governments cannot gain suitable financing, or the costs of issuing bonds raises too high, many of these entities will suffer.

More importantly, however, it was the insurance of more risky debt obligations that has significantly threatened the market as a whole. Some critics allege that it was pressure on these firms from shareholders to produce unrealistic profits that forced them to venture into more risky areas of insurance, and have only resulted in their failure. Their exposure to CDOs has brought about an overall downgrading of the industry as a whole; in 2007 there were seven insurers rated triple-A by the three major rating agencies, but today none of them enjoys this rating.

Many of these firms have since exited the municipal insurance business or significantly curtailed their exposure; the merger of FSA and Assured Guaranty means that there is now only one significant bond insurer. There is now a lack of competition within the municipal bond insurance industry, and this cannot but be detrimental to consumers and taxpayers. Even prior to the present crisis, competition was somewhat constrained with only a small number of insurers, especially those with higher credit ratings. Yields between top-rated and lower-rated debt have widened, making it more expensive for issuers to access the insurance they need to sell their bonds. The flight to quality that has ensued from the general economic decline has exacerbated this, making it either impossible or prohibitively expensive for small issuers with lower ratings to access capital markets.

Returning to Dexia, one must wonder whether they should have been in the insurance business in the first place, given their core business as a lender to local governments. To a large degree, this represents at least a potential conflict of interest. The scope and swiftness of the bailout itself and its cross-border nature illustrates the importance of Dexia to local governments. Perhaps Dexia was too big to fail, as the world's largest provider of public financing, and that is not confined solely to the European region. Dexia, though, did provide financing to over half of France's local governments, and there is no way to tell what the devastation might have been like if these agencies were subsequently forced into failure.

While it may not have been in the business of underwriting municipal bonds, a role most often played by investment banks, there was still a significant 'spillover' in the core businesses of Dexia and FSA such that exposure by one may have played a large role in the crippling of the other. Like its rivals, FSA insured riskier debt issues and suffered at the hands of the rising pace of defaults that swept the US. Dexia's bailout of FSA caused it to incur additional losses and to extend millions in credit in order to keep its subsidiary afloat, and it was revealed that FSA had itself invested heavily in subprime assets in its own portfolio. Taxpayers and shareholders would ultimately bear the burden of these heavy losses.

> *"The worse a situation becomes the less it takes to turn it around, the bigger the upside".*
>
> **George Soros**

Conclusion

The bailout of Dexia presents an interesting case, not because of size but because of complexity. As this chapter has shown, Dexia was neither the first nor the biggest Belgian bank to come under pressure as a result of the mounting credit crisis. Dexia, however, succumbed to the panic that gripped global markets in the wake of the collapse and bankruptcy of Lehman Brothers as well as the failure of US lawmakers to swiftly deal with the crisis and secure a bailout package to stop the bleeding. The 'Bear Flu' that brought down Lehman and on the same weekend led to the emergency acquisition of Merrill Lynch by Bank of America quickly spread across the Atlantic to Europe; as Dexia shows, we have yet to adequately right the ship.

Dexia's bailout was significant because of the amount of cross-border and multi-party cooperation that it necessitated. Dexia's ownership structure was unique, given its position as one of the first multinational mergers in the banking sector in Europe. It is noteworthy that all of the shareholders and national governments could agree so quickly and comprehensively, and the fact that they did so is evident of the 'too big to fail' moniker that has been applied to Dexia.

However, what the Dexia bailout also illustrates is the relative absence of the ECB, in comparison to the Federal Reserve in the US, or the

Bank of England in the UK. The ECB does not possess '*lender of last resort*' facilities, and up to this point its mandate has been limited to fighting inflation. It has played a significant role in ensuring that liquidity—perhaps more than any other, the one factor that can calm a bank panic—has been present and available. The statutory limitations in this respect have also meant a corresponding inability—or at least reluctance—to take on the critical task of cleansing bank balance sheets.

As the advancing pace of European integration reveals, it is perhaps time that monetary union takes this further step. The ECB is presently not capitalised in the same sense as the Fed or the Bank of England, and without revisions to the statutes governing European Union more generally, there is as yet no way that the ECB could itself be recapitalised. In the US and the UK, this is not the case. This though, also reveals the limits on central bank action and the differences that presently exist between the US and much of Europe.

Some of those differences, of course, reflect the different '*targets*' of these central banks. Even though the Fed and the ECB, for example, both have the primary role of fighting inflation, they have divergent views over what that means. They should recall the words of Martin Feldstein: *"Domestic inflation reflects domestic monetary policy."*

Whereas the US was quick to cut lending rates in order to aid the economy, the ECB was often criticised for not acting quickly enough. Without policy convergence in this critical area, it is doubtful that a truly coordinated effort can emerge. As the ECB president has noted, however, some of the facilities available to the Fed are simply not an option in Europe, given the differing capital structures and funding sources that prevail on each side of the pond.

It seems, though, that the interconnected nature of our world economies and global markets now necessitates such a coordinated effort. We simply cannot afford to pursue divergent policies! In many respects this is not about which one is right, and certainly these disagreements will persist until a fundamentally new process for global financial regulation is undertaken.

Dexia's departure from the bond insurance business, through its subsidiary FSA, might have removed a potential conflict of interest, but it is impossible to say whether or to what extent this might have insulated the firm from further decline. What is clearly evident, however, is that the ***profit-chasing behaviour of the bond insurance industry negated the very insurance that they should have provided, and that their clients paid for!***

The economic value of bond insurance, important to issuers and investors alike, has since been diminished; without potential further public involvement, this lack of competition will likely continue to result in a higher cost of funds.

As we've seen, this has also resulted in significantly curtailed access to capital markets for many local governments, particularly the smaller ones that simply don't have the revenue base to command higher credit ratings of their own. The bond insurance industry allowed them to gain better access to capital at lower prices, but this has now come to an abrupt end, and it is not clear that a successor system is yet in the offering.

The important thing to consider, of course, is how this will affect the lives of taxpayers. As a result of Dexia's bailout, taxpayers in Belgium and France will have to shoulder the burden of not just their own losses but also those that came as a result of failures across the Atlantic. Despite its much smaller size, this shows how size *doesn't* matter when it comes to systemic risk. Indeed, nobody could have foreseen the sweeping effects of the downgrading of creditworthiness of the bond insurers and how this quickly leapt across to the European banks. The bankruptcy of Lehman Brothers further threatened Dexia's financial security, and in turn, the loss of Dexia could have threatened the public financing system across the globe.

The effect on local taxpayers—the 'consumers' of local government debt—is nearly impossible to estimate as well. It is too soon to tell what the economic effects of this limited or curtailed access to capital markets might be. The effective 'loss' of the bond insurance market is surely not remedied by the lack of competition, given that FSA and Assured Guaranty have now been combined into a single firm. Competition is an essential characteristic of the modern economic system, and is necessary in order to ensure proper pricing. At present, the bond market itself shows that adequate pricing is absent, as the yield spreads between high-rated issuers and lower-rated entities has doubled from just a few years earlier. Even though these rates have come down significantly from just a few months earlier, they are still at persistently high rates, which can only have negative consequences for all.

Those negative consequences have already played themselves out in many localities, where bond issuers were effectively frozen out of capital markets. We saw these even earlier than Dexia's bailout, as auction-based bond markets used by many municipalities began to fail in the fall of 2007. Many issuers were dependent upon these long-term bonds to fund their daily operations, but because the interest rates that they paid were periodically set at auction, they could be treated as short-term securities by investors, and were usually used for cash management purposes. At the same time, investment banks began to face intensifying pressures of their own, as write-downs from mortgage-related losses began to threaten their own balance sheets. When credit markets began to seize and the investment banks were no longer willing—or able—to support the auctions by buying up excess supply, auctions began to fail in rapid succession.

When auctions of this type fail, rates must adjust upward. This penalised the issuers, who could not afford to pay exorbitant borrowing costs, and the fears of further failure became self-fulfilling. By the spring of 2008, the entire market had virtually ground to a halt; investors were unable to redeem their securities, as the entire market turned illiquid. Many issuers faced significant difficulty as a result of the new, higher borrowing costs—the New York Port Authority was forced to pay upwards of 20% until liquidity was restored. These problems stemmed from the perception that these 'cash-like' securities were no longer safe, and a virtual bank run ensued.

Even though these bonds were not the equivalent of money market funds, they enjoyed high credit ratings and were treated as such by investment banks and investors alike, and the failure of this market has put significant pressure on all parties as a result. The spillover from other areas of the market damaged the auction-rate securities market, which in turn made it more difficult for bond markets in general to function normally. Municipal bond markets in particular suffered, as they once enjoyed almost default-free status. This, however, was soon replaced with a new and crippling panic mindset that has threatened the very functioning of not just the municipal bond market itself but the survival of the issuers themselves. In this sense, what started as a brushfire has turned into a threat to the entire forest, and it has yet to be fully extinguished. The forced sale of Dexia's FSA unit will only make this downward spiral more difficult to escape from, as the virtual failure of bond insurance itself makes it harder and more costly for issuers to borrow funds.

Dexia shows how systemic risk can easily overwhelm even the best efforts of our regulators. In this sense, it is not size that matters but the complexity of the institution that should dictate the extent of the intervention by fiscal and monetary authorities. Dexia also shows what is missing in our present system, and this is perhaps the most critical point to consider in this discussion. Within the Eurozone, the ECB does not yet have the mandate to pursue many of the critical tasks that fall to the Fed in the US. Between the ECB and the Fed, there is a lack of communication, cooperation and policy convergence that has effectively curtailed a swift response to the global credit crisis. Unless and until these problems are solved, it is doubtful that the responses to the next crisis will unfold any differently. The ECB is in its infancy compared to the central banks that support it. It is time the lessons of history flowed upwards.

> *"There is no such thing as failure. There are only results".*
> **Tony Robbins**

In this chapter we have looked at the link between banks, insurance and ratings agencies. In **Chapter 19** we will look at the link between investment banks and corporate bonds. *Are corporate bonds the safe, high yielding haven we all presume them to be? Let's see.*

Chapter 19

October 2008—Rag & Bone Men:
Junking the Market!

"Where there's muck there's brass"

Anonymous

October 2008—On the 8th October 2008 Central Banks cut rates in a co-ordinated effort to aid world economy.

What are junk bonds? And what impact did they have on the Credit Crunch?

The Price of Rubbish: As a result of the global financial crisis which started in 2007 and may be petering out in 2010, the phrase "junk status" has regained currency. As a result of some highly questionable public accounting, Greece was allowed to join the group of nations using the single European currency, the Euro, a decade ago in 2000. As part of the convergence criteria for the Euro, Eurozone countries had to ensure that their national deficits did not exceed 3% of their gross domestic product (GDP) and their GDP to debt ratio could not exceed 60%. During the global financial crisis, it emerged that previous Greek governments had incorrectly reported the true state of Greece's finances. This caused the current Greek administration extreme embarrassment, to put it mildly. The fiscal deficit was determined to be at least 13.6% of GDP and the debt burden was in excess of 115% of GDP. Ultimately, the credit ratings agencies Moody's and Standard and Poor's downgraded the credit worthiness of Greek government bonds to "junk status" which meant that the Greek government had to offer substantially higher interest on its bonds to attract investors. In this chapter, we will investigate the rise of the junk bond market, some of the characters behind it and its part in the Credit Crunch.

The History of Junk Bonds

"My experience indicates that most people who've accumulated a great deal of wealth haven't had that as their goal at all. Wealth is only a by-product, not the original motivation."
Mike Milken

The term "junk bond" became popularised in the 1970s and 80s. It referred to the issuance of a bond that was not deemed to be of "investment grade"; a bond is simply a promise to pay back an investment at a stated date with agreed interest payments being made over the lifetime of the bond. In the main, government bonds are regarded as very secure investment vehicles which have a negligible risk of being defaulted on. Governments use bonds to finance public borrowing and because, with some notable exceptions, the perceived risk of a default is low, the yields associated with these vehicles are usually modest, but higher than the interest payable on a deposit account with similar drawing conditions.

In the case of a junk bond, the issuer of the bond is perceived to be at a higher risk of defaulting than would be the case for an investment grade bond. As a consequence of this higher risk, the yields associated with junk bonds are substantially higher than for investment grade bonds. Of course, there is a risk associated with any bond and some companies have defaulted on their bonds, despite the fact that they were of investment grade because the financial situation of the corporation has deteriorated in the meantime. On the other hand, most junk bonds reach maturity and pay back their investors fully. It is important not to confuse the concept of risk with a guarantee of failure: if a junk bond was certain to fail, nobody would invest in it.

It is probably less pejorative to refer to a junk bond as a "high yield" bond and to characterise them as being of a "speculative" or "below-investment-grade" issue. As such, junk bonds have been around for a very long time indeed.

The Development of Modern Junk Bonds

"Junk bonds are the Holy Grail for hostile takeovers."
Roger Miller

The 1980s saw one of the world's greatest bull runs, but it was built upon some radical changes that took place in the 1970s in the aftermath of the collapse of the Bretton Woods agreement. As we have seen earlier, the Bretton Woods agreement was designed to regulate international trade in the aftermath of the Second World War and at its heart, had established the dollar as a *de facto* world currency which could, in principal at least, be converted into gold. The demise of the Bretton Woods agreement inevitably led to increasing inflationary pressure and much higher interest rates than markets had become accustomed to.

In the thirty years since the end of the Second World War, interest rates had been stable and, consequently, predictable. By the middle of the 1970s, after the Bretton Woods collapse, interest rates had *doubled for short-term borrowing within just a couple of years*.

The 1970s also saw two major price hikes in the price of crude oil as Middle Eastern producers first flexed their muscles for political and economic reasons. The first of these oil price shocks triggered a recession which saw more than 40% wiped off the value of US companies traded on the stock market. In a response to the crisis, banks restricted their lending to all but their creditworthy customers, to minimise their exposure to companies that might be forced into bankruptcy. The interest rates that the banks could offer had been capped since 1966 under regulation Q which was designed to help the Savings and Loan institutes (see Chapter 10). Since savers could get better returns from the financial markets from bonds, for instance, money flowed out of the banks and into the markets. This meant that financing for small to medium businesses became even harder to come by, particularly if they lacked an established, good credit history, and consequently, an opportunity was created.

In the 1970s, even the most dynamic and innovative of companies were finding it hard to obtain the capital to start-up, develop or expand because of the perceived risk of investing in them in uncertain times. At that time, less than 5% of US corporations qualified to have any bonds that they might issue to be considered as "investment-grade" vehicles. Issuing debt to finance expansion or other business ventures was just not a viable possibility for the vast majority of firms at the start of the decade. Additionally, higher inflation levels meant that investors were seeing their profits eaten into by the rising tide of inflation and consequently, many were looking for higher returns which would offset the losses due to inflation.

The solution to the problem was to make financing these companies more appealing by offering substantial returns on investment and so the junk bond was re-invented. A substantive difference between junk bonds and other financial vehicles which were then available was that the junk bonds could be readily traded. The typical junk bond had a life to maturity of between 10 and 15 years.

A Brief History of Drexel Burnham Lambert

"In financing growing companies, we always looked for human value that didn't appear on the balance sheet, the quality of management, especially its entrepreneurial drive."
Michael Milken

The name of Drexel is synonymous with Michael Milken. The junk bond boom of the 80s is seen as a recent phenomenon in the public imagination, but it has a much longer pedigree. The firm was founded in 1838 by Francis Drexel and initially was involved with activities stemming from the California Gold Rush. It was also involved in business activities with the Rothschild family and J. P. Morgan. At one stage, Drexel was part of the largest bank in the world; Drexel Morgan & Co.

Following changes in US Federal regulations in 1933, which separated commercial and investment banking, the company was broken up. The banking arm became subsumed into the Morgan bank and the investment arm, Drexel, concentrated on securities. However, the fortunes of this part of the company did not thrive after the enforced split.

To maintain an adequate capitalisation and an adequate business profile, Drexel engaged upon a series of mergers. They merged with Harriman Ripley in 1965 to become Drexel Firestone. A further merger with Burnham in 1973 was necessary to provide additional cash for Drexel Firestone and it provided Burnham, a successful investment bank in its own right, with the caché of the Drexel name, creating Drexel Burnham. The last merger took place in 1976 and involved one of Europe's oldest banking families, the Lamberts of Brussels, forming Drexel, Burnham Lambert which was the incarnation of the company eventually declared bankrupt in 1990; but that is getting ahead of the story.

Michael Milken

For many people, Michael Milken is credited as being the father of the modern Junk Bond; indeed, he is often referred to as The Junk Bond King, much to his evident annoyance. As Milken himself pointed out, he had not invented the high yield (higher risk) bond: the American government had been using them two centuries earlier. It was estimated that in the 1920s bull market, 15 to 20% of corporate bond issue was of "non-investment" grade. This figure didn't include the contribution from "fallen angels", the poetic term applied to investment grade bonds that had fallen on hard times when their corporate issuers got into financial problems. Reduced to junk status, the fallen angels were still appealing to investors since the bonds were selling for pennies on the dollar giving them a good yield despite their modest coupon values. The interest was payable against the original value of the bond, rather than the sum for which it was trading when purchased; so as long as the company didn't actually go bankrupt and default on the bond, there was always a market for these "fallen angels".

Milken was born in 1946 in Encino, California into a Jewish family as a second generation American. His paternal grandparents had immigrated to the USA from Poland. Milken was educated at Berkley, University of California where he took an undergraduate degree in business studies in 1968. He went on to obtain an MBA from Wharton, University of

Pennsylvania and it was during this period that he first became involved with Drexel, Harriman and Ripley, an investment bank and securities firm that he had first started to work for as a summer job whilst at Wharton.

During his MBA which involved the study of corporate structure, Milken had become interested in the work of W. Braddock Hickman, then President of the Federal Reserve Bank of Cleveland. Hickman had written about credit studies and had observed that non-investment grade bonds could offer greater returns than those accruing from an investment grade portfolio since they offered "risk-adjusted" i.e. high yield, returns. It was an old debate that had gone on since the beginning of the century. It had been re-launched during the 1920s Bull Run by Arthur Stone Dewing in 1926. Dewing argued that investors had irrationally eschewed lower-rated, i.e. non-investment grade, bonds which typically outperformed their investment grade cousins; allowing more level-headed individuals to profit from them.

Milken became interested in the capital structure of a company and convinced of the importance of research into the details of a company to understand its asset base more fully. He concluded that a company's capital structure could be calculated in a number of different ways and that there was no single right way to do so. He considered a company's cash flow to be more important than their reported earnings, presumably because it provided a tool to consider their economic activity more accurately, and also considered "human capital". He was convinced that by carefully assembling a portfolio of high yield bonds, i.e. junk, one could find a basket which posed only slightly greater risk than the "blue chips", but offered higher returns. Eventually, the idea would be to offer the basket to the market as an investment vehicle where risk was spread; in exactly the same way as mortgage debt is "securitised".

He was asked to join Drexel when he completed his MBA at the start of the seventies. At this stage, Drexel's strategy was to look after the smaller companies and those with less than stellar credit ratings which had been spurned by the major Wall Street investment houses. Milken took an interest in identifying investments that had "fallen on hard times", analogous to "fallen angels": convertible bonds; preferred stock and real estate investment trusts. Milken believed that these were hidden gems since the underlying assets that they related to remained unchanged, meaning that these vehicles had inherent worth. The philosophy meant that Drexel had to put effort into researching these companies which inevitably distracted from traditional sales, in the short term, generating some friction towards Milken at the time. However, the strategy paid off and he earned Drexel a fortune through these endeavours.

As we have noted above, the timing for an alternative to traditional finance was perfect. Following Drexel's merger with Burnham in 1973, Milken was made responsible for the non-investment grade bonds marketing and by 1976, he was reputed to be earning $5 million a year, such was the market for this type of product.

The initial customers for Milken's junk bonds, of which he was initially just a broker, were mutual funds and insurance companies and less well established firms which wanted to increase their returns. A number of these early clients were Wall Street outsiders, often excluded from the Street's syndicates of debt purchasers, making Drexel's products all the more appealing.

New money was looking for good returns with low perceived risk and Milken proved very adept at providing it. The next logical step was for Drexel to underwrite debt directly. The idea was not new; Lehman Brothers' Kuhn Loeb had been experimenting with mechanisms whereby "troubled" client companies could originate debt, that is borrow further money. Drexel was already trading in such debt, albeit largely in the form of "fallen angel" type vehicles after all.

The market was clearly there: corporations which were deemed to be non-investment grade companies, and hence were being shunned by larger investment houses, that wished to borrow money—potentially, a vast pool of new customers. Milken persuaded Drexel to undertake this new direction and they issued their first underwritten junk bond, to Texas International, in April 1977. This was the start of a financial revolution in that it opened the bond market to firms that would previously never have been given any consideration. It allowed these companies access to a vast network of funds both domestically and internationally that they had never had before and offered investors access to high yield returns that Milken insisted were only slightly riskier than traditional bonds.

As the first company to offer and then underwrite junk bonds, Drexel became the undisputed market leader in this area of finance. Milken was perceived by some as a genius and others as a man with the Midas touch. Drexel's star was in the ascendant.

Within ten years, Drexel and Milken issued over a thousand new junk bonds and continued to finance corporations that had fallen on hard times and could no longer attract funding elsewhere. At the height of the market for junk bonds in the 80s, Drexel's high yield investment department, under Milken's direction, was estimated to be responsible for the underwriting of half of the junk bond market. In 1983, junk bonds made up approximately one third of all bond issues in the USA. It was a colossal market. In 1979, the market was worth $10 billion; by 1989 it had exploded in value to $189 billion representing an annualized growth in the market of 34%.

Baring in mind what we said about the paucity of funding possibilities for entrepreneurs in the 1970s, it will come as no surprise that the provision of funding through the issuance of junk bonds did create many new start-ups, permit expansion of companies that had been stymied for lack of funding and create jobs. It has been suggested that this financial vehicle was responsible for creating millions of new jobs between the start of the seventies and the end of the eighties, simply through the funding of dynamic medium-sized companies and smaller companies that had been denied funding through traditional, conservative channels.

Between 1980 and '86, junk bonds provided much needed liquidity and this accounted for 82% of the job growth in small and medium publicly listed companies at that time. New start-ups funded with venture capital provided by junk bonds were able to recruit at six times the average rate typical for their industries.

As a consequence of the perception that junk bonds created growth and jobs, they enjoyed a window of popular approval between 1978 and 1985, being viewed in much the same light as venture capital. It wasn't to last.

Uses and Abuses of Junk Bonds

"The only time to buy these is on a day with no 'y' in it!
Warren Buffett (on junk Bonds)

Interestingly, the major investors in "junk" bonds were financial institutions; according to Drexel Burnham, these investors held between 80 and 90% of the total holdings of this class of investment. Savings and Loan institutes accounted for approximately 7% of junk bond holdings although they were forced to abandon this instrument by Federal law in 1989, under the legislation that brought in FIRREA; junk bonds amounted to less than 2% of industry wide investments of the thrifts industry. Other institutional holders of junk bonds included pension funds; insurance companies and commercial banks in addition to investment banks.

Whilst the returns on junk bonds were often very substantially higher than for investment grade bonds, the risks were also greater. In the period from 1974 to 1985, the average default rate for junk bonds was 1.5% per annum. This compares to a figure of 0.09% for traditional, investment-grade bonds. Whilst in real terms, a default rate of 1.5% is pretty low; it is nevertheless almost 17 times higher than for the traditional vehicle.

The junk bond was very much the child of its time. The '70s and '80s saw the rise of a predator called the corporate raider. The popular conception of corporate raiders is strongly negative, however, as with anything, there are always two sides. The raiders liked to portray themselves as champions of the stock holder, earning them extra value from revamping over-sized and moribund corporations that had often diversified into illogical, non-core, ventures and stripping them of ineffectual senior management. It was their mission to pick apart these behemoths and allow a "leaner and meaner" company to emerge.

Of course, they made themselves fabulously wealthy in the process! Their detractors, on the other hand, saw them as nothing short of smash and grab pirates who took control of a corporation that may have been decades in the making and broke it up for scrap, taking the money and running, leaving others to clean up the mess that they had made. As usual, there is a degree of truth in both versions and reality was often more complex in any event.

The chosen weapon of the corporate raider for their mergers and acquisition targets was often the junk bond. Certainly, this was the usage of the junk bond which caught the public imagination. Michael Milken is quick to point out on his website, however, that junk bonds financed only a small part of the frenetic mergers and acquisitions activities seen during this period, suggesting that it accounted for only 5% of the financing of such activities. According to Milken, the remaining 95% came from traditional financial sources.

Michael Milken and Drexel Burnham started to offer junk bonds to finance leveraged buy-outs in 1981. A "leveraged buy-out" is the term used to describe the acquisition of a company using borrowed money to obtain a majority position, thus a controlling interest, of its stock. The equity that needs to be put up to borrow the money for the leveraged buy-out is often only 10% of the loan. This means that a leveraged buy-out is a tool that can be used to make a large acquisition without the principals being required to invest a very large sum, relative to the total loan, of course. Most leveraged buy-outs were executed by senior management within the company itself, usually in concert with a pool of investors assembled by a financial institution. When a leveraged buy-out succeeds, the management team has a considerably larger personal stake in the fortunes of the company than previously and so has a greater incentive to see it succeed. A second consequence is that the company now has a substantially greater debt burden resulting from borrowing the money that was required to gain control of the stock.

Between 1983 and 1988, roughly a fifth of leveraged buy-outs were motivated by a desire to concentrate ownership of the company, by taking it private, in order to avoid the disadvantages of being a public company. The perceived disadvantages of being a publicly listed company are that a public corporation must meet Stock Exchange Commission rules on financial accounting; it is subject to potential stock holder pressures for short-term gain i.e. higher dividends, over longer-term growth and runs the risk of a hostile take-over. However, the majority of leveraged buy-outs during this period was altogether different and involved a much more radical restructuring of the target corporation: the hostile take-over by corporate raiders.

In 1983, Drexel was the first company to make the bold move to use junk bonds to finance a hostile take-over through leveraged buy-outs. In a hostile take-over, the sitting board of the target corporation opposes the acquisition or merger activity. Milken was well aware that funding corporate raiders would be likely to generate a lot of bad feeling within traditional Wall Street financial circles, with potential fallout on the junk bond market that he had done so much to create. His initial championing of the junk bond had been in order to champion the financing of mid-size companies and start-ups, but the genie had been let out of the bottle. Whatever his reservations, Milken quickly set about arranging "war chests" of funding which were made available to leading corporate raiders such as T. Boone Pickens, a Texas oil and gas magnate, and Carl Icahn, for their hostile takeovers, the first of which was completed in 1985.

The use of junk bonds to finance a hostile take-over was a complete innovation. Before 1985, a hostile take-over was relatively rare, since only large, well—established corporations could garner the support from large investment houses to mount the attack. All of this changed once Drexel had demonstrated that such a coup could be financed with junk. Drexel was charging a 4% commission for underwriting a junk bond issue, making a very healthy profit for the firm from the corporate raids they helped to finance.

Milken and Drexel would facilitate certain of these hostile take-over's to the extent that they provided the seed money for a corporate raider to provide an initial stake and then encourage the Drexel syndicate of buyers to commit themselves to buying the debt that Drexel was underwriting. This permitted Drexel to announce that it had the money to back the hostile take-over; despite the fact that no external factor had put up any money. The next stage was that Milken would issue an infamous "highly confident" letter in which he stated that he was highly confident that the money borrowed to buy the stock needed could be placed amongst buyers. In effect he was stating in advance that the junk bond that he was issuing would be successful. Such was Milken's reputation that these "highly confident" letters were all it took to attract the involvement of banks and other investors. According to an article in Time (26/02/90), Milken would charge up to $3.5 million for producing one of these letters. When Carl Icahn made his raid against Phillips Petroleum in 1985, Milken was able to raise the astounding sum of $1.5 billion within 48 hours; such was his clout at that time. In the end, Icahn was thwarted in his raid on Phillips: the board voted to buy stock in their own company at a premium to prevent his take-over. As a result of the stocks he held, Icahn walked away from the episode $50 million richer.

Phillips wasn't the only hostile take-over target that dug deep into its pockets to prevent a leveraged buy-out. One way of financing this was to obtain a junk bond to fight the raiders off with. Drexel and other companies that joined the junk bond market had no particular scruples about whom the bonds were sold to and so made money on both sides of the street. A serious criticism of the junk bond phenomenon was that it hugely increased indebtedness as corporations made themselves less attractive as take-over targets.

It has been estimated that the total value of hostile take-over transactions between 1985 and 1990 was approximately $140 billion. In 1987, it is believed that Milken made an income of $550 million for his expertise.

The End of Empire

> *"The foundation of empire is art and science. Remove them or degrade them, and the empire is no more. Empire follows art and not vice versa as Englishmen suppose."*
> **William Blake**

Michael Milken is a figure who seems to divide opinion, even today. It seems to be common ground that he was to be credited with the re-invention of high yield bonds and that this development did create very many jobs and create new wealth through providing cash for entrepreneurs and managers to develop their ideas. The extension of junk bonds to be used as a tool for leveraged buy-outs by management was also regarded as being a largely positive event. It meant that corporations could take themselves back into private ownership; provide funding for restructuring and give management and staff a greater feeling of involvement with their company.

The role of junk bonds as a mechanism to help mount a hostile take-over is a more controversial area. The tool allowed certain corporate raiders to make vast fortunes by breaking up large corporations and divesting them of assets that were not relevant to the core business. It was claimed that this unlocked value within these corporations and increased the value to shareholders. However, it also resulted in many redundancies and the saddling of the corporation with very substantial and new debts that had to be serviced. There is very little to suggest that corporate raiders ever acted altruistically; although in some cases, the outcome of the raid could be viewed as being beneficial.

Drexel and Milken were intimately involved with some of the leveraged buy-outs and inevitably this led to accusations of impropriety on their part. Whilst Milken's "highly confident" letters were never the subject of criminal scrutiny, the fact that they were apparently issued, in some cases, without any capital being raised nor firm promises of support being obtained, would be enough in certain jurisdictions to warrant an allegation of fraud. However, such was Milken's influence at the height of the junk bond market that he probably could have been "highly confident" of the success of a bond designed to underwrite the selling of snow to the Eskimos.

In the end, Milken and Drexel were subject to charges from both the SEC and the legal authorities. The thread began to unwind as early as 1986 when a Drexel banker, Dennis Levine, pleaded guilty to charges of insider trading. Insider trading is the term used when a broker learns of information which will drastically alter the value of a stock and uses that knowledge for their personal gain. Brokers are supposed to be above such abuses in order to preserve trust in the markets that they work in; consequently it is a criminal act.

Levine had set up an insider trader network before joining Drexel. The scam involved collecting information from a wide range of sources in law firms and brokerage houses, minimising, or so he thought, the risk that the SEC would find out. The network used a trading house in Geneva, originally, but the company became suspicious and asked Levine to close his account. The network then used an offshore branch of a Swiss bank in the Bahamas which was instructed not to contact Levine in writing or orally—the bank thought nothing of this which was probably a sad testimony to how commonplace insider trading was in the 1980s. The account was only identified by a number; a common practice with Swiss investment banks. Over the six years that the scam ran, Levine was believed to have made profits of at least $13.6 million based on inside knowledge. One of those involved in the network was Ivan Boesky.

Levine was eventually undone because an agent executing orders for the Bahamian bank noticed that the account successfully anticipated many mergers. That broker set up a mimic account so that he too could profit from these transactions and he mentioned his suspicions to a colleague (who also set up a mimic account!). Eventually they were denounced anonymously to the SEC who set up an investigation. The traders were fired but not charged with any criminality, presumably because they were not directly privy to inside information. What they did was not criminal, merely immoral. Levine was eventually charged with insider trading in 54 stocks and was sentenced to two years in jail after agreeing to name others involved in his network—including Boesky. He also had to repay $11.6 million in illegal profits from his trading activities. At the time of his disgrace, Levine was a managing director at Drexel.

Ivan Boesky was working as an arbitrage broker, somebody who works in arbitrage buys stocks and then sells them on immediately at a higher price taking advantage of price differences between different markets e.g. domestic and international markets. Boesky specialised in companies that were likely to be taken-over. Boesky invested money on behalf of his clients. This type of activity was perfectly legal, so long as the trading was based on information which was in the public domain—a detail overlooked by Boesky.

Boesky was a Drexel client and one of the leading arbitrage brokers when he pled guilty to charges of fraud in 1987. He actively assisted the Federal government enquiry into insider trading and in return got a lighter sentence. This assistance included Boesky's agreeing to wear a wire such that his conversations with other brokers and financiers could be taped. Boesky had some $2 billion worth of investments in his portfolio at the time and the SEC permitted him to unload $440 million worth of these holdings before news of his involvement was released. The justification given for this was that Boesky would have been forced to unload most of his positions once the news broke which would have caused worse downward pressure on the markets than was seen. As it was, the revelations were blamed for causing the fourth largest one-day drop ever seen on the Dow, at the time. It was alleged that Boesky agreed to allow Levine to share in the profits of his insider trading and a one-off payment of $2.4 million and that Levine wasn't Boesky's only source of insider tips. Boesky was jailed for three and a half years, banned from trading for life and ordered to pay fines of $100 million.

Based, at least in part, on allegations made by Ivan Boesky, the SEC brought charges against Drexel in September 1988, alleging insider trading, stock manipulations and assistance in tax avoidance. These were civil rather than criminal charges. In December, Drexel agreed to plead guilty to six criminal charges of mail and securities fraud. The settlement required the firm to pay $650 million in fines and to remove Michael Milken from his position. The charges were filed in January 1989 and eventually a settlement was formally reached between Drexel and the SEC in April 1989. The following month, Milken had challenged the aspects of Drexel's plea bargain which required him to forego his earnings for 1988 and his dismissal.

Milken was indicted by a Federal Grand Jury in March 1989 to answer charges of criminal racketeering and $1.8 billion were demanded in forfeits against Milken and other defendants. The charges were brought under legislation enacted in 1970 to tackle organised crime; the RICO (Racketeer Influenced and Corrupt Organizations) statute. In total, some 98 charges were put forward which could have carried a 28 year prison term had he been convicted on them. The prosecution was led by Rudolph Giuliani, who subsequently was elected to the office of Mayor of New York and ran unsuccessfully for the Republican Party Presidential Nomination in 2008. At first, Michael Milken strenuously declared himself to be innocent of any wrong-doing and planned a vigorous defence. Ultimately, Milken entered into a plea bargain whereby he admitted his guilt on six charges related to securities fraud and tax violations. He was sentenced to ten years imprisonment and ordered to pay a sum of $600 million, at that time, the heaviest fine ever levied against an individual.

Milken also agreed to a lifetime bar on his working in the securities industry and to pay $500 million to settle civil lawsuits against Drexel. At the time of Milken's trial, he would have become eligible for parole after serving a third of his sentence. The law changed subsequently and no longer permitted parole in such cases. However, the trial judge later reduced his sentence to two years on the grounds that he had helped federal prosecutors in other cases and had mentored other prisoners in the minimum security facility in California where he served his sentence.

Inevitably, supporters of Milken claimed that he had been made a scapegoat and was the victim of an over-zealous prosecutor with political aspirations. They argue that the six crimes that he pled guilty to were in fact "technical infractions" and that the use of the RICO statute was a tool to force him to accept a deal rather than risk a lengthier jail term and confiscation of a much larger proportion of his assets. Milken's own website points out that nobody had ever faced criminal charges over these infractions before or since his own trial. Of course, he pleaded guilty to them in order to avoid other charges and a lengthy trial—some argue that the Federal case was weak and would not have resulted in a conviction. Certainly Milken could have afforded the very best criminal defence in the land, but chose to take the deal and pay out over $1 billion.

By the late 1980s, the junk bond market was worth $200 billion. However, it suffered a downturn as the decade drew to a close. A number of factors conspired to take the gloss off the junk market, not least of which were the revelations at Drexel and the charges laid against Milken, including Federal legislation requiring the thrift industry to divest themselves of junk bonds; a rising default rate and a general slowing of the economy. These factors saw the trading values of some junk bonds fall by half since the autumn of 1989. The final demise for Drexel was largely caused by the collapse of its $1 billion junk bond portfolio in addition to the $650 million fine that it had had to pay to the Securities Exchange Commission. Drexel declared bankruptcy in February 1990. It was at the time the biggest ever failure of a Wall Street investment firm and cost 5,300 people their jobs. Drexel staff owned 54% of stock in the company.

Conclusion

> *"I am turned into a sort of machine for observing facts and grinding out conclusions."*
>
> **Charles Darwin**

On the surface junk bonds, Drexel Burnham and Mike Milken had little real influence on the 2007 Credit Crunch. The era of junk bond supremacy had passed, Drexel Burnham was just another ghostly name from the Wall Street graveyard and Mike Milken had been reinvented as one of Americas leading philanthropists and a financial icon.

The relationship between the two eras lies in the argument relating to securitisation. The argument put forward by supporters of junk bonds is that when you assemble a portfolio of these bonds then you obtain a higher return i.e. yield, than you would get on conventional low risk bonds. The risk of default is higher but this is offset by the fact you get a higher return. Indeed supporters of these bonds say that the risk can be further alleviated the greater the diversification of the portfolio. Their argument is not without merit. It comes down to the human element—picking the right bonds. As Mike Milken always correctly pointed out you should always undertake intensive research on the company *actually issuing the bond!*

Twenty years later the same argument resurfaced in respect of the securitisation of mortgage products. Wall Street bankers argued that by "dicing and slicing" mortgage debt and then placing them in bonds of variable quality and in tranches of various grades then the risk attached to holding lower quality mortgages i.e. sub-prime could be alleviated by the diversification of the mortgages within the bond. The theory looked at in isolation is correct.

Unfortunately the new generation forgot Mike Milken's cardinal rule—they did not do the research on the underlying mortgages contained within the bond. This is no different to researching a company issuing a junk bond. Nobody checked or could be bothered to investigate fully the underlying quality of the product or in layman's terms; *who was going to be paying the mortgage and did they have the ability to do so!*

The lessons of the 1980s were forgotten by the latest generation of Wall Street whiz kids!

> *"Memory is deceptive because it is colored by today's events."*
> **Albert Einstein**

In Chapter 20 we look at how the banking industry developed in Medieval Europe and how those early points of development influence our current structure some 500 year later; *let's look at the Medici's!*

Chapter 20

November 2008—Florence to Milan: The History of Art-Full Lending

"We need a renaissance of wonder. We need to renew, in our hearts and in our souls, the deathless dream, the eternal poetry, the perennial sense that life is miracle and magic."

E. Merrill Root

November 2008—Italy's top bank UniCredit and its nearest rival Intesa Sanpaolo both saw trading in their shares suspended on the Milan Stock Exchange.

The Renaissance;—*French for "rebirth"; Italian: Rinascimento, from re—"again" and nascere "be born"—was a cultural movement that spanned roughly the 14th to the 17th century, beginning in Florence in the Late Middle Ages and later spreading to the rest of Europe.*

Why is it when you are at the top there is only one way to go? Is history a record, a memory or a mirror?

History is not a savior just a teacher—**Italian Banking;** In the fall of 2008 shares of Italy's two top banks, UniCredit and Intesa Sanpaolo, were suspended from trading on the Milan Stock Exchange. The suspensions were due to excessive fluctuations during the morning trading session October 1, 2009, but possibly in part triggered by the recent narrowing of permitted fluctuation limits.

The Milan Stock Exchange, known as the Borsa Italiana S.p.A. is Italy's main stock exchange. It was privatised in 1997 and acquired by the London Stock exchange in 2007. Borsa Italiana S.p.A. is responsible for the organisation and management of the Italian stock exchange. Their primary objective is to ensure the development of the markets, maximising their liquidity, transparency and competitiveness while pursuing high levels of efficiency.

Trading halts on the Italian exchange are either discretionary or non discretionary. A discretionary halt is when the suspension is called by an exchange official under specific circumstances that are defined in the market rulebook. For example, if there are rumours regarding a security, an official may stop trading and simultaneously request the issuer of the security, to provide the market with complete information. A halt is non-discretionary when it is triggered by a specific event, regulated by a market rulebook provision. For example, the Exchange may halt or suspend the trading of a stock if the stock's price moves more than 10% from the previous close or more than 5% from the last price.

These two banks, UniCredit and Intesa Sanpaolo, are the two largest banks in Italy and rank among the world's largest banks. According to Forbes Global 200 in 2008, UniCredit ranked ninth in the world and Intesa Sanpaolo ranked thirty-first. UniCredit is a pan-European bank with over 40 million customers in 22 countries. They have 10,000 branches and employ somewhere in the region of 170,000 people. UniCredit is a major international financial institution and a leader in Central and Eastern Europe with a market share that is double that of its closest competitors. They pride themselves on having a strong European identity, extensive international presence and broad customer base.

Intesa Sanpaolo was created in January 2007 through the merger of two leading Italian banks, Banca Intesa and Sanpaolo IMI. It is considered to be the second largest bank in Italy. It has leadership in the Italian market and a strong international presence focused on Central-Eastern Europe and the Mediterranean basin.

Prior to the trading suspension, Thomson Financial News reported on September 29, 2008 that, *"Italy's central bank sought to calm market jitters on Monday by saying liquidity in the banking system was 'satisfactory and adequate' after shares in Italian lender UniCredit were briefly suspended for excessive losses."* UniCredit's shares were down 9.32% having hit a 10-year low before beginning to climb back up. At the time, UniCredit was the Italian bank most exposed to the global credit crunch. Half of UniCredit's revenue was coming from outside of Italy's conservative lending market. With fears in regards to liquidity, among other things, Italian banks had been making headlines around the world for quite some time.

> *"There will always be speculation of some kind. If you throw it out of an organised exchange, you throw it out into the street."*
>
> **H. C. Emery**

Specifically in regards to the trading suspension, UniCredit declared that it was being damaged by market speculation even though it was well capitalised. Due to recent stock declines, the regulators of the Italian stock exchange operator, Borsa Italiana, requested a statement from UniCredit, thus indicating that it was a discretionary halt. UniCredit stated that it would sell some property assets to raise its capital ratio. Specifically, UniCredit said it would spin off the real estate holdings to raise its capital ratio indicating financial strength. The shares of UniCredit were suspended because they had opened sharply lower on October 1. The shares had already fallen 22% that week.

Claiming that the suspension was a result of the stock exchange's recently implemented volatility rules, Marcello Berni, head of media relations for UniCredit vouched for the company's viability. Marcello Berni continued to defend stating that, *"Nobody knows why the price has fallen . . . There are no concrete elements for the recent stock price decline."* Berni attributed the slide to rumours. One other key point is that the top Italian financial market regulators said the *"fallout from the United States' financial crisis on Italian lenders and insurers was 'contained' and their liquidity levels were 'adequate'."* Brokers said that UniCredit had been a target of selling by US funds explaining some of the volatility. UniCredit in particular seemed to be more exposed to US investors than other firms. Brokers were mixed as to whether Intesa Sanpaolo would benefit from this or that the entire Italian banking system is at risk.

On October 1, 2009 a press release stated: *"Concerns over liquidity have already led to government bailouts of German, Icelandic, Benelux, Franco-Belgian and British banks in recent days—as concerns over the recent events in the US have left banks more reluctant to lend to each other."*

> **"You may be deceived if you trust too much, but you will live in torment if you don't trust enough."**
>
> **Frank Crane**

On Sunday October 5, 2008 UniCredit's board met to discuss the steps it would take to raise at least €5bn to bolster the bank's financial levels. The meeting was in response to UniCredit's largest shareholders agreeing to back extraordinary measures following a tumultuous week where UniCredit's stock plunged to a 10-year low amid liquidity concerns.

The trading suspensions caused quite a stir in the media—clearly not a blip in the normal, everyday frenzy in the financial world. Nor were the suspensions believed to be solely due to the new volatility restrictions enforced by the Italian exchange. The press release on October 6, 2008 stated: **"UniCredit shares were suspended after they slid 14% on Monday following the bank's abrupt U-turn to boost capital by 6.6 billion euro's amid what it called unprecedented market turmoil."**

The article went on to state that Alessandro Profumo, Chief Executive of UniCredit insisted that there were no surprises and that regardless of its exposure to international markets, UniCredit, was solid. The volatility was due to market deterioration rather than weakness in the bank. However, UniCredit was battered by investors to second place in Italy, by stock market value, below Intesa Sanpaolo. Furthermore, UniCredit derives over half of its revenue outside of Italy's ultra-conservative lending markets thus making it is the most exposed to the global financial crisis. This turmoil in the financial markets then prompted regulators to step in and ban short selling. Italy's Prime Minister Silvio Berlusconi, enraged with the situation, vowed he would not tolerate the speculative attacks on his country's banks.

By October 9, 2008 things seemed to have calmed down and Economy Minister Giulio Tremonti ruled out the possibility of any Italian bank failing. This followed Berlusconi's cabinet approving a decree offering the banks the option of a public cash injection in return for non-voting shares. Rome insisted on keeping its banks privately run even if the government takes a stake—a key word in the decree is *"option."* Economists in Italy noted that the details on the plan were thin and interpreted it to mean that if there is trouble, they will be ready for it *and that it's possible that there is no trouble as of yet!*

Tremonti further assured the public that Italian banks, in addition to conservative strategies, had sufficient levels of capitalisation to weather the storm. However, despite the uplifting press, Tremonti did remind parliament that while Italy's economy is far from the third largest in the world, the Italian public debt is. Overall, the calming actions were enough to restore some stability and shares of UniCredit and Intesa Sanpaolo moved up 3.58% and .45% respectively.

It is this point that we wish to highlight in this chapter: *more than anything else, the Italian banking system has exhibited strength and stability that belies much of its modern history*.

As Italy headed into European Union, it faced significant economic and political challenges in terms of the demands placed upon it to modernise. When we delve into its past, we see that its Italy's "pre-modern" history that sets it apart; in many respects, the notion of banking was conceived and perfected by Italy's famous merchant families. In the pages that follow, we will show how the concept of money itself was translated into this pre-modern system of banking. We will also demonstrate how the lessons of the past are still applicable today, and how Italy's influence in this regard is still being felt—*and will continue to be felt in the years to come, as the global economy emerges from crisis*.

A Brief History of Banking

"A bank is a place that will lend you money if you can prove you definitely don't need it!"

Bob Hope

Before we can look at the history of banking, we need to have a basic understanding on what money is. Over time, many different things have been used as money: amber, shells, drums, ivory, jade, leather, and vodka just to name a few. The function of money, by simple definition, is to provide a concrete medium of exchange. In his book *A History of Money*, Glyn Davies concludes that, *"Money is anything that is widely used for making payments and accounting for debts and credits."*

Interestingly, the invention of banking preceded that of actual coinage. The first banks were religious temples. Well-built and constantly attended, temples were seen as the safest refuge for storage. Furthermore, as sacred places, temples would have likely deterred thieves. Before the deposits of precious metals, deposits consisted of cattle, grain and other crops. In Egypt and Ancient Mesopotamia, gold was deposited in temples for safekeeping. In the 18th century BC in Babylon, a city-state of ancient Mesopotamia, modern day Iraq, at the time of Hammurabi, the sixth king of Babylon, there are records of loans made by the priests of the temple.

Around five thousand years ago in ancient Mesopotamia, clay tablets were used to record transactions involving agricultural goods such as barley or wool. A great many of the clay tablets survived. This tells us that when human beings first started producing written records, it was not to write history, poetry or philosophy. *Human beings began writing to do business.*

One of the tablets that was especially well preserved came from the town of Sippar that is modern day Tell Abu Habbah in Iraq. This tablet dates back to the reign of King Ammi-ditana, which was 1683-1647 BC. It states that, *"its bearer should receive a specific amount of barley at harvest time"*. The relationship between borrower and lender is recorded and the concept of banking has arrived.

The concept of interest also became apparent during this period. Rates were often as high as twenty percent and mathematical exercises from the reign of Hammurabi (1792-1750 BC) suggest something similar to compound interest being charged on long-term loans. The foundation for interest hinges on the credibility of the borrower's promise to repay. Despite the Laws of Hammurabi stating that debt would be forgiven every three years, public and private lending expanded; thus indicating that the creditors generally collected their debts. This however, was not the beginning of credit as these loans were simple advances. Nevertheless, the foundation of lending and borrowing and the relationships between creditors and debtors were important developments.

Jumping forward to the 4th century BC, we note that the early banking activities of Greek financiers were more varied and sophisticated than in any previous society. Private entrepreneurs, temples and public bodies were all involved in the financial system, actively partaking in deposits, loans, currency conversion and validation of coinage, being the testing of coins for weight and purity. This early system even included book transactions where moneylenders would accept payment in one Greek city and arrange for credit in another, eliminating the need to transport large sums of coins.

By the 2nd century AD, the Romans had adopted and regularised the banking practices of the Greeks, nearly perfecting all recognised administrative aspects. Charging interest on loans and paying interest on deposits became more developed and public notaries were appointed to register debt repayment transactions. After the fall of the Roman Empire and the subsequent collapse of trade, the need for bankers was greatly diminished. The demise of the bankers was hastened by the ascent of Christianity and the belief that charging interest was immoral. This, the concept of usury, is discussed further below. Banking was, for the most part abandoned in Western Europe and did not reemerge until the 12th century AD.

> *"Then I consulted with myself, and I rebuked the nobles, and the rulers, and said unto them, Ye exact usury, every one of his brother. And I set a great assembly against them."*
> **The Bible**

The original meaning of usury was the charging of interest, or at least excessive interest, on loans. After many countries fixed a set limit on the interest rate, usury became known as an interest rate greater than the legal limit. In today's terms, usury is considered to mean the charging of an unreasonable interest rate. The concept of interest may initially have been derived from the natural increase of a herd of livestock. Ancient societies in the Middle East appreciated the reproductive capabilities of plants, animals and people. Hence, if you lent food as money or monetary tokens of any kind, it was legitimate to charge interest.

In ancient times, usury was associated with lending and could be applied not only to money, but also to anything that could be counted, measured or weighted. The interpretation of usury from biblical texts from both the Old Testament and the New Testament tended to be an unresolved issue. One thing that concerned Christians was that in biblical text, the usurer was interpreted to expect to receive back more than was given which underlies the sinful intention of the usurer.

Theological historian John Noonan argues that, *"the doctrine [of usury] was enunciated by popes, expressed by three ecumenical councils, proclaimed by bishops, and taught unanimously by theologians"*. Over time, various councils and religious figures decreed, forbade and condemned usury citing biblical text. Specifically, in March of 1179 the Third Lateran Council excommunicated usurers and in 1311 the Council of Vienna determined, arguing that usury was not a sin, that it was heresy. Christians engaging in usury activities had to make restitution to the Church before they could be buried on hallow ground. Suffice it to say that charging interest based on the social undertones, that it was unjust and discriminatory, was not encouraged by those of the Christian faith. The taboo of usury was deeply entrenched, as witnessed in the fresco by Domenico di Michelino in Florence's Duomo where there is a special part in the seventh circle of Hell reserved for usurers.

In the early 1200s, Northern Italy was subdivided into multiple feuding states. The region was plagued with remnants of the defunct Roman Empire, including a numerical system not suited to complex mathematical calculations let alone capable of supporting the growing need of commerce. At the time, merchants in Pisa were trying to deal with multiple forms of coinage in circulation. By comparison, economic life in the Eastern world had been more advanced since the time of Charlemagne.

The contribution to the development of banking made by Leonardo of Pisa, or Fibonacci (1170-1250), was significant. Fibonacci is credited with importing the ideas of modern finance from the east. Perhaps most important of Fibonacci's introductions was that of Hindu-Arabic numerals giving Europe the decimal system. He also demonstrated concepts of commercial bookkeeping, currency conversion and the calculation of interest. Pisa and nearby Florence became a place where finance flourished. However, above all, it was Venice, more exposed to Oriental influences, which became the center of finance in Italy.

The Jewish presence in Venice dates to around 1509. In 1497 Jews forced to adopt Christianity sought refuge in the Ottoman Empire. Jews then established trading relationships with Venice from the ports in Constantinople and other Ottoman ports. The Jews who first arrived in Venice were seeking refuge from the War of the League of Cambria—a Holy War where Pope Julius II was intending to curb Venetian influence in Northern Italy. The Jews arriving from Mestre, a town in Northern Italy, were not welcomed with open arms. The Venetian government was reluctant to accept the refugees but then realised that it could be to their benefit. Not only could the government tax the Jews, they also saw the potential benefit of financial services.

As discussed above, the Christian faith prohibited usury. This provided an opportunity for bankers of another religion, specifically the Jewish faith. Although the Torah and later sections of the Hebrew Bible frowned upon interest taking, Biblical interpretations varied. One example in particular from the Old Testament book of Deuteronomy states, *"Unto a stranger thou mayest lend upon usury: but unto thy brother thou shalt not lend upon usury"*. This was interpreted to mean that Jews were forbidden to charge interest on loans made to other Jews, but were allowed to charge interest on transactions with non-Jews, specifically the Christians in Venice. However, the price of charging interest was social exclusion.

In 1516, Venetian authorities secluded the Jews to a specific area at the site of an old iron foundry, which came to be known as the *Ghetto Nuovo*. Throughout the 16th century, Jews in Venice encountered hardship and fought for basic rights and although they eventually were able to practice their religion freely, Jews were ostracised from most professions by the Church and not allowed to join guilds or to engage in trade. Thus, the Jews were forced into what were at the time socially inferior marginal occupations such as tax and rent collecting and money lending.

The Jewish money lenders did their business in the cramped ghetto, a distance from the city over simple tables while sitting on basic benches—a far cry from the lavishly decorated financial houses of today. With the provision of financial services becoming increasingly important, the Jews played an important role in the expansion of European trade and commerce and the business of money lending proved to be lucrative.

Interest

> *"I don't believe in principle, but I do in interest."*
> **James Russell Lowell**

There are interesting tales in literature that help us to understand the early beginnings of and concepts behind interest in a way that relate to today. Consider not just the economic and political aspects of money lending, but also the cultural aspects as well. As mentioned earlier, it was Venice, with its Oriental influence, which became Europe's great money lending Mecca. Shakespeare's play *The Merchant of Venice*, based on the 14th century book *Il Pecorone (The Dunce)*, tells us the way things were, in the same fashion that art history itself can be accurately reflective of various historical periods.

Il Pecorone is a collection of tales and anecdotes written in 1378 by Giovanni Fiorentino, but it was not published until 1565. Shakespeare drew his inspiration from the tale of a wealthy woman who married a young upstanding gentleman. Her husband, Bassanio, was in need of money and his erstwhile and eager friend Antonio goes to a moneylender to borrow money on his behalf. The moneylender, known as Shylock the Jew in Shakespeare's retelling, agreed to lend the money to Bassanio on the strength of Antonio's reputation as a *"good"* man and respected merchant. In Shylock's view, a good man is not that Antonio is virtuous or possessing of good character; *being a good man is a reference that Antonio actually has sufficient credit.*

Regardless of this, however, Shylock demands a pound of flesh as security or payment if the money is not paid back. The pound of flesh would, of course, mean Antonio's life. The reason for Shylock's term is because lending money to merchants, or in this case to their friends, can be a risky venture. At this time, Antonio had many ships at sea and scattered across the world, which meant to Shylock that his wealth was tied up: ships were "mere boards" and sailors "just men." The possibility of damage or loss to Antonio's fleet, whether on land or at sea could destroy the backbone of his fortune.

This helps to demonstrate why anyone who lends money demands compensation for it. That compensation comes in the form of interest—an amount paid to the lender above and beyond the amount of the loan, which of course is known as principal. In Shakespeare's story, Shylock's demand for a pound of flesh if the debt is not paid seems exorbitant, but in this era, the reason behind it is that ethnic minorities were very vulnerable to hostile debtors from the majority population.

In this tale, Antonio becomes unable to pay his debt and the case goes to the courts. Our parallel today is that lending needs to be regulated and enforced by strong legalities. Even though the courts recognised the right for Shylock to insist on the repayment of his bond, the law also prohibited him from killing Antonio. Unfortunately for the lender, the law required that he lose his goods and indeed his life for plotting to kill a Christian. In the end, Shylock escapes by converting to Christianity.

While today, this is no longer seen to be a requirement, defaulting on credit certainly has its disadvantages; as we shall see, it is a two-way street, and can harm creditors just as much as lenders if adequate safeguards are not in place.

The Medici Banking Empire

"How beautiful is youth, that is always slipping away! Whoever wants to be happy, let him be so: of tomorrow there's no knowing."

Lorenzo De'Medici

In the 1400s, Florence was the center of the Renaissance and by no accident; it was also the center of banking. At the center of banking sat the all powerful Medici family. The Medici was the first princely dynasty to win their status not through warfare, marriage or inheritance. *They earned their status through commerce.*

They were a political dynasty, banking family and later a ducal house, though officially, they remained simply citizens rather than monarchs.

The Medici came to Florence in the 12th century from the nearby countryside of Mugello in the region of Tuscany. Over the next two centuries, the family amassed a fortune through banking and trade thus making them not only prominent in Florence's political life, but also politically powerful throughout Italy and later on in Europe. Their initial wealth came from land holdings in Mugello and later from the textile trade guided by the Arte Della Lana—the wool guild of Florence.

The Medici family may have made an imprint on the Italian Renaissance greater than any other family in that gilded age. With their great political clout in Florence, the Medici family were able to create an environment where art and humanism could flourish. Along with other families, the Medici inspired the period of great cultural change in Europe from roughly the 13th through to the 16th centuries. Furthermore, the Medici family produced two Popes of the Catholic Church, Leo X and Clement, two Queens of France, Catherine and Marie, and three became dukes of Florence, Nemours and Tuscany.

With the exception of a couple interruptions, the Medici basically ran Florence for almost 400 years. The power of the Medici family emanated from the family bank. The Medici Bank (1397-1494) was the most international, most prosperous and the most respected bank in Europe during the 15th century. The Medici family were not only bankers but also innovators in accounting, and managed most of the great fortunes in the world from merchants to royalty. One of the most notable contributions to the accounting profession by the Medici was the development of the double-entry booking system, discussed in greater detail below. They were so prevalent in Europe, that at one point, the Medici currency was the preferred currency throughout Europe. It was estimated that, for a period of time, the Medici family was the wealthiest family in Europe owning priceless art, land, gold and much more.

Of course the other side to all of this great achievement is the means by which the Medici did so: ***"Prior to the 1390s, it might be legitimately suggested, the Medici were more gangsters than bankers: a small time clan, notable more for low violence than for high finance. Between 1343 and 1360 no fewer than five Medici were sentenced to death for capital crimes."***

Although the Medici policy was always aimed at encouraging democratic aspirations, the basic intention of the family was to turn those aspirations to their own advantage and to exploit them in their own interest. The Medici family, sometimes referred to as the Godfathers of the Renaissance, were known to be ruthlessly ambitious: ***"They clawed their way to the top, sometimes through bribery, corruption and violence. Those who stood in their way could end up humiliated—or dead. And the Medici exploited a network of "friends of friends"—hangers on who would do anything to stay close to the family . . . The power of the Medici stretched all the way to Rome, where even the papacy was something to be bought and sold."***

There was a number of Medici whose contributions are of interest to us in regards to the Medici Banking Empire and the development of banking in general from the 14th through the 16th centuries. We begin with Giovanni di Bicci de' Medici—the founder of the Medici Bank and the man responsible for laying the foundation of the great Medici Empire.

Giovanni's Era: 1360-1400

Giovanni di Bicci de' Medici (1360-1429) was the first historically relevant member of the Medici family in regards to their banking empire. His aim was to make the Medici family legitimate. Through hard work, sober living and careful calculation, he was successful. Giovanni is credited with achieving the special status the Medici enjoyed and was the founder of the Medici Bank.

Giovanni was a skillful banker and an intelligent businessman. He was thoughtful, reserved and began with little money. Generally uninterested in politics unless it pertained to his bank, Giovanni preferred to pay a fine rather than participate in the Florentine government. The Medici bank was founded in 1397 when Giovanni separated his bank from his nephew's and moved his branch from Rome to Florence. The choice of moving his bank to Florence was prescient. At the time, other banks had recently failed, leaving a void and great opportunity for Giovanni.

Prior to moving to Florence, Giovanni built up his reputation as a currency trader in Rome. At the time, there were many different types of currency, multiple systems of coinage, gold, silver, base minerals, flowing in and out of the Vatican. This made the papacy the ideal client for Giovanni. Giovanni demanded loyalty and profits thus, characteristically, he took a gamble on an old friend, Baldassare Cossa, and supported Cossa's bid to become Pope. The risk paid off and in 1410 ex-pirate Cossa was elected Pope John XXIII. Loyal to Giovanni, Cossa handed over the entire Papal account to the Medici bank and Giovanni became "God's banker".

Having the Vatican as a client proved lucrative. It was a major, instrumental, tremendous development in the Medici Banking Empire. It is phenomenal when one stops to really consider the scope of that relationship. An interesting aspect to consider in the development of the Medici-Papal relationship is that at the time, the great Bardi and Peruzzi banking houses in 14th century Italy had more branches and probably more power than the Medici. It was the international scope of the Medici Bank and most importantly, the long term relationship between Giovanni and Cossa that landed the Vatican as a client for the Medici.

The immense power and wealth that ensued as a result of the Medici's relationship with the Vatican is unfathomable. One source of funding came from the Medici collecting 10% of everyone's earnings for the Church with the penalty for not paying being excommunication. This, along with the following example, showed the Medici's power resulting from their papal relationship. The nomination of a new bishop was delayed until his father, a Cardinal, repaid his debts to the Medici. In contrast to the overindulgent presumptuous display of wealth we see at today's financial services firms, the Medici's Rome "branch", earning half the bank's revenue in 1434, was little more that a mobile outfit following the Pope around the world.

As a shrewd trader, Giovanni used the bills of exchange developed in the Middle Age to make profits. Essentially acting as a broker, Giovanni would profit on merchant to merchant transactions by offering a discounted amount of cash upon completion of a transaction. For example, if Bob owed John 100 coins but Bob wouldn't have the money until sometime in the future, John would go to the bank and draw a bill on Bob. John, the creditor could either use the bill as payment or take a discounted rate of cash from the bank.

Yet another way Giovanni made profits, still avoiding the condemned sin of usury, was by offering depositors *discrezione*—a portion of the firm's annual profits. Giovanni also established an early multinational company with banking branches in Rome, Florence, Venice, Geneva, Pisa, London and Avignon as well as two wool factories in Florence. It was diversification and decentralisation—and not size—that proved to be the strong foundation for the Medici Bank. Other banks were monolithic structures that were easily brought down by one defaulting debtor. As a smart businessman, Giovanni also protected the bank's wealth by banning loans to princes and kings who were notoriously risky investments.

Giovanni also diversified the family business by expanding the two wool factories in Florence into a profitable division. The Medici then got into silk and later secured a near-monopoly on trading in supplies vital to the textile industry. Giovanni set his family on the path to becoming one of the richest dynasties in Europe. In fact, when Giovanni died in 1429, not unlike the financial giants of today, he had amassed great person wealth as well. It has been said that Giovanni's fortune was around 180,000 gold florins. To understand how great that was, consider that in 1402 the Medici Bank had capital of 20,000 florins and on average; the bank profited 6,326 florins per year with a 32% rate of return on profits.

More significant then Giovanni's accumulated wealth upon his death is how the pope referred to him: ***"Political questions are settled at his house. The man he chooses holds office . . . He it is who decided peace and war and controls the laws . . . He is King in everything but name . . . Beneath a veil of apparent disinterest, he concealed a tenacious, intelligent will to accumulate wealth, so that his patrimony might become an instrument of political power in his hands and in those of his successors."***

Cosimo's Era: 1360-1400

With a demeanor like that of his father, simple, patient and modest, Cosimo also had the determination to become more than a rich banker with political influence. Cosimo had his sights set on political power. Within a few years of being in control, Cosimo absorbed the majority of the thirty-nine Florentine banks. He used his economic clout to support his political ambitions, which naturally enraged other merchant bankers, who immediately became Cosimo's enemies. These new enemies, the Strozzi, Pazzi, Acciailoli and above all the Albizzi, eventually had Cosimo exiled but he then returned a year later and governed for thirty years.

Truth in Art

Anyone who has visited Italy or studied art, even at an introductory level, likely owes the experience to the patronage of the Medici commercial empire. As the merchant class generated more wealth during the 15th century, and rather than spending their wealth on lavish lifestyles, many chose to contribute to the community by providing financial support to gifted artists. Cosimo, for example, effectively took control of the city in 1434 and thus began his legacy as a patron of the arts; he had an eye for talent and tactfully dealt with many great artists. Alberti, Brunelleschi, Luca Della Robbia, Fra Angelico and Filippo Lippi all flourished under his patronage. Some of the finest buildings in Florence are a testimony to Cosimo's tastes; Cosimo commissioned Brunelleschi to do an extensive renovation of the Church of San Lorenzo as well as the Nativity by Fra Angelico.

The contribution of the Medici family continued under Cosimo's grandson, Lorenzo. Under his rule from 1469 to 1492, Florence became the epicenter of the Renaissance. Such artists as Michelangelo, Botticelli and Ghirlandaio all benefited from further Medici patronage. His contributions made him known as the greatest and most generous patron of Florence, and his support and commitment to the backbone of the Renaissance earned him the name Lorenzo the Magnificent.

It is important to realise that this type of patronage is not as selfless as it sounds. In the case of the Medici, private patronage became increasingly effective in manifesting the family's affluence. Through their artistic self-promotion, the Medici also gained a political following in Florence. Government offices were filled with their supporters, which enabled the banking family to become *de facto* rulers of the city. As they did not abuse their power or privilege in relation to those they supported, their contributions greatly benefited the people and city of Florence. Perhaps we are seeing a similar pattern emerging today.

Conclusion

Perhaps more than any other, it was the Medici dynasty that laid the foundations for modern banking as we know it today. They were the first bankers to make the transition from heredity to profit as the primary determinant of financial success. The Medici showed us that it was not size that mattered so much as it was performance, and in doing so, they catapulted themselves not just to the front of the financial line, but also increased their political clout as well.

In finance, small is seldom beautiful. With the Medici, we've seen how their relative size at the outset was not a limiting factor. They were able to grow through performance, rather than simply politics, as had usually been the case in their day. The Medici commercial empire grew larger and gained prominence precisely because they understood that it was necessary to diversify where others did not; they spread their risk geographically and engaged in currency trading in order to reduce their vulnerability to lending default.

It was a prescient development, and indeed, has significant consequences for banking today. The Medici model became the dominant model for most of Europe in the process. Beyond this, the Medici also showed us what some of the necessary conditions for success should be; however, many of these conditions would prove to be insufficient on their own. The inherent weakness of the lender is its exposure to large-scale default by even a small minority of their clientele, and without sufficient controls on these operations, that risk can spread like wildfire.

It was also here that we first learned how credit was not simply the institution of mathematical models. The notion of moral hazard, in which individuals or institutions are said to take on additional risk because they have little incentive to share in the consequences of default, originated with this pre-modern banking system. The extension of credit originated "outside" the law, in as much as it was the domain of the "shylock." It is easy to see how the modern-day credit score evolved from this, and instilled in us the fear of harm should we "choose" the default route. Today, it is also a business model in itself, although in light of our recent experiences, we see that harm can indeed come to both parties.

In order to dilute these risks, banks are effectively obligated to increase their size. The Medici concept of diversification was therefore to limit their exposure to default by one large debtor. In the process, they amassed great personal wealth, although this was at the time an integral part of their banking and merchant activities. This showed us how the concept of reserve banking came to pass, but also shows how the fortunes of the creditor are inextricably bound to the fates of the

445

debtor—a notion that would be painfully demonstrated hundreds of years later and many times over.

In practical terms, the notion of interest charged by the creditor as compensation for the risk of default on the part of the debtor is highly evident. While this allowed them to accumulate great wealth, what we see today is how quickly that wealth can evaporate. The Medici enterprises were successful where others failed because they were able to ensure that it was not simply the charging of interest that was the sole determinant of their success.

Today, we see that much the same still applies. While certainly not immune from the devastation of the credit crisis, UniCredit has suffered the damage well, precisely because it has been imbued with the same notions of diversification and risk management. With nearly a third of its revenues derived from its consumer banking division, it has weathered the storm in much the same manner as France's stronger banks, and indeed, now stands in a position to extend its reach should it choose to do so. What's more, it has spread its risk geographically and into different business areas, such as commercial banking in Eastern Europe, which has thus far been less damaged by the present downturn. In a somewhat reversal of fortunes, it is Eastern Europe that may prove to be the savior for the core European countries, who have been harder hit as a result of the credit crisis.

Perhaps the most interesting outgrowth of Italy's experience of late has been the extent to which these same factors of success have been prevalent in the Italian state as well. As we've seen with the Medici, size matters, but not in the same way as most might think. To be sure, a country or a bank requires a critical mass in order to function, but what we've seen from the saga in the US and other countries was that size can also be a limitation, if it is not accompanied by adequate controls. Italy has previously lagged behind its European counterparts in terms of economic stability, with high rates of inflation and unemployment.

Today it is proving that size *doesn't* matter, and perhaps small *can* be beautiful. Italy is far from being the largest economy and has depended in large part upon its political power in the run-up to European Union, for example, but now the state seems to be in a better position by virtue of its relative strength and stability. Much like the Medici in the pre-modern day, Italy now stands in a better light than many of its larger neighbours, and may even be in the position to potentially influence the way this *"new world"* emerges from the present crisis.

Much of this, of course, has been because the Italian government took swift action and appropriate measures to calm the crisis before it spread. As we saw earlier, they were successful in stabilising the banking sector, even declaring that no Italian bank would fail, and that no Italian saver would be at risk. It seems they have thus far been proven correct, and as a consequence, the country may be in a stronger position to help rewrite the rules as we transition to a new global economic regime. Like his banking counterparts, Italian Prime Minister Berlusconi has been pushing the EU for a more coordinated response and to be more inclusive of emerging nations.

Whether this emboldened stance will have the same success as the Medici's did five centuries earlier remains to be seen, but it seems that the nation is on the right track.

Clearly, history is apt to repeat itself, although perhaps not exactly as laid out in Shakespeare's brilliant narratives. What many failed to realise with respect to credit is that lending poses a risk to both parties. *No longer is the credit score, the modern day equivalent of Shylock's pound of flesh, enough to ward off default on its own*.

The risk of default has proven to be extraordinarily far-reaching; in many ways, even the earning of interest in order to compensate the lender for risking their capital has not been enough, for as widespread as the credit crisis was; it has endangered not just profits but the very business of many lenders. Thus, much like in Shylock's story, this reversal of fortune threatens the welfare of both creditors and debtors. Today, it is tough to say who is extracting that pound of flesh from whom.

History also seems to be repeating itself in the virtuosity of Italy's bankers today. Whereas the recklessness and abuse that have characterised the behaviour of bankers the world over has without a doubt inflicted great damage upon the community, Italy's more responsible lending practices may just be its saving grace. Indeed, it seems as though Italy's bankers have not provoked the ire of the political class in the same manner as they have it the UK or the United States, where calls to limit executive compensation through punitive actions and legislation have become commonplace. Italian politicians have not had the same reticence in coming to the rescue of their bankers as has been the case elsewhere in the world. Realising that the relationship between bankers and clients is indeed a two way street, perhaps in the same sense, we are now seeing somewhat of a renaissance in banking today.

From the potential of a renaissance in banking led by Italy we turn in Chapter 21 to a more sinister aspect of the credit crisis. We turn to the phenomena of the fraudster and swindler: a feature that grows more prevalent during boom times and is often frighteningly exposed when markets turn downwards. We turn our attention to the maggots on the credit corpse: from pirates to Ponzis!

Chapter 21

December 2008—Pirates to Ponzis

"Rather fail with honor than succeed by fraud."

Sophocles

December 2008—FBI questions Victor Madoff regarding his US$65 billion fraud.

Fraud / frôd/ • n. wrongful or criminal deception intended to result in financial or personal gain: *he was convicted of fraud| prosecutions for social security frauds.* ■—person or thing intended to deceive others, typically by unjustifiably claiming or being credited with accomplishments or qualities: *mediums exposed as tricksters and frauds.*

Why are there more fraudsters in good times than bad? Why do such intelligent people take the wrong path? Is it nature or nurture?

Pirates and Ponzis; the stock markets have always been cyclical beasts. Anybody who watches the news or glimpses at the financial pages will have seen periods when the value of the stock markets only seem to be moving in one direction. In the halcyon days of the 1990s tech stocks bubble, all technology or internet shares seemed to be moving in just one direction; upwards. Of course, eventually the bubble burst. Currently, we are now entering the recovery phase after the worst global recession since the Wall Street Crash and the Great Depression of the 1930s. Between May 2007 and until the second quarter of 2009, stock market values seemed to be almost in freefall.

"Where there is a sea, there are pirates!"

Greek Proverb

In optimistic times, some people will always delude themselves into the belief that markets will continue to rise indefinitely and all that they need to do is select an appropriate basket of stocks, sit back and get rich. A rising market, where the general view of traders is positive, is known as a bull market and those taking an upbeat view of a particular sector or stock are said to be "bullish". There is a technical criterion used to define a bull market; it is when the market value has risen by 20% above a certain arbitrary timing reference point. The other side of the coin is when market prices start to tumble and confidence is at low ebb. Then a market is said to be a bear market, and, as you'd imagine, it is defined technically as the period when stock market prices have fallen by 20% below an arbitrary timing reference point. Traders who think that the market will stay flat or continue to decline are said to be "bearish" about it.

Whilst it is obvious that investors stand to make money in a bull market, it is entirely possible to make a fortune in a bear market also. The maxim "buy low, sell high" always applies, it is really a matter of knowledge, nerve and timing. However, in this chapter, we will explore how some famous and infamous investors have made fortunes during bull market runs—by fair means or foul!

Corporate Raiders

"None has more frequent conversations with a disagreeable self than the man of pleasure; his enthusiasms are but few and transient; his appetites, like angry creditors, are continually making fruitless demands for what he is unable to pay; and the greater his former pleasures, the more strong his regret, the more impatient his expectations. A life of pleasure is, therefore, the most unpleasing life."

Sir James Goldsmith

A *corporate raid* is a term used to describe the take-over of a company from the outside, rather than by management, through the purchase of a large amount of the company's stock. The result is that the "raider" gets decisive voting rights on the company's board of governors. Armed with control of the board, the corporate raider is then free to decide on which assets and employees can be disposed of with a view to increasing the company's share value and, with it, the value of their own investment. Obviously, the corporate raider is looking to find a business that is asset-rich and at the time of the take-over under-valued.

Although corporate raiding still goes on today, the heyday of the corporate raider was the 1970s and 1980s. Part of the reason for this is that during this time, the world's stock exchanges enjoyed one of the greatest bull runs in their history. Many businesses made huge profits during this period and had very substantial disposable cash reserves. In some cases, the profits were re-invested in diversification of the business base, rather than being returned to the shareholders as profits. In 1986 alone, there were more than 3000 corporate mergers and buyouts in the USA worth a staggering $130 billion dollars; *in those days, a billion dollars was actually worth a billion dollars!*

Whilst many of these diversification plans were logical and well thought-out, others were less so, with companies acquiring businesses that had little or nothing to do with their core activities and often paying a premium price. A consequence of this expansion was that some of these conglomerates were badly mismanaged and were hemorrhaging money from the parent business. These companies were ripe targets for the corporate raiders. In the next section, we will look at some of the stars of the golden days of corporate raiding.

James Goldsmith (1933-97)

"If you see a bandwagon, it's too late."
Sir James Goldsmith

James Goldsmith was born in Paris to a French mother and German father, but he grew up for many years in the United Kingdom. His father managed a luxury hotel chain based in France and was at one time a Conservative MP. They were related to the Goldschmidt banking dynasty and his family was prosperous, permitting the young Goldsmith to be educated at Eton.

Goldsmith's first business venture was to found a pharmaceutical manufacturing company, Laboratories Cassene, with his brother in 1955, but he was forced to sell it two years later because of over-ambitious expansion plans. He became a more conservative businessman on the back of this experience and continued in the same field with a company called Gustin-Milical, gradually diversifying into other businesses including the UK pharmaceutical industry and a chain of children's furniture stores, which eventually developed into the highly successful Mothercare chain in the early 1960s.

He founded Cavenham Foods in the UK in 1964 and began to acquire some of the best known UK food brands. In 1971, Goldsmith succeeded in a hostile takeover bid for a well established and respected British food company, Bovril. However, the battle generated a very substantial debt which Goldsmith repaid by restructuring the new acquisition and selling off its subsidiaries for a substantial profit. The move cemented James Goldsmith's reputation as an astute financier and marked the first episode of what became known as his "corporate raiding" activities.

A simplistic view of Goldsmith would focus on the fact that he acquired businesses for a relatively low price, dismembered them and sold off the rump business for substantially more than he had paid for them—a sort of latter day robber baron. This was not how Goldsmith saw himself and his view is backed up by the judgment of history.

James Goldsmith took over two US timber companies Diamond International Corporation in 1982, eventually disposing of it in 1987, and Crown Zellerbach in 1985, involving an investment of some $580million on the part of the financier. He had started to acquire Diamond International stock in 1978 which shows that Goldsmith was no mere "asset stripper"; a charge often laid against him in the media.

He attempted to gain control of a third timber and paper-making company, St Regis, but was thwarted as he could not obtain enough shares for a take-over. However, he sold out his stake for a very handsome profit. The appeal of these timber companies was that they had diversified away from their core business activities into non-related areas. Diamond International's traditional business was the manufacture of matches, but the demand for the product, once very substantial, was already diminishing by the 1960s. The company had indulged in a spree of acquisitions in the seventies, for instance acquiring a papier-mâché egg carton plant, Diamond Fiber, and a retail lumber chain. Whilst on the face of it, this might seem a logical extension of the core business; the trees that these businesses used were not compatible, so there were no synergisms to be gained. Diamond International's spending spree ran to $400million whilst the earnings of the company halved during the 1970s.

Goldsmith started to divest the company of these acquisitions shortly after he gained overall control of the company. This has been likened to carefully unpacking a case rather than bulldozer flattening a cherished landmark. The components of the conglomerate were sold off and flourished with their renewed independence, freed from the bureaucracy of Diamond International's heavy corporate oversight. For instance, Diamond Fiber was privatised following a leveraged buyout by its management, releasing it from three layers of bureaucracy. Decisions could be taken and acted upon at once in the new company in contrast to the months required before. The new owners had a direct stake in the company's profitability which provided excellent motivation. Although 25 of 300 jobs were lost, the company moved from being at the brink of closure to being a stable and profitable company following the restructuring of Diamond International.

Goldsmith also decided that he could not justify keeping the corporation's headquarters, or the managerial staff that went with it, so the restructuring process was certainly not without casualties. Amongst other assets, the acquisition of Diamond International gave Goldsmith rights to 96,000 acres of land in New York's Adirondack Park. He eventually sold this to a French utility and telecommunications company, CGE, when disposing of his interests in the company. CGE sold on the land to a company that had interests both in timber management and development. The sale angered the environmental movement who inevitably laid the blame at Goldsmith's door. It was suggested that the profit made from Diamond International by Cavenham was $500 million.

James Goldsmith was also famously involved in an "unsuccessful" corporate raid on Goodyear Tyres in 1987, but he still walked away from the venture $90 million richer. Although mainly recalled for his corporate raiding activities, Goldsmith built Grand Union up to be the third largest supermarket chain in the USA. He also saw the writing on the wall when the bull run of the 80s came to an end and liquidated his most vulnerable holdings. It was suggested that he made over a billion dollars just before the stock market crash of 1987. When he died in 1997, he was a multi-billionaire and one of the world's richest men.

Carl Icahn (1936-To Present)

"You learn in this business: It you want a friend, get a dog"
Carl Icahn

Carl Icahn is said by Forbes to be the 43rd richest man in the world with a net worth last year of $9 billion. Born in New York City in 1936, his mother was a teacher and his father a cantor. He was educated at Princeton University, where he read philosophy, and began his Wall Street career in 1961.

Much of Icahn's fortune came from corporate raiding activities in the 1980s, during the Bull Run. Like James Goldsmith, he was convinced that his actions were for the good of shareholders and he styles himself as a "shareholder activist", keeping the managers of major corporations accountable to those who own the company stock. That's not a view that his detractors would endorse.

In the '80s some of Icahn's fortune was created through "greenmail". Greenmail is the name given to the buyout of a hostile shareholder by the board of the corporation that they are targeting. The "greenmailer" gets a handsome dividend on their investment and then leaves the board in peace to go about their business. Obviously, the share volume that the greenmailer must have acquired has to be sufficiently large to give them a say on the board or a powerful voice at shareholder meetings, so they need to have invested a substantial sum in the first place. Icahn was credited with pioneering the tactic in 1984 for his raid on BF Goodrich, a conglomerate founded on rubber manufacture, which was probably undervalued at the time. He had acquired a 4.9% stake in the company, investing $30.8 million, and announced his intention to a company director to obtain 20 to 25% of the stock and a seat on the board in what clearly amounted to a take-over bid. Shares were then trading at about $28 and Icahn offered to walk away and agree not to make any further Goodrich stock purchases for five years if the company would pay him a 25% premium on his investment. Fearing that Icahn would engineer a hostile takeover of the company, the board agreed to his terms and paid him $41 million for his stock. Whilst he made a fortune from the abortive takeover, the ordinary shareholders did not make money from it; indeed, the funds to pay off Icahn ultimately came out of the dividends they would have earned.

Carl Icahn has honed the skill of spotting companies whose assets far outstrip their share value, the traditional target of the corporate raider; their market capitalisation. His preferred targets are companies with hard, tangible assets, such as timberland; real estate; oil reserves and so on; although he has developed expertise in prospecting for pharmaceutical companies with promising drugs in the pipeline but high costs.

During the 1980s, Icahn was involved in two other famous corporate raids; TWA and Texaco. In 1985, he started to acquire stock in TWA, amassing a 20% stake. Eventually, Icahn took over the control of TWA. He was responsible for taking the company into private ownership in a deal rumoured to have netted him $469 million and to have saddled TWA with $540 million worth of debt. In 1991, he sold off TWA's lucrative London routes to rival American Airlines in a deal worth a further $445 million. It was a killer blow. In 1992, the airline filed for bankruptcy protection, emerging in 1993 with its creditors owning 55% of the company—Icahn's own slice of this debt was worth a further $190 million. He eventually resigned as chairman of TWA in 1993 and came to a deal with the company in 1995 in respect of the debt owed him. He negotiated an arrangement for a period of 8 years whereby he could purchase any TWA fare that connected through St Louis for

55% of its face cost and sell them on at a discounted price over the full fare cost. Although the arrangement prevented Icahn from selling the fares through travel agents, it did not take into account sales over the internet, which was still in its commercial infancy then, so he set up a company Lowestfare.com to take advantage of the deal and in doing so, further crippled TWA. The company was taken over by American Airlines in 2001 and ceased trading in its own name in the aftermath of the 9/11 attacks.

Carl Icahn made an abortive attempt to takeover Texaco Oil Company in the late 1980s. He bought stock at an average of $38 a share, amassing a 17.3% stake in the company. The shares were sold off in 1989 at $49 each and he netted a $4 dividend on each share as well. His profit on the raid was estimated to have been $630 million.

Carl Icahn remains a very successful and active businessman today and his name can probably strike fear into the heart of any boardroom around the world!

*

Ron Perelman (1943-to Present)

To date, Ron Perelman has been involved in the acquisition of more than 50 businesses and his personal worth is said to be in excess of $11.5 billion. He too, came to prominence during the bull run of the 1980s and is probably best known for his takeover of the Revlon cosmetics company in 1988.

Ron Perelman was born and raised in Philadelphia. He studied at Wharton College, University of Pennsylvania and then started to work at his father's metals conglomerate. At the age of 35, he hungered for a change and using $2 million provided through his first wife, he bought a 40% controlling stake in a retail jewellery and distribution business, Cohen-Hatfield Industries. The business was mismanaged, in his view, but had substantial assets in the shape of the jewellery stock. Perelman sold its assets off, including the retail locations, a year later, in 1979, for a $15 million profit. He retained the profitable watch distribution business.

The break-up of Cohen-Hatfield was Perelman's first solo foray into raiding; a practice that he has mastered. The template of the acquisition and disposal was one which he followed with great success over the years. The strategy was simple; identify a suitable company that has over-reached itself by expanding into areas divorced from the core activity; sell off the superfluous divisions, reducing the debt burden and generating profits; refocus the business on its core activities and then dispose of it or retain the company for cash flow.

The next target for Perelman, in 1980, was a liquorice extract and chocolate business, MacAndrews and Forbes. He obtained a controlling interest for $50 million and then sold off the chocolate side of the company for $45 million which enabled him to repay his loan. MacAndrews and Forbes obtained their supplies of liquorice from Afghanistan and Iran. Perelman was able to source the commodity from more stable countries and added spices to the portfolio which could also be obtained from the new suppliers. In 1983 Perelman bought all the remaining stock in the company and ultimately, he used MacAndrews and Forbes as a holding company.

Also in 1983, Perelman got control of film company Technicolor and sold off five of its divisions for $68 million. Under his control, the remaining divisions were able to increase annual profitability from $3.4 million to $100 million within a five year period.

In 1985 Perelman took control of a Florida based company Pantry Pride which was interested in obtaining Revlon, whose fortunes had been failing. He sold Pantry Pride assets to buy up Revlon stock and in a deal worth $2.7 billion, managed to get control of Revlon. He then sold off the non-cosmetic side of the company for $1.5 billion recovering a substantial part of the funding that he had needed for the acquisition. He was able to restore Revlon to its position of power within the cosmetics marketplace in the space of five years. In doing so, he acquired Max Factor and the cosmetics and fragrance products of Yves St Laurent. This is another illustration of the fact that the best of the corporate raiders were not just asset strippers out to make a fast buck, but skilled and astute businessmen.

Ponzi's

"Dishonest man can always be trusted to be dishonest. Honestly it's the honest ones you ought to watch out for, because you never know when they are going to do something incredibly stupid!

Pirates of the Caribbean,
Curse of the Black Pearl

Whilst some people found the actions of the corporate raiders to be highly distasteful, *nothing that these men did was against the law; indeed they were well within the prevailing legal framework and showed they had a greater understanding of it than the companies they absorbed!* As we have shown, it can be argued that many of their actions were to the ultimate benefit of the shareholders in the companies that they took control of.

In the next section of this chapter, we will look at some famous individuals that crossed the line from legal to illegal activities to make or sustain their fortunes.

Carlo Ponzi (1882-1949)

"Behind every great fortune there is a crime."
Honoré de Balzac

The man who gave his name to what has become the best known fraudulent scheme of the twenty-first century was born in Italy. Carlo Ponzi was a crook from the very first. He immigrated to America when he was just 17 and spent several years in jails in Canada and the USA for crimes running from forgery to people smuggling, in his case illegal Italian immigrants into the USA.

In 1919, Ponzi set up a company called the Securities Exchange Company as a vehicle to defraud investors of their money. The mechanism was very simple. Ponzi offered his investors a fifty percent return on their money after 45 days if they left it on deposit with him, or they could double their money if they left it in his care for 90 days. The supposed investment commodity was international reply coupons (IRC) which could be purchased in one country and redeemed in the USA for their face value. The function of the IRC scheme was that a correspondent in country A could enclose an IRC with his letter to an individual in country B and that person could then use the IRC to reply to the original letter at no cost. Since the face value of an IRC was higher in the USA than in many European countries in the aftermath of the Great War, a profit could be turned—a perfectly legal process known as arbitrage.

If an investor asked for their money back after 45 or 90 days, Ponzi paid them with the money that other investors had put into the fraud. Seeing that their money grew so quickly, many investors left their money in the scheme and more and more people were attracted to it. Within a few months, he had made $30,000, a fortune in 1920s America. So great was the demand for this novel investment tool that he hired agents to help him rake in the cash.

By May 1920, Ponzi's returns were in excess of $420,000 and by the summer, they ran into millions. The influx of new money was more than enough to pay those investors that wanted to take their money out.

Inevitably, the house of cards had to fall. The first crack happened when a Boston based financial writer questioned how Ponzi could deliver such high returns in so short a time. Ponzi countered with a libel action and won $500,000, effectively silencing all criticism for a while, but raising doubts. The next blow was delivered by a furniture dealer who sued Ponzi for money owed to him, in the hope of cashing in on Ponzi's bonanza. Again, the action was unsuccessful, but it resulted in many questions being asked as to how Ponzi could get from being penniless to a millionaire in so short a time. The disquiet caused a run on the Securities Exchange Company with investors demanding their money back. Ponzi paid these investors in full and ended the run. At that time, it was estimated that Ponzi was receiving $250,000 per day in new investment.

Eventually, The Boston Post contacted a financial expert, Clarence Barron, to look into the scheme. He noted that it was strange that Ponzi himself was not an investor in the scheme and calculated that for the venture to work, some 160 million postal reply coupons needed to be in circulation whereas the actual number was only 27,000. The US postal service confirmed that these coupons were not being purchased in large numbers in the US or overseas. Whilst the theoretical gain from the arbitrage was indeed substantial, the overheads involved in redeeming the coupons were so high that the scheme would be bound to run at a loss. A second run on the Securities Exchange Company ensued, following publication of the story. Once more Ponzi calmed the investors by disbursing $2 million to his investors in just three days. By that stage the end had become inevitable. Ponzi had hired William McMasters, a publicity agent, to help him. However, McMasters discovered documents which revealed the nature of the scam and went to the Boston Post with the story for which he was paid $5,000.

An audit was commissioned by the US Attorney for the district of Massachusetts which revealed that Ponzi had debts of $7 million. The bank commissioner, Joseph Allen, then put a block on Ponzi's funds at the Hanover Trust bank and bankruptcy proceedings were started. On the 11th of August, the Post printed a story about Ponzi's criminal past and the following day he surrendered to federal authorities. He was charged with mail fraud since he had sent letters to his investors telling them that their investments had matured. He plead guilty to a count of mail fraud, he was charged with 86, and was sentenced to five years in jail. Upon his release, after three and a half years, he was re-arrested and charged with larceny by the State of Massachusetts and was eventually sentenced to an additional seven to nine years in jail.

The investors in the Ponzi fraud were the victims, of course. Many lost very substantially and were only able to recover 30 cents on the dollar of the monies that they had entrusted to him. In the aftermath of the scandal, five Boston banks failed in addition to Hanover Trust.

Ivar Kreuger (1880-1932)

*"The more gross the fraud the more glibly will it go down,
and the more greedily be swallowed, since folly will always
find faith where impostors will find imprudence."*

Charles Caleb Colton

Ivar Kreuger, a Swedish national was perhaps better known by the moniker "the Match King". Kreuger won control of match concessions in many countries by offering loans to their governments when funding was otherwise hard to come by. He came to greatest prominence during the roaring twenties when Europe was still recovering from the Great War. In his day, he was regarded as a financial superstar and was the guest and advisor of presidents, kings and prime ministers.

Kreuger was born in Kalmar, Sweden into a family that owned several match making concerns in the region. He graduated from the Royal Institute of Technology, Stockholm with a master's degree in both civil and mechanical engineering at the remarkably early age of 20.

In 1907, he returned to Sweden after seven years of foreign travel and working overseas armed with the rights to represent the Julius Kahn system for re-enforced steel construction in Germany and Sweden where the method was unknown. He established businesses in Sweden and Germany to exploit the new technology the following year, but it took a few years for the technology to become established before they flourished.

Kreuger became drawn into the family business a few years later in 1911. The business was in financial difficulty and Ivar was advised by his banker to generate capital from the stock by offering the business publicly. Using the family business as its foundation, Kreuger founded a Swedish corporation *AB Kalmar-Mönsterås Tändsticksfabrik* in 1912. Over the next few years, Kreuger oversaw the mergers of many small Swedish match making concerns with his corporation. He also took control of companies involved in the raw materials production. In 1917, Kreuger engineered a merger with the largest Swedish match company and had gained control of the largest producers in both Norway and Finland.

Kreuger is credited with pioneering the large international corporations that are the bedrock of modern global capitalism today. He championed new concepts such as large scale production and efficiency gains in distribution, sales organisation and administration. Thanks to his efforts, the Scandinavian match industry was able to compete with any other large scale producers worldwide. His efforts to secure government created monopolies made his company one of the largest match manufacturers in the world. Kreuger formed the International Match Corporation through an affiliate in the USA and the New York company; Lee, Higginson and Co. The International Match Corporation was eventually able to control 75% of the global match production. At the height of his success, his match business was selling an astonishing 20 billion boxes of matches a year.

In the aftermath of the Great War, much of Europe was in need of reconstruction. For Ivar Kreuger, this was a golden opportunity. Kreuger's businesses were able to make loans, which were secured by the granting of concessions for his match making business, to these governments. The concessions might encompass production, distribution and sales or a total monopoly within the territory in question. The USA was awash with cash at that time and it was principally to the US that Kreuger turned to raise the money for these loans. The cash came through a series of share and bond issues along with the issuance of debentures. The loans to the nation states he helped provided only modest returns, for example only 6% in the case of a loan to Germany, but to attract investors, the Swede offered returns as high as 25%. The difference in the rates was explained away as stemming from the additional income his corporation would garner from the match monopolies in the countries receiving the loans, but this was never the case and Kreuger had crossed the line from legitimate business man to crook of epic proportions. It has been estimated that over the five year period between 1925 and 1930, Kreuger lent $387 million to various governments around the world.

The Swede did not restrict his business empire to construction and match-making. He held a very diverse portfolio of companies including Ericson Telephones; mining concerns; cellulose; timber; banking; ball bearing manufacture and construction. His business empire expanded to include over 200 companies and this allowed the Match King to perform certain legerdemain with his accounting and cash-flow needs. It was a much simpler and less regulated age and, of course, all record keeping was done by hand. Ivar Kreuger demanded absolute obedience from his underlings and was famously quoted as saying that the secret of his success was *"silence, more silence, and even more silence."* In addition to all the sharp practices of the day, Kreuger utilised some unorthodox accounting tools such as creating "non-voting" shares; leaving liabilities off the balance sheet; reporting fictitious profits and attracting new investment by paying generous dividends or plundering the cash from existing ones. He also made extensive use of a network of holding companies and subsidiaries which made tracing funds almost impossible. At the time of the Wall Street crash, Kreuger stocks and bond were the most widely held securities in the USA and worldwide. It was estimated that at the height of his business empire, prior to the crash, Kreuger's personal wealth was the equivalent of $100 billion today.

Just a few days before the great bull run of the 1920s came to a spectacular end with the Wall Street crash of October 1929, Kreuger finalised a loan worth $125 million to Germany. In return, Germany would ban the import of Russian matches; as Kreuger's company already had 70% market share in Germany, this was the equivalent of granting him a monopoly. Despite not having the assurance of backing from his American counterparts, Kreuger went ahead with the arrangement. With the financial world in crisis, it was impossible for him to get funds from the usual sources and he was pushed into a corner from which he would never properly emerge. Kreuger miscalculated the extent of the Wall Street crash, believing that the downturn would be short-lived and over within a year. In order to drive up interest in his stocks, Kreuger continued to pay good dividends throughout the period following the crash and to acquire businesses, depleting his own cash reserves. In 1943, an investigation of Kreuger's holding company, Kreuger and

Toll AB revealed that almost four times more money was being paid out in dividends than was being generated in profits.

In early 1931, Kreuger scraped together the funding for a second phase of his German loan being $15 million. He made a further stock offering in Kreuger and Toll AB, but it was not well received in a very bearish market. Desperate for funds that he could not secure elsewhere after making the second tranche of the German loan, Kreuger personally oversaw the forgery of Italian government bonds with a face value of thirty million pounds sterling—they were not good fakes. He hand-signed the papers once they had been printed. It was evident that they would not stand even them most cursory scrutiny. His intention was to use them as collateral to obtain further financing; they were to play a role in his ultimate demise and subsequent disgrace.

By 1931, rumours were circulating that Kreuger's business empire was unstable. He had asked for a large loan from the Sveriges Riksbank which had required a probe into the financial health of his interests, since the total value of his loans was roughly half of the Swedish national reserve and it was beginning to affect the value of the Swedish kroner. The audit suggested that the finances of his group were far too weak to risk further capital on.

The event that ultimately led to the collapse of his financial empire involved a deal between his Ericsson Company and International Telephone and Telegraph Company (ITT). The deal involved an exchange of stock between the two and opened up Kreuger's corporation to the scrutiny of J. P. Morgan. Morgan engaged accountancy firm Price Waterhouse and Co to look at Ericsson's books early in 1932. Numerous discrepancies were uncovered which implied that Kreuger had seriously misreported Ericsson's financial position. The upshot was that the deal in which ITT provided Ericsson with an $11 million loan was rescinded and ITT wanted its money back.

Ivar Kreuger was found dead in his Paris apartment on 12 March 1932. The official version of his death was that he committed suicide by shooting himself in the chest. Inevitably, conspiracy theories abound that he was murdered, but suicide remains the official conclusion. The total debt of Kreuger's empire was believed to outstrip the Swedish national debt of 1.8bn Swedish Kroner.

Bernard Madoff (1938-to Present)

"Rather fail with honour than succeed by fraud."
Sophocles

It is not so often that the goings-on of a financier make headline news, but the Madoff story was one of the biggest news stories of 2008.

Bernard Madoff founded Bernard L. Madoff Investment Securities (BLMIS) on Wall Street in 1960 with $5,000 that he had managed to save. BLMIS started trading in over-the-counter penny shares. The firm was initially a market maker, quoting bid and asking prices and making a profit from the spread between the two prices. Madoff offered his customers, brokers, a perfectly legal commission when trading with him in an attempt to attract big trades to the firm; a practice known as payment for order flow.

When the laws changed in the seventies, Madoff was allowed to trade in blue chips and continued the practice of payment for order flow—whilst this was distasteful to the established stock broking businesses it was legal. Madoff started to get good trading volumes and was fast to adopt new technologies which also gave him an edge over more traditional brokerages. At one stage BLMIS was the largest market maker on the NASDAQ and the sixth largest on Wall Street. BLMIS expanded to offer investment management and advisory services and this was the vehicle Madoff used to perpetrate his fraud.

In the early seventies, Madoff started to court regulators in key positions which helped, ultimately, to expand his influence and acceptability within the financial community. His typical return for monies invested with him was in excess of ten percent; year in and year out. Bernard Madoff was elected for three one year terms to serve as chairman of the NASDAQ stock exchange, 1990-93, and also served as a board member of the National Association of Securities Dealers. He was also a leading light of the Jewish community and known ironically for his philanthropic activities. Some of the charities that he worked with trusted him with their funds and became victims in probably the biggest single fraud in history.

The fraud, for which he was jailed for 150 years in 2009, only began in the nineteen nineties and was worth approximately $65 billion when it was uncovered in December 2008. The story is that Bernard Madoff told his sons about the con he had been running for so many years and they reported the matter to the authorities. Madoff has always insisted that he acted alone. It is suggested that over the years that BLMIS was trading, $170 billion may have passed through the company's accounts. The fraud Madoff perpetrated was a classic Ponzi scheme, as discussed above in the section on Carl Ponzi; if needed, the money to pay investor A was taken out of the deposit made by investor B. Intriguingly, there seems nothing to suggest that Madoff acted fraudulently until the 1990s by which time he was a very wealthy individual in his own right.

Robert Maxwell (1923-1991)

> *"You are as safe with me as you would be in the Bank of England."*
>
> **Robert Maxwell**

This larger than life character better known to the world as Robert Maxwell, was born Ján Ludvík Hoch in Czechoslovakia in 1923. As Nazi Germany moved against his country, Maxwell fought in the resistance until the country was defeated whereupon he joined the French Foreign Legion. After the fall of France in 1940, he escaped to Britain and joined the British Army Pioneer Corps in 1941; adopting the name Ian Robert Maxwell; the War Office insisted that foreign nationals fighting for Britain assumed an alias to protect them in case of capture. Maxwell fought with bravery and was promoted from private to corporal. He participated in the D-Day landings and fought his way across Europe, winning the Military Cross and eventually earning promotion to the rank of captain.

It was in the aftermath of World War 11 that Maxwell embarked on the course that was to make his fortune and lead to his ultimate disgrace. He worked as a newspaper censor for the British army in Berlin. By 1946, he was involved in publishing ***Der Berliner***, and in the process learned about the publishing industry and international business. By 1947, he was selling scientific literature to the USA and the UK through a deal with German publisher, Springer. Two years later, Maxwell set up his own publisher, Pergamon, as a vehicle to publish scientific journals, textbooks and scientific papers, at the time, it was a niche market. He was very successful at getting scientific papers from the Soviet Union published.

Maxwell took Pergamon public in the 1950s and tried to sell the group to a US concern in 1969, but the deal unraveled amid accusations that Maxwell had inflated the profitability of a part of the group, an encyclopedia concern, over the preceding three years. This had been achieved by making transactions between Maxwell's private, family companies and Pergamon in order to inflate its share value. Maxwell was censured by the UK Department of Trade and Industry; the report concluding *"We regret having to conclude that, notwithstanding Mr. Maxwell's acknowledged abilities and energy, he is not in our opinion a person who can be relied on to exercise proper stewardship of a publicly quoted company."* At that time, the investigators lacked any authority to take any action against him.

Maxwell re-organised Pergamon in 1974 which by then was seriously in debt, taking a controlling interest again, through his holding company, the Maxwell Foundation.

In 1981, Maxwell purchased a controlling interest in the troubled British Printing Corporation, the largest printer in the UK at the time. Maxwell renamed the business as Maxwell Communications and managed to turn around the company's fortunes by rationalising the business through selling off assets that were superfluous. It was a corporate raiding strategy that Maxwell had mastered and frequently applied. One dubious mechanism that he used to generate income was to use shareholder's funds to speculate on international currency dealing and short-term investments in the stock markets.

Three years later, in 1984, he took over the newspaper concern, The Mirror Group and set about revolutionising the technical side of British Journalism which was painfully outdated at the time. His media empire extended to include interests in British cable TV; European MTV; Macmillan (publishers) and Official Airline Guides amongst others. He also extended his newspaper empire into Eastern Europe, buying the English edition of Moscow News in 1988 and two Hungarian newspapers, *Esti Hirlap* and *Magyar Hirlap* amongst other newspaper concerns around the world.

Maxwell had borrowed heavily to expand his empire, to the tune of $3 billion, particularly the acquisition of the Macmillan group in the USA. Much of this expenditure happened just as the bull run of the 1980s came to an end with the 1987 crash. Under pressure to raise cash, Maxwell floated the Mirror group on the stock market in 1991, knowing that its prospectus seriously overplayed the worth of the group. He also raided the Mirror group pension fund, defrauding it of £400 million, destroying the pension provision of 32,000 employees. The pension fund was under Maxwell's control and money was "lent" to Maxwell's other companies. Maxwell sought to inflate the share value by trading shares within his business empire to make it look as if the issue was in demand, thereby inflating its value. As the financial mess was unpicked, it emerged that Maxwell had borrowed money using the same collateral repeatedly in assembling his conglomerate.

At the height of his business empire, Maxwell's conglomerate consisted of 400 interconnected companies, but it all came crashing down in 1991 just weeks after Robert Maxwell fell overboard from his yacht and drowned as it became clear that the group's debts far outweighed its assets. There was much speculation that Robert Maxwell took his own life and there were the inevitably more fanciful explanations suggesting that he had been murdered. The official verdict into his death cited accidental drowning as the cause. The following year, Maxwell Communications filed for bankruptcy protection.

Conclusion

The top end of any bull markets always generates excesses and larger than life financiers. In some cases those individuals act for the benefit of society, in the case of corporate raiders who whilst legitimately lining their own pockets also released value to other shareholders. On the flip side others, such as Ponzi and Maxwell, use the complexities and euphoria of bull markets to deceive and rob others with less financial acumen.

The common factor, despite the polar opposites of the motivations involved, is the weight of money available in the market place during any bull run. To carry out corporate raiding or indeed fraud it requires the use of other people's money in large quantities. In downturns the instinct of most people is to save and only release the purse strings when prosperity appears to be beckoning to all. The later stages of any bull run tend to be the main feeding grounds of crooks and fraudsters. The general public having seen "easy pickings" being achieved in the early stages of burgeoning prosperity increasingly and somewhat greedily look for higher returns than can credibly be achieved. They are of course then susceptible to the conman who can offer them the world . . . . *in return for their hard earned cash!*

>*"There are sharks all over, up and down the whole entire Gulf Coast . . . How do you warn someone that there are sharks out there all the time anyway?"*
>
>**Bob Clark**

Excess liquidity in our financial system is like blood in the water . . . . it brings the sharks!

In Chapter 22 we turn back the clock and visit a venerable old world empire, the Austro-Hungarian and look at the founding of the Rothschild family banking dynasty . . . . *and how it changed the world of banking forever.*

Chapter 22

January 2009—Marchia Orientalis:
Last Man Standing

"A banker is a man who lends you an umbrella when the weather is fair, and takes it away from you when it rains."
Anonymous

January 2009—Austrian National Bank (OeNB) Governor Ewald Nowotny said today liquidity was the key to resolving the banking crisis.

Bank: a business that keeps and lends money and provides other financial services.

Who is the grandfather of modern banking? Why do some live in the world and others change it forever?

   Rothschild; the name of Rothschild has become a synonym for wealth and influence. The family fortune was derived from banking activities that had their origins in Frankfurt-am-Main, in what is now modern day Germany. What started in 1765 was to lay the foundations for the greatest banking dynasty the world has known.

"The Rothschilds can start or prevent wars. Their word could make or break empires!"
Chicago Evening American

The family business that was to become the Rothschild banking dynasty was established by Mayer Amschel Rothschild in the Jewish ghetto of Frankfurt-am-Main. His father had a money lending and counting house business. The family's original name was Bauer, but Mayer adopted the symbol of a Roman eagle on a red shield as a trademark placed over his businesses. The family's adoptive name is derived from the red shield (rot schild).

Mayer spent some years working for the Oppenheimer bank in Hannover rising to become a junior partner. During this time, he encountered General von Estorff who eventually became attached to the court of Prince Frederick of Hesse-Hannau. Through this association, Mayer became a court agent for the Prince in 1769. The prince was a very influential figure of the time. He was a grandson of King George II of England; cousin to George III; a nephew to the King of Denmark and brother-in-law to the King of Sweden. Upon his death in 1785, his son, Prince William IX, inherited one of the largest fortunes in Europe. Much of the fortune stemmed from the hiring-out of Hessian mercenaries to fight in foreign wars (for example for the British government was a valued customer, engaging 16,000 Hessian soldiers to fight in the American war of independence).

This period of history was a very turbulent time for Europe as Napoleon was engaged in his wars of empire. He made it known that he wished to see Prince William deposed causing William to exile himself to Denmark in 1806. In doing so William entrusted a substantial part of his wealth into the hands of Mayer, his father's advisor, who he made responsible for recovering taxes due to his estate and interest on any loans outstanding. This was to be a critical development in the creation of the Rothschild dynasty.

Formation of the Dynasty

"Give me control of a nation's money and I care not who makes the laws!"

Mayer Amschel Rothschild

Mayer married Gutele Schnapper in 1770 and the couple had five sons and five daughters together. The male children were the key to the formation of the Rothschild dynasty. The banking empire was very much a family business. It is often said that Mayer sent his sons off to exploit the rising tide of capitalism and international trade; Nathan was sent to Manchester in 1798 to exploit the textiles trade; James went to Paris in 1812; Saloman was sent to Vienna in 1820; Carl went to Naples and the eldest child, Amschel, remained in Germany. Since some of these events took place after Mayer's death in 1812, it is incorrect to say that this was done at his direct behest. However, there is evidence to suggest that the family worked closely together and obviously the original vision was Mayer's.

When Prince William entrusted his fortune to Mayer in 1806, Nathan was already established in England as a merchant of textiles and a money lender. Within two years of the Prince's assets passing to Mayer, Nathan had established a fully fledged financial services business in London which became his sole concern. In 1809, it moved to its new headquarters in New Court where it remains today.

Some accounts suggest that Mayer hid the Prince's assets from Napoleon's soldiers in wine barrels; others that he gave the whole sum to Nathan to invest, which is much more probable. The Napoleonic wars were certainly instrumental in establishing the Rothschild fortune. Nathan was responsible for providing funds for the allied armies and Wellington's army. According to the family website, the British Government asked him to raise the funds to defeat Napoleon. Other sources claim that the family couldn't lose since they were also funding Napoleon's army!

It seems likely that the company was engaged in smuggling gold coins across Europe at the time, taking advantage of differential exchange rates. Whilst technically illegal, it seems that this was sanctioned by the British government to a greater or lesser extent. In effect, Rothschild became the paymaster to the British forces and their allies and payment for these services certainly swelled the family coffers. This also marked the Rothschild's long involvement in gold bullion trading.

One thing that seems to be certain is that the family used whatever means was at their disposal to communicate with each other rapidly and that they gathered intelligence on unfolding events—all of this in an age before modern telecommunications and efficient transport. The family had a network of agents throughout the continent keeping them abreast of relevant news. They utilised fast boats, coded messages and carrier pigeons to get information before other players knew what was going on. The Rothschilds were amongst the first to realise that knowledge is power and offers an enormous commercial advantage.

The accounts as to how Nathan Rothschild pulled off his coup in the immediate aftermath of the Battle of Waterloo in 1814 differ. By some accounts he had advance news through his network of agents that the Duke of Wellington had won the day; others that it was a master stroke of bluffing, but what is sure is that he went to the stock market and sold a lot of stocks. Such was his reputation by then that many others followed suit on the assumption that the battle was lost, generating further selling and a freefall in the stock prices. Nathan then bought back into the market when the prices were low, before news of the Duke's victory reached London. It was suggested that his "confidence trick" netted the Rothschilds a 20 fold increase in their wealth.

Again, stories of the fate of Prince William's fortune vary. In some accounts, the Rothschilds simply steal the fortune and use it to establish their dynasty. In other versions, the "Jewish Rag-and-Bone" man hid it in wine barrels and returned it to his patron when the latter returned from exile. The semi-official Rothschild's website version is that Mayer was engaged as an "asset manager" for the Prince who was no doubt delighted that the investment of the £550,000 sum "proved extremely lucrative . . . and accrued considerable interest" by the time he returned from exile. The site credits Nathan with generating the profits from investment in British Government securities and gold bullion and concludes that "The Rothschild's reputation for trustworthiness and astute financial management was firmly established" through the episode. Given the connections and importance of William it is not conceivable that the Rothschild family would bilk him, nor is it likely that he would have stood still for such a fact. ***Indeed, part of the Rothschild philosophy***

has always been that it is better to take a small profit today to build a strong and rewarding partnership for tomorrow.

The Rothschilds were credited with becoming the prime money-lenders to many European nations; clearly a very profitable profession, something that required states to believe in their integrity. In 1818 Nathan Rothschild was responsible for organising a loan of £5 million to the government of Prussia. It was the first loan of a business that would last for more than a century; providing loans to sovereign governments.

The family have been credited with popularising, or possibly inventing, a tool that remains a mainstay of government finance to this day; the government bond. The idea of a bond is that it can be used to raise the capital that a government needs for a specific project or, these days, to fund its current borrowing. The bond guarantees that at its expiry, the investor will recoup their money in full and that during its lifetime it will bear regular fixed interest, commonly this is paid twice per annum. Since the bond is issued by a sovereign state, there is little danger on the issuer defaulting on the payments. As interest rates rise and fall, such bonds may rise or fall in value, but will always pay the face value upon maturity; furthermore, they could be redeemed by selling them on to a third party before maturity. The bonds proved very popular with governments and investors alike. On the back of UK bond issues, major projects such as the Suez Canal, railway expansion and the industrial revolution could be funded. Of course, the Rothschilds got a cut of everything and would almost certainly have had advanced knowledge of the major projects that the bonds were to fund. This would give them ample opportunity to assess the profitability of the venture and invest at the outset.

The Austrian Branch

> ***"Banking was conceived in iniquity and was born in sin. The bankers own the earth. Take it away from them, but leave them the power to create deposits, and with the flick of the pen they will create enough deposits to buy it back again. However, take it away from them, and all the great fortunes***

like mine will disappear and they ought to disappear, for this would be a happier and better world to live in. But, if you wish to remain the slaves of Bankers and pay the cost of your own slavery, let them continue to create deposits."

Sir Josiah Stamp

Salomon Rothschild was the second eldest of Mayer's sons. He was born in 1774 in Frankfurt-am-Main. When his brother James set up the French arm of the Rothschild's European banking dynasty in 1817, Salomon was made a major shareholder. Salomon had been trained in finance and was very experienced by that stage.

In 1820 he established the S.M. von Rothschild bank in Vienna, capital city of the Austro-Hungarian Empire, and remained its director until the revolution in 1848. The intention behind establishing the bank was to provide formalisation of existing Rothschild involvement in projects with the country. The bank played a leading role in raising funds for, and investing in, Austria's first railway network for the Austrian Emperor Kaiser Ferdinand in 1836. It was also responsible for financing other ventures needing a large amount of capital. The bank organised loans to Austria in 1823, 1829 and 1842. The brothers were ennobled by the Kaiser for services to the state with hereditary baronies in 1822.

Salomon's son, Anselem, was responsible for establishing the bank that eventually became to be known as Creditanstalt in 1855. This very successful bank established branches in many parts of the Austro-Hungarian Empire: Prague, Budapest, Brno, Trieste, Kronstadt and Lemberg.

With Creditanstalt's close ties to the Rothschild banking dynasty, it enjoyed more privileged conditions in the world's great financial centres than any other bank in central Europe or Germany. The bank became the first European bank to be listed on the New York Stock Exchange in 1927 and more than half of its stock was owned by foreign investors, including 130 of the most important foreign banks, mostly in America and the United Kingdom. The board of directors included several well known foreign bankers and businessmen. Creditanstalt had excellent standing in the eyes of the financial world. The bank had interests in eleven other banks and some forty industrial businesses drawn from the former Austro-Hungarian Empire. It was heavily involved in all the fields of industrial activity held to be of greatest importance to Austria at the time: mining and metallurgy; engineering and metal-working; textiles; timber; beer-brewing; construction; chemical industry, electrical industry, leather and shoe making and paper.

By the time of the Wall Street Crash in 1929, Creditanstalt had become the biggest bank in central Europe. When the bank failed in 1931, it triggered a crisis in European banking which was a major contributing factor to the duration of the Great Depression.

The failure of Creditanstalt was not an isolated event that just depended on the actions of the bank's directors, but was due to the inter-relationship between banks and the weaknesses in the gold standard system stemming from unresolved issues from the Great War, as we shall see. In order to understand what happened when Creditanstalt failed, it is important to understand the history of international trade to some extent.

The Gold Standard

"Accursed thirst for gold? What dost thou not compel mortals to do?"

Virgil

The power of gold and its link to the monetary system are covered in detail in Chapter 4 but we need to look at it again. If you take a look at a UK bank note, you will notice that it contains a promise on it, for example; "I promise to pay the bearer on demand the sum of twenty pounds" appears on the £20 note. The promise is made on behalf of the Bank of England. For this reason, paper money was known as "promissory notes" and could, in principle, but no longer in practice, be exchanged for the equivalent value in gold coins or specie.

We owe the existence of the "pound sterling" to the French who introduced a metallic currency to Britain, a year or so after the Norman Conquest in 1066 AD. The pound was originally a unit of weight of silver.

Gold has been given value since antiquity and artifacts made from the precious metal have been dated as far back in history as 4000 years BC. Artifacts made from gold were produced by a culture dating from this period in what is now known as Eastern Europe; the gold was probably mined in the Transylvanian Alps. Indeed, gold was the first *de facto* international currency since it held value in both the importing and exporting countries. Evidence for the international value for gold can be traced back to Nubia, in modern day Egypt, in the year 1500 BC. The Shekel was a coin made from an alloy of gold and silver which was used extensively for trade within the Middle East from this time. It incorporated approximately 11.3 grams of gold per coin.

Pure gold coins first began to circulate in Asia Minor in 560 BC, in the kingdom of Lydia. In 50 BC, the Roman Empire started to use a gold coin, the Aureus, extending use of a "single currency" throughout their empire.

In England Sir Isaac Newton, the celebrated physicist, was master of the Royal Mint. He was responsible for establishing a fixed price for gold in Britain as 84 shillings, 11.5 pence per troy ounce in 1700. The gold was alloyed with silver with a ratio of 16 parts of gold to one part of silver. The valuation stood for more than two centuries.

In 1816, Britain created a gold standard by specifying the value of one pound against a specific quantity of gold. A year later, the country minted the gold sovereign which at the time was worth one pound.

Eventually, modern international trade became based on the value of what a currency was worth in terms of gold. Obviously, it would be impractical to trade in gold for global commerce, but the tie-in to a gold standard meant that "fiat" money, i.e. any money declared by a state to be legal tender, could be traded as if it were gold. It must be remembered that, at the time of the Great Depresssion, the holder of a promissory note could redeem it for its face value in gold—the value of which was agreed internationally and not subject to the speculative gains that one sees nowadays.

There were three different arrangements of the gold standard over time; the gold standard; the gold exchange standard and the gold bullion standard.

The gold (specie) standard related the currencies that subscribed to it to a set weight of gold and therefore ensured a fixed rate of inter-convertibility between the currencies used in the global market place. Ultimately, trade imbalances between nations were settled by the transfer of gold between vaults. The advantage of a gold standard to which all currencies were, *de facto*, pegged meant that there was no foreign exchange in reality. This meant that entrepreneurs could build factories to produce goods for an export market with confidence about the end value when those products were sold—irrespective of the currency used. Since banknotes could be exchanged for gold, nations could not simply print money to pay for things internationally. A nation's money supply was linked to the amount of gold it held in its treasury. By 1870 almost all nations had adopted the gold standard. Gold flowed from country to country on the basis of imports, exports and loans. Gold provided the confidence behind international trade as the industrial revolution took hold and international trade exploded in the 19th and 20th centuries. By 1914 it is estimated that 40% of the UK's national capital was invested abroad.

The fate of the gold (specie) standard was sealed by the outbreak of hostilities in the Great War because demand for the metal outstripped its supply—in essence, the system "ran out" of money. This is referred to as a liquidity problem and, again, has some echoes in the current global financial turmoil.

The Gold Bullion Standard (1926-1931) system effectively put an end to individuals being able to use gold as money. Currency could still be exchanged for gold, but only in gold ingots, denominations suitable for paying large international transactions. The system also allowed other currencies to be traded for British Pounds or US Dollars rather than directly for gold. The gold exchange system allowed for foreign exchange deficits to be run up since the physical transfer of gold was no longer required and also permitted inflations in the value of the Pound and Dollar to occur. As the Sterling balances increased in treasuries around the world, the risk of a loss of confidence in the system put the whole edifice in danger of collapse. ***The trigger for this was the failure of Rothschild's Creditanstalt in Austria in 1931***.

Global Factors

The Wall Street Crash happened after one of the longest bull runs on record, during the roaring twenties. As so often happens, when the values of stocks rise for an extended period of time, many people convince themselves that the market will continue to rise indefinitely and that they only have to get on-board the gravy train and fabulous wealth awaits them. A proportion of investors went to the banks to borrow the money to speculate on the markets since interest rates on bank loans were affordable.

To a certain extent, success does breed success within the stock markets. When a market is rising, new players will enter the system attracted by the lure or rising value which stimulates more people to hop onto the bandwagon. The new demand pushes stock prices even higher and attracts still more people into the market. However, the value of stock in a company is tied to real world factors such as its profitability, production costs, expansion plans, and its market capitalisation and so on. The inflation of stock market values beyond any level justified by market fundamentals is known as a stock market bubble.

The newly formed US Federal Reserve had tried to rein in excessive stock market speculation in 1928 and again in 1929 by raising interest rates making the cost of speculative investment borrowing higher and therefore less attractive. This triggered an initial recession because the move caught businesses by surprise and, in response, they cut back their purchases of durable goods. In turn, this reaction caused durable goods producers to cut back production and lay off staff. The consequence of this development in turn harmed consumer confidence as buyers put off non-essential purchases fearing that they may become unemployed, exacerbating the problems that durable goods manufacturers faced and worsening the problem which rapidly spread to other areas as confidence ebbed away.

The drop in demand caused price deflation in the economy, by as much as 10% per annum. Producers, keen to sell their products, dropped their prices in the hope of attracting customers. This caused another vicious circle to start; investors saw that by delaying their investment, their funds would go further at a future date, enabling them to buy more stock for the same capital. This prompted investors to stay out of the market.

The Bankruptcy of Creditanstalt

The seeds of doom for the Austrian banking sector were sown in the aftermath of the Great War. The defeated nations, Germany, Austria, Hungary and Bulgaria, and additionally Poland and Czechoslovakia, needed finance to rebuild their economies and consequently, Eastern Europe attracted substantial capital investment from Britain, France, the Netherlands, Belgium, Italy, the USA and Switzerland. This resulted in substantial foreign interest in, or even ownership of, many banks in those nations. The governments in these countries were in need of foreign investment and supported the internationalisation of their banking systems.

The early 1920's were characterised by severe inflation in the region and this required Austrian banks to attract foreign bank participation in their equity; be able to access their hard currency accounts or act as mediators for foreign loans such that they could meet the industrial demand for credit at home and for the foreign loans that they continued to offer. The Austrian banks required that businesses demonstrated their liquidity before loans were granted; however, it had become common practice for businesses to hide losses and even to continue paying dividends at the same time. This situation inevitably led to bad debts being accrued. The banks also took interests in some of the industrial businesses that came to them for credit—even in what subsequently transpired to be insolvent concerns. Between 1924 and 1930, Austrian foreign debt tripled.

Against the backdrop of a lack of confidence in world stock markets and the ensuring global economic recession, the failure of Creditanstalt on 11 May 1931 caused a crisis in international banking that reverberated around the world and probably prolonged the Great Depression by several years. *At the time of its crash, Creditanstalt was the largest bank in central Europe.*

The failure of the Creditanstalt was triggered, in part, by some industrial loans which were defaulted on, and because it had been obliged to merge with the *Allgemeine Oesterreichische Boden Credit Anstalt* (BCA) in 1929. BCA had, in its turn, had to absorb some savings banks which were in danger of defaulting in 1926 by the Austrian government because the depositors were mainly private individuals. It had been the second largest bank in Austria after Creditanstalt before the merger and almost half of its stock was in foreign ownership. In October 1929, BCA was suffering a major liquidity crises due to a loss of customer confidence following some poor financial decisions and political instability. The same factors were still in play in May 1931 when the merged bank failed in its turn.

It needs to be remembered that the bull run of the 1920's was well and truly over and the world had entered a recession by the time Creditanstalt got into difficulties. People who had any savings were, naturally, very keen to preserve them in a period of economic turmoil and high unemployment. One credible suggestion as to why Creditanstalt failed when it did is that the bank had just published its balance sheet for 1930 which showed enormous losses; 140 million schillings; the equivalent of 85% of the bank's equity. It is argued that a new director of the bank refused to sign off on accounts that misrepresented the bank's gold reserve; a practice that had probably gone on for at least the previous six years to 1925. The rosier picture of the bank's financial position would have bolstered business with, and investment in, the bank. The explanation does go some way to explain the massive losses that Creditanstalt made in a very short period, if the true financial position of the bank had been misrepresented for years prior to the collapse.

The release of the true balance sheet led to a loss of confidence in Creditanstalt, despite the fact that a "rescue" package was announced simultaneously. The rescue package had been put together in just three days after the bank had presented its balance sheet to the Austrian authorities on 8 May 1931. The plan, which was orchestrated by Baron

Louis von Rothschild, involved funding from the Austrian National Bank; Rothschild's Dutch bank in Amsterdam and the Austrian government who contributed 30 million; 22.5 million and 10 million schillings respectively. The sum should have been enough to cover the losses reported on Creitanstalt's balance sheet and ensure the bank's liquidity when taken in conjunction with assets at the bank's disposal. The additional backing should have been enough to restore confidence in the bank. *It didn't*.

The public release of the details of the rescue plan and rumours about the balance sheet led to a run on the bank and other Austrian banks. By this stage, confidence in Austrian banking was at low ebb because of a number of banking failures. When the run started on Creditanstalt in Vienna, depositors withdrew 16% of the funds on deposit at the bank within 48 hours. Within two weeks, 30% of the deposits had been withdrawn.

Between March and August 1931, current account deposits at the bank fell by 80% and savings fell by 74%. The bank had held 16% of the nation's checking and savings account business before the balance sheet was published. Within the space of four months, this figure had declined to just 4%. Following the crisis, savings and current accounts in Austria fell by 390 million schillings with Creditanstalt bearing two thirds of this loss alone. Much of this money left the country; or rather fled the Austrian currency, the schilling, through conversion to gold—real money.

The Austrian National Bank stepped in to prevent Creditanstalt from becoming illiquid, essentially guaranteeing that it would honour the bank's debts, but the debt was substantially larger than Creditanstalt had said. The government authorised the Austrian National Bank to increase interest rates in an attempt to stem the outward flow of capital, but although the rate eventually increased to 10%, it had little effect. In June of 1931, it was clear that the Austrian National Bank needed help to stem the massive loss of gold and foreign exchange which was haemorrhaging from its vaults. The Bank of England gave it a 150 million schilling credit, despite having refused a request to support the original rescue plan in May. This was followed by a loan from the Bank for International Settlements in Basel, to whom Austria had turned after the initial Bank of England refusal, of a further 100 million schillings. An additional funding of 250 million schillings was granted by the League of Nations in August. By October 1931, the Austrian National Bank had disbursed more than 700 million schillings and the Austrian government was forced to introduce currency controls. It took until January of 1933 before Creditanstalt could be placed on a secure financial footing. It eventually emerged that the true level of indebtedness of Creditanstalt was more than seven times higher than the figure disclosed on the balance sheet of May 1931.

"Bankruptcy is a legal proceeding in which you put your money in your pants pocket and give your coat to your creditors."

Joey Adams

At the time of the bankruptcy, Creditanstalt was the bank for 69% of Austrian limited companies and 14% of these businesses were deeply in debt to the bank. Its balance sheet was about the same size as the Austrian state's expenditure at the time. Stock in the Creditanstalt was listed on twelve major foreign stock exchanges and more than half of the company was in foreign hands at the time of its collapse. This meant that the fate of the bank would inevitably have consequences beyond the borders of Austria and outside the former Austro-Hungarian Empire. The failure led to runs on banks in Hungary, Czechoslovakia, Poland, Germany, France, the USA, the UK and elsewhere.

Within a few months of the bankruptcy of Creditanstalt, most nations had been forced to abandon the gold standard permanently. It set the scene for the creation of foreign currency exchanges and, arguably, the creation of the national deficit as a tool to help nations manage their finances.

The collapse of Creditanstalt, high unemployment, inflationary pressure and the perceived unfairness of the armistice treaty from the Great War all contributed to the rise of fascism in Germany and Austria. Following the "Anschluss" of Austria with Germany in 1938, the Rothschild family were forced to sell their Austrian based banking business for a fraction of its worth. Laws were passed within the Third Reich that forbade Jews from owning any businesses and following on from the Anschluss, life in Austria was made intolerable for Jewish business people; as history tells, far worse was to follow as the lunatic Hitler tried to implement his *"final solution"* for the Jewish people.

The Rothschild family fled from Austria, but Baron Louis von Rothschild was detained by the authorities and only released after a year of detention against the payment of a substantial ransom by the family, rumoured to be several million US dollars.

Rothschild Dynasty Post World War II

Probably, the golden era for the Rothschild family ended as the Great War began, but certainly in the aftermath of the Second World War the sway that the family once had over much of Europe was gone for good. Many of the fabulous homes and art collections the family had acquired had been seized or taken into State ownership. In the immediate post war period the Rochschild business was focused on the London and Paris branches.

In the 1960s, the family finally got a lasting foothold in the American market with the establishment of Rothschild Incorporate. The London branch became involved in the emerging Eurobond market. A Swiss arm of the family was established in 1963 by Edmond de Rothschild which established itself as an investment bank, a source of venture capital and an asset management company. Indeed, asset management is the main thrust of the Rothschild family today.

Conclusion

> *"History is the essence of innumerable biographies."*
> Thomas Carlyle

The echoes of the Great Depression can still be heard in the global financial crisis that the world is slowing emerging from eighty years later. The financial world has become ever more inter-connected as global investment and global commerce have sought good yields wherever they can be found on the planet. The sub-prime lending crisis, which was predominantly an American problem, has led to many banks being over-extended. The result was a collapse in confidence within the financial sector world-wide and a choking off of liquidity, meaning that even good financial risks found it hard to obtain finance. Ultimately, it has taken massive underwriting and stimulus measures from governments around the world to head off a second Great Depression.

In Chapter 23 we look at how businnesses that fall outside the law have coped with the Credit Cruch. *Are people more or less interested in sex and drugs when they are losing money?*

Note

The Rothschild family are Jewish and have been immensely wealthy for more than 200 years. When the dynasty was started and for much of its existence, anti-Semitism has been a powerful force and many people readily believed in the "Jewish Conspiracy": an idea that the Jews planned to take over the world. When you add to this mixture the accumulated sands of time since the dynasty was born and the inevitable colouring of jealousy, any account of the dynasty is bound to encounter contradictory information. Equally, other accounts are uncritically flattering to the Rothschilds. The above account is based on cross-referencing several sources and the judgment of probability; for instance, several accounts paint the father of the dynasty as an ill-educated rag-and-bone man and moneylender—surely such a person would not have gained the confidence of Europe's richest man! Had he not done so, there would not have been a Rothschild dynasty. However, the image fits in well with the stereotype of the "dirty Jewish money lender". Several accounts attribute the granting of the status of Court Agent in 1769 to William IX Hesse-Kassel. However, although he played an important role in the Rothschild story, since he was not born until 1787, this is incorrect. The honour was actually conferred by his father, Prince Frederick.

Chapter 23

February 2009—Sex, Drugs, Rocky Markets & Rolling Indexes!

"The big difference between sex for money and sex for free is that sex for money usually costs a lot less."

Brendan Francis

February 2009—The UK Home Office has admitted that the street price of both cocaine and heroin has fallen by nearly half in the last ten years.

What is the connection between financial collapse and the illegal professions? Are they affected like normal business or are they immune to financial pressure?

""I believe that sex is one of the most beautiful, natural, wholesome things that money can buy."

Tom Clancy

The Oldest Profession; Men, and, to a lesser extent, women are often willing to pay for sexual gratification. Where demand exists, businesses will become established to meet the need; transactional sex is no exception. Whether one talks about the street corner, hands-on "owner operator" or up-market clubs where décor, location and cost place a thin veneer of respectability on the transactions that go on within, sex is a multi-billion dollar enterprise globally. This section looks at the sex industry around the world and its economic links with the financial arena. Furthermore we dip into the spectrum of activity from legitimate, regulated business to exploitative, overt criminality and international crime.

Women have exchanged sexual favours for money or other commodities since before the dawn of recorded time. The Hammurabi is regarded as the first surviving example of written law and dates from circa 1790 BC. The text makes reference to the inheritance rights of prostitutes, so it is clear that prostitution pre-dates this period and probably by a very long time! In 600 BC, the Greeks defined three classes of prostitute: *pornai* or slave prostitutes; free-born street prostitutes and *hetaera* who were educated female prostitutes and entertainers who enjoyed considerable influence in society. In Greek society, both male and female prostitutes were able to offer their services. The Greeks also introduced common brothels, priced such that even poor men could afford to use the services on offer.

Whilst prostitution was legal during the Greek and Roman empires, it has been controversial for religious or social reasons for much of its history—and a source of considerable sexual inequality. One of the earliest known bans was established in 590 AD by Reccared, the King of Spain on the basis of his interpretation of Christian teaching. Men using prostitutes suffered no penalty under the law whereas the women who supplied them could be whipped and exiled if caught.

In Venice, prostitution was considered to be "indispensible" in 1358. Most major Italian cities had government-funded brothels in the 14 and 15th centuries.

The Catholic Church was so opposed to prostitution that Pope Sixtus mandated the death penalty for prostitutes during his papacy in 1586, although his decree was not widely implemented.

In the modern world, attitudes to prostitution and its legal status vary from country to country and even from state to state within the USA. It is safe to say that there is a demand for the activity in every country, even within the Islamic world where it is not officially tolerated and where even adultery with one man can result in a death sentence in some nations.

Some western sociologists and psychologists regard all prostitution as violence against women. They argue that even women who choose to become sex workers of their own free choice do so purely because of the lack of other viable options. Further, they suggest that male clients of these women are perpetrators of sexual violence and just stop short of suggesting that they are rapists. Certainly, the issue is complicated, but there seems to be abundant evidence that many people engaged in prostitution do so freely because of the financial rewards that can be made. *It is just as certain that a proportion of sex workers are forced to do so under enormous duress.*

Crime and Prostitution

> *"These can never be true friends: Hope, dice, a prostitute, a robber, a cheat, a goldsmith, a monkey, a doctor, a distiller."*
> **Indian Proverb**

In many areas of the world aspects of transactional sex are illegal, or any form of prostitution is against the law. However, the laws controlling prostitution are often complicated. For instance, in the UK it is legal for consenting adults being over the age of 18, to buy and sell sexual activity, but it is against the law to solicit for sex on the street; either the client or the prostitute commits an offence by doing so. An individual can sell sex from their home, but if two or more people do so from the same address it constitutes a brothel. Keeping a brothel is illegal in the UK and can result in up to 7 years in jail. The maximum penal tariff for this crime in the UK was recently increased from six months under government legislation. It is illegal to control somebody for the purposes of prostitution, known as pimping, and under changes to UK law in 2009, a client can be prosecuted if they have sex with somebody acting under the control of another—even unwittingly. The intention was to provide some protection for those caught up in sex trafficking, but also to drive demand down by criminalising clients.

Of course, there is no law, in Western Countries, at least, which prohibits consensual sex between adults that is not for financial gain. As a consequence of this, where prostitution is criminalised, it is often forced to act from beneath a façade, such as a massage parlour or escort agency business, for instance, which is perfectly legal. Should the client and the service provider decide to have spontaneous sex at the conclusion of the other services, then clearly it is a private matter for the individuals involved. This type of strategy makes successful prosecution of those involved very difficult—but not impossible.

It is difficult to place a value on an unregulated sex trade by the very nature of the activity. However, estimates suggest that sex workers in the UK make £1bn in untaxed earnings every year. Some individuals working as high-class call-girls can charge hundreds of pounds an hour for their services, or even more. Often, these women are well educated, attractive individuals who have come from good family backgrounds such as "Belle de Jour," Dr Brooke Magnanti, a 34 year-old research scientist who famously documented her exploits as a high-class call-girl.

The going rate for a "full" sexual encounter in the UK can run from as little as £15 up to the stratospheric fees charged by those at the top of the market. According to The Poppy Project, there are more than 900 brothels in the UK and a third of these will offer unprotected sex.

> *"There are a number of mechanical devices which increase sexual arousal, particularly in women. Chief among these is the Mercedes-Benz 380SL."*
>
> **Lynn Lavner**

Going "on the game" as a business, requires no investment or qualifications and it is certain that some people involved in prostitution have been drawn into it in desperation as a relatively easy mechanism to make money to live or pay debts. Such people can easily be preyed upon by criminals who seek to exploit them. Since soliciting is a criminal offence, those involved in sex work within the UK are highly unlikely to pay taxes or keep financial records of their business activities. They are also under no obligation to have regular health checks and therefore, their clients are at a higher risk of contracting a sexually transmitted disease when having intercourse than they would be in a country where prostitution is regulated.

Government statistics suggest that some 80,000 people work as prostitutes in the UK and claim that of these, 90% are class "A" drug users and 70% were coerced into becoming prostitutes. The same report indicated that 8.9% of UK men had visited a prostitute in the past five years.

According to the English Collective of Prostitutes, 70% of female prostitutes are mothers, often single mothers, drawn into prostitution to feed their families. They also suggest that the figure of 80,000 sex workers is a substantial under-estimate of the numbers involved in UK prostitution as it ignores off-street prostitution, part-time and casual sex workers. The Collective hotly disputes the idea that the vast majority of prostitutes are working in the sex industry to support their drug habits. They point out that the statistics are derived from women presenting themselves at Home Office funded projects that hand out free condoms and that many sex workers plying their trade on the streets would wish to remain anonymous and not come to the attention of the authorities. It is also likely that a client who perceived a prostitute to be on drugs or in the throes of withdrawal would find the whole venture less appealing, driving down demand. Whatever the truth of the matter, it illustrates how facts and figures can be adjusted to support a specific point of view.

Human Trafficking

"Freedom suppressed and again regained bites with keener fangs than freedom never endangered."

Cicero

Migrant smuggling, in general, is the smuggling of people across international borders from poor countries to richer ones by organised groups for profit. The people being smuggled are usually seeking to improve their lot by finding work in countries where they perceive the economic prospects are much better for them but where they would not be granted the chance of legal migration. These people are "volunteers" who often pay criminal gangs substantial sums of money to get them into a richer country. They are regarded as economic migrants and are subject to detention prior to repatriation when caught by the authorities.

The United Nations agency with responsibility for human trafficking is UNODC (United Nations Office on Drugs and Crime) which is based in Vienna, Austria. According to UNODC, human trafficking is regarded as a crime against humanity and it can be described as follows:

> *"Human trafficking is the acquisition of people by improper means such as force, fraud or deception, with the aim of exploiting them. Smuggling migrants involves the procurement for financial or other material benefit of illegal entry of a person into a State of which that person is not a national or resident."*

According to the broader definition of human trafficking, that UNODC uses, the scourge of human trafficking affects almost every nation in the world. The organisation explains the differences between migrant smuggling and human trafficking in the following way:

> *Consent—migrant smuggling, while often undertaken in dangerous or degrading conditions, involves consent. Trafficking victims, on the other hand, have either never consented or if they initially consented, that consent has been rendered meaningless by the coercive, deceptive or abusive action of the traffickers.*

> *Exploitation—migrant smuggling ends with the migrants' arrival at their destination, whereas trafficking involves the ongoing exploitation of the victim.*

> *Transnationality—smuggling is always transnational, whereas trafficking may not be. Trafficking can occur regardless of whether victims are taken to another state or moved within a state's borders.*

> *Source of profits—in smuggling cases profits are derived from the transportation and facilitation of the illegal entry or stay of a person into another county, while in trafficking cases profits are derived from exploitation.*

UNODC estimates that human trafficking probably involves more than 2.5 million people at any one time and that the global criminal proceeds from the activity run into tens of billions of dollars. Nations can be affected by being the origin or destination of the trade in human trafficking, or simply a nation through which the victims transit. Obviously, by its very nature, the scale and profitability of human trafficking is difficult to gauge with any real accuracy. The majority of human trafficking is conducted by organised crime.

The deplorable activity of "human trafficking" of vulnerable women and children to work in the sex industry against their will has received a lot of publicity lately. Women who fall prey to the scheme can be lured to the target country on promises of gainful employment in innocuous areas such as waitressing, cleaning, domestic help or hairdressing only to find that they are spirited away to be forced to work in a brothel either under duress or on the pretext of repaying the costs of their travel. It seems to be a fairly common occurrence that these victims are often brutalized and repeatedly raped in order to cow them into compliance. According to UNODC, almost four fifths of human trafficking is for the purposes of sexual exploitation. Much of the remainder (18%) is estimated to be for forced labour; the modern form of slavery! The victims of sexual exploitation are often to be seen in some city centres and along highways openly working as prostitutes. The agency cautions that the overall picture of sexual exploitation may be affected by statistical bias since it is the most visible form of exploitation through human trafficking.

The USA Department of Health and Human Services identifies four mechanisms through which victims are trafficked into the sex industry:

- *A promise of a good job in another country*

492

- *A false marriage proposal turned into a bondage situation*

- *Being sold into the sex trade by parents, husbands, boyfriends*

- *Being kidnapped by traffickers*

The victims of such crimes may have very limited knowledge of English or the language of the country where they find themselves, and are often in the country illegally, meaning that they may fear the consequences of going to the authorities. Amongst the mechanisms that the Department has identified as being used to condition the victims into compliance with their captor's wishes are; starvation; physical and verbal abuse; rape; gang rape; threats of violence against their families and forced drug use. Other areas of sex work that victims may be forced to engage in include pornography; stripping; lap dancing; live-sex shows even "mail order" brides. Since the victims are essentially slaves and therefore have no rights and nobody to protect them, they can end up being forced to participate in the most exploitative forms of commercial sex activities.

Rightly, there is much public revulsion at human trafficking and many governments have taken strong stances against it. It has become a sensitive political issue. In the UK, the country's 55 regional police forces worked in concert in two operations aimed at targeting human trafficking for the sex industry; Pentameter 1 and 2. At the time, the operations were claimed as making significant progress against organised crime and in helping the victims of this appalling crime. However, one of the UK's major national newspapers, The Guardian, obtained a confidential police report which suggested that the problem of sex trafficking to the UK was being greatly overstated for political reasons. Of the 528 individuals arrested as a result of the Pentameter operation, 122 arrests never took place; of the 230 women arrested most were not implicated in sex trafficking; 106 people were released without charge; 47 were given a police caution for minor offences and released. 67 people were charged with offences relating to human trafficking, but only 22 of these cases ended with a trial, including two women who had originally been "rescued" in the operation, and seven of the accused were acquitted of the charges against them. Five people were convicted specifically for human trafficking and forced prostitution, although none of the convictions stemmed directly from Pentameter. Chief constable for North Yorkshire, Grahame Maxwell is the head of the UK Human Trafficking Centre. He was quoted as saying: *"It's not where you go down on every street corner in every street in Britain, and there's a trafficked individual. There are more people trafficked for labour exploitation than there are for sexual exploitation. We need to redress the balance here. People just seem to grab figures from the air."*

Indeed, it seems that the extent of the problem within the UK has been exaggerated. Figures have been bandied about, even in Parliament, suggesting that as many as 25000 "sex slaves" were working in the UK sex industry. It seems that this figure, subsequently repeated in the press and taken up elsewhere, has no basis in fact. A report produced in 2000 by two UK academics, Liz Kelley and Linda Regan of the University of North London may have been the original seed from which the numbers grew. Based on a hard fact that 71 people had been trafficked for sex in 1998, according to the police, the report made a number of clearly stated assumptions and extrapolations before concluding that the number of people trafficked for sex in the UK could range from 142 to 1420. It also took the broadest definition of trafficked possible. The report, stripped of all explanations and caveats was taken to confirm "at least"1420 sex slaves were working in the UK. Like a snowball running down the hill, the numbers grew. A second report put the number at 3812, but was based on assumptions such that all foreign women in the "walk-up" flats in Soho had been trafficked; 75% of females in other flats in the UK and 10% of all foreign workers in escort agencies had also been trafficked. Clearly these figures are absurd, but were seemingly only intended to provide a worst case scenario number. The figure was rapidly rounded to 4000 and taken to be a factual estimate. Taken together with the real number of sex slaves freed by Pentameter, it is clear that the problem has been exaggerated by those with a political or religious mandate, but it is just as clear that even one woman forced to endure this horror is too much for a civilised society to ignore.

Other Aspects of the Sex Industry

The true value of the sex industry is incalculable. It covers a very broad spectrum of activities from the relatively harmless including phone sex lines for instance to the exploitation discussed above. Between these extremes, many people make a living.

With the advent of the swinging sixties, sex outside of marriage moved from being a dirty, smutty activity to something accepted and increasingly mainstream. In the western world today, it is the case that couples entering into married life together without sexual knowledge of each other, or a previous partner, are in a minority. This change in attitude has led to the growth of a network of supporting industries which invades everybody's life to a greater or lesser extent.

With liberalisation of attitudes to sex and changes in the laws governing what can be purchased in supermarkets, a wide range of condoms can be purchased with your groceries. Intimate massage gels, arousing creams, love beads and vibrators can also be purchased in supermarkets in certain countries, just as casually as purchasing toothpaste. In any newsagent and many a petrol station, magazines can be bought offering semi- to fully nude models of either sex and a vast array of erotic writings, of highly varied literary merit! Magazines, such as Cosmopolitan, providing advice on how to improve your sex-life, obtain better and more plentiful orgasms and how to manage your relationships are now considered to be mainstream publications. Sex sells and the publishing industry has not been slow to capitalise on it in products for general consumption—this extends down to the problems pages in many magazines and newspapers and also many of the personal adds they contain.

With the changing of attitudes has come a plethora of "hard core" publications with explicit images of men and women. These and the merely titillating publications require printers, photographers, editors, writers and, of course, models before the final product can be sold. This illustrates that the sex industry employs a large number of people who do not engage in any sexual acts to earn their pay. Again, laws in different lands will dictate what is regarded as being beyond the legal pail in terms of hardcore pornography. A visit to a sex shop in Amsterdam would no doubt provide access to publications which are prohibited under UK law, for instance. One area where all civilised nations find agreement is the banning of all publications involving sex with children—however, magazines with models who have just reached their legal majority are very popular.

There has also been an explosive growth in the production of pornographic movies recently. In the late 1970s, only a hundred or so 35mm adult movies were produced each year. Currently, over 10,000 adult movies are produced commercially each year, providing a living for a substantial number of people apart from the "acting talent" on display in the films. The advent of the internet has also led to an avalanche of sexually related material covering the gamut of human sexual activity. Money can be made from the digital equivalents of on-line pornographic magazines and video output to explicit "cam" sites and dating sites. It is quite impossible to have an accurate estimate of the value of the market for sex on the internet, but back in 1998, "adult content" was estimated to be worth $1 billion. In the twelve years since that figure was produced, internet use has grown from 147 million to 1734 million users as of September 2009. Since many more sex-related sites have come on-line in the intervening period it is highly likely that growth in adult content sales value will have outstripped the increase of users, so a figure of $10 billion is likely to be very conservative. It is currently believed that internet dating sites is the largest growth area in cyberspace.

In 1995, For Your Eyes Only, the first lap-dancing club opened its doors in the UK. In just thirteen years, the industry had expanded to 300 clubs with the number doubling over the last four years to 2008. These clubs make money from their entrance fees, but also through bar sales, restaurant activities, special evenings, stag and, surprisingly, hen nights, and stage shows. In the USA, up-market strip clubs are multi-million dollar businesses—some are even listed on the stock market.

The UK now has more than 90 licensed sex shops, not counting chains, offering a wide range of products designed to stimulate libido and enhance your love-life. It is big business. The Anne Summer's chain is orientated towards women and concentrates on lingerie and sex toys. The chain's revenue in 2007-8 was in excess of £117 million. The industry claims to employ 2000 people directly with a further 5000 engaged in indirect work, such as manufacturing some of the products they sell. Industry representatives claim that the industry is under severe pressure from on-line sex shops that are not following UK guidelines with respect to pornographic DVDs and quality standards. The licence fees for trading in the UK are set by the local councils but typically cost several thousand pounds.

Other ancillary areas of the sex industry include dating agencies and escort agencies; "sauna clubs" and massage parlors—both of which have counterparts offering a strict business service that has nothing to do with transactional sex; fetish supplies and sex workers ready to oblige and the BDSM milieu.

We are sexual creatures and we live in a materialistic, capitalist world. Unless these factors were to change, it seems clear that commercial sex is here to stay, no matter what politicians, moralists and religious leaders think about it.

The Drugs Trade

What Are Drugs And Where Do They Come From?

By definition, a drug is a substance which affects the processes of the mind or body; a drug can be used in the prevention; treatment or diagnosis of disease; a drug can be a substance used recreationally for its effect on the central nervous system such as alcohol, tobacco, cannabis, heroin etc. Drug misuse is not a modern invention nor is it a modern problem.

Most drugs have their origins in extracts made from various plants or trees. For instance, Aspirin is derived from the bark of the willow tree from a naturally occurring compound called salicin. Use of this natural product can be traced back as far as the ancient Greeks. Whilst the vast majority of drugs can be linked back to their plant origins, modern pharmaceuticals attempt to improve on what nature has to offer by altering the active molecules, using synthetic chemistry techniques to change functional groups and to alter the stereochemistry, shape, of the compound to improve efficacy or reduce unwanted side-effects.

The history of using natural substances to produce states of euphoria can be traced far back into human history. The use of opium has been traced back to the Samarian civilisation in 5000 BC; brewing of alcohol was referred to in Egyptian texts dating back to 3500 BC; use of marijuana for medicinal purposes is recorded in China in 2737 BC. Since drugs tend to cause behavioral changes whilst a user is taking them which may include reduction of inhibitions, violent or psychotic behavior and so on, the record of attempts and dictates to prohibit their use can also be traced back into the mists of time. One of the earliest examples of this is drawn from Egypt where a priest forbids his acolytes to use alcohol; the text dates from 2000 BC.

A Brief History of UK Drug Legislation

Within the UK, the history of regulation of drugs is relatively recent. Although certain groups of people e.g. Methodists refused to consume alcohol because of their religious beliefs, it has never been banned. This is unlike the USA where a law prohibiting the sale, production and consumption of alcohol was on the statute books between 1920 and 1933.

The Poisons Act (1858) is regarded as the first general UK legislation aimed at curbing access to certain substances. Building on the Arsenic Act (1856), it was designed to restrict access to substances which could be used by criminals for the purposes of murder since many poisons were very difficult to trace, making them excellent tools of murder.

In 1860, the Treaty of Peking was signed by the Chinese, British and American governments, bringing to an end the second opium war. One concession of this treaty, won by the British, was that it legalised the opium trade from India into China, arguably making Britain the first national sponsor of the international narcotics trade. The British ended the trade 50 years later, in 1910.

Britain signed the convention stemming from the First International Opium Conference in The Hague, 1912. It was the first international drug control treaty and aimed to ensure that the production, distribution, import, export and selling of "morphine, cocaine and their respective salts" was controlled. The UK finally passed the relevant legislation into law in 1920

In 1916, the Defence of the Realm act was passed without debate in parliament as an emergency war-time measure. Regulation 40b of this act effectively implemented the Opium Conference accords, by placing the legal sale, distribution and possession of opium and cocaine under the control of the Home Office. Part of the justification for this was the reports of "crazed soldiers" acting under the influence of cocaine. The legislation reflected a hardening attitude the use of "narcotics" although cocaine is a central nerves system stimulant rather than a narcotic, in the medical sense of the word that was gaining ground, notably in the States.

Between 1920 and 1923, the Dangerous Drugs Act and its amendments went through parliament. This act is regarded as the UK's first specific drug control legislation. It brought in controls on tincture of cannabis; a full ban came in the 1928 amendment to the act; dihydrocodeine and banned cocaine use. The law made it an offence for an occupier to permit smoking of opium on their premises; it also gave the police enhanced search powers.

The Dangerous Drugs Act was amended in 1964 and 1967. It gave police stop and search rights for suspected drug possession; prohibited LSD; required notification of addicts coming before the courts to the Home Office; curtailed the medical prescription of heroin and cocaine to addicts and brought in the use of heroin substitute methadone as a treatment for heroin addicts.

In 1971, the government signed the Misuse of Drugs act into law. This law broadened the scope of legislation to include synthetic drugs, such as LSD, amphetamines and MDMA, and brought in the "schedule" system for drug classification. Use of MDMA (Ecstasy) was largely unknown in 1971 and this drug was included in an amendment to the act in 1977.

In 1985, the Controlled Drugs (Penalties) Act passed into law and permits a sentence of life-imprisonment to be imposed for drugs trafficking in the UK.

Under current UK law, all recreational drugs including cannabis; Ecstasy; cocaine; heroin; amphetamines; barbiturates etc are illegal although the police may use their discretion if the amounts in question are clearly for personal use but they are not obliged to.

Trends in the price of illegal drugs within the UK

DrugScope is a UK registered charity which aims to be an independent centre of information and expertise on drugs. They conducted a survey on the price of street drugs in the UK over the period from 2006 to 2009 and the following table is taken from their survey:

Drug Type	2006	2007	2008	2009
Herbal cannabis (standard quality)	£70 per ounce	£87 per ounce	£89 per ounce	**£31 per quarter ounce** *
Herbal cannabis (good quality)	£121	£134	£131	**£40 per quarter ounce***
Resin cannabis	£54	£55	£51	**£21 per quarter ounce***
Cocaine per gram	£43	£43	£42	£39
Ecstasy pill	£3	£2	£2	£2
MDMA powder per gram	£40	£38	£39	£36
Amphetamine per gram	£10	£10	£9	£9
Ketamine per gram	£28	£25	£20	£22
Diazepam per 10mg tablet			£1	£1

*NOTE: For the 2009 survey, cannabis prices were recorded per quarter ounce for the first time as this is the most common amount dealt on the street drug market. The 2006-2008 surveys refer to prices for an ounce of cannabis so are not directly comparable.

The survey was drawn up from data obtained in 20 towns and cities across the UK. It also concluded that the purity of the drugs on offer was declining. After all, drug consumers can hardly complain to their local trading standards agency about the quality of the product that they had purchased. DrugScope conclude that this adulteration might be causing users to experiment with mixtures of drugs. With any commodity, there is a relationship between its demand and supply. When supplies are plentiful, the price will usually fall; conversely restricted supply pushes the price of a commodity higher. If the number of consumers increases, prices will generally rise too.

Drugs and Crime

In the UK, all recreational drugs are illegal. Their possession, use or supply can result in unlimited fines and, potentially, life-imprisonment, but users that are not also suppliers are unlikely to face such draconian punishment. This is not surprising when you consider that UK government estimates suggest that a third of the population have taken drugs during their lifetime.

Many drugs that are used recreationally such as heroin and crack cocaine are highly addictive and relatively expensive. As a consequence of this, some drug users turn to crime to obtain the money they need to maintain their drug habit. It is also true that a proportion of people with an existing criminal record subsequently develop a drug habit. They may continue to use their criminal activity to fund their addiction. However, it would be completely wrong to suggest that all drug users turn to acquisitive crime because of their use of drugs. As we saw in the previous section, the suggestion that 90% of prostitutes are drug addicts is probably a wild exaggeration, but certainly some addicts turn to prostitution as a method of paying for drugs. Apart from the fact that their use of recreational drugs is, of itself, a criminal act, the majorities of drug users are law abiding and have the funds to pay for their recreational drugs use from working in mainstream employment.

It is notoriously difficult to put an accurate price on the costs to society stemming from illegal drugs since the numbers of people involved are unknown and the reasons behind a crime may not be simply linked to maintaining a drug habit—even criminal addicts have "straight" living costs such as accommodation; food; clothing; transport; entertainment etc.

Transform, a charity which runs a think tank that advocates changing drug policy from prohibition to "effective, just and humane governmental control and regulation" has estimated that illegal drugs cost the UK almost £17 billion a year. This figure takes into account costs stemming from crime, health unemployment, social services, criminal justice and costs relating to drug prohibition programs. The charity believes that the position it advocates could save the hard-pressed British tax payer almost £11 billion a year, if drugs were to be decriminalized and properly regulated.

According to the UK's Serious Organised Crime Agency (SOCA), the value of the UK illicit drug market in 2004 was worth somewhere between £4 billion to £6.6 billion. The market is served both by British organised crime and foreign criminals. Some of the foreign gangs have ethnic ties to producing regions. The criminal activity covers all phases from importation to street level distribution.

Drug Geographical Origins

The heroin and cocaine consumed in the UK comes mainly from two producing regions. SOCA believes that 90% of heroin consumed in the UK originates in Afghanistan. Afghan opium is transported via Iran to Turkey and then enters the EU overland via the Balkans. Much of the heroin destined for the UK market passes through The Netherlands.

More than 2/3 of the cocaine sold in the UK originates in Columbia or its bordering regions with Ecuador and Venezuela, with the remainder coming from Peru and Bolivia. The UK is one of the largest European markets for cocaine. Traditionally, the drug entered the EU by boat into Spain, but new routes via West Africa are increasingly used.

Once drug shipments have arrived in the UK, they are usually distributed from major cities such as London, Birmingham and Liverpool before filtering down to other cities and larger towns. The drugs tend to be moved in bulk until they filter down to the level of the local dealer.

Why Do People Take Illegal Drugs?

Much of the information on drug use naturally stems from organisations which wish to put an end to it; after all, it is certain that drugs can blight lives by causing health problems and even death; social problems and criminality. UK government statistics suggest that 10% of the UK population aged between 16 and 59 have taken recreational drugs during the past 12 months being approximately 4 million people. *So why do they do it?*

Part of the reason stems from the fact that drug taking is enjoyable; drugs that do not produce enjoyment are not abused. A treatment used for addicts with heroin withdrawal symptoms is to give them methadone. Whilst methadone helps with the symptoms of withdrawal, it does not produce feelings of euphoria. Consequently, it is not a drug that people abuse—what would b the point? On a physiological level, drugs have an effect on the chemistry of the brain and are known to trigger dopamine release, a naturally occurring substance which is associated with feelings of pleasure.

Another factor which is often cited as a trigger for drug taking is peer group pressure. If a person has friends who embrace the drug culture, they may feel pressured to try drugs to fit in with them—particularly younger people—and obtain the elusive quality of being "cool". Linked in with this are elements of curiosity and daring. Some people want to know what all the fuss is about and have their first experience with drugs to satisfy this desire. Others perceive drug taking as being daring; rebellion against the establishments and parents and dabble with drugs for this reason. It is highly likely that the motivations behind drug taking will differ with different educational and social backgrounds.

Linked to this in certain groups are attempts to escape from boredom and feelings of hopelessness over the future and job prospects.

Problematic Drug Use

It has been estimated that class "A" drug abuse costs the UK something like £15 billion per year, according to a Home Office report. It concludes that 99% of the costs stem from 327000 "problematic" drug users; about £44200 each. The report estimates that 90% of the cost stems from drug-related crime associated with this group. The Home Office attributes more than half (56%) of the 56 million, or so, crimes committed in the UK each year to being drug-motivated. They estimate that this is responsible for £19 billion, roughly a third, of the cost of crime within the UK. Problematic drug users are estimated to be about 3% of the drug using population; implying that the UK has roughly 11 million drug users—more than two and a half times the previous Home Office estimate cited above!. As the charity Transform points out, 97% of drug users are not problematic and some thought ought to be given to the consequences of decriminalising and controlling drug use.

Drug Profits

According to a Home Office report, the street price for heroin and cocaine in the UK represent a mark-up of 16,800 and 15,800% over the supply chain from the producers respectively. Possibly, up to 4,000 people within the UK are involved in the trafficking of large quantities of drugs. The value of the UK drug market is believed to be between £3.9 to 8.5 billion per year, based upon seizures made by the police and customs services.

Money from drug profits is laundered to break any clear association between the cash and the criminals engaged in the trade. According to SOCA, this is achieved with varying degrees of sophistication from moving the proceeds abroad to using it to purchase legitimate, often cash rich, assets, such as casinos. The United Arab Emirates, Hong Kong, Singapore, Shanghai and Spain have all proved attractive to money launderers. There are a relatively small number of specialist criminal enterprises that handle money laundering, but they are responsible for handling a significant proportion of the proceeds from all crime.

There is big money associated with the darker side of human activity. It is difficult, for obvious reasons to estimate the true money flows from these enterprises but as we can see from the above areas of criminal activity they seem relatively immune to the effects of the credit crunch. Indeed in the case of the drugs industry it would appear the street cost has actually risen indicating an increase in demand or perhaps worse the inelastic nature of the product!

In Chapter 24 we will look at legitimate trade and commerce. We will see how Wall Street meets Main Street over 3,000 years!

> *"Commerce links all mankind in one common brotherhood of mutual dependence and interests".*
>
> **James A Garfield**

Chapter 24

March 2009—Slippery Road: Oxford Brogues to Silk Slippers

"By virtue of exchange, one man's prosperity is beneficial to all others."

Frederic Bastiat

March 2009—World Trade organisation announces 9% decrease in global trade due to the Credit Crisis.

What is the link between trade and finance? How quickly does the real world follow the financial world?

The History Of Trade; Essentially, humankind is a co-operative species. Trade, in one form or another, has been going on for many thousands of years and it predates any kind of monetary system. The original currency of trade was barter; items of value to "buyer and seller" were simply exchanged at a mutually accepted worth. The origins of trade are lost in the mists of human pre-history, but evidence for its existence has been discovered by archaeologists where artifacts produced remotely have been found at excavations which are suggestive of trade.

Trade routes are ancient links between cultures which facilitated contact and trade between distant communities. Some of the earliest examples of these highways of commerce date back to 1800 BC. At this time, there was a trade in incense, a mixture of resins, gum and herbs that produces a pleasant smell when burned. The ancient Egyptian civilisation used incense in religious ceremonies and to mark victory in battle. Incense was also used in Jewish religious ceremonies and by the Greeks and Romans to celebrate victories, for religious purposes and in funeral rites amongst other uses.

Clearly, incense was much in demand in ancient times. A trade route was established which linked the Indies, Saudi Arabia and Egypt. The route ran for approximately 2400 km and dates from 1800BC, but may have existed well before that date. It continued to be an important artery of commerce for many centuries. Indian spices would be transported to the port of Arabia Aden and then the Arabians would transport it to the city of Petra by camel train from where it would be taken, originally, to Egypt and Syria by traders. The route provided access to Indian spices and silks, African wood and gold and myrrh and frankincense from the Middle East in addition to pearls, precious stones and textiles. The Arabs grew rich from acting as middlemen in the trade. Others obtained income from levying taxes for passage, or for the use of wells along the route. Fortresses, sophisticated irrigation systems and urbanisation, developed along part of the route in the Negev desert, gave rise to four ancient cities to serve the route as it passed through the region; such was its importance to the ancient world.

By its nature, trade involves the movement of desirable, valuable commodities and consequently, trade routes were raided by robbers and fought over by nations. The Incense Route was no exception to this and was controlled at different times by the Assyrians, the Persians, the Greeks and the Romans.

> *"Agriculture, manufacturers, commerce, and navigation, the four pillars of our prosperity, are then most thriving when left most free to individual enterprise."*
> **Thomas Jefferson**

The Arabs were demanding payment in gold or silver for transshipment of incense and other goods through their lands when the Roman Empire took an interest in the trade route. The Romans original solution to this problem was to circumvent the Arabian Peninsula entirely; hiring Greek sailors to ply the route direct to the Indies by sea for them. This was a perilous sea journey of its own right, but made more dangerous by raids from pirates keen to seize the goods being transported. The sea route provides an early linkage between trade and technological advancement. The Greeks altered the traditional design of their ships to make them stronger and better able to cope with the rigours of the voyage by changing the way the craft were constructed. These craft were up to 180 feet in length and could hold a cargo of almost a thousand tons. It has been estimated that the cost of seaborne transport were a sixtieth of the costs involved of shipping the same quantity of goods by land.

Probably the most famous of all trade routes is the Silk Road which eventually linked China to Rome, some 11,000 km. Silk was first produced in China in about 3000 BC. Although silk is a natural product produced by silkworms, the Chinese were the first to weave fabric from it; a secret they guarded jealously for thousands of years. The fabric was very highly prized and was actually used as a form of currency within the Chinese Empire. The material was also highly valuable outside of China; indeed silk was found on an Egyptian mummy that dated to 1070 BC, indicating that it was being traded by then, if not earlier. The secret of silk production eventually leaked out and it was known in Korea in 200 BC and had reached India by 300 AD.

The Silk Road came into existence in 200 BC under the rule of Emperor Han Wu-ti. It is likely that he wanted expanded trade to allow him to bolster the defenses of his Empire against the Xiongnu. He sent an emissary, Chang Ch'ien, to form an alliance against the Xiongnu with one of the central Asian tribes. This mission ended up as a ten year odyssey, but when Chang Ch'ien did return to the Emperor, he persuaded him to expand trade with the central Asian tribes and form strong alliances with the nomadic people of the region. The Chinese traded their silk for horses, cattle, furs and hides with the central Asians.

The Emperor Han Wu-ti also dispatched emissaries to Mesopotamia and Persia with gifts of silk, opening up trading to the region. By 100 BC, trade links had been established with the Roman Empire although silk may have arrived via the Incense Route from India initially.

In view of the enormous length of the Silk Road, few people ever travelled from one end to the other of it, but goods travelled along it in a series of relays. Chinese exports were not limited to silk, but included things such as ceramics; jade; bronze objects; furs and iron. Goods travelling in the opposite direction included gold; silver; ivory precious stones and glass, once the Chinese started fabrication of glass in the fifth century.

The Silk Road had its heyday in the Tang dynasty during the eighth century AD. Chanang, the seat of the dynasty, burgeoned to a population said to be two million and was home to 5,000 foreigners, according to a contemporary census.

Marco Polo (1254-1324)

Was Marco Polo the first European to travel extensively in Asia and China and did he serve the court of the first Mongol Emperor of China, Kublai Khan?

What is certain is that Marco Polo was the son of a merchant and that he grew up in Venice. It is also agreed that he dictated his account of his travels to China and his service to Kublai Khan whilst he was a prisoner of war, held in Genoa, to a fellow prisoner, Rustichello. The manuscript that was produced was known as *"The Description of the World"* or *"The Travels of Marco Polo"*. Rustichello was an author of romantic fiction. The manuscript dates from 1299 and the earliest known surviving manuscript is written in a blend of French and Italian; a vernacular tongue which would have made the manuscript accessible at the time, but there is no certainty that this was the original account penned by Rustichello.

Marco Polo is considered to be the first European to have travelled extensively in Asia and gained an insight into China. The fact that the story he tells recounts that his father and uncle had left him as a young boy, in 1260, to travel to the far East and met Kublai Khan during their trip underlines the fact that this is not so. His father, Niccilo, and his uncle, Maffeo, returned to Venice after nine years in Asia. The Khan had asked them, or so the story goes, to meet with the Pope and ask him to obtain oil from the lamp at the Holy Sepulchre at Jerusalem; and arrange for 100 learned men to teach his people about Christianity. Just how likely it is that a pair of Venetian merchants and explorers could gain an audience with the head of the Roman Catholic Church, at the time, is difficult to judge.

Marco Polo returned to Asia with his father and uncle in 1269 to visit Kublai Khan. According to his account, Marco became a favourite of Kublai Khan and was granted high posts in his administration. He also travelled to India, Burma and China on special missions on behalf of Kublai Khan. The Polos were reputed to have spent 17 years at the court of Kublai Khan and to have left with great wealth in jewels and gold. Indeed Kublai Khan was so attached to them that he only allowed them to leave his court to escort a Mongol princess who was to marry a Persian prince.

The tales of his exploits proved extremely popular, once published by Rustichello. They were translated into Latin and other languages and it is entirely possible that they were embellished down through the years. The memoire tells of men with tails; frequent encounters with cannibals; a bird large enough to carry an elephant, drop it from a height and feed from its carcass. Polo's account contains some accurate accounts of the region and its history; a first western description of asbestos; use of paper money; and the Imperial postal service, for instance. It also has some glaring omissions, the most striking of which is the absence of any remarks about the Great Wall of China which has impressed many a modern-day visitor and should have left an indelible impression on the "first European" to see it.

The Italian version of his memoire became known as **"*Il Milione*"**; the modern Italian translation of the phrase is "the million"—this was supposed to relate to the many fanciful tales in Polo's account. It is entirely possible that Marco Polo did not make the journey or carry out the exploits that he claimed. Perhaps he drew on other accounts of the region from Persian and Arabic sources or from encounters with non-Europeans who had travelled to the region. Whatever the truth of the matter, the work does represent the most accurate account of China and Asia that was available at the time and became one of the most popular works of medieval literature.

Explorers That Paved the Way for Modern Trade

Prince Henry, the Navigator (1394-1460)

Prince Henry was the third son of King João I of Portugal. Although he did not undertake any voyages of discovery himself, he was responsible for the Portuguese exploration of the African west coast. Under his sponsorship, the Portuguese developed a new type of ship, the caravel, which was better suited to long voyages of exploration; two of Christopher Columbus' ships, the *Nina* and the *Pinta* were caravels. Henry was also reputed to have encouraged and patronised cartography and navigation skills and tools including the quadrant and mathematical tables to determine latitude. The explorations that he sponsored discovered and claimed islands in the Atlantic Ocean—Madeira; Porto Santo and the Azores—and pushed down the African coast below Cape Bojador, eventually exploring as far south as the Gambia. These voyages of exploration brought with them trade links and new colonies for the Portuguese.

Christopher Columbus (1451-1506)

One true explorer who was to have a profound influence on trade may have been influenced by the stories of Marco Polo, written 152 years before his birth. That man was the Genoese sailor Christopher Columbus. The European seafaring nations were interested in using maritime routes to exploit the spice trade from the Indies, at that time, a term that meant anywhere east of the Indus River in Asia. The Portuguese were interested in a sea route around Africa, but some scholars thought that the Indies could be reached by sailing west across the Atlantic Ocean. Columbus was convinced of the existence of a westerly route to the Indies and sought a sponsor for his expedition, eventually securing the support of the King and Queen of Spain. His expedition made landfall in the Caribbean in 1492 and ultimately led to the colonisation of the Americas. Columbus was convinced that he had discovered a sea route to the Indies. Ten years after his original landfall, Europeans finally realised the significance of his discovery; Columbus had discovered the New World.

Vasco da Gama (1460-1524)

Vasco da Gama was born in Portugal. In 1497, he set off on an expedition to reach the Indies by rounding the Cape of Good Hope. The voyage followed the route of another Portuguese expedition, led by Bartolomeu Dias that had rounded the Cape of Good Hope and returned safely to Portugal. Vasco da Gama's voyage continued on beyond the route charted by Dias, voyaging into areas never before sailed by Europeans. He made landfall on the East African coast at various points: Mozambique; Mombasa; and Malinda. From Malinda, da Gama crossed the Indian Ocean, with the aid of a pilot who knew about the monsoon winds, making landfall at Calicut on the south western coast of India. Vasco de Gama returned to Portugal in 1499 with valuable concessions for the spice trade which proved to be very valuable to the Portuguese economy, however, this was ultimately achieved with considerable bloodshed. Vasco da Gama played a very important role in helping his nation to become a major colonial power.

Slave Trade

> *"So enormous, so dreadful, so irremediable did the Trade's wickedness appear that my own mind was completely made up for Abolition. Let the consequences be what they would, I from this time determined that I would never rest until I had effected its abolition."*
>
> **William Wilberforce**

The slave trade is regarded with deep revulsion from the perspective of 21st century morality, but slavery can be traced deep into mankind's history to biblical times. In the wake of the European explorers and the discovery of the New World, a commodity trade was established between the Old and New Worlds that needed a lot of manpower. This need was met by the establishment of the slave trade which continued from the 16th to the 19th centuries. The slave trade even received the blessing of the Roman Catholic Church during the middle ages, *just as long as no Christians were enslaved.*

The slaves were mainly taken from western and central Africa to labour in the Americas on sugar, cocoa, coffee and cotton plantations; in gold and silver mines and as domestic servants, as well as other roles. The principle first world nations involved in the trade were the Portuguese, the British, the French, the Spanish, the Dutch, in order of their involvement. The Brazilians and the Americans were also engaged in the trade. Estimates suggest that between 9 and 12 million people were brought to slavery in the Americas—this figure does not take into account the attrition rates on the voyage which were as high as 10% to 30%. The slaves were mainly traded for goods in Africa in transactions with Kings, Chiefs and other dignitaries; in other words, Africans were responsible for selling slaves to the European powers, although some slaves were seized by the traders directly.

The British ports of Bristol and Liverpool had grown prosperous from the slave trade by the 18th century. Trade goods were shipped to Africa and the ships returned with their human cargoes. The slaves were then sent to the Americas to work on the plantations and in mines and the ships returned laden with sugar, molasses, timber, other raw materials and cash.

During the years of the slave trade, many people considered that the trade was a moral one since it introduced heathens to the benefits of civilisation and Christianity. It was an argument that did not bear close scrutiny and by the end of the 18th century, abolitionism was gaining strength in Britain. The movement was led by the Quakers and championed in Parliament by William Wilberforce and the British involvement in the slave trade was abolished in 1808. However, it took a further 26 years before the Abolition of Slavery Act was passed into law in Britain. The slave trade ended in 1860 with the signing of various international treaties which outlawed it.

Despite the ending of this horrific practice 150 years ago, the United Nations believe that 27 million people could be considered to be modern day slaves, forced to work in a wide range of activities from forced labour to forced sexual exploitation.

Regulation of International Trade

In 1860, Britain entered into a free trade agreement with France, the Cobden-Chevalier Treaty. This treaty was born in an age of international tension between Britain and France from a suggestion that it would be better to establish a free trade agreement with the French rather than spend money on armaments to repel a possible French invasion. The overture came from the British, but was rapidly adopted by the French side and came into force within a year of the original question being raised in the Commons. As a result of the treaty, most British manufactured goods attracted duties below 30% in France and the British reciprocated with reduced duties on French goods including wine and brandy and removal of duty on other items such as silks, carpets, lace and shawls; just about the only commodity that Britain levied protective duties on and all of greatest relevance to trade with the French. Whereas the British concessions were offered to all her trading partners, the French restricted their accord to the British market.

One of the terms of the Cobden-Chevalier Treaty was that it bestowed "most favoured nation" status on Britain. In effect, this meant that the UK had to offer all other countries with whom it enjoyed the status the goods covered by the Anglo-French agreement at the same reduced level of duty. The idea behind this is that free trade is encouraged amongst the nations sharing most favoured nation status and bureaucracy is reduced since the same conditions will pertain to an exporter sending goods to all nations within the group.

The Cobden-Chevalier Treaty proved a catalyst to the establishment of free trade agreements within Europe, involving either France or Britain, or indeed accords between other nations. Similar agreements were signed covering a range of trade issues between: France and Belgium (1862); France and Italy (1863); France and Switzerland (1864); France and Sweden, Norway, Spain and Holland respectively (1865); France and Austria (1866) and France with Portugal (1867).

Britain secured treaties with Belgium, Italy and Austria in the period from 1862 to 1865.

An additional effect of the low or free trade agreements was that it led to a greater degree of co-operation between states on non-trade issues that would lead to facilitation of international trade, such as accords on railways, canals, telegraphs, postal communications and the like. In 1868, the river Rhine was designated as a freeway for ships from all nations. The Rhine rises in Switzerland, forms the Franco German border in places, flows through Germany and exits into the North Sea in Holland. The river is still an important commercial freight route even today.

The Bretton Woods Agreement

As the Second World War was drawing to a close, a critical meeting took place in the town of Bretton Woods in New Hampshire, USA. Just less than a month after the Allies had splashed ashore in the blood and carnage of the D-day landings, gaining a foothold in Nazi occupied Europe, representatives from 44 allied nations met to set out the post-war economic structure of the world. The war in Europe would rage on for ten months and victory against the Imperial Japanese forces would not be achieved until September of 1945, but a new world financial order was being mapped out in this small New Hampshire resort.

The Bank of International Settlement had been established in Bassel, Switzerland, in 1930, as a bank to handle the war reparations imposed on Germany in the Treaty of Versailles, in line with the Young plan. The treaty established the peace settlements at the end of the Great War and required that Germany take sole responsibility for the hostilities, amongst other things. The war reparations that Germany was to pay were set in 1919 at £6.6 billion; had the schedule been adhered to, it would have taken Germany until 1988 to pay off this sum. Historians believe that the terms of the Versailles Treaty were partially responsible for allowing the rise of National Socialism and Adolf Hitler in Germany during the 1930s and so sowing the seeds of the Second World War.

Ultimately, the Bank of International Settlement took on the role of helping the co-ordination of central banks and other agencies interested in monetary and financial stability. As we have seen, the bank played a role in the provision of emergency funding during the crash of Creditanstalt in 1931 and provided financial support to both Austria and Germany. Critically, the BIS continued to take interest payments from Germany on this loan during the war, amounting to 3.7 tonnes of gold. It transpired that the Nazis had simply helped themselves to this gold from the central banks of Belgium and the Netherlands, countries which they occupied at the time. This led to accusations of collusion in war crimes against BIS and to demands for its cessation, led by Norway and some other European nations and supported by the Americans, during the Bretton Woods conference. Indeed, against British objections, it was decided to dissolve BIS, but this never happened. After President Roosevelt died, his successor President Truman reversed the decision and BIS continues today.

However, the Bretton Woods accord was about much more than the fate of the Bank of International Settlement. The ground work had, astonishingly, been done between 1942 and the conference date between American and British Treasury officials—whilst the outcome of the war was very far from certain. The officials analysed the mistakes that had been made in the interwar years and factors involved in the Great Depression of the 1930s. Their primary conclusion was that a system of international payments was needed that would allow international trade to continue without the fear of a sudden currency depreciation or wild fluctuation of value. With this in place, international free trade could flourish, they concluded. Protectionist measures imposed by nation states to protect their exports whilst limiting imports were widely seen as contributing to the misery and duration of the Great Depression.

As an outcome of the Bretton Woods conference, the US dollar emerged as the world's reserve currency. The value of gold was set as $35 dollars per ounce and the American government pledged to redeem its currency against gold, if required. The US dollar was to be the only currency that could be converted to gold. The national currencies were pegged to a gold (US dollar) value and it was agreed that the value would be maintained within 1% of this value, the national currency's trading band, through the buying or selling of dollars. The dollar was more flexible than gold in practical terms and could also attract interest. The move, naturally, led to international trade being conducted in terms of US dollar value.

Bretton Woods laid the foundations for the establishment of the International Monetary Fund (IMF) which had the mandate to oversee that currencies were maintained within their agreed bands. Only with the agreement of the IMF could these rates be altered and only then to correct a "fundamental disequilibrium" in the balance of payments of the nation in question. The IMF was established in 1945 and took up functional duties in 1947.

A sister institution to the IMF was also mandated by Bretton Woods; the International Bank for Reconstruction and Development (IBRD). The initial aim of IBRD (now a part of the World Bank) was to facilitate the recovery of Europe from the aftermath of World War II through the provision of finance; the first beneficiary of an IBRD loan was France which borrowed $250 million for post-war reconstruction in 1947. It was also to foster economic development in developing countries. IBRD was responsible for managing the system of fixed exchanges agreed at Bretton Woods. These concepts and institutions are explored more fully in Chapter 7.

As a consequence of Bretton Woods and the dire state of Europe after World War II, a triangular system of trade emerged. The US traded with developing nations through the convertible financial system at tremendous profit, permitting her to acquire raw materials and expand her industrial base. The surplus dollars were sent to Europe through schemes such as the Marshall plan, to help rebuild European economies permitting them to sell to the US. The income then allowed Europe to purchase raw materials from the Third World in their turn. When this triangle became destabilised, the resulting crisis led to the eventual failure of the accord.

A factor in the ultimate demise of the Bretton Woods agreement which led to the US pulling out of the system was gold bullion trading, largely organised through London being 80% of the market. Gold outside of the Bretton Woods system could be bought and sold and the price was fixed on a daily basis in London. As the gold price rose above the US dollar peg of $35 dollars an ounce, there was increasing temptation for traders to buy gold from central banks and sell it on the open market. This was a particular problem at times of world crises; during the Cuban Missile crisis of 1963, open market gold spiked at $40 an ounce, a nominal profit of 25% over the peg price. A run on Sterling and gold in 1967 forced the UK to devalue the pound, putting a strain on the system.

The US had started to run a trade balance deficit. If it attempted to correct the situation by imposing strict fiscal control at home, it risked triggering a liquidity crisis. If nothing was done, the US risked seeing confidence slip away from the dollar. The US deficit grew as it funded the war in Vietnam and there was increasing pressure on the accord as some states sought to convert their dollar holdings into gold as allowed for under the Bretton Woods agreement.

In 1971, in a move that came to be known as the Nixon shock, the US president announced that the USA had abandoned the convertibility of dollars into gold. As a consequence, other nations were obliged to float their own currencies against the dollar and other currencies. By 1976, the foreign exchange stability afforded by the Bretton Woods agreement was dead.

The General Agreement on Tariffs and Trade (GATT)

"No nation was ever ruined by trade."
Benjamin Franklin

The Bretton Woods conference had one notable failure. It had been the intention to establish a body that would be responsible for trade in the aftermath of the Second World War. This body was to be known as the International Trade Organisation (ITO), but it was not to be. Preparative work was done to establish the ITO and the finishing touches were applied in Havana, Cuba. However, the American government could not get the US Congress to pass the necessary legislation to ratify it and in 1950, President Truman announced that he would cease trying to get Congress to pass it, effectively ending the initiative.

In the interim, 15 nations had met together in December 1945 with the aim of reducing and fixing customs tariffs which were seen as an impediment to free trade. The initial accord resulted in the creation of a package of trade rules. Some 45,000 tariff concessions were affected in 1948, around $10 billion of trade, roughly a fifth of the total of world trade at the time. A deal was signed in October 1947 by which time the group had expanded to 23 nations all of whom were involved in ITO discussions. This agreement became known as the General Agreement on Trade and Tariffs and was to have been subsumed into ITO when it became established.

GATT functioned by means of rolling "trade rounds" which lasted for several years each. There were eight rounds in the 47 years of the body's existence. Initial rounds were focussed on reduction of tariffs and trade barriers. The so-called Kennedy round in the 1960s brought about an anti-dumping accord and included a section on developing trade. In the seventies, the Tokyo round looked at reform of GATT and talking trade barriers that were not in the form of tariffs. The final round, the Uruguay round, lasted for seven and a half years and laid the foundations for the establishment of the World Trade Organisation (WTO) and a new set of agreements. The WTO was established in 1995 and is based in Geneva.

The World Trade Organisation

The WTO came into being in 1995 to take over and expand the mandate that had been handled by GATT since 1947. It is the sole international organisation with a remit to handle the rules of trade between nation states with the aim of helping producers of goods and services, exporters and importers to conduct their businesses. The agreements have been signed by the majority of the world's trading nations and have been ratified by their respective parliaments. There are currently 153 member states of the WTO and the organisational budget for 2009 was $180 million. There are 16 separate multilateral trade agreements which have been adopted by all WTO member states and two so-called "plurilateral" agreements which only some countries have signed up to. WTO decisions are usually taken on the basis of a consensus of all members and all Member States must agree to follow all WTO rules; an agreement known as the single undertaking.

According to the WTO's Director-General, Pascal Lamay, the WTO's main activities are as follows:

—negotiating the reduction or elimination of obstacles to trade (import tariffs, other barriers to trade) and agreeing on rules governing the conduct of international trade (e.g. antidumping, subsidies, product standards, etc.)

—administering and monitoring the application of the WTO's agreed rules for trade in goods, trade in services, and trade-related intellectual property rights

—monitoring and reviewing the trade policies of our members, as well as ensuring transparency of regional and bilateral trade agreements

—settling disputes among our members regarding the interpretation and application of the agreements

—building capacity of developing country government officials in international trade matters

—assisting the process of accession of some 30 countries who are not yet members of the organization

—conducting economic research and collecting and disseminating trade data in support of the WTO's other main activities

—explaining to and educating the public about the WTO, its mission and its activities.

The Director-General expresses the view that ***"The opening of national markets to international trade, with justifiable exceptions or with adequate flexibilities, will encourage and contribute to sustainable development, raise people's welfare, reduce poverty, and foster peace and stability."***

The WTO has an Economic Research and Statistics Division which is responsible for helping to produce short-term forecasts for global trade growth, amongst other things. It is responsible for preparing the annual World Trade Report and its outputs are released at about the same time those of the Organisation for Economic Cooperation and Development (OECD) and the International Monetary Fund (IMF). The OECD and the IMF are regarded as the leading macroeconomic forecasters amongst the international organisations. The WTO forecasts relate to their year of issue and the year ahead.

In 2009, the WTO predicted that there would be a 9% decrease in world trade as a consequence of the global recession that was triggered by the financial crisis. The trade decline lagged behind the triggering event, as liquidity in the global markets evaporated and confidence ebbed away. The collapse in global demand was the worst seen since the Second World War. The effects were more pronounced in the developed world, where export trade volumes were down by 10%, than in the developing world which saw a 2 to 3% decline in trade volumes. However, the developing world is reliant upon trade to fuel development, so the impact could be more keenly felt there. World trade had still managed to post positive growth for the full year in 2008 at 2%; a third of the level seen in 2007 as the storm clouds of the financial crisis began to gather. World output in 2008 fell to 1.7%, less than half the value seen in the previous year and the worst performance since the Great Depression.

On the bright side, a report issued by the WTO this year predicts that world trade will increase by 9.5% this year (2010). Director-General Lamay believes that WTO rules that have prevented nations from adopting the protectionist measures that would have offered short-term respite at home have but worsened the global situation. The WTO believes that export trade volumes in the developed world will rise by

7.5% this year whilst the rest of the world should see volumes rise by 11%. **The true figure for the contraction of global trade was 12.2% rather than the 9% that the organisation had predicted.**

It seems to be the case that the global recovery is strongest in China and the rest of Asia at the moment. China has overtaken Germany as the world's leading exporting nation and has now replaced Japan as the world's second largest economy in 2010. **2200 years after it was first created, trade from the home of the Silk Road has established itself as the most important nexus of commerce for the 21st century.**

Conclusion

October 2009—A Circle Has No End!

"Insanity: doing the same thing over and over again and expecting different results."

Albert Einstein

"The danger already exists that the mathematicians have made a covenant with the devil to darken the spirit and to confine man in the bonds of Hell."

Saint Augustine of Hippo

"I may not have gone where I intended to go but I think I have ended up where I intended to be."

Douglas Adams

The End; If you have opened this chapter either you have valiantly ploughed through the previous twenty four sections or you are sneaking a peek in the book shop to see if you want to make a purchase. Either way you are to be congratulated—especially those who buy the book!

Those of you who have read through the previous chapters will have spent a considerable span of time reading and will agree or disagree with my conclusions in this chapter based on the book verses your own experiences. Those of you who just flick through to the back have to make an instant judgment. This differing outlook based on time is one of the key differences between a trader and an investor.

Time itself can be distorted by our own relative view of it when we appear within the period under review. Time seems slow and endless whilst being enjoyed during our lifespan yet would seem almost instantaneous when compared to the full span of humanity's history. This was brought in to sharp perspective the other day when I was reading an excellent book on Anthony & Cleopatra by Adrian Goldsworthy. He so rightly points out that Cleopatra and her star crossed lover lived closer to our generation than they did to the original builders of the pyramids!

How does that bending of time reflect on the Credit Crunch of 2007?

Well, we always compare things to our own experiences. Thus for us this event is a transformational financial event. Those who experienced the 1929 Wall Street Crash and the subsequent Great Depression were marked. Successful businessmen who lived through that era were characterised by a risk aversion principal that they subsequently stuck too after experiencing firsthand the financial hardships of the thirties. It is too early yet to see what characteristics will emerge from this experience but I suspect risk aversion will still not be as prominent in our generation.

The rather depressing and obvious conclusion I have reached on my research, which travels across time and geographic borders, is that we are, as a species, unable, up to now, to prevent financial crashes. *The good news is that we are still here!*

The good news must be tempered and contextual.

I am always keen to point out to my students that we human beings are very resilient and resourceful. We are the alpha species on the planet and manage to exist in nearly every condition and environment. Across the last five millenniums many great cities that still exist today have been sacked, burnt and pillaged yet have been able to rise from the ashes to restore their former greatness. A lesson from which we can all take heart! Yet for those countless thousands who experienced the not so tender mercies of an Attila, a Genghis Khan, a Napoleon, a Hitler, a Caesar or even an Alexander; who were raped, pillaged and sold into slavery, the fact that their cities would once again rise to prominence was of little or no consolation.

Thus the additional two questions to consider, over and above just whether *"Credit Crunches"* are inevitable are:-

Do these financial crises serve any purpose that is good and which truly benefits humanity?

And

If they do serve a useful purpose, is it possible to achieve the same results without the pain?

To answer the questions in order we need to look at whether these financial crashes serve any benefit to us first. That means detaching ourselves from the horror of job loss, redundancy, foreclosure, forfeiture, repossession and bankruptcy whilst focusing on the bigger picture. The flip side is simple. Does the current financial structure serve any purpose? The essence of banking should be the provision and matching of savings with investments so that the economy, whether local, national or international, grows at a rate which increases the real standard of living of the population. Its secondary function should be the provision of funding to allow the populace to acquire their own property—if they so desire—at rates and ratios which are safe to *both* lender and borrower.

The history of financial crashes always throws up a pivotal point at which banks have deviated from this function. They have strayed from their true path.

> *"To forget one's purpose is the commonest form of stupidity"*
> **Friedrich Nietzsche**

Over 80% of all UK bank lending is made directly or indirectly against property. This would seem a massive distortion of what should actually be going on. At the same time lending to small and medium firms, who generate the most growth in the short time frame, is at an all time low in real terms. The same is true in the United States whereby cash funds held on banks' balance sheets are the highest since the Second World War and yet good firms are being strangled to death due to lack of lending facilities. Banks have clearly moved from their true purpose. There is a simple reason for this transition.

The lines between investment banking and retail banking are blurred not only by legislation but in the minds of those that operate those institutions. We discussed in earlier chapters the repeal of the Glass Steagall Act 1933 which was overturned by President Bill Clinton on November 12, 1999. This allowed banks to carry out both retail and investment functions under the same corporate umbrella. Simultaneously the leaders of both forms of banking looked over the fence, assumed the grass was greener and stepped into their neighbor's garden.

In general these big wave crises like 1929 and 2007 are linked to the banks blurring their true functions. It is important for society that we have a financial and banking system in place. It facilitates trade and commerce—simple, easy and acceptable to all. Retail banks can make a very nice living out of the oligarchic nature of the sector. When they become greedy by leveraging themselves into the stock market, as in 1929, or the housing market in 2007 that is when the greatest damage occurs. Thus the Banks need to be put back in their boxes and quickly.

Will it happen? *It is down to political will and the jury is out on that one!*

So, returning to the original question—are crashes good? The answer is, unfortunately, yes. They serve the purpose of rebalancing the financial system. In the same way that burning crop residue in fields at the end of autumn is ecologically and environmentally bad and yet is still carried out. Crop residue burning helps growers stay competitive as it is an inexpensive and effective method to remove excess residue. It harms the environment and kills numerous small mammals and birds yet in the United States it is still carried out in fifty states.

Thus we must suffer the crash in order to flush clean the system— *however unpleasant the short term effects may be!*

The second question was—if they do serve a useful purpose, is it possible to achieve the same results without the pain? After reading the above I am sure you will be able to answer this yourself. They definitely serve a useful purpose but it is somewhat painful. What is the alternative? We have what central bankers call a *soft landing* whereby through their diligent and prudent actions we are bought back from the abyss.

It never happens! As soon as people hear those words they make all sorts of assumptions and dash for the exits. The very thing that everybody is trying to prevent then occurs more rapidly and earlier than it would otherwise do.

The answer is that, as in the medical industry—*prevention is always better than cure!* We must not let the financial system get to the point of needing a financial crisis to bring it to heel.

As a writer it is always possible to criticise everybody and not be called upon to present solutions—I think those species of writers are called journalists! However I would be delighted if you would indulge me a little longer whilst I list out my own solutions. These solutions primarily focus on the United States on the premise it is the world's largest nation by GDP and the dollar is holding on to its position as the world's reserve currency. Thus any changes would have greatest effect on the global economy. The solution proposed below can obviously be enacted by nearly all other governments / nations similarly afflicted.

Banking

- Banking functions should be split. Retail banking should not be involved in investment products.

- Retail banking should be a state hybrid corporation. It should make profits but how it makes them should be clearly defined. For example, banks should lend money for people to acquire homes but under simple fixed formulas—three times salary, a certain salary to monthly repayment ratio and the elimination of interest only mortgages and tax relief on payments.

- Global profits should be taxable in the country of domicile.

- Central banks would have a "golden share" that out votes all others. Its primary purpose is the selection of high level officers to ensure the Board functions correctly.

Given the quasi-monopoly nature of retail banking all banks would have to redistribute a high percentage of profits as dividends.

Investment Banks

- Investment banks would not be allowed to indulge directly or indirectly in retail banking business.

- The balance sheet gearing allowed on their balance sheets would be limited by Central Banks.

- All company officers of investment banks would be personally liable for any loses their banks make. I am sure many would say that is unfair but if we have a situation when people can become multi-millionaires or indeed billionaires from working at such companies in good times and yet pass the buck to tax payers in the bad times. They must be accountable for their actions. At a minimum it will focus the mind clearly on where their firms are committing their capital.

Central Banks

- The Federal Reserve System would be acquired by the US Treasury.

- All US Government debt owned by other departments of the US Government would be cancelled. Bizarrely, yes other departments own their government's debt to the tune of 8% of the total outstanding debt.

- Even more bizarre is that the Federal Reserve is a large buyer of its own debt. This too would be cancelled.

- Estimates of overseas owners of US Government debt, the largest being China and Japan, range from 44% to 50%. All domestically held US Government debt would be redeemed immediately at face value. Not able to do it under the terms of debt issue? Well, just pass the required legislation. The payment for this proportion of the redemption is covered in the Money Supply section below.

- How is the redemption of US debt to be paid for? Well by the one proper use of the printing press! Create new money and send it to the former owners of the debt. Bad news, you cry—highly inflationary, etc. This is what is going to happen in the future anyway, just bring it forward and let's save the interest burden. The former owners will then be left with cash but no home to put it in. That is where the newly tidied up retail banks come in. They will offer long term deposit accounts into which these monies can be deposited, thus creating funds available to support normal economic lending activity and residential property purchase.

Residential Mortgage Sector

- A single sweeping measure. In the US the Government would carry out by degree the redemption of *all* residential mortgages in full by a one-off payment. How would this be done? Quite simply the Government would issue the funds required. The major recipients would be the banks. Simultaneously the Government would significantly increase the proportion of money to be placed by the banks with the central bank—the ratio would be high enough to absorb a significant proportion, if not all, of the monies initially created to repay the mortgages. These monies held on deposit by the central banks would be the guarantee against any new lending by the retails banks. As previously stated any future borrowing on residential mortgages would be strictly limited, based on multiples of earnings and a much lower loan to value ratio possibly around 50%.

Money Supply

- The argument is that these measures would greatly increase the money in circulation and would be inflationary. My counterarguments and proposed measures are:-

• This money is going to get into the system anyway over the next few years so we are just bringing it forward in order to affect a solution.

• Money from redemption of US Government debt will either go into investment in industry or will flood into deposit accounts at banks—both good, although the former is better than the later.

• Money from redemption of domestic mortgage products would be placed back on deposit with the newly formed Central Bank—a replacement to the Fed run by the Government on behalf of the people it serves, not just those in the banking arena.

• The Government would then replace the old dollar with a new dollar by a ratio of 10 to 1 thus increasing the value of existing dollars tenfold and reducing the dollars in circulation by 90%.

• The Government will run a policy of reducing the money supply in circulation by way of a levy on the deposits of retail banks held at the Central Bank. As the levy operates a percentage of the money held would be cancelled.

• As US Government debt held by overseas / foreign governments falls due this would be paid from a second levy on the deposits of retail banks held at the Central Bank—as with the money supply reduction. As the levy operates a percentage of the money held would be cancelled.

- All remaining residual money from retail banks then held by the new Central Bank would be drawn down over 10 years for expenditure on domestic infrastructure projects.

The effect of the last three measures is to alleviate the debt burden currently resting on the shoulders of the population. It shrinks the money supply effectively, whilst drawing in and tightly controlling mortgage lending by the retail banking sector. It clears all remaining Government debt meaning the country starts with a clean sheet. At the same time expenditure on infrastructure over a sustained period will replace much of the dilapidated infrastructure in place whilst placing money back into the economy in a controlled formula.

- The dollar would then be linked to either silver or gold or a combination of both. This would effectively put the country back on the "Gold Standard" reversing and putting a full stop on the monetary madness that has taken place since 15th August 1971.

Government Control

- The simple frame of reference is that from this point on the Government must run a balanced budget i.e. there would be no borrowing—all expenditure must be met from tax revenue. For this I would adopt the simple Warren Buffett solution which is to make politicians personally accountable for any shortfall that arises. This would certainly focus their mind!

Three key questions come to mind:-

Is it fair?

Would it work?

Will it be done?

The speed dating answer to those questions is—No, it is not fair. Some people and companies would benefit disproportionately. Well, hey, life is not fair and we are talking fixing a broken system here not sticking a band aid on a grazed knee! The alternative—*well see below!*

Would it work? Yes it would work. By splitting the roles of the banks you remove temptation. By removing the Fed to Government control, the country's Central Bank works for the people not the bankers. If you make banking officers and politicians accountable for their actions you make them act cautiously and diligently. By removing the yoke of debt from the country you free the people to prosper!

Will it be done? No, it will not be done. When politicians' campaign funds are supported by major interest groups and, in particular, the financial services sector there is no real reason to effect lasting change. The easiest solution is to serve the hand that feeds you by putting in place measures that superficially placate the masses without upsetting your wallet holder too much. A politician's view is that the best thing to do is to find fairly lame measures and then promote ineffective regulations thus pushing the problem forward for another generation of politicians to deal with. The time to have taken charge of the banks and the monetary system was when the banks were reeling during the middle of the credit crunch. At that time they would have agreed to any form of control and restrictions just in order to get under their Centrals Bank's protective umbrella. *Now only a few years later we cannot even control the bonuses they pay their officers!*

> *NO true change will happen until after the ultimate financial apocalypse has taken place!*

The End is in Sight!

"The time to stop a revolution is at the beginning, not the end!"

Adlai Stevenson

The good news / bad news conclusion is that I must end with the view that we are unable to prevent traumatic financial expansion and contractions whilst the historic and current structure of our monetary and economic system prevails.

The monetary and economic structure in place was no modern day assemblage of disparate threads. It evolved from the day we left the caves and moved in to primitive communities. Commerce and capitalism, with a small c, did not solely evolve as a system to service the direct wants of communities. The pressure that distorted it and subsequently shaped its final form is a trait that we do not like to acknowledge. Deep down we are innately selfish creatures. Thus, what we do is driven by personal desires not community desires!

It is only when we have satisfied our own wants that our umbrella of support / empathy / love is allowed to flow out in waves: a sort of emotional waterfall normally starting with family, then friends, then people we know and then eventually people we are aware of who exist but are not in our range of physical experience, the true essence of charity and overseas aid.

We have to face the raw truth that we as a species are driven by our own wants. This starting point manifests itself into greed and jealousy. The easy flip interpretation of my words is that I am saying all billionaires and millionaires are greedy, selfish human beings. This is not the case as many, indeed nearly all rich individuals are the first to acknowledge that they owe something back to society and are the greatest contributors to charity. Many of them have also built business that support hundreds, thousands and millions of people by giving them valid employment.

What I am saying is that this attribute has, like an out of control hormone, warped both the speed of growth of financial markets and their final shaping. This book points the finger of blame at many different individuals over many market collapses but no *single* individual created a total market collapse. *Although blame must be proportional the shocking conclusion was that it was all of us!*

We all need to shoulder some of the blame, not equally and often unfairly but that is how it is. As a *society* we let it happen. For ninety nine percent of the people this was due to passivity whilst for the other one per cent it was due to what one might term affirmative action. To make you feel better let me say that the blame is spread even thinner because it must be spread across the generations. Every generation has experienced a financial turmoil and yet has not had the strength to make any long term changes to the system. ***Why not, you cry!***

Simple!

The system is inside us. We seek to improve our own situation thus overlooking / ignoring / concealing those factors which may harm others. We unconsciously ignore the threat of systemic collapse in order to take advantage of market circumstances for our own selfish and short term desires. The greedy person is not the faceless banker, the anonymous mortgage broker, the corrupt politician, the incompetent overseer, the overreaching landlord, the Ponzi scheme operator it is sadly . . . . *the person in the mirror!*

In case you think me an opera critic it must include authors, writers, speakers, lecturers, journalists who are in a better place than most to push for *real* change. It is said that a nation gets the government it deserves. The saying could be extended to say that humans get the economic arrangement, and its symbiotic twin the financial organism, it deserves.

These are harsh words. A bit like watching a crime thriller and finding the kindly police inspector played by your favourite heart throb is in fact the terrifying masked serial killer. Those who have skipped to the end may well feel that I am making excuses for all those who are directly involved. I am not. They should suffer for their faults and failures; the essence of capitalism. If they broke the law and created untold misery, like Madoff, then incarceration unto death is fair. If you read the book from cover to cover then you will know I am no apologist. Blame has been directed with the aim of a sniper and the effect of a missile. No prominent nut, or nutter, has remained uncracked by this sledgehammer!

"How many psychiatrists does it take to change a light bulb—one but the light bulb must want to change."

The bad news is that the real financial tsunami remains out there; below the horizon and hidden from view. I am not a scientist but quick studies of this natural phenomena reveal a few interesting characteristics.

A tsunami which causes damage far away from its source is sometimes called a teletsunami. A tsunami behaves very differently in deep water than in shallow water. In deep ocean water, tsunami waves form only a small hump, barely noticeable and harmless; in shallow water near coastlines, a tsunami slows but in doing so forms large destructive waves.

What we have in the monetary world is a seismic event about to take place that most of the world's population remains unaware of. In the course of the next few years, may be as long as a decade or two, there will be another upheaval of the financial tectonic plates that govern all economic activity on this planet. The joy and pain of it is that the actual cause will be indeterminable until we are in the event or immediately after.

The shocker is that we have created our own shallow water. By leveraging assets and cash flow to the max, by adding synthetic instruments on top of this already unstable structure we have made our economic coastal shallows no deeper than bath water whilst a Tsunami of Boxing Day 2004 proportion builds momentum offshore.

> *"Wild, dark times are rumbling toward us, and the prophet who wishes to write a new apocalypse will have to invent entirely new beasts, and beasts so terrible that the ancient animal symbols of St. John will seem like cooing doves and cupids in comparison."*
> **HEINRICH HEINE,**
> **Augsburg Gazette, 1842**

Humanity will survive the shock of the financial *"big one"* and possibly it will cleanse the system. I am quietly confident that a better system will be created and our species will emerge stronger for the lesson.

So humanity will survive but the key question you need to ask is . . . . will you?

Neil Chapman-Blench—Profile

Neil has had many careers including banker, investor, business builder, share trader and property owner. Across this diversified range of vocations there have been many highs and a few dramatic lows but the professions he is most proud of are author, financial educator and futurist.

Neil worked in the investment banking industry from 1979 to 1992. Initially starting at Samuel Montagu & Co he worked in the back up operations before moving up to the trading desk where he traded gold, currency markets and Eurobonds. The trading desk was an integral part of the investment management division, which then became a management buyout called MIM Britannia. Later on he focused on UK stocks and options. In 1985 he was head hunted to set up the non-US trading desks for Fidelity Investments, the world's largest fund management company. In 1987 he was appointed a main board director of Fidelity International and also served on the boards of the stock broking subsidiary as well as the fund management companies.

In 1992 he left to set up his own business. For the next seven years he built up a fund management company that focused on developing bespoke property portfolios in the student housing market in Cardiff, Manchester, Nottingham and Lincoln. This grew to £10 million of property under management but the company was subsequently broken up following a partnership dispute.

Like most successful entrepreneurs Neil has had a few brushes with disaster and as a result of the company breaking up and the partnership dispute he went into bankruptcy. He views this as one of the most valuable business lessons he has had over his career and it significantly shaped his subsequent success and business outlook.

After this Neil built up a company called Personal Risk Management Ltd with three partners. PRM specialised in background screening for banks, insurance companies, the pharmaceutical industry and airline security with a focus on fraud, food and industrial terrorism. Neil was head of Operations and Finance and controlled the international offices in the UK, India and Poland. This was sold to Kroll, the world's largest private investigation company, in 2003. He worked for Kroll for two further years during the period of an earn out, which was successful. He left in 2005 and became a private property and stock market investor.

Parallel to this he built up a highly successful commercial property investment company in Katowice in Poland with four partners. This company was profitably sold in 2007.

Neil is an educational speaker for a number of wealth creation companies including Tigrent, the Rich Dad Organisation and Martin Roberts in property, business and shares where he often works alongside his co-author Alistair Crooks. He has co-founded—**The Wisdom of Wealth**—an online financial education company, part of the Unlock the Future Inspirational Learning Group.

He is the author and co-author of a number of books and articles including—**The Madness of Money** and **The Pathway**.

To read more about Neil please visit his Web Sites at the following links:-

www.TheMadnessofMoney.com

www.TheMadnessofMoney.co.uk

www.TheWisdomofWealth.com

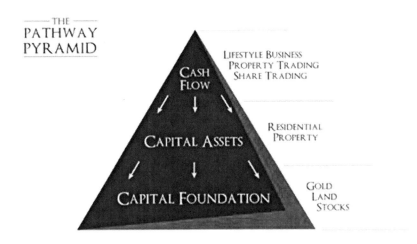

Lightning Source UK Ltd.
Milton Keynes UK
UKOW030944210712

196357UK00002B/2/P